PENGUIN BOOKS

THE GREEK REVOLUTION

Mark Mazower is the Ira D. Wallach Professor of History at Columbia University. He is the author of *Governing the World*, *Hitler's Empire*, and *The Balkans: A Short History*, winner of the Wolfson Prize for History, among other books. He lives in New York City.

Praise for *The Greek Revolution*

Winner of the Duff Cooper Prize

"[A] superb new history of the rebellion and its broader implications. . . . A compelling story—full of conflicting characters, rivalries, massacres, betrayals, enslavements—all of which [Mazower] narrates with earned authority and exceptional power. . . . He achieves more clarity on this tangled subject than other historians in English have managed before."
—*The Wall Street Journal*

"Elegant and rigorous . . . [*The Greek Revolution*] holds lessons for modern geopolitics: about the galvanizing effects of violence, the role of foreign intervention, and the design flaws in dreams."
—*The Economist*

"[A] rich, illuminating, and imposing history of [a] paradigm-shifting conflict. . . . An expert storyteller, Mazower unravels a Gordian knot of local, regional, and international factionalisms."
—Claire Messud, *Harper's Magazine*

"[A] pulsating narrative . . . rich with social history and the luminaries of the age . . . *The Greek Revolution* causes us to think more deeply about the role of the nation-state in a global context. . . . It is hard to imagine it being surpassed any time soon as the definitive English-language account of the Greek Revolution."
—*The New York Times Book Review*

THE GREEK REVOLUTION

1821 and the Making of Modern Europe

MARK MAZOWER

PENGUIN BOOKS

PENGUIN BOOKS

An imprint of Penguin Random House LLC
penguinrandomhouse.com

First published in the United States of America by Penguin Press,
an imprint of Penguin Random House LLC, 2021
Published in Penguin Books 2022

ISBN 9780143110934 (paperback)

THE LIBRARY OF CONGRESS HAS CATALOGED THE HARDCOVER EDITION AS FOLLOWS:
Names: Mazower, Mark, author.
Title: The Greek Revolution : 1821 and the making of modern Europe / Mark Mazower.
Other titles: 1821 and the making of modern Europe
Description: New York : Penguin Press, 2021. | Includes bibliographical references and index.
Identifiers: LCCN 2021029233 (print) | LCCN 2021029234 (ebook) |
ISBN 9781591847335 (hardcover) | ISBN 9780698163980 (ebook)
Subjects: LCSH: Greece—History—War of Independence, 1821–1829. |
Europe—History—1815–1848.
Classification: LCC DF805 .M39 2021 (print) | LCC DF805 (ebook) |
DDC 949.5/06—dc23
LC record available at https://lccn.loc.gov/2021029233
LC ebook record available at https://lccn.loc.gov/2021029234

Printed in the United States of America
2nd Printing

CONTENTS

PART I
In the Great Morning of the World

PART 2
International Interventions

Acknowledgments

Research has been transformed out of all recognition by digitization and I am conscious of my debt to those many anonymous souls who have over the past few years scanned hundreds of books and journal articles and thousands of pages of documents. The range of primary materials now available online for this subject is breathtaking. But my research has also depended upon the kindness and generosity of friends and colleagues, scholars and booksellers. In the first place let me therefore acknowledge my debt in what is essentially a work of synthesis to two extraordinary generations of historians, notably: Denys Barau, Simos Bozikis, Antonis Diakakis, Dimitris Dimitropoulos, Maria Efthymiou, Haken Erdem, Athanasios Fotopoulos, Gelina Harlaftis, Marios Hatzopoulos, Georgios Kalpadakis, Giannis Kokkonas, Christina Koulouri, Sofia Laïou, Christos Loukos, Hervé Mazurel, Georgios Nikolaou, Vassilis Panayiotopoulos, Petros Pizanias, Charles Stewart, and Dionysios Tzakis. And also to the booksellers who came to my rescue at a time when books could reach places that humans could not: Efi Flindri, Dimitris Retsas, George Stathopoulos, and Lakis Vouyioukas in Athens and Vladimiros Voïnas on Tinos. I'd especially like to thank the following individuals for their help in various ways with the writing of this book: Antonis Hadzikyriakou, Gelina Harlaftis, Aristides Hatzis, Marios Hatzopoulos, George Kalpadakis, Kostas Kostis, Costas Kouremenos, Leonora Navari, and Vasia Theodoropoulou in Athens, along with my forbearing publishers Takis Fragoulis and Victoria Lekka; Father Markos Foskolos, Vangelis Kontizas, Memi Papakonstantopoulou, George Sitaras, and Marinos Souranis on Tinos; Simon Golding and CRASSH in Cambridge and Andrew Kahn in Oxford; James Allen, Brune Biebuyck, Marie d'Origny, and Eve Grinstead in Paris; Dimitris Antoniou, Lee Bollinger, Afroditi Giovanopoulou, Susan Glancy, Rashid Khalidi, Yanni Kotsonis, Paul LeClerc, Charis Marantzidou, Daniel Sun Shao, Christina Shelby, Adam Tooze, Karen Van Dyck, Stelios Vassilakis, and Konstantina Zanou in New York. I owe a special debt to Peter

Mandler and Kostis Karpozilos for their thoughtful comments on an earlier draft; to my mother and my brothers for their support; and to Scott Moyers and Simon Winder for the all-round pleasure and privilege of working with them. Neil Gower crafted the two beautiful maps with which the book begins and ends. Costas Kouremenos and Richard Mason went beyond the call of duty in saving me from errors and infelicities and tolerating my last-minute authorial interventions. My children Selma and Jed uncomplainingly put up with piles of books on the kitchen table and added their own. Julie Fry not only made the writing of this one an immensely happy experience in a very difficult time but also improved it in innumerable ways; there is no page of this book that has not benefited from her discerning eye. Many years ago, Fay Zika and her mother gave me their friendship and introduced me to Greece: this book is dedicated in gratitude to Fay and, in fond memory, to Calliope Bourdara.

Note on Names

Transliteration is a pedant's dream and a perfectionist's nightmare. In this book, I have tended to use "k" for the Greek letter "kappa" and "y" for "ypsilon"—thus Kefalonia and Ypsilantis rather than Cefalonia and Ipsilantis; on the other hand, I have generally retained the conventional English form of well-known names—thus Capodistrias and Hydra. By the same token, I prefer Athens, Corfu, Jannina, and Crete to less common variants. Greek place-names have undergone dramatic changes over the years and I have generally gone with names in common use at the time such as Navarino (rather than Pylos), Vostitsa (rather than Aigion), Modon, Jassy, Salona, and Constantinople, though I drew the line at Napoli di Romania, which few readers would associate with the Peloponnesian port of Nafplion, and I have kept Syros rather than Syra, Kythera over Cerigo, and have always preferred Evvia to Euboea. Ottoman Tripolitsa was to all intents and purposes a different town from Greek Tripolis, which today stands in its stead; Mesolonghi is a more faithful transliteration than Missolonghi. Where there are names in alternative variants in the sources, I have generally remained faithful to the original.

Topography creates more problems. I generally refer to the Cyclades and the islands of the east Aegean rather than to the Archipelago, which is how contemporaries commonly referred to them all or to the Isles of the White Sea, which was the Ottoman term. The Morea is a well-known synonym for the Peloponnese but some readers may be unfamiliar with the use of Rumeli for the mainland north of the Gulf of Corinth; it was, however, a term used by both Greeks and Turks. Speaking of which, while I do use the term "Greek," meaning Orthodox Christians who spoke Greek, I try—for reasons explained in the Introduction—to avoid the term "Turk" unless it appears in an original source or cannot otherwise be avoided.

The Orthodox Christians of the Ottoman Empire still used the Julian calendar in the 1820s and Greece would not move to the Gregorian calendar, in general use in the rest of Europe, until 1923, sometime after the Ottoman Empire (1917) and Russia (1918). In the period in question, the Julian calendar was twelve days behind the Gregorian. The approach taken in this book is to refer to the Julian calendar for events inside Greece, the Ottoman Empire, and Russia, and to the Gregorian for events taking place in western and central Europe; in one or two places, I give both to avoid possible confusion.

List of Illustrations

Photographic credits are shown in parentheses. Every effort has been made to contact all rights holders. The publishers will be pleased to amend in future editions any errors or omissions brought to their attention.

Page 1

View of Istanbul, ca. 1789, watercolor by Jean-Baptiste Hilaire. (*Pera Museum, Istanbul, Turkey*)

Sultan Mahmud II, ca. 1825, print by Josef Kriehuber after Höchle, ca. 1825.

Phanariot Mihail Soutzos, illustration by Louis Dupré, from *Voyage à Athènes et à Constantinople*, 1825. (*Hellenic Library, Alexander S. Onassis Public Benefit Foundation*)

Page 2

The Congress of Vienna, 1814, print by Friedrich Campe. (*Wien Museum, Vienna*)

Emmanuil Xanthos, print by an unknown artist.

Christoforos Perraivos. (*National History Museum, Athens*)

Page 3

Prince Alexandros Ypsilantis, from a chromolithograph by I. K. Nerantzis, Leipzig.

Prince Dimitrios Ypsilantis, illustration by Adam de Friedel, from *The Greeks: Twenty-four Portraits of the Principal Leaders and Personages*, 1832. (The Gennadius Library, the American School of Classical Studies at Athens)

Greek Filiki Etaireia survivors of the Danubian campaign, Switzerland, 1822, lithograph by Joseph Brodtmann. (*Swiss National Museum, Zürich (Inv. No. LM-39454)*)

Page 4

View of Jannina, ca. 1833, by Clarkson Stanfield. (*Private collection*)

Khurshid Pasha, illustration by Adam de Friedel, from *The Greeks: Twenty-four Portraits of the Principal Leaders and Personages*, 1832. (*The Gennadius Library, the American School of Classical Studies at Athens*)

Georgios Karaïskakis, portrait by Karl Krazeisen, from *Portraits of Famous Greeks and Philellenes*, 1828–31. (*Collection of the Society for Hellenism and Philhellenism (www.eefshp.org) and the Philhellenism Museum (www.phmus.org)*)

Greeks After a Defeat, 1826, painting by Henri Decaisne. (*Benaki Museum, Athens (photograph: Bridgeman Images)*)

Page 10

Mehmed Ali, Pasha of Egypt, 1840, portrait by Louis-Charles-Auguste Couder. (*Château de Versailles, France (photograph: Bridgeman Images)*)

Soliman Pasha al-Faransawi, illustration by Louis Dupré, from *Voyage à Athènes et à Constantinople*, 1825.

Ibrahim Pasha in Pylos, 1828, by Eugène Peytier. (*Stephen Vagliano Collection*)

Page 11

The slave market in Cairo, illustration from Robert Hay, *Illustrations of Cairo*, 1840. (*The Gennadius Library, the American School of Classical Studies at Athens*)

Women from the Peloponnese in a makeshift tent, ca. 1828, illustration by Théodore Leblanc, from *Sketches from Life Made during a Three-year Journey in Greece and the Levant*, 1833–34. (*The Gennadius Library, the American School of Classical Studies at Athens*)

Pages 12–13

Greek Soldiers during the Insurrections of 1829, watercolor by Théodore Leblanc, ca. 1829. (*Anne S. K. Brown Military Collection, Brown Digital Repository, Brown University Library*)

Page 14

The Battle of Navarino, 1827, lithograph by George Philip Reinagle.

The assassination of Capodistrias in Nafplion, 1831, by an unknown artist. (*Benaki Museum, Athens (photograph: Bridgeman Images)*)

Page 15

Otto, King of Greece, 1832, portrait by Joseph Stieler. (*Benaki Museum, Athens (photograph: akg-images)*)

The port of Ermoupolis, Syros, 1833, from *Marchebeus, Voyage de Paris à Constantinople par bateau à vapeur: nouvel itinéraire*, 1839.

Page 16

The Ottoman Balkans, 1820

Legend:

- ○ Place of birth of Filiki Etaireia members (more than 5)
- **12%** % of Filiki Etaireia members by place of birth
- ◎ Place of recruitment of Filiki Etaireia members (more than 5)
- **12%** % of Filiki Etaireia members by place of recruitment
- Area under Ali Pasha's control

Russian Empire

Habsburg Empire

Jassy · Kishinev · Odessa

17.5%

MOLDAVIA

19%

Ismail

Galati

WALLACHIA

5.5% Bucharest

River Danube

Principality of Serbia

Black Sea

EASTERN RUMELIA

Varna
Burgas

Plovdiv

2%

Bosporus

CONSTANTINOPLE

5% **17.5%**

MACEDONIA

2% Salonica

ASIA MINOR

EPIROS

10.5%

THESSALY

6% Larissa

Volos

Mitylene

3%

Corfu · Jannina · Arta

Preveza

Chios

Smyrna

RUMELI

4%

Cefalonia

Patras · Corinth

Tripolitsa · Argos

15%

Zakynthos

Hydra

Spetses

CYCLADES

Rhodes

MOREA

Mani

IONIAN ISLANDS

12% **7.5%**

37% **20%**

CRETE

Mediterranean Sea

| 0 | 50 | 100 | 150 | 200 miles |
| 0 | 100 | 200 | 300 km |

N

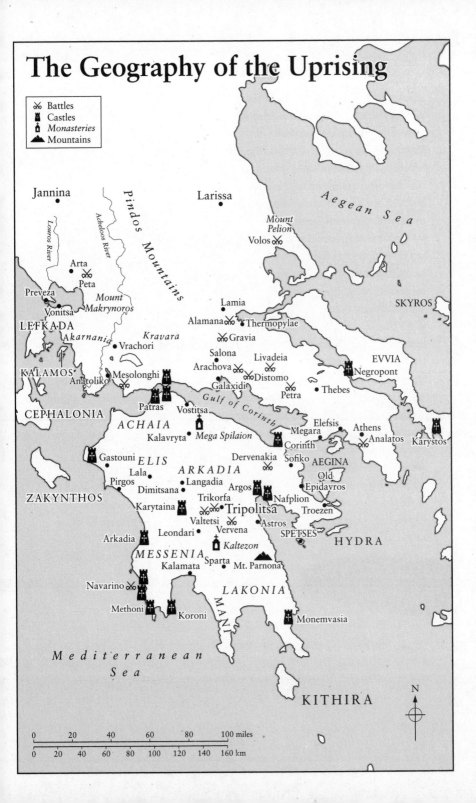

The Geography of the Uprising

Legend:
- ⚔ Battles
- 🏰 Castles
- ⛪ *Monasteries*
- ▲ Mountains

Jannina

Pindos Mountains

Larissa

Aegean Sea

Louros River

Acheloos River

Arta

Peta ⚔

Mount Pelion

Volos ⚔

Preveza

Vonitsa

Mount Makrynoros

Lamia

Alamana ⚔ Thermopylae

SKYROS

LEFKADA

Akarnania

Kravara

Vrachori

⚔ Gravia

Salona

Livadeia

EVVIA

KALAMOS

Anatoliko

Mesolonghi

Arachova ⚔ ⚔ Distomo

Galaxidi

Petra ⚔

Thebes

Negropont 🏰

CEPHALONIA

Anatoliko

Patras 🏰

Vostitsa

Gulf of Corinth

Megara

Elefsis

Athens

Karystos 🏰

ACHAIA

Kalavryta

Mega Spilaion ⛪

Corinth 🏰

Analatos

Gastouni 🏰

ELIS

Lala

Pirgos

ARKADIA

Dervenakia ⚔

Sofiko

AEGINA

Langadia

Argos 🏰

Nafplion 🏰

Old Epidavros

ZAKYNTHOS

Dimitsana

Karytaina 🏰

Trikorfa ⚔ ⚔ Tripolitsa

Troezen

Valtetsi ⚔

Astros

HYDRA

Arkadia 🏰

Leondari

Vervena

Kaltezon ⛪

SPETSES

MESSENIA

Kalamata

Sparta

Mt. Parnona ▲

LAKONIA

Navarino ⚔ 🏰

MANI

Methoni 🏰

Koroni 🏰

Monemvasia 🏰

Mediterranean Sea

KITHIRA

N

0   20   40   60   80   100 miles

0 20 40 60 80 100 120 140 160 km

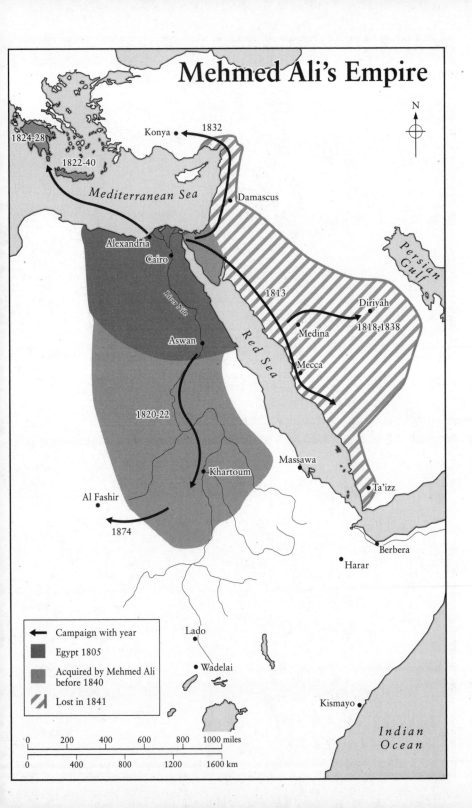

Mehmed Ali's Empire

N

1824-28

1832 Konya •

1822-40

Mediterranean Sea

Damascus •

Alexandria •

Cairo •

Persian Gulf

River Nile

1813

Diriyah •

1818, 1838

Medina •

Aswan •

Mecca •

Red Sea

1820-22

Massawa •

Khartoum •

Al Fashir •

Ta'izz •

1874

Berbera •

Harar •

Lado •

Campaign with year

Egypt 1805

Wadelai •

Acquired by Mehmed Ali
before 1840

Lost in 1841

Kismayo •

0   200   400   600   800   1000 miles

Indian Ocean

0   400   800   1200   1600 km

EUROPE and
the OTTOMAN EMPIRE
after 1815

APULIA

RUMELI

Salonica

Naoussa

Jannina

Larissa

Volos

Arta

Preveza

CORFU

IONIAN ISLANDS (under British protection)

KEFALONIA

ZAKYNTHOS

PINDOS

Mesolonghi

Salona

Galaxidi

Thebes

Patras

Vostitsa

Corinth

MOREA

Argos

AEGINA

Tripolitsa

Nafplion

HYDRA

Navarino

Kalamata

Methoni

MANI

Monemvasia

CERIGO

Grabousa

The World of the
OTTOMAN GREEKS
in 1821

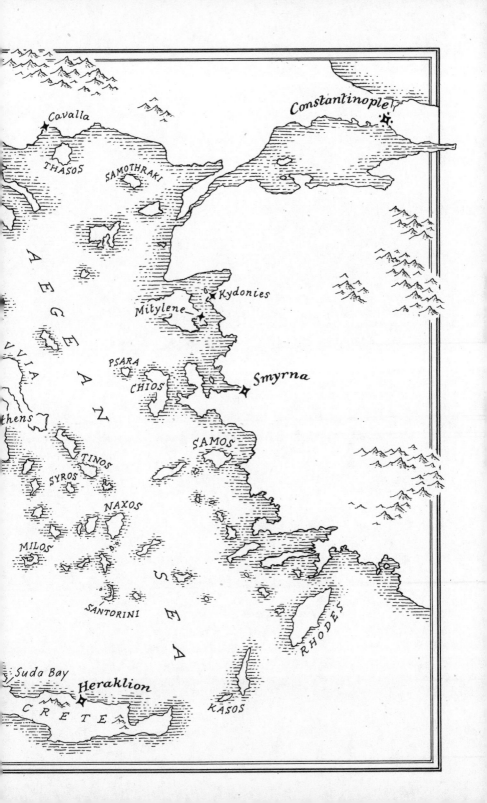

INTRODUCTION: ON HEROES, GREEKS, AND TURKS

What did the people of Greece want to do in 1821? . . . I will proclaim it concisely. They wanted to establish the reign of the Greeks. Why? I run to the Church for an answer. I leaf through the holy scripture and what do I discover? God made man in His image according to His likeness. And He made him master of the earth, its animals, plants and so on . . . Power has authority, the state virtue, when it is founded in the holy attributes of His image. [When it is not], the scepter shrivels in the hand of the ruler . . . The people of Greece wanted to restore the reign of that image in those heroic days when we cried for joy.

Georgios Tertsetis, 1855[1]

Located along the harbor wall in the port of Ermoupolis, the terrace of the Hermes hotel shelters guests from the summer *meltemi*, the north wind that sends the waves crashing onto the shingle beach below and keeps all but the most intrepid swimmers from venturing out. Tall stone mansions line the bay; the hill beyond is crowned by the blue dome of the church of Ayios Nikolaos. The island of Syros in the Cyclades, just over a hundred miles southeast of Athens, is a busy shipping hub for Mykonos, Naxos, Santorini, and other tourist destinations, and in the port the ferries come and go from morning to night. But round midday the shops along the front close up, the quayside empties, and the tavernas set out their tables in the shade of the back alleys.

It might seem as if this beautiful town has been there for centuries. Yet before the Greek war of independence there was little on this shoreline besides sand and marsh: since Roman times, the seas had been too unsafe and the threat from pirates too great to settle down by the water-front. There were a few scattered buildings along the bay—a small church, some storerooms, and a tiny café on whose wooden boards travelers occasionally passed the night waiting for their boat. The main town was set back at a remove from the shore, clinging to the sides of a craggy hill a good mile away, its narrow medieval lanes crowned by a Catholic cathedral. Known now as Upper Syros, it remains a largely unspoiled example of a medieval settlement, well worth a visit but a steep and arduous walk in the summer heat, and almost crowded out from view by the modern town that has sprung up at its feet.

The port of Ermoupolis was born out of a wartime catastrophe when Ottoman irregulars crushed a Greek uprising in 1822, on the island of Chios barely a hundred miles to the northeast, massacring the inhabitants amid scenes that horrified Europe. Of the thousands of survivors who fled, some arrived on Syros: bringing their mercantile skills to what had formerly been a farming island, they created the modern town and named it after Hermes—the god of trade and prosperity. "Syra is a place of mushroom growth," wrote a young American philhellene who visited in 1826 on the paddle steamer *Karteria*, a sight that drew crowds along the front. "It contains thirty thousand inhabitants while three years ago there were but five or six shops along the shore." By the middle of the nineteenth century, no less than one-third of all the shipping of the Kingdom of Greece was based there and the population around the port vastly outnumbered that of the old town up on the hill.[2]

A steam frigate—not only the first steamship to visit the islands but the first to be deployed in hostilities anywhere in the world—the *Karteria* had been a portent of the coming of capitalism and industry that followed independence. The great shipyards that lined the southern side of the harbor reflected Ermoupolis's emergence as a key refueling stop in the eastern Mediterranean. Cables laid by the Levant Submarine Telegraph Company linked the town to Athens, Chios, and Constantinople. An elegant central square lined with porticoes, palm trees, and a small Italianate opera house testified to its embrace of modern bourgeois culture. Such profound changes shaped not just Syros but Greece as a whole: the country that tourists visit today was born to a large extent out of the revolution of 1821. In the Peloponnese, devastated settlements were rebuilt with rectilinear avenues and neoclassical villas in a Western style. In a previously quiet Ottoman backwater that had been left in ruins by the fighting—Athens—a new capital arose with wide boulevards, hotels, a parliament, a university, and a palace. Across the new kingdom, an older, largely agrarian way of life came under the spell of a society run by banks, newspapers, clocks, and private property rights. And just as the gap between Syros's new Orthodox port and the older Catholic town on the hill gradually narrowed, so the country's numerous distinctive local and regional cultures gave way to a larger sense of national belonging. This transformation of a society, a polity, and an economy was the product of a peasant uprising that turned into a revolution and created a nation. What the Greeks fought for, and won, was a harbinger of Europe's future in which new states would be carved out of pre-national empires to emerge as sovereign nations within a global capitalist order. Driven by the desire for freedom, the Greek struggle inevitably became a search for the meaning of statehood in the modern world.

The uprising of 1821 came near the end of a half century of revolutions. This epoch of global transformation had begun with the United States successfully shaking off colonial power and it continued with the French overthrow of their monarchy and Haiti's bid for freedom.[3] As the Greeks rose up, the Spanish colonies in South America were fighting for independence, and much of southern Europe was in turmoil. The American independence movements had the advantage of being an ocean's remove from their oppressors, but the European revolutionaries were not so lucky and uprisings in Spain, Sicily, Naples, and Piedmont were easily suppressed. Only the Greeks fought on and, against the odds, prevailed.

What they accomplished thereby was unique, not merely eradicating the power of the Ottoman state in their lands, but also sweeping away an entire ruling philosophy and the institutions that had supported it. Not the legitimacy of dynasties, but nation, faith, capitalism and constitutional representation were the watchwords of this new order. The fundamental principle, wrote Lord Acton in his 1862 essay on "Nationality," was that "nations would not be governed by foreigners": it was this principle that marked the Greek war out from the other revolutions of southern Europe and helps explain why it was sustained and widespread, and also unusually brutal and violent. Members of other oppressed peoples—such as Italians, Poles, and Germans—flocked to join the struggle, seeing in the success of the Greeks a promise of their own future.

And though it took longer than many of them anticipated for that future to come, they were right to do so. The Greek revolution, wrote an economist in 1910, was "the first manifestation of that theory of nationalities which would dominate the nineteenth century." And the twentieth, too: Europe's principalities, composite monarchies and land-based empires— some of which had lasted nearly as long as the Ottomans—gave way to new states based on the same principles of ethnic homogeneity and democratic rule that had emerged in Greece. This was the world of nation states, the world in which we live, which has survived even late twentieth-century globalization.[4]

But that is only one side of the story, for along with the nation-state came a new way of thinking about international affairs that would reshape Europe and beyond. Writing in 1916, the British political theorist and publisher Leonard Woolf discerned in the "conferences which settled the question of Greek independence . . . the central point of a new, if rudimentary, international system." For Woolf, and for many others, those far-off diplomatic conferences provided a model of how to manage the peace of the world, and indeed the spread of the principle of national self-determination at the end of the First World War went hand in hand with the founding of the League of Nations—the precursor of the United Nations and the landscape of international organizations that we inhabit today. It is thus not only nationalism's triumph but that of the very idea of an internationally organized society of states whose origins may be found here, conjoined, in the story of 1821.[5]

The war on Syros was one of diplomatic maneuvers and shrewd commercialism, not battlefield heroics. When the Ottoman fleet moored offshore, the notables rowed out to present the imperial admiral—the *kapudan pasha*—with the customary gifts. They paid their taxes and for some years managed to maintain a unique kind of neutrality. Down in the port, the main source of its prosperity was a thriving market in plunder and pirate loot that included captives and slaves along with church bells, clothes, precious metals, weapons, and other valuables. When the insurgents made their appearance, it was in the shape of a private flotilla of armed men who mixed political slogans with outright robbery and from whom the islanders defended themselves with all the means at their disposal.[6]

What a contrast with the conventional depiction of the Greek war of independence as an epic drama of national unity starring fighters such

as Odysseus Androutsos and Giorgios Karaïskakis, "Old Man" Kolokotronis and Nikitaras "the Turk-eater." Warriors whose mustaches and
fierce gaze testify to their manliness and courage, they still stare down
from the walls of *kafeneia* and schoolrooms, their yataghan (sword) or
rifle raised high, leading the struggle against the turbaned barbarians. A
subject for popular lithographs ever since Peter von Hess, a Bavarian
painter with a fondness for set pieces, romanticized them for Greece's
first king, Otto, many of the heroes of 1821 had in reality loathed,
maligned, ousted, betrayed, and even occasionally killed one another.
Yet with time they became emblems of moral virtue, inspirations and
models of patriotic self-sacrifice for future generations. The most famous
of them all, Theodoros Kolokotronis, made the leap from brigand to
national hero thanks not only to his wartime exploits but also to the
works of a small circle of veterans who burnished his image through
the written word with such success that in a 2008 national poll to find the
greatest Greek of all time he came third, bested only by Alexander
the Great and Georgios Papanikolaou, cancer specialist and hero in a
different kind of war.[7]

Heroes come with certain drawbacks. They populate static tableaux
designed to illustrate immortal values; they do not exist in a historical
landscape whose meaning changes with time and perspective. Moreover, the heroic drama highlights one group and one set of mostly
martial virtues at the expense of others that were in reality no less
important. The politicians involved in Greece's struggle have fewer
admirers even though they were just as influential upon events and no
more morally flawed, self-interested, cowardly, or mercenary than the
leading chieftains. The men with swords, cutting through moral com-
plexity as readily as they lopped off heads, have overshadowed the
landowners and the merchants who bankrolled them, not to mention
the farmers whose olives, vines, sheep, and goats fed them. It goes without saying that they have overshadowed the women as well, save the
few who feature in the popular telling as honorary men.[8]

Yet heroes have their uses too, and in the Greeks' struggle with a far
mightier foe, heroism had been at the heart of revolutionary thinking.
Heroes had been needed in 1821 because despite the evident burdens
borne by all Christians in a polity based upon the sultan's wishes and
the unquestioned primacy of Islam, many who endured those indigni-
ties did not favor rebellion. Some Greeks were "disposed to fly from the

calamities which they groaned under"; over the preceding decades they had colonized Minorca and Corsica, British Florida and Russian Alaska. Others had undeniably prospered by staying. The large landowning dynasties, whose leaders controlled districts of the Peloponnese, hesitated to embark on a struggle that was unlikely to leave them better off than they already were. Tax breaks and imperial privileges gave prosperous shipowners pause too. The most important Greek chieftain in the western Pindos declared for the revolution late and soon returned to the Ottoman fold. In the spring of 1821 insurgents waited impatiently for weeks for the townspeople of Mesolonghi and the islanders of Hydra to join them, castigated the Chiots for their lack of revolutionary zeal, and at one point even impersonated a Russian general in an effort to whip up enthusiasm.[9]

Those to whom the prospect of revolution did appeal included sea captains bankrupted by the downturn in trade after the Napoleonic Wars; brigands driven from their homes into precarious exile; and bright young men studying republican ideas in universities abroad. All these groups were prominent within the conspiratorial society that popularized the idea of taking up arms in the run-up to 1821.[10] Once the machine had been prepared, in the words of its activists, the question was how to set it in motion. This is why they appealed for heroes. They demanded men who sought to emulate the ancients, who would heed the call of the fatherland without reckoning the risks since that, as one of the revolution's leaders later observed, would have doomed the cause from the start. "Better one hour of freedom than forty years of slavery," in the words of the most famous revolutionary song of the time: that was their calculation. The war's emblematic figures were thus men whose greatest deeds were acts of almost foolhardy bravery.

Just how foolhardy can be measured. The population of the Ottoman Empire in 1820 was probably about 24 million, and while there were possibly 3 million or so Greeks scattered throughout the empire, the number of them living in the provinces directly affected by the fighting was probably around 1 million at most. In terms of money, organization, and resources the mismatch was even greater. The sultan of the Ottoman Empire had at his disposal one of the world's great bureaucracies to govern a realm that extended from the Ukraine to the Sudan, from the Persian frontier to Tunis. His navy and his armies were far larger, better organized, and more easily replenished than the small forces of the Greeks. The latter could with difficulty raise 15,000 to 20,000 men, few of whom would move far from their homes; the sultan could raise four, five, or six times that number. He could wipe out communities with impunity—as he had in the past, with devastating consequences. This is why so many well-informed Greeks regarded the prospect of fighting as worse than foolish and why those who instigated the revolution promised anyone who would listen that the uprising was supported by the Russian czar. In fact, it was not, but the fiction bolstered what otherwise seemed a hopeless cause.

But while the czar hesitated, much of Europe was enraptured. It saw ancient heroes come back to life in the descendants who were emulating their achievements and displaying their virtues. The Greeks recognized this European obsession with the past and capitalized on it. Chieftains from the mountains of the Peloponnese were urged to rival Themistokles and Leonidas. The same more or less illiterate chieftains, through their educated young secretaries, made grandiloquent appeals to the peoples of Europe to help the new "Spartans" shake off the shackles of servitude. The talk of heroes was endless, part of that special appeal that the Greek cause held for educated men and women on both sides of the Atlantic. But there was always something slightly unreal about it too. One evening in 1825 a young English volunteer fighter in the mountains began declaiming Homer in the English fashion to the warriors he was spending the night with. He paused after a few lines. The chieftains were flummoxed: "What language is that?" one of them quietly asked.[11]

"My family came originally from Epirus: my father settled at Chios." Sketching the parameters of an unfamiliar Greek world for an English audience, this was the opening sentence of one of the literary sensations of 1819, the anonymously published novel entitled *Anastasius: or Memoirs of a Greek Written at the Close of the Eighteenth Century*. Its narrator is an antihero—an amoral young adventurer who impregnates a young woman and then flees his native island as he embarks on a picaresque odyssey through the world of the Ottoman Levant, changing identities and faiths with every voyage. Anastasius is a Greek deprived of the possibility of heroism precisely because he is degraded by servitude, a moral degeneration that he struggles to escape. When Byron was asked if he had written the tale, he replied he would have given two of his poems to have done so. It was soon revealed to be the work of the remarkable Anglo-Dutch banker Thomas Hope, a wealthy aesthete who had lived for several years in the Ottoman lands.

But it was not only Byron who was envious: Shelley, Delacroix, and Prince Metternich all devoured Hope's story. What made it so unusual was its portrayal of the Greeks in their contemporary Ottoman environment. The truth is that even more than today, Europeans at that time lived in the past where the Greeks were concerned, and travelers to the region took with them not a modern guidebook (there were none), but a fake ancient one, a bizarre eighteenth-century travelogue that purported to describe the journeyings of a young Scythian in the fourth century BC. *The Travels of the Young Anacharsis in Greece*, unlike *Anastasius*, has nothing to say about the dragomans, janissaries, imams, and pashas whom any real voyager was likely to encounter in some form. Early nineteenth-century maps, even the most precise, lived in the past in a similar way, using the classical place-names and mostly guessing at the layout of the mountainous interior that lay behind the region's neatly drawn coastlines. As the "Citoyen Grec," author of the pioneering 1826 *Résumé Géographique de la Grèce et de la Turquie d'Europe*, noted: "Of all the parts of Europe, it is Greece whose geography is the least known."[12]

Over the centuries, commerce and the Church had extended the Greek language and the reach of Orthodoxy far beyond the lands familiar to readers of the ancient classics. The "Citoyen Grec" states that Greece "must be considered, like Spain and Italy, as a great peninsula," and goes on to delineate an astonishingly large region stretching from Bosnia, the Danubian lands and the Black Sea in the north to Cape Matapan in the south: it is, in fact, the territory that later generations would call the Balkans. At the same time, an attentive reader may note a "little Greece" hidden inside his book as well, occupying a much smaller area around the city-states of classical antiquity. It was at the very northern limits of the vast Balkan "Greece," next to Russia, that the insurrection broke out first in February 1821, yet it was pledged to bring "freedom to the classical soil of Greece," and after the fighting fizzled out in the north it continued in those regions one thousand miles to the south, which eventually became the heartland of the new independent state.[13]

As this suggests, Greece's geographical extent was surprisingly indeterminate even in the minds of the Greeks themselves who did not in fact launch their uprising with very specific territorial demands in mind. They lived in a largely pre-national era, one shaped by the example of empire and inspired by the promise of redemption and deliverance rather than by land and boundaries. The peoples of the peninsula included not only Greeks but also Serbs and Albanians, Bosnians and Romanians, an assortment of Orthodox, Catholics, Muslims, and Jews. To call this enormous area Greece was less to pay homage to the past than to lay a kind of claim to an imagined future in which the Muslim Ottomans had been replaced by a new Christian domain. Could all these disparate peoples ever form part of Greece? Some Enlightenment radicals imagined that they could—even the Muslims. In 1797 the revolutionary Greek intellectual Rhigas Velestinlis had appealed to all the empire's inhabitants—"Bulgarians and Albanians, Armenians and *Romioi*, blacks and whites"—to fight for freedom under the sign of the cross. He defined the people "descended from the Greeks" as the inhabitants of "Rumeli, Asia Minor, the Mediterranean islands, Vlacho-Moldavia" and all those who suffered under the "unbearable tyranny" of the Ottoman despotism—"all, I say, Christians and Turks, without any distinction of religion (since all are made in God's image)."

Once the fighting broke out in 1821, however, the magnificently ecumenical horizons of Enlightenment republicanism vanished and faith became an existential dividing line. Indeed, one reason why the Greek war of independence reached levels of violence unseen in the other revolts in southern Europe was that it assumed at the outset the character of a religious clash. The educated Greeks who studied abroad and dreamed of Enlightenment might refer to their struggle in the terminology of a "revolution," but this was an elite vocabulary that reflected the influence of secular European republicanism and it had overlaid a much older and deeply entrenched popular oracular and prophetic tradition: it was this latter vein of Orthodoxy that spoke most directly to the ordinary illiterate villagers who rose up and fought.

For decades if not centuries, Christians under Ottoman rule had understood themselves to be waiting. Their bishops told them it was God's will that they endure the rule of a Muslim sultan—his punishment for their sins. Patience was a virtue; submission to the Ottomans was divinely enjoined. At some point in an ill-defined future, however, their waiting would come to an end and their yearning for freedom would be answered. What they longed for was the liberation of Constantinople, and through this the triumph of Christ and his true believers. Prophets preached the eventual overthrow of the sultan, a figure who embodied the twin principles of tyranny and the antichrist. Widely circulated oracular texts predicted intervention by the Russian czar, or by the allied Christian monarchs of Europe.

This great imagined moment was called the *romeïko* and it had been on the horizon of expectation for as long as people could remember. In the words of a folk song: "Let the *romeïko* take place, to end the tyranny." At some point in the decades preceding 1821, the idea of the *romeïko* made the all-important shift from being an event brought about solely by outside intervention to something that might conceivably involve the participation of ordinary Christians themselves. When the uprising began, therefore, it was widely identified with this long-awaited moment of political agency. A colloquial expression among the insurgent peasantry for what was happening in the spring of 1821 was thus that they were "making the *romeïko*." They did so in the belief that outside powers had made their decision and were on their side. "Francia [meaning Europe] supports the *romeïko*," a handbill claimed two days into the uprising. Letters went out to community elders assuring them that "the kings have decided to make the *romeïko*."[14]

The *romeïko* conveyed the triumph of Christ and the dream of the resurrection of imperial Byzantium through the overthrow of the sultan in Constantinople; it had nothing at all to do with the ancient Greece that so entranced Europe. In Paris, the great Enlightenment Greek savant Adamantios Korais had worked hard to popularize the terms "Hellene" and "Greek" (*Graikos*) among the literate classes, to wean Greeks off the Church and bring them back to the values of the ancients. For the word "Hellene" (*Ellinas*), which is how Greeks today generally refer to themselves, originally denoted the ancient Greeks exclusively. By far the commonest way Greek villagers referred to themselves before 1821 was as *Romioi*—meaning literally "Romans" but in fact simply Orthodox Christians. In some Orthodox eyes, the Hellenes were not fit ancestors for modern believers because they had been pagans, yet in the eyes of Europe and of Greece's intellectuals, they were the ancestors who mattered the most. Thanks above all to the educated young revolutionaries who drafted the hundreds of decrees, proclamations, and instructions that were the output of the wartime provisional governments, "Hellene" triumphed. As it lost its originally exclusive reference to the distant pagan past and came to refer to their descendants, the modern Greeks, so the uprising itself ceased to be seen as the fulfillment of the *romeïko* and came to be viewed as the resurrection of an ancient nation. It was the war itself that popularized this new vision of a political community, one based less on a shared allegiance to the patriarch of the empire and more upon genealogy. "You Greeks have something grand in your heads," the all-powerful Pasha of Jannina is said to have said to Christians in his service. "You no longer baptize your children Ioannis, Petros and Kostas but Leonidas, Themistocles and Aristides! You must be cooking up something." Thus what started out as the *romeïko* ended up as a struggle for the political independence of the Hellenes.[15]

Using the term "Greek" may not have been straightforward in the early 1820s, but the term "Turk" was even more problematic. Common in European parlance and in Greek as well, it was seldom used by Muslims inside the Ottoman Empire. A contemporary narrative of the uprising in the Morea written by an Ottoman official there, Yusuf el-Moravi, does not once mention the term. "Turk" might denote an Anatolian peasant but certainly not the Georgian ex-slave who was the first commander of the imperial forces in the Morea, Khurshid Pasha, nor the man he defeated, the Albanian Ali Pasha of Jannina. The so-called Turks fighting for the Ottoman armies included Egyptians, Bosnians and many who were not Muslims at all—Zaporozhian Cossack fishermen from the Danube, Catholic warriors from the Albanian highlands, conscripted Christians from Epiros. They even included Greeks.[16] Actually, to encounter men from Asia Minor was, for some Greeks, a surprising and noteworthy event. The siege of Patras, wrote one fighter, was the first time that they encountered "the eastern Turks." Christians and Muslims from the Peloponnese and Rumeli shared certain terms for these strangers—*chaldoupides, doudoumides,* and *kaklamanous*—that were unmistakably derogatory and marked them out as foreigners.[17]

Perhaps the most important thing to realize about the war of 1821 is that it was not really a two-way Greco-Turkish struggle at all: if one thing was perfectly obvious at the time, it was the exceptionally large and often decisive role played in the conflict by the Albanians, both Christian and Muslim. "I like the Albanians much," Byron had written in the winter of 1809 on a visit to their most prominent provincial ruler, Ali Pasha. "Some tribes are Christians, but their religion makes little difference in their manner or conduct; they are esteemed the best troops in the Turkish service." Byron had identified the two key features of the Albanians in this story—the relative unimportance of faith in determining their allegiances and their reputation as fighters. Their language was spoken over a swath of mountainous territory from Montenegro down into the Peloponnese by Catholics, Orthodox Christians, and Muslims alike, and it gave many so-called Greeks and Turks a common means of communication as well as a sense of solidarity reinforced by their shared experience of Ali Pasha's decades in power. After Ali was killed in 1822, some Albanians chose to serve the sultan and others went with the Greeks. Ottoman armies in the Balkans relied on Albanian units, both Christian and Muslim, and the Porte (the central government of the Ottoman Empire) fretted endlessly about their reliability. "They are such people that for five or ten *gurush* they can kill their own mothers and fathers," one Ottoman official reported. "It is impossible to expect service and loyalty from them."[18] On the Greek side, there were the Christian Albanian Souliot bands, hardened mountain fighters based around clan leaders who gradually became integrated into the national war effort. There were also the Albanian-speaking seamen of Hydra and Spetses who provided not only the core of the Greek fleet but also leading members of the Greek government—including one wartime president—who occasionally used Albanian among themselves to prevent others on their own side from reading their correspondence.[19]

In this pre-national world, language barriers were low and no one, a handful of intellectuals aside, worried about linguistic purity. A maritime folk, the Greeks spoke a language rich in words from Arabic, Spanish, Albanian, Turkish, and Slavic. At sea the strongest influence was Italian: they sailed the *gallotta*, *saccoleva* or the larger *briki* or *polacca* on which they might carry a *passangieris* or two along with their *karikon* (cargo), or they might go on the *kourso* (piracy) or fit out a dreaded *burloto* (fireship). On land, they relied on Turkish words like *ordi* (encampment), *loufes* (a soldier's wage), *tophanas* (arsenal), *toufeki* (rifle), or *tambouri* (entrenchment), which reflected the Ottoman martial tradition, with the occasional Italian term—*resalto* (assault), *incontro* (opportunity), or the *munitziones* (munitions) needed for an *ekspeditzion*—as a reminder of Venice's long hold over the region. In the hills of the Peloponnese in 1821, one found an astonishing assortment of titles borne by high-ranking fighters on the Greek side alone—*Izpravnik* (Russian-Romanian), *beïzade* (Turco-Persian), *Milord* (English), and *Prince* (French).[20]

The entire spectrum of Orthodox society within the Ottoman world was drawn into the fighting: princely families from Constantinople, deeply enmeshed in imperial court politics; provincial notables, martial bishops and revolutionary priests; polished young men dreaming of Rousseau and rough, semiliterate chieftains like Theodoros Kolokotronis, the charismatic brigand whose homespun skill with words, arms, and politicking smoothed his rise to become commander of the Greek armed forces in the Peloponnese. What is noteworthy is that none dominated either sociologically or individually. Indeed, after the revolution began contemporaries were struck by its failure to throw up a unifying personality—a Washington or a Napoleon. Leading figures flit across the stage for a minute and then vanish, while others suddenly emerge from obscurity. The man who led the initial uprising, Alexandros Ypsilantis, never set foot in the lands that eventually became independent Greece; the country's first monarch, Prince Otto of Bavaria, was six years old when the fighting began and arrived in his new kingdom at the age of seventeen after it was over. Kolokotronis and Karaïskakis—the two fighters most familiar to Greeks today—both played important roles, but the former followed his most remarkable exploits against the Turks by fomenting civil war while the latter actually worked with the Turks before going to war against them. Neither could be compared to Washington, who led his side's armies throughout their independence struggle and then became head of state.[21]

The landscapes against which the struggle played itself out were no less varied than the cast of characters. Athens became the new national capital in 1834 but nothing of much consequence happened in that small and rather unimportant Ottoman town until late in the war. The Peloponnese was the center of action for much of the time, and the heartland of the insurgency, but critical conflicts also took place in the Danubian Principalities, the mountains of Epiros, central Greece, and the Aegean. The densely populated Ionian Islands remained under quasi-colonial British rule throughout, a vital source of goods, manpower, intelligence, and money; Egypt was both the home of a rapidly growing Greek community and a key Ottoman ally. This was thus not so much a single war as a set of interconnected regional struggles where local topography, traditions, and power structures deeply affected events and only gradually converged. This book is structured accordingly, moving from the mountains and the islands to encompass the perspective from Vienna and Odessa, Marseille, Constantinople, London, Alexandria, St. Petersburg, and Paris—that variegated post-Napoleonic Europe which came to matter as much as, and sometimes a lot more than, anything that was going on in the heartlands of the Ottoman Empire.

By 1828 it was evident that the Greeks had wrested some kind of independence from the sultan. But exactly what the nature of that triumph was and when it was achieved would be argued over for decades. Servitude to the sultan and Islam ended. What the sultan had regarded as an absurdity—a Greek state—had emerged. The insurgency won the Greeks new political rights and religious freedoms. Yet it is surely telling that, while there is no real argument about when the rising began, historians do not agree on when it ended: some finish the story when Count Ioannis Capodistrias established his presidency in 1828 and secured European recognition; others opt for the establishment of the Bavarian monarchy and the arrival of the first king, Otto, in 1833. The fighter and historian George Finlay concluded that the rising ended with the revolution of 1843, which forced upon the monarchy one of the most democratic constitutions in Europe. The disagreement points to something important: for Greece the realization of independence was not instantaneous and lasted for years, if not decades. Freedom from Ottoman rule was one thing; securing national sovereignty was something quite different and took much longer to achieve. Indeed, in some ways the struggle continues to this day.

I started working on this book a decade ago, in the midst of a global debt crisis that saw Greece's economy placed under international surveillance. At that time it seemed as if the price for Greece's remaining in the Eurozone might well be the loss of its independence. Was Europe living through the end of the sovereign nation-state? What indeed was independence really and what had it meant for a country like Greece? Such questions pushed me to go back to the era when both Greece's and Europe's embrace of the nation-state began. The desire for freedom was age-old in 1821, but the aspiration to exercise freedom through a national government ruling in the name of its people was new. I wanted to understand how this aspiration had emerged, and in particular how national emancipation came, from the very start, to be bound up with capitalism in the form of foreign loans, international indebtedness, and financial speculation.

Twenty-first-century Greece was already impoverished by austerity when it was faced with another challenge: the refugee crisis. In 2013,

3,485 refugees were granted asylum there; the number rose to over 46,000 in 2016 and over 80,000 three years later. Having lived through the *katastrofi* of 1922—when hundreds of thousands had been forced to flee Asia Minor—as well as the vast internal displacements of the civil war of the late 1940s, the Greeks were as familiar as any in Europe with what it means to lose your home and make a new life elsewhere. A century before the *katastrofi*, Greece itself had emerged from a conflict that had uprooted perhaps one-quarter of the entire population of the Peloponnese alone. The tragic aftermath of the siege of Mesolonghi, when thousands of Greek women and children had been sold into slavery, galvanized the sympathies of Europe. It was such upheavals as much as any victories that not only accompanied the end of Ottoman rule but—by throwing people out of their older, more settled ways of life—created a new kind of political community around the resources and policies of a centralized national state.

The wider role and responsibilities of the historian in telling this story were brought home when the Greek prime minister Kyriakos Mitsotakis established a committee to oversee the impending bicentennial of the revolution and shape its commemoration. A government spokesman talked about using the celebrations to help restore pride in the country, encouraging Greeks to reconnect with their national identity.[22] When I first read about this initiative in the papers, I confess I remembered how a century earlier, in 1921, a Central Committee for the Centennial of the Greek Revolution had met and come up with any number of ideas before being overtaken by the Asia Minor disaster and completely forgotten.[23] More worryingly, conservatives in France in particular had been going on for years about the need for a new national narrative that would restore pride in the country and its past, and in the French case this had turned into a kind of right-wing rationale for exclusion and excision. Historians mostly see themselves as a profession dedicated to dispelling nationalist myths, not propping them up. So when I was asked to join the committee, my initial reaction was to hesitate. But then I thought again: was it unreasonable—given the divisions that had opened up in Greece as a result of the years of austerity—to try to figure out what might bring people together in an understanding of the past that was inclusionary not exclusionary? Was that not better than acquiescing in the kind of political polarization that had torn Greece apart in the past?

If this invitation thus made me reassess my stance toward the subject, what I really wanted to say about it became evident only during the coronavirus pandemic. Living in Manhattan at an epicenter of the catastrophe, I followed Greece's response in those first months, which formed such a contrast to that of the United States. The two governments could scarcely have taken more different approaches. But the real differences lay deeper. There is nothing like a public health emergency to illuminate the degree of a people's trust in their state. The pandemic revealed the US to be a starkly divided country whose attitude to government is in profound crisis. In Greece, on the other hand, the state was able to enforce one of the most pervasive lockdowns in Europe because people trusted it and were willing to go along. Greek society turned out to be capable of enduring things that American society could not; it was remarkably resilient—as indeed arguably it had been throughout all the immense challenges of the past decade.

As in fact it had been two centuries earlier. I started to see that the revolution of 1821 had succeeded because beyond the epic and oft-celebrated moments of individual bravery and self-sacrifice, it was fundamentally a story of social endurance in the face of systemic upheaval. It was not so much their victories that gave the Greeks independence as it was their refusal to accept defeat. This was because what we call a war was in fact an insurgency in which all the weaker side could really do was to hold out and hope. The promised assistance from Russia never materialized, yet the struggle went on for year after year. The strength of the ordinary villagers and islanders—who faced not only the incursions of Turkish and Egyptian armies but constant plundering and pillaging by their own armed countrymen—was the vital element. To go beyond the heroes is important, then, not to suggest that they had feet of clay, but to give a fuller picture of the forces that the uprising set in motion and which propelled it forward. The wartime commander Makriyannis put it best, at the conclusion of his memoirs:

> Do you know when a man should say "I"? When he has fought alone, and either created or destroyed, then he may say "I." But when many people have fought and created, then let them say "we."[24]

PART 1

IN THE
GREAT MORNING
OF THE WORLD

In the Great Morning of the World
The Spirit of God with might unfurled
The flag of Freedom over chaos,
And all its banded Anarchs fled . . .

Percy Bysshe Shelley, *Hellas: A Lyrical*
Drama (1821), lines 46–9[1]

1

OUT OF RUSSIA

In my opinion, the French revolution and Napoleon opened the eyes of the world. Before that the nations did not recognize themselves, and people thought kings were gods on earth and said whatever they did was good. For that reason, it is harder to rule a people today.

Theodoros Kolokotronis, *Apomnimonevmata*, 49

3 403α3αη9ωγηα3α23 *(The decision has been taken!)*
Anthimos Gazis, February 22, 1821[1]

It all started with the defeat of Napoleon. In 1814, after more than two decades of war across Europe, the French emperor was sent into exile on Elba while the victors celebrated and prepared to convene the peace congress in Vienna that would settle the fate of the continent. Czar Alexander I, ruler of Russia and commander of Europe's largest army, was staying in his mother-in-law's castle at Bruchsal en route to the Austrian capital when, at the end of a day filled with formal presentations and heavy meals, he enjoyed a quiet tête-à-tête with one of his wife's maids of honor. "Since you treat me with such kindness, Sire, I owe you my profession of faith," Roxandra Stourdza told him. "In the depth of my soul, I am a republican, I detest courts and have never attached the slightest importance to those distinctions of rank and birth that give me the chills and bore me to death. But please don't betray my secret here or I could pay dearly." "No, no," the czar replied with a smile. "Have no fear. And to return frankness with frankness . . . *I think absolutely as you do.*"[2]

The men he was about to meet in Vienna would have been horrified at the thought that the czar of Russia was a closet republican. The presiding genius of the Congress, Prince Metternich of Austria, saw the threat of subversion everywhere, and regarded monarchy as the chief defense against it. Castlereagh, the British Foreign Secretary, took legitimism so far that he refused to sign the treaty ending the war on the grounds that Napoleon was a usurper. Between them, these two men were determined to impose a conservative order upon a continent convulsed by the French Revolution. Neither of them had much time for talk of the rights of peoples or nations. Defending the erasure of the centuries-old republic of Genoa from the map of Europe against the evident wishes of its inhabitants, Castlereagh pronounced that "the prejudices of a people" could be taken into account only if "greater objects did not stand in their way."[3]

In reality, the czar was no republican either. At Vienna he and his fellow monarchs returned ousted Bourbon monarchs to their thrones, put the Catholic Belgians under the Dutch king, abolished the ancient republic of Venice and dashed hopes that Poland might be resurrected as an independent state. At the same time, he wanted a settlement that would uphold the "sacred rights of humanity," and unlike Metternich, he sought to be liked rather than feared. "That boy is a mass of contradictions," his grandmother, Catherine the Great, is said to have remarked. Having come to the throne in the midst of the Napoleonic Wars, Alexander insisted that defeating the French required a higher moral purpose. He fought for constitutional rule in the Ionian Islands and Sardinia, he recognized the Spanish constitution in 1812, and he favored imposing one on the Bourbons in France. His sensitive soul thrilled with the idea that he was destined to bring peace to Europe and he listened to Germany's leading mystics who told him that he was a kind of messiah and that his defeat of the antichrist Bonaparte would lead the continent under Russian guidance to a spiritual rebirth. This conviction crystallized in his extraordinary scheme for Christian monarchs to band together in a Holy Alliance.[4]

At Vienna the czar felt in need of a soulmate, someone who understood his own blend of piety and Enlightenment rationalism, a man who would help him, as he saw it, fight for constitutionalism and stand up to Metternich and his more reactionary instincts. He had been impressed by a brilliant young Greek-born diplomat in his entourage, and so he ordered him to join the negotiations: it was thus that the thirty-eight-year-old Ioannis Capodistrias entered the limelight at the Congress, becoming deeply involved in crafting the post-Napoleonic future for Europe (and—years later—the first president of independent Greece). "Two factions are opposing each other all over the world," Metternich said, "the Capodistrias and the Metternichs."[5] The two men were agreed that the coalition of states that had won the war should guarantee the coming peace. But they differed on the nature of that peace and the principles that would help it endure: Metternich believed the radical forces unleashed by the French across Europe must be vigorously combatted and suppressed; Capodistrias felt they should be understood. "This war has not been fought by sovereigns but by nations," he told an interlocutor shortly after his arrival in Vienna. "Since Napoleon has been tumbled from power, one has forgotten the interest of nations and been concerned solely with the interest of princes."[6]

One reason for Capodistrias's sensitivity to the power of nationalism was that he hailed from the Ionian Islands, where a largely Greek-speaking population had been ruled by the Venetians for centuries before enjoying a brief period of self-rule under joint Russian-Ottoman occupation. Founded in 1800, during the Napoleonic Wars, the so-called Septinsular Republic was effectively the first independent Greek state in modern times, only nominally subservient to the Ottoman sultan. Capodistrias's father, a member of the Corfiot aristocracy, had helped craft its constitution before the son took over the task of making it work, a task that brought him into contact with a range of Greek patriots including bishops, scholars, merchants, and armed fighters who had fled the Ottoman mainland for the safety of the islands. After the French dissolved the Septinsular Republic, Capodistrias left his native island of Corfu and entered Russian service, but he retained his contacts with these men and shared their dreams of freedom. When the czar summoned him to Vienna in 1814, Capodistrias openly wondered whether his ties to the Greeks might not be problematic. "I respect your feelings for your fatherland and for Greece," Alexander reassured him. "And it is because I know how you feel that I wish to have you close by. Nothing could be more appropriate nor more useful than that the Greeks have you near me as their advocate."[7]

Russo-Ottoman antagonism had been building up for more than half a century. Even during their common struggle against the French, the two empires had gone to war, barely patching things up on the eve of

Napoleon's invasion of Russia in 1812. The last thing the other powers wanted after Napoleon's defeat was more discord, and Metternich and Castlereagh sought to get Sultan Mahmud II to join them in Vienna at the Congress so that his differences with Russia could be settled peacefully. But the sultan refused—remaining adamantly opposed to any European intervention, however well intended, in his own internal affairs for the next decade and more. His refusal meant that the great powers could not bring the Ottoman lands within the territorial guarantee they planned to provide for the European political settlement; the next best solution, from the British and Austrian viewpoint, was to ensure no official discussion of the Ottoman Empire in Vienna at all.[8]

Metternich did his best to keep the subject off limits. His police blocked the emissaries of subject peoples of the Ottoman Balkans from coming to Vienna. They also attempted to suppress a pamphlet by a German professor that called for Europe's armies to drive the Turks out of Europe. But the Austrians could not prevent a good deal of talk of Christian solidarity with the Serbs, the Greeks, and others. Reports of "scenes of carnage" in Ottoman Serbia were reaching the capital. As for the Greeks, their supporters were in Vienna in force, seeing the Congress as a chance to bring their plight to the attention of Europe. There were salons and memoranda and speeches. Exiled archbishops pleaded for Russian assistance. Richard Church, a British army officer who had trained Greek fighters in the Ionian Islands, told anyone who would listen about the "free men" ready to "defend their liberty against the Turks." Russians in the imperial delegation sympathized. Their empire had been expanding southward at Ottoman expense for decades and they were happy to use Orthodox solidarity as a reason to continue: their army had seen off Napoleon and was not likely to be checked by the sultan's. Austrian secret police reported that the Russians were speaking like "Masters of the Universe": "They inflame the Greeks again and make them hope for their resurrection . . . The Greeks abandon themselves to these ideas . . . Several leading figures speak of the liberation of Epiros, Morea, and a Greek fatherland which Russia will ensure is reborn."[9]

The truth of the matter was that, whatever the Greeks dreamed the czar would do for them, their liberation came a long way down his list of priorities. In Vienna, Alexander's overriding priority was to hold together the wartime coalition that had defeated Napoleon. He understood that none of his partners shared the Russian receptiveness to the cause of the fellow Orthodox Christians in the Ottoman lands, and his basic view therefore was that the peace congress was not the right place to help the Greeks. When Capodistrias begged him to consider bringing the Ionian Islands back under Russian protection, the czar refused: British troops had taken them over and he had no wish to antagonize allies. The only support he was willing to give was on a much smaller scale. Alexander patronized a new learned society—the Friends of the Muses— that Capodistrias established for the cultural improvement of the Greeks, and the czar attended Sunday service in a Greek Orthodox church in Vienna that was used by Christian worshippers from the Ottoman lands. When his presence there was applauded, however, Alexander became upset that what he had intended as a private gesture of support had been misinterpreted.

In Vienna, diplomacy and social display were intertwined as never before. "Doubtless, at no time of the world's history had more grave and complex interests been discussed amidst so many fêtes," remembered one of those present. "A kingdom was cut into bits or enlarged at a ball: an indemnity was granted in the course of a dinner; a constitution was planned during a hunt." It was in this glamorous milieu that Capodistrias and the czar set up their Greek cultural society. Yet for the Greeks what did all the courtly glitz, the gossip and chatter really matter when Metternich was to be heard bluntly saying that he recognized no such thing as a Greek nation, only Ottoman subjects? The czar was not willing to jeopardize the coalition to counter him because his fear of revolution trumped his sense of Christian solidarity. It dawned upon the Greeks of the Ottoman Empire that they could not look to Europe's leaders for liberation and it was at this point that a group of them, hundreds of miles away from the Habsburg capital, decided to take matters into their own hands.[10]

"'Athena Gallery' is a modern shopping center in the heart of Odessa," a Ukrainian tourist website informs visitors to the Black Sea port. "On seven floors there are more than 200 shops, services and restaurants. The shopping center is located in the heart of the city, close to Deribasovskaya Street with a convenient access to the center, underground parking and excellent transport interchange at any time of the day or night." The mall's name, its well-preserved neoclassical facade (now dwarfed by a multistory glass addition), and its address on Hrets'ka—Greek

Square—indicate that this is where the original Greek market was built at the start of the nineteenth century, when the town was in its infancy, a product of the Russian Empire's push south to the Black Sea. A far cry from the splendors of imperial Vienna and a tenth its size, Odessa in 1820 was a settlement less than three decades old and based on the coming and going of goods. The Greek market was in its commercial center, amid importers' stores where carts transported dried fruits, olive oil, walnuts and tobacco, salted fish, carob, incense, and wine the short distance to and from the port.

In a tree-lined street in the shadow of the mall, a row of three modest early nineteenth-century town houses survives to this day. The middle one has the layout commonly found in the neighborhood—a ground-floor shop, an entrance to the inner courtyard to unload goods, and residential rooms upstairs with a balcony overlooking the street. It was here, at number 18 Krasni Perulok, then owned by a prosperous Greek merchant, that "some Greeks of very obscure class" banded together at the end of 1814 to found a fraternal society of their own. Humbler than its illustrious Vienna equivalent, their Filiki Etaireia (Friendly Society) would turn out to be the catalyst for Europe's first successful national revolution, ultimately forcing kings and diplomats to change their entire approach to the management of the European peace.[11]

They were just three men at the start: a commercial clerk, a former student, and an artisan, whose lives until then had been nothing but stops and starts. Emmanouil Xanthos was a merchant's factor from the island of Patmos, who had been traveling in the Balkans when he joined the Freemasons and was inspired to found a similar organization in Odessa to bring Greeks together to work for the overthrow of Ottoman tyranny. Athanasios Tsakalof, the son of a fur trader based in Moscow, had studied in Paris and joined a Greek cultural society there before coming to Russia for work. Nikolaos Skoufas was a hatmaker. The three of them may not have been rich but they were literate, well traveled, and politically engaged. When they met in late 1814, they were upset about the Congress of Vienna. They knew about the German professor calling for a European war against the Ottomans and they were outraged that Metternich had not only tried to suppress that pamphlet but had also had the effrontery to deny the Greeks were "to be found in the catalog of nations." Faced with the prospect that Europe would henceforth oppose revolution of any kind, Xanthos, Tsakalof, and Skoufas agreed to try to "gather the select and brave men of the race so that they could work, by themselves, to gain that which they vainly hoped to receive, over so many years, from the philanthropy of Christian kings." To work for their own liberation: that was the vital decision.[12]

That these three men met in Odessa was scarcely an accident. Thanks to the 1774 Treaty of Kuchuk-Kainardji, the Russian Empire had acquired a recognition of its interest in the treatment of Orthodox populations in the Ottoman lands. Moreover, Catherine the Great, Czar Alexander I's strong-willed grandmother, had been obsessed with the Greeks. She had named a new summer palace after Alexander the Great's birthplace to inspire her elder grandson. She dreamed of his younger brother sitting on the throne in Constantinople; she built a replica of its great Byzantine church, Ayia Sofia, on the grounds of her estate at Tsarskoe Selo, and she also provided support for the Greeks under Ottoman rule as well: it is as though, ancient or modern, to Catherine the Greeks were one. "The empress discoursed with me the other day on the ancient Greeks; of their alacrity and the superiority of their genius, and the same character being still extant in the modern ones," wrote the English ambassador in 1779.[13] Once Russia conquered the Crimea, that entire region was wrested from Ottoman rule. Establishing a vast new southern province of New Russia—an area larger than France—the government welcomed settlers, among them many families from the Greek islands, with free land, subsidies, and tax exemptions. A small Tatar village on the Black Sea became the new settlement of Odessa, whose population grew tenfold in three decades. By the late 1820s it numbered over 30,000 and was expanding quickly. It was a place, wrote the young Alexander Pushkin, where "everything breathes Europe." A city of foreigners, on its way to becoming the third-largest city of the empire, Odessa was an astounding commercial success and the Greek community was at its heart.[14]

Capodistrias had excelled in the imperial service but he was by no means alone: the governor of Bessarabia was a fellow Greek, for example, and so was the chief of police in St. Petersburg. "Christian Orthodox, Greek by birth, faithful subject and—I dare say—devoted servant of the Emperor": these words summed up their overlapping allegiances. Members of Greek princely families who had fled Ottoman rule and found refuge in the czar's service included the czarina's aforementioned maid of honor, Roxandra Stourdza, granddaughter of a former imperial Dragoman and *hospodar* (governor) of Moldavia; her brother, Alexander, a diplomat who served as Capodistrias's secretary; and a dashing young aide to the czar, Prince Alexander Ypsilantis, who had lost his right arm fighting the French at Dresden. When the czar prayed in the Greek church in Vienna—a church founded by Stourdza's family—they were all in attendance, Capodistrias and Ypsilantis sitting with the Greeks, their noble faces displaying a melancholy, recalled Stourdza, "that seemed to foretell the misfortunes and future destiny of Greece."[15]

Lower down the social scale but no less wealthy or powerful in Russian society were the Greek merchants who spearheaded the expansion of imperial power into the south, many of them self-made men who were dominant in the grain trade that fueled Odessa's growth. A Greek hero of Russia's 1769 war with the Ottomans, the sea captain Ioannis Varvakis made a fortune exporting caviar from the Caspian Sea and later spent it bankrolling the Greek cause: it was in the monastery that Varvakis built at Taganrog that the funeral service for Czar Alexander would be held after his untimely death there in 1825. Greeks from all kinds of backgrounds came to Russia to find riches and even when they did not, they found something else: a new political consciousness. One village boy from the Peloponnese was packed off to Bessarabian Kishinev by his worried parents at the age of fifteen to enter a trading house and keep out of trouble. When he returned home seven years later, he looked like a European: he was speaking Russian and wearing European dress and scouting out the state of Ottoman fortifications for the Etaireia. Later he became one of the foremost chroniclers of the Greek uprising.[16]

Being in Russia thus helped to foster a sense of Greek national allegiance. As often happens with emigrants from peasant societies, it was in their new home that they ceased to talk solely about their native village or island as their "fatherland" and heard the term used instead to describe a community uniting all those who spoke the same language and worshipped in the same church. Regional pride was strong but so increasingly was something closer to a modern sense of national belonging. In Odessa there were Greek neighborhoods with their own schools, churches, benevolent societies and theater; the first modern Greek drama, *The Death of Demosthenes*, was staged in 1818, followed by a ballet, *The Souliots at Jannina*. This newly expansive sense of identity coursed through a commercial network that connected the Greeks of southern Russia not only with the Danubian Principalities and the Ottoman

Aegean, but with trading houses established across Europe and Asia. According to an English traveler writing from Odessa in 1821: "The Greeks are very intelligent and artful; they have agents of their own country in all parts to which they trade; they form, as it were, one large family and manage to lay their neighbors under contribution."[17]

There was from the start a close connection between the world of trade and the workings of the Etaireia. It is not just that many of its members—a majority, in fact—were in commerce, and often victims of its uncertainties. It is also that the business life provided them with useful cover. When the Etaireia sent a man abroad to recruit among Greeks in the Arab lands, for instance, his journeying from Constantinople to Egypt and Cyprus appeared to be a normal commercial voyage. Business provided them with a ready-made secret language. "Friend," the usual term of solidarity within the Etaireia, was a common way of referring to business associates. One of the leadership wrote about the need to prepare for the coming "great fair" (*panayiri*: the uprising) and itemized the areas "supplied with sufficient products to bring to market" when he was really talking about the recruitment of armed men ready to fight. Code names, encrypted messages, and jargon were all adapted from the world of commerce to the needs of conspiracy. Armed forces (*stratevmata*) were "accounts" (*logariasmoi*); war (*polemos*) "balance sheet" (*bilantzon*); commercial vessels were "camels" and large ships "elephants." The czar was "the Philanthropist" (*Filanthropos*), the family of Napoleon were "the Blessed" (*Makaritai*), the patriarch was "the Most Ancient" (*Palaioteros*), and the sultan was "Apathetic" (*Apathis*). Peoples got code names too: the Serbs were "Failures" (*Apotychontes*), the Italians "Sweet" (*Glykeis*), the Turks "Foreign Residents" (*Metoikoi*), the Muslim Albanians "Relatives by Marriage" (*Sympetheroi*).[18]

Within the Etaireia, whose members recognized one another by secret signs, there was a hierarchical brotherhood, entirely male (women were not permitted to join) and exclusive, in the sense that in theory at least members were not permitted to join other organizations. In its structure it resembled the Freemasons; in its liturgy it was heavily impregnated with the atmosphere of the church and indeed a priest was supposed to supervise the oath of membership. The lowest grade of the so-called *Adelfopoiton* (Fraternized) was for the "simple and the illiterate"; members of the second grade, the *Systemenon* (Recommended Ones), knew little more than that the goal of the society was "the improvement of the fatherland." Only the *Iereis* (Priests) and *Poimenes* (Shepherds), the third and fourth grades, could recruit others into the movement: they knew that "the society is formed of genuine Greeks who are lovers of the fatherland and it is named the Filiki Etaireia. Their purpose is the improvement of the nation (*ethnos*) and, if God permits, their liberty." Yet there was nothing to indicate how this was to be achieved, nor any more precise articulation of the political goal.[19] Membership of the Etaireia's Supreme Authority (*Anotati Archi*) was a closely guarded secret. Lesser ranks were given to understand that it was led by men of great eminence, perhaps even by the czar himself. In fact, it was a collective of varying size—generally about eight or nine— of the earliest and most trusted members. But the secret was functional: it allowed all kinds of rumors to flourish about who was backing them, and it gave the entire organization a mystique. As one recalled: "some believed [the Supreme Authority's] headquarters was in Russia, others in France, England, America and elsewhere."[20]

The Freemasons were the major secret society of late eighteenth-century Europe. But after Napoleon's defeat many new clandestine and conspiratorial organizations arose with avowedly constitutionalist or revolutionary political aims. There was the Italian *Carbonari*, whose name sent shivers down the spines of Bourbon loyalists; there were also numerous long-forgotten shadowy groupings—the *Patrioti Europei*, the *Charbonnerie*, the *Filadelfi*, the *Decisi*, the *Cavalieri Guelfi*, the *Indipendentisti*—not to mention the imaginary ones, like the secret Egyptian sect said to be operating in the Ionian Islands and stirring up mischief. To Chancellor Metternich, and to the secret policemen under him on the lookout for any sign of "the tumultuous spirit of the century," they all formed part of a vast network aimed at troubling the "tranquility of Europe" with "the fantastic project of national independence." The Etaireia had no contacts with any of these, despite what Metternich and others later assumed, but it shared with them a revolutionary disposition and dramaturgy, a skill at underground political work and a capacity to alarm the powerful. It was certainly not the largest of them— the Carbonari had probably more than ten times the membership—but the Etaireia was, out of them all, far and away the most successful.[21]

These secret societies were in turn an aspect of a fundamental feature of the politicization of European culture after 1815—the rise of mass politics through associations and societies of all kinds, most of them highly visible and perfectly respectable yet engaged in shaping a new force that was ultimately even more threatening to Metternich and the Holy Alliance than underground radicals: public opinion. Alongside abolitionism, it was the cause of Greece that was to reveal for the first time in modern history the transformative international power of public opinion expressed in print and fueled through associational life.[22]

Not a few of these new societies were driven by the European infatuation with the Greeks, as the examples of Capodistrias's Society of Friends of the Muses suggested. Europe's new archaeological museums, learned societies, antiquarians, philologists, and political philosophers all testified to the wide impact of Hellenism. In the Ottoman lands, too, schools disseminated Enlightenment learning among the Greeks of the empire, with remarkable effectiveness. The erudite Dimitrios Galanos, who went out to Dacca and Bombay and became a pioneering scholar of Sanskrit, acquired his philological expertise from nowhere more illustrious than schools in Ottoman Athens, Mesolonghi, and Patmos. Anthimos Gazis started out as a poor village boy studying logic, science, and philosophy at a school in Ottoman Zagora. In Vienna, where he attended the Congress, he preached in the Greek church, helped run the Greek cultural society founded by Capodistrias and the czar, wrote articles and translated learned works before returning to his homeland in Thessaly to teach. Such men contributed to the revival of learning in the Ottoman lands but they also did something more: they popularized the idea that Greece might one day be reborn as a political community.[23]

Between the respectable learned and cultural societies on the one hand, and the revolutionaries in the Filiki Etaireia on the other, the differences ran deeper however than simply an opposition between public and clandestine. Some, like Gazis, bridged the two. But for most there was a real difference of outlook. The cultural societies tended to disseminate the learning of the Enlightenment and reflected its secularism and its endless absorption with the ancients. The Etaireia was immersed in the world of Orthodoxy and spoke to the literature of prophecy and eschatology that circulated among believers and foretold a coming cosmic struggle with the forces of the antichrist and the eventual triumph of Christianity over Islam. The two kinds of societies thus differed sharply in their sense of the time that would be needed to bring about real change: the scholars and intellectuals placed their trust in cultural transformation and believed it would take years and perhaps decades before the Greeks were ready for freedom. They feared haste and worried at the cost in blood of those "untimely and irrational enthusiasms" that could bring "the greatest harm to the fatherland." The radicals did not worry—all that mattered, to use the metaphor then in vogue, was getting the machine to move: "The means we have today are enough. The machine, after all, is perfected! Nothing is needed now beyond someone starting it up, and then it will work by itself." They were confident, in the words of a newspaper of 1820, that "our age is one of miracles and we must be prepared for any eventuality."[24] The clash between these two approaches would not end even with the outbreak of the uprising itself.[25]

No sooner had the three Greeks set up their secret group in Odessa than Skoufas and Tsakalof left for Moscow while Xanthos took a boat to Constantinople, where he found a job as a merchant clerk. Before going their various ways, they gave each other coded initials. But there was no real program, nor any plan of organization, and their preliminary recruitment efforts were greeted with disdain: the prosperous Moscow merchants Skoufas approached made it clear they wanted nothing to do with him. In fact, when Skoufas and Tsakalov later returned to Odessa and chose the name Filiki Etaireia (Friendly Society) for their secret organization, they had fewer than twenty members, mostly traders, sea captains, and sailors who had fallen on hard times. One described himself as "a bankrupt merchant." "The fall in the price of wheat has ruined me," wrote another. "As long as commerce is dead, I am ruined," stated a third. "The reason I am not at sea is that I owe 10,000 grosia and can't find work to pay my debt off." By 1817 only forty-two had joined up, many of them jobless; revolution was no nearer.[26]

Things had not progressed far when a smooth-talking dandy from Ithaca, dressed in the uniform of the Ionian National Guard, appeared in Odessa. Making little effort at discretion and claiming noble ancestry and kinship with Capodistrias himself, Nikolaos Galatis talked himself into the Etaireia inner circle and then headed north to meet the Russian foreign minister. Capodistrias formed an instantly unfavorable impression of the young adventurer. No sooner had Galatis begun to describe the Etaireia and his hope that Capodistrias would lead it than the furious minister cut him short:

You must be out of your senses, Sir, to dream of such a project. No one could dare communicate such a thing to me in this house, where I have the honour to serve a great and powerful sovereign, except a young man like you, straight from the rocks of Ithaca and carried away by some sort of blind passion . . . The only advice I can give you is . . . to return immediately where you have come from, and to tell those who sent you that unless they want to destroy themselves and their innocent and unhappy nation with them, they must abandon their revolutionary course and continue to live as before under their present governments until Providence decrees otherwise.[27]

Under Capodistrias's orders, the Russian police deported Galatis across the river Pruth into the Ottoman province of Moldavia, where the Russian consul was instructed to keep an eye on him.[28] Over the coming months, Galatis proselytized widely and somewhat indiscriminately in Moldavia and neighboring Wallachia, bringing many new members into the Etaireia in a fashion that would be vital to its future course. At the same time, he behaved in ways that alarmed the founders. Strutting one day down the main street in the Moldavian capital, Jassy in a Russian officer's uniform, Galatis accosted the passengers of a carriage that he claimed had bothered him as it drove past. When they protested, he snatched the whip from the hands of the coachman and began to beat them. That his victims were from prominent Moldavian families only angered him the more, and he told them in no uncertain terms that "they ought to know that those who went on foot were much better than they were."[29] The anecdote highlights not just Galatis's quick temper and vanity but more importantly the tension generated within the hierarchical world of Ottoman Christianity—with its landed elite, its peasants and its emerging middle classes—by the dawn of an entirely new kind of political association, one premised on radical ideas of self-sacrifice, individual agency, and equality in the cause of national rebirth.

When Capodistrias mentioned his meeting with Galatis to the czar, it appears to have been the first time either of them had heard about the Etaireia and they worried that it could lead to "catastrophe" for the Christians under Ottoman rule. Eventually, however, they concluded they could do little and Capodistrias confined himself to writing to prominent Greeks in the Russian lands, warning them off the conspirators.[30] Meanwhile Galatis—"loose-tongued, restless in his mind and greedy for money"—was creating confusion. When he came to Constantinople to see the Etaireia leadership, he started making wild demands and threatened to betray them to the Ottoman authorities. These were men who took their oath seriously, and their security too, and after much soul-searching and efforts to get him to change his ways, they sent him off on a mission to the Peloponnese where, entirely unsuspecting, he was eventually shot at close range by one of his companions in a deserted spot near some ruins on the coast. He took fifteen minutes to die, while his assassin sat by him in tears, bemoaning the behavior that had led Galatis to such an awful end. The Etaireia might have been small but its leaders were passionately committed men. On a commemorative plaque in Galatis's home village on Ithaca are engraved what were supposedly his last words: "What did I do to you?"[31]

It was in 1818 when the society's base of operations shifted to the Ottoman capital that its operations were suddenly transformed. A newly recruited well-off Constantinople merchant called Panayiotis Sekeris took matters in hand and found himself effectively running the organization. The want of an orderly centralized administration had led to accusations of corruption and chaos. Sekeris entered details of the new recruits and their contributions; he tracked finances; he stopped attempts at extortion and blackmail. It was Sekeris who gave the Etaireia entrée into the wealthy Greek society of the Ottoman capital, recruiting some powerful figures from the Peloponnese in particular, and Sekeris who funded it so extensively that he eventually impoverished himself. When one of the founders, Skoufas, died penniless at the age of thirty-nine, it was Sekeris who paid for the funeral.[32]

The Etaireia's move to the very heart of the Ottoman state was a sign of remarkable confidence, and Sekeris's administrative reforms were backed by an ambitious and extensive recruiting drive. Before his death, Skoufas had suggested appointing so-called apostles to different regions and the obvious candidates—a number of outstanding Greek *kapetans* with military experience—now presented themselves. They were soldiers, veterans of the Napoleonic Wars, who had fought for the Russians in the Ionian Islands and had come to Russia to collect their wages. Capodistrias himself knew them: they had originally come to see him, and he warned them off the Etaireia and urged them to stay in Russia. But they headed south and joined it anyway. To the leadership of the Etaireia they came as a godsend, as "apostles"—a title with both

Christian and Jacobin associations—and they began to recruit very effectively in the Greek lands.

One powerful figure who joined as a result of their efforts was Petros Mavromihalis, the so-called Bey of the Mani, whose rule over the remote rocky peninsula in the south of the Peloponnese gave the Etaireia a potential base for its future operations. Less powerful but equally important later on was Theodoros Kolokotronis, a well-known former *kleft* (brigand) in exile on Zakynthos since 1806, who would end up returning to the Peloponnese and becoming the revolutionary commander there. The apostle Anagnostaras is reckoned to have recruited nearly fifty men, among them Kolokotronis; the latter in turn recruited perhaps as many as eleven, including several of his numerous godsons. One of them, a young watchmaker from Tripolitsa, claims he recruited twenty more. The numbers may be mythical but it was in this fashion that the Etaireia's influence spread rapidly into the Peloponnese, the Aegean, Epiros, and the Ionian Islands, while the northern Balkans, Egypt, and Italy were also brought into the net. A polished young Russian diplomat of Greek descent became the apostle for Russia, opening up the upper echelons of Russo-Greek society. Sekeris's register shows that 168 new members joined in 1818 and over 330 the following year. By 1821 most of the wealthy merchants of southern Russia were donating to the cause and there were so many new members that protocols were no longer being observed, central leadership could not track everyone and secrecy was becoming unsustainable. "I began to bring every Greek into the Filiki Etaireia," recalled one. "Within twenty-four hours it was known to all the Greeks in Odessa and they came to my room and I swore in as many as came."[33]

Perhaps because it was easy to confuse the Friendly Society with the very different Society of Friends of the Muses that Capodistrias had founded in Vienna in 1814—a confusion that may have been deliberately fostered when the Etaireia's founders chose its name—Russia's foreign minister was widely believed to be the Etaireia's leader. Indeed, the assumption that the Etaireia was backed by the czar and the Russian state was largely responsible for its success. Neither Capodistrias nor the czar seem to have felt they could do much about these rumors. They were much more concerned about conspiratorial activities within the Russian army and the czar for one probably cared little about what the Greeks were doing. Capodistrias, who cared more, was keeping an eye on their activities. One of his aides was an Etairist; and Capodistrias's older brother on Corfu joined up.[34] Yet although he was on close terms with many members, Capodistrias himself was always extremely careful to keep his distance and to remain faithful to the czar, and we have many indications that he advised Greeks to avoid joining the Etaireia and no evidence that he ever encouraged them. When the Etairist founder Xanthos tried to get him to change his mind and accept the leadership, he got nowhere.[35]

There was, however, another leadership option for the Etairists—a Greek officer of elevated birth who was an aide-de-camp to the czar and whose name had already been circulating as a possible alternative. This was the aforementioned Prince Alexander Konstantinovich Ypsilantis, who had been in Vienna with Capodistrias and the czar and was well known to them both. A man of action rather than a diplomat, Ypsilantis possessed the ideal résumé—aristocratic, revolutionary, and military, he was well respected by his fellow officers in the Russian army. His family were Phanariot nobility—one of those enormously wealthy Greek princely families who had for decades occupied the most senior positions open to Christians in the service of the sultan. His father had been the Ottoman governor, *hospodar*, in the Danubian Principalities at the end of the eighteenth century before he had been forced to flee into Russia. Alexander was the eldest son, a general in the imperial Hussars, esteemed for his courage and for the fortitude he had shown after losing his right arm fighting the French.[36]

When Xanthos met with the prince in early 1820 and told him how much the Greeks were suffering under Ottoman rule, Ypsilantis asked why, if their ordeal was so great, they were doing so little about it. "How can the poor Greeks of the Ottoman Empire do anything when they have been abandoned by those who could lead them," Xanthos shot back. "All the good families flee to foreign parts and leave their fellow Greeks [*omogeneis*] orphans." Xanthos gradually led the prince to the main point, revealing to him at a second meeting the existence of the Friendly Society and offering him the leadership. In fact, Ypsilantis must have known something about the Etaireia as three of his brothers had already joined. The prince accepted the offer and threw himself headlong into the cause. Less than a year elapsed between his decision and the start of the uprising.[37]

Ypsilantis's motives for accepting the leadership of the Etaireia have long been disputed. Some say he was driven by ambition and the desire for glory. Others note a monetary factor: his family's extensive properties in Moldavia had been expropriated by the sultan after his father's flight, and they were fighting for compensation. In an apologia written years afterward, when he was close to death, Ypsilantis denied that he had been swayed by personal considerations. According to him, it had been a question of patriotism: the danger facing the Greek people had been obvious to him and he had felt it was important not to let the Etaireia collapse in recriminations and feuds.

Ypsilantis claimed too that he had been assured of Russia's support, though the evidence scarcely bears him out. He did meet with Capodistrias, and according to Ypsilantis, Capodistrias heartily approved his ideas. But Capodistrias says quite the opposite—that he warned Ypsilantis against "such foolish projects," which were the work of "miserable merchants' clerks" who acted like spokesmen for the Greek nation but threatened it with danger. Ypsilantis was refused a meeting with the czar, although in fact they too did meet, accidentally, in the garden of the imperial country palace. While Ypsilantis claims the czar encouraged him and expressed his own deep sympathy for the Greeks, a more trustworthy account tells us that Alexander resisted being drawn into a conversation on the topic. "You are young and eager, as always, my friend," the czar is said to have told him, "but you can see that Europe is at peace."[38] This rings true: the best assessment is that when Ypsilantis assumed the leadership of the Etaireia, he knew—or should have known—he did not have the czar's backing. But he was, in the words of a contemporary, "a man of romantic and unbalanced temperament" who, as events would show, had a highly developed capacity to hear what he wanted. The chief Russian counterinsurgency expert regarded him as "fundamentally frivolous," while a diplomat who knew Ypsilantis well saw him as "a noble soul, full of warmth, but deprived of intelligence—one of those mediocre spirits which perversity strains, vanity intoxicates and who believe themselves to be the motors of great initiatives . . ." Subsequent events would reveal the prince to be impetuous, careless, and a poor judge of character.[39]

Formally, the collective leadership of the Etaireia had not been abandoned and Ypsilantis was given the code name "The Good One" (*Kalos*) the initials AR for correspondence, and a new title—the "General Representative of the Supreme Authority" (*Genikos Epitropos tis Archis*)—which allowed the Etaireia both to keep its collective character and to preserve the widespread belief that someone even more important was in charge above him. But Ypsilantis had only limited interest in collective decision making; he was, after all, an aristocrat and an officer. He swiftly made the Etaireia more hierarchical, nepotistic, and military, creating a neo-medieval initiation ceremony, knighting his brothers and bringing them into positions of prominence. There was an influx of Phanariot princes. As one observer from that milieu noted: "After his appointment, members of the better families joined the Etaireia." A split began to emerge between some of the earlier members, who were risking their lives on a daily basis in Ottoman Constantinople, and a new circle of aides clustered around the prince in Russia. The former were more cautious than the newcomers and also more experienced administrators. Increasingly, however, they felt sidelined as the center of action in late 1820 moved back from Constantinople to Russia's Black Sea shore.[40]

This turbulence within the Etaireia contributed to the confusion that bedeviled its planning for the uprising. It is naturally hard for historians to figure out how key decisions were made within a secretive conspiratorial organization, and there are few questions more difficult to answer in the whole saga of 1821 than how and when Ypsilantis decided to embark upon the uprising: the process, a story of stops and starts, remains obscure and contentious. "Everything was disorderly in Ypsilantis's council," wrote someone who tried dealing with him. "No systematic planning, no organization, no foresight, no semblance of efficiency."[41] Decisions were having to be made too against a fast-moving background in international affairs: a constitutionalist coup in Spain that spread to Naples and later Piedmont; in Epiros, an embryonic Ottoman civil war as the sultan's generals besieged the powerful Ali Pasha of Jannina; simmmering tensions in Serbia. While raising funds and recruits in Odessa, Ypsilantis had a sense already by September that the Greeks needed to move fast.[42]

Two hundred miles southwest of Odessa, the remote little Bessarabian border town of Ismail was a recent Russian acquisition, located on the edge of the Danube delta, on the Ottoman frontier. Ypsilantis arrived there on October 1, 1820, and stayed for about a week in the house of a Greek merchant in order to meet the Etaireia's leading figures. For many of them, it was their first opportunity to forge a personal bond with their new leader and tell him about their activities. For Ypsilantis this was the moment at which he took command. For the Etaireia it was a turning point, the moment it made the move from organizational growth to the task of preparing for the uprising itself.

Lacking records, we cannot be sure whether there were meetings on one day or over several, who all the attendees were or what exactly was said. We do know that there were a dozen or more participants, that discussions were led by Ypsilantis, and that they revolved around the date and place of the uprising. The urgent question was how close the Peloponnese—at the center of the Etaireia's strategic thinking for some time—was to being ready to rise up. Some warned that the Peloponnesian notables were wary and that weaponry was still in short supply. Others disagreed, saying there would never be an ideal time. The prince sided with them and the outcome of the Ismail meeting was an agreement that the uprising should take place soon. Working on the basis of the so-called Great Plan, it was agreed that Ypsilantis would sail down to the Mani to lead the Greeks in the Peloponnese. Agents would coordinate with Ali Pasha in Epiros to tie up Ottoman troops there, synchronize revolts elsewhere in the Balkans and—perhaps most spectacularly—strike terror into Constantinople itself in order to kill the "beast" in the head rather than in "the tail" or "the feet." They talked of setting fire to the Ottoman fleet in order to protect the islands and the Peloponnese from the sultan's vengeance and in later versions— which kept changing—assassinating the sultan himself. All this was to be put into effect before the year ended, and instructions immediately went out to Spetses for a boat to be sent to await Ypsilantis at Trieste. Other emissaries armed with proclamations and letters of authorization left to pave the way for his arrival in the Peloponnese and to notify supporters around the Aegean.[43]

One small problem needed immediate resolution, however. The key to the Etaireia's plans was the Mani, the remote, semiautonomous rocky peninsula in the south of the Peloponnese from where the insurrection would be launched. Its effective ruler in the Ottoman governance system was its bey, Petros Mavromihalis. He was a canny and cautious man who had joined the Etaireia but he had also sent someone to Capodistrias to find out whether the Etaireia's stories of Russian support were true. In St. Petersburg, Capodistrias gave Mavromihalis's emissary, a merchant called Kamarinos, a letter confirming that the imperial government did *not* favor an uprising and prized the peace with its Ottoman neighbor.[44] This was a potentially explosive document and

Kamarinos's behavior added to the Etairist worries. As Ypsilantis made his way south to Odessa in the summer of 1820, Kamarinos was not far behind him, announcing to all and sundry that he had written proof that the czar was not supportive of an uprising, that Ypsilantis was lying, and that the Etaireia would end up sacrificing the Greek people for its daydreams of revolution. What to do about Kamarinos must have been on Ypsilantis's mind during the Ismail meeting, and the decision made there to move rapidly ahead with the uprising made it more critical than ever that Mavromihalis's backing should be ensured. When Ypsilantis demanded Capodistrias's letter, Kamarinos, himself a member of the Etaireia, refused to hand it over. The prince then took an extreme step. Contacting one of the men he had met at Ismail, a zealous Ionian sea captain, he ordered Kamarinos to be killed. Two other trusted Etairists were also recruited, fellow Ionians who disguised themselves as sailors. One was a hard-drinking former soldier called Vasilios Karavias, who was keen to prove himself as a Greek patriot and would shortly play an even more vital role in the uprising; he had once worked for Ypsilantis's father, and he was currently in charge of the town guard in the small south Moldavian port of Galati on the Danube. The three Etairists embarked on a small Danube barge together with the presumably unsuspecting Kamarinos as he headed for Galati to catch a boat home; he never arrived. His body was apparently tossed overboard, his papers were sent to Ypsilantis, and the whole business was more or less hushed up. The prince penned a letter to Mavromihalis lauding his courage and consigned one of his most experienced aides to make sure the Mani remained faithful to the Etaireia. Mavromihalis remained in the dark for many months about the fate of his envoy and the realities of Russian policy. It was the second such officially sanctioned assassination in the Etaireia's brief history.[45]

Around the time of the murder of Kamarinos, barely two weeks after the Ismail meeting, Ypsilantis changed his plans radically and without any warning opted for a completely different strategy. He decided to launch the revolt from across the Russian border rather than from the Peloponnese. The reasons probably had nothing to do with Kamarinos's death: Ypsilantis told associates that he was worried the journey across Habsburg territory to Trieste had become too risky. Instead, he would lead an expeditionary force into Ottoman Moldavia and Wallachia and then link up with the Serbs before heading south to join the Greeks overland. The already tight time frame was further compressed: Ypsilantis told the Serb Milos Obrenovic, whom he counted on joining him, that he had given instructions to "all the parts of Greece from the Morea to the Danube" to be ready to attack the Ottomans on November 15, in less than a month's time. He would, he assured Obrenovic, be in Serbia by November 25; perhaps he still planned to head south in time to join the Greeks at the end of the year. Ypsilantis said they needed to move fast; he had apparently come to believe that once the sultan had finished dealing with his other security problems, he was bound to turn his attention to the Greeks in the spring.[46]

The two semiautonomous Danubian Principalities of Moldavia and Wallachia, which featured so centrally in Ypsilantis's new thinking, were in the far north of the Ottoman Empire. Squeezed between the Habsburgs and Russians, they occupied a unique place in imperial governance that gave them obvious advantages in the eyes of the Etairist planners. For one thing, no Muslims could live in them without special permission—these were very largely Christian lands. For another, treaty obligations meant that the sultan could not send in troops without Russian consent. It mattered too that the two principalities were ruled not by Muslim pachas but by Christian princely governors (hospodars), who were drawn from the elite Greek Phanariot families of Constantinople; both Ypsilantis's father and grandfather had occupied these positions and he knew the incumbents. The two principalities had in fact been occupied by Russian troops during the Russo-Turkish war of 1806–12 and temporarily unified under the rule of his father, Constantine. The troops had been withdrawn but the Ypsilantis name remained. The only drawback was that he could not count on the majority of the population, Romanian peasants or petty nobility who regarded the Phanariot Greeks as corrupt and Greeks in general as foreigners.[47]

Ypsilantis's change of heart was surely also influenced by Moldavia's proximity to the southwestern borderlands of the Russian Empire that had become his center of operations. Orders from Moscow and St. Petersburg could take weeks if not months to reach Kishinev or Odessa; thus local and regional officials had more independence as well as less knowledge of the czar's actual wishes than their counterparts in the center of power. Distance created a uniquely supportive environment for wishful thinking both by Ypsilantis and by his Russian colleagues. The governor of Odessa allowed the town to be turned into a recruiting ground for the Greeks, believing mistakenly—or so he later claimed—that the Etaireia had the czar's secret support. Military officers in the region regarded Ypsilantis as a friend and a war hero. The commander of the 16th Infantry Division, Mikhail Orlov, whose troops were stationed at the border on the river Pruth, was a radical who savored the thought of a quick war that might allow constitutionalists to seize power in Russia. The governor of Bessarabia, Konstantin Katakazis, was a wealthy Greek landowner who happened to be married to Ypsilantis's sister. The local bureaucracy provided passports, gave Etairists useful postings, and turned a blind eye to the increased traffic of agents and munitions across the border into Ottoman Moldavia.[48]

Sensing the excitement in the air was a youthful foreign ministry protegé of Capodistrias called Alexander Pushkin. The czar had ordered him to Siberia because of his subversive verses, but Capodistrias managed to get him posted instead to the Bessarabian backwater of Kishinev, which happened to be Ypsilantis's center of operations. Capodistrias's letter of recommendation, approved by the emperor himself, noted the young poet's remarkable talents but warned of his attraction to "that system of anarchy which bad faith calls the System of Human Rights, Liberty and the Independence of Peoples." Kishinev scarcely offered a calming environment. Pushkin befriended the Etairists there as well as the Russian officers who they mingled with, and even wrote a poem for the uprising that everyone was talking about and that he intended to join:

> War! The revolt is finally under way:
> The banners of warlike honor are unfurled!
> Blood I behold; I see the feast of vengeance.[49]

Ypsilantis remained committed to the Moldavian option from this point on. But it must have soon become evident that planning a complex uprising in three weeks on the verge of winter was asking for disaster, so on November 1, he decided to postpone it until the spring. The additional months would allow him to secure political and military support inside the Danubian Principalities themselves, give his emissaries more time to make their preparations, and recruit a few experienced military commanders for the march south in the spring. His priority was to get the backing of Moldavia's *hospodar*, a cautious and wily Phanariot prince called Michalis Soutsos whose family were in the imperial capital. As he was surrounded by spies, Soutsos could not afford to take risks, at least not without the prospect of commensurate rewards. "Oinoplouton" (Rich in Wine), as the Etairists dubbed Soutsos, demanded to know who would protect his province once Ypsilantis's forces had moved off southward toward the Greek lands; he wanted to be named commander of the forces in Moldavia itself, and finally, he wanted Ypsilantis's support for his claim to lead the province if and when it fell to the czar to decide its fate. Soutsos was still bargaining when the *hospodar* of neighboring Wallachia, a relative of his, died suddenly in January. Soutsos's reaction was to add a new request: to be made prince of both provinces under Russian protection.

It is from early 1821 that the surviving Etaireia documents start to give the sense of events accelerating, not to say spiraling, out of control. No clear date had yet been fixed for the spring—at least none is mentioned in any of the documents—although it is a commonplace of Greek historiography that everyone was working toward the Feast of the Annunciation at the end of March. But the chances of word getting out were rapidly increasing with the mass recruitments in Odessa and elsewhere in southern Russia. Meanwhile internal disagreements were widening as action approached. Some key Etairists did not bother to hide their view that the Greeks were woefully unprepared; others in Moscow were impatient for Ypsilantis to accelerate his plans.

The Balkan environment too was changing by the day. For one thing, the Serbs could not now be relied upon to rise up in support. For another, an uprising led by a native Romanian *boyar* (minor nobility) called Tudor Vladimirescu had transfixed Wallachia and although the Etaireia enjoyed very close relations with him and promised him its support, they were anxious lest the Ottoman army move against him before they were ready.[50] It seemed too only a matter of time before the Ottoman authorities realized what was brewing and moved against the entire organization, especially after a key Etaireia agent in the Balkans was arrested with compromising papers. Meanwhile, in the inns of the Moldavian capital, Jassy, the Etaireia's recruitment drive was creating more problems: Albanian fighters were openly boasting that when spring came they planned to go and liberate their homeland, and Soutsos was increasingly alarmed by the amateurish and disorganized way Ypsilantis's men were hiring mercenaries.[51]

By mid-February the impending invasion had become common knowledge, the *hospodar*'s role in the plotting was publicly discussed, and secrecy had gone out of the window. Soutsos's chief minister wrote to Ypsilantis angrily that "the entire secret of the Fraternity is known to all the locals."[52] In mid-February, Ypsilantis made what Soutsos's secretary called "a sudden resolution" to go ahead. He ordered meat in Jassy for several hundred troops, gave Soutsos just enough time to tell his relatives to flee Constantinople, and ordered the trusted Etairist Vasilios Karavias in Galati on the Danube, the gateway to the province from the south, to "raise the flag of liberty" there in four days' time. Ypsilantis himself would cross the Pruth the following day.[53]

And so it came about that it was in a small Danubian port—hundreds of miles away from the Peloponnese where Ypsilantis's arrival was still expected—that the Greek revolution began on February 21, 1821. That morning, Karavias's militia, reinforced by sailors from the Ionian Islands and hired Albanian fighters, attacked the headquarters of the tiny Ottoman customs guard in Galati, setting it ablaze and killing those inside. The Etairists plundered shops and warehouses, seized several Ottoman ships moored along the Danube, and massacred the town's few Muslims in what was probably a deliberate effort to provoke Ottoman reprisals and thus secure Russian intervention. It is striking that whether or not Ypsilantis had ordered this, he evidently did not disapprove because Karavias was promoted shortly afterward. The Etaireia fighters had taken an oath to exterminate the enemy and the killing was a signal: There was no turning back.[54]

That same afternoon, about one hundred miles or so to the north, Ypsilantis set out with a small group of his close aides and bodyguards from Kishinev, and shortly after noon on February 22 they presented their passports at the border post on the Pruth and were allowed through by the Russian customs guards. Across the river, they were on Ottoman territory. It was a mere twelve miles to Jassy and they were joined along the way by an escort of two hundred Albanians sent by Soutsos to greet him. Yet Ypsilantis's mood was anything but euphoric and in a message he sent to the Etaireia leadership he complained of feeling abandoned by them. It was an odd rebuke to make at that moment to men who had risked their lives for years, but it revealed the disconnect at the top of the organization and the deep doubts within it about the path the prince had chosen. The entry into Moldavia could not have been easier, but complications lay ahead.[55]

*

In Jassy, Ypsilantis took over. One of the first things he did was to send instructions to the Etaireia's leaders in Constantinople to seize the shipyards, burn the capital and, if possible, capture the sultan himself; sent by the obliging Russian consul in the Moldavian capital to his minister in Constantinople, these orders never reached their recipients. After huddling in confidential talks with the *hospodar*, his adviser, and the Russian consul, the prince then emerged to review the hundreds of armed men who were gathering from all over the Balkans to serve under him. As word got out that he had arrived, even the *hospodar*'s bodyguards left their posts to join him and the atmosphere in the streets of Jassy became euphoric. "You have no idea of the enthusiasm here among the Christians," the *hospodar*'s wife wrote to her father. "Hundreds are coming in from Odessa, many on foot, others from German regions . . . Surely God has extended his hand over this business and will see it succeed." A service was held in the cathedral at which the metropolitan blessed their standards and all present unsheathed their swords and swore to defend the revolution.[56]

Before setting out Ypsilantis had written to Odessa urging his agents to drum up support not only among the Greeks there but also among any "good French officers of Napoleon's army," Italians with military training, and Serb and Bulgarian warriors. Many of the Greeks in Russia were sending in money or arming themselves to go and fight. In Odessa, wrote Pushkin, the news had led to "rapture." Everyone thought of "the independence of the ancient fatherland . . . everybody was talking about Leonidas, about Themistokles." They were selling everything to buy "sabers, rifles, pistols" before they headed off to Jassy. An Austrian agent in the Moldavian capital sent a report to his superiors in Vienna. "The Greek Nation," he wrote, "had apparently for many years been planning to cast off the Turkish yoke and replace it with its own State, the state of its ancestors." A secret brotherhood, led by unknown figures and guarded by solemn oaths of secrecy, had spread among "the chosen leaders of the Nation" into "Thessaly, Macedonia, Serbia, Albania, Bulgaria, Rumeli, and the Aegean islands." The group's leaders were unknown but their representative was "the son of Constantine Ypsilantis."[57]

The first proclamation Ypsilantis issued on Ottoman soil was to the Romanian-speaking Moldavian majority. The prince had planned to announce the abolition of all feudal due in the province, but the *hospodar*'s secretary warned him off such a dangerously radical step.

Ypsilantis therefore told the locals simply that "all Greece" (*apasa i Graikia*) had risen up to throw off "the yoke of tyranny" and that he and his men were headed south to fight for freedom. The Moldavians were urged to remain obedient to their *hospodar*. Should the Turks come in, Ypsilantis indicated that "a strong power" was ready to punish them, a clear reference to the Russians whom he implied would intervene if the Ottoman army breached its treaty agreements and entered the province. It was an act of staggering diplomatic folly that killed off any residual instinct the czar might have felt for wanting to intervene; by publicly compromising Russia in this way, Ypsilantis had made it utterly impossible for him to act. To the Romanian nobles who came to pay homage, Ypsilantis claimed to be acting in the name of the czar. He behaved rather imperiously toward them—as though he were already the king of Greece, one observer acidly commented. It was not behavior calculated to gain the support of the population upon whom he would depend for the coming weeks and it was another early indication of his political ineptitude.

To his fellow Greeks, whom he addressed next, his tone was very different. Ypsilantis called upon them to rise up for their faith and their fatherland and told them that Europe was looking on and awaiting miracles while tyrants trembled. He publicly pledged to set his camp "between Macedonia and Thermopylae"—evidently hoping to head south to meet the Greeks coming from the Peloponnese—and he hinted once again that the Russians would protect them all.[58] Thousands of Russian infantry had indeed taken up positions on the other side of the Pruth, and a supporting invasion was regarded by many as imminent. There were rumors that the emperors of the Holy Alliance, then meeting at the Austrian town of Laibach, had decided the time had come to chase the Turks out of Europe.[59]

But this euphoria took only days to dissipate. On paper the Etaireia's army had been organized by Ypsilantis's brother, Nikolaos, with a command structure, a symbol—the Phoenix, rising from the ashes—and a tricolor flag—white for the purity of their enterprise, black for their willingness to sacrifice their lives for freedom, and red for the autonomy of the Greeks and the resurrection of their fatherland. But as the history of the Greek war of independence would reveal on numerous occasions, between paper plans and the reality of combat there was a vast gulf and this was scarcely an army in the modern sense of the word at all. Men of arms and volunteers had flocked to the Etairist banner and after nearly a week in Jassy the prince started out with about 4,500 men, a number that swelled along the way to perhaps as many as 7,000. Despite the lack of artillery, this was not an insignificant number and they were initially well-fed and supplied, thanks to the funds that had poured in from Greeks in Russia. But they lacked unity and discipline and strong leadership, and they were grouped under separate chieftains, each with their own banner. They came, too, from all over the Balkans. Only about 2,500 of the original force were Greeks; the rest were Russians and Ukrainians, Serbs, Montenegrins, Albanians, and Bulgarians. Ypsilantis had led the Romanian nobles to expect the Russian army but seems never to have questioned whether, in the absence of the czar's support, a province inhabited mostly by Romanian speakers would support an uprising in the name of Greece, especially as many of his troops were really mercenaries who, as his aide Prince George Kantakuzinos wrote contemptuously, were "men skilled in idleness, intemperateness and plundering." They turned into such a nuisance that local Etaireia officials ordered them out of Jassy entirely and told them to "be careful to leave without causing any further disorders."[60]

On Kantakuzinos's urging, a regular unit was established from Greek volunteers—the so-called Sacred Battalion: relatively disciplined, dressed in the Etaireia's black uniform and committed to the cause, they were later to achieve a kind of mythical fame in postindependence Greece. But men with real command experience were in short supply: Tsakalof, who had none, was named adjutant, and Karavias was placed in charge of the cavalry, which was not his specialty. Among the irregulars, the looting, drinking, and even killings that had been seen in Galati and Jassy continued and eroded any sympathy for the revolt among the Romanians. On the road, as a Greek participant later recorded, "we constantly saw the inhabitants of the villages and towns on our route fleeing in fear, looking for safety."[61]

Ypsilantis had wasted days in Jassy before marching south and joining up with Karavias, whom he found to his dismay had only 360 poorly armed men instead of the thousand or so he had pledged to recruit.[62] Advancing slowly toward Bucharest, the prince's resolve, impatience, and energy drained away and he seems to have realized early on that the expedition was in difficulties. He proposed to Kantakuzinos before March was out that they make their way in secret to Trieste and sail to the Morea, and he gave up the idea only when his aide pointed out that this meant abandoning the men who had chosen to follow them. They did, however, decide to send his brother Dimitris in April, accompanied by Kantakuzinos's brother Alexandros, thereby ensuring princely leadership in the Peloponnese. For Ypsilantis, the revolution was, from start to finish, a family matter.[63]

The killer blow that deflated the expedition's expectations came from Europe. The czar had been meeting with the other members of the Holy Alliance at Laibach in Habsburg Slovenia since January, focused on the anti-Bourbon rebellions in Italy and Spain. Conservative fears of internationally coordinated revolution were at their height and Russia, Austria, and Prussia had issued a declaration underscoring the right and duty of the great powers to suppress *any* revolutionary movement that they deemed a threat to the peace of Europe. The spring of 1821 was thus about the worst moment imaginable to mount an uprising and to ask for Russian assistance.

Yet this is what Ypsilantis now did in a letter he sent the czar from Jassy. He could scarcely have crafted something more calculated to alarm the Russian emperor. A "secret society" had organized the campaign that he had felt obliged to lead out of patriotic and filial devotion, he told Alexander, adding for good measure that "the generous impulses of nations come from God" and that the uprising was divinely inspired. He urged the czar to play the role of liberator of the Greeks. Accompanying his missive was a more practical letter from Soutsos, the *hospodar* of Moldavia, worried about the fate of his province and requesting Russian troops to safeguard it.[64]

Capodistrias was with the czar in Laibach, and he was thunderstruck when he learned of the news of Ypsilantis's expedition; in despair, he foresaw that it would condemn the Greeks to Ottoman reprisals and that Russia and Europe would do nothing to help. If anything, there was the danger of a conservative intervention on the Ottoman side. Capodistrias wrote to his aide: "How can one not recognize in that which has broken out in the two principalities the identical effect of the same subversive principles, the same intrigues, which attract the calamities of war . . . the most dreadful plague of demagogic despotism." The czar was especially furious that a Russian army officer, a former aide, had compromised him in the eyes of his allies, and the lie of Russian backing was finally and brutally exposed when Capodistrias himself, replying to

Ypsilantis in the czar's name, denounced the prince and his brothers and ordered them never to return to Russia. "Russia," the minister stated, "is at peace with the Ottoman state. The outbreak of revolution in Moldavia in no way justifies any break between our two states." The anger seeped out between the lines: "No help, either direct or indirect, will be accorded you by the Emperor, since—we repeat—it would be unworthy of Him to undermine the foundations of the Turkish Empire by the shameful and blameworthy action of a secret society." The sole advice was that Ypsilantis seek some way to repair the damage he had done. A more emphatic repudiation was impossible to imagine. Metternich was jubilant. The Etaireia seemed by its own actions to have effectively ended any chance of precipitating a new Russian-Ottoman war.[65]

In Moldavia, the Romanian population turned wholly against the Greeks and the *hospodar* Soutsos fled to safety across the Russian border. Galati was retaken by Ottoman forces after a struggle; an Etairist unit fought bravely but was overwhelmed. In Wallachia the Etairists put Vladimirescu to death for treachery—he had been trying to contact the sultan to surrender—before their massively outnumbered force was pushed back by an Ottoman army toward the Austrian and Russian borders. Several hundred Greeks made a gallant last-ditch defense on the banks of the Pruth on June 16, some swimming across, others dying under the eyes of the Russian soldiers stationed on the opposing bank from where Ypsilantis had departed with such hopes four months before. The Sacred Battalion made its final stand at the village of Dragaşani. Poorly led, impetuous, and courageous, the Greeks were cut to pieces by the Ottoman cavalry.

It was not Ypsilantis's finest hour. He first denounced his own men for cowardice and then fled across the Habsburg border. The Russians proposed allowing him to head for Hamburg and exile in North America, but Metternich wanted him under lock and key and so Ypsilantis began the years of captivity that would end only on the eve of his death in Vienna in January 1828. The remnants of the ragtag Etaireia army dispersed, many of them heading back into Bessarabia where Pushkin saw them sitting quietly in the coffeehouses of Kishinev with their now idle yataghans and pistols. The poet had wisely refrained from joining them but he lapped up their stories—of their time with Ali Pasha, of their ruthless drowning of Muslim families in the waters of the Danube, of their euphoric arrival in Jassy, of the final defeat. Many of them died destitute; some would eventually trek hundreds of miles through Poland, Germany, Switzerland, and France and find passage to Greece.[66]

The first person in the Ottoman capital to learn the news of the uprising may have been the Russian ambassador, Baron Stroganov, whom a courier from Jassy reached with the letter from Ypsilantis on March 3. The prince alerted Stroganov to his "unforeseen movement" across the Pruth and asked him to protest any possible Ottoman troop incursion into the two Danubian Provinces. Apparently unconcerned about compromising the Russian diplomat, he also enclosed letters to be forwarded to senior Etairists instructing them to set fire to the city and seize the sultan. There were other messages to be passed on to elite Greeks to warn them to leave. Stroganov, who regarded Ypsilantis's behavior as unbelievably irresponsible, was placed in an impossible position. He quietly tried to help Greeks left exposed by Ypsilantis's actions while at the same time informing the Ottoman authorities of the correspondence he had received and denying any prior knowledge of what was happening to the north.[67]

To the sultan and his advisers, the revolt in the Danubian Principalities "occurred as suddenly as a bolt of lightning." When the news of the massacre of Muslims in Galati reached them at the start of March, their disbelieving assumption was that the whole affair was a Russian plot. Even after the czar had denounced Ypsilantis—news that reached Constantinople at the start of April—Ottoman ministers continued to believe it was impossible for a Russian officer to have mounted such an expedition without official backing. Their real fear was a war with Russia, which would not only pose a military threat to the empire but would inevitably jeopardize the food supply to the capital and test its defenses. Yet ironically, their own actions brought such a war much closer.[68]

For two weeks there was little reaction from the Porte beyond a decision to replace the *hospodar* of Moldavia, and a notification to the Russians that Ottoman troops would be sent into the province. But as investigations revealed the scale of the uprising, the furious sultan betrayed more draconian impulses. He even toyed with the idea of having all the Greeks of the empire put to death, an idea that his longtime favorite at court, Halet Efendi, backed. But the sheykh-ul-islam, the supreme Muslim religious authority, bravely objected, saying it would be against the *sharia* to lump together the innocent with the guilty, and the grand vizier too advised against it. Both men were dismissed from office, but the sultan heeded what they said and on March 18 he addressed the empire's Muslims instead: they had grown soft in ease; it was time to return to the virtues of their nomadic ancestors, carry arms at all times, and behave as battle-ready defenders of the faith. This was more than moral exhortation; it was an open invitation for indiscriminate violence, especially after several thousand rifles were distributed in Constantinople to janissaries and guards who began raiding Christian homes and inns to search for weapons. Any relief that might have been brought by the news that the czar had denounced Ypsilantis was erased when the first reports reached the city at the start of April that the Greeks had risen up in the Morea as well.[69]

The illustrious Phanariot brothers Konstantinos and Nikolaos Mourouzis, who occupied two of the most senior ministerial positions available to Christians in the empire, were among the first to be executed. Konstantinos was accused of involvement in the conspiracy. Nikolaos's death sentence, as the placard hung publicly on his corpse stated, was explicitly connected to the killing of innocent Muslims in Jassy and Galati. In the sultan's court, Ypsilantis was invariably referred to as "the son of Ypsilantis the fugitive" to underline the theme of Phanariot betrayal. The influence of the Greek princely families in Ottoman government never recovered, and those families that did not manage to flee were sent into exile and their properties were expropriated. A few continued to serve in diplomatic positions, but the Phanariots were thereafter a remnant of their former glory.[70]

On April 10 came the most sensational execution of all—the hanging of the Patriarch Gregorios V. As head of the Orthodox Christian community in the empire, the patriarch, who had kept his doubts about the Etaireia to himself, bore by virtue of his position the ultimate responsibility for the Greeks' loyalty; nevertheless, the manner of his killing was unprecedented in its brutality. The frail, eighty-four-year-old Gregorios had concluded Easter Sunday service in the cathedral when he was arrested in his residence, deposed, and sentenced to death. He was left to die painfully in public, his body dangling over the main doorway where it remained for several days. The usual placard was placed around his neck: it accused him of treachery and explicitly alluded to his origins in the Peloponnese and his connection with the "great sins" being carried out by "misguided brigands" in the region. News of his execution, and of the despoiling of his corpse, which was dragged humiliatingly down to the water's edge, circulated around the Black Sea and the eastern Mediterranean and provoked consternation in Europe.

There was no letup after that. On the contrary, a new grand vizier was appointed with explicit instructions to intensify the repression, and the arrests and executions multiplied: the sultan denounced the incumbent for his excessively humane attitude to the non-Muslims, and a mob attacked the patriarchate. Three other senior clerics were hanged in public places around the city on the same day as the patriarch; many others were arrested and killed in the days that followed. In Constantinople it became dangerous for foreigners to venture into the streets, lest they be accosted, robbed, beaten, and spat at. As armed janissaries roamed the streets, Greeks were killed in cold blood. Out for a walk, the chaplain at the British embassy saw someone strolling just ahead of him up a narrow alley casually stab a man to death with a single strike: watching the victim fall, the killer then wiped his yataghan and went into a café for a quiet smoke. Another Greek, richly dressed, struggled with two assailants, losing his turban and slipper as he was dragged through the mud, forced onto his knees, and beheaded. Constantinos Oikonomos, a renowned scholar and teacher, managed to flee by boat to Odessa after hiding for three days, terrified "throughout those frightful hours" by the screams in the streets. He was eventually rescued by an Etairist wine merchant who concealed him and some other fugitives on one of his ships. A few days after Oikonomos's arrival in Odessa, another Greek ship docked there with the corpse of the patriarch, which had been found floating in the waters of the Golden Horn; the body was given a solemn burial and Oikonomos delivered a powerful funeral oration.[71]

About 230 Greeks died in the Ottoman capital in April, followed by about 100 more in May and another 100 in the first half of June: it was a summer of killing. Greeks fled the capital, shipping was carefully checked, and commerce was brought almost to a standstill.[72] Constantinople resembled an armed camp. "This government perseveres in its endeavors to strike terror into the minds of its Greek subjects," reported the British ambassador, Lord Strangford. "An armed and licentious population, wandering through the streets of this capital and its suburbs, daily commit such excesses as destroy all confidence on the part of the *reaya* in the security of their lives and property."[73] Despite occasional official admonitions, the killing continued over the coming weeks, not only in the capital but also in Edirne, Smyrna, Salonica, and other places besides. The sultan warned his subjects not to attack the innocent but at the same time he congratulated instigators of a massacre at Aivalik in June and continued to equate zeal with slaughter.[74]

The violence of the official Ottoman reaction shocked European diplomats deeply. It was a first indication that the imperial response might fare worse in their estimation than the Greek uprising itself, and it began a slow and ultimately fatal erosion of the sultan's legitimacy in the judgment of European public opinion. More than 40,000 refugees fled not only Constantinople but also the Danubian Principalities where Ottoman troops carried out massacres of their own, testing to the limit Russia's tolerance for their presence there. In Russia, a major humanitarian effort was mounted and pressure grew to use the country's vast army to take action against the Ottomans. At the head of this war party was Capodistrias, who had been marginalized in February but now gained in influence. In June the Russian ambassador denounced what he described as the Porte's mission to "exterminate anyone bearing the name of a Christian in Turkey."[75] Later that month, Capodistrias drafted an ultimatum that accused the sultan of having declared war on his own Christian subjects and warned that "Christendom" might not be willing to stand by indefinitely to watch "the extermination of a Christian people." The idea of justifying a possible intervention in the internal affairs of another state on humanitarian grounds was perhaps a first in international affairs, certainly for a leading member of the Holy Alliance. Alexander Stourdza, Capodistrias's secretary, argued that the sheer extent of the Greek insurrection demonstrated the revolt was quite unlike the revolts in Spain and Naples: it was not merely the work of a Jacobin conspiracy in Paris but the expression of deeply rooted grievances among wide swaths of the Christian population of the empire.[76]

Yet the Congress system of the European powers held together in rejecting this argument. The British wanted peace and the French valued their traditional ties with the sultan. The cynical Metternich did not believe what happened in the Ottoman lands should affect Europe at all. "Beyond our eastern frontiers," he wrote that spring, "three or four hundred thousand hanged, strangled, or impaled do not count for much." He talked extensively with the czar to wean him of any residual sympathies for the Greek cause. "Today I had a long conversation with the Emperor Alexander," he noted on May 9, a few days before the end of the Congress of Laibach. "If ever anyone turned from black to white, it is he." But Metternich's abundant confidence in his own brilliance led him astray, for the czar had needed no persuading of the dangers of revolution. Convinced the Etaireia was a pernicious radical organization connected to troublemakers elsewhere, Alexander told Capodistrias in August he believed there was a "directing committee" in Paris behind all the upheavals that had been taking place in southern Europe. The following year, Capodistrias was sidelined from the foreign ministry. Although he stayed on the imperial payroll, he left Russia and retreated into a kind of semiprivate existence in Switzerland, where he would remain for the next five years.[77]

From the sultan's viewpoint, the violence was starting to have the desired effect. The rebellion in the Danubian Principalities was crushed, its leaders were excommunicated, killed, or exiled, and the Ottoman army managed to reoccupy the provinces without triggering hostilities: the Russian minister left Constantinople in protest but war was averted and the capital's food supply was ensured. Another imperial decree was issued in August reminding officials across the Ottoman realm of the importance of treating Christians fairly. In Odessa, the Etaireia survived for a time as a philanthropic organization before the Russian authorities shut it down. It seemed as though all those who had expressed their reservations about the planned national uprising had been proven right. It would bring enormous suffering to Ottoman Christians and it would not succeed. From the Habsburg town of Czernowitz a commentator wrote what was, for that time, a plausible prognosis: "'Greek Carbonarism' is approaching its end."[78]

2

ALI PASHA'S
ANCIEN RÉGIME

"My father," said Haydée, raising her head, "was that illustrious man known in Europe under the name of Ali Tepelini, pasha of Yanina, and before whom Turkey trembled."
Alexandre Dumas, *The Count of Monte Cristo*, ch. 77

In the spring of 1821, Sultan Mahmud II's principal headache was not the Greek expedition into the Danubian Principalities but a white-bearded eighty-year-old Albanian pasha hundreds of miles away who had tyrannized the western Balkans for decades. What to do about this frustratingly durable despot in the heart of his European provinces had been on the sultan's mind for a long time. "[Though] the creation of an independent power in the midst of its territory, is no new or extraordinary fact in the Turkish empire," wrote one visitor, "none of them perhaps have attained the stability and extent of power which characterizes the government of Ali Pasha; nor has any one acquired the same importance in the political condition of Europe." A wily, complex figure, whose crocodile tears were as familiar to his associates as his fearsome punishments were to his enemies, he was dubbed the "Mahometan Bonaparte" by Byron while Alexandre Dumas, who knew a sensational story when he saw one, described him as "if not one of the most brilliant, at least one of the most singular [figures] in contemporary history." Dumas included Ali's life in a selection of celebrated criminals and wove the "illustrious Albanese chief" into the plot of *The Count of Monte Cristo*.[1]

In the history of the Greek revolution, Ali Pasha was to play a vital role, though not the one he had wanted. The Etaireia's agents, with whom he had typically duplicitous dealings, gave him the code name "Father-in-Law," which summed up all the intimate ambiguities of their relationship. They understood his importance in the eyes of the Ottoman government and his value as a distraction. Without the priority attached by the sultan to eliminating the hated upstart, the fate of the Greek uprising would have been very different. The Ottoman authorities firmly believed Ali Pasha was their chief threat in the region and when they got wind of the Etaireia's plans for an uprising in the Peloponnese they believed he was behind that too. In this way they underestimated the Greeks and for so long as Ali remained alive, the sultan's attention and his military effort remained fixed on the mountains of the western Balkans and the pasha's base in the town of Jannina.

With its serene lakeside location beneath the snow-covered peaks of the Pindos mountains, Jannina still bears the imprint of the Ottoman past in its formidable castle walls, mosques, and well-preserved mansions—a mere forty-five minutes by plane from Athens but a world away. Ali Pasha, who parleyed with Napoleon and treated English diplomats as if he were the equal of the Prince Regent, had risen from humble beginnings in the mountains of southern Albania. Having entered the sultan's service as guardian of one of the passes in the Pindos, he eventually became pasha, crushing the power of his rivals and bringing vast territories under his control on both sides of the mountains and down into the Peloponnese. He suppressed the banditry that had been the scourge of peasant life in the region for decades, improved the local roads, and encouraged learning—there were at least two renowned Greek schools in Jannina. At the same time, his agents tracked potential opposition, opened post from abroad, and assassinated rivals. Henchmen under his chief of police confiscated merchants' property at whim—many fled to the Ionian Islands, Vienna, Trieste, or Russia—and imposed forced labor upon the peasants. Those who crossed him faced the prospect of imprisonment, torture, and a painful death.

One thing that took newcomers by surprise was the openness Ali manifested toward the Greeks: his doctor, two of his secretaries, and several bodyguards were all Greeks as was his youthful wife Kyra Vasiliki, whose brother Georgios Kitsos would later play a significant role in the uprising.[2] Whether or not it is true that his family had converted from Christianity only a few generations earlier, or whether it was the influence of Bektashism, Ali manifested a relative indifference to confessional boundaries that effectively allowed him to maximize the benefits of the ethnically fluid society of the western Balkans. He ruled through his sons as well as via a network of Albanian beys and Greek notables and chieftains: known to other Greeks as "Ali Pasha's men" (*Alipashalides*), their long and intimate knowledge of one another survived his death, crossed religious divides, and shaped the course of the Greek uprising. To European visitors, he seemed a gentle old man, wrapped in his furs by the fire, curious and accessible; but his reputation for cruelty and cunning preceded him. It was believed that he had amassed a legendary treasure in his palace in Jannina, and this wealth was the foundation of his security and the secret of his endurance.

At the start of 1820, Ali seemed to be at the height of his power. When the British government appointed a new consul general, his letter of appointment was addressed to "His Highness Ali Pasha." Consul William Meyer arrived loaded with presents: a large silver sandwich service, a silver telescope (with the Prince Regent's royal arms on one side and the insignia of Ali Pasha on the other), cut-glass goblets, and several large silver watches. Two rings, one mounted with a large emerald, the other with a ruby, were for the pasha's two Greek secretaries—Manthos Oikonomou and Spiros Kolovos, who were among the most powerful figures at his court.[3]

Yet Meyer had already heard rumors that Ali Pasha's relations with the sultan were "in a most critical and alarming state," and so they were. The sultan had mistrusted his ambition for some time and coveted his riches, but what tipped things over the edge was when Ali arranged to have one of his rivals assassinated in the Ottoman capital—and not just in the capital but in the vicinity of the sultan's seraglio itself. Although the intended victim escaped, shots were fired, the assassins were arrested, and Ali Pasha's role instigating the plot was quickly uncovered. It was an outrageous breach of security and protocol and it precipitated his downfall.[4] By April or May the rupture with the sultan was common knowledge. Meyer reported that the pasha and his family were "exposed to the most imminent perils" and were uncertain how to respond. The Ottoman fleet was sent out to reclaim the coastal fortresses under Ali's control on the Epiros coast, key provincial posts were handed over to men loyal to the sultan, and a large army was assembled at Monastir to march on Jannina.

As the rift with the sultan widened, Ali wondered how he could use the Greeks for his own protection. Some of Ali's Greek aides were members of the Etaireia and he asked them for more information about the organization. He seems to have believed, as most people did, that the Etaireia was a Russian instrument and so he also approached the Russians to see if they would lend him their support, using an Etairist emissary who went off to Constantinople and reported his approach. Yet typically, even as he tried to win them over, Ali was sharing what he knew of the Greeks' plotting with their enemies. That April he asked an English officer in a private conversation whether "we had ever heard of a Society established for the liberation of Greece, of which Count Capodistrias was the head, and who was after such liberation to be king of Greece." He had his secretary, Kolovos, hand them over a list with the names of two dozen members of the Etaireia. He passed the same information to the sultan, hoping to ingratiate himself. But the Etaireia was not a priority for the British, and the Greeks were not taken very seriously as a threat in Constantinople.[5]

As the summer went on, therefore, Ali returned to the Russian option and with it the Etaireia. He clearly hoped at this point he might be able to hold out against the sultan and his forces until a new Russian war changed everything. One idea of his was purportedly that the Russians should back him as a ruler of the western Balkans, along with the creation of a small new Greek state in the Peloponnese that would be under his protection. At the same time, Ali reached out to the Greeks themselves within his provinces: his policy toward them suddenly became milder, and he showed marks of favor to the Greek chieftains and their bands. He allowed them to fly the cross on their banners and even, as a special courtesy, invited the leading chieftains to dine with him. By June, as he was restoring the fortifications around Jannina and bringing in stores of arms and provisions in readiness for a siege, the "topic of the emancipation of the Greeks" under his flag was being widely discussed in the region. Etairists in Constantinople were interested enough to sound him out.[6]

Faced with the wrath of Sultan Mahmud II, however, Ali's power was shrinking with unexpected speed, and his hold over his provinces was loosening as thousands of the sultan's troops started arriving in the region. By June his control of the granary of Thessaly and the ports south of Parga had become precarious: a last convoy of 8,000 horseloads of grain reached Jannina from Trikkala in early July. Within the town, feeling against the pasha was rising, spurred on by requisitions, the ill discipline of his troops, and the forced labor he was demanding. Ali's best hope was that the sultan might wish merely to leave him greatly weakened, in charge of the Jannina region. But the proclamation from the sultan when it came called on the faithful to join together against his "impudent and scandalous disobedience" and made it clear the pasha was now an outlaw.[7] Many of Ali's remaining supporters deserted him and the chieftains guarding critical mountain passes took their men home. Most of the Etairists in his entourage abandoned him as well, some even going over to the sultan's side. After some delay in recruiting soldiers from the Peloponnese, a large Ottoman fleet took over key forts such as Lepanto and blockaded the coast, preventing supplies reaching the pasha by sea. As the Ottoman forces began to lay siege to Jannina, Ali set fire to the town and withdrew to his fortress stronghold on the lakeside, supported by a garrison of several thousand men. More and more detachments of the sultan's army marched into Rumeli to the east: all that remained was to defeat the old man. Writing to the Foreign Office in London, Meyer underlined the rapid "revolution" in the affairs of the province that had, in the course of just three months—from May to August—seen Ali reduced from ruling some 2 million people to being declared a rebel, abandoned and isolated.[8]

The pasha remained, however, even in these extreme circumstances, a master of Ottoman realities. He knew that, while outright resistance to the sultan could not succeed, there was little more than a month remaining for the besieging army to bring up field guns and lay in supplies before the winter set in; at that point, if he was still uncaptured, it would not be until the following spring that hostilities could resume. Impatient for word from the Russians, Ali sent off another messenger to St. Petersburg to ask again for help. He knew that in the meantime an occupation force needed to live off the land and thereby risked making itself unpopular and provoking a backlash. He retained good contacts with his subordinates in the hills on either side of the Pindos, both Muslim and Greek, many of whom remained loyal. And finally, he had at his disposal an ample treasury, built up over decades, and there were rumors he was bribing senior commanders in the sultan's army.

Bereft of artillery or ordnance, poorly commanded, the sultan's army eventually amassed an enormous number of men but could make no real impression on the fortress. The numbers were deceptive; the problem was the soldiers' motivation, organization, and leadership. A Greek family fleeing the fighting in Jannina passed one of the Ottoman detachments heading into the town—first the sound of the drums of the horsemen with their red uniforms and their high head coverings, in two rows of thirty horses each, then the pasha alone, and behind him the armed infantry. To the onlookers' astonishment, the foot soldiers were all Greeks. Short of manpower, the Ottomans as well as Ali were giving weapons to the Greeks of the region and drawing them into the fighting. It was, as the Russian ambassador in Constantinople noted in a dispatch, quite extraordinary: in what he termed a civil war between the sultan and Ali, both sides were appealing to the Greeks—not only Ali himself, but even more remarkably, the sultan, whose officials in the region were now proclaiming a general rising of the Christians against a rebel Muslim.[9]

It was a clear sign of imperial disarray that even organizing the downfall of a rebellious pasha was placing such a strain on the logistical apparatus of the Ottoman state. Dozens of buffalo died in the effort to drag heavy guns up from the coast, and it took weeks to construct the large rafts needed to patrol the lake and prevent Ali's men from communicating with their allies outside. Sure enough, the besiegers themselves started to feel the lack of food and had to send their horses down into the plains for the winter. Jealousies among the six pashas in the besieging army reached such a pitch that the sultan had to step in to order them to cooperate. By late October 1820 the local Albanian chieftains were waiting to see which way the struggle would go, and by December some of them were beginning to move back into Ali's camp. Among the population in Epiros, not a few were now wondering whether the province could bear the burden of feeding the sultan's soldiers and began to look back nostalgically to the era of the pasha's rule. Above all, thanks to the war, arms were circulating among the Christian population in unprecedented quantities. In Meyer's words:

> It is understood that the Albanians and Greeks are now ready to rise en masse, the moment they can see a favorable opportunity for it, and place themselves under a provisional government of their own formation until the proper appeals can be made to the Sultan on the subject of those causes which may have compelled them for their own preservation to take such a course . . . This state of things has been brought about chiefly by the impolitic measures pursued by the pachas who have been employed

to act against Aly Pacha. The country has been outraged by the rapacity, the violence and the contempt of all rights with which they have acted. The present situation has become intolerable to the people.[10]

Realizing that his campaign was in danger of faltering, the sultan overhauled the entire operation and used the winter interval to bring in a far more formidable figure as commander in chief.

A brilliant and experienced general, Khurshid Pasha had traveled by sea from Aleppo to Nafplion and had just taken up his assignment in late 1820 as governor of the Morea when the sultan ordered him north to Jannina, several hundred miles away. The Muslim beys in the Peloponnese who watched the newly arrived Khurshid head off again warned him of rumors of an imminent Greek uprising. But Khurshid was inclined to take his lead from Constantinople, which regarded all security considerations in the region as secondary to the defeat of Ali Pasha. In retrospect, had Khurshid stayed in the Peloponnese a few more months, or had he managed to crush Ali as quickly as he had hoped in the summer of 1821, the history of the Greek war of independence would have been very different: indeed, there might not have been much of a war at all. But instead Khurshid proceeded to the town of Larissa to oversee the provisioning of his army, and his advance detachments reached Jannina in March just as the Greek insurgency erupted in the south.

While the sultan was making his preparations for the spring offensive against Ali under Khurshid Pasha's command, the Etaireia was hoping to bolster the pasha's resistance. In late January, new instructions went out from Kishinev to support him, stipulating that this should be done in such a way as to give the Greeks access to his legendary wealth and to prevent him from ever again becoming the force he had been before the war. The Greeks should make Ali think they were fighting the Ottomans on his behalf and should profess the greatest respect for and loyalty to him. In this way, they would be able to expel the Ottoman forces from the region so that "at the first trumpet blast" they could declare themselves to be free.[11]

Ypsilantis sent these instructions to Kolokotronis, but the former brigand was already in the Peloponnese. Instead, the task was undertaken by Christoforos Perraivos, who was rightly regarded by the British consul Meyer as "one of the most active and important members of the

Etaireia." A lifelong revolutionary, teacher, and intellectual, nearly fifty years old, Perraivos was a link between the Etaireia and an earlier generation of Balkan radicals. He had been a comrade of the almost mythical Rhigas Ferraios before the latter's arrest and execution in 1798. Since then Perraivos had formed a close bond with the Souliots, the exiled Christian Albanian tribes who had suffered greatly at the hands of Ali Pasha. He was a longtime advocate for their cause and wrote their first history. Through Perraivos, the Etaireia hoped to reach out to the Souliots, turn Ali Pasha's former victims into his allies, and realize their marriage of convenience with the pasha in Jannina.[12]

Leaving the Peloponnese by ship the week before the uprising there broke out, Perraivos arrived in Epiros to find things moving in the right direction: the Souliots had already returned to the mainland from their exile in the Ionian Islands and were now ready to fight for their old enemy Ali Pasha in order to get back their ancestral lands. As the Souliot chieftains knew nothing about the Etaireia, Perraivos decided to confide what he called "the great purpose of the race" to them and produced a letter written by Ypsilantis and addressed to "the brave leaders of the Greek armies" in which, in his usual lofty way, the prince urged the Souliots to show the world they were descendants "of the glorious heroes of Marathon and Thermopylae." In fact, nationalism was an entirely alien concept to these Christian Albanians and they certainly did not see themselves as leading "Greek armies": the following year they would even tell the Russian czar—in a confidential message begging for assistance—that "we don't have anything in common with the other Greeks." They generally felt closer to their fellow Albanian Muslims than they did to the Greeks, and Ypsilantis's rhetoric surely counted for less than the trust the Souliots placed in Perraivos himself.[13]

The Etaireia was relying not only on the Souliots. The idea that the Greeks should themselves feign support for Ali Pasha also fell on fertile ground. After years under his rule, many Greeks on either side of the Gulf of Corinth found it hard to imagine life without him. They listened to the rumors that the pasha had converted to Christianity, that he had pledged a constitution to deliver the Greeks from Ottoman tyranny, and that banners bearing four crosses had been glimpsed flying from his castle. In fact, many Greeks favored backing Ali for real. One young Etairist remembered visiting Patras, the main port on the northwestern Peloponnese, and being astonished at the townspeople there: "These people . . . wanted Ali Pasha to win and deliver them: Him! Ali Pasha the tyrant, to aid the cause of Greece, and bring freedom to our country, this man who, had he gained the day, would not have left us our nostrils to breathe with!" Such sentiments were encouraged by Ali's Greek aides, who were in conversation with their countrymen and urging them to continue to support him.[14]

For his part, Ali proclaimed his love of the Greeks but complained that they had so far let him down. His every move, he wrote to Perraivos from Jannina, had been made out of a desire "to redeem that unfortunate race," but sadly they had not shown any signs of wanting to help him. Despite his advanced age, he had sortied out—like Leonidas, he said—at the head of his men to take on the foe; if the Greeks had followed his example, the siege would be over. Ali expressed the hope that they would all now realize their common need. One historian has described the Greek uprising as Ali Pasha's "last gamble." And so it was: but it turned out to have a life of its own.[15]

For the Ottoman position, as a few observers discerned at the time, was in reality no more secure than Ali Pasha's. A few days before the uprising broke out in the Peloponnese in March 1821, the British consul in Preveza noted that the influence of the Filiki Etaireia, which had previously been curbed by Ali's reign of terror, was spreading rapidly—he estimated it had 200,000 members, a vast exaggeration that testified only to its success and its renown—and was now "in the greatest state of activity." Rumors of the coming insurrection were everywhere. "What struck my ears, in Ioannina, at home, in Grammenon, in Arta," recollected a Greek from Epiros, "was always the phrase: 'The romeïko will happen.'" The consul Meyer saw nothing in the Ottoman system of government that could still this ferment. Whatever happened to Ali—and Meyer believed his downfall was only a matter of time—his view was that the sultan was far from secure in his position in the Greek lands too. Any sudden crisis might find his power dissolving "more suddenly than is generally imagined."[16] It was a perceptive assessment.

THE LAST DAYS OF
THE OTTOMAN MOREA

I will never become reaya, *nor kneel down to the Turks
Nor kneel down to the notables and the* kodzabashis.

"Stergios, or The Unconquered *Kleft*,"
folk song from the Peloponnese[1]

When Khurshid Pasha left the Peloponnese to march north against Ali
Pasha in the winter of 1820–21, he could have been forgiven for thinking
there was little to worry about. Compared with Serbia, where he had
successfully crushed a rebellion some years earlier, not to mention the turbulent eastern marchlands of Anatolia where war was about to break out
against the Persians, the Morea (as the Peloponnese had been known since
medieval times) was a haven of tranquility in an empire under constant
threat. Over the preceding century Ottoman power there had been largely
unchallenged, for with the notable exception of one Russian-inspired
uprising in 1770, the peninsula had escaped serious unrest. The Ottomans
had inherited from the Venetians a ring of well-constructed castles that
guarded the coastline. Discounting the prospect of danger from within,
they had moved the regional capital from heavily fortified Nafplion on the
sea to the landlocked town of Tripolitsa, which was conveniently located
in the center of the peninsula but at the end of a long supply line should
reinforcements be needed, and barely protected by its makeshift walls.[2]

Although Khurshid Pasha tried to reassure the local Muslim leaders
that they had nothing to worry about, they knew how precariously balanced the Ottoman system in the region really was. For one thing, only
one-tenth of the peninsula's 400,000 or so inhabitants were Muslims,
leaving the most overwhelming concentration of Greek-speaking Christians in the Balkans. Muslims predominated in Tripolitsa and the

fortified Venetian coastal towns but with the exception of two regions in the south and the west, the villages and the countryside were overwhelmingly Christian, which helps explain why the Greeks were able to take over the thinly guarded peninsula with such speed in the spring of 1821.[3] The regional military balance favored the Greeks too. According to the Etaireia's estimates, there were more than 30,000 Greeks under arms in 1820, compared with only 12,800 Muslims. This was an exaggeration and the real disparity was smaller because the Muslim troops were much better armed and more of them were professional soldiers, but they were still outnumbered in almost all districts.[4]

In economic terms, a tiny minority of Muslim landowners owned a staggering 60 percent of the property in the region, much of it in the hands of just two powerful families whose presence dated back to the end of Venetian rule. They were the regional versions of the great provincial potentates—the so-called *ayans*—whose rise was a feature of the eighteenth-century Ottoman Empire as exemplified most remarkably in the emergence of figures like Ali Pasha of Jannina. Yet unlike Ali, the Moreot landowners had surprisingly weak forces at their disposal; even the wealthiest of them all, Kiamil Bey—who was said to control more than one hundred villages from his base in Corinth—did not possess a large fighting force of his own: he could count in fact on barely four hundred men, fewer than some of the Christian notables. The beys' relative weakness, which probably reflected the lack of cheap and available Muslim manpower in the region, was glimpsed in 1770, when they were easily brushed aside by the insurgents, and was to be revealed again in 1821. In short, the economic predominance of the Muslim notables disguised their military vulnerability.[5]

Politically too the position of these beys was precarious for they were the servants of a capricious imperial system whose master, the sultan, was acutely conscious of his own limited reach and endlessly suspicious of their power, especially the tendency to incorporate entire villages into their vast domains. Unlike Ali Pasha, they did not hold the reins of government in their hands. On the contrary, the administrative apparatus of the central Ottoman state was as much their watchdog as their support—especially the *Mora valesi*, the governor of the region, the embodiment of the sultan's will—the position to which Khurshid had been appointed: this was a centrally appointed official whose seat was in Tripolitsa and who was charged in particular with the regulation of taxes and public order, the two priorities of the imperial government. To advise him the governor had two councils—one consisting of his own officials, the other a small advisory body of the most important Muslim and Christian notables of the region. It was the members of this latter group, the Christian landowning equivalents of the beys, who were both the principal rivals and the main collaborators of men like Kiamil Bey.[6]

The Greek notables of the Morea, the *kodzabashis*, are among the most important and ambivalent protagonists of the entire saga of 1821. For the truly striking feature of this region, which marked it out from most of the rest of the Balkans, was the surprising degree of autonomy that was granted under imperial rule to its Christian population in general and to its most powerful families in particular. Some of them would play leading roles in the war, securing political dynasties that endured into the twentieth century. Their memoirists extol the indispensable contribution of these "visionary men, thoughtful, highly competent with great patriotism and unshakable principles." Others, however, described them very differently: to many Greeks then and later, they were nothing more than Turk-lovers and worse—collaborators, to use the charged vocabulary of a later age.[7]

The value of these Christian notables to the sultan rested upon their capacity to raise revenues from the land and from those who worked it. The Peloponnese was divided into twenty-four districts called *kazas*, each of which was under the authority of a Muslim district governor and a Christian *kodzabashi*; the latter was charged, among other things, with assigning and collecting taxes from Christians on behalf of the Ottoman government. The *kodzabashi* was chosen annually by an assembly of the headmen of the villages in each district. In turn, the *kodzabashis* met together to choose two of their members to sit with their Muslim counterparts on the pasha's council. Estimates of the number of notable Greek families from which the *kodzabashis* were drawn range from eighty to nearly two hundred, but there were perhaps twenty-five or so who were to play a key political role in the uprising, and of these there were two—the Londos and Deliyannis clans—who led the factions that had come to dominate in the years before it. The power of such families was dynastic, secured by marriages and under the overall authority of a paterfamilias who ruled a large network of relatives. Kanellos Deliyannis was one of nine siblings, mostly male; Petros Mavromihalis, the Bey of the Mani (known as Petrobey), had five sons and six brothers, all of whom, one of his henchmen tells us, "had a religious submission to his commands." Great households such as these could easily number dozens of members and as many servants.[8]

This unusual form of local government had allowed the Greeks of the region to develop a significant tradition of collective deliberation under Ottoman rule: in the Mani, which was administered separately from the *pashalik* (province) of the Morea, this amounted virtually to self-government under their bey, who was always drawn from one of the great families of the peninsula. The Moreot Greeks had other rights as well, such as the privilege of sending agents to represent their grievances at the sultan's court in Constantinople (something denied to the Muslims); their judicial system was largely autonomous of the Ottoman state, and run by their bishops according to Byzantine ecclesiastical law; they even enjoyed the right to choose the Muslim judge (the *kadi*) and the governor (*voyvoda*) for their district. Some observers were so struck by these arrangements and the power they gave the local Christian leadership that, as the French consul wrote about the town of Kalamata in 1788, they understood them to be a form of "aristocratic democracy subordinated to the Sultan."[9]

This "aristocratic democracy," however, formed part of a hierarchical social structure with the poor villagers who sowed and harvested the crops firmly at the bottom: the largest single social category, the Christian peasants of the Morea, were the ones who would rise up in 1821, form the bulk of the first fighting formations, and support the insurgency over the years that followed. Their lives were arduous at the best of times because much of the Peloponnese was mountainous and relatively poor in farming land. In the last decades of the eighteenth century, however, the fiscal crisis of the Ottoman state, especially during the Napoleonic Wars, brought with it a growing burden of taxation that many villagers simply could not endure. One way out was brigandage, and another emigration, which is why many peasants left the Ottoman lands to find an easier and more prosperous life elsewhere, in the process emptying out entire villages. For those who stayed, indebtedness was virtually inescapable; moneylending became as lucrative as tax-farming for the Muslim and Christian notables whose grip upon the villagers was thus tightened. There was a fourth way out as well: conversion to Islam. This gained acceptance in the late eighteenth century especially in the west, in Albanian-speaking villages around Gastouni and Phanari, and in the south, near Mistra. A complex web of dealings thus bound together notables and peasants, Muslims and Christians.[10]

It is not surprising in these circumstances, where the numerical dominance of the Greeks was counterbalanced by the political dominance of the Ottoman Muslims, that there was a good deal of interaction between the two communities. How could it have been otherwise? Life tilling the fields created ties that bridged the confessional divide. In the hinterland of Monemvasia, a Greek chronicler tells us, Muslim and Christian farmers lived "in peace." The former had "more or less turned into Greeks," speaking Greek and no longer wearing Muslim dress. "Nor was their rule tyrannical and barbaric." Ottoman manners especially shaped the habits and behavior of the Greek notables, who dressed and behaved so much like Muslim grandees that in the eyes of the poorer Greeks there was not much difference between them. The fighter Fotakos, who was himself from a humble background, tells us: "The notable imitated the Turk in his dress, his external deportment and in his home. His ease of living was like the Turk's, and only the name differed so that they called him Yanni not Hasan and he went to church not the mosque."[11] The phrase the peasants had for these notables was *to gounariko*—the "fur-clad lot," meaning those who wore luxurious robes in the Ottoman style. One of the key symbolic steps undertaken by the notables in the first days of the uprising would be to give up their "Asiatic" finery in favor of Greek peasant dress, as if to bolster their national credentials.[12]

Christian and Muslim households were also bound together in intimate ways that were later forgotten or passed over in silence. When Petros Mavromihalis was appointed Bey of the Mani in 1816, making him the Ottoman official responsible for the area, the rumors circulated that he had got the position only because the imperial officer sent out to make the nomination, Sukur Bey, was in fact his uncle Ioannis's son Georgios who had been taken as a boy to Constantinople as a hostage decades earlier and converted to Islam. Lower down the social scale, two of Theodoros Kolokotronis's younger brothers were captured and sold into slavery during the Ottoman army raid that targeted the clan and killed their father in the early 1780s. Kolokotronis—for whom family was of supreme importance—tells us he managed to redeem his brothers later. What is not mentioned in his memoirs, but is described by his secretary, is that a sister of his had also been captured at the same time and ended up in Albania, a convert to Islam and married to an imam. When Kolokotronis visited her there more than two decades later, they embraced in tears but could not easily communicate as she had forgotten Greek.[13] Kolokotronis also had very close ties with local Albanian Muslims, cemented mostly through blood-brotherhood (*adel-fopoiisi*). His grandfather had been thus linked with an Albanian bey in the Morea, and Kolokotronis himself was so close to the bey's grandson, a notable called Ali Farmakis, that he twice risked his life for him: once to help him fight Ottoman troops, and once after he died, by going and paying his condolences to Ali's widow in person. Folk songs commemorated their friendship.[14]

Yet such stories of confessional coexistence should not obscure the acute asymmetries of power under Ottoman rule. Muslims might have been in the minority, but the Christians were unmistakably inferior. Fotakos tells us that any Christian meeting a Muslim on the road had to dismount as a mark of respect. Because Ottoman administrators were concerned about public order in general, they supported the Church and were willing to discipline corrupt or unpopular Muslim officials. But while Christian violence against Muslims was always taken very seriously, the Ottoman state was less concerned about the reverse, nor did it necessarily regard Christian violence against fellow Christians as its concern: in this sense Christian lives simply mattered less in the eyes of the state. "Being always armed, [the Turks] treat the miserable Greeks as a conquered people," wrote the author of an early analysis of the revolution. Lacking overwhelming might, the Ottoman state relied on other techniques such as hostage taking and the threat of draconian collective punishment to ensure obedience to its wishes.[15]

The precarious nature of these arrangements first became evident in 1770, when with Russia's encouragement the Greeks rose up, thus putting an end to what Kanellos Deliyannis in his memoirs described as "an era of great tranquility and great contentment [which] our ancestors called . . . the good times."[16] The uprising collapsed because the Russian reinforcements were too few to make much difference to the Greeks, but to crush it the Ottomans in the Morea were forced to call in thousands of Albanian mercenaries who came down from the north and rampaged across the country. For the Russians the uprising was an episode in a larger war that ended with major gains; for the Greeks of the Peloponnese it was an unprecedented tragedy and tens of thousands of people lost their lives in the years of massacre, plague, and looting that followed.

The memory of these events was fresh half a century later and one reason why people greeted the Filiki Etaireia's claims of Russian backing with suspicion: "What are they thinking of, my friend," Muslim notables reminded a Greek cleric at the start of the uprising. "Look, there's Rumeli, a hop, skip and a jump away . . . In twenty days, one hundred thousand Turks can invade the Morea. Let them remember the other fiasco [i.e., the revolt of 1770], what they did and what they suffered."[17]

Once the revolt of 1770 had been suppressed, the Ottoman state had faced a larger problem, namely, reestablishing its authority over the Albanian fighters. Betraying the fundamental weakness of the empire in a crisis, the Turks realized that the only way to drive them out was by soliciting the help of the Greeks themselves. As elsewhere in the Balkans, Christian as well as Muslim robbers and highwaymen had pursued their way of life over many decades, plundering farmers and travelers, and sometimes crossing the line into a more settled, lawful line of work by accepting positions as guardians of public order. These brigands, known as *klefts*, became the nuclei of the Greek forces that temporarily fought alongside the Ottomans to crush the Albanians.[18]

The decades after 1779 thus turned into a kind of brief golden age for the klefts of the Morea, a period that would later be idealized as a moment of resistance to Ottoman rule. In fact, the freedom klefts valued was primarily their own. "Three villages bemoan us / Three towns" begins a folk ballad about Zacharias Barbitsiotis, perhaps the most feared kleftic leader of them all. It paints a far from romantic picture of his men's brutal behavior toward the peasantry and conveys the blend of terror and admiration his name evoked:

> And a priest from Ayios Petros
> What did I do to him, the cuckold, that he cries about me?
> Did I slaughter his oxen, or his sheep?
> I gave the bride a kiss, and his two daughters,
> I killed one of his sons, and seized the other
> And took five hundred and two florins to give him back.
> All in soldiers' pay I doled them out, pay for the pallikaria,
> And kept nothing at all for myself.[19]

"Fleet-footed, well-built, medium-height," with black, curly hair, a wound on his right eyebrow "that made him handsome" and a powerful voice, Zacharias took his "independence to such a degree that he never in his entire life recognized anyone as his superior"—or so we are told by a Greek notable who remembered him. The stories about him ranged from his physical prowess—he could wrestle every man in his band to the ground—to his flag, supposedly bearing the inscription "Freedom or Death." He was as likely to blackmail Greek *kodzabashis* for money as he was the Muslim beys—although the wealthy Kiamil Bey was said to be on friendly terms with him. The deeds of Zacharias were legendary, but even some of his chroniclers felt compelled to acknowledge his fondness for the bottle, his notorious cruelty, and his tendency to mistreat women. When he was betrayed and killed by a Maniot chieftain, it is said the deed was prompted partly by Ottoman pressure and partly by the liberties Zacharias had been taking with the chieftain's female relative.[20]

The swaggering disdain of the klefts for settled village society, their use of plunder to finance the continued existence of their bands, their nonconformism and boldness were all in evidence when the revolution of 1821 began and helped to turn them into national heroes later on. Among them was Kolokotronis's father, ensuring a certain family renown that would pass down to Theodoros, who became a kleft in his turn. When he was ten, his father was killed; he fought under Zacharias later. But eventually the Ottoman government coordinated a drive against the bands, enlisting the support of the Orthodox patriarch in Constantinople who issued a fiery decree commanding all good Christians to help rid the province of the "evildoers and klefts." Many of them were wiped out. Kolokotronis himself narrowly escaped, went into hiding, and reached the safety of the Ionian Islands where he was to spend most of the next fifteen years, returning to the Peloponnese only occasionally at the risk of his life.[21]

By 1806, the klefts had been all but crushed, and the notables' power was as great as ever. When they faced increased taxes and controls because of the Napoleonic Wars, they fought back and after Ali Pasha engineered the appointment of his son, Veli Pasha, as governor of the Morea, Christian and Muslim notables began scheming together to evict him. In an extraordinary initiative, they even appealed collectively to Napoleon to take the Peloponnese under French protection, laying out a blueprint for a political condominium in which they would rule the region together. The proposal went nowhere but it remained, in the shocked eyes of later Greek historians, "a mindless, false combination" of the Cross and the Crescent. A better way to look at it would be as the expression of an elite regional class solidarity more powerful than any differences of faith.[22] Yet this strong sense of class feeling was accompanied by intense rivalries and infighting. There were two fairly entrenched factions of notables—one supporting Veli Pasha, the other opposing him—both involving close alliances between Christian and Muslim clans. Such politicking was increasingly lethal: the Greek leaders of the two factions were both executed as a result of their activities. By 1820, the notables of the Peloponnese thus found themselves locked in a deadly game that required expensive lobbying at the imperial court for ever more uncertain rewards.

As for the surviving klefts, banished from the mainland, they turned their exile on the Ionian Islands during the Napoleonic Wars to good use. Few Christians outside the Mani were skilled in the use of arms, but several thousand of them now acquired military training and combat experience through their participation in volunteer regiments that were established on the islands at various times by the French, Russians, and British. It was by serving in such units that the klefts from the Morea met their counterparts from farther north, Greek and Albanian, Christian and in some cases Muslim, laying the foundations for the personal attachments that would help the Etaireia to grow very rapidly a few years later. Many found themselves under the command of a British career soldier, Richard Church, who liked to pose in his *fustanella* (white kilt) as commanding officer of the 1st Regiment Greek Light Infantry. Kolokotronis was a junior officer in this unit and his relationship with Church remained strong even after the unit was disbanded at the end of the Napoleonic Wars: a decade later they would fight together again when Church was invited back to Greece as commander of the revolutionary army.

But in 1816–17 these Greek men of arms faced an impasse of their own: they were among the estimated 2.5 million veterans dismissed all over Europe at the war's end. Church went off to fight for the Bourbons in Naples, while some Greeks made their way to Russia for the back pay they were owed before joining up with the Etaireia. Keeping his red regimental dragoon-style officer's helmet, Kolokotronis settled down reluctantly on Zakynthos in a small house with his wife and children, working as a butcher and occasionally sitting in on his sons' lessons with their tutor. Other comrades returned to their mainland lairs but for Kolokotronis the Peloponnese remained dangerous. To a fellow chieftain back in the mountains he wrote enviously from exile: "You have gained your fatherland and you eat meat without weighing it . . . I have neither found it, nor is it likely that I am going to." Unsuited to civilian life, men like him responded eagerly to the Etaireia's call for it gave them a chance not merely to return, but to do so in a new and more positive guise—that of the patriot.[23]

Among the lesser-known figures who did make it back to the Peloponnese before 1821 were Kolokotronis's nephew Nikitaras and his cousin Dimitris Koliopoulos, commonly known as Plapoutas. By 1818 Plapoutas was a *kapo* (armed retainer) for the immensely powerful Deliyannis family, which like the other major clans kept dozens of armed men on its payroll. That summer, on the feast day of Ayia Paraskevi, he and Nikitaras were involved in a drunken village brawl in the hills to the west of Tripolitsa that nearly cost Kanellos Deliyannis his life and shone a vivid light on the social relations that existed in the pre-revolutionary Peloponnese between four key groups—Ottoman government officials, the Greek notables, the men of arms and, not least, the all-but-nameless Greek peasantry.

Plapoutas, Nikitaras, and some others had been escorting Deliyannis and a fellow notable through the mountains to a meeting with the Ottoman governor in Tripolitsa; leaving their two masters to make the last stage of the journey into the town alone, Plapoutas and Nikitaras had headed back, passing the village of Alonistaina, known to be the haunt of some Muslim hotheads. Foreseeing trouble, especially on a feast day, Deliyannis had warned Plapoutas not to enter it, an order he and his men duly ignored; sure enough, the dancing and drinking in the summer heat led quickly to a brawl that ended with two of the Muslim rowdies shot dead and others wounded. The villagers panicked, knowing that they would be held responsible by the Ottoman authorities, and they chased out Plapoutas and his men, firing on them as they fled and wounding Plapoutas in the foot; he was then carried off to safety through the woods on Nikitaras's shoulders.

When the news reached Tripolitsa that two Muslims had been killed by Christians in a village in the hills, a mob assembled in front of the mosque and called for vengeance. A massacre loomed and acute danger threatened Kanellos Deliyannis and his traveling companion, who were staying in the town that night. Fortunately, they had already been alerted thanks to a messenger who had rushed in before dawn and their friend-ships with local Muslim notables bought them time. The pasha himself hid his two important Greek guests near the women's quarters in his palace, ordered the angry crowd to disperse, and announced that the men responsible would be identified and punished. The two Greek nota-bles were protected by a large Ottoman guard while a unit of fifty men was sent out to bring back the heads of the culprits.

Yet Plapoutas was Deliyannis's henchman and son of the strongest and most fearless kapo in the region, a "*kapobashi* [head of a group of kapos] and *kleftokapetanios* [head of a band of klefts]" (in the words of an admiring folk song), a rough former shepherd whose massive tower can still be seen in his stronghold of Paloumba. Long-standing ties united the two families and only a few years earlier Plapoutas's family had helped shelter some of the Deliyannis men in a moment of danger: it was therefore inconceivable for Deliyannis to give Plapoutas up to the authorities to be killed. Sure enough, when the Ottoman detachment returned to Tripolitsa some days later with a couple of severed heads to show the crowd that the men responsible had been killed, the heads belonged not to the murderers but to two unfortunate Christian shep-herds who had been working in the fields. Almost no one there could recognize Plapoutas by sight; honor was satisfied and the matter was settled. Deliyannis in his memoirs says the two innocent men were killed by the Turks. Other sources suggest they were actually killed on his orders and handed over to the Ottoman commander along with a bribe to keep quiet. Money had certainly been involved: writing years later, Deliyannis was furious not only that his henchman's actions had nearly cost him his life but also that he himself had been forced to spend 20,000 *grossia* in blood money to pay off the families of the two dead Turks, plus another 50,000 on gifts for the pasha, his officials, and other Muslim notables.[24] Deliyannis would later play a critical leadership role in the war in the Peloponnese; Plapoutas himself became a prominent military leader, and later on senator and aide to the king. As for the two villagers who had lost their lives, their names were known locally and the graves where their headless bodies lay buried survived to the end of the nineteenth century. Deliyannis refers to them in his memoirs merely as "two poor guys" (*dyo ptoxous*)—unfortunates in the wrong place at the wrong time.[25]

*

The Etaireia's emissaries to the region were mostly drawn from the fighting class and they recruited into the organization many klefts and kapetans from the regiments on the islands, men who would form the backbone of the military leadership during the uprising. The notables dismissed these men, however, as their social inferiors; Deliyannis, for instance, describes the emissary Anagnostaras as "an opportunist and entirely unimportant," and claims his approaches were rebuffed by other notables.[26] Despite this ambivalence, which persisted on both sides, almost all the great families not only joined up but recruited others—had they not done so, the revolution would never have got off the ground: at least such a conclusion is suggested by the much slower and more partial engagement of other regions, such as western Greece, or the islands of Hydra and Chios, whose notables were far more cautious and reserved than they were in the Morea. By the summer of 1820 there was a large and sprawling Etaireia network across the Peloponnese. This created considerable unease among the *kodzabashis* due to their relative lack of control over a conspiratorial organization whose very existence had the capacity, should it become known to the Ottomans, to ruin them and destroy their own position. Unsure of the organization's extent, of the identity of its leaders or even of its plans, they took steps therefore to preserve their traditional authority. In "Thoughts of the Peloponnesians concerning the Forming of a System"— a document they sent off to the Etaireia in Russia in the spring of 1820 for its still anonymous leadership there—they suggested the Etaireia should allow them to create a regional administration to control the funds they raised in the Morea and compel obedience among its members. Ypsilantis, newly unveiled as the Etaireia's leader, agreed to allow this but insisted that their representatives—made up in the scheme of three bishops and at least five notables—should recognize his ultimate authority. On this basis, they went ahead.[27]

Ypsilantis's chief emissary to the Peloponnese was a priest called Grigoris Dikaios, better known to the Greeks as Papaflessas. The grandson of a kleft from Messenia, Papaflessas was a smart, sharp-tongued, indiscreet, and ambitious man whose life had been one long series of quarrels. His insult of a Turkish official when he was a boy at school had led his family to place him in a monastery for his own safety; a clash with the abbot had produced a move to another. He ended up heading to Constantinople with a letter of recommendation that, as he found when he opened it, described him as immoral and untrustworthy. He threw the letter away and before long he was an archimandrite in the service of the patriarch in the Ottoman capital, and a member of the Etaireia.[28]

The kind of man to push events forward by whatever means required, Papaflessas proselytized heavily for the Etaireia over many months in the Danubian Principalities before returning to Constantinople, where he forced the man who had recruited him to admit him into the most senior rank, waving a knife in front of him and threatening to go to the sultan if he did not get his way. Behavior that had got Galatis killed instead got Papaflessas promoted, and when Ypsilantis was put in charge of the Etaireia, Papaflessas impressed the prince with his energy and resolve. At the Ismail meeting in October 1820 he was one of the most outspoken advocates for immediate action in the Peloponnese—a region he had not visited for three years—and Ypsilantis showed his approval by offering him valuable gifts as well as entrusting him with the mission of informing the Greeks in the Peloponnese about his impending arrival.

Papaflessas's temper got the better of him one last time before his departure from Constantinople. Lathering his beard one morning, he was so infuriated when his servant accidentally washed the soap off too soon that he hit the man across the face. The servant, a Muslim Tatar, went off to the local police chief and said that his master was at the heart of a plot against the sultan and that there were frequent comings and goings in the house and talk of violence. "What sort of man are you that you have Muslim slaves and roam here and there, stirring up the Christians against my master?" the Ottoman official berated Papaflessas. Papaflessas protested he was merely a monk who traveled to spead God's word and had tried to look after a poor man as an act of charity. "These are my weapons," he said, taking a book of prayers out of his coat. A bribe secured his release, but the episode encouraged the Etaireia leadership, along with the patriarch, to get Papaflessas on his way south to deliver the message that Ypsilantis was coming.[29]

When he set sail, in late 1820, carrying a considerable sum in Etaireia funds, Papaflessas must have already known that the uprising would not happen before the spring. But unaccountably he had not yet heard that Ypsilantis had committed to the Danubian option instead and so he was still expecting the prince to arrive in the Peloponnese to take command. Papaflessas sailed to the coast of Asia Minor to commission a shipment of munitions, called in at Hydra and Spetses to whip up support for the revolution, and arrived off the Peloponnese shortly before Christmas, expecting Ypsilantis to be not far behind him. While the Moreot notables argued among themselves over who should run the business of coordinating their activities and securing contributions, Papaflessas sent them an utterly fantastical scheme calling on them to create an army of "only twenty-five thousand men," experienced in arms and organized into units with officers, ready for action when Ypsilantis arrived. This was typical of his lack of realism. Learning who the Etaireia's new emissary was, one *kodzabashi* who knew him was horrified: "Papaflessas? Po-po: we're done for!"[30]

A critical secret meeting took place at the end of January 1821 between Papaflessas and the most eminent of the Etaireia's members in the Peloponnese. Gathered at Vostitsa on the Gulf of Corinth, the region's leading notables and bishops were told for the first time that Ypsilantis was expected to arrive shortly to assume command. They were unhappy for many reasons. For one thing, they had no desire to place themselves under the directions of a Phanariot prince. For another, they remained deeply worried about whether Russian backing was really assured. The meeting only exacerbated their worries. Papaflessas was crass, unpersuasive, thuggish, and headstrong, unable to answer the tough questions they threw at him: Was the Etaireia's plan to rise up only in the Peloponnese or elsewhere as well? Why now when Europe was at peace? What would the attitude be of the European powers? Would Russia intervene and in what way? Were there any military preparations at all? They were not impressed by his blustering answers nor by his threat that if they refused his orders, he would use his funds to hire mercenaries from the Mani to start a war and then leave them to fend off the Turks themselves.[31] Disbelieving his assurances of Russian support, they waited for their own emissaries to Moscow to confirm what he said. From what we can tell from the sources, they agreed to work to prepare the peninsula for Ypsilantis's arrival and to aim for a late March uprising but with the possibility of pushing it back to April 23—St. George's Day—or even, in the worst case, to May, if they had still not heard from Russia before then. They were not to meet again as a group before the insurrection began.[32]

It must have been in early February, some days after the meeting at Vostitsa, that a young Etairist from Tripolitsa went out into the hills early one morning pretending to be going hunting; in fact, he had a secret rendezvous with an agent who turned out to be none other than Papaflessas himself. Disguised as a beggar, Papaflessas was initially nervous, mistaking the armed young Greek for a Turk, but once the misunderstanding was cleared up, they exchanged secret Etairist codes and embraced, and Papaflessas revealed who he was. He explained he had come "from the source of the revolution—Russia," and wanted to know the state of preparations in Tripolitsa and the south. He went on to say that the local Greeks there should be ready to rise up any day, that 10,000 men would very shortly be appearing in the hills above the town, and that a musket fusillade from a nearby mountaintop would be the signal for the Etairists to take up arms and head into the streets to fight. The result, we are told, was that the conspirators in Tripolitsa got excited and immediately readied themselves, taking their arms out of hiding and preparing for the great day. "However, many days passed and we saw no army arrive nor news from abroad and we fell back into inactivity, unsure what was happening and what we should do." The testimony is crucial because it makes clear that Papaflessas was following his original orders from Ypsilantis, which were to hold things in a state of readiness for his arrival: no specific date had been set either in Russia or elsewhere afterward for when the rising should take place. Indeed, it was only a week or two after this that Papaflessas sent off a series of almost hysterical letters complaining he had been left without instructions since November, seeking to find out why Ypsilantis was taking so long and warning they had no time to lose.[33]

The resolution during the meeting at Vostitsa in January had been, so one of the participants tells us, "to preserve great secrecy and discipline and if the secret should be betrayed, to take up arms."[34] When they heard that preparations for insurrection were being conducted openly on the island of Spetses, the notables reminded the islanders to keep things quiet. They also conferred with shipowners on Hydra to see if they knew what the Russians' intentions really were; the shipowners there were skeptical and refused to believe the Etaireia's claims. In fact, they sent word to the headquarters in Constantinople that they would support an uprising only if the imperial fleet was destroyed first; they were not prepared to risk the destruction of their own ships for less.

The trouble with the notables' caution was that they were no longer in control: talk of an uprising was spreading so fast it was turning into a self-fulfilling prophecy. One source estimates the Etaireia had 20,000 people associated with it by the end of 1820 and even if this figure is inaccurate, it is clear that insurrectionary rumors were circulating widely in early 1821. In Dimitsana, in the heart of the Peloponnese, the Greeks had started up gunpowder mills under the noses of the local Muslims. In the Mani, Kolokotronis was in discussion with the kapetans. Not only Papaflessas but other Etairists assured Petrobey that the Russians were coming, and that Ypsilantis was on his way to the Mani, with a vast treasure. Four decades later Fotakos summed it up starkly: "God had got men drunk so that they believed lies to be truths; and if we now try to figure the whole thing out, it began with lies and ended with lies and the lies are still all around us."[35]

Awaiting Ypsilantis, Perraivos was worried. He had never shared Papaflessas's gung-ho attitude: he regarded his entire approach as amateurish and dangerous. "The Greeks could not have been more lacking in weapons, nor had they any overall plan of where, when and how to begin the war," he wrote. "Rather each district or town rivaled the other to kick things off and to become the exemplar." Weapons and explosives were still scarce; few men had any kind of training and a clampdown by the Ottoman authorities could have cost hundreds or thousands of lives. Not only was there no clear command; the real trouble, Perraivos wrote, was that people would no longer listen: "A thousand Demosthenes would not have succeeded in calming their spirits, but would instead have risked their lives. To argue against immediate action exposed one to the accusation of being 'a Turk worshipper' [tourkolatris]."[36]

As confirmation of how far things had gone, in early 1821 a message from Capodistrias actually did get through warning the Greeks not to launch the uprising before Russia had declared war on Turkey. The news should have dampened the excitement but it had little effect. Reaching Tripolitsa—whose Greek inhabitants were most immediately exposed to possible Ottoman vengeance—the message plunged the local Etairists into gloom because they saw no way out. If they rose up, they would be crushed; if they did not, they would probably suffer awful collective punishment and the loss of their leaders. They were all the more worried because they saw how some peasants had noticed the unmistakable preparations for insurrection and might notify Ottoman officials in order to escape blame. The Etairists therefore decided to ignore Capodistrias's instruction and go ahead anyway. In the noise and excitement of those months, its import was drowned out—there are few references to it in other accounts—and the belief that the Russians were on their way remained an article of faith.[37]

Word of the Greeks' activities had indeed reached the Ottoman authorities. They learned some details from informers, got scattered information from villagers, and noticed a newly assertive attitude among the Christians. They tried to figure out whether attacks on tax collectors were the work of klefts or portended a rising. A Greek notable in Tripolitsa rejected an invitation to join the Etaireia, refused to swear an oath of secrecy, and promptly went off to inform the Ottomans that something was brewing. Seized documents were scrutinized by Ottoman officials, who needed Greeks to help try to work out their meaning, and thus misread them as the work of Freemasons plotting foreign invasion. Spies were sent out. One, masquerading as a Greek, was sent to the archbishop in Arkadia to ask him whether the stories of a planned uprising were true. It was only after the spy failed to recognize the secret signs of the Etaireia that the archbishop, who was a member, realized the danger. The Etairists meantime did their best to pretend nothing was amiss. One day, the watchmaker Stefanopoulos tells us, "some of the Turks in Tripolitsa were passing the time at their favorite café and they were saying that 'not all is well with the Christian folk, they are buying flints, cartridges, pistols, rifles,' and so they invited me over and willingly or no I went and they complained about all this, and even so I managed easily to persuade them that these were all rumors of friends of Ali Pasha."[38] This was the Greeks' preferred rebuttal, helped by the fact that it corresponded to the official Ottoman view in Constantinople.

Nevertheless, worried by the signs of impending trouble, Khurshid Pasha's deputy got a small detachment of troops sent back to the Morea at the start of 1821, and he even received orders to be ready to kill the Greek leadership if necessary, orders that remained secret for the time being. Then, at the start of March, the Ottoman authorities ordered more than twenty bishops and notables to come to Tripolitsa, effectively to serve as hostages. Those summoned included nine senior clerics and twelve primates; Mavromihalis's son, who was already being held there, was now joined by one of the Deliyannis brothers and other members of the leading families of the Morea. Proof of the very real dangers that faced the notable class under Ottoman rule, their presence in Tripolitsa temporarily allayed the worries that had begun to circulate among members of the Muslim elite. The hostages would remain for months, held in increasingly harsh and crowded conditions, where most of them died before the town fell to the Greeks in September.

But in the northwest of the Peloponnese this development acted as a kind of catalyst upon plans for the rising. A few of those notables who had been summoned failed to obey, pleading illness or other excuses, and they met in the Ayia Lavra monastery, dejectedly hoping either for good news from Russia or for the arrival of Ypsilantis. They briefly contemplated fleeing overseas before realizing this would simply leave the remaining Greeks in the region to the mercy of the Ottoman authorities. It was a lesser-known notable from the town of Kalavryta, Asimakis Fotylas, who made them realize that things had proceeded to the point where they now really had no choice:

> We have done what we could until now, and drawn things out, but from now on, the Turks won't believe us however much we try to fool them. Thus as things are now, they will cut off our heads and not only ours, but those of all the Christians, and God knows if they will not send our women and children to Asia . . . So my view is we should take up arms and God help us, and what will happen will happen.[39]

ON OR AROUND
MARCH 25, 1821

Praise be to God! We've won the romeïko, *brothers, we've won it!*
A messenger on the Greek side passes on the news: April 1821[1]

Some years after Greece's independence had been won, it was decided to make March 25 a national holiday to commemorate the start of the insurrection. Other possibilities had included March 22, when fighting broke out in Patras, and February 26, when a cathedral mass had been held in Jassy at the start of Ypsilantis's expedition into the Danubian Principalities. But the logic behind the choice of March 25 was compelling: by connecting the Annunciation to the Virgin Mary with the emergence of the Greek nation, it turned the birth of Greece into a quasi-divine event, and at the same time relegated the Etaireia's failed Danubian adventure to the status of a prequel.[2]

It did not, however, have much to do with historical veracity. The March 25 date may have been earmarked at some point by Ypsilantis; it may also have been adopted by the notables at Vostitsa. But the evidence in both cases is surprisingly slim and mostly after the event, and whether or not the date had been discussed, it had not in fact been followed. The Peloponnesians had actually sent a letter on March 24 to the shipowners on Hydra and Spetses, apologizing that the uprising had gone off prematurely. The Romantic painting by the Greek painter Theodoros Vryzakis, depicting the Metropolitan Germanos blessing the Greek flag in the monastery of Ayia Lavra on March 25, is a magnificent reconstruction of a scene that cannot have taken place since Germanos—who has left us his memoirs of that time—was many miles away on the day in question in Patras, together with the other regional leaders. What the postindependence inauguration of a national holiday did very successfully was to create a fixation with the precise date of the uprising's start. From the time the first accounts of the uprising appeared, many of them written by former participants, there was intense competition to identify *the* specific moment in which the armed struggle in the Peloponnese erupted.[3]

"Dear Episcopal Vicar Frantzis," wrote the magnate Kanellos Deliyannis in 1840, in a long letter to the author of a valuable early account:

> Mistakenly, or from ignorance you write on page 146, that Soliotis and the Petmezades killed Ottomans on the 14th and 16th March, that the rebellion [*apostasia*] first appeared on 20 March in Kalavryta and Old Patras, and on the 23rd in Kalamata. The truth is that on the 18th for the first time the inhabitants of Lapata near Kalavryta killed 6 of the Tsipoglaioi tax collectors, on the 19th the villagers of Sopoto killed the *moukapelentsides* Asim Agha and Dervis Agha and their two guards; on the 19th horsemen, officials, revenue collectors . . . and any other Turks found in the villages of Akova and the mountains were arrested on my orders, disarmed, bound and brought to Langadia where . . . 48 of them were killed on my orders . . . while in Kalamata not even a pistol was fired for a long time.[4]

Deliyannis was disputing the accolade usually given either to the revolutionaries in the northwest or to Mavromihalis, who had helped to organize the assault on the southern town of Kalamata and the largely bloodless surrender of its Ottoman garrison. These days there are at least half a dozen "birthplaces of the revolution" that vie for primacy on the internet. Some hail the raising of the flag in the Mani. Others give pride of place to Patras or Kalavryta. But history is not a competition and amid all the claims and counterclaims two things are clear: First, that several months of preparation and spreading the word, both through the Etaireia and outside it, had created an atmosphere of such intense expectation, fear, and rumor during the last fortnight in March that violent clashes became inevitable. Second, that because everyone was still waiting for the arrival of Ypsilantis, there was no overall leader and hence no real plan. What matters is not who was first but the fact that the uprising occurred in so many places more or less at once. It is this that shows the Etaireia had achieved an important goal— disseminating the message of revolution widely across the entire Peloponnese. To do this, they had worked through members who could take advantage of the established networks of patronage and authority that existed among the Greeks, networks that would remain operative and structure the apparent chaos of the first weeks of the uprising in the absence of any central command.[5]

The man whose account Deliyannis found fault with, Ambrosios Frantzis, had been the episcopal vicar—bishop's deputy—in the small coastal town of Arkadia when the uprising started. Both Frantzis and his bishop were Etairists who had attended the meeting with Papaflessas in Vostitsa. Some time after the bishop was summoned to Tripolitsa in March, worried local Ottoman officials in Arkadia consulted Frantzis. They were scared by a rumor that warships had moored in the Gulf of Sparta, with European troops sent by Christian kings in order to slaughter them. They issued instructions to the local farmers to bring in their pack animals so they could leave, clearly worried Muslims were no longer safe staying in the town, before another rumor sent them rushing for the safety of the ruined castle. After a sleepless night, the Muslim notables decided to escort their families to more secure forts farther along the coast, and they ordered Frantzis to go and calm the Greek peasants in the villages.

Frantzis raced off through the olive groves on horseback, keen to see for himself what was happening, and he rode so fast into a gathering of armed villagers that they mistook him for a Turk and nearly shot him. There were about 160 *palikaria* (young men) from one village known for its warlike traditions, and behind them were 600 more led by fellow Etairists, one of them carrying a flag made of a white sheet fastened to a long reed. Frantzis's first reaction was to ask why they had disobeyed his orders by coming out with their weapons when this could lead to a massacre. They told him that they had learned the Turks wanted to kill the villagers anyway. They had come to guard him because they feared the Turks would take him away. The rumors multiplied, as someone arrived with a proclamation from Papaflessas and Kolokotronis telling the Greeks that "the hour has come" and that they were on their way with an army of 10,000 to help them send the Turks "to Hell." Learning that some men had just gone off to kill the Turks collecting pack animals in the villages, Frantzis ordered them back, reminding them not only that it was a sin to murder but that the villagers of the neighboring settlements would suffer the Turks' revenge. He then sat down and wrote a remarkable message to the Muslim notables in town:

Most noble *aghas*, I salute you . . . I arrived at Kefalari near Soulima and found so many hopeless things I cannot describe them to you, things I never saw even in my dreams. Men have in general gone mad and don't know what they are doing. They listen to the words and views of anyone. Which charlatan led them to this I cannot say; the plains and mountains are full of armed men.[6]

Frantzis was seeking to preserve his standing with the Ottoman authorities even as he assumed command of the rebels, and he wanted to encourage the Muslims to leave the town peacefully for somewhere safer by warning them of what was happening. In Arkadia, however, the Christian townspeople were alarmed about what would happen if their Muslim neighbors left and so begged them to stay, and even asked for a letter attesting to their loyalty to the sultan, in case of trouble. "Who cannot shed a tear at that tragic exodus," wrote Frantzis:

Elders, aghas, womenfolk—wives and young girls—ran not only on foot (since they had loaded up the animals with their belongings) but barefoot for the most part, since the fine slippers which they wore did not stay on their feet. It was remarkable to see those Muslim women bid farewell to their Greek friends and embracing them . . . and to shed floods of tears at their parting. One saw the same thing between Muslim and Christian men who accompanied the departing Muslims for half an hour, the ones saying "Farewell neighbor" to the Greeks with tears and sighs, and the others replying: "Farewell, may God bring us to meet again."[7]

Frantzis's moving and fast-paced account of the days and hours leading up to the outbreak of the revolution on the western coast of the Peloponnese illuminates several features of the situation. First, there was the omnipresent fear: the Muslims felt outnumbered and feared the Greeks; the latter feared their masters and their revenge. Remembering 1770, prudent men on both sides anticipated a bloodbath and did what they could to avert it. Second, it was not so much bloodthirstiness as rumor that drove events toward violence. In Galaxidi we know that Etairists deliberately spread stories about the Russian army and navy coming to help from the north to get the *romeïko* under way, and similar rumors were traveling through the Morea, even if there were no parallels to the enterprising Etairist who dressed up as a Russian general to give the stories credibility.[8] News and stories of far-off developments were reaching these small towns and villages, and most decisions were having to be made on the spot fast. Thus the Muslims decided first to take refuge in the ruined castle above the town and then to leave completely. Frantzis, who in his bishop's absence was the natural authority figure for the Greeks in the area, had to tread very carefully so as to protect the lives of the Christian inhabitants of the area. The armed young men from the villages had to decide whether to obey his instructions or to take up arms to come and find him. The Etaireia had been highly effective in spreading the insurrectionary message among the Greek population. But it was not as though everyone had suddenly decided they could not live with their Muslim neighbors. Some villagers were clearly ready to fight to the death. But in the town, in particular, where Muslims and Christians were neighbors, who ate and bathed together, borrowed from one another and knew one another from childhood, there was evidently much sorrow in a parting that was destined to be permanent.

The second half of March was thus when a pattern of sporadic and episodic violence turned into uprisings at either end of the Peloponnese. In the now volatile atmosphere, there were disparate triggers. In the north, where several kapos and village units had already begun to murder a number of locally prominent Muslims, a wider rising was precipitated by the hostage crisis: the notables of Achaia, having refused to surrender themselves to the Ottoman authorities in Tripolitsa, and sensing that time had run out, gave the signal to the kleft-kapetans in their service to besiege the town of Kalavryta, whose garrison surrendered on March 21. Nearby Patras was next and fighting on its streets soon followed.

In the south, it was on or around March 15 that a ship arrived in the Mani peninsula bringing the astonishing information that Alexandros Ypsilantis had already launched the revolt three weeks earlier by crossing the river Pruth into Moldavia. In the frenzy of the moment Ypsilantis had forgotten to alert the emissaries he had sent out around the Aegean. It was left to the level-headed Emmanuil Xanthos to find a Greek ship docked at Ismail on the Danube, whose captain was willing to make the risky journey south through the straits. Only now did the Greeks in the Mani learn that the leader of the Filiki Etaireia was not coming, and realize that the revolution had already begun. Historians have not generally connected this news to the start of the uprising in the southern

Peloponnese, but it is hard to see how it could not have been a spur to action and Xanthos himself clearly believed it had been.[9]

Mavromihalis was still waiting for confirmation of Russian support, and his natural reluctance to jeopardize his official Ottoman position as bey had been increased by the fact that he had not one but two sons being held as hostages, one in Tripolitsa, and the other, Georgios, in Constantinople. But he was being pushed into action by events. He learned the Etairists had spirited Georgios away from the Patriarchate where he had been lodged, thereby neatly both putting Mavromihalis in their debt and compromising him (and the patriarch) in the eyes of the Ottoman authorities. Next came a crisis at the nearby town of Kalamata whose worried governor learned about a large mule train that had been spotted leaving the coast and heading inland. He was right to be concerned: it was loaded with munitions that had arrived for the revolutionaries. When the governor took the Greek notables of the town hostage, the situation escalated rapidly: Maniot troops under Mavromihalis entered Kalamata and the Turkish garrison surrendered without a fight on March 23. Even then Mavromihalis was still trying to keep his options open, claiming implausibly he had acted merely to save the town from "brigands," and sending word to Tripolitsa proposing to exchange the voyvoda of Kalamata for his son, continuing secret but fruitless negotiations for some weeks before they were accidentally discovered by other revolutionaries and brought to a halt. At the same time, a grandiloquent proclamation prepared by his Etairist advisers went out in his name seeking Europe's help for his army of "Spartans" in their revolt against tyranny. In such ambiguous fashion did the revolt in the south begin. With no one in overall command, decisions were made in rapid conclave on the spot: some bands dispersed across Messenia to attack the Ottoman fortresses of the southwest, while Kolokotronis, Nikitaras, and Papaflessas marched north toward Tripolitsa. On March 25, Kolokotronis laid siege to Karytaina and by the end of that week Greek forces controlled much of the center of the Peloponnese.

Contemporary observers found it hard to believe the Greeks had taken the initiative alone. Czar Alexander and Metternich had assumed that behind the insurrection in the Danubian Principalities there must have been the guiding hand of a secret international revolutionary organization, and they did not abandon this attitude when the Morea erupted into violence. The sultan, for his part, assumed the Russians were behind it. Even many Greeks linked the fighting to the long-promised intervention of foreign kings. It is as though no one could grasp two essential features of the revolutionary wave of that spring: first, that it was the work of the Greeks themselves, and second, that it had happened in the absence of its expected leader. Yet the very fact that events took place almost simultaneously at either end of the peninsula—a journey of several days at a minimum—shows that decisions were being made locally and that there was no overall plan beyond what had been rather tentatively agreed upon back in January at Vostitsa. "The Peloponnese moved, not being sure that they were on the move in other parts," writes Anagnostis Kontakis. "The bad thing was that there was no preparation, no leader: but each district rose up and mobilized its own leadership: the only guide was danger, our leader and salvation." Naturally some refused indignantly to take up arms, like the Corinth notable who cursed those who "took the world by the throat" and risked bringing down bloodshed on the Greeks as the rebels had done half a century earlier.[10] Others hesitated. Konstantinos Papazafeiropoulos, a powerful figure from the village of Lasta, went to talk to the primate Kanellos Deliyannis to suggest they join forces to attack Tripolitsa, only for Deliyannis to ask him to wait a few days while he tried to liberate his brother who was among the hostages in the town. But this was no longer something that could be stemmed. On the contrary, as each encounter brought news of the unthinkable—Turks killed or put to flight by Greeks bearing arms—so the uprising spread.[11]

The Etaireia's impact was felt in several ways. First, the false story of Russian support fueled that unstoppable wave of enthusiasm and anticipation that generated its own dynamic since everyone was aware of Russia's enormous value as an ally. Second, its members recruited volunteers to fight from the Ionian and Aegean Islands, from the coast of Asia Minor, and from even farther afield. Third, it fostered cooperation among Greeks not only of different regions but also of different classes: blood grudges between former klefts and those who had chased them years before were temporarily forgotten, so were rifts of long standing among the notables. A certain class resentment of the landowners, fueled by earlier revolutionary radicalism, never left the minds of many Etairists, but for a few weeks it took second place to the need to defeat the Ottomans.

The truly astonishing result was that in little more than one week virtually the entire Peloponnese, with the exception of a few fortified coastal towns, the capital Tripolitsa, and the hill country of Lala in the west, fell into the hands of the Greeks. On March 23–24 the Muslims of Argos departed for Nafplion; on March 26–27 they fled from other districts to the safety of the coastal forts or Tripolitsa. There was a little fighting in one or two areas where the Muslims had flocked together, but overall what was most remarkable was the speed of the capitulation. The sense of euphoria among the Greeks was surely extraordinary and we catch glimpses of it in the sources, before it all came to be seen as pre-ordained and inevitable. In late April the Greeks of Argos sent a messenger to Corinth with a letter for Papaflessas. The messenger, who must have been a Christian Albanian, drank heavily along the way and by the time he reached the town it had fallen to Ottoman Albanian reinforcements sent in from the north. Not realizing he had crossed over onto the enemy side, he hailed the sentries with the excited, joyous words: "We've won the *romeïko*, brothers, we've won it!"[12]

Yet the reasons that had led the magnates to hesitate remained valid. The Greeks possessed no military organization at all; one would have to be improvised from the highly localized and personalized levies of man-power that had emerged in March. No systematic thought had been given to the supply situation and there was an acute scarcity of arms. Above all, relatively few Christians had any real knowledge of fighting. The inhabitants of Argos, Anastasios Orlandos tells us, were "neophytes in the arts of war" who had "taken no measures to protect themselves or their families." The primates of Mistra grieved at the "lack of forethought and disorder of our forces." "This was the commencement of our warfare and they did not know how to fight," Kolokotronis acknowledged in his memoirs. "At first the kapetans treated their men like brothers," writes Fotakos, "trying to teach them what revolution meant, and with them still unaware of who was in charge of whom." They were unfamiliar with killing: even he, a committed young revolutionary, confessed to being upset by the sight of a mound of bodies after one of the early clashes. Any setback immediately evoked memories of 1770 and caused villagers to flee into the hills.[13]

Deliyannis's memoirs give an account from the perspective of one of the chief Peloponnesian notables of how the insurgency was organized locally at the start and how precariously balanced it all seemed. Orders went out on his authority in March for men to join bands under well-known kapos. Within a couple of weeks there were hundreds at his disposal and his own stronghold (*patrida*) of Langadia became a provisioning and mustering center whose Muslim inhabitants were themselves detained as hostages. What had been hidden, writes Fotakos, was now happening in plain sight. Armed kapetans were flocking to the fortified houses of the notables to receive weapons and money. Women and children were filling cartridges and baking bread. When Kolokotronis arrived from the south, with 300 men mostly provided by Maniot chieftains, he was given some troops to command but he started out as one of a number of kapetans whose cooperation—for food and supplies—was entirely improvised. Papaflessas had been dishing out military ranks to local commanders, but the impression they gave of formal organization was spurious. Deliyannis himself was new to the military life: as he admits, it was only a few days earlier that he had set aside his customary robes, furs, and "all those Asian clothes" and put on the Greek *foustanella*, the shepherd's cap, and shoes. Other notables were doing the same thing, abandoning the visible signs of their former rank.[14]

Initially, the villagers had been astonished to see Turks surrender to them; it was, an observer says, "a great wonder." But they remained instinctively obedient to the voice of the *agha* (a local Muslim man of standing), revealing a fear, according to Fotakos, that was "rooted from childhood in the souls of men." Nor did they immediately take to the military life: The Greeks' first efforts to besiege Muslim-held fortresses were desultory and interrupted by other concerns. Outside Koroni, the local peasants abandoned the siege lines to farm their fields, leaving the siege to the Maniots who were not much better at it, since they returned regularly to their families; over a few months the siege gradually disintegrated. Badly disciplined, poorly armed peasant bands also failed to prevent reinforcements reaching the besieged Muslims of Karytaina; when the Ottoman troops approached, the Greek peasants simply melted away.[15]

Because many Greeks lived in terror of Ottoman reprisals for weeks after the uprising began, the temptation to capitulate was always present. The headmen of one village hid some Turks who were in danger of being killed by insurgents and then appealed to the Ottoman authorities for a formal acknowledgment of their loyalty.[16] In the village that was his family stronghold, Deliyannis was shocked to find the same defeatist mood and took extreme measures in response. Before leaving for the attack on Karytaina, he had disarmed the forty Muslim families of the village and put them under the guard of their Christian neighbors. But the latter thought he and the other fighters had fled to Zakynthos and decided in their absence to free the Muslim hostages and to go with them to Tripolitsa to announce their submission and seek an amnesty for the entire region. "Terror and despair seized me and my brothers," Deliyannis writes. When he heard about it, he turned to his companions and explained there was only one thing to do: "Send orders without any delay to kill all the Muslims that remain in Langadia, men, women and children, some three hundred in all, and to burn down the mosque . . . And then we will have surely saved the fatherland; otherwise we and the nation are lost!" He thus sent off his younger brother Konstantaki with 150 armed men and they entered Langadia at dawn the next morning and carried out his orders, killing all the Muslims they could find and burning down the village mosque. As was the intention, the Christian villagers were appalled and terrified: the killing of the Turks was for them a completely unprecedented act. Deliyannis told them sternly that he forgave them; the main thing was that "it was impossible henceforth for us to live together with Turks." For the insurrection to succeed meant convincing the peasantry there was no point in thinking any longer of surrender: in short, they were starting to understand the grim implications of a popular revolutionary insurgency.[17]

The Peloponnese had never been heavily garrisoned. There were usually perhaps some 12,000 Ottoman soldiers guarding it in normal times but when Khurshid Pasha departed to head north for the campaign against Ali Pasha, he took many of these with him. In early 1821 the Muslim notables requested him to send back several thousand men in case of problems but he initially provided far fewer, assuring them that at the slightest hint of trouble from the Greeks he would instantly respond in force. As late as April 1821, a full month after the uprising had spread to the Peloponnese, the Grand Vizier's advice was still to bear in mind the two imperial priorities—Ali Pasha in Epiros and the revolt in the Danubian Principalities.[18]

Nevertheless, two contingents of Turkish reinforcements arrived that month which looked as though they might turn the tide. The first came about by accident after Khurshid dismissed one of the commanders with him, Yusuf Pasha, and ordered him to go to the island of Evvia. It happened that Yusuf Pasha's route led him and his men through Patras, after the fighting broke out there. They arrived on April 3 and stayed to shore up the Ottoman position in the northwest Peloponnese, strategically vital for communications with Rumeli. By holding onto Patras, Yusuf Pasha was also able to rescue many Muslim villagers from the surrounding hills and he retained such an effective grip on the fortress, despite acute provisioning and financial difficulties, that it remained in Ottoman hands throughout the entire war. Had Patras fallen, the Greek claim to independence would have been immeasurably strengthened. But it never did.[19]

Tripolitsa, the administrative capital, also received reinforcements. The town was an obvious target for the Greeks because its walls were scarcely fifteen feet high, it lacked water, and it was overlooked on three sides by mountains; the Ottomans had clearly discounted any serious internal threat for decades. Located in a landlocked plain where the temperature can soar to above 100 degrees in summer, it was also crowded with Muslim refugees from the villages in the hills. Khurshid Pasha sent Mustafa, his chief of staff (Kehayia Bey), south with 3,000 men in April to help it hold out, and this force entered the Peloponnese in the middle of the month and marched along the southern shore of the Gulf of Corinth, crushing all opposition, until it reached Corinth and Argos. In Nafplion the local Muslims told Kehayia Bey he should evacuate the inhabitants of Tripolitsa. But such a move would have looked very much like a sign of defeat, so he marched inland, clearly expecting to have no difficulty wiping out the uprising entirely. At first Kehayia Bey's confidence seemed warranted: through late April and into early May his successes along the northern edge of the Peloponnese were repeated in no fewer than four victorious encounters with the poorly organized and easily intimidated Greek bands massing outside Tripolitsa.

Under the impact of these Ottoman counterattacks, however, the Greek leaders started to coordinate. On April 28, Kolokotronis was made military commander for the Karytaina district and a few days later another experienced kapetan was put in charge of the camp at Vervena. In both places, committees were appointed to supervise administration, supplies, and communications, and conscription was given over to men who were known to the villagers in their area. Of critical importance was the decision by the Deliyannis family to hand over the military direction of the war to former kapos and klefts. Elsewhere the kapetans were made to swear an oath of allegiance to the notables, much as they always had done. But around Tripolitsa, the new commanders were empowered, their legitimacy deriving now not from their obedience to the great landowning clans but from the collective will of their region, or as was stated in Kolokotronis's letter of appointment, "by the entire Race of the district of Karytaina." In this way the revolutionary war undermined the old quasi-feudal order in the countryside and laid the foundations for a different kind of politics.[20]

In the spring and summer of 1821, we are just at the beginning of the rise of Greek military men, of whom Kolokotronis would become the best known. Later mythmaking exaggerates his stature during these early weeks of the uprising. As a notorious former kleft, Kolokotronis was important enough back in February for the Ottoman authorities to have been alarmed by a report that he was returning from Zakynthos to participate in an uprising. Yet when he landed with a single companion on the shore of the Mani, his position was dependent on the will of his Maniot hosts and he was very far from being, as a later historian wrote, "the real commander-in-chief [*pragmatikos archistratigos*]"—a rank he would gain only a year and a half later. Mavromihalis's longtime bodyguard later wrote to correct the postwar Kolokotronis cult: "How many men did Kolokotronis have in the Mani? . . . Who would have dared to rise up in the Mani or in the Peloponnese if the Chief [*Archigos*] of the Mani did not want to move?"[21] It had been the Maniots who sheltered Kolokotronis from the Ottoman authorities and who gave him men to march with into Kalamata while in Gortynia, his next destination, "the entire district . . . operated by will of Kanellos Deliyannis."[22] For long afterward, the Deliyannis family still regarded Kolokotronis as their social inferior and in some sense beholden to them.

Yet to their credit, they understood they needed him too. Kanellos Deliyannis's blessing put the old kleft in charge of the men being gathered from the central Peloponnese; under his leadership, the soldiers were mustered every two days in the hills around Tripolitsa, and desertion was ruthlessly punished. In May this work paid off when Greek forces successfully fought off an Ottoman attack at Valtetsi and then fell upon the retreating troops, carrying off large quantities of booty and supplies: it was their first major victory in the Morea and both a psychological and military turning point. Unable to use their cavalry effectively, Ottoman excursions into the hills dropped away. The Greeks gradually tightened the siege around Tripolitsa, pushing their lines ever closer while remaining within the safety of the hills, and the number under arms grew from fewer than 6,000 in April to more than 10,000. A series of smaller victories followed, and then at the end of June the Muslim Albanians of Lala retreated to Patras, in effect leaving the rebels in control of most of the western Peloponnese. With the approach of summer the Greek tactics were simple: avoid direct confrontation and force their enemy into the hills where the terrain suited the Greeks. They were playing a waiting game, cutting Tripolitsa off and trusting to time and the heat to do their work. As the Turks sent out foraging parties to feed the town, they came under attack by the besieging bands who would pick off their pack animals as well as the horses that the Turks let graze in the nearby fields.

Beyond this increasingly effective military strategy, however, there lurked the fundamental political questions that one of the notables had put at Vostitsa back in January to the Etairist emissary, Papaflessas: "As for us here, once we have killed the Turks, to whom do we surrender? Whom will we have over us? As soon as the people [o rayias] take up arms, they won't listen to us or respect us, and we will fall into the hands of men *like that* (the speaker pointed to Papaflessas's brother Nikitas) who a little while ago could not even use a fork to eat."[23] The question betrayed the anxieties of the landowning class, but it was true that the Etaireia had begun without any clear political goal beyond that of disarming the Muslims and nullifying the threat they posed. By the early summer, the Greeks not only knew that Alexandros Ypsilantis had opted for Moldavia rather than the Morea; rumors were also reaching them that he was now at the head of a large army advancing southward through the Danubian Principalities toward Edirne in the direction of Constantinople itself. (In fact, the rumors were entirely baseless: he was days away from a catastrophic defeat at Dragaşani nearly one hundred miles north of the Danube.) The news only rendered the question of political leadership in the Morea more acute, especially as some of the Etairist agents in the region were worrying that the revolution was in jeopardy from a "lack of regular direction and by a tumultuous disorder."[24]

If the young Etairist agents saw the *kodzabashis* and their tendency to equate the nation's interest with their own as the root of the disarray, the notables saw themselves rather as the solution and were naturally focused on preserving the power they had accumulated under the Ottomans. Thus their response to Ypsilantis's absence was—after a little prodding from some of their political advisers—to create a regional administration of their own. Convened initially in the monastery of Kaltezes in the hills south of Tripolitsa, their so-called Peloponnesian Senate was essentially a vehicle for them to control the continued direction of the war. We know little about what was decided there, other than that Mavromihalis was given the largely honorific title of commander in chief of the forces in the Morea—no one familiar with the wary and cautious Bey of the Mani could have mistaken him for a dynamic wartime leader—and that the participants agreed the overall question of how to run the insurgency should be revisited once Tripolitsa had fallen. Several key notables were not present and neither were there any representatives of the islands, nor most of the important military chieftains, who remained occupied with the ongoing struggle. The Senate was important symbolically as an assertion of the will of the landowners and a reminder that what counted for them was the preservation of their regional power.

But the Peloponnesian Senate had been in existence for barely three weeks when astonishing news transformed the political landscape and brought the Etaireia's leadership back into the picture. A boat from Trieste had docked at the island of Hydra in June with an Ypsilantis prince on board—not Alexandros but his younger brother Dimitrios. Announcing himself as the emissary of "the commander-in-chief of the Race," he declared grandly that he had come to "most beloved Greece" as "plenipotentiary commander-in-chief of the Peloponnese and the other regions."[25]

Back in March, when the difficulties of the Moldavia expedition were becoming evident to Alexandros Ypsilantis, he had decided to send his younger brother to the Peloponnese in his place. Unable to risk the Black Sea passage through Constantinople, the alternative was a hazardous journey through the Habsburg lands. The long-time Etairist Panayiotis Anagnostopoulos led the small group in the guise of a Russian merchant: Dimitrios Ypsilantis was in disguise as his "servant"; his bodyguard made a third. After some narrow escapes they reached Trieste at the start of June, undetected by Metternich's much-feared police.[26] Prince Alexandros Kantakuzinos, who had gone ahead of them to divert attention, contact sympathizers, and raise funds, arrived some days earlier with considerable fanfare and caused so much excitement

among the local Greeks that the police hardly registered when Anagnostopoulos's small group arrived. They did remark that the two
servants ate with their supposed master, and that in general their bearing and behavior suggested they were "anything other than servants."
But their passports seemed in order and they were allowed on board the
Fidelissimo, a brig that had been secretly placed at Dimitrios Ypsilantis's disposal by its owner, a Greek merchant in Trieste, and which sailed
with its twenty-eight passengers out of the port under the Russian flag
at dusk on May 28/ June 9. It carried a cargo including a printing press
(the first to reach the Greek mainland), weapons, ammunition, and
food. A week later the Trieste police chief faced the wrath of Metternich
and the emperor when they learned, too late, that one of the notorious
Ypsilantis princes had slipped through their fingers.[27]

When the *Fidelissimo* reached its destination, Hydra, on June 8/20,
great hopes rested on the shoulders of this slight and sickly aristocrat,
whose Greek name disguised the fact that he was a product of the military academy in Paris and the imperial court of St. Petersburg. Dimitrios
Ypsilantis's arrival was widely believed to herald the Russian reinforcements from the north that would help the Greeks complete their
conquest of the Peloponnese; notables, chieftains, and their men jour-
neyed to the coastal town of Astros to welcome him. As one of his
secretaries later put it, his arrival was "exceptional, even unique, in the
chronicles of Greece. There appeared to the Greeks on that day no foreign representative of Rome, Venice or Turkey, but a Greek of a princely
and always patriotic family, Greek in flesh and bone."[28] To the peasants,
Ypsilantis was their long-prophesied prince from overseas. Many of
them saw him as the ruler who would liberate them not only from the
Turks but from the *kodzabashis* they loathed.

Although the landowners looked forward to greeting him too, their
reception was very different from what they had expected. Invited on
board, they found a small, unimposing man seated stiffly on a throne; to
their greetings, Dimitrios Ypsilantis responded "like a hospodar" with a
slight incline of his head—a typical Phanariot, comments Deliyannis—as
if they were his underlings. They were startled and outraged that he
behaved much more warmly toward Kolokotronis and the local Etairists,
their social inferiors, embracing them and kissing them. They suspected
that some of his Etairist advisers saw the landowners as the foe, little better than the Turks, and that Ypsilantis shared their views.[29]

After the Greek leaders escorted their new guest to their encampment in the hills, and the feasting and celebrations gave way to talks, the tensions between the Etaireia leadership and the Peloponnesian landowners quickly exploded. The latter had not thrown their weight behind the revolution in order to see it undercut their own privileges: their vision of freedom for the Greeks was a regime that would function much as before except without Ottoman oversight. Dimitrios Ypsilantis, a man who had never set foot in the Peloponnese until this moment, evidently envisaged something very different—a kind of replica of the system in the Danubian Principalities, in which grateful peasants were ruled by a powerful prince who could keep the local landowners in check. Ypsilantis now demanded the dissolution of the Peloponnesian Senate, so that he could exercise power unimpeded in the name of the Supreme Authority of the Etaireia. Naturally, the magnates pushed back, suspecting him of seeking to undermine them so as to become "dictator" and "highest leader of the Nation." His unfortunate habit of giving his subordinates Danubian titles such as *izpravnik,* which were unknown in the Morea, intensified the concern that he had come to turn the Peloponnese into a kind of Moldavo-Wallachian hospodarate with himself as its ruler. It did not help when one of his aides, Konstantinos Kantiotis, the Etairist agent who had formerly served Capodistrias in the Russian foreign ministry, threatened the Peloponnesian notables that if they did not do as they were told, 12,000 Russian troops would arrive "and then you'll see what fate awaits you." Let them come and kill me first, the urbane and unflappable Andreas Zaimis, one of the most powerful landowners of the northern Peloponnese, is said to have responded. "What matters is the salvation of the fatherland."[30]

A different man from Dimitrios Ypsilantis would have taken on the notables, for the newly arrived prince certainly enjoyed the support of the ordinary soldiers and their kapetans. Instead of confrontation, however, Ypsilantis withdrew from the talks and without telling anyone he left the Greek camp suddenly. The *Fidelissimo*—the ship that had brought him—was at anchor off Kalamata and when his departure was discovered, the soldiers accused the notables of trying to chase the prince out of Greece for their own "tyrannical reasons." There was an uproar as hundreds of villagers gathered in the camp, shouting "We want Ypsilantis!" and "Kill the Turk-loving bosses." They quickly surrounded the house in which Mavromihalis was meeting with Kolokotronis, Deliyannis, and others to discuss what to do, and for a moment the notables were in acute danger: it was one of the few moments in the war when we glimpse the unmistakable class anger felt by the ordinary peasants of the Peloponnese toward the *kodzabashis*, an anger that the Etairists were happy to whip up.

The Etairists perhaps—but not Kolokotronis, who declared he would talk with the protesters. The landowners were not sure where his allegiances lay and were terrified he was going to take the side of the mob: after all, the notables' disdain for their former men of arms was matched only by the latter's reciprocal mistrust of them. But in fact, Kolokotronis was a political realist who likened the revolution to a tripod held up by three institutions—the notables, the clergy, and the fighters like himself—so he now charged off into the midst of the mob, shouting to them to follow. He was determined to defuse the situation and the crowd was willing to listen to the old kleft. Standing on some rocks, he promised them he would bring Ypsilantis back. But they should remember: they had vowed to kill Turks, not fellow Greeks. Their uprising against their tyrants had attracted the admiration of Europe. If they killed the notables, what would the world say? That they had not risen up for fatherland and freedom, that they were no better than "Carbonari, rebels and troublemakers" and no one would want to help them. In that case, the great powers would help the Turks, and their lot would be worse than before. Otherwise, they should disperse and leave him to bring the prince back. In a country that valued rhetoric, Kolokotronis's plain speaking—rich, direct, and pithy—brought the insurgency back from the brink.[31]

After that, an effort was made on both sides to patch things up. Dimitrios Ypsilantis was named commander in chief of the war effort and agreed to share power for one year with the Peloponnesian Senate. The deal reserved him some additional powers but, because decisions depended upon votes rather than executive fiat, it implied a clear shift away from the kind of princely authority Ypsilantis would have preferred and became a precedent for the political arrangements that were forged later in the year through the founding of Greece's first national assembly. Written off by some historians as merely a sign of regionalism— which it certainly was—the Peloponnesian Senate turned out to be not only the embodiment of the resistance of the region's landowning class to the Etairists from Russia but also the first incarnation of a new kind of national politics, the expression of a preference for representative government that constituted a stark contrast between the Greeks and the Ottomans.[32]

Dimitrios Ypsilantis's authority never stood as high again. In truth, it had depended heavily on reports of the success of his brother Alexandros to the north, which he tried his best to exploit. In an effort to end the siege of Tripolitsa, Dimitrios wrote to the Muslim beys warning them that his brother's 80,000-strong army had reached Edirne and offering them, as his emissary, to guarantee their safe passage to Anatolia. He told the most powerful shipowner in the Greek islands, Lazaros Koundouriotis on Hydra, that war had been declared between Russia and the Ottomans. Gradually it became known that none of this was true: the Russians had held back from war and there was no 80,000-strong Greek army. On the contrary, by the middle of August, news had reached the Peloponnese of the real fate of the expedition into the Danubian Principalities. The *romeïko* in its traditional conception—a Christian king restored to the throne of Constantinople by foreign intercession—was clearly over. The result was corrosive for Dimitrios Ypsilantis's long-term political future, and for the fate of the Etaireia in Greece.[33]

On his own, the younger Ypsilantis was not a sufficiently commanding figure to be able to turn his widespread support among the Greek villagers into a more permanent power. Although the position had been his for the taking, he failed to become the national leader the revolution wanted and that—unlike its American and French precursors—it never acquired. He had accepted his brother's mandate but lacked the strength of character to carry it out and as for the money he had brought with him, it was quite inadequate for the purpose. A French artillery officer who had arrived to fight with the Greeks, Maxime Raybaud, has left us a vivid but damning portrait: stiff in his personal interactions, physically unimposing, and prematurely balding, Dimitrios Ypsilantis was a man who was courageous on the battlefield but otherwise indecisive. Fond of talking in French with visitors and reminiscing about his days in Paris, his experience in the Russian army when he was nineteen had given him, in Raybaud's words, "a sprinkling of military knowledge [*une légère teinture de l'art de la guerre*]." But he lacked political sophistication, held the assumptions of his class, and was unwilling to impose himself except rhetorically. His personal courage was clear, but Raybaud was not the only one to question whether he had the temperament of a revolutionary. Those who had come with Ypsilantis from Trieste remained outfitted in their black Etaireia uniforms with the death's head on their caps, increasingly sidelined. When a young Englishman reached his camp, he found "the most stupid inactivity": "The Greeks walked about with their pipes in their mouths, the prince slept twelve and frequently fourteen hours in the twenty-four, seldom came out of his hut, and was chiefly employed in writing letters and issuing orders that were never obeyed." He was a figurehead for an army in which "there was no authority or command."[34]

The need for some kind of political centralization thus remained. Around Tripolitsa, every village had its own would-be leaders who had a say in when the villagers would fight and what supplies to provide. "I told them often," Deliyannis recalled, "I beseeched, I urged them, I advised them to concentrate politically and militarily, to create a provincial system of their own, but it proved impossible." In the hills above Tripolitsa, the Peloponnesian notables looked forward to "the establishment of a national system, and to good order among the local bodies."[35] To avoid further political dissension, they decided to wait until Tripolitsa was taken in order to convene a national assembly. But for them, "national" still meant primarily and predominantly a system with the Peloponnese, and themselves, at its heart.

The population of the besieged town was more than double its usual size of 15,000–16,000, swollen by the presence of refugees from around the region and the several thousand additional troops sent in by Khurshid Pasha that spring. By July 1821 shortages of food and water were beginning to tell and many of the remaining Christian inhabitants were forced out to conserve supplies. Inside, the newly arrived Albanian soldiers positioned themselves by the wells to make people pay them for access. At night they bought food from the Greek troops outside, which they sold on within the town. In the no-man's-land outside the walls, cheese, figs, and butter were swapped for fine clothes, guns, and knives. Greek soldiers were even let into the town, hauled up the walls by rope. The Albanians within the town had their counterpart among the Maniot fighters outside it who plundered their own bread convoys coming from the mountains for the Greek troops and then sold on the bread.[36] Inside Tripolitsa, the Ottoman leadership was divided over what to do. The local Muslim beys wanted to negotiate an end to the siege; those from elsewhere, mostly government appointees, wanted to fight their way to the coast; and the Albanian military contingent, whose leader Elmaz Bey was a longtime servant of Ali Pasha, wanted to negotiate a separate surrender for themselves.

Dimitrios Ypsilantis was especially adamant that the profits of any negotiation should be put to general use and on September 11 he brokered an agreement with the other Greek leaders on how to divide the spoils: in the event of a negotiated surrender, the soldiers were to receive two-thirds, and the public treasury one-third; if the city was taken by attack, the proportions were to be three-quarters and one-quarter. The other leaders of the insurgency disagreed with his insistence on treating Muslims humanely and even more with his idea of taking control of the plunder in the name of the nation. His emissary—the highly capable Prince Alexandros Kantakuzinos—had already supervised the peaceful surrender of the fortress of Monemvasia to the south, securing the safe passage of the Muslims while the booty they left behind was appropriated in the name of the national struggle, leaving the local chieftains outraged. If there was one thing almost everyone else could agree on, it was not allowing Ypsilantis to assume control of the treasure that awaited them in Tripolitsa, and when news came that an Ottoman relief force had entered the Gulf of Corinth, they encouraged the young prince to go to the aid of the insurgents there. Had he truly appreciated what was at stake he would not have left; his decision to depart the siege smoothed his path into irrelevance. In Raybaud's words: "the greatest advantage which could have resulted from the fall of Tripolitsa, the formation of a national exchequer, was at that moment lost."[37]

At dawn on the same day Dimitrios Ypsilantis left, a crowd of Muslim women and children emerged from the town, forced out by hunger. Searched by the Albanians for any hidden valuables, they ended up under Greek guard alongside the road to Kalavryta where they scavenged for weeds in the summer heat. Many died of hunger in the coming days; others were hunted down. A few hours later they were followed by a very different group—a negotiating committee of five Ottoman delegates, mounted on Arab steeds and attended by slaves—who seated themselves under canvas in no-man's-land for talks. Joining them there were the Greeks speaking for the revolutionaries: Mavromihalis, Deliyannis, the Metropolitan of Old Patras, Kolokotronis, and a couple more. One of the less conspicuous figures among them was the thirty-one-year-old Etairist Anagnostopoulos—the same man who had accompanied Ypsilantis on his journey from southern Russia to Hydra; he was there as the prince's representative and his recently unearthed protocols of the meeting are a precious source for this encounter.

"Tell us in the name of your God what is going on, and what are the causes?" the Turks began. "Are you Peloponnesians acting alone, or the entire Nation [*ethnos*]? Is any other Power behind you and has that Power empowered you, or are you acting alone?" To which the Greeks replied: "Unable to endure any longer our sufferings at your hands, we have decided upon this, and Europe, seeing the justness of our cause, has decided to help us." The Turks: "That is all well but are you subordinated to any power?" At this point Anagnostopoulos intervened, aware of the delicacy of the question of who was in charge: "Aghas! . . . We have come according to the instruction of the Prince [Ypsilantis] and by the will of all [the Greeks]." He went on to say that they had the support of Russia and Europe behind them. They had decided to rise up on receiving the news of the killing of the patriarch in Constantinople; all the kings of Europe were meeting in Vienna and their support for the Greeks would soon be manifested. Such were the preliminaries. But when the dealing began, Kolokotronis insisted upon stiff conditions and the delegates withdrew to the town for further consultation. By September 16 their discussions had broken down and desultory fighting broke out again.[38]

Among the Ottoman delegates was the leader of the Albanian troops, Elmaz Bey—"one of the most handsome Turks I'd seen," writes Raybaud, who was in the Greek encampment. "He was dressed with all the extravagance of the Albanian style." When his bejeweled fingers aroused the attention of the Maniots, he ignored their glances, smiling "with the disdainful and tranquil irony of a man accustomed to command and unafraid of personal attacks. With his air of ease and security, one would hardly have imagined that he found himself among his enemies." Elmaz Bey had reason for feeling confident: on September 18 he brokered a safe passage for himself and his men with Kolokotronis. The Greek had very close contacts with Albanian chieftains that dated back years and he now gave Elmaz Bey his personal oath—that *besa* which all men of honor in Ottoman Balkan society recognized as the sign of noble character and the basis of mutual respect—to guarantee their way back home safely through the Greek lines. The next day, the bey sent thirteen large treasure chests for safekeeping under Kolokotronis's watch.[39] Some of the wealthiest Muslim and Jewish families were also making their way to the Greek tents to conclude deals of protection while the Spetsiot shipowner, the widow Bouboulina, entered the town to negotiate with the women of Khurshid Pasha's harem. After dark, a stream of heavily guarded pack animals brought silver and other precious objects into the encampments of the major chieftains. Tripolitsa was not only the center of Ottoman power in the region, it was also by far the repository of the greatest riches. Such secret deals thus offered a chance for enormous private gain.[40]

These comings and goings were not lost upon the Greek rank and file who now feared they were about to be cheated of the city's fabulous treasure. Anagnostopoulos, who as an old Etairist was sympathetic to their worries, recorded the dissent that began to surface:

> 22nd Thursday. Kolokotronis began to confer very secretly with the Albanians, the Bey [i.e., Petrobey] with Kiamilbey, and other Turkish notables. After these private conversations, they continued in public calling us into the discussion and all the other kapetans together who were there. Kapetan Konstantinos Valsamis, Kapetan Panayiotakis Zafeiropoulos . . . began to shout while they were talking, saying they will prove that they are Greeks, and no lower than the others. Old Anagnostaras, being smart, realized their error and told the others that he foresaw widespread anger on the part of the other kapetans and the people, to which they [i.e., Kolokotronis and the notables] answered: "Which People is that?"[41]

"Which People is that?" So much for Kolokotronis, the man of the People, beloved by later generations! At this juncture the real cleavage was between the Greeks' leaders and the men that followed them, and nothing could express the anarchically democratic nature of the insurgency better than the events that grew out of that mistrust, ending the siege not as the result of a concerted attack but almost by accident, in a moment of improvisation and greed.

September 23: a brilliant, hot morning opened the day on which a key meeting was to take place inside the serail so that the divided Ottoman leadership of the town could decide what to do. Outside in the hills there was silence. Suddenly it was broken by an indistinct noise and then by the sound of cannons. As the besieging troops around the town quickly learned, a few Greek soldiers had scaled one of the walls on their own initiative without meeting any opposition. Later it transpired that in all likelihood they had told the Turkish soldiers they wanted to come up in the usual way for business and had been pulled up by rope after which the guards had paid them little attention. Led by one of the numerous lesser kapetans who feared being cheated of the spoils, this small group managed to open one of the town gates to their fellows: the word spread, the other gates were opened, and all discipline broke down as thousands of fighters poured in, encountering little resistance because the Albanians had withdrawn into the citadel to await their safe passage out. The Frenchman Raybaud decided to follow them into the town.

The first thing he noticed were armed groups roaming the streets looking for victims to rob and murder. Corpses lay underfoot. "It was a hell of iron and blood, in which the crash of falling houses, the blast of artillery shells, the noise of the fusillade which never ceased, the cries of the dying and the strange yells of the victors ran together to form a terrifying concert." Shots flew. Women and children were thrown from windows. Soldiers argued at the entrance to the wealthiest houses and tried to force their way in. Inside one mosque, apparently as yet unransacked, a slight noise betrayed the hiding place of someone still alive. Much of the city was on fire and the heat was almost unbearable. Raybaud was struck by the victors' ululations—"the cry of the man-tiger, man devouring man"—in the moment of killing.[42]

Taken by surprise, Kolokotronis and the other commanders lost no time in rushing in. It was too late for them to tame their own men. But they knew they needed to secure the lives of the Albanians; if attacked, the latter could inflict enormous casualties on the undisciplined Greeks. The Greek leaders were also anxious to ensure the safety of the main Ottoman notables, all of whom were worth more alive than dead—and, the most important of all, Khurshid Pasha's wives. Kolokotronis's men protected Elmaz Bey's men and marched them out of the city through the Kalavryta gate to the safety of a nearby encampment.

As the serail went up in flames, the women of the governor's harem and dozens of their servants, along with the most important Muslim officials and about fifty of their finest horses, were ushered out into the gardens by Greek guards and then hurried into a fortified mansion nearby, where they were protected from the mayhem outside. Deliyannis—who two years earlier had nearly been put to death himself in the town—describes the scene in his memoirs:

> They asked me who I was and I said that I am Kanellos Deliyannis. They ran straight over to me, shouting and crying, and then told the two wives of the Vezirs and they too ran over and grabbed my clothes shouting in Turkish: "Save us, Kapetan! In the name of God, for the love of God! Have mercy! Have compassion!" . . . I gave them my word of honor that I would save them and took them all into the garden which was walled around in the Turkish style, and I immediately set a guard around them and gave strict orders they were not to let other soldiers approach and Papatsonis and I spent the entire night there.[43]

This was the provincial notable exulting in his power. But the destruction of Ottoman authority and Tripolitsa's collapse also signaled the rise of the former kleft, Kolokotronis, at the head of the military, and arguments among the Greeks broke out even while the fighting was going on. When the revolutionary leaders were brought together to divide up the spoils by Mavromihalis in the house of one of the leading Muslim beys, they all agreed it was important to keep the hostages safe and to allow the women to keep their valuables and their servants. Dissension arose over their horses however. Kyriakoulis Mavromihalis, the bey's younger brother, was starting to apportion them among the different chieftains when Kolokotronis intervened and said he was owed all the horses due to the district of Karytaina. The younger Mavromihalis told him that was the domain of the Deliyannides, insults and curses were exchanged, and he then hit Kolokotronis, telling him angrily: "Shit-Vlach! You want me to make you a big chief, you old kleft?" The two men had to be pulled apart by the other leaders until tempers had calmed down.[44]

"I'm no friend of that kleft, and I don't fear him anymore," another of the Deliyannis brothers bragged. For his part, Kolokotronis seemed indifferent: "Calm down, it's nothing," he told Fotakos who was outraged, "They're right, kid, because they see these corpses here of those with whom they once shared power. Now the nation has taken it." At least in the telling, Kolokotronis was keen to assert a revolutionary new order of things. When he and his brave but boorish second son, Gennaios, called upon the richest captive Muslim of them all, the worldly Kiamil Bey, the sixteen-year-old Gennaios greeted him with unbecoming familiarity: "*Geia sou* [Hey there], Kiamil." The bey, reclining at ease on the divan of the house of a Greek friend, betrayed no sign of offense at this astonishing breach of etiquette and replied similarly. "Don't be surprised by my greeting, Bey," Gennaios went on. "Now the time has come for the Greeks to greet you as you used to greet the *rayiades* [Christians]. We are all equal: *geia sou*, Gennaios, *geia sou*, Kiamil." Fotakos tells us they all laughed. Kiamil Bey asked who the boy was and being told he was Kolokotronis's son, he got up and petted him gently and told him he was brave and would grow up to be a great man, but he should remember to behave courteously and to keep his promises. Kiamil Bey was under the protection of Kolokotronis; so were the wealthy Tripolitsa landowners, the Arnavutoglous. The Greek chieftain was too late to save another friend of his, sheyk El-Haj Ahmed Necib, who was the mufti of the town and who died defending his dervish *tekke* (place of worship) with a large force; the sheyk's sons survived, however, in the care of the Deliyannis brothers who later allowed them to go to Egypt in return for a large ransom. At least a dozen of the top Ottoman officials were captured alive.[45]

In the streets outside, all control had broken down, and as the fighting raged for many hours, Muslim families desperately defended themselves from inside their homes. The widely loathed Ali Tsekouras, a man who had bedeviled the lives of the Greeks for years with his greed and cruelty, barricaded himself with his family and some companions and fought for two days to the death. But it was not only Muslims who lost their lives. Most members of the city's small Jewish community were killed; only a handful of well-protected individuals survived the collective blood lust.[46] Another victim was the Greek primate of the Tripolitsa district, Sotiris Kouyias. Formerly one of the most prominent notables in the Morea, he had remained in the town throughout the siege and was accused of having been a traitor, then tortured and killed by a notoriously rapacious Greek kapetan. Greeks who lacked weapons now armed themselves; some went around decked out in luxurious robes and valuables that they had seized from the Muslims or received in payment for looking after them. Nikolaos Kasomoulis, a fighter from the north, who had come to Tripolitsa to seek help for the uprising back home, was shocked:

> Entering the gate, what did I see? Noises, disturbances, yells and tussles among the soldiers . . . We were just about able to emerge unscathed from

the throng of different bands all avid for booty. Along the streets I saw the windows of houses with painted signs of St. George, with Panayias, with Crosses, with St. Dimitrioses, with St. Nikolaoses, according to the whim of each band leader among the Greeks, with the doors blocked up from inside with stones, each guarding his loot so that others should not enter and take it.[47]

Kolokotronis, a man of the hills by tradition and by upbringing, had never liked towns and had a special revulsion for Tripolitsa. On entering it, he is said to have stood a moment in front of the great old plane tree near the market where many years earlier the heads of his relatives and friends had been displayed during the great campaign against the klefts. This, after fifteen years, was his return and his triumph, as much over the primates as over the Ottomans themselves. Ordering the tree to be chopped down, he installed himself in an Ottoman mansion where Kasomoulis witnessed him and his son mocking the absent Dimitrios Ypsilantis before scrambling to find more Muslim houses to claim so that their men should not be left out of the general plundering. It was then that Kasomoulis, as he wrote later, started "to figure out the sort of people I had come to."[48]

The fighting, butchery, and looting went on for three days until, on September 26, heralds announced an end to the killing and patrols were established. When the soldiers who had been with Ypsilantis returned to Tripolitsa, there were further arguments over the spoils. Weeks later, with the streets still strewn with corpses, the subject was unresolved. But Ypsilantis could do nothing for his men. On October 12, now back in the town, he wrote a letter to soldiers guarding the passes against possible attack from the north, to sympathize with their grievances: "My brothers! The complaints of those done out of their share of the spoils have been going on continuously for the twelve days now that I have been in Tripolitsa. I grieve that those who ought to have enjoyed recompense for their troubles took nothing but that others, strangers, or working little for the fatherland, plundered and looted all of Tripolitsa and all of that happened in my absence and they left everything upside down. This is why there is now great disorder . . . You are not the only ones to have been hard done by. You have many others in your position." But the gratitude of the fatherland, which is all he offered them, was small compensation and a confession of his weakness.[49]

Kolokotronis and Dimitrios Ypsilantis stood for very different principles—not merely personal gain versus collective solidarity, as Raybaud moralized, but perhaps more importantly two visions of political and military mobilization. Kolokotronis's prestige was inherently personal; it did not depend on his holding any special office but was based primarily on stories of his own bravery and exploits and on his ability to secure the means to pay his men. Although he had, temporarily, melded the armed bands of the Morea into a sufficiently coherent organization to mount the siege, his power base was a local one, concentrated on the area around Karytaina. He was known to "love" the Peloponnese and had little interest in what lay beyond the Gulf of Corinth. A widower, he was wiry and plainspoken, sharp-eyed and watchful. Used to life outdoors, he ate sparingly and slept lightly. Despite his years of service with the British in the Ionian Islands, he had no interest in European-style methods of warfare or military organization, and he relied for success on the time-honored methods of irregulars in the Balkans—keeping behind cover, avoiding pitched battles on flat ground, and using ambush and surprise raids to devastating effect. Although he paid lip service to Ypsilantis when it served him, he basically had no respect for the "foreigners" who—in the words of his aide Fotakos—had come to Greece "wanting only to rule, cheating the natives, whose simplicity and sincerity they judged to be ignorance and stupidity."[50]

Ypsilantis, on the other hand, was a man educated in a European court, an army officer, and an aristocrat. He too was not wanting in courage, but that was where any resemblance with Kolokotronis ended. In the summer of 1821 he was undoubtedly the most important of those foreign-born Greeks who had come to join the struggle. But Russia's failure to declare war on the Ottoman Empire weakened his standing and his brother's failure further damaged it. Status-conscious, he tried to preserve the pomp he felt his position required. Lacking a local power base, he was increasingly aware that neither his family name nor his office within the Etaireia would automatically produce the deference he expected. He had attempted and failed to take charge of the Greek war effort; his absence from the first great triumph of the insurgency testified to his political obtuseness.

Kolokotronis had better understood what drove those fighting. Yet it was Ypsilantis and the Etairists around him who grasped the larger political context and the need to organize the administration of the uprising more formally if it was to prevail. That task had already proved to be beyond him. It was to be realized not by him but by another member of the Phanariot princely class who arrived in Greece the month after he did—and without the blessing of the Etaireia behind him: this was the figure of Alexandros Mavrokordatos, who was to become one of the most important protagonists in the leadership of the Greek cause.

THE PISA CIRCLE

Fate wanted this thoughtless movement to happen. Now that those who are without the requisite experience, practice and preparation, have seized the tiller, and realize they are leading the ship into terrible danger, precisely now is when we are needed, who have some idea about sailing, to take the helm and to captain the ship with all our strength, to prevent an irreversible shipwreck.

Panayiotis Kodrikas to Nikolaos Postolakas,
Le Havre, August 22, 1821[1]

"I know," said Mr. Niebuhr, "that the whole revolution broke out too soon, and against the wishes of the best leaders of the whole affair. Nothing is so difficult, in matters of this kind as to have the rare moral power of waiting, and also the penetration and character to say: 'Now is the time.' Besides, it is hardly ever possible to keep from the best-planned mines political clowns who put the match to them, or make them otherwise explode, before the proper moment. Then is the time to show the man; and few of those who plan the most judiciously are possessed of that combination of powers which invents at the instant new means for every emergency. This requires not only political wisdom but political genius."

F. Lieber, *Reminiscences of an Intercourse with Mr. Niebuhr the Historian* (Philadelphia, PA, 1835), 106–7

It was in 1819 that the Swiss botanist Augustin Pyramus de Candolle found his attention shifting from plants to the human species and in particular to some new arrivals in his home city of Geneva—a "singular class of men, half princes, half individuals, half Asiatic, half European, half civilized, half barbarian." This was the entourage of the former Phanariot hospodar of Wallachia, Prince Karatzas, an affable and handsome man who had fled to Europe to enjoy the riches he had plundered from the province. (Behind him he left a Romanian saying—"Theft as in the time of Karatzas"—to testify to his impact on its population.) Aside from their picturesque Ottoman garb, the prince and his companions failed to sustain de Candolle's interest—except for one man, Karatzas's nephew, "Prince Mavrocordato . . . a remarkably well-educated and deep-thinking man, gayer, livelier and less solemn than all the others." De Candolle asked the young Phanariot to run through the great princely families for him: "Oh! I'll tell you," he answered in front of Prince Karatzas. "First of all there is mine! That is the first: then come the Ypsilantis, the Soutzos etc., and then the Karatzas and so on."[2]

Not yet thirty, Alexandros Mavrokordatos was among the most intriguing and important figures thrown up by the Greek struggle for independence. Formidably educated and hardworking, reputed to be conversant in ten languages, he was a product of the Enlightenment and a believer in the power of letters. Teachers and scholars were among his valued correspondents, and his inner circle comprised bright young men up to date with the latest works in Paris and Geneva. His Swiss bookseller was kept busy: Mavrokordatos read omnivorously in the fields of history, education, political commentary, and strategy, and he wrote too. Fleeing a Turkish foray outside Patras, he would lose an unfinished draft of a history he had been writing on the Ottoman invasions of Europe. If, like any aristocrat, he was acutely conscious of lineage, title, and the power of a name, he was a personality in his own right with extraordinary intellectual energy and charm to spare.[3]

Barely into his twenties when his uncle was appointed prince of Wallachia, Mavrokordatos had served for several years as his chief minister—the Great Postelnik (o *megas postelnikos*)—which afforded him a vast range of high-level contacts in European diplomatic circles. In exile in Geneva he stood out because of his turban and the rest of his Phanariot garb, but once in Greece he switched to European dress and was instantly recognizable among the chieftains by his black frock coat, cravat, his long hair, fob watch, and glasses.[4]

It was, in its way, a statement of intent and even defiance, for the warlords with their unrefined manners and crude language called Mavrokordatos "four-eyes" and liked to write him off as a "pen-pusher," a "foreigner," and worst of all a "Phanariot," as if he was the only schemer intent on power. Their hatred of him reflected his growing influence over the revolution. It also reflected their dawning suspicion that he had understood something vital, something that eluded them until it was too late. For what Mavrokordatos recognized was that in order to achieve independence, the Greeks could never rely on the class of men who had started the uprising. These men were either, like the leaders of the Filiki Etaireia, too associated with revolutionary radical-ism and too detached from the realities of power; or, like the kapetans and the primates, too enmeshed in the old Ottoman world, being its beneficiaries to such an extent as to be unable to conceive of real change. What the power brokers of the revolution wanted, as Mav-rokordatos once put it, was merely a change of dynasty, which would leave them as masters in their own domains. Their horizons were too narrow, their conception of power too personalized, to allow them to coordinate an effective national challenge to what was, after all, still one of the great empires of the day. For that, something else was needed, something more. The truth was that the Greeks would never, in his view, achieve independence on their own: they would need the support and intervention of the European powers. This in turn necessarily entailed understanding the political theories and expectations of the day and presenting the struggle in terms that European diplomats could respond to.

This is why Mavrokordatos believed it essential to introduce into the insurgency the idea of a centralized administration to run the war effort—an administration whose legitimacy would not be questioned in European eyes because behind it there would be an entire system of parliamentary assembly, popular representation, rights and constitutions, legislature and executive. The kapetans of the mountains, however, did not talk this language nor really understand it. Polite in their discourse, novel in their ideas, Mavrokordatos and his circle surely did not think it was really possible to inaugurate a fully functioning Enlightenment polity in the midst of a national revolution, but they understood that the plausible semblance of one was necessary to secure the international backing needed to bring them victory. In short, what Mavrokordatos brought the Greeks was—in the modern sense—politics. He was the first politician of the revolution and possibly the most adept and successful. For many it was an unforgivable achievement.

When Prince Karatzas and his family left Geneva in 1819 to settle in the north Italian town of Pisa, Mavrokordatos went with them. Under the benign rule of Ferdinand III, the Grand Duchy of Tuscany remained an enclave of liberal thought in a peninsula—and a continent—ruled by reactionary powers. It also had a small but vibrant Greek diaspora that in Pisa revolved around the remarkable and much-traveled figure of the Orthodox metropolitan Ignatios. A man of vast experience and considerable insight, Ignatios had been bishop of Arta in western Greece in Ali Pasha's heyday, before fleeing to the Ionian Islands during the Napoleonic Wars. He had served as adviser to the Russians and guide to two generations of Greek nationalists, and he had firsthand experience of both Ottoman and Russian rule. After the Napoleonic Wars, Ignatios settled finally in Pisa where he became a magnet for young Greeks abroad. The "venerable Ignazio" enjoyed close ties with everyone from Kolokotronis to Capodistrias and the czar. Equally at home in analyzing the court politics of Ali Pasha, the sentiments of European bankers, and the needs of Lord Byron, the bishop was one of the leading figures of the Greek diaspora in Europe. For Mavrokordatos, he was quickly to become a mentor, and the prestige of Ignatios's name and recommendation were to be critical assets for the younger man when he launched himself into the Greek cause.[5]

Two of the senior Etairists visited Ignatios and Mavrokordatos in Pisa. The Etaireia's central committee wanted to enlist them and to sound them out on the path forward—these were the critical months just before Alexandros Ypsilantis was invited to become the Etaireia's leader and basic questions of approach and strategy remained to be decided. Athanasios Tsakalof, one of the three founders, was the first to arrive, in late 1819; Panayiotis Anagnostopoulos, the man who two years later would bring Dimitrios Ypsilantis (disguised as his "servant") into Greece, reached the town the following spring where he briefed Ignatios fully on the Etaireia's history. The Etaireia had hoped Ignatios might help persuade Capodistrias to become the organization's supreme head until the news arrived from Russia in 1820 that Capodistrias had rejected the idea and Alexandros Ypsilantis had been chosen instead. Almost certainly Ignatios and Mavrokordatos felt that this development confirmed the need for caution and realized there would be difficulties ahead. Thus, having agreed to join the main Etaireia committee, they suggested form- ing an advisory council to temper the impatience of Prince Ypsilantis and to ensure sensible collective decision making. Because Ypsilantis went the other way—making the organization more hierarchical and hastening preparations for the uprising—neither Ignatios nor Mavrokordatos ever played a significant role in the Etaireia's planning. The mutual dislike between the Ypsilantis family on the one hand and Mavrokordatos in particular never dissipated. But Ignatios was no less critical of the Etaireia's impulsive young leader. Looking back in October 1821, the bishop observed acerbically to a Swiss philhellene that the Greeks had been working for years through learning and education to build a better future for themselves, when a "secret Society made up of poorly schooled, opportunistic and brainless youngsters with Prince Ypsilantis at their head gave the signal for the national uprising . . . whose results have been so fatal in all the major Greek urban centers where the inhabitants are without arms and exposed to the evil of their Turkish oppressors."[6]

Pisa was a town filled with radicals, Romantics, and adventurers, and at the end of 1820 Mavrokordatos started teaching Greek to Mary Shelley, whose *Frankenstein* had been published two years earlier. The Shelleys had settled in Pisa in January 1820 after unhappy peregrina- tions across northern Italy and they were introduced to Mavrokordatos by an Italian professor who taught physics at the university in Pisa— part of a circle that Shelley himself thought of as a ray of light amid the darkness of Metternich's Europe. The Shelleys were impressed by this exotic, learned, argumentative figure, and the poet dedicated *Hellas*, his remarkable 1821 poem about the Greek uprising, to "His Excellency Prince Alexander Mavrocordato, late Secretary for foreign affairs to the Hospodar of Wallachia."[7]

Their acquaintance blossomed against the backdrop of dramatic news from Piedmont some 350 kilometers to the northwest, where a constitutionalist revolt was inspired by similar struggles against royal absolutism in Spain and Naples. "The South of Europe was in a state of great political excitement at the beginning of the year 1821," Mary Shelley recollected. "Shelley, as well as every other lover of liberty, looked upon the struggles in Spain and Italy as decisive of the destinies of the world, probably for centuries to come."[8] In his *Ode to Liberty*, written in 1820 in response to the revolution in Spain, Shelley idealized the spirit of freedom that had once created Athens and was now about to return after so many centuries. In *Hellas*, he imagined the Sultan Mahmud's fitful slumber, as the Greeks rose up and his "sinking empire" disintegrated.

While Shelley's imagination ran across eternity, Mavrokordatos was writing a briefing paper. The poet's Romantic radicalism was less alien to Mavrokordatos than one might have supposed, yet the latter was a political thinker par excellence and in a memorandum he drafted that he hoped might reach the desk of Metternich, he penned an extraordinary analysis of the state of the Ottoman Empire. It was basically a warning that European policy needed to change. What worried him was the tendency in Restoration Europe to prop up the Ottomans for the sake of stability: He wanted the great powers to see that the empire was doomed and to alert the Austrians in particular that if they did not do something concerted in response to this decline, the sole beneficiary would be Russia. It was an argument he would continue to make for the next seven years as the Greek insurgency entered the vortex of international power politics.

According to Mavrokordatos, most European commentators on the sultan's empire lacked basic statistical and other factual information, and so they were unable to do more than trade in clichés. In contrast what he offered was unique—an argument authored for a European audience by a man with firsthand experience of high-level Ottoman governance. He started off with two simple questions: "What is the weight of the Ottoman Empire such as it finds itself to be today in the political balance of Europe? What should one hope for, what may one fear?" Summarizing the challenges the rulers of the empire faced, Mavrokordatos went on to explain in his memorandum that Turkey was a "despotic absolutism" that could scarcely be compared with other regimes. Its collapse was inevitable because it was "a power without an army, without resources, without means, composed of heterogeneous elements which are mutually antagonistic, whose weight in the balance of power is nil." Only English and Austrian support kept it alive; militarily it could be crushed easily by the Russians. Were the latter to invade, the sultan could scarcely hope to lead "a war of nationality," for the simple reason that his population was too diverse.

Mavrokordatos saw a political future for the Greeks of the Ottoman Empire in a way he admitted for no other confessional or ethnic group.

The Greeks had degenerated, he conceded in his memorandum, and whether or not they would one day prove themselves worthy of their ancestors it was hard to say. Yet the Greeks' love of learning was making them conscious of their fallen state and they had shown already in the recent past their desire for independence. Despite the failure of the uprising of 1770, they had not given up. "Those who know them must be persuaded that they will again seize the first opportunity which presents itself to renew their efforts and to finally reconquer their liberty through any sacrifice necessary." Noting that there were some four hundred Greeks studying in the universities of western Europe, Mavrokordatos predicted their eventual return and success. In the Balkans, the Greeks were "more numerous, more active, more intelligent than the Turks. The national spirit, however compromised, has never been extinguished." They were rapidly advancing on the path of civilization and would not long remain "in submission." Yet like other Greek notables, Mavrokordatos was thinking of a process that would take years not months. "If I take for the sake of argument, the most distant date, I am persuaded that if Russia does not pre-empt all calculations—which she probably will—the Ottoman empire will collapse in no more than forty years, under the blows which the efforts of the Greeks alone will inflict upon it." Writing in 1820, Mavrokordatos did not however predict—nor even in a sense want—the revolution of the following year.[9]

Any reader of Mavrokordatos's extensive correspondence quickly becomes familiar with his circle of trusted friends, confidants, disciples, and emissaries—educated, worldly young men like himself. Georgios Praïdis had taught Greek in Bucharest before going to Pisa and then Paris to study. Also in the French capital was Konstantinos Polychroniades, who provided lengthy analyses of political sentiment across Europe. Spiros Trikoupis, private secretary to the philhellenic Earl of Guilford, was the brilliant and wealthy son of a merchant from Mesolonghi who later became Mavrokordatos's brother-in-law, prime minister many times over, and a notable historian of the revolution. This rather studious group loved writing—often preferring French to Greek—and found any interruption to their communications with one another agonizing: "I was annoyed to learn," Praïdis wrote a little later to his friend Andreas Louriotis—a student who within a year or so was to be entrusted by Mavrokordatos with negotiating the first major loan to the Greeks on the Stock Exchange in London, "that your correspondence via Naples with Corfu and Epiros has been blocked so that you can only get news from the fatherland by sea . . . Don't omit to let me know, as soon as the news reaches you, whether Ali Pasha has really surrendered the fortress of Souli to the Souliots." It was entirely characteristic of the habits of this intellectual circle that Praïdis concludes his letter by summarizing the argument of a book on the importance of constitutions. They would, sooner than they realized, have the chance to put their theories into practice.

In the first months of 1821 the letters going to and fro between Paris, the port of Livorno, and nearby Pisa expressed growing apprehension and uncertainty. "What unease and what fear your soul must suffer," wrote Praïdis from Paris in early February 1821. "Every patriot must be unable to sleep these days."[10] We are fortunate that none other than Mary Shelley has left us a record of how Mavrokordatos reacted to news of the uprising in the principalities:

> He often intimated the possibility of an insurrection in Greece; but we had no idea of its being so near at hand when, on the 1st of April 1821, he called on Shelley, bringing the proclamation of his cousin, Prince Ypsilanti, and radiant with exultation and delight, declared that henceforth Greece would be free.

As for the uprising in the Peloponnese, a letter has survived in Mavrokordatos's archive dated March 26, which contained the essentials. It was sent from Corfu and brought by sea from Patras to Pisa:

> The *Romaioi* have rebelled against the Turks who have taken refuge in the fortresses. More than 10,000 Maniots are up in arms and all the Greeks . . . They have separated to blockade the fortresses which will soon surrender for lack of supplies. The day of the Evangelismos was set for these big events. All the foreigners have fled. The notables have sent their families away by boat . . . The ships from Hydra and Spetses are ready . . . Now of course Ali Pasha too has taken heart because with this news the imperial army will soon dissolve.[11]

A few days later, Mavrokordatos was still trying to sift fact from rumor and was as yet uncertain what to do. Fake reports spread by Etairist agents in order to get more Greeks to rise up added to the uncertainty: one handbill from the town of Galaxidi in the Gulf of

Corinth claimed that an army of 200,000 Russians had crossed the Balkans and was marching straight on Constantinople, that another 100,000 were coming by sea in an enormous fleet, that five Russian ships had already arrived with soldiers in the Mani, and that the "Moreots" had taken Tripolitsa.[12]

As it became clear that many of these rumors were false—the Russians had not in fact crossed the Pruth let alone the Danube, nor was any army advancing upon Constantinople—some of Mavrokordatos's confidants urged caution: maybe there had been no uprising in the Peloponnese either; or perhaps the sultan and Ali Pasha would come to some agreement and turn on the Greeks. From Paris, the prudent Praïdis wrote on April 17: "It seems yet very foolish to us and dangerous to trumpet our freedom before we have risen up." Yet once news of the spread of the revolt in the Morea was confirmed, Mavrokordatos decided to make the journey to Greece. He sent money to Praïdis in Paris to purchase a printing press—a demonstration of the importance he attached to a means of political communication that was still virtually unknown in the Ottoman lands.

A Hydra merchant who was a member of the Etaireia had put his brig, the *Baron Stroganoff*, at the disposal of the Greeks in Pisa: flying the Russian flag, it had left Hydra on March 15 for Pisa, its captain having been given instructions to do whatever Bishop Ignatios there decreed; after several adventures along the way, it arrived in Livorno two months later. Ignatios remained in Pisa and placed Mavrokordatos in charge of the vessel that sailed on to Marseille, where it picked up about eighty passengers. They were mainly Greeks but they also included five French army officers, and some Piedmontese, fleeing the fallout after their own abortive revolt earlier in the year.[13] Departing the French port on July 18, their destination was the port of Patras which, so the newspapers had reported before their departure, had fallen to the Greeks. In fact, when they approached it, they learned from a passing boat that the Ottomans were still in command of the fortress, and Mavrokordatos decided they should head instead for Mesolonghi, northwest of the Gulf of Corinth. Thus, by chance, did he make one of the most important decisions of his life. Had he landed in the Peloponnese, he would inevitably—as he himself realized shortly after—have been swallowed up in the bitter internecine feuds there between the *kodzabashis* and the kapetans. Instead, he was able to establish his headquarters in western Greece, where the political and military situation was very different.

The strip of land that runs down the Balkan peninsula between the Ionian Sea and the western edge of the Pindus mountains, from Albania to the Gulf of Corinth, had long been under the control of Ali Pasha and his sons. Because of its geographical and political peculiarities, it was destined to play a quite different role from the Morea in the Greek uprising. For one thing, it was more ethnically mixed and contained sizable Muslim populations. Around Mesolonghi and north to the Gulf of Arta, the peasantry were mostly Greeks. But from Arta northward, the population was increasingly Albanian in speech and soon one was in what the Greeks knew as "Arvanitia" (the land of the Albanians) with both Christian and Muslim populations, the erstwhile heartland of Ali Pasha but now contested by a large Ottoman army.

This ethnically indistinct terrain, impossible to map onto any kind of clear Christian-Muslim divide, was rendered even more ambiguous by the region's unique power structure. There were no dominant Greek landowning families—no equivalents of the powerful *kodzabashis*—as there were in the Morea, and few urban notables with anything more than purely local influence. This was, for the most part, a poor, rough land with few cash crops and large herds that wandered across its high mountain ranges. Order was maintained by hereditary Christian chieftains known as *armatoles* who enjoyed immense power over dozens of villages, collecting their taxes and levying their menfolk for forced works or armed service. In the spring of 1821 there were about a dozen major armatoliks (a region under the control of an armatole), each under the authority of a Greek clan; extensive intermarriage further cemented the power of what some called "the aristocracy of the knife" (*machairiki aristokratia*). Far more powerful than the klefts of the Peloponnese, ensconced in their ancestral and inaccessible strongholds, the armatoles could raise hundreds of armed men each and constituted a serious military force in their own right.

Although Greeks, these men were Ottoman appointees, but more precisely they were Ali Pasha's men—the *alipashalides,* as they were known—rivalrous and combative. They had depended for years on Ali's patronage and had close connections to Jannina in the north. Most of them had also joined the Etaireia, apparently through one of Ali's trusted Greek secretaries: the Etaireia's instructions allowed the armatoles to continue serving the pasha. In British-controlled Lefkada they had met in conference in January 1821 to agree upon a common plan of action with the kapetans in the Peloponnese, and the armatoles were also aware of the uprising planned for that spring. But the situation that faced them was far more complex than the one farther south. For one thing, an Ottoman army was already fanning out across the region for the campaign against Ali Pasha and was demanding their allegiance. For another, Ali himself remained alive and was at that point mounting a rather successful resistance in Jannina, and so was very much a force in their minds: breaking with him was not something to be undertaken lightly either. The armatoles' choice was thus not a simple binary—to rise up against the sultan or not—but whether to support the sultan, the Greek rising, or Ali, their former master.[14]

In eastern Greece, the armatole Odysseus Androutsos, who it had been agreed in Lefkada would lead the insurgency there, soon began attacking Ottoman troops. There was heavy fighting in the mountains, where Greek chieftains took control of the town of Salona, defending key passes against a large Ottoman force. But in the west, to Androutsos's annoyance, the leading armatoles hesitated to declare themselves for the Greek cause—and week after week went by without them moving. Long after the sound of the fighting in Patras could be heard across the gulf, merchants and sea captains based in Mesolonghi were still selling supplies to the Ottoman forces and ferrying them over to the Peloponnese. Tensions rose with nearby Galaxidi. While that coastal town with its large fleet declared for the Greek cause early, as late as mid-May, Khurshid Pasha was congratulating the townspeople of Mesolonghi on their loyalty and urged them to remain faithful to the sultan.[15] But by then some of the local Muslim families were already moving out of Mesolonghi and on May 20, Greek ships were seen flying the revolutionary flag in the Gulf of Patras; a few days later, led by the local chieftain, a former butcher called Dimitrios Makris, Mesolonghi's inhabitants seized the main Ottoman municipal officers, killed many of the Muslim men who had stayed behind, and held the women and children captive.[16]

This was the febrile and finely balanced situation in the hinterland, which awaited the unwitting Mavrokordatos when he arrived in Mesolonghi in the summer of 1821. Ferried through the lagoon in the primeval shallow boats—some of them mere dugouts—that the inhabitants used, he and his fellow passengers stepped ashore in the town to be greeted by a celebratory volley of muskets and cries of "Long live Freedom!" The French artillery officer Maxime Raybaud, who was with the party, was struck by the enthusiasm and relief on the faces of the crowd, who were exhilarated by the arrival of such a distinguished visitor as the prince. It was, wrote Raybaud, as if they needed this confirmation of the validity of their cause, as if "these men free but a day, having been slaves before, were still astonished not to feel the weight of their chains and in the still confused instinct of their new political existence, needed guides and supporters." Raybaud wandered through the twisting unpaved alleys of what was a rather small and undistinguished town built on damp ground and could not but notice amid these drab and makeshift surroundings the heavily armed and lavishly costumed chieftains, surrounded by their numerous escorts, who came to greet the distinguished new arrival.[17]

The political challenge for Mavrokordatos was to persuade such men that despite his lack of weapons or indeed funds, they should heed what he had to say. The most powerful of them all was characteristically absent: Georgios Varnakiotis, first among equals of the armatoles of western Rumeli, who ruled the shepherds and farmers of the so-called Dry Land (Xiromero) from his stronghold in the hills much farther north along the coast. A man of around forty, patient, farsighted, Varnakiotis hailed from an established clan with close familial and friendship ties to numerous other kapetans and officials of the old Ali Pasha order.[18] He was the grandson of a renowned Rumeliot chieftain who had fought for the Russians in 1770, and the early death of his father had brought Varnakiotis the command of his armatole from an early age. He knew both Bishop Ignatios and Count Capodistrias and had been present at a famous meeting of the armatoles and kapetans on Lefkada back in 1807 at which the two men had sought help to defend the island against Ali Pasha. Much had changed since then, to be sure, and Varnakiotis had returned to the mainland and been reappointed by the pasha. When the Greek uprising erupted, Varnakiotis hesitated for as long as possible. Given the three-way choice before him—the sultan's cause, the Greeks, or Ali Pasha—logic dictated putting off a decision until it was clearer who would prevail; the armatoles' entire training and outlook also inclined them not only to keep their options open but to switch when necessary from one to another. As all-or-nothing options were unappealing to them, Mavrokordatos understood that such men could not be relied upon to put the cause of the nation above their own interests and local outlook. Yet without their backing he was just another volunteer.

Aware that much of the population of Rumeli was unsure about the Greek cause, Etairists had been spreading rumors that a Russian force was on its way. In one town their agent had gone so far as to impersonate a Russian general. Varnakiotis was too shrewd a man to be taken in by such tricks, and an Etairist sent from Wallachia had to resort to threats. On May 25, having learned that Khurshid Pasha was planning to send a force to attack him, Varnakiotis had finally issued a call to his fellow notables in the hills of western Greece. He appealed to their love for their region and to their precious "Greek name." He told them the Morea was entirely liberated, that "the leader of our Race" Prince Ypsilantis was the master of Edirne and about to take Constantinople itself, that all the other provinces had been freed from the enemy. It was noticeable that he did not mention the Etaireia itself and Varnakiotis stressed how much he had tried to avoid any conflict; it sounded rather as if he had been forced into action. He strenuously avoided mentioning Ali Pasha also. In short, he had made one choice, which was to take on the Ottomans, but whether he was calling on the Greeks to fight for their own sake or for Ali Pasha was unclear. His forces laid siege to the Ottoman provisional center, a small inland town called Vrachori, and took it over in June. Farther north, armatole bands blocked the key passes across the Pindos mountains and pinned down Ottoman troops in Arta. The revolution was spreading in western Greece, but in contrast to the speed of events in the Peloponnese in late March it was spreading slowly.[19]

Compared with the Morea, the influence of the Filiki Etaireia in western Greece had never been great and it was diminished further by Mavrokordatos's arrival. Dimitrios Ypsilantis's emissary to the region, a man called Ivos Rigas, had made little impact; months later, one of the Etairists noted that he was scorned locally as "someone who had presented himself as a great emissary but showed himself to be the smallest and least of men."[20] Mavrokordatos simply ignored Rigas and behaving as if the Etaireia had nothing to do with him, he took his own steps to create a new kind of administration, based in Mesolonghi and resting on an alliance with Varnakiotis and the other armatoles.[21]

After several days of intense talks, Mavrokordatos persuaded a coalition of town notables and chieftains to sign an extraordinary document. Strikingly, it made no reference at all either to Alexandros Ypsilantis or to the Filiki Etaireia. Addressed to "the absent other brother kapetans and notables from Xiromero, Valtos, and Vonitsa," the signatories invited them to join in setting up "an administration" under a "worthy leader," with one or more representatives drawn from each place with powers to speak for their inhabitants and for the benefit of the "fatherland." The document specified that the chieftains would have their old rank and retain their existing power and they would support the new administration as needed. They would also agree to provide men as required and to obey its orders. The administration expected obedience from its subjects and could punish anyone who disobeyed. Those infringing this agreement could be declared an "enemy of the fatherland."[22]

Through this document, Mavrokordatos introduced into the hills of Akarnania (the region from the Gulf of Corinth to the Ambrakian Gulf) the language of Western political theory, systems, and abstract principles. Whereas Dimitrios Ypsilantis had invited participants to serve under his personal command, this document said nothing about any specific individual at all. What mattered was to establish the fatherland through an impersonal institution—"the administration"—that was to be led by an unnamed leader and whose powers rested not upon force but upon the legitimacy of its representatives. Treading delicately on the ground of the armatoles and their private armies, which it recognized, the agreement nevertheless established that it was the civilian leadership that had the right to dispose of the military power. For a man who had stepped ashore only days earlier, with no claim beyond his name as backing, this was a remarkable achievement.

Wooed not only by Mavrokordatos but by Ypsilantis as well, Varnakiotis was keeping his distance. Casually calling him "kapetán," Ypsilantis wrote to Varnakiotis from the Peloponnese inviting him to join in the struggle under his brother's banner. In his message, Mavrokordatos showed more sensitivity. He used the more formal title "general" as if to conjure into being through titles the state he dreamed of. His language to Varnakiotis was simpler than Ypsilantis's and so was his stated purpose, which was, as he wrote, just to notify him of the agreement reached with the others in Mesolonghi, and to offer his friendship and assistance, signing off from "the patriot and your friend A. Mavrokordatos."[23]

Mavrokordatos knew Varnakiotis would make him wait for an answer. He knew too that, although Varnakiotis might be the most powerful figure in western Greece, the real center of revolutionary power was in the Morea. He therefore left his associates in Mesolonghi to continue discussions with the cautious armatole and headed across the Gulf of Corinth for the Greek camp outside Tripolitsa. Bishop Ignatios had been urging the Moreots for several months to form a national government and Mavrokordatos intended to accelerate the process. He was joined along the way by an old friend, the son of Prince Karatzas, who had arrived in the Peloponnese from Italy bringing more badly needed supplies, and by another Phanariot, Theodoros Negris, who had been en route to Paris to serve as Ottoman minister there before deciding to join the revolutionary cause.

In the Peloponnese, there was growing hostility to the influx of these Phanariot newcomers. For his part, Mavrokordatos was disturbed by the unproductive atmosphere and the bitter rivalries among the uprising's leaders: "The disagreement of those here is indescribable," he wrote. The deficiencies of Dimitrios Ypsilantis were becoming evident and he was losing supporters; Prince Alexandros Kantakuzinos, who had accompanied him from Trieste, now moved into Mavrokordatos's camp, conscious of the latter's superior political capacity. Mavrokordatos himself had never had any respect for the Ypsilantis brothers but he had to behave as if he did because he had come for just one thing: to get the prince's backing for his idea of a regional assembly of Rumeliot Greeks. Once Dimitrios Ypsilantis had given his consent, Mavrokordatos saw no reason to stay and he, Negris, and Karatzas departed almost immediately from the Greek camp above Tripolitsa, waited two days for horses, and headed back north across the Gulf of Corinth.[24]

The three Phanariots now took the initiative. Going much further than a shocked Dimitrios Ypsilantis had ever imagined they would, they issued a proclamation not only to the population of western Rumeli but to central and eastern Rumeli as well, to choose representatives to govern them regionally and to participate in the impending national assembly. Mavrokordatos's Assembly of Western Continental Greece, originally scheduled to meet in October, finally convened in Mesolonghi at the start of the following month. Talks with Varnakiotis had been delicate and protracted; he did not show up but did send a representative. What Mavrokordatos had created was an organization that looked and sounded like an institution of representative government but realistically preserved most of the existing local power structures. It created a Senate of ten men, to govern the region internally, each representing a district for a year; Mavrokordatos himself became president. How centrally appointed civilian bureaucrats would work alongside the regional armatoles remained to be seen but this was an arrangement that both could live with. A week later, the grandly entitled Areios Pagos of Eastern Continental Greece emerged thanks to the efforts of Mavrokordatos's fellow Phanariot, Theodoros Negris. Like its western Greek equivalent, it provided for regional representation, but it gave even greater formal powers to the local kapetans and fewer to the new civilian prefects. Unlike its western Greek counterpart, however, the Areios Pagos, electing Negris as president, declared itself autonomous of any eventual national government, even stipulating that its permission had to be sought before any armed forces could enter its territory. In effect Negris had created something Mavrokordatos did not aspire to—an autonomous mini-state within the Greek struggle with its own constitution. Mavrokordatos had his eye on a bigger prize: the creation of a provisional national government whose authority would encompass the entire area under the rule of the insurgents and unify their actions.

While these two assemblies were being formed, Dimitrios Ypsilantis was trying to take advantage of what was left of his popularity among the peasantry of the Peloponnese in order to outflank the Peloponnesian Senate and the landowners he had clashed with in the summer. His own political shortcomings were, however, as much in evidence as ever. Proclaiming the convocation of a national assembly, Ypsilantis emphasized his own person in a way that Mavrokordatos would never have done: "I, Dimitri Ypsilanti, am come hither to fight for your liberty," he grandly pronounced in October from Tripolitsa, not long after the conquest of the town. "I am come to defend your rights, honor, lives and goods; I am come to give you just laws and equitable tribunals." With the *kodzabashis* clearly in mind, he spoke pointedly of ending *all* tyranny, not only that of the Turks but also that of "those individuals who, sharing the sentiments of the Turks, wish to oppress the people." "I am your father who heard your groans even in the heart of Russia," he declared as if he, from a Phanariot princely family himself, was the savior of the common people. He offered not a vision of representative democracy but rather the prospect of a kind of enlightened paternalism, with the prince—"your chief and father"—as the czar of his own mini-kingdom. This announcement came after the Etaireia's defeat in the Danubian Principalities had become known; only a man with complete confidence in his family name, and with little political sensitivity, could have signed off, as Dimitrios Ypsilantis did, as the plenipotentiary of his elder brother.[25]

Distinguished Greeks abroad were by this point openly urging the formation of a provisional national government. The revolution had, against the odds, lasted several months; but it was an open question whether it could survive much longer without real internal organization. Capodistrias weighed in, writing that the Greeks' fate lay in their own hands. Allowing anarchy to prevail would simply guarantee they were abandoned by the European powers. The creation, on the other hand, of an administration that could plausibly claim to speak in the name of the nation and that proclaimed itself defender of the rights of the race (*ta dikaiomata tou genous*) would mean that Greece had in some important and critical sense already come into existence and could not be allowed by the great powers to be exterminated. In short, in the words of Capodistrias's brother, which accompanied the letter: "Why the devil do our people delay setting up a general administration of the Nation, and not subordinate all and everyone at once to it?"[26]

It was equally necessary—at least when viewed from abroad—that this consolidation of the leadership of the revolution take place without reference to the Etaireia; given the conservative leadership of Europe— where the Holy Alliance had crushed rebellions in Piedmont and Naples and were threatening Spain's constitutionalists—any taint of radicalism was undesirable. To the influential Archbishop Germanos of Old Patras, Bishop Ignatios wrote from Pisa: "The fatherland will be endangered if we do not establish a National Administration . . . and one not only acceptable to the Race but also to the foreign powers who think the peace of peoples is disturbed by any novel system. They view your system as a Carbonari system (*systima Karvounarikon*) . . . because this is what Ypsilantis declared at the start and so long as they see no proper administration [*Dioikisi*] they are right to think what they think and to say what they say." To Dimitrios Ypsilantis in the Peloponnese, Ignatios wrote bluntly that his brother Alexandros—whose Etaireia code name had been "Kalos" (Good)—had really been "Kakistos" (the Worst). From Paris, the astute Konstantinos Polychroniades wrote that the very word

"Etaireia" made the great powers shudder. It was best, he wrote, to avoid all reference to it, or to that unfortunate failure in the Danubian Principalities, and to call the uprising what it was and needed to become: a "national" matter.[27]

Mavrokordatos had of course long regarded Alexandros Ypsilantis's leadership of the Filiki Etaireia as a disaster—a view confirmed in August by the dismal news from the Danubian Principalities—and he saw no reason to accept his younger brother's orders any longer than was necessary. When he heard the latter had been criticizing him for exceeding his instructions, Mavrokordatos fired back a detailed and excoriating letter that articulated his thinking better perhaps than anything else he ever wrote. Everywhere in Greece, he wrote to Ypsilantis, there was anarchy. Terrified by the Ottoman armies and the presence of the imperial navy, the armatoles and primates of Rumeli were tempted either to submit to the sultan or to accept the return of Ali Pasha; they needed therefore to be encouraged to resist and they needed to agree on the establishment of a "political system" that would enable them to participate in a national assembly. He explained to Ypsilantis in the kind of detail the latter could never have mastered exactly how he was setting about this. But Mavrokordatos did more. Throwing diplomacy to the winds, he castigated "the guilty ones" who had led men to disaster in the Danubian Principalities; he accused Alexandros Ypsilantis of having harmed the Greek cause by ridiculous proclamations that had alarmed the European powers. He had invoked the name of Russia, when the Russians wanted to remain aloof; he had proclaimed that Greece was ready to take up arms when in fact "in many areas it sleeps the deepest sleep." In short, "not even their worst enemies could have made so many unforgivable political errors."[28] Mavrokordatos might technically have been Ypsilantis's plenipotentiary, but he was ready to push the prince aside for the sake of what he knew Greece needed most: a national government.

The Greeks did not require foreign-educated Enlightenment intellectuals for them to appreciate the importance of deliberative collective government—their traditions of local self-government under the Ottomans provided robust and durable models, and thus the idea of a representative assembly was not in itself new. A Messenian Assembly had been set up in Kalamata in the southern Peloponnese at the end of March 1821; the much more important Peloponnesian Senate was established in May at the Kaltezes monastery and acted as a de facto government in the region for months afterward: Dimitrios Ypsilantis was elected its president near the end of the year. What they had never had, however, was a national assembly. To achieve this, Mavrokordatos decided it was necessary to break the logjam of Peloponnesian wrangling by bringing in spokesmen from other regions as a counterweight. That was the rationale for his organizational work in western Rumeli and for his support of Negris's plans in eastern Rumeli. But in the complicated internal political jousting that accompanied the revolution in its first months, there was one other regional power center emerging as well. During his brief stay in the Greek camp, Mavrokordatos had spoken with the powerful shipowner Giorgios Koundouriotis from the island of Hydra, and the two men remained in touch in the weeks that followed.

Mavrokordatos told Koundouriotis that the islands were critical to the formation of an effective national government. Such a government could have no other headquarters than in the Peloponnese, he wrote, but the islands' inclusion would be indispensable. Moreover, a national government could help them too since it would provide the legitimacy to enforce sharing the financial burdens of the war: in this way, the contribution of the island ships to the Greek fleet could be acknowledged and repaid, a matter of considerable concern to the ships' money-conscious owners. Mavrokordatos was building up what would become a key ally and the means of his ascent to power. He told the Hydriots that the fall of Tripolitsa should make it easier to establish the proposed national assembly, and he urged them to put pressure on the leaders of the Peloponnese to accelerate the larger convocation. Preparations for the assembly went ahead but because of the epidemics afflicting Tripolitsa after its sack in September, it was agreed to hold it during December in Argos in the northern Peloponnese. When that town filled up with armed bands, and became crowded, the meetings were moved into the countryside to a village just outside ancient Epidavros to the east.[29] By this point, no fewer than three regional assemblies had already met and drawn up constitutions of their own—in Mesolonghi and Salona and at Epidavros itself where twenty-four notables had just finished deliberating in the Peloponnesian Senate under the presidency of Dimitrios Ypsilantis. The national assembly was thus the fourth constitutional meeting held since the outbreak of the revolution but it was the first whose outcome would be a government ruling in the name of all Greeks.

When the assembly started its deliberations at the village of Piada, amid the pine woods not far from the ruins of the great classical theater, the delegates included representatives from not only the Peloponnese but also from western Rumeli, the shipowning islands of Hydra, Spetses, and Psara, as well as eastern Greece and Thessaly. No rules seem to have governed how many delegates each assembly could send—scarcely surprising in such times, for elections had been similarly chaotic in the first years of the French Revolution—and many were there under their own auspices. Dimitrios Ypsilantis attended, along with warlords such as Kolokotronis and Plapoutas. There were longtime Etairist activists such as Christoforos Perraivos, accompanied by some of the Souliot chieftains, Peloponnesian landowners, Rumeliot armatoles, and a young student called Anastasios Polyzoidis, not yet twenty years of age, who had returned to Greece from his studies in Germany to fight and who now played a major role in drafting the provisional constitution— Greece's first—which was adopted by the assembly at the beginning of January 1822.

Mavrokordatos had attended in his capacity as president of the assembly of western Greece. But he had been chosen to preside over the national assembly at Piada too, and when its deliberations ended, he was elected president of Greece's first provisional government. Barely six months since he had first landed in Mesolonghi, this was an astonishing ascent, one that reflected not only Mavrokordatos's own undeniable talents but also an oft-neglected aspect of the leadership class of the revolution more generally—their political realism, willingness to compromise, and respect for governing expertise. It no doubt helped too that as an outsider with no hereditary regional base of his own, he did not represent a threat to the established interests. Sidelined, Dimitrios Ypsilantis had been chosen to preside over the new legislature, a consolation prize, and he departed, aggrieved, to supervise the surrender of the Ottoman garrison in the fortress of Corinth. On January 28, 1822, President Mavrokordatos brought the proceedings to a close and the executive began its work. On paper, at least, Greece now had a national administration.

At Epidavros, the key players were not the fighters who had driven the Turks out of the Morea nor the Etairists who had planned the uprising, although both groups were there in the assembly in significant numbers. They were the Phanariot newcomers Negris and Mavrokordatos, along with the notables of the Peloponnese. The latter had played their hand with characteristic skill: comparing the list of leading families in the two main political factions that had existed in the Ottoman Morea with the names of the Peloponnesian delegates to the assembly, there is a striking degree of overlap. This was largely because the Peloponnesian Senate not only remained in existence with significant powers of its own but also claimed the right to name the region's deputies to Epidavros. Indeed, the powers of the new national government were significantly limited so far as the Peloponnese was concerned; it was the older Senate that named a commander in chief for the region, for instance, and controlled taxes. The bifurcation of the overall war effort—between the forces of the Morea on the one hand and, on the other, the alliance of the Rumeliots and the islanders—began here, with these decisions. Much as the Peloponnesian notables had intended, it precluded the formation of an effective central command, a problem that would linger throughout the revolution.[30] The regional assemblies themselves survived another year before they were wound up. However imperfectly, the revolution acquired a political dimension at the national level, which it would never, henceforth, lose.[31]

Intellectuals had an outsize influence at Epidavros as well, notably on the drafting of the constitution. An Italian radical lawyer, Vincenzo Gallina, a former leader of the Carbonari, "had brought into Greece a book containing the most modern constitutions," wrote a skeptical observer later. "It was a treasure which never left its owner's side, an oracle that was often consulted."[32] In discussions that drew in Mavrokordatos, Polyzoidis, Gallina, and many other keen students of contemporary constitutionalism, what emerged was a distinctive adaptation of Enlightenment principles to Greek conditions. There was, for one thing, a clear assertion of civil supremacy over the military—a blow against the new power of upcoming men like Kolokotronis, whose followers could be heard muttering about the need for a *governo militare* for months afterward. At the same time, the new constitution opened by declaring Orthodox Christianity to be the ruling faith of the Greek state and said that all its Christian inhabitants were to be regarded as Greeks enjoying equal political rights before the law. It established a provisional government, divided into a legislature and an executive branch: representatives to the latter would have to be at least thirty years old and would serve as government ministers. No fewer than eight ministries were created. Thus the pattern was set of an approach that first, highlighted the importance of written constitutional law to the Greeks; second, prioritized equality among citizens; and third, avoided the establishment of a powerful executive branch. It reflected the Greeks' interest in the French and American revolutionary models, though less in any specific details than in the desire to launch their struggle by constitutional means and their assertion of the importance of founding a state under law that would define and defend the rights of the citizen. It goes without saying that this marked a radical break not merely with Ottoman political tradition but with the elements of ecclesiastical and Byzantine law that continued to survive at the local level. On the other hand, only Christians could be Greek citizens, a testimony to the limited appeal of Enlightenment secularism. The sense of religious solidarity this reflected should not be underestimated: one of the striking features of the Greek uprising was the relative lack of bloodletting among Greeks. There was, for instance, no parallel to the Reign of Terror during the French Revolution, and in general, extreme violence against Muslims was accompanied by relative forbearance against other Greeks, even at the height of the civil war later on. It is hard not to attribute this to the sense of a shared faith.[33]

In the 1950s, the Algerian revolutionaries fighting the French were struck by the sudden realization that national independence was something to be claimed not bestowed: this was the approach that the Greeks had adopted more than a century earlier at Epidavros. A declaration of independence at the start of 1822, accompanying the new constitution, stated simply that "the Greek nation [*to ellinikon ethnos*]" had been unable to bear any longer the "yoke of tyranny" of the "terrible Ottoman dynasty," and having overthrown it at great sacrifice, "declares today through its legal representatives in a national assembly, before God and Man, its political existence and independence." The document highlighted the importance of Orthodoxy, and it was even prefaced by the words "In the Name of the Holy and Indissoluble Trinity"; yet what was even more striking was its repeated invocation of "Greece" (*Ellas*) and the Greek nation (*to ellinikon ethnos*). It is with good reason that it has been called the starting point of modern Greek consciousness. Henceforth, a term that had primarily referred to the ancient Greeks connoted their modern descendants as well. All reference to the Greeks as *Romaioi* was downplayed, no doubt because of its Ottoman connotations. It was hard to imagine that only thirty years earlier, a Phanariot intellectual had insisted "it is a thing unworthy of a *Romios* Christian" to be called a "Hellene."[34]

The authors of the declaration of independence were well aware they were fashioning a diplomatic and political weapon for use abroad. Conscious of the Holy Alliance's express disapproval of revolution, they were careful to avoid any reference to the Etaireia. It is very striking that despite the fact that nearly a half of the delegates at Epidavros were members, and despite employing a former leading member of the Carbonari as their adviser, all mention of the Etaireia vanished. They scrapped the Etairist flag with its black, red, and white, and decreed the national colors would henceforth be blue and white. In short, as Bishop Ignatios and others had urged, Mavrokordatos and the Pisa circle did everything they could to distinguish the Greek struggle from the other uprisings in southern Europe and to assert its national not socially radical goals. "After years of slavery," they wrote:

> we have finally been compelled to take up arms, to avenge ourselves and our country against a tyranny so frightful and in its very essence unjust as to be neither equal nor even comparable to any other. The war we are waging against the Turks, far from being founded in demagoguery, seditiousness or the selfish interests of any one part of the Greek nation, is a national and holy war, the object of which is to reconquer our rights to individual liberty, property and honor, rights enjoyed by all the civilized neighboring peoples of Europe.

The Greeks were identified as "the descendants of the wise and philanthropic nation of the Hellenes (*Ellenes*)," who had found Ottoman rule insufferable, relying "despotically not on the word but the will as law." This was an argument crafted for Europe about the fundamental illegitimacy of the Ottoman system of rule and the revival of the values of ancient Greece. Independence would allow the Greeks to take their place as a free nation alongside the other peoples of the world.

6

KHURSHID PASHA'S HAREM

Grand Vizier by the grace of God, he made his enemies obey with the edge of his sword. One so favored by fortune will not exist again before the second coming ...

From Khurshid Pasha's epitaph[1]

"Greek versus Turk," "Christian versus Muslim": these were the stark oppositions upon which the logic of revolutionary nationalism was based, and they remain the categories by which people today generally try to make sense of 1821. But the reality was both less simple and more interesting, and especially north of the Gulf of Corinth in the regions once ruled by Ali Pasha there was an equally important distinction in play that cut across the others—that between locals and outsiders. Julius Millingen, a young British surgeon who had the distinction of serving both Byron and later Sultan Mahmud II himself, was struck while in Mesolonghi by the close ties that existed between the Greek armatoles and the Albanian beys. They were "enemies only in appearance," wrote Millingen. "A tacit agreement existed between them not to oppose one another's depredations; and in several instances they even protected their respective properties and gave proof of their attachment that made them forgetful of the duties they owed both to their nation and their religion."[2]

Millingen noted as an example the friendship between the Muslim Albanian governor of Preveza and Tsongas, a Greek armatole in the mountains nearby—a mutual understanding that served as a kind of insurance designed to preserve both men's wealth and power. "Whenever the Albanian wished to preserve his flocks from the rapacity of the [Ottoman] troops encamped in the neighbourhood of Prevesa [*sic*], he sent them to his friend, who never failed to receive and punctually to return them; and when the slightest apprehension of an invasion of Acarnania prevailed, Zonga [sic] placed, in the same manner, all his cattle in safety, by sending them to Vonitza, where they continued to graze undisturbed till the danger was over."[3] This was not a unique case and even as the conflict to the south in the Peloponnese turned into a kind of existential struggle, the ties between Muslim and Greek chieftains across much of Rumeli remained strong. The bonds among men who had known one another for years and even decades counted for as much as confessional boundaries or national claims.[4]

At the center of a network of these relationships was the Muslim Albanian commander Omer Vryonis Pasha. He had started off as an Ali Pasha loyalist before switching sides to join the sultan's forces, earning the pashalik of Berat as his reward and becoming one of the most important Ottoman generals in the region, heavily involved in fighting on both sides of the Pindos range. Omer knew most if not all of the leading Greek chieftains of western Rumeli. To Giannis Rangos, an armatole who had once worked under him, Omer wrote an affectionate letter praising him for his bravery and even claiming the credit: "My dear Yiannaki, I learned that you've become a kapetan and a brave warrior and it is certainly true that whoever eats my bread becomes a fighter." Omer's letter offered the Greek leniency if he surrendered, and also reminded him who really controlled the region. "Yiannaki," he wrote. "Know that first God, and then the Porte and my co-religionists gave me these mountains, and that these days these mountains are mine, and such is God's will." Omer's relationship was equally close with the most important of the region's armatoles, Georgios Varnakiotis. "My most beloved kapetan Georgaki," Omer began one of his confidential letters (in Greek) to Varnakiotis. "Know that as I was before for you, so I still am." That was the key: in a world where men regarded switching allegiances as prudence rather than betrayal, personal constancy was precious. In a region where the result of the struggle being waged between Ali Pasha and the forces of the sultan remained in the balance, it was indispensable. However, where that left the Greek national cause and its very different and much less ambiguous conception of loyalty was unclear.[5]

The bewildering twists and turns of local leaders in the region shadowed Ali Pasha's shifting fortunes. Three of his most trusted Albanian lieutenants switched to fight for the sultan, and then against him, and then for him again, all within the space of a year. They had their

Greek counterparts, men such as Georgios Karaïskakis and Odysseus Androutsos, both later hailed as heroes of the revolution. The Souliot chieftain Markos Botsaris, a former commander under Ali Pasha and a blood brother of Kolokotronis, turned against Ali and declared for the sultan, then changed his mind again, and was fighting for Ali once more when the Greek insurrection erupted. All these men sought to adjust to a struggle complicated by a new element—nationalism: all were united by an overriding sense of local and regional attachments that did not easily accommodate the new demands made on them and where personal trust provided safety in case they bet on the wrong horse.

If there was one allegiance that united them for months across the confessional divide it was to the elderly figure who had ruled them for so long that it was hard to imagine the world without him, the man they referred to as "the vesir Ali Pasha." At the beginning of September 1821, their regional cooperation reached its apogee when Muslim Albanian beys, Christian Souliot chieftains, and Greek armatoles pledged to fight in a common front to defend Ali against the sultan's army. Indeed, they went further and declared their solidarity with one another in the event that Ali himself recovered enough to harm members of their "alliance." The following month they met together and declared "brotherly" unity. The Muslim Agos Muhurdar made his position crystal clear: "We should place no trust in the Sultan, nor do we have anything in common with the *chaldoupides* [a word of contempt for Ottoman Muslims not from Albania]. As for me, I am and I will always be with the Greeks [*Romaious*] and whatever the regime—European, Greek, or Russian [*frangkiko, romaïko, moskoviko*]—I am with you."[6]

This mind-boggling arrangement has been described by some Greek historians as a "pseudo-alliance," as if the Greek signatories had no real intention of fighting for Ali Pasha and signed merely out of expediency. Perhaps it depends what is meant by expediency. Mavrokordatos, for one, believed that the Greek armatoles had not given up their cherished idea of declaring Ali Pasha—in his words—"roi de l'Albanie, de l'Épire et de toute la Thessalie."[7] But in fact their alliance was underpinned by something more solid even than political solidarity—the prospect of plunder, because the immediate target for their alliance that autumn was the prosperous town of Arta in the northwest, which had been taken over by the sultan's troops. The besieging forces gathered around it, swelling from 4,000 to over 10,000 men, and in November 1821

Arta was stormed by armed bands, Muslims and Christians, Albanians and Greeks united in their pillaging. Knowing they were not the real target, the Ottoman soldiers did nothing but look down from the safety of the Byzantine ramparts while churches, mosques, stores and shops were indiscriminately looted. Some of the Greek bands not only plundered the homes of Christians but stripped them of their belongings and even tortured their owners in boiling oil to make them reveal where their valuables were hidden. As one of the Greek band leaders later admitted: "We plundered all those wretched people and left them in misery."[8]

By this point, however, the Ottoman siege of Ali Pasha in Jannina, seventy kilometers to the north of Arta, was tightening and at the same time some of the Albanian Muslim leaders were learning about events in the Morea and starting to have doubts about the Greeks and where their allegiances really lay. Taher Ambatzis was an Albanian leader who had formerly been in charge of Ali Pasha's police force and was especially trusted by him; he was well known to the Greek kapetans and Souliots with whom he was in alliance.[9] In October he visited Mesolonghi at Mavrokordatos's invitation to see how the Greeks were faring. As he and his aides were shown around, it became clear to him that many of the Greeks were not now fighting, as he had thought, simply to help Ali Pasha. When Mesolonghi had declared for the revolution, it had driven out, killed, or enslaved the remaining Muslims: mass killings had been ordered by the local Greek armatole Dimitrios Makris, according to the British consul in Preveza, William Meyer, "with a view to committing the whole population and of thereby pledging them to a desperate resistance in the event of their being attacked by the Turks." A devout man, Ambatzis was shocked to see mosques that had been razed to the ground and befouled and to learn that Muslim girls had been forcibly baptized. On the outskirts of the town, the corpses of mutilated Muslims still lay under the olive trees.[10] Ambatzis's belated understanding that the Greeks were now fighting a different kind of war was confirmed when Elmaz Bey, who had just got back from Tripolitsa, told him that on their way home some of his soldiers had been strangled by the Greeks and left on a riverbed near Komboti. No more was needed by way of confirmation and the Muslim Albanian leaders broke finally with the Christian Souliots: "Souliots! Until today we were servants of Ali Pasha and your allies . . . thinking that we were fighting together to free him. But we were deceived because now we see clearly that both you and your co-religionists fight for your faith and your freedom. Your war for faith and freedom is clearly a war against our faith and ruler."[11]

The Muslim Albanians now abandoned not only their pact with the Greeks but also Ali Pasha himself in order to fight for the sultan. Ambatzis and the others approached the Ottoman commander in chief, Khurshid Pasha, asking for his pardon and pledging to help him kill Ali and drive out the Greeks.[12] For the next four years, Ambatzis and Agos Muhurdar would fight in Ottoman armies against the Greeks although, true to their traditions, throughout that time they kept open their communications with the other side. Neither Khurshid nor the sultan himself trusted the Albanians and resented them all the more for having to rely on them. But for the time being they had no choice.

The implications of the collapse of the Albanian-Greek alliance were far-reaching. Over the summer of 1821 this coalition had effectively checked the power of the sultan's armies and placed Khurshid Pasha in a delicate position, threatening his rear even as he tried to defeat Ali Pasha in Jannina. By hindering the passage of his armies south, and by facilitating the defection of the Albanian garrison in Tripolitsa, the strange alliance had contributed to the Greek victory in the Peloponnese. That July, the British consul had even predicted that "the whole power of the country" might once again fall into the hands of Ali Pasha. Within a few months, all this was shown to be false.[13]

By the end of 1821, all the signs pointed to Ali Pasha's imminent demise. Most of his men had deserted him and he had withdrawn with a guard of only seventy men and his wife Kyra Vasiliki to the citadel in the southeastern corner of Jannina's fortress. In the basement his men had readied barrels of gunpowder in case they needed to blow the fortress up. It was there, supposedly seated on one of the barrels, that Ali received an emissary from the sultan's commander, Khurshid Pasha. Ali offered him coffee, smoked his pipe, and laid out his demands: to be allowed to go to the capital to lay himself and his treasure at the feet of the sultan. Khurshid promised to relay the message to Constantinople and in the meantime issued Ali a safe pass signed by himself and the other pashas. But Khurshid, who knew the sultan's wishes, had no intention of passing on Ali's request and instead sent him back a fake imperial decree instructing him to leave the fortress while his request was being studied, and to make himself comfortable anywhere else he pleased. Unwillingly, and tormented by the fear that he was being deceived, Ali left the palace for the island in the middle of the lake where together with his wife, his entourage, and his bodyguards, he settled into the monastery of Ayios Panteleimon. To amuse him, Khurshid Pasha sent over food and musicians.[14]

After a few weeks had passed, Ali was visited by a group of pashas and senior officials; although he suspected a trap, their meeting passed without incident. Some days later, their boats returned, and this time a senior official, Kiosé Mehmed Pasha, disembarked carrying the imperial order for Ali's execution. Ali shouted out he was not to come closer until he was able to read it. The officer ignored the request, unfurled the edict, and ordered Ali to comply; Ali fired his pistol at him, Kiosé fired back, and their bodyguards joined in until a shot mortally wounded Ali. His last instinct was to order one of his men to kill his wife Kyra Vasiliki—a renowned beauty nearly half a century his junior—but this was ignored: once he was dead, the fight was over.[15]

Presented with Ali's head, Khurshid Pasha is said to have gazed on it and wept. It was handed to his bodyguards who wrapped it in a cloth, mounted it on a silver platter, and rode with it through the streets of Jannina, entering the town's mansions to prove to its notables—both Muslims and Christians—that the sultan's will had prevailed. Demanding the usual *bakshish* (tribute), they barged into the residence of the archbishop, who was at dinner with friends, and set the head on the table: The metropolitan said a prayer for the soul of the dead man and handed over a bag of gold coins. The headless corpse was buried in the precinct of a mosque within the citadel, while the head was sent in the usual way to Constantinople to be displayed in the sultan's serail.

Stuffed and perfectly preserved, it bore a close resemblance, in the view of the British chaplain who went to look at it, to the head of John the Baptist. "The countenance was pallid but plump, not collapsed but full and expressive of character. It was large and comely, evidently belonging to a portly man of commanding presence; it had the appearance of openness and good humor—covering as I thought under a smooth exterior, a ferocious and faithless heart." Bald, except for the long tuft of gray hair behind in the Albanian style, and a silver-gray beard, the head was set on a revolving dish for public viewing in a courtyard of the palace. It narrowly escaped being exhibited in London and found its burial spot some time afterward, when the sultan ordered the execution of Ali Pasha's three sons and grandson: the tombs of all five were set side by side outside the Selvyria gate in the imperial capital.[16] "The lawless activities which this man carried out were such as have never before been heard of or seen," ran the official notice of the reasons for his execution. "He was never tranquil. Wherever there was revolution or revolt, he was whether obviously or secretly the originator, taking part and feeding it either with money or with his plots." It is clear that for Ottoman officialdom, the Greek uprising remained something that had essentially been conjured into being by Ali Pasha. With his death, they expected that suppressing it would be only a matter of time.[17]

The man who had defeated Ali, Khurshid Pasha, who was honored by the sultan with the title of "khan" for his success, was one of the most impressive and experienced Ottoman commanders of his era. Born into a poor Christian family in Georgia, he had been sold as a boy into slavery, entering the household of a well-connected pasha where he converted to Islam and rose rapidly in the Ottoman service. By 1820 he was a hardened troubleshooter who had served amid turbulent conditions in Egypt, Serbia, Bosnia, and Syria. Appointed as governor of the Morea, Khurshid and his family had come over from Aleppo and no sooner settled in Tripolitsa than he was instructed to take over the campaign against Ali Pasha. The British consul in Preveza, who had seen many senior Ottoman officials, regarded Khurshid's promotion as entirely deserved and praised what he described as his "transcendent talents and merits."[18]

Khurshid Pasha was also a fond and worried husband. Departing Tripolitsa, he had left behind his three wives and his personal household and they had remained there throughout the siege. After the town fell, the Greek leaders had—as we have seen—attached great importance to the safety of the pasha's harem and had moved very fast to secure this, eventually placing the womenfolk under the personal protection of Petros Mavromihalis's son Georgios, the so-called *beyzadé* (in Ottoman parlance, the "son of the Bey"), a young man who spoke Turkish and knew Constantinople. Their plight weighed on Khurshid Pasha's mind and no sooner did he learn they had been captured than he dispatched agents with letters for them. One of these survives as a remarkable example of the personal expression of the feelings of an Ottoman pasha toward his womenfolk. Couched in the formulaic language of consolation and patience, it makes clear his affection and his desire to see them again:

My dear Esma *hanum*, Hadizé *hanum* and Aysé *hanum*: With my greetings I let you know that I have heard that the *Romaioi* of the Morea have
captured you at Tripolitsa. Thus it was decreed by God and in no way
should you be saddened. Thus was your fate written by the will of God . . .
With the will of God I will bring you either to the East, or to Corfu or to
Rumeli. However, I did not learn where you are or in whose hands and to
learn where you are I am sending this letter with a man from the Bishop
of Jannina. By the will of God, write to me back by the same man where
you are and in whose hands, either in the Romaic [i.e., Greek] or in Turkish, and do not fear anything, nor be sad . . . If you need money where you
are, take loans and let me know . . . Are you all in the same place? Don't
worry. Let me know quickly and in your plight again don't be sad . . .
With the aid of God no harm will come to you, nor any grief.[19]

While the pasha sent off his own agents, the intermediary who eventually
secured their release was a resourceful thirty-year-old Greek from the
Ionian island of Zakynthos. From a trading family, Panayiotis Marinos
Stefanou had studied medicine in Paris and possessed polished manners,
education, courage, and patience. He was probably recommended to the
pasha by the British high commissioner of the Ionian Islands, who also
provided ships for the transfer. Stefanou traveled to Argos in November
to visit Khurshid's wives, returning with valuables that they had entrusted
to him for safekeeping. It was the beginning of several months of complex talks through the winter of 1821–22 that continued even in the
midst of Khurshid's deadly game of wits with Ali in Jannina.

The terms that were eventually agreed to by the two sides involved
exchanging the pasha's wives for some important Greek and Souliot
captives, along with a handsome sum that Khurshid agreed to throw
in—he had, after all, just defeated Ali and gained access to his fabled
fortune—and in April 1822 the valuable Ottoman prisoners were
escorted to the north coast of the Peloponnese for the handover, which
was carefully orchestrated by Stefanou. The women and more than a
hundred of their servants—Khurshid Pasha was known for the splendor of his household—were brought down to a beach near Corinth
and embarked on a British brig. At the last moment there was nearly a
hitch when Georgios Mavromihalis demanded compensation for the
cost of looking after them and threatened to call the deal off. He was
overruled and the swap took place, but what looked like a last-minute

extortion effort left behind a residue of suspicion and recrimination that was to cause trouble later on.[20]

When Khurshid Pasha arrived at the small port of Preveza on the west coast of Epiros to greet his wives, he was accompanied by no fewer than 4,000 soldiers. Taking up his quarters in the old seraglio, he received a stream of guests. The Greeks and Souliot families being sent south as part of the deal, including the children, were sent up to thank the pasha, receiving gold coins from him as a gift, along with a little lecture on the importance of remaining faithful to the Porte. The Greeks should not, he told the men, place their trust in Russia, for the czar was committed to living in peace with the sultan and they should remain loyal to him too. "I believe Signor Gentz himself could not have laid down the principles of legitimacy clearer than His Highness," wrote the British consul Meyer the next day, alluding to Metternich's legendary counselor, "and the duties of subjects to their government." In conversation with the consul, Khurshid discussed the crushing of the Greek revolt in Naoussa across the mountains and confided that he planned to attack the Morea and to defeat the Greeks before the year was out.[21]

There is an apocryphal story that his wives had not been happy to leave the Morea and that one or more of them had fallen in love with their handsome young captor, Georgios the Beyzadé. In one version, some of them were even allegedly pregnant and hence fearful of the punishment in store on their return: and indeed the pasha himself was allegedly furious to discover the evidence of their infidelity and tied them up in sacks and had them drowned. One can see the attractiveness of the myth to the Greek side. The victors of the sack of Tripolitsa are transformed from bloodthirsty killers into seductive young men; the Turks were not only defeated, they were cuckolded as well. In reality, the women were—not surprisingly—said to be in a "very sad and drooping state" when they were first visited at the end of 1821: captivity was no fun even in the hands of a young sprig of the Mavromihalis family.[22] More important, in the holdings of the Greek Literary and Historical Archive in Athens there is a file entitled "The Harem of Khurshid Pasha," which forms part of the papers of the Stefanou family. We can therefore read the correspondence between the Greek leaders in the Peloponnese and Khurshid Pasha in Jannina, track the dealings of the good doctor Stefanou, and understand something of the aftermath.

Contrary to the legend, the pasha's wives lived for many years. We know this because over the following decades a long wrangle ensued between them (and their heirs) in Constantinople and Stefanou himself.[23] Although the women had handed over to him their most precious valuables for safekeeping when he arrived in Tripolitsa at the end of 1821, they had never got them back. It was probably all the fault of Georgios Mavromihalis and those last-minute extra charges he had tried to extort. When his harem had been returned to him, Khurshid Pasha had shown his gratitude to the doctor from Zakynthos in gifts and in words—his letter of thanks is effusive in its praise—but he had not reacted well to being presented with a new bill for 150,000 piastres (nearly £5,000 sterling) to cover the expenses demanded by the young Mavromihalis. In fact, in a rare moment of anger, Khurshid had torn it up on the spot. Stefanou—who claimed he had given the money to Mavromihalis and was thus out of pocket—refused to return the harem jewels until he was recompensed. Because the women had written them down item by item when they gave the valuables to Stefanou, we know precisely what they were. Hadizé *hanum*'s items included "a pair of bracelets of small pearls and diamonds; a pearl chain; a diamond pin; a pair of emerald earrings; two diamond rings; a gold musical tobacco box; a small golden watch; a repeating watch with small diamonds; a tobacco box containing two rings." That was modest compared with Esma *hanum*'s diamond and ruby rings, multiple sets of gold earrings, and her diamond chains and flowers and brooches. Their total value ran into thousands of pounds sterling. Once the women had returned to Constantinople, a case was brought against Stefanou in the Ottoman courts that dragged the British embassy into its coils and continued for decades in Dickensian fashion even beyond the doctor's death in 1863 at the age of seventy-two.[24]

In an era in which women had little agency or visibility in public affairs, personal valuables were one of the most important forms of female wealth and protecting their right to them was also a way to safeguard their own independent standing. The litigiousness of the pasha's wives was not unusual. Ottoman courts in general gave women far more scope to be heard than their Christian counterparts in Europe tended to enjoy; indeed, within the empire, Christian women in the Greek lands sometimes turned to Ottoman judges to obtain satisfaction where their own communal law fell short. The decades they spent in the courts could thus be seen as a further expression of the power of these once powerless women, a determination to turn the tables on the men who had supposedly liberated them. And as we shall see below, it was not only Khurshid's wives who showed a remarkable capacity to defend their interests.[25]

With Ali's head en route to Constantinople, Khurshid Pasha was free to focus on the Greeks at last. Even before news of Ali's death was confirmed, one of Mavrokordatos's closest aides wrote worriedly from Mesolonghi: "Anyone can figure out now what our enemies can do unhindered by any obstacle and with such wealth in their hands." The British consul Meyer believed that the insurrection, at least in western Greece, was "in a rapid decline." An observer in Corfu predicted that "[Ali's death] will prompt a serious disturbance in the affairs of the Greeks."[26] The Porte was in a mood for vengeance, outraged by the reports of atrocities committed against Muslims in the Morea and determined to crush the revolt within the year.

With the Christian-Muslim alliance in western Rumeli in disarray, the Ottoman army retook Arta without difficulty. In the traumatic exodus that followed, the Christian townspeople, stripped of their possessions, many of them barefoot, walked into the hills to escape the Turkish soldiers. Local armed bands under the sway of Greek warlords offered no protection, robbing them and cutting their fingers off to take their rings. "I became disgusted with the Greek cause," the chieftain Ioannis Makriyannis writes, "because we were a lot of cannibals." As disease decimated the lice-ridden refugees, he tried to lead the survivors to safety until he fell ill himself and was carried away by his brother to the safety of his village.[27]

A large Ottoman army now assembled in Arta to clear the Greeks out of western Greece entirely. Mavrokordatos moved a small force up from the south to block them, occupying a position in the hills only a few kilometers away and hoping to advance northward. But at the battle of Peta in July 1822, the Ottoman troops inflicted a crushing blow on him and his men, wiping out the battalion of philhellenes formed specially to fight under his command. At the same time, Khurshid's men also eliminated the threat from the Souliots, forcing them to leave their homelands for good. Beating off efforts by the Greeks to come to the Souliots' aid, the Ottoman army was now effectively in control of all of western Greece—only Mesolonghi lay between it and the Peloponnese.

*

The Peloponnese could of course be reached by Ottoman armies from either side of the Pindos mountains and once Ali Pasha was dead, Sultan Mahmud II resolved to send other forces down the east coast to make for Corinth and the mountain passes that led into the Morea's interior. After the shocks of the previous year, the spring of 1822 was a time of Ottoman rebuilding and resolve, punctuated by the massacres that wiped out the insurgency in northern Greece and in the eastern Aegean, where the island of Chios would become the site of killings that shocked Europe.[28] The sultan was undeterred by the outcry abroad. At the start of the summer he appointed a commander to invade the Peloponnese, Mahmud Dramali Pasha, who set out with a vast army of more than 20,000 men, including approximately 8,000 cavalry—easily the largest force the insurgents in the Morea had faced. Despite the overwhelming numbers, however, Dramali Pasha was not a leader of the same caliber as Khurshid: irascible, proud, and fabulously wealthy, he lacked Khurshid's experience and patience in the field and he had been lulled by easy victories against Greeks in Thessaly the previous year. Dramali's confidence grew as he encountered no significant resistance on his march southward, but as his men razed Thebes and passed through the half-destroyed towns en route to the isthmus, other difficulties quickly became apparent. In the summer heat, the scarcity of food and water soon told, provisions lagged, medical help was virtually nonexistent, and soldiers began falling ill and dying. At the start of July, the Greeks abandoned the fortress of Acrocorinth that guarded the entrance to the Morea; Dramali's forces took possession and found the widow of Kiamil Bey mourning the corpse of the fabulously wealthy Muslim landowner. The bey had been killed in his prison cell by a soldier as the Greeks fled. The Peloponnese lay wide open.[29]

The wisest course for Dramali Pasha, in retrospect, would have been to wait in Corinth, build up his supplies, and establish communications with the imperial fleet before moving south again: such a strategy might have taken a few more months but it could well have ended the Greek insurgency entirely, especially as Dramali had a significant additional force of hardened soldiers in the fortress at Patras to draw upon whom the Greeks had not managed to defeat. Instead, ignoring the advice of more experienced commanders, and buoyed by overconfidence and contempt for the Greeks, he pushed down through the passes toward the plain of Argos, counting on the imperial fleet to meet him at Nafplion with supplies.

Reports that a huge Ottoman army had entered the Peloponnese terrified the Greeks. Many believed this was the end of their uprising and the members of the newly formed provisional government fled from Argos, abandoning papers and archives and taking to the boats while men from the Mani enriched themselves amid the general lawlessness. In the panic, only a small force commanded by Dimitrios Ypsilantis stayed to block the way to Dramali Pasha and his army by making a stand in the town's castle. There the prince showed his remarkable courage and stalled the Ottoman troops for nearly two weeks. Kolokotronis, who had been appointed commander in chief by the panicked government, managed in the meantime to raise a force of several thousand men that mustered in the hills to the north. The Greeks were hugely outnumbered—there were perhaps seven hundred men with Ypsilantis in Argos, and around 6,000 with Kolokotronis. But they understood the terrain and they were defending their homes. They started burning the crops and despoiling the wells in the fields around the Ottoman army. Dramali's soldiers were mostly irregulars who had joined in the expectation of easy plunder: exhausted by the scorching summer heat in the plain, they began to go hungry and wanted to abandon the fight. With no sign of help from the fleet, an Albanian unit sent messengers secretly to let the Greeks in the castle know they were ready to reach an understanding, and one night in late July they allowed the defenders of Argos to slip through their lines unhindered. The next morning Dramali Pasha was told by his men that he could have the fortress but that they were heading home, leaving him no alternative but to retreat. In the narrows of the Dervenakia pass, the Greek bands led by Kolokotronis were waiting for them. They fell on the exhausted soldiers, surrounding them as they tried to cut their way through and slaughtering them in their thousands. Dispersed and disoriented, the remnants of Dramali Pasha's army eventually made it back across the mountains to Corinth where, ill and exhausted, Dramali himself died in November: the few thousand survivors eventually staggered into the fortress at Patras. Khurshid Pasha headed south from Larissa to help but appears to have concluded there was nothing to be done so late in the year, so he returned to his headquarters. Nafplion surrendered days later. Thanks to the combination of Ypsilantis's bravery and Kolokotronis's levelheadedness, resolve, and cunning, the revolution had not only survived its most formidable military challenge: it had achieved its greatest victory.

Dramali Pasha's defeat was a major blow to Ottoman efforts to crush the Greek rebellion in its infancy and it did not reflect especially well on Khurshid who had seen the second season of campaigns end in failure. Khurshid had not disguised his resentment at being excluded from the command of the expedition, but nevertheless he remained the outstanding figure on the Ottoman side and what happened next took everyone by surprise. At the end of November 1822, imperial messengers arrived at his camp in Larissa. The precise content of the orders they brought remains unknown because Khurshid Pasha said nothing to anyone else around him but simply asked the messengers for a couple of days to arrange his affairs. He sent a large sum of money to his wives, called in his advisers, and told them of his impending death so that they should not find fault with his doctors. Without making any comments against the sultan, Khurshid then took poison. It took him several days to die, amid the sustained hemorrhaging of blood.

A few days after Khurshid's burial, imperial messengers are said to have disinterred the corpse to cut off his head, which was ceremonially conveyed to Constantinople. His body was buried beside the river in Larissa in a splendid tomb that was erected, following his own instructions, with marble brought in from the palace of one of Ali Pasha's sons. An inscription in Arabic commemorated the resting place of "He who was known as Khurshid Pasha the just, the unbreakable, the most faithful, the dedicated servant of Farouk Osman, he who was a lion in battle, a noble fighter, by the will of the Prophet, at whose death heaven and earth suddenly darkened . . ."[30]

If the manner of Khurshid's death was striking in its stoicism, its impact was instantaneous and catastrophic. The political challenge of mobilizing coalitions of the rivalrous, double-dealing pashas and beys of the southern Balkans into a coherent military force was immense, and few other Ottoman officials had Khurshid Pasha's diplomatic skills, experience, or judgment. "All parties now seem to feel that the Porte cannot reduce these provinces to submission by the troops which march from her Asiatic dominions; and she can no longer rely on the levies made in her European provinces," noted Meyer. As if agreeing with this judgment, some of the Greek armatoles in Rumeli now rejoined the insurgents. One of them was a future leader of the Greek forces, Giorgios Karaïskakis, whose decision was based at least in part on the news of Khurshid Pasha's death. The Albanian beys too, who had gathered around the pasha and the sultan's banner, now began to think again. Meyer's prognosis was grim for the Ottomans:

> It is certain that the talents and personal character of this Seraskier [commander in chief], so well known throughout the Empire and so much esteemed in these provinces during the last two years, alone checked the progress of the Greek insurrection and the rebellious factions among the native pachas and beys. This only check has now been removed and with it, as I have before remarked, the only authority of the Porte which remained in these provinces, in which a new and general crisis cannot long be delayed.

Saved from the renewed tyranny of Ali Pasha, the Greeks were now—thanks to the sultan's decree—spared the wrath of Khurshid, his victor. The revolution in the Morea had gained a breathing space.[31]

The British consul in Preveza was not the only one to wonder what could have caused the sultan to "deprive his Government at this great crisis of the support of this most distinguished Prince in his Empire." Some said he was accused of being too lenient toward the Greeks; others wondered if the sultan had been angered by the amount of time Khurshid had devoted to the rescue of his wives and the consequent delay of his spring offensive against the Souliots. Was he a victim of imperial court politics, targeted for his association with the wrong faction? Or was the real motive money? Khurshid Pasha had "a passion for splendor and magnificence," and the sultan is said to have settled the pasha's huge debts with his bankers in Constantinople as a mark of favor.[32] There was also the compromising legacy of Ali Pasha's legendary fortune, estimates of which had reached astronomic proportions. After Ali's death an accountant had been sent in immediately to itemize and evaluate the treasure. What he found amounted to a huge sum for the time—30 million grossia (300,000 Turkish lira) of which half was sent to the Porte and the rest accounted for in other ways by the needs of the campaign against Ali. But had there perhaps been even more? Had the sultan perhaps suspected Khurshid Pasha of dishonesty, maybe of having used more than he should on the redemption of his womenfolk? At least one source suggests that it was Ali Pasha's widow in Constantinople, Kyra Vasiliki, who avenged her husband by planting the seeds of doubt in the sultan's mind that he had been cheated.[33]

*

In 1962 a Greek publisher in Larissa published a grainy black-and-white photograph of a smiling middle-aged lady with a bouffant hairdo and sunglasses pointing to a badly bricked-up wall in a corner of a garden. It was all that was left of Khurshid Pasha's once magnificent tomb. It had remained more or less intact in a neighborhood known as the Pera Machala even after the town was incorporated into Greece in 1881. "I came across it one day on a ramble along the banks of the Peneios, on the left bank, a few paces left of the bridge, deliberately enclosed within a walled garden with openings protected by iron bars," wrote a local man in 1891. "Recently the tomb has begun to suffer damage, though I believe it to be of great value for the traveler and for the lover of history, a value which will only increase with time." The main wall survived until after the Second World War, but postwar urban development was more pernicious than complicit and a century later only scattered remnants survived. Today's residential buildings appear to have entirely obliterated what was left.[34]

In death, the body of Ali Pasha fared better than his rival's, secure in its grave in the courtyard of the Fethiye mosque overlooking the lake in Jannina. The young Benjamin Disraeli paid a visit and in 1854, when John Murray published his pioneering *Handbook for Travellers in Greece*, the tomb featured as one of the sights in a town that had not recovered the prosperity it had known forty years earlier. The tomb may still be seen. As for Ali Pasha's Christian wife Kyra Vasiliki, who was with him until the moment of his death, and who may have avenged him after it, she was released eventually into the care of the patriarch in Constantinople. In 1830, still reputedly in possession of the beauty that had so struck Ali, she was allowed to return to Greece. Four years later she died of dysentery, not yet fifty, in a small town not far from Mesolonghi. Today her grave can still be seen in a nearby churchyard; its inscription makes no reference at all to her husband.

7

THE WAR IN
THE ISLANDS

*The sea itself, the one we see and love, is the great document of
its past existence.*

Fernand Braudel, *The Mediterranean and the
Mediterranean World in the Age of Philip II*

"Three insignificant little islands stood up successfully for the freedom
of the whole of Greece against a great and old empire, and overpowered
fleets a thousand times and more powerful with only their merchant
shipping, and only the funds of their inhabitants," wrote Spyridon Trikoupis in 1853 in his monumental history of the revolution. This
statement rather underplayed the sheer size of the Greek merchant
marine, which amounted to nearly one thousand well-built seagoing
vessels and countless smaller coastal craft, based in dozens of ports. Yet
Trikoupis was right that the odds against the Greeks were nevertheless
immense. Not only were the islands themselves open to easy and devastating attack, as the 1824 destruction of Psara was to show, but even
their largest brigs carried a quarter or less the firepower of the Ottoman
three-deckers. To complicate things, Greek ships were privately owned
and their crews were volunteers who could not be coerced and had to
be paid. Falling initially on the pockets of shipowners themselves, the
burden of creating, outfitting, and maintaining a war fleet in such circumstances posed thorny questions of governance and financing that
eventually brought a new and distinctive regional interest into the
already complex political calculus of the revolution. This interest
focused upon the maritime islands whose fleets provided the core of the
Greek navy: Psara, Spetses, and—first among equals—Hydra.[1]

Perhaps best-known today as the picturesque vacation spot that inspired the singer-poet Leonard Cohen, the isle of Hydra lies a few miles off the eastern coast of the Peloponnese, a pine-clad rock whose terraced stone houses rise in an amphitheater above a well-protected harbor. In the spring of 1821 its population was about ten times its present size and its wealthy magnates, grown rich over the previous decades, owned dozens of ships manned by thousands of sailors. Although the men of the island spoke Greek, their forefathers were mostly Albanian settlers, and Albanian remained the tongue in which they spoke with one another and sang their songs at sea. (Many women spoke only Albanian.) Administered under the aegis of the Kapudan Pasha (admiral of the imperial navy), whose fleet they supplied with crews, the island was governed in what Trikoupis described as an "aristocratic" system by a small class of notables in conjunction with a local man, Nikolaos Kokovilas, who had been appointed governor by the Porte some years before.[2]

For the Etaireia, the importance of Hydra's ships to the Greek cause was obvious. Papalessas and other emissaries stopped there en route to the Peloponnese, alternately praising and threatening the shipowners, in the hope of getting their support, even warning them that their ships would be seized if they refused.[3] But the shipowners were as unimpressed as the landowners on the mainland with the Etaireia's half-baked preparations and they were not men to be swayed by wild promises. "Hearing the kind of wondrous tales some of the Etairist apostles brought to the island, for instance that we will have the help of an American fleet, that we have Russia as a protector of the revolution . . . that many powerful Turks in Constantinople and elsewhere are in fact secret Christians," one recalled, "they hesitated, remembering the catastrophes and the terrible aftermath of 1769 and the Russians' inhuman abandonment of the revolutionaries."[4] The Hydriots' caution was in striking contrast to the island leaders of neighboring Spetses, who embraced the revolution from early on, and it was a worry to those planning the insurrection in the Morea. At the end of January 1821, the Peloponnesian notables sent an emissary; a few weeks later, the Etairist intellectual Anthimos Gazis wrote enthusiastic letters to the Hydriot leaders, telling them to get ready for "the bridegroom" and not to stint in their patriotic duties. None of this moved them; they had already made clear to the Etaireia months earlier that they needed the Ottoman fleet to be destroyed and confirmation of Russian backing before they would support the revolution. On March 24, "the notables of the Peloponnese" wrote to the "most well-born notables and brothers of Hydra and Spetses," admitting it might seem as though they had been hasty in rising up, but explaining that they had feared waiting any longer. They begged the islanders to put aside their misgivings and set sail to prevent the arrival of Ottoman reinforcements. But remembering the disappointments of the past, Hydra's notables waited on events and ignored the ever more desperate entreaties that followed.[5]

Etairists had organized three caïques to run between Hydra and the mainland to keep in touch with developments in the Morea. In this relatively safe setting where there were no Muslims nearby, some of the Etairists were so unguarded about what they were doing that around the start of March the notables on Hydra had taken them aside and told them to act more prudently; one or two of the young revolutionaries had resented being chastised and there were angry words. Among the local conspirators there was an unemployed sea captain called Antonios Oikonomou. He had lost his ship at sea some years earlier, joined the Etaireia in Constantinople, met Papaflessas, and embraced the revolutionary cause. The two men were alike in temperament and even Oikonomou's defenders agree he was hot-tempered and single-minded; it is perhaps fitting that the commemorative bust of him that today overlooks the quay on Hydra glares somewhat fiercely over the scene of his fame. He and some comrades were gathering volunteers to go and fight on the mainland when a boat brought the news, around sunset on March 27, that the uprising in the Morea had begun.[6]

We will probably never know exactly what happened over the next twenty-four hours, but Oikonomou's actions changed the entire course of the insurgency. To those who later hailed him as a hero, it was the courage and bravery of such "decisive democrats" that forced Hydra's notables into the war and thereby contributed to the success of the revolution. For those who were more sympathetic to the shipowners, he was an ambitious and disreputable troublemaker who nearly started a civil war. It is a partisan of the second group who tells us that when Oikonomou heard the news of the uprising in the Morea, over a glass of rum in a tavern on the waterfront, he began denouncing the island's elite for their lack of patriotism. As men gathered around, he is said to have told them it was shameful that their brothers across the water were embarking on the revolution, while on the island they were prevented from helping "because our Turko-bosses [*tourkoproestoi mas*] are stopping us." "What should we do?" someone shouted. "Kill them," he is reported to have responded: was it right that they hoard their wealth instead of fighting for freedom?[7]

Whether or not he really whipped them up in that way, what is not in question is that Oikonomou assembled a large mob and seized the moment as word spread of the extraordinary events taking place on the mainland. That night his excited followers rang the bell in the port church of the Panayia—a signal for townspeople to assemble, traditionally used only in the event of danger—sent criers through the streets calling the citizens to arms, boarded the ships docked in the harbor, and seized their weapons. At dawn the next day a crowd armed with guns, knives, and staves entered the offices of the island government, the so-called chancellery, deposed Kokovilas, the representative of the Ottoman state, and tore down the imperial flag. Having in this way dismantled the visible symbols of Ottoman power, Oikonomou and his men now turned their attention to the real rulers of the island—the notables.[8]

Acute class differences divided the tiny island and deep resentments simmered below the organized surface of communal life. The sailors had only to lift their eyes from the quay to see the great mansion of "the bey" Georgios Voulgaris: with its sheer walls, guard tower, and lavishly decorated and cavernous reception halls, it resembled the Constantinopolitan palace of a great Ottoman potentate. Confidant of the imperial Kapudan Pasha, a respected figure at court, Voulgaris had helped to ensure the island's extraordinary prosperity during the Napoleonic Wars. The Tombazis and Koundouriotis mansions not far away were equally grand.[9] Yet only a few hundred yards separated them from the crowded, poorer neighborhoods inhabited by the men in Oikonomou's mob. For them, times were very hard. The decades of economic boom had brought Hydra the largest single Greek shipping fleet in the Aegean; fortunes had been made, while sailors had been able to marry young and create large families of their own. But trade had collapsed around 1815 and many of those now following Oikonomou had already rioted two years earlier because their families were starving and work was scarce. Since then, with many of the island's ships laid up, things had got worse. Skilled seamen, tough and quick with a knife, they were—wrote a Swiss doctor who stayed with them in 1820—"like werewolves" and their anger against the notables was easily roused.[10]

With the island chancellery in his power, Oikonomou now told the notables that all he really wanted was for them to help the starving poor of Hydra and support the revolution. The island's most prominent ship-owner, Lazaros Koundouriotis, was a wily, well-informed merchant who had been in business from the age of fourteen. Possessing more than a dozen large vessels, he headed the island's pro-Russian faction and he would emerge as one of the most powerful behind-the-scenes figures of the entire revolution. At a disadvantage in the face of the mob, and shut up for safety in his mansion, he and the other notables who traditionally ran the island's government promised funds for those in need and the next day these were distributed to the sailors—the largest portion being donated by Koundouriotis and his brother Georgios. Oikonomou proposed to Lazaros Koundouriotis that the two of them govern together but the latter refused, preferring to marshal the other notables behind the idea of allowing Oikonomou to rule alone: Koundouriotis was a man who knew how to wait. The notables thus signed over the powers of government of the island to "our most honorable patriot, master captain Antonios Oikonomou" on March 31. It was a huge change in the management of the island's affairs. Previous announcements had been signed by "the notables of the island of Hydra"; later ones declared them to be "the inhabitants of the island of Hydra." In this way, says historian Antonios Maioulis, scion of one of the leading families, the island passed from aristocracy to democracy. Some talked rather less enthusiastically about the imposition of a revolutionary dictatorship.[11]

But as Koundouriotis had surely understood, while Oikonomou had been given vast powers on paper, getting the notables to distribute funds to disperse the mob was one thing, and getting their crews ready and risking their ships was quite another. In fact, not one ship left for days, and in practical terms the island remained aloof from the struggle: the ships would not sail until their captains were prepared to set out to sea, and the captains worked closely with the shipowners. Oikonomou's ineffectiveness is evident in the series of appeals for help that were sent to the island from the Peloponnese. Chieftains, notables, and bishops all wrote to tell the Hydriots they could not understand why they had not provided any boats, and urged them to hurry before people on the mainland got discouraged. More than two weeks went by. On Spetses, where the Etaireia influence was much stronger, the revolutionary flag was run up on April 2 or 3, and some say it was only the sight of Spetsiot brigs sailing past Hydra carrying booty, flying the revolutionary flag, and firing their cannons that eventually tipped the balance. On Hydra it was not until April 15 that a church service finally blessed the island's participation in the national struggle and the colors of the revolution flew above the chancellery. Although this suggested that the two sides had come to terms, such was not the case. The notables had regained the initiative, released their ships, and were waiting for the moment to strike. After the capture of a wealthy Ottoman prize triggered off angry scenes over how to share out the proceeds, they sensed the popular mood turning against Oikonomou and had him and the other troublemakers sent off the island and handed over to the care of Peloponnesian notables. He was held in semi-captivity for some months in a succession of monasteries before making his escape. On the eve of the national assembly in Argos, Koundouriotis made it clear that the island's ships would cease to sail for the revolution unless Oikonomou was found and eliminated. He was tracked down and assassinated by a hired band of armed men on a roadside outside Argos. The wealthy shipowners were not forgiving men and did not take kindly to threats. But Oikonomou had achieved his objective: Hydra had entered the war.[12]

If the shipping magnates hesitated to break with the Ottoman system, it was not only because of the failed risings of the past; they and their islands had done very well under the sultans. Greeks were heavily involved in the south Russian wheat trade, and by 1800 they dominated commercial activity in much of the Levant. Ottoman policy under Sultan Selim III (1789–1807) had deliberately fostered this by giving concessions to Ottoman subjects, Christian as well as Muslim. There was virtually no imperial presence on the islands and the Ottoman authorities were not even overly bothered by what flag the islanders flew on their vessels, many of which ran under Russian colors. By comparison with the situation facing Christians on the mainland, this was rule with a light touch. The result was the transformation of Greek shipping and the emergence of a class of men with experiences and resources that could, with a little modification and some persuasion, be put to use in war.

By 1821, the Greeks as a whole possessed a commercial fleet of about 1,000 medium-sized vessels, many of them armed with between ten and fifteen cannons, manned by a total of approximately 18,000 experienced seamen. Among them were oceangoing brigs capable of long-distance travel: the Hydra captain Dimitrios Tsamados had sailed as far as Montevideo in South America; a certain Giannis had made the run from Constantinople to Calcutta and the Philippines.[13] The largest fleets belonged to Hydra and Spetses in the Saronic Gulf, Psara and Kasos in the eastern Aegean, and the port of Galaxidi in the Gulf of Corinth; the Ionian Islands, under British rule, owned at least 200 more ships. But there were no fewer than forty islands or coastal towns that owned more than local craft, and about twenty of these, with roughly 13,000 sailors among them, took part in the revolution. Yet mercantile activity did not stop just because some of the ships were deployed for fighting; had it done so, there would have been even less money available for the cause than there was. Many vessels continued trading throughout the conflict too and only 10 percent of the total shipping in the hands of the Greeks was ever converted for war use: even many of the well-known ships involved in the fighting were deployed for only a few months before returning to commercial traffic. Throughout the war, the route through Constantinople to the Black Sea ports remained open to Greek-owned ships; they continued to call into Ottoman ports, and many even went on supplying besieged Ottoman forts.[14]

The Greeks were unquestionably remarkable sailors and the Ottoman navy relied on its standing complement of Hydriots in particular. The Ottomans were badly affected, therefore, when they were forced to replace them with costly Neapolitans less familiar with the Aegean.[15] With its dozens of islands, unpredictable currents, and seasonal winds, the eastern Mediterranean is a test of maritime ability—the summer *meltemi* can reach gale force; sudden storms may be followed by calms that last for days—and the Greeks had an unrivaled knowledge of the sea and its vagaries. Alongside their daring and belief in their cause, their experience, skill, and confidence in handling small but highly maneuverable vessels went a long way toward balancing the gap in resources between them and their imperial foe. The Ottoman navy may have been better armed, almost impregnable, yet it was manned for the first two or three years of the revolution by inexperienced crews and risk-averse commanders with predictably poor results.

Etaireia agents had been recruiting across the Aegean since 1818 and making preparations for an uprising from early in 1821. But it was not only on Hydra that there was hesitation. On Psara, learning in the New Year of the decisions made by the Etaireia leadership, the local island government decided to stop sailing into the Black Sea lest their ships be cut off and unable to return, and it then sent a message asking the Etaireia for further instructions. Learning of the uprising in the Danubian Principalities, it deferred the moment of decision, reassuring the Ottoman governor on nearby Chios of Psara's continued loyalty to the sultan, and resisting pressure from Etairists on the island to tear down the signs of Ottoman authority. Only after a Spetsiot vessel appeared on Good Friday flying the new revolutionary flag of a red cross standing on a crescent did Psara follow suit, adding to the customary greeting of "Christ is Risen" (*Christos anesti*) a new one—"Greece is Risen" (*Ellas anesti*)—and adapting the Spetsiot flag. The crew of an Ottoman merchant ship were ashore at the time: the Psara *dimogerontia* (assembly) ordered they were not to be harmed, escorted them onto their vessel, and allowed them to depart. They were lucky. The Spetsiots surprised an Ottoman corvette and a brig off Milos in the southern Cyclades, killed the crews, and seized the ships as prizes.[16]

Once Hydra declared for the revolution, it prepared an expeditionary force under Iakovos Tombazis. His ship, the *Themistoklis*, was owned by the Koundouriotis brothers and was typical of the Hydriot brigs: armed with sixteen guns, it was neither large nor powerful, but it was superbly maneuverable and crewed by experienced sailors. Tombazis himself was empowered to use all means compatible with "legitimate warfare" for the cause of national independence.[17] On April 18, a proclamation was issued for the first time in the name of "the Greek fleet" on behalf of the three key islands—Spetses, Hydra, and Psara—announcing their intention to fight for the independence of the nation from "our Ottoman tyrants." The announcement did not mean there was yet any national direction nor even much coordination between the three islands. The oath Tombazis swore associated his island's fleet with those of Spetses and Psara and committed him to cooperating with them. But the rivalry between Hydra and Spetses was notorious and each was jealous of their prerogatives: the Spetses admirals were not placed under Hydriot command, and indeed in June 1822 the two fleets nearly turned on one another. When the provisional government was established under Alexandros Mavrokordatos in January 1822, the ministry of marine was shared three ways since Spetses, Hydra, and Psara each insisted on having a representative.[18]

The war at sea thus displayed many of the virtues and vices of the whole Greek war effort in embryo. Not only was there no unified command over the "fleet," there was nothing that Europeans or Americans would have recognized as a structure of command on board either; the Royal Navy, for instance, with its press gangs and its draconian punishments, had no equivalent in the Greek islands. There were of course different ranks of sailors, who earned different wages, but there was great freedom of expression and a practice of consultation among them. "The sight of a vessel of war conducted without what is commonly called discipline would probably have been to most persons in the United States a greater novelty than it was to me," writes a young Greek who volunteered to be ship's secretary under the Hydriot commander, Admiral Miaoulis. The men, he noted, mostly knew one another and were often connected by family ties so that what held them together was "obedience enforced by force of opinion and the value of character." "There was no compulsion, and in fact there was no discipline on board in the common meaning of the word. Each man had voluntarily entered the vessel; each was at perfect liberty to go when he pleased. While on board, each had a voice in every question relating to the voyage, management and movement of the vessel."[19] The log of another Hydriot brig, the *Kimon*, confirms that, after the captains conferred with one another, they typically consulted their crews. On June 11, the captain of the *Kimon* announced to his men: "Boys! All of us captains have agreed to stay to burn the enemy's ships and to do whatever else we can [to them] . . . What is your view?" Twenty-two members of the crew protested and insisted on being put ashore to head back to Hydra directly by land. Such an action could have left the brig undermanned; yet only the force of opinion of their shipmates could be brought to bear upon dissenters and that was not always enough. Maritime democracy was, to put it mildly, a major limitation for the Greeks in executing a sustained and effective naval strategy.[20]

Money was an even bigger headache. Traditionally, earnings were shared out among owners, captains, and crew, and in addition, once a ship had set sail, its itinerary was often a matter of negotiation between the captain and his crew that depended on the balance of patriotism and profit. Most sailors were reluctant to remain very long at sea, and because the means of paying them were unpredictable, the needs of national strategy often took second place to more mercenary considerations: seamen usually demanded to be paid up front—sometimes for an initial three months, sometimes monthly—and would turn the ship for home several days before their wages were due to run out. Even when they had been paid, they might be tempted by opportunities to earn more from raiding. Those in charge of the Greek naval effort understood the danger. In an uncertain economic environment, where there were limited funds for noncommercial work, it was impossible to eradicate the temptations of piracy. That first proclamation made on behalf of "the Greek fleet" declared—somewhat defensively—that "the war which we are waging on our impious tyrants is not thievery [kleftikos] but for our entire Nation." It warned crews against interfering with fellow Greeks or Greek ships, or those of other powers: "we fight none other than our Ottoman tyrants." This was the language of classic republicanism, but it was not one most of the sailors and their captains understood.

The temptations of piracy combined with the murderous imperatives of religious war, making a lethal maritime cocktail whose consequences were visible in the very first Hydriot expedition into the eastern Aegean. It had set sail to try to persuade the island of Chios to enter the war and had run up not only against the islanders' reluctance but the distractions of easy plunder. It was while they were off Chios that two captains from the expedition seized an unimaginably rich prize—a ship carrying the new mullah of Egypt along with his family, his household servants, and rich gifts from the sultan to Mehmet Ali of Egypt. In what the Ottoman authorities understood to be an act of revenge for the execution of the patriarch in Constantinople, the Greek sailors were reported to have landed the passengers and crew on a deserted islet, slaughtered them, and then tortured the mullah's wife in front of her husband, before killing them both and hanging his body from the yardarm. It was an early example of what was to become a practice of both sides at sea—the flaunting of corpses and heads to indicate resolve and the power of their cause: the Ottoman navy treated captured Greek crews the same way. The account given in the ship's diary of the Hydriot commander of the squadron is very brief—noting only that "some of them were killed" and giving more details about a much more consequential matter—the astonishing prize that was worth more than 6 million grossia, including "many brilliants and other diamonds, twelve silver candlesticks, six gold and three large mirrors framed with precious stones." The plunder from the mullah's ship was so great that when the two Hydriot ships refused to share their prize with the other crews, the rest of the fleet accompanied them home for fear of losing out on the spoils. The episode led to what an early historian describes as "great discord" among the Greeks, not over the killings but about the division of the loot, and it showed how easily the crews could be distracted from their political mission. These arguments pitted the sailors against Hydra's ruler, Antonios Oikonomou, who wanted to ensure that a share of the loot went to the public chest; it was this dispute that gave Hydra's notables the opening they needed to get him out.[21]

The Greek fleet went on to attack other boatloads of pilgrims—this was the season of the hajj and many were making their way to Mecca—spreading alarm along the Asia Minor coast: writing home from Smyrna, an Algerian called El-Hadj Khelil deplored the frequent assaults on devout Muslims by these "miscreants."[22] The raids deeply worried the Sultan and his ministers; not only did they strike a blow at his title of Defender of the Holy Places of Islam but they brought home the frailty of the empire's control of the seas, the limited naval resources at its disposal, and the liberty the rebels enjoyed.[23]

The Greek sailors' sense of a religious war may have been intensified by the news of the hanging of the patriarch in Constantinople, but an ardent French philhellene who worked at the consulate in Smyrna was nonetheless shocked by the cruelty they had displayed; their murderous treatment of the Muslim passengers and crews they captured could not, he wrote, be excused by the heat of battle since they were invariably carried out in cold blood.[24] Those fighting had gone to sea—in the words of a Patmos sea captain's written pledge—to fight "the Muslims, the enemies of our race."[25] Yet religious hatred was not the only reason for violence. Greek vessels on the corso—sailors used the Italian word for a pirate raid—often beat, killed or drowned their unfortunate victims even when they turned out to be Christians, indeed even Greeks. Off Rhodes a Cypriot volunteer on his way to fight encountered some Greek pirates at sea whom he and his comrades fought off at gunpoint. A few days later they all met up again on land on Syros, in the middle of the Cyclades, and the pirates cheerfully admitted to their intended victims that they would have slit their throats had they caught them. In the seas near Tzia, also in the Cyclades, a passenger asked nervously whether a rapidly approaching craft was Turkish. "Please God, they are just Turks," was the Greek captain's response as his crew got ready to dive and swim for the shore.[26]

Despite the noble sentiments of the proclamation of April 18, the dividing line between piracy and prosecuting the war was blurred, especially as many of the Greek sea captains and their hard-up crews did not always observe the sanctity of neutral flags. The resulting diplomatic frictions became a major political problem for the revolution from the outset. In April, a brig out of Spetses captained by a certain Argyris Stemitziotis, called into the island of Tinos to pick up volunteer fighters for the Peloponnese. By coincidence, goods belonging to an Ottoman pasha were being loaded at that moment onto an Austrian vessel bound for Smyrna. The Austrians were especially loathed by the Greek seamen because of Metternich's pro-Ottoman diplomacy, so Stemitziotis's men ignored the flag, seized the goods and took the crew—eighteen north Africans—captive. When another two escaped, there was a manhunt through the town.

Tinos was a busy port with traffic across the Aegean, and as if the plight of the two fugitive north African sailors was not enough, another boat now entered port carrying the agha, the chief Ottoman official of the island. It had come from the imperial capital, and on learning what the Spetsiots had done, its Tiniot captain immediately ran up the French flag for protection. Stemitziotis ignored it too and demanded that the agha be handed over. The islanders' notables objected, fearing that this would immediately expose them to the threat of Ottoman reprisals, so they brokered a deal, handing over the agha's property to the sailors and managing to get the official and his family into the safety of the house of the French consul and eventually onto a French ship bound for Rhodes.[27] When the news of Stemitziotis's activities reached Spetses, the island's leaders realized the likely damage to the revolutionary cause should their ships ignore the rights of major European powers, so they sent their political adviser to Hydra to confer. It was agreed that Stemitziotis should return what he had seized and allow the Habsburg vessel to leave freely. Metternich's Austria was a Great Power and such behavior could do immense harm to the Greeks at a time when they were trying to persuade Europe of the justice of their struggle.

The Hydra admiral, Tombazis, headed for Tinos to help sort things out, but ironically his arrival only made things worse because one of his own sailors assaulted a local girl and was then killed by her menfolk in retaliation. The Hydriot crew rampaged through the town looking for the killers and when they were unable to find them, they started firing the ship's cannons into the town, ignoring Tombazis's pleas to stop.[28] The revolution had been proclaimed on Tinos just days earlier with a procession in the main town and a show of enthusiasm as local Etairists assembled a force of several hundred volunteers keen to go and fight; now, local opinion began to sour, and it was the turn of the Spetsiots to become peacemakers. Eventually, financial compensation was agreed for the dead Hydriot's family and only then could the fleet sail off and get on with its original task of taking the war to the Ottoman foe.[29]

All the islands of the Aegean were having to weigh up whether and when to break with their Ottoman masters. For administrative or naval centers of imperial power like Mitylene and Rhodes close to Asia Minor, openly declaring for the revolution was out of the question: it would have been suicidal. But although there was only a minimal Muslim presence on most of the other islands, they too were essentially defenseless against any Ottoman retaliation and in any case they were closely linked commercially with Constantinople, Smyrna and Alexandria. Moreover, the Ottoman authorities took pains to remind them where their loyalty was supposed to lie. After the first attacks on the hajj pilgrims, an imperial decree warned the islanders that the price of insubordination was the confiscation of their property and captivity or death for communities who supported the rebels. To the inhabitants of the island of Symi, the governor of nearby Rhodes offered amnesty and pardon for any who had strayed but warned them to confirm their allegiance to the sultan. The message was backed up by a letter from the archbishop of Rhodes.[30]

The Cyclades were closer to the Hydra and Spetses fleets than islands like Symi, yet the Ottomans sent out reminders to the islanders there too. Gasparis Delagrammatikas, the imperial agent for Andros, wrote to his countrymen from Constantinople urging them to reaffirm their loyalty. In October 1821 an Ottoman emissary called Raktivan Agasi Halil Bey disembarked at Syros after a long and dangerous voyage from Constantinople carrying instructions for the notables of the archipelago: we can assume these were a blend of promises and threats.[31] Among the documents was probably advice from the new patriarch, Evgenios II, reminding the islanders to stay faithful to the sultan, and calling on those who had taken up arms to throw them away as they were the "sources of your common ruin." "Brother-Christians, and my sons, of our Church," Evgenios wrote a few months later:

You who live in the Morea and the islands of the Archipelago, as well those who sail on the sea as those who dwell on land, and, in brief, you all who are in error and have embraced the accursed plague of rebellion, throw away those arms from your hands—listen to my fatherly voice which proceeds from my paternal affection . . . cast away from your thoughts the diabolical attempt of revolt, cast away, I repeat, those arms, the cause of your destruction, return to obedience and submission and ask forgiveness of the Lord God our Savior, in order to regain the love and protection of the sultan, by such celestial intercession.[32]

Among the agents of the devil—at least in the Patriarch's eyes—were the two Etairist emissaries who had been sent out by Alexandros Ypsilantis at the start of 1821 to prime the Aegean Islands for the uprising. Both men had participated with him in the key planning conference at Ismail back in October 1820: one of them was an impoverished Ionian sea captain called Evangelis Matzarakis, who had family connections in Santorini in the southern Aegean; the other was Dimitrios Themelis from Patmos. The two of them had worked effectively to create a network of members across most of the islands, who responded to news from the mainland by proclaiming revolution and gathering arms and volunteers ready to go and fight.[33]

Caught between two competing demands for unconditional loyalty—from the Ottomans on the one hand, and the Etaireia on the other—island society in the Cyclades split much as it had done on Hydra. While enthusiasts for the revolution mobilized through the Etaireia, others remained ambivalent and hesitant, worried at the cost of disloyalty to the Sultan. On Sifnos, the revolution was greeted with enthusiasm; on Serifos, on the other hand, where some islanders were insisting on remaining aloof, a local Etairist raised the flag of the cross "to shift the simple People toward helping the Race." On Andros, some of the island's notables prepared to receive the Kapudan Pasha, provoking a peasant backlash and something akin to an island class war.[34]

It was a sign of the islanders' generally lukewarm response to the revolution that when he arrived on Hydra in early June, Dimitrios Ypsilantis felt obliged to advise his agents to rely on persuasion rather than threats and other "tyrannical means."[35] His arrival was accompanied by the usual Ypsilantis fondness for pomp and titles: Themelis announced the arrival of "His Excellency Dimitris [sic] Ypsilantis, Commissioner and Commander-in-Chief of the Southern Greek Army with his Highness and Brother Prince and General Alexandros Ypsilantis, the Commissioner-General of the Nation"; for good measure, Themelis now proclaimed himself "*ispravnik* Dimitris, Commissioner by the Grace of God for the White Sea" (i.e., the islands of the Aegean). But grandiose rhetoric was not enough to win the islanders over. When an Etairist agent reported Ypsilantis's arrival to the inhabitants of remote Kastellorizo, scarcely a mile off the Anatolian coast, he found the islanders—while glad the prince had appeared—disappointed that none of the Moreot fortresses had yet been captured and interested chiefly in organizing raids on Ottoman shipping. These had already netted the islanders rich catches of coins, clothes, wheat, timber, and weapons that they were arguing over. When the agent's boat docked, the small community had already split into two groups sitting in separate areas of the harbor, refusing to cooperate. He reminded the islanders that this was a time for unity not squabbling, and he made the two-day voyage back to Symi a somewhat disillusioned man.[36]

During that summer of 1821, the lines of revolutionary authority in the Aegean between the Etairia and the shipping islands were beginning to overlap and become blurred: put simply, Hydra rather than Dimitrios Ypsilantis was turning into the point of reference for other islanders. Richly endowed in men and weapons and with a long tradition of self-government, the shipping islands, with Hydra at their center, were quickly developing a political ascendancy among the Greeks. Ypsilantis hoped to see the revolutionary wave spread by voluntary means; yet his own agents were aware of the impediments and outright resistance, and it was to the shipping islands that they turned for help.

The other islands mostly looked to them for the protection that they required in order to come out on the Greek side, especially as a stream of refugees brought home the awful cost of disloyalty to the sultan. On Skyros that summer, ships from Psara disembarked more than 2,500 refugees who had escaped massacre in Aivalik on the Asia Minor coast; 1,000 more arrived from Evvia fleeing the advancing Ottoman troops. The notables of Skyros, who feared the sultan's men were headed for them next, wrote to Spetses for reinforcements.[37] Serifos needed gunpowder and the islanders were collecting funds and animals to send back as payment. Santorini sent a consignment of one hundred barrels of wine for the fleet, and asked for gunpowder too, "since we won't find it elsewhere. We will repay it as quickly as we can. Please don't leave us without it."[38] The Etaireia's authority did not suddenly vanish overnight but it was being superseded, a process that accelerated after late August when islanders from Milos passed on the news that the revolt in the Danubian Principalities had failed, and that in Constantinople things were calm again. As disappointment with the Etaireia grew, its influence dwindled.[39]

It could, however, claim one unquestionable success in the Aegean in that first summer of the war: the creation of a revolutionary authority on the wooded island of Samos, just off the coast of Asia Minor, a thorn in the side of Ottoman power. It had all begun in mid-April, when two Spetsiot ships had sunk an Ottoman brig offshore that had been sent by the governor of Rhodes to keep order there. Their exploit had effectively prevented Ottoman troop reinforcements being sent to suppress the revolt in the Peloponnese—a decisive illustration of the importance of Greek sea power. But it had also "electrified the freedom-loving people of Samos," alarmed the Ottoman authorities on the mainland, and led to weeks of random violence on the streets of Smyrna and other towns along the coast. "The unexpected revolt of this island," wrote a French consular official on the mainland opposite:

> has excited the Turks to a pitch of ferocity it is difficult to calm . . . For several days, the Samos narrows have been infested by two large vessels armed with cannons. They are said to be from Spetses. They have already captured several boats of different nations coming from Egypt, and they have put to death the Turkish crews. The conduct of these rogues has alarmed the entire region.[40]

Samos, a stone's throw from the Anatolian mainland, was to become the center of the most effective insurgency in the eastern Aegean thanks to the combination of Greek supremacy at sea and the work of one remarkable Etairist agent.

Giving himself the nom de guerre Lykourgos Logothetis—Lykourgos the Minister—the Samiot Georgios Paplomatas had served Phanariot households in the Danubian Principalities and had been sentenced to death twice by the sultan for his political activities. Even before his return to Samos, revolutionaries led by a local Etairist, a veteran of Napoleon's army in Egypt, had killed eighteen Muslim merchants there and declared for the Greek cause. Samos was an island with a long history of factional politicking and the insurgents' opponents immediately contacted the Ottoman authorities on the mainland for help, protesting their own loyalty. The Etaireia's emissary Themelis appointed Logothetis as commander and he arrived on Samos in the second week of May. He was a capable and ruthless revolutionary leader, familiar with the island's bitter internal feuds, and he created a centralized administration with a strong executive that he termed the "Military-Political System of Samos" (*Stratopolitikon Systima Samou*): with minor modifications this remained in force for more than ten years, in itself an extraordinary and unique achievement.[41] In all that time, Samos was undefeated, thanks to the degree of military organization that Logothetis introduced along European lines. He got the few men on the island with experience of the Napoleonic Wars to train several thousand men in European-style tactics—a number that grew several times over as a result of Asia Minor Greeks fleeing to Samos for shelter. Boats from Psara unloaded a few cannons and munitions, and soon new fortifications were being raised around the capital Vathy and other strategic points.[42]

The position of the insurgents was strengthened by the arrival of seven more boats from Psara that entered the Gulf of Smyrna, alarming the Ottoman authorities and preventing other troops from departing for the Peloponnese. This was momentous enough but more was to follow. At the start of June a relatively small Ottoman flotilla sailed out of the Dardanelles: it comprised two ships of the line, three frigates, and three corvettes. Against these large vessels, the Greeks could do little: their cannonballs often simply bounced off the sides. Then they remembered a technique from the Russo-Turkish war—the fireship, or *brulot*. An old ship would be chosen and gunpowder laid down in a line from the stern, with small kegs of powder set under the hatches. More trains of gunpowder led to the rigging, which was caulked with grease and resin, and down below deck where wood and other combustible materials were stacked. Behind the fireship came the rowboat for the crew to make their escape. It was a means of attack that required enormous courage as well as good fortune and a fair wind, and more often than not a fireship would be set ablaze but then fail to make contact with its target. When it did, however, the results could be spectacular and terrifying. When the Greeks prepared three of them, the first two failed. With the third, however, they managed to blow up one of the Ottoman warships and in this way a ship crewed by eighteen men managed to utterly destroy a vessel several times its size along with the lives of hundreds of its crew. The Greeks had found the weapon they needed. Over the seven years of the war at sea, they would prepare—by one recent estimate—112 fireships; and even though it was an extremely unpredictable weapon—Kanaris, the Psaran "bruloteer" who was the legendary ace of the craft, had three successes in twelve ventures—it struck terror into the enemy and the Ottoman navy became even more battle averse than it had been before. When a French captain encountered the Hydriot fleet a few weeks later, he was told that they had converted many of their vessels into *brulots*: their approach was now not to engage the enemy but to burn their ships down. Commercial traffic with Egypt and Anatolia dwindled, and many merchants waited in Rhodes, the main Ottoman base in the region, to see what would happen.[43] A second Ottoman effort against Samos was beaten off and the Greeks' maritime superiority protected the island. Credited with a brilliant defense system, Logothetis had himself proclaimed commander in chief (*archistratigos*).[44]

In thinking about the war's impact on the Aegean Islands, a useful distinction can be made between food-deficit and food-surplus regions. The seafaring islands were in the former category and it was no coincidence that they focused upon shipping—there was virtually no other means of livelihood open to them. But the islands that could grow their own food were in a very different situation: their populations were mostly farmers or traders, and their fleets were not large and mostly small craft. Tinos, for instance, had a relatively insignificant fleet of its own but a prosperous peasantry and a busy port through which it exported its abundant produce; Santorini, Naxos, Paros, and Milos were all chiefly farming islands, and when they needed gunpowder from the Spetsiots they had crops to offer in return. It is not by chance that on these islands there was plenty of resistance to the revolutionaries' efforts to enlist them: they faced no economic crisis and many of the islanders mistrusted demands by a new power that was in some ways more arbitrary and intrusive in their lives than the Ottoman state. They might like the idea of freedom, but that did not mean they wanted to be told what to do by Hydriot or Spetsiot sailors, and they were acutely conscious that the Ottoman fleet could punish them when it chose to.

This ambivalence about the revolution was seen most clearly on the most important food-surplus island of them all—fertile Chios, which in population, wealth, and resources easily outweighed the others. Vulnerably close to the Anatolian mainland, it had an enormous population of 100,000 Christians and no more than 2,000 Muslims. As the shipping islands struggled with how to fund their fleet, the question of the resources and allegiance of Chios became a decisive issue for the revolution. As early as April 18, 1821, only a few days after they themselves had entered the war, Hydra's notables had singled it out: already sounding the alarm about funding and warning that "the three so-called maritime islands of the nation cannot bear the costs of such a fleet," they insisted that "Chios should show the most keen and largest contribution as it is wealthier than other towns and islands."[45] But when they tried to get its inhabitants to declare for the revolution, they were rebuffed. To further ensure Chios's loyalty to the empire, the pasha governing the island ordered the bishop and other leading Greek notables to be held as hostages within the citadel.[46]

Among the advisers to Dimitrios Ypsilantis there were several enthusiastic Chiots who dreamed of getting involved. On Samos, Logothetis's agents claimed the Chiots would back the Greek cause and this message was reinforced by another of those veterans of the Napoleonic Wars who recur throughout this story, a Chiot revolutionary called Antonios Bournias. Logothetis himself had several reasons for pushing his large neighbor of an island into the struggle. Bringing Chios in would leave Samos itself less isolated. Its riches would help him pay the several thousand armed men defending the revolution on Samos. For the historian Giannis Vlachoyannis there was a purely mercenary motivation: "The expedition hid the irregulars' quenchless thirst for enrichment. The irregulars from Samos in no way differed from the other Greek irregulars in their uncontainable desire for loot."[47]

On March 9, 1822, an expeditionary force under Lykourgos's command sailed from Samos, reaching the coast of Chios the next day and disembarking before dawn on March 11. It totalled several thousand soldiers, a surprisingly large force though lacking in weaponry: according to one source, they had "six small cannon, two barrels of gunpowder and whatever cartridges his men were carrying." Easily repelling an outnumbered Ottoman troop detachment of some five hundred men sent out to check them, they advanced quickly on the main town, forcing the governor and his troops to take refuge in the citadel, which now came under siege. At three in the afternoon a flag with the cross was paraded through the main street amid cries of "Long live Liberty!" Lykourgos ordered a lavish service in the cathedral and according to at least one source, he had himself crowned and hailed as the island's "Prince." His offer of capitulation having been rejected by the pasha, he had his men drag a cannon up a nearby hill, but the citadel was out of range and suffered little damage; the defenders' response was to bombard the town while Greek peasants from the villages came in and began pillaging the abandoned shops and houses. Some of the Samiots stripped the lead off the roofs of the mosques for ammunition and started to take the loot back to their boats.[48]

Lykourgos was later to deplore the "great indifference" with which the Chiots had met them, "and worse than indifference, pro-Turkish sentiment." But even among the revolutionaries there was dissension over how to continue. The Chiot veteran Bournias, who had arrived with the Samiots, now declared himself the commander (*archistratigos*) of the island and between the two men there began a fierce rivalry for leadership. While the Samiots under Lykourgos were fighting the enemy, Bournias—or so Lykourgos alleged—was leading his men in an orgy of plundering "irrespective of whether the property belonged to Christian or Turk."[49] This dispute went beyond personal ambition: Lykourgos argued in terms of national necessity and centralized command, whereas Bournias stood for local patriotism—each island in charge of its own destiny, presenting himself as a Chiot and arguing that the island needed its own force not one subservient to the Samiots. Both men started handing out titles and decorations and when their followers tussled over control of the few cannons available, they nearly began shooting at one another.[50]

As the revolution descended into anarchy, many Chiots fled before the inevitable arrival of the Turkish reinforcements while the peasants, whom Lykourgos was assured had been supplied with weapons, descended on the town with cudgels, farm tools, and a few old muskets for which they had no shot. Lykourgos admits that what basically drove them was the desire to loot. He claims he was on the verge of breaking the siege of the citadel when the Ottoman fleet arrived, but this claim has to be taken with a grain of salt, made by a man responsible for cataclysmic errors of judgment. From Smyrna, the editor of *Le Spectateur Oriental* was apprehensive for the Greeks living not only on the island but up and down the Asia Minor coastline. "When the insurrection broke out on

Samos," he wrote, "it was singularly fatal to our country, and much blood was shed at different times. And yet what is Samos next to Chios?"

That the sultan was preparing a drastic response was no secret: he had determined to prevent the Greek uprising spreading any farther that spring and there were reports that a large naval force was being outfitted in Constantinople. When the imperial fleet reached Chios on March 30, 1822, the line of ships stretched across the horizon, more than thirty of them under the command of the Kapudan Pasha himself, as well as 7,000 men in troop carriers. Thousands more irregulars were waiting in Smyrna and Chesmé to be ferried across. *Le Spectateur Oriental* reported from Smyrna that news of the rising on Chios had "produced an extraordinary sensation," which had "put the whole of Anatolia into movement. It looks like an armed camp. Troops are marching in from all sides, in and around us . . . The event on Chios has once again embittered the Muslims against the Greeks and reopened the wounds which had begun to heal."[51]

Within hours of the first landings, the remaining Samiots had retreated, leaving the town to the Ottoman irregulars who killed, plundered, and looted with abandon, knowing they had official sanction for their actions. Churches and graves were despoiled in the search for valuables and soon much of the town was in flames. The slaughter continued unabated as more soldiers arrived from Chesmé: within a week an estimated 30,000 irregulars were on the island and the port of Smyrna was reported to be almost empty—most of the Muslim men were on Chios. The Greek hostages in the citadel there were now taken out and hanged from trees in the main square of the town. Survivors hid out for days, hearing the killings around them, afraid to move or to scavenge for food. Only the foreign consulates, sanctuaries to which hundreds of Christians had fled, remained safe. Virtually everywhere else was at the mercy of the irregulars who roamed unchecked for nearly two weeks with the blessing of the Ottoman governor. His orders were simple: put to death any male inhabitants they found. The women and children were to be sold into slavery.

"We recognize our error and we request forgiveness," Lykourgos's men wrote to Hydra and Spetses on April 8 in a plea for help. They got a frosty response—the ships were being fitted out and would shortly sail—accompanied by an admonition: "Your expedition against Chios has brought the greatest harm to the Race." But the unfolding tragedy had revealed not only the irresponsibility of some of the Etairist revolutionaries but also the shortcomings of the Greek system of war at sea and its incapacity to respond rapidly in a crisis. In fact, it was only in late April that the flotilla finally sailed out to patrol the straits around Chios, too late and with too small a force to alter its fate: as the islanders of Psara admitted, the enemy was just too powerful. The best the Greeks could hope for at that stage was to keep their own fleet together, since without it "the entire race would be in peril." The Greek fleet thus mostly stayed moored in Psara, while half a dozen brigs circled Chios, helped extract survivors, and kept an eye on the Ottoman fleet.[52]

In the space of a few weeks, the Ottoman forces slaughtered thousands of Chiots in an orgy of violence and enslaved thousands more. By the time the Kapudan Pasha managed to get the governor sent off the island and reestablished some kind of discipline, around 25,000 Greeks had been killed and an estimated 45,000 shipped into slavery—more than half of the original population of 100,000–120,000. These were extraordinary numbers even by the standards of a notably violent war waged chiefly against civilians. By the middle of May there were probably fewer than 20,000 people left on Chios, excluding the Turkish soldiers. The town was a mass of corpse-strewn ruins, and apart from the mastic villages in the south, which for a time enjoyed a semi-protected status because of their unique crop, most of the other forty villages were uninhabitable.[53]

Eugène Delacroix's famous painting of the massacre, exhibited in Paris two years later, was thus not far from the truth. Thousands of prisoners were beheaded; others were held in the ruins of the town while their new owners waited for export permits to ship them off. From Chesmé on the mainland, caravans of captive women and children departed for the slave markets in Smyrna, Constantinople, and Aleppo. Europe was shocked at the news. But disbelief at the scale of what had happened was felt locally as well: it was almost beyond human comprehension and some referred to it as "the catastrophe of catastrophes." "Maybe we should confess," wrote the historian Anastasios Orlandos in 1869 in a kind of apologia for the shipping islands and their inability to help, "that the catastrophe on Chios took place according to God's intention . . . because it scattered the Chiots across the face of the earth, and through their commercial skill allowed them to show themselves once again in only a few years as wealthy and thus honoring their Greek origin and becoming more useful to Greece thereafter."[54]

Admiral Miaoulis, the Hydriot commander, had been able to do little at the time. Standing off for several days, he eventually launched several fireships that burned themselves out in vain; disappointed, his flotilla returned to Psara. But that was not the end of the Greeks' naval efforts. At Eid-al-Fitr, the celebrations marking the end of Ramadan, the victorious Kapudan Pasha Kara Ali prepared a feast on board his huge eighty-gun flagship, which was illuminated in the port of Chios for the occasion. The Muslims of Smyrna had been in their mosques at prayer when shortly after midnight they saw the sky light up for more than half an hour from the direction of Chios. Soon the news reached them of a tremendous explosion and its cause: in what was one of the most daring exploits of the war, the Psaran captain Konstantine Kanaris had steered his fireship undetected in the darkness right up to the Ottoman man-of-war and the flames had detonated its powder magazine. The ship had been totally destroyed and an estimated 2,000 men, including the admiral, perished. Kara Ali's body was washed up on the shore of the island; to this day his ornate tomb survives in the small Ottoman cemetery in the citadel. The reaction on the streets of Smyrna was muted. According to one report, none other than the imam in the main mosque attributed the admiral's death to the crimes and injustices committed by Ottoman forces.[55]

An eight-year-old Greek boy was watching from the balcony of the British consulate in Chios as Kara Ali's flagship burned; later, he remembered his feelings of joy as "suddenly that floating Pandemonium burst like a Volcano." Christoforos Castanis's memoir gives us a remarkable glimpse of a child survivor's few months in hell. From a wealthy and cultivated Chiot family, he had been captured one day in the street: under guard, he watched soldiers vandalize his family's house, collect scores of prisoners, and execute many men before taking their heads and ears for payment from the pasha's accountants; he had even seen the soldiers kill one another over the spoils. He had eventually been sold to a mullah, who went off plundering, bringing back valuables and more captives, including girls kept for sex until they were sold. Meantime, little Castanis was ordered to play with the family children and, renamed Mustafa, was sent to school to learn Turkish, before being passed on to a new owner, an executioner from Aleppo who used the boy as a pipe-bearer. When his new master fell ill, Castanis fled. He spent some months in hiding on the island disguised as a Frank before escaping to Syros. After a brush with pirates, he made it to Nafplion at the end of 1822.[56]

The sheer number of people trying to flee Chios created a refugee crisis of unprecedented proportions across the Aegean. Many sailors helped out of sympathy but some of the Psara boats seem to have been charging an average of 50 piastres a head, payable in advance, for the passage to safety. The French naval captain Philippe Jourdain noted: "It was by weight in gold that they sold their help." A row erupted when one captain took clothes and silverware in payment from some of his passengers and another demanded his share—as if they had been prizes. They had to be reminded that it was one thing to seize the property of Turks and another when it belonged to Greeks. One survivor from the prosperous Argenti family wrote that he and his relatives had been lucky: they had found a boat from Mykonos for "a bagatelle," paying 15 or 30 *grossia* per person, whereas those who went via Psara paid as much as 500, 1,000, or even 1,500 *grossia*. By the end of April an estimated 12,000–15,000 refugees had fled Chios for the other islands, and more followed; many of them lived in the open air, on beaches and hillsides, where they made rudimentary shelters out of rushes. Conditions were so grim in many places that by June some were already reportedly considering returning to Chios. On crowded Tinos many refugees made their way across to a small harbor on the north shore from where they hoped to be able to find a boat home. According to a sea captain from there, they complained that "it would be better for them to die in their fatherland under the savage sword of the Turks and thus be liberated from their present unbearable trials, than be thus mistreated by their fellow Greeks."[57]

Although the Ottoman authorities appear initially to have toyed with the idea of encouraging Muslims to settle on Chios, they soon realized they needed the Christians back. The harvest was moldering in the fields: workers had to be shipped over from the mainland to collect the crops. Bands of sailors from Psara helped themselves to fruit and livestock, which they brought back to their more barren island. But a stream of imperial firmans designed to encourage the return of Greek survivors had little immediate impact: terror and uncertainty along with a raging epidemic kept people away. Only 2,500 Greeks had reportedly returned by early October; more joined them as the winter approached. In the coming years others would follow. Yet no Ottoman incentives could make up the damage: a century later, the population of Chios remained well below what it had been before the massacre; indeed, it has never recovered.[58]

On April 7, 1822, as the extent of the disaster facing Chios became clear, the notables of Hydra sent a message to Mykonos in the Cyclades. Although the Ottoman fleet threatened them all, the Hydriots had no more money to crew their ships. They had approached the provisional government for help but it had said it could not find the funds in time. They were therefore putting the islands on notice that unless they started contributing financially to the national cause, there was absolutely nothing they could do for them.[59] "Bear in mind that our island has been conducting the war against the tyrant out of its own pocket," they cautioned in a response to pleas for help from Samos:

> Our wealth is used up and that of the tyrant barely tapped, and if in future the Nation does not contribute, there will no longer be a Greek fleet . . . If each island does not contribute money for the establishment of a national account for the maintenance of the fleet, as the Greeks of the mainland spend on the preservation of their armies, then surely all the islands will pass this summer unprotected and the enemy will destroy them one by one.[60]

A week later, on April 14, the Hydra authorities sent out another message. They had scraped together the funds to fit out a few boats for one month. But in return they needed the islanders to hand over their annual taxes promptly to the newly established provisional government of Alexandros Mavrokordatos. More generally, they should follow its orders, accept its representatives, and thus unite themselves with the "political body of Greece." "Organized as a well-ordered Nation," the Greeks would thereby prove themselves worthy of independence in the eyes of Europe. In this way the Chios tragedy presaged the beginnings of a fiscal and financial revolution.[61]

The commitment to a national fleet was one of the linchpins of Mavrokordatos's provisional government, a precondition for his alliance with the Hydriots that allowed him to counterbalance his opponents in the Peloponnese and to provide essential naval support for the ongoing war in western Greece as well as in the islands. His government declared its intention to "form a national fleet out of privately owned fighting vessels," aiming for a core force of sixty vessels that could be called upon at all times. Yet one estimate put the amount needed for the fleet's monthly wage bill alone at 1 million *grossia*—an immense sum that was approximately equivalent to the total monthly revenues from the Peloponnese in peacetime. The question was: How and where was this money to be found?[62]

Unlike the Peloponnesians, whose notables and chieftains were largely financing their armies with revenues from lands and properties under their own immediate control, the owners of Greek ships of war needed the national government to help them extract funds from the other islands. Maintaining the boats, fitting them out, and finding wages for the men were all major expenses. While the Morea was essentially self-governing, the interests of the Hydriots and the provisional government thus converged, since both wanted the establishment of a central state that could legitimately extract resources from one part of the country and use them more systematically for the war effort in another. They wanted—in that striking phrase—to unify "the political body of Greece." The result was a flurry of institutional legislation, laying the foundations of Greece's future administrative apparatus in order to prosecute the war.[63]

Bureaucratic organization is not the most glamorous of subjects for the historian. And yet, as any student of Napoleon's Europe or Stalin's Russia will appreciate, few subjects are more important in understanding the modern state and its power. At the end of April 1822, the Mavrokordatos government embarked upon an organizational revolution, creating a centralized structure of prefects and subprefects responsible to the government, and specifying the duties of the officials attached to each office. "The Greek land is divided into prefectures" was the decree's uncompromising opening clause. This was the start of the country's long-standing system of nationwide prefectural rule modeled on the European, and especially the French, example.[64]

Because the immediate task at hand was to raise funds for a national navy, the three shipping islands, Hydra, Spetses, and Psara, were rather strikingly exempted in this decree: unlike all the other islands, they were to be allowed to govern themselves. The government's focus on the Cyclades prompted the creation of a so-called Commission, a four-man body whose delegates toured the Aegean in the coming months to supervise the implementation of the new reforms. The Commission was not something that the law on regions had foreseen but it was needed: in the weeks after the Chios disaster, the Aegean was in a fever pitch of anxiety and any effort to try to appoint new representatives of the Greek state and levy taxes was bound to meet with opposition and to arouse fears of violent Ottoman countermeasures.

Wisely anticipating trouble, the commissioners left Hydra with a force of forty handpicked Kefalonian sailors and soldiers aboard a sixteen-gun brig and a four-gun schooner. Starting on Naxos, the largest of the Cyclades, they spent nearly a year traveling through the archipelago, helping the new prefects to raise revenues and advising on local government reforms. From the late spring of 1822 the money began to come in, and the paperwork too—dozens of handwritten lists that documented the islanders' contributions in Spanish thaler, *kolonata*, *roumpiedes*, *machmoutiedes*, *misiriotika*, and *psiloi parades*, the whole melange of Mediterranean monies that circulated in the maritime economy of the Ottoman Levant. Sometimes the sums raised were handed over by the headmen of each village; in other cases they were levied on individuals. Payments in kind included silverware, sometimes from churches—presumably from booty returning soldiers or merchants had picked up elsewhere—as well as fruit, silk, wines, and other commodities. This was the modest start of Greece's system of nationwide taxation and local government.

The critical role anticipated for the islands in this fledgling national economy emerges from some of the first official budgetary estimates that we possess. For 1823 it was anticipated that the islands would be second only to the Peloponnese in the amount of revenue raised. True, the total envisaged would be barely enough to cover one month's wages for the fleet, but it was nevertheless important since only the archipelago was a net contributor: in every other region—the Peloponnese, central Greece, and Crete—the government estimated that the costs of fighting would exceed anticipated revenues.[65]

Yet the effort to raise taxes was bound to pit the representatives of the revolution against those local elites who had formerly run the islands in the Ottoman system. The former aspired to a centralized system that would funnel revenues to the three shipping islands; local communities, many of them Catholic, prized the autonomy they had enjoyed under the sultan and were reluctant to give this up. Even those who favored the revolution did not like to be ordered around by some of the emissaries sent out by the Etaireia or the government. The result was that in the spring and summer of 1822, before the dismayed eyes of the commissioners, protest turned to unrest as one island after another questioned the revenue-raising powers of the new provisional government. The imposition of a new tax system thus brought with it the first national tax revolts.

Arriving on Naxos in May, the commissioners began by emphasizing that the islands' revenues were needed to help keep the Greek fleet at sea. They quietly abandoned the more ambitious provisions of the new administrative law—realizing it was better to deal with the existing village headmen rather than confuse matters further by trying to elect new officials. But they still faced serious opposition from two local members of the Etaireia. One was the archbishop of Naxos, a proselyte for the revolution and a radical who wanted to emancipate the island's peasantry. The other was a landowner whose family ruled from one of the imposing fortified towers that can still be seen in the fertile center of Naxos. Claiming to speak for the villagers in his district, he too opposed any requisitions by outsiders, including men coming from the island's main town. The protesting villagers sent in a petition that cited a clash between "the constitution of the Town of Naxos and the constitution of all the villages of Naxos." The landowner saw a struggle between oligarchy and democracy.[66] Everyone on the island seemed an expert in political theory, no one wanted to pay up, and the matter dragged on for months before the representatives of the government got their way. It was a first indication of the difficulties ahead.

In Santorini, the Etaireia's representative Evangelis Matzarakis had been appointed prefect by the government. But he was not a natural diplomat and by the time the commissioners arrived in July, the island was in an "explosive situation," roiled by rumors that the Morea had just been conquered by Dramali Pasha. Some islanders said the government had sold out the revolution; others claimed that the Ottoman navy was going to attack Spetses and Hydra. A large amount of money—twice what had been collected on Naxos—was eventually raised in revenues, but Matzarakis was so loathed locally that he had to hire bodyguards, his tax collectors resigned, and by the winter Santorini was in open revolt. Despairingly, he sent out word that the islanders were in need of "political re-education": they had become used to the low taxes demanded by their Ottoman master; they did not yet understand that they now needed to pay more to support the "Struggle."[67]

The commissioners were pretty uncompromising men. Two of them had been appointed to represent the interests of Hydra and Spetses. The other two were more wide-ranging in their goals, capable of seeing the larger picture and defending the need for a national effort. One of them, from Kefalonia—the largest of the Ionian Islands—was a twenty-nine-year-old Etairist volunteer called Konstantinos Metaxas, a well-educated man with a tendency to self-promotion; he had studied law in Italy, fought in the Peloponnese and been named minister of justice in the Mavrokordatos government. Acknowledging that the lack of a judicial infrastructure in the Peloponnese and the ongoing war made his job meaningless, Metaxas had taken on the additional role of commissioner. Alongside him was an older man, a very distinguished cleric and pedagogue called Benjamin of Lesvos: much-traveled, worldly, intelligent, and notorious for his sharp tongue.[68]

Neither man was the sort to give ground easily nor to be intimidated by island notables, and in the face of a clear reluctance to support the revolution they resorted to extreme measures: as in the Peloponnese the previous year, Muslim captives became pawns in a mortal struggle against signs of defeatism. Metaxas took charge of some thirty pilgrims captured at sea, distributed four or five of them around each of the islands, and arranged for them to be guarded at the islanders' expense. He foresaw that the notables would take care of them but that this would enrage the poorer villagers whom the "friends of the revolution" could stir up. Once the captives had been killed, the entire island would be rendered culpable in Ottoman eyes, and the struggle for their loyalty would be over. Class tension would generate ethnic war and the result would be commitment. And indeed, according to Metaxas, "one saw no more of those petitions, and the notables became the principal sponsors of the revolution. This course of action was cruel, I admit, but when the liberty and existence of an entire people is at stake, the judgments of history cannot be too severe."[69]

Despite such extreme steps, the islanders' fear of the sultan remained strong. With the Ottoman navy making periodic voyages through the archipelago, the memory of Chios could lead not only to defeatism but even to outright anger against those leading the Greek struggle. When the imperial fleet appeared off Santorini in the weeks following the Chios massacres, at least two villages declared they were ready to surrender. The island's notables even arrested Metaxas, intending to hand him over to the Turks to demonstrate their loyalty, and he was saved only by the intervention of his armed Ionian sailors. In the summer of 1823, with the Kapudan Pasha nearby, the inhabitants of Milos sent an extraordinary message of reproach to the leaders of the three main shipping islands. "Look," they wrote:

> that fateful hour has struck when the innocent bodies of the islanders will become victims. The fleet is at Milos: hour by hour we await our pitiful end! And we go as martyrs martyred by your tyranny because when you did not intend to protect us you should not have played with our lives.

They were not attacked, but their panic was felt by inhabitants of other islands who lacked the means to defend themselves.[70] Resistance to the tax-raising efforts of the revolutionary leaders did not drop away. On the contrary, as late as 1826 it was reported that unidentified men were traveling through the Cyclades telling the islanders that it was time to "throw off the yoke of Hydra."[71]

"The yoke of Hydra"—a striking phrase—had been weighing on many of the islands for several years. Matzarakis finally fled Santorini in the face of a revolt, alleging his life was in danger. On Andros, there was a full-blown uprising, in which angry peasants targeted the wealthy notables of the island, burning their houses, even carrying out murders and refusing to hand over any money to the government. The commissioner—Metaxas—again had to call in a shipment of troops from Psara to disband the proclaimed "revolutionaries" and reassert the government's authority.[72] On Mykonos, the inhabitants rioted, plundered the wheat that had been gathered for export, and announced their desire to be placed under the protection of the French consul; the deputy prefect on the island could not leave his house, so great was the anger against him. On Skopelos, the delegates were expelled. On Amorgos, townspeople of Aiyiali, led by their priest, said they saw no point in hearing all the latest news or being forced to participate in public gatherings in the main town. They preferred to remain in their villages "to continue their efforts for the Struggle." Having chosen their own representatives, they declared themselves willing to make contributions to the war effort and deplored their enemies' efforts to accuse them of being pro-Turkish. They were reminded that it was not up to them who represented them, or who was empowered to collect taxes that were going to support the Greek fleet, which "fights for all equally."[73]

The lengths that the government, and the notables of Hydra in particular, would go to make the other islands pay for a Greek naval presence was nowhere revealed more starkly than on the island of Syros, in the heart of the Cyclades. It was something of an anomaly—the one island that the commissioners had not been tasked to visit—and indeed it had not even been incorporated within the 1822 legislation that established a governmental administration across the archipelago. The reason for these omissions was a kind of de facto recognition by the Greek authorities of the island's neutrality in the conflict. Its notables were continuing to openly pay taxes to the Ottoman state, much though others resented this: the *Spectateur Oriental* in Smyrna commented that "the Greeks would have made Syra [*sic*] pay dearly for its loyalty to their sovereign if they could."[74]

On Christmas Eve 1822 they tried to do this when six ships flying a variety of flags sailed into Syros under the command of an Ionian sea captain called Nestor Faziolis and trained their cannons on the town. Described by his friend, the prefect of Tinos, as an "ardent patriot," Faziolis led twenty men armed with pistols and cutlasses onshore. Acting "in the name of the revolution," they killed one of the harbor policemen, looted warehouses, and set fire to buildings by the waterfront. So far as the islanders were concerned, this was mere piracy since Faziolis lacked any formal authorization from the government. Fortunately for them, the town was out of cannon range, and after the intervention of some of the consuls, he sailed away. Two months later Faziolis tried again, this time bringing several hundred men with him. They were about to disembark when a French schooner forming part of the Levant squadron intervened to stop them, and its sailors detained Faziolis and put him in irons. Admiral de Rigny, commander of the squadron, eventually allowed him to go free but forced him and his men to sail off. The French had arrived because Syros was a Catholic island, one of several in the archipelago, and they wanted to give it some kind of protection. Yet the inhabitants were not French subjects, the legal arguments were not clear-cut, and despite the evident opposition of the French, the Hydriots were determined to persist. In April 1823 a Hydriot flotilla arrived and gave the inhabitants twenty-four hours to pay the money they claimed they owed the Greeks in taxes. When they were told this was impossible, the Hydriots responded with an all too credible threat to loot the town. They sailed back with the money, livestock, wine, and honey. The French government and even the Vatican protested, but the Greeks insisted they had fiscal authority over the island.[75]

That summer Faziolis even returned for a third time, now with confirmation of his appointment as official commander of the garrison (*politarchis*). This was too much for de Rigny, who seized him and shipped him off to Smyrna where he was tried and jailed in a consular court. To the notables of Hydra he protested at their support for a man who, "while from Zakynthos and thus a British subject, took every nationality and used every flag and who came to Syra [*sic*] to satisfy his desire for revenge." The island's neutrality remained sufficiently intact for the Ottoman fleet to pay its annual visit in 1823 as well.[76]

One of the reasons Syros was important enough to the Hydriots to risk an international incident was that it had become—thanks to its special status—the key market in the Aegean for the buying and selling of all kinds of goods, especially stolen or looted. It was, according to one source, "the principal place of deposit for plunder—a great deal of which is sold openly in the market." In a struggle where money itself was generally scarce, there was plenty to be had on the island. According to another source, "it is in the port of Syra [*sic*] that all the pirates of the Archipelago meet once they have accomplished their mission." Politics took a backseat to business: after the Ottoman attack on Psara in 1824, which devastated the island and left it deserted, sailors from Hydra and Spetses sold off the church bells, cannons, and other valuables that had been abandoned there. The Syros communal authorities purchased Muslim captives from merchants and sea captains in order to demonstrate their continued loyalty to the Ottomans, and the Kapudan Pasha came by to pick them up. But there was money to be made from the traffic in prisoners too: one consul on the island netted 80,000 piastres in two months by buying captives and selling them on at a profit to their families; the member of a notable Spetses family even recorded his purchase of six Ottomans from a Greek privateer before a notary. The 1823 constitution prohibited slavery, but a public auction two years later brought in thirty piastres a head from some ninety-six pilgrims who had been captured off Karpathos in the Dodecanese Islands en route to Mecca.[77]

The importance of the market on Syros, more lucrative than any other in the Aegean, fueled the extraordinary growth of its new port, Ermoupolis. Mostly populated by refugees from Chios and elsewhere, it not only transformed the rural Catholic society of the island through the establishment of its powerful and increasingly wealthy Orthodox merchants, but it generated customs revenues that became a vital source of support for the Greek fleet. A new prefect was appointed by the national government—itself by then based in Hydra and headed by the shipowner Georgios Koundouriotis. By 1825 the Ottomans had begun to count Syros among the enemy islands.[78]

ARMATOLES AND CONSTITUTIONS

In January 1822, Alexandros Mavrokordatos had been elected president of Greece's first provisional government. But it was western Greece that had been his springboard for national leadership and the region remained vitally important for him. Mavrokordatos understood that for an outsider like himself, a *heterochthon* in the new language of the day, the strength of his position depended on at least two things: a soldiery that was loyal to him and a viable regional base. For most of the revolution's leaders, after all, the two went together. With his new authority as president of the government, he therefore worked to establish a modus vivendi with the armatoles in western Rumeli and in March 1822 the Senate of Western Greece, over which he also presided, gave the most important of these, Georgios Varnakiotis, a veto over its dealings. Mavrokordatos later made him the supreme military authority within western Greece, and Varnakiotis sent a stirring message to the inhabitants of his district, assuring them that "from now on there is no armatole, no *reaya*: we are all Greeks": the new administration was "comparable with those of the civilized nations of Europe."[1]

In reality Varnakiotis, for all the honors paid him, could offer no more than lip service to the idea of Mavrokordatos's European-style state. The two men had completely different views and experiences of politics and their endless professions of mutual confidence and trust belied their uneasy relationship. Varnakiotis complained more than once of being undermined by his president, provoking Mavrokordatos to write in exasperation: "Again you tell me that you think I believe you indifferent to the good of the Fatherland. Good God! Once and for all abandon such suspicions, and be assured that in no one do I have, nor could I have, such confidence as in your Excellency."[2]

In fact, it was precisely because he knew he could not count on

Varnakiotis and his irregulars that Mavrokordatos lost no time in assembling a soldiery of his own out of the remnants of the regular detachments that Dimitrios Ypsilantis had started to build up the previous year. Mavrokordatos understood that the resurgence of Ottoman power under Khurshid Pasha in the summer of 1822 was testing the armatoles' loyalties. That is why on his return to Mesolonghi from the national assembly he brought with him 700 men from Corinth, many of them European volunteers under the leadership of European officers. Mavrokordatos chose to command them, which was a mistake as he had no real military competence, and he led them north himself toward the critical battle that would determine the fate of the revolution in the region. They were from the outset too few in number to make the decisive difference Mavrokordatos hoped they could and he was still reliant on the armatoles and their irregulars. When the imperial army left Arta in the northwest in July 1822 and advanced on the Greek positions in the village of Peta, some seven kilometers away, the Ottomans had more than 6,000 infantry and 1,000 cavalry. Facing them were the philhellenes, who probably amounted by this time to some 500 men, together with another 1,000 or so Greek fighters alongside them, mustered under some of the armatoles, a detachment from the Ionian Islands, and Souliots under Markos Botsaris. At the start, the Greeks fought well. But another armatole, Gogos Bakolas, had arranged a secret deal of his own with the Ottomans—the usual behind-the-scenes offer of help in exchange for the sultan's favor—and quite unexpectedly in the middle of the battle he withdrew his men into the mountains, leaving the philhellenes exposed and surrounded. The impact was catastrophic. A dozen or so Poles fought to the death inside a church; a French lieutenant from Marseille perished after killing several Turks. By the end of the day most of the European volunteers were dead. The defeat at Peta was a crushing blow to the Greek hold over western Rumeli and more or less the end of the philhellene detachments as a military force. But Bakolas's betrayal had another target: by destroying the philhellenes, he and his men had undermined Mavrokordatos himself, whose efforts to create a new kind of administration directly threatened their own power. The logic of the armatoles had prevailed over the effort to establish an army based on national allegiances.[3]

Fortunately for the Greeks—in the long run at any rate—the double-dealing ran both ways. Khurshid Pasha had entrusted the Ottoman campaign against them in Rumeli principally to two military command-ers. The experienced Albanian general Omer Vryonis Pasha was one; the other was the formidable Mehmed Reshid Pasha—generally known as Kütahı Pasha, after the Anatolian town where he had served as governor. The former, as we have seen, was on close terms with many of the arma-toles, and their knowledge of each other went back many years. Unlike Omer Vryonis, Kütahı Pasha had no ties either to the Ali Pasha court or the region. He was a man of extraordinary energy and dedication, entrusted with the task of reconquering western Greece precisely because of the difficulty of trusting the Albanians. After the Greek defeat at Peta, he warned Varnakiotis that he was ready to lay waste to western Greece and that he too should submit if he wished to save his region.[4] A month later, in August 1822, Varnakiotis won a victory at the battle of Aetos, but that was his last significant achievement on the Greek side. It was clear after Peta that the full force of the Ottoman state was about to descend on the Greeks in western Rumeli. Mavrokordatos fell back southward toward Mesolonghi, giving Varnakiotis as supreme regional commander the authority to use the death penalty for desertion and the right to burn the homes of anyone refusing to take up arms.[5] Even so, thousands of peasants simply fled Akarnania on the Ionian coast ahead of the expected Ottoman offensive, abandoning their fields, and trailing huge flocks of sheep and goats behind them, as they made their way to the safety of the nearby islands, leaving much of the countryside south of the Gulf of Arta deserted. Varnakiotis witnessed the rural society that was the base of his power evaporating before his eyes. From Arta, his old friend Omer Vry-onis passed a message to him: it was time to choose sides.

The Greek plight in western Rumeli in the autumn of 1822 seemed acute—so acute that Mavrokordatos himself proposed to Varnakiotis that he reach out to Omer Vryonis Pasha, making use of their friendship to win some time so that reinforcements could be brought in from the Peloponnese. There followed a spectacular case study in duplicity in which who was using whom, and to what end, may never be satisfacto-rily settled. Varnakiotis wanted an assurance from the Greek leadership that his contacts with Omer Vryonis would not be used against him and he therefore obtained a formal letter empowering him to enter into negotiations. Did he use this letter as cover for the capitulation he then made? Or did Mavrokordatos set up the powerful armatole chieftain so that he could get rid of him once and for all and send a message that the old arrangements were no longer possible? Had Varnakiotis really gone to plea with the Turks with the interests of the Greeks in mind, or only his own? The most searching recent study concludes that Varnakiotis, despite his later protestations, had in fact surrendered, agreeing to disarm and to pay the taxes he owed the sultan in order to save his regional power base.[6] What we do know is that while the Greek armatole was in Arta talking to Omer Vryonis, an Ottoman offer of amnesty circulated among the inhabitants of Akarnania, and other chieftains and their troops also gave up the fight: Greek soldiers besieging the town of Vonitsa melted away. Varnakiotis stayed in Arta and was denounced by Mavrokordatos for his betrayal. The armatoles were being forced to choose sides, and the most important of them all had not opted for the Greeks.

As a result, nothing now prevented more than 10,000 Ottoman troops converging on Mesolonghi, and by November, Mavrokordatos was preparing to defend the town where he had landed in such different circumstances. Eighteen months after his arrival from Italy, Ali Pasha was dead, and the Ottoman reconquest of Rumeli appeared to be close at hand. As the assembled forces of Kütahı and Vryonis Pasha encamped outside the town's pitiful defenses, Varnakiotis was with them, along with the main Greek armatole-chieftains of Akarnania. The local bands had melted away; the few remaining philhellenes, those who had survived the debacle at Peta, were in poor shape. The situation seemed hopeless, yet Mavrokordatos felt compelled to defend the town; the alternative was to do nothing to prevent the Ottomans sending thousands of Albanians down into the Peloponnese, crushing the Greeks just as they had done fifty years earlier.

Fringed by the lagoon, Mesolonghi was a "little town, built on a mud bank, level with the waves, protected merely by an unfinished ditch, seven feet wide and five deep, with a parapet of stones and earth four feet high and two and a half in thickness."[7] In addition to the inadequacy of the fortifications, Mavrokordatos had also to contend with the lack of troops—only a few hundred men were with him, mostly Souliots and foreigners, along with fourteen old guns. Since many of the inhabitants had fled to the Peloponnese, their homes were demolished for timber to shore up the walls. Discovering a store of bayonets, the defenders fixed these on stakes and poked them above the parapet in a desperate effort to fool the besieging army; they also brought herds of livestock to graze on the open ground inside the walls to ensure they would not run short of food. The town was in the hands of two "foreigners"— Mavrokordatos himself and the Souliot chieftain Markos Botsaris— because the Greek chieftains had mostly left and gone over to the enemy. Had the two Ottoman commanders—Kütahı Pasha and Omer Vryonis Pasha—attacked immediately, the town would certainly have fallen.

Instead, typically preferring a negotiated resolution to a frontal assault, they opened negotiations with Botsaris, a man Omer Vryonis knew well. Guaranteed safe conduct, the fearless Souliot scaled the walls alone for their first meeting and walked toward the enemy line where he was met by the two pashas. Seated on a carpet in the plain, the three leaders talked, watched from a distance by their troops. After the first encounter, which went on for three hours, Botsaris returned and told his soldiers with a smile that the Ottoman generals had asked him how many men he had. Playing for time, he had exaggerated the size of the defense and telling Omer Vryonis that it was no simple matter to persuade his comrades to surrender, he successfully dragged out their discussions until help could arrive. In late November it did: reinforcements sent from the Peloponnese by Petros Mavromihalis more than doubled the defending force, and others followed.[8]

The besiegers had arrived too late in the year for a long siege and time was not on the Ottoman side: the pashas' armies started to come under attack from the Greek bands in the hills, and heavy autumn rains spread disease. It was about this time that they would also have heard about Khurshid Pasha's unexpected death. When some of the Albanian units started for home, loath to linger after St. Dimitrios's Day at the end of October, the Ottoman commanders resolved to attack and end the siege. They planned their assault for Christmas Eve, a time when they believed the Greeks would be distracted. In fact, the defenders learned of their planned attack from the fisherman who provided the pashas with fresh fish, and they prepared so effectively for it that when the attack came, it was repelled with relatively little loss of life on the Greek side while hundreds of Ottoman soldiers died trapped under deadly fire in the ditch below the walls. Two weeks later, informed that the armatoles had changed sides again, thus imperiling his route home, Omer Pasha suddenly withdrew from the town and after a tough march through swollen rivers and amid constant attack from Mavromihalis's

Maniots, his men eventually fought their way back north to safety. Incredibly, the siege was over and the city survived.

"The siege of Missolonghi deserves to be forever celebrated in the history of Greece," wrote an Italian philhellene who was among the defenders. "I think nothing like it ever occurred in the history of the whole world. To keep off fourteen thousand men by land, without arms, without walls, without men—only by talk . . . is I think unprecedented." Overshadowed subsequently by the far longer, more dramatic and bloodier siege of 1825–26, this first failed assault on the town was an astonishing example of the incompetence of the Ottoman campaign in Greece: incapable of securing its basic logistical needs, poorly led, the army had been unable to make its overwhelming numbers translate into victory. But the problem went deeper. After starting well, 1822 had turned into a year of disasters for the sultan: Dramali Pasha's force in the Morea had been virtually wiped out; Khurshid had been forced to commit suicide. The retreating armies of Kütahı Pasha and Omer Pasha left a wasteland behind them, the soldiers reduced to eating their horses, wild herbs, and grass. The threatened invasion of the Peloponnese had been averted once again and Mavrokordatos's reputation received a much-needed boost after the catastrophe at Peta.[9]

Varnakiotis was among those who made his way back with Omer Vryonis Pasha to Arta. Later he was invited by his friend Kolokotronis to come to Tripolitsa to defend himself, but he never did so. Later still, in response to an article in Mavrokordatos's newspaper in Mesolonghi denouncing him, Varnakiotis replied by attacking Mavrokordatos himself as the man who was endangering Greek lives and warning the Greeks not to underestimate the threats they faced from vast new Ottoman armies. Varnakiotis did not return to Greece until 1828. Even though many other armatoles played both sides in much the same way as he did and still became incorporated into the pantheon of heroes of the war, not even a dogged effort by his supporters over the next fifty years ever really revived his reputation. Varnakiotis remains a shining example, not of treachery—a term that implies allegiance to a sovereign state—but of the lingering impact of the old Ottoman system of regional governance upon the behavior of some of the leading military men of continental Greece. That was the system they had grown up with, and their actions—prompted by their own self-interest with its roots in the prosperity of the villages under their control—pointed to the power of localism that lingered in the region long after independence had been gained.[10]

Varnakiotis's counterpart in eastern Rumeli was the much better-known armatole called Odysseus Androutsos. In 1820 he had been Ali Pasha's man in the town of Livadeia. In the spring of 1821 he had been the hero of the hour, urging others to rise up and leading a small band to victory over Omer Vryonis and his much larger Ottoman army, thereby forestalling a Turkish assault across the Gulf of Corinth. But Androutsos was no more comfortable with the Mavrokordatian idea of a centralized national government than the other armatoles and he openly detested the "pen-pushers" as much as they did. Personal power buoyed up by fear, force, and a local tax base was what Androutsos was really after. In the memoirs of Byron's friend Edward Trelawny, the adventurer who found his way to Androutsos's impregnable cavern headquarters, stayed with him, and ended up marrying his half sister, Androutsos cuts a noble figure; in the popular telling in Greece he is a kind of tragic hero. But the Scottish philhellene Thomas Gordon tells another story: A physically imposing man, muscular and fleet of foot, Androutsos was also "bloodthirsty, vindictive, and as treacherous as an Arnaut." Watchful and suspicious, he shared many of the attributes and assumptions of the military men in western Greece and the logic of their behavior was his too. An expression of the very different traditions, ethnography, and military topography of Rumeli, the phenomenon of secret agreements between armatoles and the Ottomans—the *kapakia* as they were termed—was equally pervasive on the other side of the Pindos mountains, and such dealings underpinned Androutsos's dominance in eastern Greece before leading to his downfall.[11]

Androutsos aimed to consolidate his influence in Attica and Evvia, both of them prosperous farming regions that had never been part of the armatolik system. In Evvia he sent in his bands at the beginning of 1822. That spring, however, as word came in of the large new Ottoman army being assembled to march southward, tension grew between Androutsos and the regional government in eastern Rumeli, and in May 1822 two men were sent out to replace him, both known to him from the Ali Pasha days.[12] One was called Christos Palaskas, the son of an armatole and a Souliot captain who had served on the staff of Omer Vryonis before joining the Greeks. The other, Alexios Noutsos, was from a wealthy Epirote family and a former member of the Ali Pasha court; Noutsos had saved Androutsos from Ali Pasha's wrath many years earlier when the headstrong, violent young Androutsos was in the pasha's bodyguard. Noutsos had been instructed by the regional authorities in eastern Greece to oversee the administration and revenue collection, and Palaskas was to take over military duties while Androutsos was ordered to appear before the government to defend himself against allegations that had surfaced suggesting he was working with the Ottomans. Rather than comply he did something unprecedented: he had his troops kill the two as they were on their way to see him. The news of their murder shocked the region; the assembly of eastern Greece fled the safety of Livadeia for Salona, and a power vacuum opened up among the Greeks at the very moment when the army of Dramali Pasha was passing through. Androutsos took no action against it beyond possibly encouraging some Albanian chiefs to defect. The region was, in the historian George Finlay's words, in a "state of anarchy."[13]

After the rout of Dramali Pasha's men farther south, Androutsos was invited to take over Athens by the Greek soldiers who were garrisoning the Acropolis and fighting among themselves. He set up a new provincial assembly that dissolved the old 1821 Areopagus of eastern Greece and conveniently appointed him commander in chief of the region. His men milked the long-suffering citizens of Athens and began to plunder the prosperous villages in the plain of Attica. Having established the town as his base, Androutsos then contacted the Ottomans offering to make *kapaki* (a secret agreement) in return for recognition of his hereditary right to an armatolik. In November 1822 he sent the Ottoman authorities a letter presenting the Greek uprising not as a national revolution but as a matter of local grievances that could be resolved by his appointment to an official position:

Since you ask the reason of our revolt, all the inhabitants of the Sanjak of Negropont, and I among the rest, have resolved to write to your Excellency. The following are the motives which I will now point out to you: the cruelties committed without the knowledge of the Sultan's government; the injustice of the Viziers, Vayvodes, Khadis and Buloukbashis, each of whom closed the book of Mohammed and opened a book of his own. Any virgin that pleased them they took by force; any merchant in Negropont, who was making money, they beheaded and seized his goods;

any proprietor of a good estate they slew and occupied his property; and every drunken vagabond in the streets could murder respectable Greeks and was not punished for it. If it please your Excellency, write a representation to the Sultan, and obtain for us an imperial edict that we may be delivered from our ills. We will then sit quietly in our houses, looking after our private affairs, and so things will go a thousand times better than they have done. With regard to my *capitaneria*, my father inherited it from his father through his valor, and I hope to keep it in the same way.[14]

Some kind of agreement was reached among them, and Androutsos remained in charge; to judge from subsequent correspondence of his with the Ottoman commanders to the north, he seems to have sent in the necessary hostages but (unsurprisingly) failed to pay the taxes they expected. The Greek government recognized it had little choice but to acknowledge his power as well and it was as the most powerful chieftain in the region—tolerated but mistrusted by both the Ottoman and the Greek administrations—that Androutsos attended the revolution's second national assembly when it was held in the Peloponnese in March 1823.[15]

On the eve of this assembly Androutsos went to Tripolitsa to meet Kolokotronis—the two of them now the most powerful members of the new military class in Greece—in order to sound the "Old Man" out about how they should approach the formation of a new government. Androutsos was worried about allowing civilian politicians and their new institutions too much power over them. "However the *kodzabashides* treat us now when we are powerful and have weapons in our hands, tomorrow they will drag us off to the scaffold," he opened. Kolokotronis did not rise to the bait. "Ah!" he said. "You always have them on your mind. Leave them alone and they will be forgotten all by themselves." "That is all very well," Androutsos retorted. "But they will kill you first, and they will weave the rope of your noose not with the truth but with lies." "Let them do what they will," Kolokotronis replied, "I won't dirty my hands with them."[16] It sounds as if Androutsos—who had already murdered two government emissaries—identified as his real foe the landowning elite of the Peloponnese, the men who dominated the existing administration. Kolokotronis was never prepared to go as far as murder, though his followers had been talking throughout the year of the need for a *governo militare* (military dictatorship): despite his fierce appearance, he was generally loath to spill Greek blood. It is not surprising that Androutsos, who lacked such inhibitions, was feared, mistrusted, and regarded by some of the leading figures on his own side as "cunning" and "vicious."[17]

On the eve of the national assembly in March, the military chieftains were in the ascendant and they surely expected this time that the new political arrangements would acknowledge their successes. In western Rumeli, Mavrokordatos was largely dependent upon them to keep Mesolonghi safe. In the Peloponnese, the triumph of the Greek bands over the army of Dramali Pasha had redounded to the chieftains' credit. Kolokotronis enjoyed immense prestige and his authority was boosted further at the end of 1822 when Ottoman-held Nafplion surrendered. Already in de facto control of Tripolitsa, he had his son Panos named garrison commander, thus ensuring that the two most important urban centers won by the Greeks were under his personal control. Panos's engagement to Eleni, the daughter of the wealthy Spetsiot shipowner-widow Bouboulina (the name by which Laskarina Bouboulis is known to posterity), cemented the alliance between the family of the former brigand and the shipping interest.

The first national assembly that had concluded its work at the start of 1822 had authorized the provisional government to serve for just one year. A proclamation was therefore sent out calling for the election of representatives for a second assembly that would revise the constitution and choose the next administration. The delegates were supposed to be selected from among those men in each region—not only the Peloponnese, but the islands and central Greece—with "virtue and thoughtfulness" and to present themselves, together with the proof of their election signed by all the local electors and stamped by the local prefect at the assembly in December.[18] In fact, there was little rhyme or reason in their manner of appointment and no checking of credentials, and a far larger number of delegates than the year before made their way belatedly to the Peloponnese in March 1823—over 280 in total compared with the 69 who had signed the provisional constitution. Their very numbers suggested that, amid the war and in some sense thanks to it, the new form of parliamentary organization was spreading ever more widely among the Greeks. It was certainly connected with older traditions of local collective government but in its reach across regions, its linkage of Greeks into a single political unit, it was unprecedented. Most of the delegates were participating in national politics for the first time and many of them would continue by working in the government: an estimated 100 or so entered official service each year during the war, either in the parliament or in the new prefectural administrations.[19]

It was at this second national assembly that the animosity between the notables and the military leaders became so strong that it threatened the war effort. At first they could not even agree on a venue; only after much bickering did they convene at Astros on the Peloponnesian coast near where Dimitrios Ypsilantis had landed almost two years before. The landowners still predominated but the military men were starting to play politics too and were much more in evidence than they had been the year before. For the first time there was clear animosity toward the "foreign-born" (*heterochthons*)—not only Mavrokordatos but all those who had come from outside—which was to become an ever more important tension in Greek politics as the decades went on. It did not prevent the participation of Phanariots like the prince, but it marked them out as strangers, and by implication not true Greeks. The atmosphere in the meetings was tense; the rules governing the assembly stipulated that no weapons were to be worn, and security was provided by troops who ended the proceedings by demanding their wages and forcing the wealthier delegates to collect some 4,000 piastres in pay for them.[20]

What is truly striking in retrospect is that despite these intimidating circumstances, and the resentments of the military chieftains at being shut out of power, the outcome reflected a continued commitment on the part of those present to assert civilian power over the warlords. The regional assemblies were dissolved and it was agreed that prefects were to be appointed by the central government, establishing a system of national control over the provinces. The role of permanent commander in chief was declared incompatible with constitutional rule—at best such an appointment could be made for a single campaign. Thus Kolokotronis remained in command for the Peloponnese, Androutsos was named commander for eastern Greece, and the hero of Mesolonghi, Markos Botsaris, for western Greece. Laws of war were to be codified in line with those of "France, or America or other enlightened nations" to regulate the conduct of fighters on land and at sea. The power of the executive was reduced and that of the legislature enhanced with new veto powers, which made effective government even more difficult but reduced the short-term likelihood of a dictatorial takeover by Kolokotronis or anyone else.[21]

The revised constitution that was voted upon that April defined as Greeks all those "native" Christians living on its territory and opened citizenship to Greek-speaking Christian arrivals from outside. The liberal tenor of many of the existing arrangements was reaffirmed: slavery was abolished and the state was empowered to foster commerce, agriculture, and other aspects of economic life, to take charge of schooling, and to ensure the welfare of widows and orphans. One of the few practical provisions was the decision to defer another assembly for two years. But intensifying the overall commitment to a constitutional division of powers made it harder for any government to rule effectively, an unwise decision in the midst of a war but an indication of the prevailing mistrust. And despite the presence of the chieftains, top government appointments still went mostly to the Peloponnesian notables. Mavromihalis moved from the presidency of the legislature to become the new head of the executive; his predecessor, Mavrokordatos, became its secretary as well as minister of foreign affairs. There was a residual Etairist flavor: Papaflessas became minister of the interior and Perraivos became one of the three joint ministers of war for the Peloponnese. But only a single key position went to a military man.

Marginalized in this way from the administration for a second time, the chieftains increasingly saw themselves as the victims of an unholy coalition between the magnates of the Peloponnese, the islanders, and the Phanariots. When the position of supreme military commander that Kolokotronis held was abolished, he reacted angrily. Turning into something of a politician himself, he flirted with forming a rival administration and vacillated between supporting the government and threatening it. Typically he chose not to force a total break, made up his quarrel with some of the landowners, and accepted a new title as vice president of the executive. Some saw this as a positive development in that it brought into the government all those with real power. It put that government, however, firmly in the hands of men whose political horizons were limited: the Bey of the Mani, Mavromihalis, who did little as president, really had no interest besides that of keeping his family in power regionally; Kolokotronis wanted to be the power broker in the Peloponnese and did not much care what went on beyond it. When Alexandros Mavrokordatos, who had no roots in the Peloponnese, was elected president of the newly empowered national legislature alongside his other posts, it prompted Kolokotronis to issue threats against him. In protest, the entire legislature withdrew to the island of Salamis off Piraeus and made it clear that they continued to regard Mavrokordatos as their president. The latter remained for some time in jeopardy in Tripolitsa, before he was smuggled out with the help of two of the Peloponnesian notables to find refuge with the shipowners of Hydra. For some weeks, he was reduced to sleeping in his greatcoat on the floor of a room in the house of Ioannis Orlandos, Koundouriotis's brother-in-law. But a new coalition, critical to the future of Greece, was now emerging to rival the Peloponnesians. Mavrokordatos and the islanders both looked on with horror at the internecine feuding in the Peloponnese and favored a political system that established a national authority. Both of them had the connections and the perspective to seek assistance from abroad and had in fact begun the process of turning to London for political and economic assistance.[22]

Although Kolokotronis could not resist being drawn into politics, it was not a game for which the old kleft was suited. Shortly after his menacing gestures toward Mavrokordatos, a satire was pasted up on the walls of Tripolitsa—a novelty in a country where such things were unknown—mocking the chieftains (*oplarchigous*) who had "the sin to love silver and gold as much as the heroes of Homer." Kolokotronis's acquisitive side was common knowledge and there were rumors he had squirreled away a fortune after the sack of Tripolitsa with his bankers in Zakynthos. What has been called the first political satire in modern Greece must have come as a shock: no prominent Greek was used to being mocked thus in public. If not Mavrokordatos's doing—something we will likely never know—it was assuredly an expression of the political revolution he was bringing into being and a reminder to Kolokotronis that there were new ways of fighting, against which he and the other men of arms were relatively defenseless.[23]

Factional arguments were starting to break out all over the Peloponnese, and the region slid gradually into the civil war that would break out in earnest the next year. There was a kind of self-absorption about this, for it was the lack of an imminent Ottoman threat that seems to have allowed the Greeks' earlier unity of purpose to dissipate. Across the Gulf of Corinth, on the other hand, they had no such luxury. In eastern Rumeli, Androutsos was steering his own course, taking on Ottoman forces in some areas, while avoiding major confrontations

and all the time continuing to negotiate for a renewal of the understand-
ings of the previous year.[24] Farther north, in the face of a successful push
by Ottoman forces into Thessaly, another chieftain, Dimitris Karatasos, made a similar kind of deal for the region around the Gulf of Volos:
his agreement specified that one of the Greek kapetans would formally
submit to the Ottomans and receive the *vilayet* (province) of Magnesia;
another, Almyros, and so on. A third pledged to run Evvia with eight
hundred paid men on the Ottomans' behalf.[25]

Ottoman armies were also threatening the approaches to Mesolonghi
once again and their commanders offered the chieftains in western
Rumeli unusually favorable terms to surrender: only a tiny Ottoman
garrison would be stationed in Mesolonghi and the chieftains could
have their old armatoliks back. Then, they went on, the Ottoman army
would descend into the Morea, and best of all, the Rumeliot armatoles
could bring their men with them, help pacify the region, and enrich
themselves. A few Greek chieftains resisted but they felt abandoned,
helpless, and in desperate need of support. They were bitter that the
Peloponnesians, now that they were safe again, seemed to have forgotten the larger national purpose. They begged the islanders too to send
ships to their aid. Regionalism, always a powerful force, was threatening
to tear the Greek cause apart. "By ourselves . . . we cannot wage war on
Sultan Mahmud," the chieftains of Rumeli wrote to the shipowners on
Hydra and Spetses. "And instead of those bloody Moreots laughing at
us and seeing the enslavement of our lands, let us enjoy watching them
being taken to Albania, and let us rejoice that they will be lost first, since
they want our downfall, and let God judge us."[26]

"Moreots" versus "Rumeliots"; "notables" versus "chieftains"; "local-
born Greeks" versus "outsiders": by 1823 the Greek government existed
in name only and the effort to construct a unified national effort was
waning. The regional assemblies might have been wound up but local
privileges were still jealously guarded: indeed as late as 1827, the communal authority on Hydra was still declaring its absolute authority over
foreign as well as domestic matters. The rift between the national executive and the legislature became unbridgeable and at the end of 1823 a
second executive was formed by the legislature. The Greeks now had two
governments—the one led by Petros Mavromihalis that had succeeded
Mavrokordatos's and been in power since the spring with very little to
show for it; and the new one linked to the legislature, which one of the

Koundouriotis brothers, Georgios, was invited to head and which fell increasingly under the island influence. The path to the outright civil war that would dominate Greek affairs in 1824 lay ahead.[27]

Among the few matters that remained impervious to this infighting was the increasingly ubiquitous language of government itself. One of the first official announcements from the Mavrokordatos administration in the spring of 1822 had been to establish a naval blockade along the Ottoman-controlled littoral of Greece and the islands. "The Greek Nation," it began, had proclaimed its desire for independence and there-fore set up a central administration in accordance with the law of nations and of Europe. Details of its blockade, it went on, "will be communi-cated to all the consuls of friendly powers that may be found within the diverse parts of the Greek state." Dated Corinth, March 13, 1822, it was signed by "The President of the Executive A. Mavrokordatos" and "The Minister Chief Secretary of the State and for Foreign Affairs Th. Negris."[28]

All that flowery phraseology, those titles and ranks: no wonder men like Fotakos thought the foreign-born Greeks were ruining the uprising with their intellectualism and verbosity. The Pisa circle, attuned to how things looked abroad, nonetheless worried about the pretension. Bishop Ignatios asked why the Greeks needed a "minister for foreign affairs" before the government enjoyed diplomatic relations with anyone. From Paris, Konstantinos Polychroniades decried "this diarrhea of minis-ters."[29] Many more such documents and titles were to follow, more ministers and civil servants, prefects and secretaries—scores of them—producing a profusion of texts: the *Archives of the Greek Renaissance* issued by the Greek parliament amount to more than a dozen weighty volumes, each several hundred pages long. To some this was alarming; to others, especially at the start, it was a very positive sign that the revo-lution was bringing a newly united Greek nation into being. Entering the Peloponnese, the fighter Nikolaos Kasomoulis arrived at Vostitsa in the Gulf of Corinth where, as he put it, "from this point I began to see 'systematic nationalism' [*ethnismon systimatikon*]," meaning a better organization of communications and administration.[30]

The evidence of the time is clear enough, however: in many areas, what was written on paper in the name of the government counted for little in 1822 and even less in 1823. "Nothing could be more melancholy than the internal administration of the different prefectures," wrote

Julius Millingen about western Rumeli. "Vain were all attempts to lessen the evil by sending *Eparchs* (prefects) to separate civil from military power. What amelioration could an unassisted stranger bring against an armed capitano?"[31] When Ioannis Kolettis was sent out as prefect (*eparchos*) to Evvia in May 1823, his instructions were clear: get the inhabitants to understand the new constitutional system so that "the nation can understand it has need of administration, and that without administration the nation does not exist in name or reality." In fact, whether in Evvia, the rest of central Rumeli, or the Peloponnese, the government's writ scarcely ran outside the major towns and often not even there.[32] Thomas Gordon, a sympathizer, was categorical: the Epidavros constitution was "excellent in theory but totally unfit for the people to whom it was addressed."[33]

While that may have been true, it missed the point of the strategy Mavrokordatos and the Pisa circle had been elaborating from the start: to look abroad, to banish the identification of the Greek cause with the Filiki Etaireia, and in this way to revise the idea of the uprising among Europe's statesmen as a national movement that sought not revolution but the defense of a people's natural rights. The insistence that theirs was a provisional constitution allowed for the possibility of revision and hence of courting foreign powers by allowing them a say in the country's future. The telling silence on the key question of whether the country should be a republic or a monarchy—not a matter of much consequence to most Greeks at this time—allowed an appeal to Europeans across the political spectrum and, when the time came, easy adjustment to the evident monarchical preferences of the European powers.

"The Greeks at Epidaurus did much to deceive Europe but little to organize Greece," writes Finlay, who was there at the time. But deceiving Europe—or more precisely, making the revolution legible to Europe so that it could help it succeed—was the point. Kolokotronis and Androutsos mistrusted this reliance upon foreigners: to them it could only indicate a desire to sell the country out. Kolokotronis, who believed Greece was "competent to her own liberation" but was comfortable with backing from Russia, was convinced Mavrokordatos wanted to push Greece into the hands of the British; Androutsos feared even the czar. "The territory we captains have dispossessed the Sultan of," Androutsos declared angrily, "our self-elected government has sold to the Russians; and with the money they are to get rid of us, to make way for a foreign king and foreign soldiers."[34] But that fear said as much about Androutsos's anxiety regarding his own future as it did about the "pen pushers." In truth, the only alternative to the sultan was a foreign king, and the only alternative to leadership by the armatoles was revolutionary politics supported from abroad. Thus fighting was not the only precondition for independence and Mavrokordatos and his circle were aware of the other one. It was, in Polychroniades's words, "European organization." That alone held out any hope of changing Europe's policy in order to internationalize the conflict and thus obtain the political and financial support the Greeks would need to win.[35]

THE NATURE OF
THE STRUGGLE

The war of the Greek Revolution was of similar duration to our own; but how unlike the conditions! how unequal the sufferings! We were three thousand miles away from our antagonist; and received his armies into our extensive country, inhabited by a people trained in the discipline of liberty, and struggling for the inalienable rights of British subjects. They rose up from four centuries of slavery under the imbruting despotism of a barbarous conqueror . . . We had the support of a powerful constitutional party in England . . . They were frowned upon by the cabinets of Europe . . .

C. C. Felton, Professor of Greek Literature,
Harvard University, 1854[1]

"Hey fellow, who are you and what are you doing assembled like this?"
"We are brigands [*klefts*]."
"Who is your kapetan?"
"There is no kapetan here, just us."
"And you want to defy the Sultan Mahmud just like that, my man? What has God put into your head?"
"This is how we have weighed it up on all sides and we've made the decision, either we'll die or you won't eat bread again."

An exchange between Ottoman and Greek soldiers,
December 1821, in E. Protopsaltis, ed.,
Istorikon archeion Alexandrou Mavrokordatou
(Athens, 1963–86), ii, 56

The Greeks were a minority of the population of the Ottoman Empire, comprising perhaps 3 million out of its 23 or 24 million people; only in a few areas—the Morea, the islands of the Aegean, and some places north of the Gulf of Corinth—did they predominate. Yet even these figures fail to give a full sense of the imbalance, for whereas the Greeks had no cavalry and found it hard to raise and arm even 15,000–20,000 fighters, the sultan could count on bringing much larger and better-armed forces into the field. After the elimination of Ali Pasha, the well-informed Alexander Kantakuzinos estimated that Sultan Mahmud II could raise 50,000–60,000 troops against the Greeks, despite significant other drains on his resources. The total manpower of the Ottoman armed forces—two or three times that amount—was not a lot compared with European armies, certainly not when set against the 800,000 or so soldiers under the czar, but more than enough in theory to have dealt with the threat the Greeks posed. However unreliable the data—and we are in a pre-statistical era where none of these figures are anything more than orders of magnitude—at the outset this looked like a very one-sided contest.[2]

The leadership of the Filiki Etaireia had wished away these seemingly insuperable odds. For one thing, they counted on the Russians coming to their assistance. For another, they dreamed of extending the struggle of the Greeks as widely as possible and their agents were active not only in what became the centers of the insurrection but also in Epiros, Macedonia, and Thrace, and throughout the eastern Mediterranean as far as the coasts of Syria and Egypt. In March 1821 an Etairist organizer called Emmanouil Pappas landed east of Salonika in the Khalkidiki peninsula with a boatload of arms and spread the revolt among the Greek villages there while armed bands mobilized in western Macedonia and Thessaly. The islands of Thasos and Samothraki in the northern Aegean were also drawn in, while the revolutionary fleet carried the message to the eastern Aegean, Crete, and Cyprus.

Faced with the prospect of revolt across an indeterminate area at a time when his forces were already stretched against Ali Pasha, the Russians and the Persians in the east, the sultan responded with ferocity, ordering massacres of Greeks not only in Constantinople but in Smyrna, Thessaloniki, Aivalik, and elsewhere. After the first onslaught, he was astonished by the Greeks' capacity to endure: "Many of them have been slaughtered and more are still being slaughtered," he stated almost admiringly in April 1821. Yet faced with a lowly foe who seemed more motivated and zealous than his own Muslim subjects, he saw no means except more killing to restore them to obedience.[3] Shocked by the uprising, he veered between wanting to continue the repression and reining it in. Contradictory orders indicated the difficulty of holding the line between massive collective punishment and a descent into chaos.[4]

It was ethnic punishment that had the upper hand in Ottoman policy. Determined to stamp out any uprisings down the Asia Minor seaboard or around the vital approaches to the Dardanelles, the sultan's troops cowed the Greeks into submission. They were empowered by the fact that once certain places had been declared rebellious, the killing of the men and the enslavement of women and children was deemed lawful in the eyes of the Ottoman state. In June, irregulars massacred townspeople in the streets of Aivalik, and a renowned center of learning in the Greek world went up in flames: about 4,000 fled by sea, but far more were either killed or enslaved. In September the islanders of Samothraki were massacred or sold into captivity, pushing neighboring Thasos to sue for clemency. The revolt in the Kassandra peninsula was crushed. Lingering unrest in Thessaly was mostly suppressed by the end of 1821 and Macedonia was shocked by the massacres that followed the reconquest of the town of Naoussa in April 1822. While fighters from those regions fled, large Greek populations remained, their communal leaders hastening to make their peace. The massacres on Chios marked the climax of the Ottoman repression and by 1823 much of the southern Balkans had reverted to Ottoman rule.[5]

It was Muslim civilians that had been the first victims of the insurrection—massacred in Galati in Moldavia in February 1821—and more were targeted by insurgent bands over the following months in the Morea, central Greece, and parts of Thessaly, many of them killed as they tried to leave the villages and towns they had long lived in. The Morea remained the center of the uprising and there the ethnic balance was reversed: Muslims were in a small minority—just over 40,000 out of a population of some 400,000. The slaughter in Tripolitsa after it fell to the Greeks must have taken the number of Muslims killed in the first months of the war to over 20,000. Dimitrios Ypsilantis and his aide Alexander Kantakuzinos had reminded the Greek fighters that "it was a law of all nations, and especially of us Christians, not to maltreat the enemy when they surrendered to us." But massacres in cold blood followed the Greek take over of Kalavryta, Neokastro, Tripolitsa, Corinth, Athens, and elsewhere.[6]

Part of the reason was obvious—the desire for revenge. The French philhellene Philippe Jourdain was not surprised that the Greeks, having been mistreated and scorned over centuries by their Ottoman masters, should have returned the favor. Muslim violence against Greeks had often gone unpunished: the notorious Tripolitsa enforcer Ali Tsekouras had combined policing, extortion, and outright sadism at the expense of the region's hapless Christians for years. Disdain toward the Christian *reaya* was widespread among the Muslim population, and the memoir of a young Greek boy enslaved in the household of a bey of Patras shows the habitual contempt addressed on a daily basis to a "Christian dog."[7] A unique wartime account allows us a glimpse inside the mind of an Ottoman cavalryman, a freelancer who served in central Rumeli and Evvia. He saw fighting the "infidel" as a combination of religious duty and moneymaking, and he records that when he cut off his first Greek head, his father congratulated him: "Let us cut off many more infidels' heads."[8]

Vengeance brought out a casual ferocity in ordinary Greeks that took aback even those whose devotion to their cause was unquestioned. A shaken Thomas Gordon described the attackers in Tripolitsa as "mad with vindictive rage": "their insatiable cruelty knew no bounds and seemed to inspire them with a superhuman energy for evil."[9] Ambrosios Frantzis, cleric and Etairist, searched to understand how people he knew could have forgotten that murder was a sin. Some, he reckoned later, killed because they remembered their own sufferings, or those of relatives, but others were simply offended by the way their captives still talked down to them as if they were inferiors: "They spoke to some of the ordinary Greeks saying 'Hey, you damn Christians!' [*Vre Romaioi!*] as if to say to them 'Slaves!' That expression '*Vre Romaioi*' the Greeks could not bear to hear." There was a widespread sense that it was time for their former masters to learn their place.[10]

The Filiki Etaireia had preached the obligation of religious hatred among its members from the start. "I swear that I will nurture in my heart irreconcilable hatred against the tyrants of my Fatherland, their supporters and those who think like them," ran the Etaireia oath, mandating that the true lover of the Greek nation had a duty to hate the Turks.[11] In the Peloponnese, they sang "No Turk shall remain in the Morea, nor in the entire world." Reports of the despoilation of the patriarch's corpse strengthened the desire to wreak collective retribution, and pamphlets circulated among the Greeks in which the dead patriarch urged the Christian faithful to commit ever greater acts of revenge.

Collective death haunted the Greek revolutionary imagination. The slogan "Freedom or Death" was a pledge to die rather than surrender, but it was also a warning that not to fight was itself tantamount to a living death. Others worried about the very real threat of annihilation. The Patriarch Gregory V had foreseen that the Etaireia's plans would lead to Greek communities being wiped out; Russian diplomats had been warning about an Ottoman "war of extermination" of the empire's Christians almost from the start. Nor was this fear entirely baseless since the sultan indicated early on that he felt within his rights in ordering the killing and enslaving of disobedient Christian populations en masse. This prospect of communal death at the hands of the Ottomans— a fear shared by Greeks in the Peloponnese, Rumeli, and Asia Minor alike—was unquestionably one of the ways in which an idea of the Greek nation emerged. It created a grouping united in its shared fate, and united too perhaps through the immortality that would be conferred by that.[12]

But the Greek imagination had also encompassed the mass killing of Muslims and had seen this as a possible corollary of the much-awaited moment of the resurrection of Orthodox Christendom. The prophecies and oracles circulating among Greeks since the eighteenth century had popularized the idea of an eventual Christian rebellion against the sultan as a collective act that would be carried out in accordance with the will of God. Whether led by the Virgin Mary, by an unnamed Christian ruler—often identified with the czar—or by "the Christian kings of Europe," it was through the death not only of the despotic sultan but of his people too that the Christians of the empire would achieve their triumph—the long-defeated *Romeïko*, converting the House of Islam back into the land of Christ. In the "Vision of kyr Daniel," the Virgin confronts the sultan in his palace and displaces him from his throne, telling him she has had enough of his injustice and tyranny and warning him that she will lead the Greeks "so they will annihilate you along with your people." The spring and summer of 1821 may thus have felt like that moment almost outside history, a moment that the Greeks had never believed would come about, the sudden end of their interminable waiting. Was this not perhaps, for some of them, therefore, an electrifying instant in which the old rules ceased to apply and new ones had not yet come into force? Something in the demeanor of the men rushing through the streets of Tripolitsa given over entirely to killing and plunder—their sense of abandon and total lack of constraint—suggests this. Such men did not share the worries of their leaders—about the impact on world opinion or the effect on the Christians elsewhere in the empire. Their world had shrunk to a space in which the killing of Muslims was divinely sanctioned.[13]

Whatever the causes, the effect was to make the continued coexistence of Greeks and Turks in the Peloponnese impossible. Elsewhere in the Ottoman lands the faiths would go on living together for another century, but not there. We read about one Muslim from Monemvasia who as late as 1850 talked longingly of returning to his home, and looked after any Greek travelers from there who came his way. But the idea that Dimitrios Ypsilantis had supposedly believed in, namely that Muslims were welcome to continue to live in the Peloponnese, was effectively dead. In the Morea the insurrection had turned into an all-or-nothing ethnic struggle, of the kind with which the world would become horribly familiar over the ensuing two centuries.[14]

According to statistics compiled under the Capodistrias government, of the 42,740 Muslims living in the Morea in 1821 only a handful remained seven years later. (Things were quite different in Attica, Evvia, and central Greece where half the estimated 13,360 had survived, or western Rumeli where 4,470 out of 5,445 were left.)[15] Along with the Muslim inhabitants, the material traces of their existence in the Morea vanished too: a recent survey of extant Ottoman architecture in Greece indicates only fifteen buildings of any significance in the region out a total of nearly 200 in the country as a whole. The Ottoman past has been eradicated more completely from the Peloponnese than anywhere else.[16] The more general problem is the absence of the Ottoman dimension from histories of the Greek revolution in general and of the Morea in particular. In many historical accounts written in the twentieth century, it is as if Muslims had never lived there. This had not been the case with the first generation of Greek memoirists who had after all grown up in an Ottoman environment themselves: not surprisingly, Muslim names and Turkish phrases are dotted throughout the recollections of figures like Kolokotronis, Fotakos, and Deliyannis. But for later generations, things were very different, and only the rise of Ottoman studies inside

Greece in the past twenty to thirty years has caused historians to turn their attention to how Muslims lived.

At the time, it was anonymous Greek villagers who registered the passing of the Ottoman Morea most immediately and movingly. The privileged role played by peasant women in commemorating the dead was a feature of modern Greek society as it had been of the ancient. As a result, one of the few subjects women made their own was the funeral lament, and the Muslim dead and the plight of those they left behind were not excluded from the genre. A ballad of the time imagined the elite Muslim women of the destroyed town of Lala, "well-educated women" in fine clothes who had once refused to let their feet touch the earth, now captives, reduced to carrying wood and pails of water. News of the killing of Kiamil Bey, the region's most powerful and wealthy Muslim notable, found its way almost at once into folk song. Captured in Tripolitsa and then courted as a captive by the Greek notables and chieftains who sought his legendary riches, Kiamil Bey had once owned scores of villages, and his four hand-painted horse-drawn carriages had been regarded by the peasants as a miracle of European technology in a land with no roads. In the summer of 1822, with Dramali Pasha's army approaching, he had been killed in captivity in the fortress in his native Corinth, taking the secret of his hidden wealth to his grave:

> *They have taken the castles, they took the passes*
> *They have taken Tripolitsa, the town of renown.*
> *The Turkish women cry in the streets, the many daughters of Emirs*
> *And the bey's wife laments the unfortunate Kiamil:*
>
> *"Where are you that I do not see you, my beloved lord?*
> *You were the pillar of the Morea, the banner of Corinth,*
> *The greatest tower of Tripolitsa . . ."*[17]

This anonymous lament, published in Paris in 1824, must have been composed shortly after Kiamil Bey's death; the words survive as a popular song, a reminder of a vanished elite. During the war much of Ottoman Corinth was burned down, together with the mosques, dervish *tekkes*, and hamams that had marked its eighteenth-century resurgence. Kiamil Bey's magnificent palace, with its separate haremlik, its bathhouse, and its lofty belvedere in the walled gardens overlooking the water, was targeted for destruction by Papaflessas in the spring of 1821. All that is left to remind visitors today of the bey and his family is a modest ruin, two-story tower with a rusting iron balustrade perched on a grassy slope above a bus stop on the coastal road running west along the Gulf of Corinth.[18]

Those Muslims—it is impossible to say how many—who managed to stay alive once the first wave of fighting in the Morea was over were mostly kept as captives to be ransomed, sold, or exchanged; many were later employed by the Greeks as servants, mule drivers, and laborers. An "Arab woman" looked after the children of one village notable faithfully throughout the war and brought them to the safety of Nafplion. A few Muslim men actually fought on the Greek side—mostly Albanians. Mustafa Ghekas headed a so-called Ottoman unit of several dozen mostly Albanian Muslims from small towns in central Greece such as Thebes and Livadeia.[19] Plapoutas's flag-bearer was a powerfully built Turk who was devoted to his kapetan. The physician of Androutsos and his thuggish lieutenant Ioannis Gouras was a Muslim surgeon from Talanti on the east coast, who remained on the Acropolis with the Greeks even when they came under siege from the Ottomans in 1826–27.[20]

The economics of ransom were an integral part of warfare, and captured members of the Ottoman elite were kept as investments because they could fetch large sums or be swapped for Christian captives held elsewhere. When Kalamata fell, for instance, the first town to do so, Mavromihalis Bey took the *voyvode* hostage, no doubt thinking of his son who was imprisoned in Tripolitsa. After Tripolitsa was taken, the notable Kontakis tells us that he "saved forty-five souls" whom he later used to bargain for Christians; Kasomoulis kept two hostages in order to win back his mother and sisters, who had been sold into slavery in the north.[21]

Muslim women were kept for other purposes too. Georgios Sisinis, one of the most powerful magnates in the west of the Peloponnese, owned a harem of captives; he was not the only one. Some women managed to forge closer, more equal bonds with Greek men. A pasha's daughter converted and became the wife of Rigas Palamidis, the secretary of the Peloponnesian Senate and a politician of some influence and power. Another well-known case was of the girl from Tripolitsa called Zafira who ended up with the armatole Karaïskakis: he took her everywhere with him and left her a substantial sum in his will when he died in 1827. Dressed in man's clothes, she cut a striking figure. "She carried over her shoulder a light Greek musket and in her girdle a brace of pistols and an ataghan," recorded an admiring Englishman. "No danger, however great, kept her from the field, and although she did not fight, still she was regardless of her life while following her lord." She acquired a new name, Marigo, but her origins were no secret.[22]

Loyal or not, these Muslims were the scattered remnants of the once-ruling caste of the region and many of them must have dreamed of escape, especially those kept as slaves. Two managed to board an Austrian vessel in Nafplion by pretending they were Christians and wearing Greek dress. When they were caught, the police recommended they should be chained around the neck and made to sweep the streets.[23] An aggrieved owner from Hydra requested help tracking down his mule driver: he was a Turkish "boy" aged between eighteen and twenty who went by the name of Georgios and had served his owner for several years before absconding with some money, helped by a couple of men from Rumeli. But escaping without Christian aid was difficult and dangerous whether by sea or on land, for any Muslims discovered traveling on their own could be robbed or killed with impunity as spies.[24]

Baptism was another way out, especially as a preliminary to marriage, and Rigas Palamidis was not the only Greek to find a wife in this way; the chieftain Nikolaos Kriezotis and the Serb fighter Hadzi Christos, who had initially come to the Morea in the service of Khurshid Pasha, also wed Muslim women who had been baptized. But the possibility of baptism made some Greeks anxious and in the first Greek parliament there was a long debate over whether there should be a cutoff age for those wishing to become Christian. The liberal-inclined legislature, welcoming baptism as a solution to the random violence against Muslims that they knew was damaging the Greek cause, wanted it to be available to all ages. The executive, however, was worried: what would then stop Kiamil Bey, they asked, or any other members of the Muslim elite, from converting, reclaiming their property, and becoming a major force within the Greek side? In the end, this was never a serious problem, though it did resurface briefly once the war was over when some baptized Muslims began to demand their property back.[25]

In a war of fluid and shifting borders, both sides tried to prevent unauthorized crossings—physical as well as metaphorical. But in practice this was next to impossible as older patterns of business, commercial life, and even tourism that connected the region as a whole continued through the fighting. A Levant merchant based in Smyrna went around the Greek archipelago adding ancient coins to his collection; a Dutch archaeologist dug up finds in Milos. Philhellenic fighters took time out to see Tiryns, the Acropolis, or the grotto at Antiparos. Greek islanders still worked as domestic servants and traders in Ottoman towns. The Asia Minor seaboard was especially porous as the example of a young Greek man from Smyrna called Petros Mengous shows: Mengous went off and fought on a Hydriot brig before deciding he needed to see his family again. Leaving his crewmates on Hydra, he sailed to Tinos, changed into European clothes so that the Turks would take him for a foreigner, and caught another ship bound for the Ottoman port where he returned to his astonished parents who had given him up for lost. Crossing between Greek and Ottoman territories, Mengous had simply needed to change his dress and find a passage.[26]

For many Greek merchants, the pull of the regional economy remained stronger than any exclusive commitment to the revolutionary cause. A consortium of Greeks and Muslims was buying prizes at auction in Constantinople in 1823—presumably Greek ships captured by the Ottomans. Greek traders and sea captains from the Ionian Islands routinely made money supplying food to Ottoman garrisons in Patras and elsewhere. Farther afield, it was actually a Chiot merchant, Georgios Tzitzinias, having moved after 1822 to the French port of Marseille, who helped Mehmed Ali, the pasha of Egypt, get his warships built in the dockyards there. Threatened with excommunication by an Orthodox archimandrite for the deal, Tzitzinias was defended strongly by his fellow Greek merchants; they even organized a boycott of the church and obtained the priest's dismissal: commerce came first.[27]

Merchants were, to be sure, not always merchants, for they shared with spies a sense for the value of information, and it was but a short step to using commerce as a cover for more shady activities often routed through Alexandria or Constantinople. The Tositsa brothers, probably the most prominent Greeks in Egypt, were said to provide intelligence to Mehmed Ali through their trading offices. Similar suspicions circled around the highly networked Xenos brothers, who grew rich in Nafplion supplying the Greek government. A Cypriot trader claimed to government investigators that he was a professional musician—another usefully peripatetic occupation—who had been moving around between western Greece and the Peloponnese, Syria, and Alexandria, intending to head home eventually to Cyprus. It turned out he was not only involved in selling on looted monastery silverware but he was being used by Mehmed Ali to report on conversations with Greeks involved in the revolution. High-level figures on the Greek side, always anxious to preserve their private lines of communication with the Ottomans, were involved in similarly shady goings-on. A web of intrigue was uncovered that was said to involve Kolokotronis and Mavromihalis Bey in moneymaking activities ranging from redeemed Muslim slaves to selling off war booty such as a library of rare Islamic books plundered from Tripolitsa. Whatever the facts of this unbelievably complicated case that was uncovered by the Greek government in the midst of the struggle, the one thing nobody could question after reading the file is that Greek insurgents and their leaders had not suddenly cut off their long-standing ties and contacts with the Muslim-Ottoman world that surrounded them.[28]

In the 1820s, information traveled at a pace that had not changed since Roman times. This explains why some people remembered the occasion before the war when a Moroccan *sheyk* had visited Ali Pasha in Jannina and presented him with a mirror of polished steel. The mirror, so the *sheyk* claimed, possessed an astonishing property: it could show whatever was happening in the world that minute.[29] Such miracles would have to await our own day to become commonplace, and even Europeans in the Levant were obliged to put up with the slow pace of news and to endure what seemed, compared with what they were used to back home, a kind of isolation. Several months after his arrival in Crete the recently appointed French consul wrote home to his minister in Paris to complain: "Since my departure from Smyrna, I have had no news, whether from Paris, or Constantinople. I am in the most complete ignorance of all the events which may have happened in Europe the past four months." Six months later he was still waiting for a reply.[30]

This was not unusual, and the slow and uncertain passage of information must be borne in mind as we understand how people tried to fathom events and how they reacted to them. It took nearly a month for news of Alexandros Ypsilantis's crossing of the river Pruth into Moldavia to reach Hydra and the Mani, for instance. That was about the norm, provided the weather behaved. The Russian fleet was becalmed in

1827 on its way into the Aegean, wasting ten days at Gibraltar, another nine at Palermo, and three in Messina, making it more than three weeks late in arriving at its destination. Contrary winds and calms notwithstanding, word traveled more quickly on the whole by sea than by land; news was passed from one boat to another, from island to island. From the log of the brig *Agamemnon*, captained by Anastasios Tsamados, which left Hydra on May 2, 1821, we learn what was gleaned: two days out, a report via a ship from Constantinople that the Russian fleet was descending from the Black Sea; a week later, by which time they were patrolling the waters off Chios, news came from a Turkish brig that Alexandros Ypsilantis and his army were reportedly making for Edirne and that the Russian and Austrian armies were readying for war.[31] Evaluating the reliability of this news was another matter: telling rumor from fact was even more difficult than it is today.

On land, travel was slow. There were no roads in the Balkans capable of bearing wheeled traffic and almost no bridges, and winter with its flooded rivers and muddy tracks could make journeys next to impossible and wear out horses, which were always in short supply. Before 1821 the Ottomans had relied upon a sophisticated system of postal relays with teams of horses stationed in the major towns, financed out of local taxes, but in the Morea the system seems to have broken down completely during the fighting, and by its latter stages even senior commanders like Kolokotronis were complaining of the scarcity of horses for their messengers. For large loads, the Ottoman armies had camels, which were highly capable and energy-efficient but slow and operating at the northern limit of their ecological tolerance: these were the very last years in which camels were deployed in the Greek lands; within a decade they would seem exotic. Horses were expensive and scarce but faster—twenty to twenty-five miles a day on average, sixty a day by post-horse; 100-plus miles in case of exceptional need. When absolutely necessary, journeys of 1,200 miles in ten days were not unknown. Thus the Ottoman postal service, if run-down compared with previous centuries, still allowed imperial officials in Rumeli to communicate efficiently by sending Tatar messengers on horseback as they had always done: the sultan had little difficulty dispatching his orders to Jannina or Larissa.

For the impoverished Greeks, however, lacking imperial access to resources, the most important means of short-distance communications by land was the foot runner (*pezos*) who was nearly as fast in the mountains as a horse, and easier to feed: without him, communications among the insurgents in the Peloponnese in particular would have been almost impossible. We know little about these men, who leave few traces in the records, but theirs was a tough and dangerous occupation that lasted, on and off, at least until the German occupation during the Second World War, the swan song of the *pezos*. We have at least one remarkable autobiography from the latter war—that written by the Cretan runner George Psychoundakis and translated by his wartime British officer, Patrick Leigh Fermor; Psychoundakis's predecessors in the 1820s had to be trustworthy as well as strong, ingenious in hiding especially sensitive notes—the lining of shoes was a favored place—and possessed of an excellent memory since the most sensitive messages were delivered only orally. Confidential agents might carry blank sheets bearing only a signature—this was how Ali Pasha operated when he sent an agent to the Russians—as a form of authorization, and there were cases of deception in which men pretended to be messengers in order to be properly housed along their journey.[32]

The key figures in wartime communications, just as invisible in the histories as the runners, were the scribe-secretaries. It was not just educated princes like Mavrokordatos, with his entourage of young Paris-educated intellectuals, who understood the importance of regular correspondence. The notables, kapetans, and armatoles all had their scribes whom they usually picked from among men they could trust—from relatives, perhaps, or youths from their village whose families were known to them. In a society with a high rate of illiteracy, the sheer volume of letters crisscrossing the mountains is staggering, and it was certainly not the fighters who were writing most of them—not even the educated ones. Some commanders, like Panos Kolokotronis, Perraivos, or Spiros Milios, had received proper schooling. But most could just about sign their names and some could not even do that. All of them employed a *grammatikos*, often several, and tried to make sure to have at least one with them at all times. Theodoros Rigopoulos was a local youth from a mountain village outside Kalavryta who had been baptized by Kolokotronis and, having learned letters at school, joined his godfather in 1821, serving him and his sons as secretary. Ready to dash off a note at any moment, he got used to writing on horseback, resting the paper on his knee or on the back of his pistol. Both *grammatikos* and *pezos* would accompany their masters every-where they went—into the thick of the fighting if needed. It was when Panos Kolokotronis stopped his horse to dictate a quick letter to Rigo-poulos for their *pezos* to carry away that he was shot dead during the civil war. After Panos's death, Kolokotronis ordered Rigopoulos to go to work instead for Panos's brother, Gennaios, but Rigopoulos found him "ill-educated" and "completely mad," and regarded him as one would "a wild beast." He spoke, Rigopoulos noted, "abruptly and insultingly, using crude and immodest words."[33]

As this suggests, a *grammatikos* did a good deal more than merely write down a chieftain's words; he recast them in acceptably courteous language, starting with the usual formal inquiry about the recipient's health, and the whole was couched in an idiom that was far from every-day speech. During the war, no figure was more important than the *grammatikos* in spreading the newly formalized version of the Greek language with its rhetorical flourishes and classical allusions, bringing it—thanks to the fighting—from the urban centers of learning into the daily life of the villages. To the chieftains and their men, who all accepted its importance, it must nevertheless have been all but incomprehensible, which put them in a position they did not like: having to trust their secretary both to explain what was meant and to communicate cor-rectly what they wanted to say. The mistrustful Odysseus Androutsos once sent Mavrokordatos a message, confessing his "weakness in writ-ing" and asking him to communicate more simply, "so that I can understand by myself what you write and answer you myself without having others explain me your letter, as they interpret it, or write you back as they want to."[34]

Only rarely do we have a scrawled comment added at the bottom of a letter in some indecipherable hand to betray how the leaders of the revolution actually addressed one another. "Gypsy, gypsy, you've got gypsy blood so look out!" Kolokotronis scribbles to his fellow chieftain Georgios Karaïskakis, whose dark skin led not only his enemies to nick-name him "the gypsy": the joke was that Kolokotronis—"swarthy, half-black, nose and eyes of an eagle"—was used to similar barbs. The insults that each side customarily hurled at the other, sometimes as a prelude to actual fighting and sometimes as a substitute for it, thus occasionally sullied the implausible *politesse* of the written page.[35]

*

In a society where the bulk of the population lived off the land, going to war was tied to the seasonal rhythms of the farming economy. Peasants manning the siege of the castle in Patras abandoned it so that they could harvest the figs; olives and currants were other crops whose needs help explain why that particular siege never worked properly and the town's Ottoman-held fort never fell. Traditional campaigning only began once horses and pack animals had been brought up from their winter grazing grounds to pasture on the first spring grasses—St. George's Day in April was the customary start—and by St. Dimitrios's Day in October, soldiers and sailors expected to be sent home since gales, flooded rivers, and snow made supplying troops almost impossible and turned camping in the open into a pointless struggle with the elements.[36] Spring rains could stop a battle since muskets and pistols would not fire when powder was wet while summer—the peak campaigning time—could bring extreme heat and make it hard to find drinkable water. "Saturday, May 27th: Pretty damn'd, considerably, particularly, uncomfortably hot," noted an American philhellene holed up in the Mani. "The musquitos [sic] were very annoying, and the heat tremendous," writes an Irish traveler, "the thermometer standing at 89° in the shade." Fotakos writes that the sun during the battle for the castle of Argos in July 1822 was so hot the Turkish besiegers were "fried."[37]

The Greek fighters had adapted to this environment: they were typically lean, frugal, and capable of going a long time on very little. Plumpness did not necessarily indicate lack of courage (both Petros Mavromihalis and Ibrahim Pasha were far from slim), but it did indicate privilege of one kind or another—access to good food and a mount—and could put men at a disadvantage in the mountains. Kolokotronis's father was "very thin, so swift of foot that a fresh steed could not overtake him." The wiry Kolokotronis himself ate sparingly, mostly meat and dry foods washed down with wine: he was ill only once before he was fifty, possessed a sharp memory and remarkable eyesight. Mengous noted the meagerness of the soldiers' rations: the fighters he was with received only a handful of flour a day, which they had to cook. In the field, they might be reduced to scrabbling for herbs and water. Perhaps this is why they often helped themselves without ceremony to any livestock unfortunate enough to cross their path. The troops "in order not to allow their warlike spirit to sleep have been shedding torrents of sheeps' blood," noted the philhellene Baron von Rheineck, later Mavrokordatos's brother-in-law. "Assuredly to be a sheep is the worst profession of all in this country."[38] But the diet was a healthy one and chieftains could remain active to an advanced age: Notis Botsaris was seventy when he led the charge through enemy lines at Mesolonghi, and the Messenian brigand Mitropetrovas was still fighting at the age of eighty; Anagnostaras, Miaoulis, and Petros Mavromihalis were around sixty; "the old man of the Morea," as Kolokotronis was known, was fifty. Karaïskakis, Androutsos, Markos Botsaris, and Plapou-tas were all around forty. On the other hand, some of the major chieftains were much younger: Kitsos Tsavellas, head of an important Souliot clan, was in his twenties, and so was Theodorakis Grivas.[39]

The fighters in the armatole bands of western Greece understood the principles of warfare in the mountains; those in the Morea soon learned them from the older klefts. Traveling light and living mostly off the land, their principal mode of attack was surprise. Night raids were a specialty, demanding familiarity with the terrain and with one another. They avoided, wherever possible, direct assault on a fortified position, and the kapetans tended to keep their men away from direct confronta-tion on open ground because this gave the advantage to the Ottoman cavalry: "They have a horror of cavalry," wrote an observer. As a result, only comparatively few battles took place in flat terrain, and these tended to result in outright defeats for the Greeks—notably in the two routs they suffered on the plains of Attica in 1827, where pressure from their own European officers drove them into disadvantageous positions. They were adept at building makeshift stone defensive fortifications, but ambushes were their preferred tactic, and it was in the narrow mountain passes that they could prevail against much larger and better-equipped Ottoman forces. One Ottoman cavalryman was told by his father: "My son, this war is not a chivalrous war. These infidels approach you from ambushes; you have never seen such a war before."[40]

Sieges were for this reason mostly drawn-out affairs in which the besieging troops, lured by the prospect of plunder but averse to risk, would set up cordons to try to starve the garrison out. The Ottoman siege of Mesolonghi in 1822 was typical in the attackers' reluctance to make a direct assault. If the defenders had cavalry, as they did in Patras, the cordon was set up so far away as to be all but useless. The Greeks' deployment of artillery was limited both because of the shortage of guns—at first all that was available was mostly ships' cannons or old Venetian pieces of uncertain reliability—and because they lacked expert gunners and tended not to heed the European artillery experts who could have helped them. It could therefore be a very long time before the defenders succumbed—and they did so either because they had run out of things to sell for food, or because water had run low, or because the attackers had actually managed the rare feat of imposing a real blockade. Since most forts held by the Ottomans were on the coast and could be supplied by sea, sieges could last months, even years. Fearing annihilation, after the bloody denouement of the earliest sieges, defenders held out to the point of starvation. "We had no more horses, donkeys or camels," recollected a soldier in the Ottoman garrison holed up in a fort in Evvia. "We had eaten them all." They went on to the cats and dogs and, he claims, some men began to eat the bodies of their dead comrades. Muslims in Nafplion were so desperate by the end of 1822 that after they had surrendered, a little girl was found eating the feet of a donkey. In Mesolonghi in 1826, dogs were cooked in olive oil and rodents, pack animals, and even corpses were said to have tempted the starving Greek defenders before their final, desperate sortie.[41]

In these long-drawn-out operations, a curious intimacy often arose between the soldiers on either side. Lines were rarely so tight that a messenger could not be dropped from the walls of a fortress to make his way through the enemy positions, or an enterprising trader allowed in with fresh produce from the surrounding countryside. When Ibrahim Pasha's Egyptians surrounded the Greek garrison in Navarino in early 1825, the besieged men got news of the outside world from a Bosnian comrade who used to talk every night with a fellow Bosnian in Ibrahim's army.[42] Attacking forces tended quickly to find out the state of the town behind the walls and to know the level of its provisions and morale. Sometimes the defenders would let in someone so that they could see how well supplied they were and spread discouragement. In Mesolonghi, they would talk—in either Greek or Albanian—across the moat: shouts and insults were common, and sometimes defenders played practical jokes to show their bravado and disdain for the other side.

Away from the ears of their kapetans or *bouloukbashis* (sergeants), the soldiers often tried to minimize the chances of a real fight so that they could all return home to their fields. "Why are you fighting us here?" Greeks shouted from the safety of their trench over to the Ottoman lines. "Go to your own province . . . Let us be friends." In Patras—where many of the Muslim garrison were villagers from the Morea who spoke Greek and Albanian—there were constant conversations between defenders and besiegers. One day a "Turk" told some of the Greeks they should bring things to an end: each side should seize their own leaders—"we our great aghas and you yours—and kill them so that we can later escape the Franks. We want this unity." But then this "Turk" was a Muslim Albanian from Lala, and his ancestral home was only a few miles away. A few days earlier the Greeks had captured several Laliots after a failed sortie and instead of killing them, they had sent them back to Patras with their greetings to say they did not wish to fight them.[43]

A case from the siege of Argos has already been mentioned briefly. The Greeks who were holed up there, fighting the Ottoman army of Dramali Pasha against enormous odds, had begun conversations with some of the Albanian soldiers besieging them. One of the latter had got the Greeks to swear not to harm him if he approached their positions, and when he was close, he whispered to one of them that they did not have much food left and wanted to retreat safely back to Corinth since they knew the Ottoman navy was not going to come and resupply them. Unfortunately, he told them, the pasha was insisting on them staying so he could have the glory of capturing the castle. He suggested the Greek defenders depart through the lines quietly at night, making sure to pass his way: he gave his word his men would say nothing. Once they were gone, there would be nothing more to fight for and the Albanians could return north again as they wanted. It worked out and two days later, Fotakos tells us, they were all gone. In light of such episodes, which were common, it is not surprising that Ottoman commanders despaired of having to rely on Albanian troops; when some presented themselves to the Ottoman commander outside Thessaloniki, they were "ordered to retire, as their motives are received with suspicion, and their assistance not required." By 1824, the Porte had decided that its efforts to crush the Greeks had failed thus far because of over-reliance on Albanian levies.[44]

The Albanian contingents in the Ottoman forces were contracted to fight on a seasonal basis—a mode of war that everyone in the region took for granted but which often surprised or shocked outsiders. In conversation with one Albanian soldier in Damietta one evening in September 1827, a British traveler was struck by his mercenary attitude. The English paid best, the Albanian claimed; the French relied on pillage. But would you, the soldier was asked by an Arab cleric, "'draw your sword for a dog, for a Christian?' 'For no man who did not pay me,'" replied the Arnaout, evading the question. A Swiss philhellene got a similar crash course in Ottoman military financing from a Souliot refugee who had served Ali Pasha: "The pasha pays good wages. When he has money, he has soldiers, but if he remains without it, they all leave him."[45]

In the Greek revolution, the economics of soldiering were of fundamental importance, and it was not just the Albanians who had money on their minds. As Byron found, the Souliots were adamant about prompt compensation. But they were not exceptional. Even in a patriotic war, all fighters expected their rations (*gemeklikia*) and their pay (*loufen*) and were prepared to bargain hard. A Greek from Corfu who boasted he was planning to raise 1,000 men to march on Tripolitsa to see if there was anything to be had was asked whether he would not fight for Greece even if there was no prospect of enrichment, and he cheerfully admitted: "Oh, *la mia borsa è la mia patria* [My purse is my fatherland]."[46] The Peloponnesians liked to say it was especially the armed bands from central Greece that fought for hire, but they behaved much the same. "We'll follow you," a Peloponnesian chieftain assured the primate, "General" Andreas Londos, as he mustered his force. "[My kapetans] confirmed that they are ready to die with me, except that they suggest that since they have five hundred soldiers with them, they desire to know where they will get the wages later on and their rations (*yemeklikia*) . . . so that they will remain by my side."[47]

Both sides were essentially outsourcing recruitment to contractors and subcontractors who gathered men around them with the pledge of compensation. The difference was that the Ottoman pashas had behind them an imperial court with the capacity to send out cash in an emergency and this put the Greeks at an acute disadvantage: throughout the conflict, shortage of coin bedeviled the efforts of the Greek leaders to keep their men in the field. "This is what we should do," burst out the member of a powerful armatole clan at a meeting in Vrachori in December 1821. "None of us move without our pay [*loufen*]. First the *groschen* should rain down and then I'll move."[48] The local notables and the appointees of the so-called Greek government might protest, but an armatole's hold over his senior chieftains (*oplarchigoi*) or kapetans was secure only so long as they were paid.

George Waddington had been "surprised to observe how little real power, with all their insolence and parade of despotism, these Capitani possess over their subjects, in consequence entirely of their notorious avarice."[49] But avarice was not exactly the point. Like piracy, plunder was a source of income during an insurgency in which the so-called government needed to promise more than it could deliver in pay if it was to keep the war going. Underpaid and underfed, its soldiers needed to loot and steal to stay alive, which also made the war a rare opportunity for unauthorized enrichment. The armed bands that were driven by the Ottomans out of their Olympos homeland took over the islands of the Sporades and lived off their terrified inhabitants; gangs of Cretans did the same in places like Tinos and Tzia, not to mention across Crete itself. In the Mani, Mavromihalis's peacetime means of financing his position as bey—the collection at agreed-upon prices of local export crops with the right to sell them on—had collapsed in the war. Keeping his predominance and that of his family meant finding other means of paying his men, and with only the arid hills of the peninsula to return to, this meant looting, chiefly from the Greek peasants in the nearby plains. During Dramali Pasha's invasion in the summer of 1822, the Maniots scared their fellow Greeks onto the waiting boats on the shore south of Nafplion with shouts that the Turks were coming—and then plundered their belongings.[50]

Towns and the riches they promised were major magnets of wealth for the poor soldiers. When two British visitors met Dimitrios Ypsilantis in Tripolitsa during the summer of 1823, they found him more or less alone, as "his funds being low most of his followers had abandoned him, to be present at the sack of Corinth, where considerable booty was anticipated."[51] Corinth was basically reduced to rubble by the end of the war and Nafplion was looted at least three times; Tripolitsa fared no better. After the sack of 1821, the roads were crowded with peasants carrying "ironware, pitchers, old looms, jars." Some cut the feet off dead horses in order to take away their shoes. In 1823, Kolokotronis's "government" men were lodged there, eating and drinking at the townspeople's expense in return for nothing more than scraps of paper, honorifically termed "receipts," which promised the bearer eventual repayment by the authorities. In Arta, Greek soldiers tortured their own countrymen to force them to reveal hidden valuables and cut fingers off women to take their rings; later in Nafplion, Grivas's men held wealthy people in torture chambers in the fortress. The soldiers were back despoiling Argos as late as January 1833, long after the fighting with the Ottomans had ended.[52]

For most of the kapetans, who lacked the revenues from the land available to the prominent notables, extracting resources was basically what allowed them to keep a band of men together: loot recycled as wages. Ioannis Fousekis-Farmakis was a poor village boy who at the age of sixteen followed his youthful chieftain, Andritsos Safakas, into the service of Ali Pasha, and at eighteen had his own band of twenty men in the mountains of central Greece north of Nafpaktos. His log enumerates 107 clashes in which he took part between 1821 and 1830: Fousekis-Farmakis was wounded seriously four times and lost his brother and another seventeen close relatives. Even allowing for the exaggeration inherent in a document drawn up as a claim for compensation, Fousekis-Farmakis had evidently been in the thick of serious fighting. What is even more striking is that by the end of his service, he claimed to have spent 30,000 *grossia* of his own money on his men; he had certainly not possessed such a sum when he started. It was plunder that had brought in the cash that was then distributed as the wages of his followers, ensuring his rising status as a kapetan.[53]

What soldiers did with their surplus gains is not clear. If they could, they sent them to safety since there was always a high risk of their being stolen by someone more powerful. After the siege of Arta, thousands of Greek fighters deserted their leaders—many claiming their feet were sore—to carry back home what they had looted. After Tripolitsa was sacked, the Maniot men got their womenfolk to take the plunder back; the following year they themselves were heading home with loot plundered from Greeks fleeing Dramali Pasha. When Kolokotronis vainly tried to turn them around to fight, they said they were ill.[54]

For soldiers far from home, the obvious solution was to make wealth portable—hence the markets set up in the main camps for the sale of captives, silverware, or animals. Soldiers spent huge sums on money belts, fine clothes, and exquisitely worked weapons. A typical chieftain's kit comprised the following: a silver-mounted musket; a pair of silver-mounted pistols; a pair of cartridge boxes; a *fousekliki* (box for pistol cartridges); a *medoullari* (box for lubricating grease); five buckles for fastening around the waist; the *silaliki* (leather pouch); a yataghan with silver sheath and handle; a ramrod for the pistols; a knife with silver chain; a small box with the image of St. George embossed on its outside, containing relics and amulets; an Albanian sword with silver sheath; eight buckles for knees and ankles and four more for the sandals.[55]

Not much was spent on their shoes, which were strong, unadorned, made of leather, ideal for hard walking. But the weapons were another matter—especially the long curved swords, the lighter yataghan, pistols, and the musket known as the *kariofili*.[56] Luxury models featured inlays in mother-of-pearl, ivory, and silver. Petros Mavromihalis's yataghan had an ivory handle and Ottoman inscriptions on the blade; he also owned a fine Persian saber. Kolokotronis had a sword with an Islamic inscription confirming God's help for the believers in Muhammed, as well as a silver *kariofili* probably captured from Egyptian troops. A fabulous pair of especially fine silvered pistols studded with diamonds and worth 4,000 thalers had supposedly come from Egypt and passed through the hands of the bishop of Modon before Kolokotronis had his son relieve the unfortunate cleric of them. Later Theodorakis Grivas cheated Kolokotronis out of them in his turn and strutted around with them in a permanent display of one-upmanship.[57]

Soldiers always struggled to keep dirt at bay: one way to distinguish the Greeks from the Turks, a British commodore was told, when visiting a battlefield on Crete strewn with more or less identical corpses, was that the Turkish fustanellas were clean, since the men were garrisoned and their clothes had just been washed, whereas the Greeks had been in the field. Yet many Greek fighters were devotees of conspicuous consumption and acutely conscious of their appearance. Some wore their hair in a long ponytail, whereas others grew it down to their shoulders applying a daily mixture of scented oil, the ringlets cascading to a finely embroidered jacket, all buttons and silk thread in gold and purple, with a white shirt open to the chest. "His dress was accurately national but formed of the most costly materials, and covered with an abundance of braiding and embroidery; whilst his pistols and silver-mounted yataghan were of exquisite design and workmanship," wrote James Emerson on meeting the young eparch of Andritsaina in 1825. "Of his dress he was particularly vain and received with evident pleasure all the praises we bestowed upon it. On such occasions he usually arose, set forward his elbow, turned out his heel, and surveying himself from top to toe, replied with evident complacency, 'Why, yes our costume is certainly pretty.'"[58]

A time to get rich fast was also a time when fortunes could be lost as quickly. In Patras, the British consul was struck by the sight of a formerly wealthy agha of the town reduced to working as a day laborer to make ends meet. But it was not only Muslim members of the elite who faced impoverishment. The vice president of the first provisional government, Peloponnesian notable Athanasios Kanakaris who had been the last representative of the Morea to the Porte, is said to have used up much of his fortune for the revolution. The remarkable Mando Mavroyenous was the daughter of one of the great Phanariot dynasties, scion of the dominant family in the Ottoman Cyclades and the great-niece of Prince Nicholas Mavroyeni, dragoman of the imperial fleet and prince of both Moldavia and Wallachia. Highly educated and fluent in French and Italian, she armed ships and bands of men for the revolution from her own funds. She would die in poverty of typhoid in Paros, her birthplace, in 1848.[59]

Other families emerged from the war, however, no worse off materially and no less powerful: this was true of quite a few of the remarkably durable landowning clans from the Morea. If avarice was remarked upon as a feature of many of the most prominent newer men who had risen up through the fighting—men like Papaflessas and Ioannis Kolettis—this was perhaps because riches were even more important to them. Nikitaras was one chieftain who had a reputation for indifference to wealth and this was often remarked upon as something unusual. The ideal was to have money to spare but not to be in thrall to it. Asked what had brought him pleasure in life, Karaïskakis answered that he had married a beautiful woman when he was young, enjoyed much feasting, won fame, and "made as much money as I needed."[60] That was the key: what critics attributed to greed was often better understood as the process of accumulating the wealth needed to preserve a major chieftain's standing and his power. Kolokotronis was the most prominent example of a warrior whose avarice was widely reputed. In fact, according to his godson Rigopoulos who had the keys to the family coffers, he was not actually enormously wealthy—some diamond rings and a large pearl and some nice weapons, the fruit of the sieges of Tripolitsa, Corinth, and Nafplion, and coin. He kept Venetian florins in his belt but gave most of what he had to his eldest son, Panos, to look after; later he lived in modest retirement.

What riches did for Kolokotronis, as for others, was to open up the possibility of a key form of power politics—the marriage alliance. The revolution was a busy time matrimonially as its leaders married off their offspring, cementing new coalitions, and establishing bonds of trust across classes and regions. The apple of Kolokotronis's eye was his first-born boy, Panos, the old kleft's main hope for social advancement. Thanks to his parents' concern, Panos had been well educated in the Ionian Islands; later he took French lessons while commanding the garrison in Nafplion. When the powerful heads of the Zaimis and Londos clans met him, they admitted they were "wrong to have thought the whole Kolokotronis family are peasants [agroikoi]."61 Panos's wedding to Eleni, the sixteen-year-old daughter of the wealthy Spetsiot widow Bouboulina, was supposed to have signaled the Kolokotronis family's wartime ascent. In fact, it turned out to cause the "Old Man" nothing but headaches because shortly after Panos was killed in 1824, his youthful widow shocked everyone by returning alone to her native island and marrying again, this time to the upcoming young chieftain from western Greece, Theodorakis Grivas. This was an extraordinary and even scandalous event, not least because Grivas had been a friend of Panos Kolokotronis and a guest in the family home. Grivas was highly avaricious and he lost no time in demanding Eleni's dowry from her first marriage back from Kolokotronis; he even briefly detained the "Old Man" in an effort to extort the valuables from him. As the vendetta between the two status-conscious chieftains spiraled out of control, it turned into a clash between Peloponnesians and Rumeliots that—as we shall see—nearly destroyed the city of Nafplion.

Kolokotronis's unruly second son Gennaios complicated things still further. Attracted to the daughter of the wealthy and powerful head of the aristocratic Notaras family, he proposed to one of his kapetans that they should kill the father and abduct the girl. He was talked out of the harebrained idea, but when his father did arrange an equally important alliance—with the powerful Souliot Tzavellas clan—Gennaios was so disappointed when he set eyes on the bride-to-be that he took off on the day of their wedding. Kolokotronis had to send his secretary Rigopoulos after his son to remind him of the dangers that would face the town from dozens of extremely angry Souliots if the match was called off. "I told him that the young woman was pretty [kali] and he had been wrong about her appearance," recalled Rigopoulos, "and that even if she wasn't so beautiful, she wasn't ugly." This seemed to work and the reluctant groom returned, cementing the alliance between the two families.[62]

Kolokotronis even got his youngest son, Kolinos, engaged to the young daughter of the wealthy magnate Kanellos Deliyannis, despite the snobbery of her family and the disapproval of the former kapo Plapoutas, his cousin: "It is insupportable," Plapoutas rebuked him. "They will make a laughing stock of you, not to mention they consider themselves well-born and see us as *klefts* and peasants." He was probably right, but Kolokotronis needed the engagement to help smooth over the friction between his followers and Deliyannis's and perhaps too to win the social acceptance he craved; in the end the marriage never took place, but Kolinos did better still, marrying into the grand Phanariot Karatzas family, an example of the war's capacity to create a new kind of Greek elite out of the old class distinctions.[63]

Kolokotronis claimed the ultimate privilege of the powerful—to dress as he pleased, hence the deliberate and notorious plainness, not to say slovenliness, of his clothing. Together with his rough manners, his great roar in battle, and his undisguised contempt for his social betters, it was part of his reputation and his mystique. These things endeared him to later nationalist historians and have survived in the popular telling to this day. His admirers spend less time dwelling on his willingness to bully anyone who stood in his way, an equally indispensable part of the power of any chieftain. In the spring of 1824, as the first round of the civil war was heating up, he warned villagers near Corinth not to disobey him: if they did, he wrote, they would find that "the *kolokotronaioi* and the men of Karytaina [his homeland] would eternally seek vengeance that would overflow rivers of the blood of their men and women . . . Stay where you are and don't meddle." That was the voice of the regional warlord, ruthless and vindictive, rarely encountered on the page. Quick to anger, with a long memory for a slight, Kolokotronis cultivated a reputation for fierceness. In fact, as those close to him knew, his temper would blow over quickly and he shied away from spilling Greek blood. But other kapetans had no such inhibitions and beat, tortured, and even killed fellow Greeks who stood in their way.[64]

The truth was that thanks to the war, the armed chieftains as a class enjoyed enormous power over the villagers under them. In the areas under their control, they often saw themselves as the real authorities, and while they craved titles and formal recognition, in everyday matters they despised the provisional government and its servants. In the remote mountain region of Kravara, about forty miles north of Nafpaktos, we have the record of a notable protesting at the impromptu execution of a local man. "With what right and according to what law did you judge [him] and take his life?" he demanded of the armatole Andritsos Safakas. "If he was guilty, you should have sent him to the government and if he was to be executed, it should have been up to the law to do it not to whomever happened along . . . What kind of magnate am I, to stand by while they slaughter my peasants like pigs without being judged by the law? How should I put up with the great crimes that go on in this district? Everywhere else a little freedom exists but in Kravvari there is greater slavery than under the Turks?"[65] "How much did the country folk suffer—and from the Greeks, not the Turks," remembered Makriyannis, reflecting with some bitterness on how he and the other chieftains had been used in the civil war to wreak violence on the peasants of the Peloponnese. "How many graves had to be dug in Tripolitsa when Grivas and Kolokotronis's clan went there?"[66]

The rural population of the Greek lands was the foundation of the entire insurgency. Shepherds and farmers provided the fighters who followed their kapetans and chieftains, as well as the produce that largely kept them alive. Yet the armed bands, like the klefts before them, preyed on those who worked the land and not even the shepherds' notoriously fierce dogs could keep them away. One fighter says that in Attica, for instance, Gouras's bands looted the peasants "without restraint."[67] The dangers ordinary villagers faced at the hands of the enemy—including indiscriminate killing and enslavement—were of course more extreme still and terrifying violence was meted out on the civilian populations of Greek towns and villages on both sides of the Aegean by Ottoman soldiers who had been given carte blanche to wreak the sultan's vengeance on infidel rebels. There were cases in which villagers committed suicide by jumping off cliffs, or drowning themselves, or were killed by family members rather than fall into the enemy's hands.

Faced with this assortment of more or less deadly enemies, all of whom targeted civilian populations and their possessions, those living in the countryside became expert at flight. At the approach of armed strangers, they quickly headed up footpaths into the mountains to places of refuge such as monasteries, isolated plateaus, or caves like the one outside Argos used by many local people to store clothes and other valuables. Those unable to escape during an Ottoman raid might have to be left behind—the elderly, who were often expected to fend for themselves, and sometimes infants. Survivors describe reentering their villages after the troops had left and finding the headless corpses of their dead relatives in the streets—headless because Ottoman troops received a bounty for heads and ears. Once, Kolokotronis's men came upon babies, wrapped in their swaddling clothes, who had been left hanging in the branches of trees for several days; the invading army had passed through and their mothers had been obliged to leave them behind. The soldiers had tried to use the babies as bait to lure the women back, and when that had not worked, they had left them where they were. Some were dead; others were so thirsty that they had sucked their fingers bloody and raw. Giving them goat milk, Kolokotronis's men sounded their trumpet and he shouted into the woods that it was safe for their mothers to return. It is a rare reminder of the war's impact on children—otherwise mostly invisible in the sources.[68]

Many well-informed observers, from Sultan Mahmud II downward, were taken by surprise at the extraordinary stamina of the Greek population and their capacity to endure enormous suffering. Indeed, given the demographic and economic superiority of the Ottoman Empire, the scanty resources at the disposal of the insurgents and their disorganized mode of fighting, it is bewildering how the insurrection managed to survive: a much likelier outcome at the outset had surely been something along the lines of what had happened in the Danubian Principalities where the uprising lasted only a few months before the sultan reestablished his control. But as we have seen, in the principalities the rural population was not supportive of the insurgents whereas farther south they were. This support was enough to expose deep-rooted weaknesses in the Ottoman imperial system and indeed to precipitate a process of reform and change that would outlast the revolution itself. For the truth is that by 1821 the Ottoman Empire, for all its might, was itself in the throes of a multifaceted crisis—military, fiscal, and logistical. Facing threats on several fronts, from Jannina to the Persian border, where it was losing a war against the Qajars and their newly modernized troops, the sultan's once formidable armed forces had declined and successive efforts at military reform had failed. The result was that the massive resources at Mahmud II's disposal translated into unreliable formations under immense logistical strain. George Finlay, both fighter and historian, suggests the sultan had done well in the first year to confine the uprising to the regions south of Thessaly. Yet his means of achieving this—massive violence targeted at Greek populations—was in its way a confession of failure. It worked in some areas but not in others, and it brought costs of its own in terms of European pressure and economic dislocation. The sultan's calls for a kind of moral crusade to match the Greeks in zeal allowed some murderous hotheads the chance to wreak havoc and to justify massacre; but most Muslims in the empire could not see the point of it and soldiers largely fought for pay or plunder. If this was an effort to raise a popular army, it failed. If it was an indication of the sultan's lack of confidence in the established forces at his disposal, on the other hand, it was amply warranted.

Sultan Mahmud II's core problem was not ideological but fiscal. Historians tell us that taxes are the sinews of war; those of the Ottomans had been atrophying for the best part of half a century. The central imperial budget had been either in balance or surplus for much of the eighteenth century, but from the 1780s onward it had been slipping into the red. As a result, the total manpower of the imperial armies (around 100,000–120,000) and navy (30,000) remained unchanged across the century at a time when rival states were expanding both. There are no budget data for the 1820s—itself a symptom of the crisis facing the Ottoman state under Mahmud—but we do not need them to see what was happening. Central administration budget deficits were being largely financed by an unprecedented depreciation in the value of the imperial *kurush* over this period, starting around 1805 and accelerating precipitously between 1820 and 1825, when it lost more than half its value against the pound sterling.[69]

A second and related issue was the Ottoman government's sense of strategic vulnerability that crystallized in the moment of the uprising in the Danubian Principalities. The safety and provisioning of Constantinople was always the ultimate priority of the sultan's government and anticipating war with Russia throughout the summer months of 1821 and beyond, it was loath to deploy the fleet too far from the imperial capital for very long. This hesitation, combined with the catastrophic short-term impact of the loss of their Greek crews and their officers, helped put the struggle for mastery in the Aegean on a much more equal footing. The government in Constantinople became anxious about

committing resources to assert its authority over the islands of the archipelago, and the naval leadership in 1821–23 was hesitant to confront the
Greek fireships. If the navy was embroiled off the coast of the Peloponnese and the Russians attacked across the Black Sea, then Istanbul could
have faced ruin. The result was that fortresses still in Ottoman hands
could no longer rely on regular provisioning by sea. It also meant that any
effort to throw large land forces into the Peloponnese or southern Rumeli
would encounter logistical difficulties that would have been eased had the
Ottoman navy continued to dominate the seas: Dramali Pasha's defeat
was the proof. The Greek land forces were small, but they were based
close to their home districts, and more highly motivated since they were
fighting to defend themselves and their families.

The third factor was the Ottoman government's reliance upon Albanian levies, both Muslim and Christian. The Porte's scathing assessment
of the Albanians reflected bitter experience. Elmaz Bey had negotiated
during the siege of Tripolitsa in 1821 as an independent agent, concerned chiefly to get his men safely home. The Albanian aghas and their
men had simply abandoned Dramali Pasha outside Argos the following
summer. In the summer of 1823, Markos Botsaris's Souliots fell on a far
larger Ottoman force outside Karpenisi in central Greece, made up
largely of Albanian Catholics from the north, and put it to flight, leaving
hundreds dead on the battlefield before Botsaris himself was killed.
Around then, Omer Vryonis scuppered a rival pasha's efforts to assemble an army of Albanians around Preveza—a region that Omer felt came
under his authority. Later that year, the pasha of Skodra, the most important of the Albanian chieftains, advanced toward Mesolonghi but then
withdrew because St. Dimitrios's Day was approaching and his soldiers
insisted they return home in time for winter. The Ottoman pashas in
command knew who they were dealing with. Sayyid Pasha described the
Albanians in 1822 as a "repugnant people"; Khurshid Pasha regarded
them as treacherous. Mehmed Emin Pasha, who got virtually nothing
done in his year in command, thought that if the Albanians had wanted
to, the war against the Greeks could have been won quickly and reckoned that many of them still remembered Ali Pasha fondly. It is striking
that as late as 1822 Kolokotronis was writing to the Albanian beys, telling him it was their fault they had let "our old grandfather" (Ali Pasha)
be killed, and inviting them on his word (besa) to join the Greeks in the
Peloponnese against the Ottomans. To Yusuf Pasha, brilliantly defending

Patras, the only solution was to bring in new troops from around his home region of Serres in the north instead. But the truth of the matter, as one general after another had to admit, was that there was no alternative to deploying the Albanian beys and their forces.[70]

The weakness of the Ottoman government meant that its armies were cobbled together from whatever groups could be assembled by the pashas it put in charge. They were unwieldy conglomerations of more or less entrepreneurial units linked through chains of military contractors; the old feudal levies played less and less of a role. Because the campaigning season ran from March to October, there was a limited window of opportunity to put together an army, get it into the field, and achieve a decisive result before the coming of winter. Quarreling at the top made matters worse. Khurshid Pasha tried to undermine Dramali Pasha and had Yusuf Pasha sent away from Jannina. Mehmed Reshid Pasha could scarcely work with Omer Vryonis, whom he rightly mistrusted. The sultan interpreted these things as a lack of spirit among his generals. Appointing a new grand vizier at the end of 1823, Mahmud II explicitly noted that "the fact that the Morea matter has not till now reached a successful conclusion is evidently owing to the lack of commitment of my servants." It would, however, be more accurate to see it as the inevitable effect of his system of divide and rule. As we shall see, once he handed supreme command over to the Egyptians in the Peloponnese, and to Mehmed Reshid Pasha in Rumeli, the Ottoman campaigns were able to advance quickly beyond their gains of early 1822. This was the most sustained and most successful example of combined leadership in the entire war. It very nearly brought the sultan victory and showed what might have been done earlier.[71]

But if the Greek insurgency survived, it was not able to obtain a decisive and lasting victory either. The hit-and-run tactics its fighters employed on both land and sea were rational given their scarcity of manpower. Yet the war could not be won from the mountains alone nor by the raiding tactics employed by the fleet, which were anyway less and less effective as time went on. Even the fireship failed much more often than it succeeded. There was also a basic problem of leadership. Dimitrios Ypsilantis had the military training but was a political failure; Mavrokordatos's political nous was not combined with a strategic sense; the chieftains who flourished in the hill warfare of 1821–22 could not rise above the factionalism and regionalism of their upbringing. Petros Mavromihalis's brother Ioannis, who liked to be known as "the king of Sparta," was notorious for never liking to leave the Mani; Kolokotronis felt similarly about the Peloponnese, and virtually the only thing that could get Lazaros Koudouriotis to even contemplate departing his native Hydra was the occasional fear of attack by mobs. Notables were too concerned about their regional power to make national leaders.

But behind the want of an overall strategic direction lay a deeper and more fundamental problem—that of revolutionary authority. Saint Dimitrios's day on October 26, 1821, was Prince Ypsilantis's name day and there was a celebratory meal at which the Greek notables came to pay their respects. When they arrived, they found to their surprise that among the guests was Kiamil Bey, the wealthy Muslim landowner they had captured at Tripolitsa the previous month. As the Greeks began to argue over dinner about the Turks, about their tyranny and their fate, a slightly drunk Kiamil Bey spoke up—in Greek, a language he spoke comfortably:

> Notables and kapetans, Turkey is not lost because of the loss of Tripolitsa and our capture. May God aid you, and may you prosper. I advise you only, as your friend even if I am a Muslim, to cease your arguing, to recognize a single leader to govern you. Believe in what I tell you, that all of you come to my chambers wanting to ask me about riches and gold. I cannot deny that I have plenty in Corinth but which among you should I confide in when you yourselves cannot trust one another and can I pass on the secret to one of you when he lacks the strength to guard me from another of his comrades? I say to you again, that I thank you all for sparing my life and that you treat me as one of you, however I counsel you as soon as possible to establish an authority, so that I can help you.[72]

Because an insurgency, by definition, emerges as a challenge to authority, it generally takes time to establish leadership structures of its own. Thus the question of who had the right to lead the Greeks was inevitably present from the start. The Filiki Etaireia had recruited on the basis of the fiction that the czar would lead the revolt, and when a face was given to its so-called Unseen Authority (*Aorati Archi*), it was that of Alexandros Ypsilantis. But the czar wanted no part of it and made that publicly known, and Ypsilantis's aura was diminished by his defeat, flight, and imprisonment. His brother Dimitrios claimed to represent him and the Etaireia to the Greeks in the Morea, but by then it was no longer enough. Turkish troops might believe that "Kolli Kotron" (Kolokotronis) was the "principal bey of the infidels," but this was not true either. Thanks to Mavrokordatos, the Greeks became accustomed to deploying the European language of government. But it would be a brave historian who claimed any of the so-called provisional governments that emerged from 1822 onward had anything resembling a monopoly of the use of armed force.[73]

On the contrary, what emerged both on land and at sea was a set of informal and poorly organized armed groupings that reflected a pervasive lack of social trust. This explains why family and locality mattered so much. Even more than marriage alliances, kinship ties generated trust in a world where this was in short supply: Ioannis Fousekis-Farmakis mentions seventeen relatives in his band—and those were just the ones who died. Grivas, a more powerful chieftain, forced to cut back his unit late in the war, proposed keeping just 200 on his payroll since they were "mostly relatives" (*oi perissoteroi syggeneis*). Kolokotronis's ambitions for his family, his former aide Fotakos tells us, were always getting in the way, "because he wanted to have his sons and other relatives at the head of the armed formations, and while they were courageous and fond of fighting, they were incapable of directing the soldiers in war or controlling them."[74]

The other basis of trust was locality, and most bands were made up of men from the same village or island clustered around kapetans and notables with the funds or the prestige to recruit and lead them. Yet they were generally reluctant to leave their region for very long or even to accept the command of a chieftain unquestioningly. "No one wanted to subordinate himself to another if he did not know him," Fotakos tells us. Each village had its own kapetan, if not more than one: "Lots of kapetans and not many men," is his pithy summary. And although the captains might recognize an overall chieftain to fight for, and beyond him even a regional commander in chief with the government's imprimatur—a title both Kolokotronis and Karaïskakis enjoyed at various points in the war—their autonomy and desire to be individually recognized in collective decisions was strong. When Karaïskakis won his great victory at Arachova near the end of the war and sent the government a triumphant message, it bore not only his signature but those of more than ninety band chiefs with him, because they all insisted on their moment of glory being recognized. In such circumstances it is not surprising that large Greek victories over significant forces were rare; rather, it is astonishing that anything more than local ambushes ever materialized. The democratic spirit was genuine among the Greeks but it made military organization impossible and led to an acute sense of rivalry that was one of the main factors in prolonging the fighting. It made it harder for the Greeks to win, even if arguably it also made it harder for them to be defeated in a single blow. Writing in 1826, a former participant noted the drawn-out quality of the conflict; it was, he wrote, one in which he could not "see any possibility of a termination, in the total absence of any man, or men, capable of directing it."[75]

Already by 1823, the two sides seemed locked in a never-ending struggle in which neither could defeat the other. The Greeks dominated the Morea but they had failed to drive the Ottomans out of the few remaining fortresses they still held, let alone managed to get the empire to sue for peace. The Ottomans could mount campaigns on an annual basis, but lacking a regular army or properly commanded navy, these could not reestablish the empire's authority. Both sides therefore began casting around for allies whose contributions might be decisive. In the Ottoman case this meant vassals such as the pasha of Egypt, Mehmed Ali, and his recently modernized armed forces; in the Greek case this meant help from the great powers and peoples of Europe. Of course in soliciting such support, both the sultan and the Greeks opened themselves up to a compromise victory—one whose spoils they would have to share in accordance with the wishes of their allies.

Yet in one critical respect their situations were not alike—and that was time. As the British foreign minister George Canning underlined to his minister in Constantinople in the summer of 1823, things had changed in Europe in just a year or two: with Spain, Naples, and France secured for the Bourbons, Metternich was losing ground, the Holy Alliance was weakening, and "the Porte may not have much time to lose." By that winter, the sultan was conscious that European diplomacy, which had so far remained respectful of his right to handle the uprising, might change course if the Greeks continued to hold out: Russia, in particular, whose czar was torn between supporting the Holy Alliance and defending the Orthodox Christians of the Ottoman Empire, could not be expected to remain aloof indefinitely. The Ottomans needed to bring the rebellion to an end without the bloodshed that had failed to date and that risked further alienating powerful European states and throwing into question the empire's treatment of its peoples. On the other hand, the Greeks needed only to avoid defeat, allowing time to do its work on the public opinion of Europe.[76]

PART 2

INTERNATIONAL INTERVENTIONS

*Mavroyeni looked thoughtful. After a little pause:
"You mistake, Anastasuis," replied he, "in thinking
the Greek of Constaninople different from the Greek
of Chio. Our nation is everywhere the same. The
same at Petersburg as at Cairo; the same now that it
was twenty centuries ago."*

I stared in my turn . . .

Thomas Hope, *Anastasuis* (London, 1819), 83

Six hundred leagues are no great distance, now that
liberalism *navigates with full sails and is making the
tour of the world.*

Gazette de France, May 26, 1821

10

KNIGHTS ERRANT

The term "Philhellene" may not mean very much today but in the early twenties of the nineteenth century it was a word to conjure with. It meant a man, generally a young man, who was ready and eager to give up ease, custom, money-getting, and go overseas to fight a savage foe among savage mountains, all for love of freedom, and of that dear land which was next in his affections to his own, the land of the imperishable Ideal.

L. E. Richards, ed., *The Letters and Journals of Samuel Gridley Howe* (Boston, MA, 1906), 21–22

George Jarvis was twenty-three years old, the son of an American consular agent in the town of Altona, near Hamburg on the river Elbe, when the news reached him of the Greek revolt. He would end up going to Greece and staying longer than almost any other volunteer, becoming "a complete Greek in dress, manners and language," fighting his way through some of the most critical battles of the war and dying a much-mourned war hero in Argos in 1828. But it all began seven years earlier, when he left home one November evening with a companion, a young sailor from Hamburg. Shouldering their baggage and weapons—their pistols, swords, and daggers alone weighed some thirty pounds—the two men trekked through the moonlight, crossed the Elbe, and continued their long journey southward on foot and by cart until they reached the French port of Marseille.[1]

Jarvis and his companion were not the only ones heading south. "It seems to me it has become quite the fashion lately," wrote a Swiss journalist in September 1821, "for young men to depart from France, Spain,

Italy and Germany for foreign armies. From such parts go young men, trouble-makers, to Greece, to fight alongside the Greeks in their struggle against the Turks."[2] On a tour of Europe, the young English lawyer Charles Tennant noted:

> . . . almost the whole of the Continent, and particularly Germany, at this time exhibited extraordinary fervor in the case of the Greeks against the Turks, and in different parts of the country I had met with numerous companies of young men on foot, with knapsacks on their backs, on their way to Marseille, there to embark for Greece. These parties appeared to be comprised chiefly of young German recruits and runaway students, and from the boisterous enthusiasm which they generally manifested, it was my endeavor always to avoid them as much as possible.

Bumping into one group in a coffeehouse in Lausanne, Tennant found himself in the midst of a violent argument after he suggested Britain might back Turkey for fear of Russia; things grew so heated that he retired to bed early, bolted his door and placed his pistols by his bedside.[3]

The surge in Europe's sympathy for the Greek cause was one of the most remarkable political and cultural phenomena of the post-Napoleonic era. Rooted in a tradition of educated veneration for ancient Greece, philhellenism metamorphosed in these years into an expression of a new kind of politics—international in its range and affiliations, popular in its origins, romantic in its sentiments, and often revolutionary in its goals. Supporting the Greeks became a way of signaling disapproval of the continent's conservative masters and their intolerance of the rights of nations. Volunteers who went to Greece were the first in a long line—stretching ahead more than a century to the Spanish Civil War—of fighters willing to sacrifice even their lives for the freedom of others. There were probably around one thousand of them and they included Finns, Danes, Poles, Swedes, and Sardinians, a real Bonaparte and an ersatz Washington and at least one African American—James Williams from Baltimore—though the largest number came from the German lands, France, and Switzerland. Although there were many points of departure, the most popular was Marseille, and the sailing of the *St. Lucie* in October 1821, carrying more than forty German, Italian, French, and Swiss volunteers, was the first of the major expeditions from the port. Eight more vessels left during 1822 and by the time the French authorities clamped down at the end of that year, somewhere over 350 philhellenes—more than half of all those reaching Greece in those months—had left Marseille.[4]

With the first reports of the uprisings in the principalities and the Morea, philhellenic committees had sprung up in places like Darmstadt, Basel, Munich, Zurich, Leipzig, and the most important—Stuttgart— under the leadership of lawyers, poets, clergymen, and professors. These towns were hotbeds of support, fueled by widespread resentment at the censorship, political monitoring, and the heavy-handed policing that had been imposed on them since the Napoleonic Wars to stamp out any sign of German nationalism. They had large student populations and influential local elites who revered the classics, and they had large numbers of educated people discontented with Austro-Russian hegemony over Europe. With limited funds and rudimentary means at their disposal—in Geneva, appeals for support were handwritten and nailed up on doors rather than printed, so as to circumvent censors—these committees raised money, passed on information, and supported volunteers as they passed through.[5]

As early as the summer of 1821, French diplomats in the Levant were already worrying about "adventurers of all nations" who were headed, wrote the consul in Corfu, for Greece, "like madmen into the midst of certain exhaustion, destitution and human suffering." Fearing that their presence would lead to reprisals against other Europeans in the empire, both consuls and merchants requested that such ne'er-do-wells be prevented from coming.[6] But officials in France decided they could not legally do this and since many of those leaving were radicals or Bonapartists, they saw good arguments for letting them go anyway.[7] Soon the number multiplied. In the first week of October, the prefect of the Bouches-de-Rhône, Count Villeneuve-Bargemont, noted the arrival of "a remarkable number of individuals, coming from different parts of Germany, wandering the streets of Marseille and attracting attention."[8] The scale of the phenomenon was suddenly becoming clear.

The center of France's Levant trading community, Marseille lived from business with the Mediterranean. Its merchants had suffered a serious downturn during the Napoleonic Wars, envied the profits made by Greek shippers, and disliked the thought that independence might increase their dominance. They were thus not overly sympathetic to the new arrivals whom they dubbed tongue-in-cheek the "Greece-savers" (*les sauvent la Grèce*). Some of these brought their own funds and stocked up for the journey: a trunk, pipe stem, overcoat, handkerchiefs, napkins, a cummerbund, a comb, a rifle, pistols, a gunpowder pouch, gunpowder, a drinking glass, and a blanket made up one philhellene's shopping list in the town.[9] Many, however, were already out of funds by the time they arrived, having mistakenly assumed, hoped, or been told that their care would be organized in Marseille. In fact, most Greek merchants did not want to know anything about them, the Swiss consul declined to help, and so (not surprisingly) did the Ottoman consul whom—because he was a Greek—they had mistaken for the organizer of the expeditions. On being told the truth, one of the volunteers responded—probably only half-humorously: "Fine, pay us and we'll go off to fight for the Turks against the Greeks, since war is what we do [*notre métier*]."[10]

In search of fame on the glorious stage of world history, they were not men to adopt a low profile. Waiting for passage, they spent their days at the Café d'Espagne, the Grand Café des Italiens, and the popular Café du Parc, which the enterprising owner quickly renamed the Ypsilanti. There was a good deal of drinking and plenty of time to read: a Danish medical student brought Sallust and Cicero; Byron's poems and the *Travels of Anacharsis* were popular. As highly conscious of image and dress as anyone in that dandyish age, they came clad in a bewildering range of outfits, a testimony to their diverse origins and outlooks. The French veteran Mignac arrived in Marseille, dressed ostentatiously in the uniform of a captain of hussars and accompanied by some Germans he had recruited who attracted attention with their shaggy sheepskin coats, their long swords, and prominently belted daggers, appearing to some like "ancient Teutons." Veterans of the Napoleonic Wars displayed their medals and paraded around the streets of the port in various threadbare uniforms; the students held on to their black gowns, at least until obliged to sell them. Many bore red ribbons, the insignia of radicalism, on their hat or epaulets or chest. One combative veteran who attracted the authorities' always ready suspicions wore a tattered overcoat adorned by a gigantic ribbon. George Jarvis was arrested for having a little cross pinned to his hat: when questioned by the police, he told them "this sign is found very often in America," eventually admitting it signified his intention of "devoting himself to the Greek cause."

The prefect worried at the presence of these men whom he described as "avid for novelty and enemies of repose."[11] They were nothing more than sensation-seekers desperate for a cause. Touchy, obsessed with rank and titles, and prone to duels, they were "unquiet" and "turbulent spirits" led astray by their "ardent imagination." There were improvident fortune-seekers like the Strasbourg officer who had "dissipated his inheritance and was looking for opportunities to change his situation."[12] Some were minors running away from home. The father of a law student from Col-mar wanted his boy stopped from leaving France. The son of a local banker headed for the Morea to flee his creditors but was unable to endure nights sleeping in the open air, nourished only by corn bread and a few wild herbs, and was home within three months.[13]

The authorities worried about the subversive potential of this mass-ing together of Italian constitutionalists, liberty-loving Poles, Germans, Neapolitans, and Piedmontese, for the times were turbulent and there had already been armed uprisings and insurrections in Grenoble and Lyon. Knowing that French conspirators, in the spirit of the Italian Car-bonari, were working on plans to overthrow the unpopular King Louis XVIII, the police could scarcely have been expected to ignore the large groups gathering in Marseille. Indeed, in January 1822 they cracked open an anti-Bourbon plot whose organizers had been fishing among the volunteers, sending them funds while trying to persuade them to "march for liberty" in France rather than abroad.[14]

The philhellenes were almost all young men under twenty-five, many of them students. But there were plenty of exceptions. In a dark café in the backstreets of Vostitsa in the spring of 1822 the German volunteer Johann Daniel Elster encountered a young boy, fully armed, drinking wine with the others: Elster was astonished when he realized the boy was really a fiery Spanish woman, Madame Toricelli, who had accom-panied her husband to Greece. She was unusual though not unique as a female fighter.[15] But the social mix was vast and besides the students one found more or less the entire span of the lower and middling strata of European society with a few aristocrats sprinkled among them: watch-makers and farmers; blacksmiths and barbers; a French fencing teacher and a Dutch dancing master; chemists, surgeons, and painters. A Bavar-ian china manufacturer hoped to open a factory in Greece; a merchant from Luxembourg wanted to extend his business there.[16]

Most numerous of all were the former soldiers. Of the 2.5 million veterans of the Napoleonic Wars in Europe, more than 1.5 million were French and many of those heading for Greece had fought in the Grande Armée before finding themselves deprived of a position or a pension by the Bourbon Restoration: they included figures like the Auvergnat Maurice Persat, who after fighting at Waterloo had seen action first with Simón Bolívar in South America and then in Naples, and François Graillard, who had battled his way through Austria, Prussia, and Russia before heading to Greece where he settled down after independence, ending up as founder of the national gendarmerie.[17] But they were not only Frenchmen by any means: Frank Abney Hastings was a veteran of Trafalgar living in France and learning the language when he seized on the idea of serving in Greece and ended up commanding the first steam frigate for the Greeks. A Pole had followed Napoleon to Elba and joined in revolutions in Piedmont and South America; there were Germans who had fought on the French side, and several Italians. Some of the volunteers venerated the emperor, others had fought against him—but all of them had grown up in his shadow.[18] It is necessary therefore to say something about the man who even in his passing marked the Greek struggle more than anyone else.

"Thus terminates in prison and exile the most extraordinary life known to political history," trumpeted *The Times* from London in that summer of 1821. The news of Napoleon's death in British captivity on the remote island of St. Helena reverberated across Europe: it happened on May 5, but the story took two months to reach the continent and the extraordinary atmosphere that followed was remembered for decades. Alfred Lemaitre recalled the strange anxious calm that befell France, the news seeming to mark the ending of "young men's hopes of emulating their fathers" on the field of battle, condemning them instead to a life of meaningless inaction under the gouty, elderly, and reactionary Bourbon king Louis XVIII. It was, wrote Lemaitre, at this very moment that the Romantic imagination seized on Byron, Shakespeare, and Walter Scott, dreaming only "of somber adventures, kidnappings, big daggers, frenzied love and prodigious exploits, one against ten"—and of rescuing the Greeks from Muslim barbarism: "the ground was too well prepared in France for the idea of coming to the help of an oppressed nation not to have electrified the great child enthusiasts of the time."[19]

It is perhaps difficult now to understand the posthumous impact of the French emperor—what Chateaubriand called the "despotism of his memory"—or how far and for how long his shadow stretched across Europe. Sightings of him were reported, supposedly accompanied by an astonishing array of troops, across much of Europe for years after. A recent history of French psychiatric institutions reveals that when Napoleon's remains were returned to France in 1840, no fewer than fourteen bogus emperors were admitted into care; there had been others before that and would be more in the following decade.[20] The news of his passing was, even more than Byron's death three years later, something that unified Europe, testified to the existence of a new public consciousness across the continent, and invested the struggle unfolding in its southeastern corner with a wider significance. "Written on Hearing the News of the Death of Napoleon," Shelley's poetic response, was sent by the poet to his publisher at the end of 1821 along with his manuscript of *Hellas*, his reaction to news of the revolution in Greece, with instructions to publish the two works together. "The two most brilliant luminaries of the nineteenth century," wrote Louise Belloc in 1825, "are Bonaparte and the Greeks."[21] She contrasted the dead emperor whose meteoric rise left nothing behind him with "the patient courage of an entire people determined to found their national existence anew." Others—including members of the emperor's own family—saw the Greek uprising on the contrary as the fulfillment of Napoleonic radicalism: we should not be surprised that at least one young relative of the emperor—his nephew Prince Paul Marie Bonaparte—died as a volunteer in Greece, nor that another nephew, the future Napoleon III, was himself an enthusiastic philhellene who had to be dissuaded several times from heading off to fight. They too were caught up in the mood. Much later, in the 1860s, the great French critic Sainte-Beuve noted of that moment: "We were young, we needed a public object for our enthusiasm: and one presented itself before us." In his words:

> To go to Greece . . . this was, for many tired souls, sated with everything, a moral awakening, the healing of unreal passions, of indeterminate boredom; for the old soldier of the great wars, it was to find again an assignment worthy of his not yet rusty sword; for the young man prey to cowardly idleness and to a gnawing sense of worthlessness, the unhoped-for realization of a beautiful dream, this time within grasp and palpable; it was baptism and consecration for a great cause.[22]

One thing above all imbued the philhellenes with the luster of heroism: they were volunteers. No one forced them to go and risk their lives; they set aside family and friends and home, and chose to go because they were free and wished others to be free as well. Hence the flamboyance of their dress, the extraordinary variety of their uniforms. Driven by sentiment rather than dogma, they believed in the cause, and they wished others to believe in it. Yet beyond that—and this was the movement's strength and the secret to its durability—there was no ideological uniformity: philhellenism brought together republicans and royalists, radical secularists and avowed Christians. Classicism fused with romantic medievalism and the language of crusade was used quite widely: many felt the allure of the chivalric epics. Several decades later, the French writer Edmond About would recall how "during the war of independence, the most ardent youth of Europe ran to the defense of Greece. These 'friends of the Greeks,' these *philhellenes*, were the last knights errant." Yet somehow these crusading visions coexisted in the minds of many of the students with ideas of freedom, equality, and the duties of humanity.[23]

Greece was in fact not the only destination that some contemplated. Major Nils Aschling, a Swedish volunteer from a wealthy family, was persuaded to go to Greece rather than revolutionary Naples: what mattered to him was simply "to be counted among those who strove for freedom and for a just cause." The old soldier Persat told the Paris chief of police he planned to go abroad: the policeman recommended Greece rather than Spain or the Americas. Former Lieutenant Lefebvre said he was headed not only for adventure but because he was in "the lucrative Cossacking business" (*le métier lucratif de cosaque*). Yet for most of them, the choice of Greece could not really be accidental, not given its outsize presence in European thought. "We are all Greeks," the poet Shelley wrote in 1821. "Our laws, our literature, our religion, our arts have their root in Greece." Independence struggles in South America attracted Europe's attention but lacked the historical and cultural allure of the Hellenic idea, or the attractions of a relatively short voyage in the Mediterranean.[24]

One of the most unusual passengers traveling from Marseille was a young Greek deaf mute of noble birth returning home. He carried with him a letter of recommendation from the committee in Stuttgart stating the bearer to be "Mr. Ziziokaeto Aivpso, a native of Argos"; it was dated March 14, 1822, and signed by "Albertios Schottios" (Albert Schott) and the other leaders of the Stuttgart philhellenic society. As he made sure his companions knew, the young man was not merely Greek, he was of princely birth from the legendary town of Argos. Before making his way with some volunteers to Marseille, he had lodged at a home for the deaf and dumb in Stuttgart, where he had been examined and his story checked. He aroused pity along the journey, and he was showered with gifts. With his companions, however, he could be difficult, flying into violent rages. Once in the Peloponnese, landing after twenty-three days at sea, they began to make inquiries and learned that no one had heard of him or his family. Greeks they met in Tripolitsa remarked he could not cross himself in the Greek fashion and then, approaching Argos, his companions were astonished when he broke into fluent German and the truth came out: "Prince Aivpso" or "Alepso" was really a nineteen-year-old watchmaker's son from Weissenburg. Having fled from home and wandering as a vagabond through Germany, he had been robbed and decided his best hope was to pretend to be a deaf mute. Because his brother was indeed deaf and dumb, he was able to fool the staff in Stuttgart, and he had played along when someone had speculated he might be Greek. Shown a map of ancient Greece so that he could indicate where he had come from, his attention had been caught by the town of Argos because it was highlighted in large letters: it seemed important and worthy of a prince. When local classicists came to test his knowledge of the language, he made up characters that they took to be modern versions of the ancient script. As the story gathered details, he found more and more people believed it and treated him with respect.[25]

His adventure could be seen as just one of the many tales of fraud, imposture, and philhellenic credulity that abounded in those years. In fact, it perfectly illustrates the blend of passion and ignorance that characterized the entire volunteer phenomenon. The liberal Stuttgart worthies whose noble sentiments drove them to work on behalf of the Greeks were so proud of their learning that they drew up letters of recommendation in Greek, signed their names in Greek, and imagined a world in which ancient Greek heroes came back to life. They were familiar with Argive princes from mythology even though in the real world any Greek living in the Peloponnese could have told them there had been no princes in Argos for centuries. They could have told them too that all difficulties of transliteration aside, there was no way that "Ziziokaeto Aivpso" could be a real Greek name: it was nonsense masquerading as Greek. Yet none of these basic truths had, it seemed, come into play before the volunteers reached Greece itself.

What is true today was even truer then: for Europeans, the familiarity they felt toward Greece came from their knowledge of the ancients. This was the other Greece, the Greece to whom, in the words of another philhellene, "Europe owes her civilization, her arts and even her spirit."[26] That other Greece was never more sought after than in the years of what the traveler Edward Dodwell called "this dilapidating mania." Obtained with the aid of judicious bribes to high-ranking Ottoman officials, the friezes of temples in Aigina, Bassae, and Figaleia were being carted away by European travelers and diplomats and auctioned off; Elgin's marbles—which Dodwell witnessed being removed from the Parthenon—had just been purchased by the British government. A French diplomat bought a statue from a peasant on the island of Milos and presented it to King Louis XVIII in the very month the Greek revolt in the Morea broke out: the Venus de Milo caused a permanent sensation. In Munich, Leiden, Paris, and London new museums were bringing the Greeks into the public eye.[27] Quatremere de Quincy, an official at the Académie des Beaux-Arts and professor of archaeology, was struck by the "passion for discovery" that was in the air.[28]

For hellenists like de Quincy, the classical ideal was as fixed and meaningful as ever: the ancients provided a standard to be imitated and an art that was "grand, noble and dignified in its character."[29] It had nothing to do with the Greeks of the present at all. From the vantage point of the royalist connoisseur, the ancients were an object of passive contemplation and European guardianship: Greece was the business of museums and galleries while the living Greeks were seen as a disappointing irrelevance if not a nuisance. The philhellenes believed in Greece just as ardently but approached it very differently and in a more radical spirit. The true miracle of ancient Greece for them was that it had suddenly come back to life and provided a moral and political compass for their own actions: Greece for them meant the example of heroic self-sacrifice, of disrupting the established order and overthrowing the bonds of tyranny. For such men, the modern Greeks were worthy successors to the ancients—to be admired for their passionate love of liberty, their love of laws, and their heroic endurance rather than their static beauty.

Reared on the classics, and keen to see the lands where the heirs to the ancient world were bringing back its glories, volunteers thus approached the Peloponnese with a thrill of anticipation that it is hard for a more jaundiced age to recapture. A young artillery officer, dedicating his work to *la jeunesse européenne*, was moved to peroration: "Greetings! O woodlands of Arkadia, land beloved by the Gods, mountains the refuge of Oreades, dells beloved by shepherds, scented plateaux where Pan, Dryads and nymphs frolic to the chants of innocent Bucolic!"[30] Disembarkation brought the first contact with reality. The young German Francis Lieber watched the sun rise over the Peloponnese and saw the snowcapped mountains as their ship moored outside the Bay of Navarino. After some smaller craft came out toward them to ask for news, a couple of English officers rowed over from a man-of-war in the port and clambered aboard: "[They] gave us a very disheartening account of the condition of the Greeks, and described them as great rogues. They pitied us, they said, and declared that we were certainly going to our destruction." Lieber and his comrades wrote these words off as of no account: they had been uttered, after all, by British officers, many of whom were believed to be notoriously unsympathetic to the Greek cause.[31] But there were other unheeded warnings, and they become a kind of trope in the contemporary memoirs. There were the generous Greek kapetans in a grove outside Kalamata who dined newcomers from Europe and told them not to go to Tripolitsa as Prince Dimitrios Ypsilantis was weak, but recommended that they stay and fight with them; there was the officer warned to keep his money out of sight and always to carry a pistol and dagger; there was the Egyptian-based Greek who warned one volunteer not to trust the Moreots but to head back to Navarino with him and his companions.[32]

Once ashore, most of the volunteers quickly found themselves in a different world from any they had imagined, one that had little or nothing to do with their ancient reveries. Kalamata was the main port in the south, and several boats headed directly for it. It was known to be under Greek control because it was from there that Petros Mavromihalis had issued a high-flown appeal for international help that March on behalf of his "Spartan fighters" and the "Messenian Assembly," a stirring appeal to classical sympathies that was widely published in Europe's press. As a result, many of the volunteers who arrived there expected to find a Greek army made up of Spartan warriors, and a political leadership in the form of a senate or assembly.[33] What they found instead was a large number of tough-looking, armed Maniots sitting about in cafés. Francis Lieber and his comrades, having braved swollen rivers and storms, found someone who spoke French and asked where the Senate was, only to be told that "he knew no more about it than anyone in Kalamatia [*sic*]."[34] The town commandant turned out to be a former merchant from Trieste who had fled to escape his creditors. One volunteer recollected his amazement: "He was old, short and very fat. He was dressed in black, with a black cap, on which were a death's head and the words Liberty or Death." The commandant did what he could to find the newcomers lodgings and food, but accommodation generally meant sleeping on a floor, and food consisting of black bread and boiled mutton.[35] A German artillery officer noted his "astonishment and amazement" at how different things were to Europe; "everything seemed so new to me": the mules and camels, the turbans, even the heat. As he and his shipmates, tired and worn out after eighteen days at sea, marched in a small column into town, in their motley variety of uniforms and civilian dress, a drummer leading the way, camels carrying their baggage, they must have made, he recollected, a "comical" sight.[36]

The Europeans who assembled in Kalamata became part of an important experiment. Thirty-one-year-old Joseph Baleste was a Greek-speaking French infantry captain, whom Dimitrios Ypsilantis had met in Trieste. Unlike most of the volunteers, Baleste could speak fluent Greek and had a good idea of what awaited him: he had grown up in Chania on Ottoman Crete—his father was a French merchant and his mother was Greek—and he had fought in Napoleon's army. As part of his effort to establish the Etairist leadership of the revolution in the southern Peloponnese, Ypsilantis had given Baleste the rank of colonel and ordered him to create a regular force around the volunteers in Kalamata that would give the prince his own troops and emancipate him from reliance on the Greek chieftains. The start was promising. The five hundred men of the Baleste regiment were fitted out with the black uniforms of the Etaireia, equipped with rifles with bayonets, and carried the phoenix as their symbol. They trained hard in French infantry techniques and had an early success when they beat back an attempted landing near Kalamata by the Turkish navy in August. However, this triumph aroused the envy and anxiety of the kapetans, who began to spread rumors that Ypsilantis had come to establish a dictatorship backed by the power of a European military. From the walls of Tripolitsa, the Turks taunted the Greeks: "You will now be made soldiers of, and be dressed like the Franks, and be more slaves than ever."[37]

The experiment to form a regular army—always implicit in the Etaireia's plans—enjoyed excellent leadership and the memoirs of participants speak highly of Baleste and his abilities. But it had no real logistical support and it suffered from one fatal weakness. Unlike the leaders of the Moreot bands, Ypsilantis lacked the money and provisions required to keep his men. As early as mid-July, his volunteers were told they would need to bring their own weapons and warned they could not anticipate regular pay. By the end of the summer, the fragility of their situation had become clear.[38] When a newly arrived Italian reached Tripolitsa shortly after the sack of the town and encountered some of Baleste's European officers, he was struck by their worn clothes and their air of ill health. The veterans laughed at him:

"We too," said they, "came to Greece well dressed, though we are now in the greatest poverty, and have only the most squalid clothing; wait a little and you will share our fate. At the very moment when we thought we should recover what we had lost we were sent on a tour round the mountains of the Morea; most days we were without food. Our soldiers are almost all naked and barefooted; our rations consist of the half of a small black loaf; our men die daily of want; such is the state of the Frankish battalion. So long as we had money, or things which we could sell, we managed to subsist tolerably well, but now that we are obliged to depend on our rations and pay, our situation is become dreadful."[39]

For their plight, many of Baleste's men blamed Kolokotronis—who did not disguise his antipathy to the regulars. Baleste went so far as to secretly recommend killing him: "No revolution can possibly succeed without bloodshed," he told Ypsilantis:

You are beloved by the people; all the Europeans are with you: you see how Colocotroni treats you ever since the capture of Tripolitza, where he took money enough to have emancipated Greece. Now is the moment: if you will only give me your permission, before the morning Colocotroni and his satellites shall be no more. You will take possession of Colocotroni's riches; you will rid the world of a villain, and will put it in your power to raise troops, and to secure the independence of your country.

Ypsilantis was reluctant to take such a drastic step and refused. But it was hard to deny Baleste's fundamental point that the only soldiers upon whom the prince could rely were the 400 half-starved men under his command. Having lost Kolokotronis's respect, Ypsilantis now began to lose his men's as well.[40] Baleste's regiment took part in two more operations—a failed attempt to storm Nafplion in December and then a more successful assault on the fortress at Acro-Corinth. Yet there too they were muscled out of the spoils by the kapetans and their bands. For Baleste, this was the last straw: he took many of the remaining men with him to Crete, where he died fighting a few months later. It is said that his severed head was hanging from the yardarm of the Ottoman admiral's flagship in the spring of 1822 when the Psaran bruloteer Kanaris blew it up off Chios.

That was not the end of the experiment to use the philhellenes as the nucleus of a national army. On the contrary, the creation of the provisional government meant that the logic of establishing a force independent of the Peloponnesian kapetans or the Rumeliot armatoles was as compelling as ever. Several hundred European volunteers were still left on the streets of Corinth, hoping for a commission, and more were on the way, so in the spring of 1822 the newly formed Greek administration under the presidency of Mavrokordatos tried to succeed where Ypsilantis had failed. An Italian colonel, Pietro Tarella, another veteran of the Grande Armée, was tasked with forming a unit around the remnants of the original Baleste regiment of 1821, adding some Greek volunteers, while keeping the majority of the Europeans together in a new battalion of philhellenes. Because many of them had to accept posts at a lower rank than they believed they were entitled to, quite a few quit. But about 180 remained, enough for two companies. The German general von Normann-Ehrenfels, who landed on the west coast of the Peloponnese in February, became chief of staff while Mavrokordatos, keen to demonstrate that he was as much a military leader as Ypsilantis, kept the position of commander in chief for himself. The men were sworn in for six months and were promised commissions in the regular Greek army once this was formed. It was a truly international force: a Piedmontese was placed in charge of one company; a Swiss headed the other, and the French and Germans were placed separately to avoid fights. Preceded by a drummer they marched out of Corinth, sailed some way along the gulf, and then continued on to Mesolonghi.[41] In total they were about seven hundred men, hardly a large enough force to exert a decisive impact. Yet Mavrokordatos sent them north to forestall the planned Ottoman advance for what was to be the first—and the last—great confrontation between the philhellenes of Europe and their enemy. Their defeat at Peta that July was not only a crushing blow to the Greek hold over western Rumeli but the end of the philhellenes as a military force.[42]

Peta was a hammerblow for the Greek cause, which carried two specific warnings for the surviving volunteers. One was the threat from the Greek bands they were fighting alongside: it was the treachery of the armatole Gogos Bakolas that ensured most of the philhellenes would die on the battlefield. The other was the very real danger of falling into Ottoman hands and the likely fate that awaited them among captors who were furious that foreigners were coming to help the Greeks at all. Monaldi was a young Italian lieutenant who had become so exhausted in the weeks before the battle that he had left one night and descended toward the Turkish lines. Taken prisoner and bound, he had been brought before Omer Vryonis Pasha in Arta. The pasha offered him coffee and chatted with him quietly about the size and composition of the forces he had just left, before having him hanged in the main square as a traitor. Some months later, a German officer fighting with Odysseus Androutsos near Livadeia in central Greece came across the remains of another former comrade, an Italian who had left to offer his services to the Turks as a military instructor. Evidently his offer had not been taken up because his head was stuck on a post in the middle of a village as a warning, until it was taken down and buried by his friend.[43] This was a far dirtier, murkier war than the philhellenes had imagined themselves fighting.

The problems that confronted the volunteers as their dreams and ideals came into contact with the realities of the war in Greece went far beyond the matter of military commissions. Landing in the Peloponnese at a time when Ottoman power had suddenly collapsed, and the Muslims of the peninsula had been confined to a few fortress towns, they found they had stumbled into a region in the grip of anarchy among people who did not seem especially appreciative of their help. A young German philhellene, Christian Müller, was robbed by a group of some thirty armed men as he and three companions made their way through the mountains from Pyrgos. When they told the brigands that they were friends "on our march to the Greek army at Kalamata," the latter hesitated a moment: however, "after having fired another shot, the latter replied laconically that this was an untruth, for people did not go to Kalamata by land, but by sea;

that we were English spies; and that, moreover, the Franks were not wanted at Kalamata." The band tied them up, shot their muleteer, and left them all to die; fortunately they managed to get free. Six months later, Francis Lieber had a similar experience: his group was trying to reach Tripolitsa when one of their drivers reappeared at the head of a band of armed peasants and took their horses at gunpoint. At this point, several of the foreigners quit, while Lieber and others who were made of stronger stuff decided to go on foot, making the journey after a two-day walk, having been forced to sell their spare clothing, watches, and even their arms. Some weeks later, a traumatized Lieber decided to leave too, and he boarded a ship for Italy.[44]

As these episodes indicate, Greeks generally assumed that Franks (their term for Europeans) were rich, and foreigners quickly learned the risks of traveling alone. George Finlay was attacked and left for a dead in a bathhouse in Nafplion; Jarvis, who carried four hundred piastres in coin in his breeches, was nearly robbed when out for a stroll in Spetses. "By experience we looked on any Greek with suspicion, and tied our mules and our horse with a long rope," writes the German Johann Daniel Elster. He had fought with Bolívar in South America but the lawlessness of Rumeli came as a shock. First he and his men were robbed by peasants; then they were captured by brigands whose chief demanded 100 piastres to save their lives. Told that Elster and the others were wounded and starving fighters in the Greek cause, his captor responded with a smile: "It was the same to him who we were and what would become of us. He waged war in that district and when it was a matter of profit he faced Turks, Greeks, Franks, all as enemies, or else he fought with them and became friends." This was the voice of the armatoles and their kapetans—one unfamiliar to the philhellenic imagination.[45]

There was also no small risk for a foreigner of being held as a spy and thereby meeting a horrible and purposeless end: the Greek priest whom one German philhellene saw unmasked as a Turkish agent outside Athens was buried in the ground with large stones up to his neck, and his face was then smeared with honey to attract insects. It took him six days to die.[46] Jarvis too was arrested as an alleged spy, but perhaps because by that point he could—unusually for a volunteer—make himself understood in Greek and explain himself, he escaped unscathed. In the case of the naive Müller, the charge of spying was not only a convenient excuse for robbery but also plausible. What innocent traveler, after all, went from Pyrgos to Kalamata by land, or visited the ancient sites in the middle of a war as he had done, making his way to Olympia even after he had been attacked? When Müller's group eventually reached their destination and found someone to complain to, they did not get the help they expected: "We met with a very cold reception, and they seemed surprised that we should complain of having been robbed in the Morea."[47]

If the foreigners' presence was not always appreciated, it was in part the result of their own behavior. Touchy in matters of honor, they remained quarrelsome and turbulent: the arguments over rank and nationality that had already taken place on the streets of Marseille repeated themselves in Kalamata, Corinth, and elsewhere. "We were constantly killing each other on the slightest provocation," remembered one. But there was also their ignorance of the country and its language. Almost none of them spoke Greek: those few, like Finlay and Mavrokordatos's French secretary Edouard Grasset, who took lessons before coming to Greece, were unusual; Jarvis learned enough to get by. The fluency of one Polish officer was remarkable. But these were exceptions. Mostly they needed interpreters, or they made do in the kind of pidgin that Edward Trelawny used with his brother-in-law, the armatole Odysseus Androutsos, whose young half sister he married—a mixture of Italian infused with English, French, Turkish, and Greek words they taught one another. The consequence was that on the one hand, the newcomers' dependence on the local Greeks was increased, while on the other, their isolation and their tendency to band together with other Europeans was intensified.[48]

Not only were the volunteers unable to communicate; they were, more significantly, often unable to pay their way. Their money went fast—there were no bankers once the Ionian Islands had been left behind—and their possessions followed. From the point of view of Greek peasants, their endless demands for food and shelter made them a burden. When a French volunteer asked for shoes for a dozen comrades, the response was: "Why didn't you bring what you need?"[49] "The Missolonghites were delighted at our departure," remembered the Italian philhellene Brengeri, at least until they came under siege. As their rations ran out, the volunteers took matters into their own hands, requisitioning lodgings and seizing sheep and cattle—behaving increasingly like the irregulars they looked down upon.[50]

Already without resources after what had often been a long journey to get even to their port of embarkation, many of the volunteers found the conditions tough to take. The exiguous diet the Greeks were used to shocked them; the climate and lack of water made things much worse as they tramped the stony mountain paths with heavy packs. A German officer remembered of his trek from Kalamata to Tripolitsa that it was the worst march he had endured in his fifteen years as a soldier.[51] Heading through the Peloponnese en route to Argos in the summer of 1822, a young French lieutenant was soon weak with thirst: "Heat and thirst annihilated nearly all our faculties." A spring of water came at a vital time: "Several of our comrades lagging behind, crippled by exhaustion and need, would otherwise have expired."[52]

There were burning hot summer days and cold mountain nights in ill-heated and often half-ruined houses. Wet clothes could not easily be dried out, and they became breeding grounds for lice and other vermin. Shoe leather was expensive and as many volunteers were soon more or less barefoot, disease—malaria, typhus, dysentery, and plague—preyed on their malnourished bodies. In Argos, where Brengeri fell seriously ill, he was delirious for over a week and the Greek who had been hired by his comrades to look after him sold off many of his possessions. A local doctor came in and bled him with leeches. The straw he slept on became putrid; his cloak was unwashed, since he feared to take it off. Then his boots were stolen. Realizing he would die if he stayed there, Brengeri crawled out of the house on all fours and collapsed on the floor of a coffee shop where a fellow soldier from the Baleste regiment found him and looked after him until he was cured. When he made his way to Corinth to join his comrades, Brengeri was so emaciated that they failed to recognize him. "We drank to the cause of liberty and to my complete restoration and banished the thought of past miseries."[53] It is not surprising that when the Frenchman Olivier Voutier returned to Greece in 1824, his sentiments were mixed. As he wrote: "It is no longer, I believe, the magic of names which touches my heart, it is the confused recollection of dangers, sufferings and disappointments which we endured."[54]

One of the most striking aspects of the philhellenes was their consciousness of a European public and its political importance. "Nationality, truth, public opinion—behold the three flags under which the world for the future is to march," the indefatigable commentator Abbé de Pradt had written in 1815; this was very much a view the volunteers shared.

Themselves part of that public and the expressions of its new force, they rightly saw public opinion as one of the few weapons at their disposal in an age when monarchs and their governments retained most of the power to shape foreign affairs. Before their departure, this consciousness had taken the form of proclamations, appeals, and pledges; on their return, it resulted in memoirs, pamphlets, and accounts of what they had seen. In the majority of cases of those who went into print, the authors were changed men, keen to testify not to Greece's resurrection but rather to the horrors of war and the moral and psychological struggles they had themselves gone through.

After his disappointing experiences in the Morea, the young German, Francis Lieber, went on to Rome where he ended up staying as a tutor to the children of the Prussian minister. Barthold Georg Niebuhr was perhaps the preeminent Roman historian of his time. The older man listened attentively to Lieber's stories and worried about his state of mind. He wrote to his sister-in-law:

> A young man has lately arrived—a Mr. Lieber, of Berlin—who had gone to Greece as a volunteer, and has returned . . . His veracity is unquestionable, and the horror which his narratives inspire is not to be described . . . We are trying to cheer his spirits by friendly treatment and to banish from his thoughts the infernal scenes which he has witnessed. He is one of the youths of the noble period of 1813 . . . who lost themselves in visions, the elements of which they drew from their own hearts; and this terrible contrast between his experience and all that he had imagined—all that impelled him into distant lands—has broken his heart.[55]

Lieber was not the first to have returned in despair nor to try to convey that despair to others. At the start of 1822, *John Bull*, an ardently anti-Whig London paper, relayed the dismaying stories of one returnee and his "wishes that all those, who with their overflowing hearts and valiant arms think of going to the Morea, may defer the execution of their purpose for a time."[56] Thomas Gordon, someone deeply committed to the Greek cause, was so appalled by what he had witnessed at Tripolitsa that he left for the Ionian Islands in the autumn of 1821 and wrote an account so dark it prompted a warning from some Greeks that it could damage their cause. Gordon understood their concern and in fact he himself later helped to hold back the publication of other stories; when Maurice Persat wrote his own devastating narrative of the sack of the town, Gordon paid him 1,000 francs not to publish it and it did not appear in print for many decades.

What was it that so horrified the philhellenes that some of them clearly suffered what we might today call a kind of post-traumatic disorder? Partly it was simply the disorienting reality they had stumbled into, and the shock that they had felt on realizing the Greeks they had come to help little resembled how they had imagined them. Jarvis describes how on catching his first glimpse of islanders on Hydra he was terrified because he took them for Turks. Byron, a much more experienced traveler, was one of the few who was happy to acknowledge that the Greeks too were products of the Ottoman world; for most, the discovery was painful and hard to absorb. "European youth, the Greeks of olden days exist no more," warned Lieutenant Louis de Bollmann.[57]

Yet more was involved than just incomprehension and surprise. The philhellenic cause was one of the earliest instances of international humanitarian intervention—an idea that the world would become familiar with as the century progressed and one that would shape global affairs into the next. This idea rested on a four-part moral distinction that divided the world into victims, perpetrators, bystanders, and those who sought to do good. Like abolitionism, the other great humanitarian cause of those years, philhellenism rested on the spread of a sensibility of sympathy, a belief in the value of understanding, and indeed feeling the suffering of others, above all of innocent victims. When news of the uprising reached Europe, it was widely assumed first, that the victims were only the insurgent Greeks, oppressed for centuries under Ottoman despotism, and second, that they were not only victims but preeminently worthy of help because of their capacity to emulate the virtues of their forebears.

There were of course Greek victims of Ottoman violence in the first year and a half of the uprising. But in the Morea, the Greeks had swept all before them in only a few weeks, and as a result it was the Muslim survivors, not the Greeks, who were more likely to strike the philhellenes as victims. The paradox therefore is that the horrors that the philhellenes of 1821–22 came across were almost without exception perpetrated by those they had come to help. The same humanitarian impulses that had expressed themselves earlier in enthusiasm and passionate solidarity with the Greeks now resulted in expressions of psychological turbulence and troubling reflection. Did speaking up for helpless Turks, defenseless women and children, really mean, as the Greeks told the philhellenes who tried to intervene, that they were saving the wrong side? Having begun to recount what he saw, Bollmann paused in his writing: "My soul, too moved by the bloody memories, has need to rest a moment."[58]

In 1826 an anonymous author, later identified as the Italian philhellene Brengeri, published a remarkable series of recollections in the *London Magazine*. They remain one of the most unsparing accounts of the cruelties of the war to be found anywhere, a testament to his own spiritual journey. Brengeri had sailed from Livorno to Kalamata, arriving there in October 1821 with the intention of fighting for "the noble cause of Greece." He was a liberal and a fair-minded observer of both his fellow volunteers and the Greeks he encountered. He admired Mavrokordatos and Dimitrios Ypsilantis, though he found the latter weak, and he disliked Kolokotronis. Brengeri respected Baleste but he condemned the unruliness and greed of some of the other philhellenes. He was certainly not a man inclined to oppose the Greek cause. Yet he was deeply affected by what he saw of the Greeks' attitude to the Turks, both living and dead.

On his approach to Tripolitsa, some weeks after the city had fallen, Brengeri noticed the bodies in the fields, stinking and attracting birds: to his surprise, the Greek muleteers "with an air of scorn and triumph" would break the skulls of the corpses with stones. Inside the city it was worse: the streets were still strewn with corpses; others lay inside houses, untouched. When he asked why they were not removed and burned to avoid disease, he was told that "they left them to show their contempt for the Turks, who were not worthy of burial." Shocked by the sight of the naked bodies of women and children, Brengeri noted that he and his companions "could not look at these innocent victims without compassion and horror."

Not all the philhellenes had the same reaction, to be sure. Brengeri and his companions were sitting under a portico one day, trying not to look at the bodies of three small Turkish boys in the street that were attracting the attention of dogs, when they were hailed by a man called Bencini, whom they knew from Italy. He was on horseback—a sign of prosperity—with two servants accompanying him. To their surprise—they knew he had only started his medical training—Bencini told them he was working as a doctor. He went on: "I am the physician of all these Turkish lords whom the chiefs have saved from the carnage in order to make more by them. They are all ill from bad food and terror as they are expected to undergo the general fate. I have an interpreter, two slaves and two beautiful Turkish girls; and I get a great deal of money."

Along with Bencini—the epitome of the foreigner scavenging in the spoils for his own personal gain—two more episodes cement the sense of mounting horror. In the first, Brengeri's party are traveling across the pass from Tripolitsa to Argos when they see the body of a Muslim on the road. He has evidently recently been killed and as there are letters scattered around him, they surmise he has been attacked by robbers. A few hundred meters away they overtake "a beautiful Turkish woman, with an infant in her arms, weeping bitterly." It turns out she is the wife of the dead man who had indeed been murdered and stripped by peasants the previous night. The philhellenes order the Greeks to give her some water. They want to take her and the child with them but are dissuaded by one of their party, an aide to Ypsilantis, who tells them: "In a revolution one must harden one's heart, as one is sure to meet with fresh objects continually to excite compassion." They give her 20 piastres instead but this turns out to be her death warrant because they have scarcely begun to move off again when they hear shots from behind them and see two peasants stripping the bodies of the woman and her child. The sight fills them with horror, and for some minutes they cannot move.

Sometime later, Brengeri made his way to Corinth where he was present at the ending of the siege in January 1822. On the day before the surrender, he watched as Greek women and children, who had been seized by the Turks, talked from the ramparts with their relatives below and awaited their liberation. "It was impossible to witness this scene without indignation," Brengeri wrote, "and at that moment I felt as if I could have willingly joined in a massacre of the Turks." Realizing the hatred the Greeks there felt for the Turks, he worried at what lay in store once the fortress was opened and did not have long to wait. As Turkish families were led down under armed escort, they were attacked and killed. Seeing one family under assault, he and his comrades ran up to defend them; too late to save the husband, two boys, and one of the slaves, they drew their sabers and bargained for the life of the woman. Fifty piastres—a high price—saved her, though there was still haggling over her fine clothes; eventually Brengeri took her back to his home and looked after her. When he left to fight in western Greece, he found an Italian sea captain to take her out of the country.

She was relatively fortunate. In the aftermath of the fall of its fortress,

Corinth was the site of buying and selling, and many young girls and women escaped death only to be sold in the market at auction where the going rate was 30 or 40 piastres, depending on their age and looks. Dimitrios Ypsilantis was powerless to do anything about what was happening as all semblance of military order had vanished. As commander in chief, he possessed little authority as more and more armed men arrived to participate in the plunder and the humiliation of the defenseless captives. Brengeri witnessed one girl with multiple stab wounds, who had crawled to the market for help, being spat on by bystanders. When he asked the minister of war to intervene, two men were sent to drag her away: they killed her with their sabers and left her body in the street. "There were now more than twenty thousand persons in Corinth, all utterly useless, and occupied only with eating and drinking. Every day the bodies of murdered Turks were found in the streets. The few who had been saved from the general massacre, were thus dispatched in detail, as it suited their plunderers."[59]

The philhellenes who witnessed such scenes in what had just become the headquarters of the new provisional government found their sympathies transformed. The same instincts that had brought them to Greece led them to intervene on behalf of captured Muslims, often turning the Greeks against them. The balance of virtue and vice, guilt and innocence, had been upset. "My enthusiasm for the Greeks had considerably cooled after the horrible sack of Tripolitsa," remembered Persat. He had rescued a Turkish family there, haggling with a group of attackers and buying them off for 20 piastres, thus ending up with a grandfather, a mother, three small children, and a thirteen-year-old girl. The older two died of dysentery and the children were killed one day while Persat was away obtaining food. That left the girl whom he lodged for safety with an Italian family in Argos. Disgusted with what he had witnessed, Persat contemplated joining Baleste and going to Crete but when "his Adèle" warned him this would mean her certain death, he took her back with him to Marseille instead. There she became something of a cause célèbre. She received a Catholic education, rejected the opportunity to return to the Ottoman Empire, and eventually became the old soldier's wife.[60]

When philhellenes intervened to defend Muslim women or children at risk of their own lives, the Greeks demanded to know why they were taking the wrong side. Some of the volunteers understood that this marked a gulf between them. "Our conduct lay in our habits," wrote

Raybaud, "and their manner of acting toward the defeated seemed to them too quite natural. It belonged in the end to the nature of men not civilized, not modified by the custom of liberal, gentle institutions." The conclusion he drew was that Greek independence was all the more worth fighting for: "more enlightened, they will become more human."[61] Similarly, for men like Brengeri, Gordon, and Persat, such behavior did not invalidate the sacred cause of national independence; but it did make it impossible to see the Greeks as they wished to be seen—as the "champions of liberty." Remaining philhellenes, most volunteers tended to explain the cruelty they had witnessed as expressions of a fallen nature. Such violence, they wrote, indicated what an impact the centuries of Ottoman rule and life had had on the Greeks. Regeneration—the transformation of attitudes and values, the whole process of civilization—would thus take far longer than they had realized: time began to stretch out before them. Some even started to wonder whether a people so degraded could achieve independence at all. Voutier wrote that the military events were secondary: "the interior situation of a people and its moral state alone can decide its independence." It was this question of national ethics that the violence levied against defenseless Muslim survivors threw into doubt.[62]

For the volunteers Greece's true backwardness was not material—poor dwellings and inadequate roads—but moral. To be a philhellene was in theory at least to be disinterested, to believe that true nobility lay in sacrifice. Evidently not all the philhellenes were free of a mercenary impulse. But what of the indications that so many of the leaders of the insurrection were acting out of avarice? Could they then be true patriots? Recent examples of successful revolutions—the American and the French—had produced leaders of stature who somehow validated by their apparent selflessness the moral preparedness of their people. The philhellenes were forced to question whether this was true for the Greeks. Ypsilantis was selfless but he was weak. As for Kolokotronis, his greed was much discussed: Raybaud was typical in seeing in him "bravery without patrotism." The volunteers' own code of conduct placed valor and the idea of a noble and sacrifical death for Greece at the heart of their actions; it was hard to reconcile this with the tactics of the Greek kapetans who were clearly devoted to saving the lives of their men, avoiding direct engagement with the enemy where possible. Many of the European volunteers discerned no leader of stature and worried that the lack of a "vigorous supreme direction" would perpetuate a state of anarchy.[63]

As philhellenes returned to Marseille with their tales of disillusionment and massacre, the authorities saw a way of deterring others from heading out to Greece. Prospective voyagers were sent to meet Maurice Persat with the result that many of them changed their minds about heading out. The prefect also encouraged the old Bonapartist to go into print, and his story ran in the local paper while Adèle's saga was turned by the French authorities into a small piece of propaganda for the Catholic faith that received her. In September 1822 a returning survivor of the battle of Peta was said to have "repented of having been one of the knights of Humanity" (*Chevaliers de l'Humanité*). The same month the prefect declared in the *Journal de Marseille* that the town was receiving the "sad debris of their crusade" and expressed the hope that the Germans still planning expeditions to Greece would renounce this "chimerical enterprise."[64]

Philhellenic circles across Europe had long been worried about counterpropaganda, and the fact that returning philhellenes were reporting atrocities that cast a bad light on the cause was, for some Greeks, a good reason to question the whole volunteer enterprise. Mavrokordatos's contact in Paris, Konstantinos Polychroniades, wrote in January 1822:

> for now foreign fighters are not only useless but harmful. Some went over to our enemies, others fuel civil war, and others, returning to civilized Europe, write against us, like the German Müller and the Englishman Gordon who—while in quarantine in Zakynthos—told the Administrator that he had been horrified by the inhumanities of the Greeks . . . Our enemies are presenting us as worse than the Turks and unworthy of pity and help.

To make matters worse, books started to appear with the same message: Christian Müller's *Journey through Greece and the Ionian Islands in June, July and August 1821* (1822) was perhaps the first to appear, but he had seen little and stayed only briefly. Lieber, Bollmann, Lessen, and Voutier all published their recollections on their return, and the first volume of Maxime Raybaud's remarkable memoir appeared in 1824—the most important firsthand account to that point. Brengeri's unsparing account ran over half a dozen or so issues of the *London Magazine* in 1826–27.[65]

Yet despite Greek fears, the truth is that these stories of disillusionment and dismay did not have much impact. The first great movement of philhellenic volunteers died away at the end of 1822, it is true, once the French clamped down on expeditions from Marseille in November, and young German and Swiss men in particular would never flock south in such numbers again. There were few expeditions of volunteers in the next three years and from Marseille they only began again in the autumn of 1825 after both the government and the king had changed. Yet as a movement of European opinion, sympathy for the Greek cause was almost protean in its forms and appearances and impervious to challenges to its most basic assumptions. We can track its persistence through the trend in the number of pro-Greek publications across Europe: 141, 216, and 125 between 1821 and 1823 and then a swelling of interest after Byron's death (1824)—194, 242, and 297 from 1824 to 1826. Concern and sympathy endured and persisted, oblivious to the accounts of disillusionment and condemnation that some of the first volunteers had penned.[66] The volunteers had not, except in the rarest of cases, had a discernible effect by their presence on the course of the war. Their real contribution and function was different: they were the mark of Europe's concern, and even though some of them came to believe it to be misplaced, a large proportion of the European public itself remained susceptible to the cause of the Greeks.

11

ENGLISH GOLD

Every loan
Is not a merely speculative hit,
But seats a nation or upsets a throne.
Republics also get involved a bit.

Byron, *Don Juan*, canto XII, verse vi

The Greek uprising began with philanthropy ranging from the often modest donations of hundreds of members of the Filiki Etaireia to large gifts from wealthy individuals.[1] Personal fortunes were spent on the cause by the Ypsilantis family and the caviar magnate Ioannis Varvakis, while Panayiotis Sekeris, who ran the Etaireia's Constantinople headquarters, more or less reduced himself to poverty. Starting with the Scottish philhellene Thomas Gordon, who arrived at Hydra in the summer of 1821, bearing substantial funds from his private wealth, a series of specially chartered consignments of supplies and materiel reached the insurgents from abroad. Sporadic at first, they were later more systematically organized by men such as the wealthy Swiss philhellene and banker Jean-Gabriel Eynard, a Geneva-based friend of Capodistrias, and by a well-connected aristocrat called Dionysios Romas, who ran an important committee from the Ionian island of Zakynthos linking bankers, relief shipments, and political agents. As philhellenism grew stronger, aid was directed to the Greeks from Paris, Amsterdam, Munich and elsewhere.[2]

But philanthropy had its limits, and so did the spoils of war. By the time the provisional government was created at the start of 1822, the riches of Tripolitsa had vanished into the pockets of the chieftains, the legendary wealth of Kiamil Bey had failed to materialize, and Dimitrios Ypsilantis had run out of money. Before the war the Morea had easily been the most important source of tax revenues in Ottoman Greece and its wealth had largely funded the initial months of the uprising there. Yet not only did the region's resources remain outside the reach of the provisional government and under the control of the Peloponnesian Senate instead. More fundamentally, its agrarian economy was increasingly disrupted by the fighting: tax receipts dropped precipitously and by the start of 1823 the leading Peloponnesian landowners were asking the Hydriot shipowners to ship in wheat on credit.[3] The latter were already finding it difficult to raise the money from the islands to fund their own naval operations. Yet they all faced an enemy capable of waging war on a very different scale and on a far more organized fiscal basis. The empire might have had its own economic issues but its resources were immense by comparison with those of the Greeks, and a loss one year could be offset by building a new fleet or raising new armies the next. Imperial revenues likely amounted to nearly 200 million *grossia* annually in the late 1820s; on the Greek side, they were likely to have been a few percent of that. Fiscally this was a contest between Goliath and David.[4]

It is not then surprising that the idea of seeking a foreign loan to underwrite the revolution started early. Alexandros Ypsilantis had mulled over a trip to his bankers in Paris almost as soon as he took on the leadership of the Etaireia; and in the summer of 1821 Tripolitsa had not yet fallen to the Greeks when Sekeris wrote from Odessa to his brother in Hydra underlining how important it was that the Greeks establish a parliament that could send delegates to seek a loan.[5] The issue came up in the regional assemblies as well. Before the end of 1821, both in eastern Greece and at a meeting of the Peloponnesian Senate, resolutions were passed affirming the importance of borrowing abroad. "Our greatest need right now is for coin," the War Council of the Senate of Western Continental Greece wrote in March 1822, "to cover the first month of the ships and the soldiers, and after that as with any government we can manage from public revenues . . . and from contributions."[6] Once Mavrokordatos's new provisional government was voted the power to contract loans, he sent abroad a number of Greeks to scout out the options in Germany and Switzerland, Russia and Italy. One of them was the son of an Arta merchant, the highly educated Andreas Louriotis, who sailed to the port of Livorno to consult with Archbishop Ignatios in Pisa.

Ignatios was a veteran fundraiser for Greek causes. "I foresaw from the start that loans would be inescapable," he reminded the Mavrokordatos government in June 1822. But the archbishop warned it would not be easy, reporting that he had already been rebuffed by Capodistrias when he had asked about money from Russia. In Italy, too, he said, the Greeks were frightened of angering the all-powerful Austrians who opposed the revolution. Political reservations aside, the problem was not lack of funds: Europe was booming in the early 1820s and investors were looking for outlets. But what guarantees or security could the Greeks offer them? The formation of a government was a vitally important step forward. But in Ignatios's view the Greeks needed also to capture the other fortresses on the Peloponnese—above all Nafplion and Patras—to make their case plausible and instill confidence abroad in their cause and their future solvency.[7]

Ignatios also told Mavrokordatos that he did not think much of Louriotis or his way of going about things. For one thing, Louriotis's activities should have remained confidential. Yet the government had sent him to the port of Livorno—where the Austrians kept track of everything that was happening—carrying so many letters with him "that not only Europe but America knows of his mission ahead of time." Ignatios, himself under constant surveillance from Austrian agents, wondered whether it was safe for Louriotis to even stay in Italy. As for another emissary, Mihalis Schinas, who had been sent to try his luck in Switzerland, Ignatios's view was that he would manage to do nothing but "drink cold water" since other Greeks had already been trying to raise funds there. The "Schinases and Louriotes" of this world were, in the archbishop's caustic view, out of their depth, or as he put it, "little animals facing big beasts."[8]

Not everyone on the Greek side thought that borrowing abroad was a good idea. This was especially true of the Peloponnesian kapetans in the revolutionary leadership, who were as fearful of the Franks as they were of the Turks and suspected the foreign-born Greeks like Mavrokordatos of wanting to turn the country into a dependency of the European powers. By early 1823 a suspicious Kolokotronis—reasoning quite correctly that foreign funds would be likely to reduce his power—was accusing those behind the search for a loan of seeking to subordinate Greece to the British. So it is worth remembering that Mavrokordatos's entourage did not start off especially anglophile. On the contrary, the

British grip on the Ionian Islands, with its overbearing colonial officials and their close relationships with both Ali Pasha and the Ottomans, made many Greeks deeply mistrustful. Louriotis himself inveighed against "those English dogs" who "fight against us secretly and openly, as much as they can." Ignatios too thought nothing could be done with the British so long as they remained opposed to the Greek struggle. It was thus somewhat remarkable not only that London would emerge as Greece's main financier, but also that it was through the radical milieu of southern Europe that Louriotis and the Greeks would get there.[9]

In the spring of 1820 a military coup led by liberal Spanish army officers had forced a constitution on the Bourbon king Ferdinand VII, and by 1822 the Holy Alliance was prepared to intervene there militarily to assist him. For a moment, Spain became the front line in the war between Europe's radicals and the conservatives of the Restoration. Among the foreigners who flocked to Madrid to help—many of whom would move later on to Greece—were an Irishman, Edward Blaquiere, who had served in the Royal Navy throughout the Napoleonic Wars, and a "young mercantile man" called John Bowring. Hearing about the Greek uprising while he was in Madrid, Bowring had helped form one of the very first philhellenic committees in Europe, and Blaquiere had joined it. Ignatios drafted a letter of introduction for Louriotis to them, and thus got rid of the young Greek by sending him to Spain to scout out the options. Styling himself "le premier Magistrat de la Grèce," Ignatios recommended his envoy to Bowring and solicited his aid for the Greeks.[10] By the time Louriotis got to Spain, however, the Spanish government was within months of its demise and Bowring had already left for London. In January 1823, therefore, Louriotis went on to the British capital where he was welcomed and helped both by Blaquiere and by the human whirlwind of a man without whom the loans—for better or worse—would have likely remained a pipe dream.[11]

John Bowring was to leave his mark on the nineteenth century through a remarkably energetic and checkered career that ended with the governorship of Hong Kong where, thanks to his passion for free trade and his well-developed egotism, he managed to start the second opium war between Britain and China. In 1823 all that lay decades in the future and the future imperialist was starting out as an enterprising young merchant in the herring and wine business, who combined a strong desire to make money with a thirst for radical philosophy, literature, and public life. A committed liberal, Bowring threw himself into supporting the constitutionalists in Spain and then the revolutionaries in Greece. He was the ultimate self-improver, reading widely not only in Spanish but also—or so he claimed in typical self-advertisement—in Russian, French, German, Dutch, Swedish, Hungarian, Serbian, and more.

Bowring's greatest passion, however, was for the ideas of Jeremy Bentham, the radical English philosopher who at that time was at the height of his fame across Europe. Bowring was energetic in his proselytizing of Bentham's works and effusive in his praise of the great man— much to Bentham's delight. "Bowring," wrote one of Bentham's young secretaries, "made Bentham quite the God of his idolatry . . . perpetually lavishing on him the warmest eulogies and adulation, often too palpable to be endured by any other than the unmercifully bespattered object of them himself."[12] Within a few months Bowring found the esteem reciprocated: Bentham deemed him "one of the most extraordinary, if not the most extraordinary man, I ever saw." Bowring moved swiftly from fan to disciple to Bentham's right-hand man, the figure at the center of a worldwide movement to preach Benthamite ideas. In the midst of all this, Bowring's irrepressible energy helped him to establish the London Greek Committee, which became the organizer of support for the cause in Britain and the force behind the drive to raise loans for the Greeks in the City of London.[13]

When the Greek revolution broke out, Jeremy Bentham was seventy-three years old. With his flowing white locks, his ready pen, and his faddishness—he was, for instance, a great believer in physical fitness and had funded the first public gymnasium in London, opened in Leicester Square—he was at the height of his influence, and his powers (as well as his confidence in those powers) were undimmed. Well known for his critique of legal traditionalism and natural law, Bentham's name was, in the caustic judgment of essayist William Hazlitt, "little known in England, better in Europe, best of all in the plains of Chili and the mines of Mexico." This was unfair but it did point to the Benthamites' almost religious belief that they had a message for the world and to their determination to get it heard: Bentham was after all the man who had coined the term "international," and he was closely attuned to the reception of his ideas beyond the Channel. After the Napoleonic Wars, the struggle against tyranny—whether against the Bourbon Restoration in southern Europe and South America or the Ottoman sultan in Greece—was regarded by Bentham and his supporters as an opportunity to demonstrate the advantages of the philosophy of utility as a guide to a rational and modern system of government. Because he regarded his teachings as universally applicable, requiring only minor adjustments to take account of local conditions, and because he regarded them as unifying science and ethics as a scheme for the general good, it was—in his mind—not only possible but desirable, indeed of supreme importance, to preach the word abroad. Mavrokordatos, an urbane man, noted when pressed that Bentham's work was "good in theory but not in practice": no insult could have been more irritating or bewildering to the master.[14] The Benthamites were, from this perspective, precursors of those late twentieth-century technocrats who fanned out across the globe from Europe and the United States, advising governments on how to manage their people's affairs. To contemporary Tory critics like those writing in *Blackwood's Edinburgh Magazine*, they were unwavering in forcing upon the Greeks—as the true price of the loan—the "visionary craziness of Jerry-benthamism."[15]

Not everyone was a devotee. Although there were many Benthamites on the London Greek Committee, its best-known member, Lord Byron, was certainly not among them. His subtle, disillusioned mind and his love not only for the Greeks but also for Ottoman society as a whole (of which he saw the Greeks as a part) made him impatient with the oversimplifications, ignorance, and intellectual narcissism of the Benthamites. Unlike Bentham, who had never been south of the Danube and did not believe local knowledge counted for very much anyway, Byron had traveled extensively in the region in the past and was deeply interested in its peoples and customs. In Mesolonghi in 1824, surrounded by Benthamites sent from London, Byron met the naval "fire-master" (engineer) William Parry, an ordnance expert sent out from London by the committee, and they forged a bond that was based in large measure on their shared sense of the preposterousness of the Bentham cult. Parry had met Bentham shortly before leaving for Greece, and his description of the elderly philosopher's unconventional behavior—not rising before three in the afternoon, then trotting so fast through St. James Park that people stared and his young secretaries had difficulty keeping up with him, meanwhile boasting of his remarkable stamina, and only being brought to a stop by catching sight of a portrait of himself in a bookstore—had Byron begging for more.[16]

The skyline of the capital: the port of Istanbul, ca.1789. Workmen load Greek antiquities for shipment to France.

Sultan Mahmud II: Padishah, Shadow of God on Earth, ca.1825.

Phanariot Mihail Soutzos: *hospodar* of Moldavia, 1819–21; reluctant Etairist.

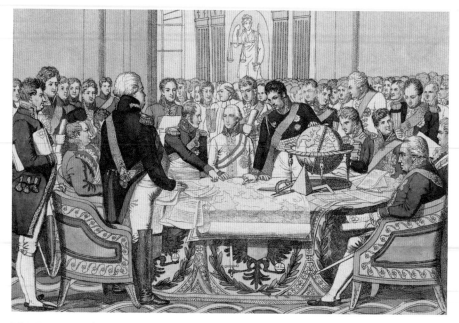

The Congress of Vienna: Czar Alexander I, Emperor Francis of Austria (in white), and the King of Prussia examine the map, 1814.

Emmanuil Xanthos: one of the founders of the Filiki Etaireia.

Christoforos Perraivos: teacher, soldier, historian, revolutionary.

Prince Alexandros Ypsilantis: commander of the failed uprisings in the Danubian Principalities and leader of the Filiki Etaireia, wearing its insignia.

Prince Dimitrios Ypsilantis, younger brother of Alexandros: Etaireia plenipotentiary and revolutionary commander in the Morea.

Survivors of the Danubian campaign: Etaireia veterans in exile in Switzerland, 1822.

Looking across the lake to the citadel of Jannina and the Fethiye mosque, remodeled by Ali Pasha and now the site of his tomb.

Khurshid Pasha: commander in chief of the Ottoman campaign against Ali Pasha, 1820–22.

The Lion of Jannina (*left*): Ali Pasha at the age of seventy-nine, 1819.

Urban life and trade in the Ionian Islands under British rule: the piazza of St. Mark, Zakynthos town, 1821.

An idealized image of cooperation between Greek fighters and European philhellenes: While Greek commanders confer, European officers inspect enemy positions.

Theodoros Kolokotronis: kleft and the son of a kleft; wartime military commander in the Peloponnese.

Petros Mavromihalis: Bey of the Mani; president of the provisional administration of Greece, 1823.

Alexandros Mavrokordatos: diplomat; politician; president of the provisional administration of Greece, 1822.

Fireship virtuoso Konstantine Kanaris attacks the Ottoman fleet off Tenedos, October 1822.

George Koundouriotis: Hydra shipowner; president of the provisional administration of Greece, 1823–26.

Lazaros Koundouriotis: elder brother of George; architect of Hydra's wartime ascendancy.

A motley group of European volunteers assemble to aid the Greeks, 1822.

Greeks and Turks in a Vienna coffeehouse, ca.1824.

Mehmed Reshid "Kütahı" Pasha: Ottoman commander in chief in Rumeli; Grand Vizier, 1829–33.

Georgios Karaïskakis: kleft; bodyguard to Ali Pasha; commander in chief of the Greek forces in western Rumeli.

Mesolonghi in flames: Henri Decaisne, *Greeks After a Defeat*, 1826.

Mehmed Ali, Pasha of Egypt (*above left*): founder of a dynasty; architect of Egyptian independence.

Soliman Pasha al-Faransawi (born Joseph Anthelme Sève) (*above*): veteran of the Napoleonic Wars; modernizer of the Egyptian army.

Ibrahim Pasha, son of Mehmed Ali (*left*): commander of the Egyptian expedition to Greece.

The slave market in Cairo where hundreds of enslaved Greeks were sold (*above*). One of them, Kalitsa Psaraki, was redeemed by and married to Robert Hay, from whose *Illustrations of Cairo* this picture is taken.

Two women and a baby living in a makeshift tent, ca.1828 (*right*). In the aftermath of the Egyptian occupation of the Morea, tens of thousands of refugees struggled to survive.

This remarkable panorama, painted at the very end of the war by French soldier-artist Théodore Leblanc, depicts Greek forces in the Morea, ca.1829.

On the left: a group of leaders including Kolokotronis and probably Nikitaras; behind them: captured camels used for transport. On the right: a small cavalry detachment; in the foreground: men resting, a priest, children, and dogs.

The Battle of Navarino, 1827: Codrington's flagship, the *Asia*, between the flagships of the Ottoman and Egyptian admirals.

The assassination of Capodistrias in Nafplion, 1831.

Otto, King of Greece at the age of seventeen, painted in 1832, the year of his ascent to the throne. He is dressed in the uniform of the Royal Bavarian Lifeguards; the Acropolis is just visible in the distance.

Capitalism arrives on Syros: by 1833, the medieval hilltop town is dwarfed by the new port of Ermoupolis. Drawn by a voyager on the first steamer cruise to the Levant.

God and his angels bless the new country: on the left, rulers of the three
Protecting Powers (Czar Nicholas, Queen Victoria, and King Louis
Philippe); on the right, King Otto and Queen Amalia flanking Greece.
From the series of paintings commissioned by Makriyannis in 1836–39.

A popular lithograph shows the revolution of 1843 in Athens: crowds
and troops gather before the royal palace to demand a constitution.

Through Bowring and others on the committee, Bentham now became extensively involved with the Greeks. He wrote four texts for them in 1823, the year of his greatest involvement, advising them on constitutional matters and warning them of the dangers of monarchy—for he and his followers tended to be ardent republicans. Into Greece there flowed a torrent of rapidly penned texts, translations, and what would today be called policy recommendations. He was a letter writer of immense energy—incapable of writing a short letter where a long one would do—and corresponded with Mavrokordatos who claimed to have brought Bentham's works with him to Greece. Mavrokordatos's protégé Anastasios Polyzoidis was translating one of them; the great savant Adamantios Korais, others. All of this, to Bentham, was as it should be. Writing in 1824 to his South American follower Bernardino Rivadavia, later the first president of Argentina, Bentham described himself as "the Master of the present age in the art of legislation," whose services were so prized by the Greeks that the arrival of his comments on their provisional constitution supposedly reduced them to tears. "Their dear father protector of Greece are the titles by which I am denominated," he wrote proudly to Rivadavia. He in turn addressed his letters to his "Dear children" and signed off "Your always affectionate Father."[17]

While it is easy to be diverted by the paternalistic arrogance and absurd self-importance of Bentham and his followers, the connection between their philosophy and the emergence of a new global regime of international capital in the 1820s is too striking to neglect. What they provided was a vision of reform that owed little or nothing to revolutionary or Napoleonic ideas. A distinctively British concept of progress lay at the heart of the Benthamite creed: the liberty to produce goods as well as ideas, through manufacturing, and through the flow of capital to enable society to become productive. It seemed logical that advocating popular liberation from tyranny, as well as the freeing of a people to enjoy the benefits of representative republican government, should go hand in hand with encouraging money and goods to circulate to where they could be most productive. We do not usually think of radical political philosophy and finance as natural bedfellows, but in the early 1820s that is what they were.

The Benthamites gave the Greek cause publicity, and under John Bowring's guidance they turned the London Greek Committee—with its meetings and pamphlets, speeches and subscriptions—into a notable example of what Tories called "these officious Associations," which expressed what was for the times a new and radical conception of political engagement. As *Blackwood's* observed with alarm, it was a model in which relations between states were no longer the monopoly of statesmen but could rather be shaped by the actions of private individuals. "In plain truth," opined the journal in October 1823, "this sort of stuff has gone a great deal too far already . . . 'The Greek Committee' may be convened in the tavern, and the Greek Committee's ambassadors may go to Tripolizza just as often as the fancy takes them—The language of every rational man will be: 'This is the affair of the state not of the pot-house.'" But if this had ever been true, it no longer applied to London in the early 1820s where resistance to Toryism in foreign affairs and to the stranglehold of the Holy Alliance was mounting by the day. It was in the capital's taverns and coffeehouses that a new front was opening in the war not only for Greece but for the fundamental political principles that would guide the international relations of Europe and the world.[18]

The Crown and Anchor tavern in the Strand was a famous dining place associated with political campaigning from the time of the French Revolution. Centrally located, it boasted a large backroom capable of holding meetings of several hundred at a time and it was favored by some of the more well-heeled Radicals. In recent years, large dinners had celebrated the cause of reform at home as well as the uprisings in Naples, Spain, and Portugal. Men such as Henry "Orator" Hunt contrasted nearby Parliament as the forum of the country's aristocracy with the Crown and Anchor as a place for "the people" to assemble and make known their views on foreign affairs. It was there that at the end of February 1823 Bowring called together nine members of Parliament, along with other leading Whigs, for the discussions that resulted in the establishment of the London Greek Committee.[19] The committee convened in the same place just over a week later, with Bowring as secretary and Lord Erskine, a distinguished philhellenic jurist, as chair.

Philhellenic enthusiasm on a popular scale had been slower to appear in England than on the continent. Within the political elite, the only noteworthy initiative prior to the formation of the committee had been Erskine's 1822 letter of protest to the Earl of Liverpool, the prime minister, publicly criticizing the latter's pro-Ottoman line. Yet when an appeal was issued for others to join the committee, more than eighty responded within days—among them members of Parliament, members of the Lords, bishops, jurists, philologists, and army officers. Byron joined as soon as he heard about it, as did two other well-known poets, Thomas Moore and Thomas Campbell. Bentham himself was a member of course. Although avowedly cross-party, the committee was chiefly Whig and Radical in its composition, reflecting the generally pro-Ottoman and anti-Greek sympathies of English Tories. In fact, despite the impressive array of names, only a small group was really guiding its activities, central among them the indefatigable Bowring.

Meeting most weeks at the Crown and Anchor, the committee began by publicizing the Greek cause and raising several thousand pounds by general subscription. Obtaining a much larger sum on the London exchange would take longer, and the organizers realized they needed two things first: a reliable assessment of the state of the country, and the arrival in England of an official mission from the Greek government with plenipotentiary powers (since Louriotis had not been formally empowered to speak on the government's behalf). It was resolved to send Louriotis back to Greece to convey this message; Edward Blaquiere would go with him to write a report for the committee on conditions in Greece. The two men set off almost immediately, landing in Corfu in April 1823 and arriving in Tripolitsa in early May. Within less than a month, the government—spurred on by Mavrokordatos—had backed the idea of a loan and begun the complicated business of choosing delegates. Returning as he had come through Italy, Blaquiere was back in London in time to read his report to the members of the committee that September on the state of affairs in Greece.

Meanwhile, it was not only in London that the Greeks were looking for money. In the summer of 1822, the Mavrokordatos administration had also instructed two emissaries to contact the papacy, hoping vaguely that the pontiff might back the idea of a new crusade against the Turks. This was an era of dreams of Christian unity and the government hoped to exploit these and present the Greek cause in a less radical and more pious guise. One of their representatives was an Ionian notable, Andreas Metaxas; the other was a French officer, Philippe Jourdain, who had been advising the Hydriots on their island defenses. Furnished with letters calling on the monarchs of Europe to help the Greeks in the struggle of Christendom against Islam, the two men arrived at Ancona only to be stuck in quarantine while their letter to the pope was forwarded to Rome. What Metaxas and Jourdain did not know was that Prince Metternich had asked the papacy to keep them in Ancona, and with Austrian troops in the Papal States, his wishes could not be ignored. When the government sent two more notables to reinforce their mission—Archbishop Germanos of Patras and Georgios Mavromihalis, the son of Petrobey of the Mani—they ended up in the lazaretto too.[20]

With the route to the papacy blocked, the Greeks decided to approach the Knights of the Order of St. John of Jerusalem—better known as the Knights of Malta. During the Napoleonic Wars the ancient crusading order had lost its historic base in Malta and Jourdain in particular was keen to create a French-speaking Catholic bulwark in the Levant since British naval strength there had grown quickly after 1815. "This power," he warned, "already mistress of Gibraltar, Malta and the Ionian Islands, has only to add to these possessions an island in the Archipelago, to have turned the Mediterranean into its imperium, and monopolize the Levant trade."[21] Islands for a loan: on this basis Jourdain was empowered to proceed to Paris where the Order's officials, having failed at the Congress of Vienna to win Corfu or anywhere else, were depressed and disheartened.[22] In return for island bases in the eastern Aegean, the Order pledged an alliance of mutual support in any "war with the Muslims." The islands of Rhodes, Karpathos, and Astypalaia would eventually be theirs, but since they inconveniently remained under Ottoman control, the Knights were to be temporarily allowed Skyros instead. The Order's officers pledged to raise up to 4 million francs for the Greeks and began discussions with bankers in London and Paris until Mavrokordatos squashed the whole idea, since he knew that the British—with whom he was keenest to reach terms—were bound to regard it as a hostile French move. The scheme rumbled on, but unsupported by the French government or anyone else, its advocates eventually gave up. Its chief function was to remind the British that the Greeks might look for money elsewhere—and in this respect it seems to have worked.[23]

In the early twenty-first century, when Greece's public finances were ripped apart by the global economic crisis, and its debt burden became unsustainable, it was the fashion among historically minded economists to trace the country's long history of debt problems back to the 1820s. Treating these loans as if they were just like the later ones, or as if the lending practices of the early nineteenth century were essentially the same as those of the twenty-first century, few stopped to wonder how the Greeks had actually been able to raise money in the City of London at a time when there was no Greek sovereign state, or what indeed it said about the lending culture of the City in those years that such loans had ever got off the ground.

One reason why they had been possible was the sheer abundance of investible capital at that time. The end of the Napoleonic Wars and of the low rates to be earned on British government bonds marked the beginning of the rise of the City of London as a global financial center. If Britain became "the world's banker" (the title of a classic work on the subject) in the nineteenth century, it was because from the early 1820s onward the British became addicted to lending their money abroad, and to the higher returns they could find there. Amsterdam, the closest to a foreign debt market in the late eighteenth century, was overtaken by London, and within the City the growth of a new sovereign bond market in the 1820s was rapid: almost no such bonds were quoted in 1820; five years later there were at least thirty-five. The rules of the new Foreign Stock Exchange were approved in March 1823 and it soon had more than 200 members. The architecture of international finance capital was being built as the Greek revolt began.[24]

The expansion of lending to foreign governments had initially catered to recognized powers such as Russia, Denmark, Austria, Naples, and Prussia, but the real takeoff into speculative risk was propelled by the emergence of the independence movements of South America. Even as Bolívar and others battled across the region, delegates from half a dozen South American countries came to London and raised significant sums. With investors buoyed by the indications that South American independence would be guaranteed, the year 1824 saw a boom in sovereign bond issues. The republic of Buenos Aires raised £1 million, Colombia £4.75 million, Mexico £3.2 million, and Peru £0.75 million. These were risky options and like the Greeks, the new governments paid heavily for the privilege: the 8.5 percent yield at issue on the first Greek loan of 1824 was not out of line with the initial yields on Peruvian, Colombian, and Mexican bonds—all of which would also end up in default before the end of the decade. British investors were even prepared to gamble on the Spanish constitutionalist government, which managed to raise more than £1 million in 1823 at a yield of over 16 percent in the face of invasion by 100,000 French troops.[25]

Then, perhaps even more than now, finance rested on fantasy and the rose-tinted prospectus for Greece that Blaquiere published after his trip for English readers in the autumn of 1823 was characteristic of a genre that owed more to travel literature than it did to accounting. But the extreme excitability of British investors at that time can best be gauged from their wild reaction to the opportunities offered by a place in Central America called Poyais. Only months before Blaquiere's report, the Edinburgh publishers William Blackwood & Sons had teamed up with the respectable London firm of Thomas Cadell to bring out A *Sketch of the Mosquito Shore, Including the Territory of Poyais*. One of the most remarkable instances of the travel-prospectus genre, it was written by Thomas Strangeways, who styled himself "Captain of the 1st Native Poyer Regiment and Aide-de-Camp to His Highness Gregor, Cazique of Poyais": although the book was advertised as "chiefly intended for the use of settlers," it was aimed as much at investors. A guide to the topography, mineral deposits ("Gold, etc."), lumber ("Mahogany, Logwood, Cedar") and other resources of the territory on the northern coast of what was later to become British Honduras, its publication formed part of a drive to bring money and settlers to the Caribbean. A Poyesian legation was established in central London in 1822 to sell parcels of land, the Bank of Scotland's printer was commissioned to make the banknotes, and bonds to the sum of £200,000 were issued, bearing 6 percent interest annually, and advertised in the pages of *The Times*. Hundreds of would-be settlers shipped out, and subscribers snapped up the bonds. And then, in a dramatic few weeks, it became clear that "his Highness Gregor" was really a Scottish adventurer called Gregor MacGregor, "Poyais" was a figment of his imagination, "Captain Thomas Strangeways" did not exist, and the bonds were a fraud. It was one of the boldest financial swindles of the century.[26]

Poyais showed up international finance as puffery. Of course, unlike the Kingdom of Poyais, Greece actually existed—or might be about to. Yet whether there existed a Greek government in anything more than name was arguable. Blaquiere's report to the London Greek Committee on the state of the country glossed over the political difficulties and scarcely bothered to seem impartial: indeed, given how much he actually learned during his time in Tripolitsa, it was positively misleading. "We continually passed through vineyards, cornfields and orchards of mulberry-trees," he wrote, portraying Greece in the idyllic shades of a pastoral by Claude Lorrain. "Groups of women and children were also seen round the wells, occupied either in washing or drawing water, as if enjoying the most perfect security. These enlivening and unexpected scenes continued while we followed the romantic and ever-winding course of the Alpheus, through the most enchanting country I ever beheld."[27]

Yet the same terrain was depicted very differently by two other Englishmen who were there at much the same time. James Hamilton Browne noticed that peasants farmed with guns slung across their shoulders, "such was the general insecurity of life and property." "The country is so poor and barren," wrote his companion Edward Trelawny, "that but for its genial climate it would be barely habitable. In the best of times there would not be plenty; but now that the war had passed over the land with fire and slaughter there was scarcely a vestigate of habitation or cultivation."[28] From Blaquiere, however, the reader gained no idea that the Peloponnese was, in the summer of 1823, undergoing the dramatic domestic political upheavals within and outside the government that would lead the following year to outright civil war among the Greeks. He came back to the committee the following week with a few facts and figures, but they were hardly an improvement: he provided unreliable estimates of the revenues from harvests around Gastouni, whose plain was "one of the finest in the world," and changed tack rapidly from dwelling on the Greeks' urgent need of funds to talking up the extraordinary opportunities that awaited the investor in what Blaquiere anticipated would become "one of the most opulent nations of Europe."[29]

A more productive outcome of Blaquiere's trip to Greece in 1823 was that England's most renowned and scandalous poet agreed to lend not only his name but his energies to the work of the London Greek Committee. Lord Byron's friend John Hobhouse, with whom he had traveled to the court of Ali Pasha many years earlier, had already told him about the committee's creation, when Blaquiere himself stopped by en route to Greece and suggested to Byron that he might be able to help the revolution. Byron had been hesitating for some time between fantasies of settling down in South America and returning to the lands that he had, in poetry at least, made his own. When he offered to go, Archbishop Ignatios was thrilled and passed word on to him that Greece would be "grateful." Byron did not have any special purpose in mind when he made his gesture of support and was as keen to escape the drift and dullness of his life in Italy as he was to do anything concrete for the Greeks. But he began informing himself about what was happening and he met returning philhellenes whose harrowing stories he summarized in reports to London. He ordered scarlet uniforms and gunpowder, mailed his banker for funds and chartered a brig, the *Hercules*. "They all say I can be of use," he wrote to his friend Trelawny, to get him to come along. "I do not know how, nor they: but at all events let us go." Ignatios advised Mavrokordatos to ensure Byron was properly treated; it was not, the canny bishop wrote, that he could do much good for the cause; but if displeased, he could certainly do harm.[30]

Originally the London Committee had intended to appoint Thomas Gordon, the professional soldier who had served in Greece in 1821, to command an expedition in its name. Gordon had helped get the preparations under way before opting out on the grounds that there was no longer an effective government in the country. He was delighted when he learned Byron had been recruited in his stead. Yet Gordon's misgivings had been well founded. By the late summer of 1823, the Greek government was so fractured that it was not clear where exactly Byron should go nor which personalities he should support. At Astros that spring, the national assembly had elected a new five-man executive headed by Petros Mavromihalis: like its president, most of its members and ministers were from the Peloponnese. Mavrokordatos had become the executive's general secretary and its de facto foreign minister, but when he was also elected head of the legislature, he was physically threatened by Kolokotronis and forced—as described in Chapter 8—to seek refuge with the island notables on Hydra. The Peloponnesians seemed to be in control, but it was the islanders and Mavrokordatos who saw most clearly the possibilities opening up in England. It was at this crucial juncture that Byron's ship reached Kefalonia and he learned that the London Greek Committee had nominated him as their representative in Greece. He made the Ionian Islands his base while he figured out what to do.

Byron was not only a great poet; he was also no one's fool. *Don Juan*, the satirical epic he was writing at this time, talks about bankers as "the true lords of Europe," so he was hardly unaware of international finance as the new instrument of state-building or, by extension, of the implications of his own role. And unlike many of the philhellenes, he not only understood something about the region but also admired and felt sympathy for the Ottoman way of life as well as for the Greeks. Conscious of the responsibility he bore, the power of his name, and the resources at his disposal, Byron began to realize how little he knew of what was actually happening and how riven the Greek leadership was. This is why he sent James Hamilton Browne and Edward Trelawny to the Peloponnese to report back to him. "Let me hear from you often," were Byron's parting words—at least as told by Trelawny. "Come back soon. If things are farcical, they will do for *Don Juan*; if heroical, you have another canto of *Childe Harold*."[31]

It is hard to think of anyone who was less suited to the task of carrying out an impartial fact-finding mission than the utterly unreliable Trelawny. The Cornishman had joined the navy at the behest of his father, fought the French on numerous occasions, visited India, married and left the first of his three wives in England, and ended up in Italy with Byron and the Shelleys. It was he who had the sad duty of identifying Shelley's body on the beach where it had been washed up after a storm at sea. Tiring of shooting ducks with Byron, Trelawny leaped at the chance to go to war, and instead of returning to him to make his report, he ended up spending months in the mountains of central Greece as lieutenant to the armatole Odysseus Androutsos. There he married Androutsos's thirteen-year-old half-sister and survived an assassination attempt and the death of his chief before returning to England, embarking on yet another marriage, and enjoying a contented old age.

In Greece, Trelawny acquired a particular dislike for Mavrokordatos and the political intellectuals around him, preferring the company of men of action such as Kolokotronis and Androutsos. Aware that Byron was on his way to Greece, and reckoning that Trelawny and others would probably persuade the poet to head for the government headquarters in the Peloponnese, Mavrokordatos ordered his closest aide, Giorgios Praïdis, to sail out to urge Byron not to make for Tripolitsa, where he would likely be in Kolokotronis's hands, but for Hydra. Barraged by requests and uncertain whom to trust, Byron did the hardest but wisest thing: nothing. "I did not come here to join a faction but a nation," he wrote in his journal in September 1823. "It will require much circumspection from me to avoid the character of a partizan." The very fact that he began writing a journal during his time in the Ionian Islands indicates Byron probably felt the need to arrange his thoughts to make sense of the choices before him. Unlike most of the philhellenes around him, he was not inclined to rush to judgment and he stands out for his willingness to try to get to grips with a complex and confused situation without idealizing any of the parties.[32]

The Greek government had approved the idea of a loan in 1823, but because of its internal divisions, getting delegates nominated to send to London took months. Choosing Louriotis was easy: he had been involved with the negotiations from the start. The second delegate was chosen for different reasons: Ioannis Orlandos was the brother-in-law of the Koundouriotis brothers, a wealthy man who represented the Hydriot shipowning interest that was allied with Mavrokordatos in its enthusiasm for the loan and similarly opposed to the power of the Peloponnesian notables. The third delegate was a sop to the latter—a member of the Zaimis notable clan who because of illness did not leave at the same time as the others and in fact arrived in London only after the loan had been agreed.

This choice of delegates left the loan negotiations in the hands of Mavrokordatos and the Hydra shipowners, a result that had not come about by chance. On the contrary, the goal of marginalizing the Peloponnesians in the government was at the center of Mavrokordatos's thinking; in his estimation, allowing them control over any future loan would do nothing to strengthen the national cause. Understanding Byron's reluctance to take sides in the Greeks' murky internal quarrels, Mavrokordatos adopted an idea—likely thrown out only half-seriously to him by Trelawny—that they should ask the poet for a loan to tide them over. There was some urgency in the request for in the autumn of 1823 Mesolonghi was once again under threat from Ottoman troops and, unlike the year before, Mavrokordatos was not there and the lack of funds meant the Hydra fleet could not bring him or any assistance to the town. Mavrokordatos thus wrote asking for Byron's help and trying to reassure him that assisting Mesolonghi would not mean picking sides: "To bring aid to this place, to save it, to save in consequence the whole of Greece, is that to declare oneself for a faction? I do not think so." Somehow he also got Petros Mavromihalis as head of the national executive to endorse the idea, which gave it the veneer of legitimacy that Byron valued, and Orlandos and Louriotis were duly empowered to make their way to Kefalonia in order to put the request to the poet. They were just in time to catch him before he left the Ionian Islands for the Peloponnese and their conversations with him, held over several days in the lazaretto in Argostoli, turned out to be decisive for the future of Greece. Not only did they get him to advance funds out of his own pocket against the future loan so that the Hydra fleet could sail; even more important, they persuaded him to change his own plans and make for Mesolonghi instead of Tripolitsa. In effect this meant the most famous philhellene of the day was opting to throw his prestige and that of the committee behind Alexandros Mavrokordatos and his allies. Byron seems to have decided that although no national government existed in reality, Mavrokordatos was more likely to help bring one into being than the Peloponnesian notables and chieftains he had been about to join. Noting that Mavrokordatos had "not only talents but integrity," he described him as a "*Washington* or *Kosciusko* kind of man"—someone with the potential to be a genuine national leader.[33]

By the time Mavrokordatos reached Mesolonghi in December 1823, the Ottoman forces had withdrawn, relieving the town, and obviating the need for military assistance. The Hydriot ships that accompanied him had left almost immediately; they had captured huge sums of money from a Turkish brig that had been carrying wage arrears for the garrison in Patras and were anxious to return home to divide up the prize. Yet Byron's own arrival in Mesolonghi in early January 1824 was far from pointless. The London Greek Committee sent out specialists to join him—including several doctors and the fire-master William Parry, with equipment and mechanics—and with their assistance Byron aspired to create a small military force that he could lead against the Ottomans. The Souliots too clustered around the rich English lord, though he found them a mixed blessing: having romanticized them as "the best and bravest of combatants," he was exhausted by their violent behavior and incessant demands, which dismayed the townspeople and eventually drove Parry's men and other volunteers away. In fact, the primary significance of Byron's time in Mesolonghi was not military but political, for he had, in effect, given the imprimatur of his presence to bolster Mavrokordatos in the looming civil war.[34]

Before he could realize his plans to campaign in the field, however, Byron suffered recurrent onsets of fever and despite or because of extensive bleeding by his doctors, he died in Mesolonghi on April 19, 1824. Nothing he had managed to achieve in the short time he spent in Mesolonghi rivaled the impact of his death. The news that the most famous poet in the world, worn down and delirious, had died as a volunteer in the Greek cause was a sensation across Europe.[35] Within Greece, it helped cast the English in a new light. Because the impression of England among the Greek revolutionaries had been largely negative up to this point, the government used Byron's death to convey a counterimage—that of the English hero who had sacrificed his life and fortune for Greece. The authorities ensured that the occasion of his death was treated with exceptional solemnity across the country and orders went out for official ceremonies of mourning. A contemporary oral account that has come down to us reveals how effectively this message was transmitted: in it, Ioannis Laganes, an otherwise unknown inhabitant of Athens, extolled the English for their material support, their courage, and their money:

> Two noble leaders come from England to help us in our rights, and they have brought treasures for our nation, they have brought ammunition, cannons and mortars, so that we may fight like worthy heroes, and check the enemy on all sides, and if we need anything else they will give us a loan again . . .[36]

"*Two* noble leaders"? One was Byron, of course. The other, less familiar today, was Colonel Leicester Stanhope, the 5th Earl of Harrington, veteran of the Third Maratha War, and an ardent—indeed fanatical—Benthamite. It is hard to imagine anyone more different in outlook from the aristocratic Byron than the "typographical Colonel," so called for his belief in the power of the press and publicity. As energetic as Bowring or as their mutual idol, Bentham, Leicester Stanhope had plenty of ideas about what the Greeks needed: he helped establish a Greek-language newspaper in Mesolonghi, under the editorship of a Swiss radical, and pursued with equal vigor the creation of a national postal service, hospitals, and schools on the Lancasterian model. Stanhope liked to boast that his experience as an officer in India had given him insight into "the character of Asiatic nations" that made him feel at home in Greece. In fact, he demonstrated far less understanding of the Greeks than Byron, who regarded him as a "crackbrained enthusiast of the regular Bentham breed . . . [He had] brought with him Nabob airs from Hindostan; and while he cajoles the people, wishes to govern them." Like Trelawny, Stanhope had a weakness for the chieftains, and he even proposed to Kolokotronis that they send little Kolinos Kolokotronis, the old man's youngest boy, to England for Bentham to educate—a mind-boggling idea that did not materialize.

Stanhope's favorite recipient of improving advice was the chieftain he came to regard not only as his friend but as the hope of Greece, the courageous but double-dealing armatole who dominated eastern Rumeli, Odysseus Androutsos. Androutsos had already acquired one admirer in Trelawny, who had joined him in his mountain cavern and formed a trusted member of his entourage and indeed his family. Stanhope encountered the chieftain in an even headier setting: Athens. Only Stanhope could have written to "General Odysseus" that he was "desirous of obtaining your sanction to the formation of a utilitarian society in Athens" that would advance "useful knowledge," generate fellow societies elsewhere in Greece, and form part of an international network of learned organizations. Watching Odysseus preside over a public election of magistrates in an olive grove outside Athens, Stanhope dreamed he saw an ancient hero come to life: he believed him to be "the most extraordinary man" in the whole of Greece. In this way the ardent Benthamite placed his hopes for the triumph of enlightened reason in a man who not only had been schooled in Ali Pasha's court, but had murdered two government emissaries and eventually patched things up with the Ottomans, marching with them across Attica. As the Peloponnesian notable Andreas Zaimis wrote in his laconic way, the colonel was "a philhellene, though simplistic and easily deceived."[37]

A lot of people could not stomach the "typographical Colonel": if one of them was Byron, another was the British foreign secretary, George Canning, who seems to have had a hand in canceling Stanhope's leave and recalling him to London as an army officer on active service. His departure in the summer of 1824 was a relief for the Greek political leaders who had been obliged to put up with the unwanted and often idiotic advice of a man who was nonetheless a powerful Englishman on close terms with the London Greek Committee and an influential voice in it after Byron's death. One can only sympathize with the passionate appeal of Mavrokordatos: "Is there a despotism more cruel than that of a foreigner who, without any right, wants to give the orders without any regard to the existing laws? . . . Have we overthrown the Ottoman yoke to succumb to another?" Could Stanhope not see, Mavrokordatos wondered, that violent chieftains, happy to kill those in their power without a moment's thought, were not "good men" simply because they humored his constitutionalism? Were those Greeks who believed a monarchy was needed to win over the European powers therefore automatically "bad men"? Mavrokordatos and others did their best to explain to Stanhope why a brand-new legal system would not work if it did not take into account the importance of the Byzantine ecclesiastical law that was still so important in the villages. They tried to convey—as Byron did too—why a time of war was not the best moment to preach total freedom of the press. Stanhope had the inhabitants of Athens write an appeal to the committee in London requesting that "the most worthy of all strangers who have visited Greece"—meaning himself—should be allowed to stay. But it took more than that to persuade the deputy adjutant general of the Horse Guards, who ordered him to return home without delay. Accompanying Byron's body back to London, Stanhope arrived there in July 1824, cross and disaffected and—as would soon become clear—keen to complicate the task of those advocating assistance for the Greeks.[38]

In London, Bowring met Foreign Secretary George Canning to plead the Greek cause. Bowring suggested to Canning—implausibly—that military successes had "decided finally the independence of Greece." According to him, Britain would soon have to choose between letting the eastern Mediterranean as a whole fall under Russian influence or establishing itself as an ally of the Greeks. The key was to raise a loan and put it in the hands of "the really virtuous party." In this way, Bowring followed the strategy that had been outlined earlier by Ignatios and Mavrokordatos: to exert diplomatic leverage in London by playing up the threat of a Russian intervention.

Too subtle a politician to be scared by such manipulative talk, Canning had for some time anyway been contemplating the possible advantages to Britain of a free Greece. After he succeeded Castlereagh as foreign secretary in September 1822, he had supported an apparently small but significant shift in policy that had led the British to recognize Greek belligerency at sea. In February 1823 a highly confidential meeting had taken place in Zante brokered by Captain Hamilton of the *Cambrian*, in which the British sounded out a representative of Mavrokordatos as to what the Greeks' aims were and offered their services to negotiate something short of a total break with the Porte: the Greek response had been to insist on full independence. A year later, when

Canning again asked Bowring what kind of regime the Greeks envisaged, Bowring reiterated that they wanted independence for a territory ending "somewhere to the south of Macedonia": as the Greeks had already done, he rejected the idea of Greece remaining a tributary power under the sultan. Canning listened; the really important thing was that he did not indicate any disapproval for the proposed loan. He was, almost imperceptibly, shifting the course of British policy around from the pro-Ottoman line of his predecessors to one that would eventually come to regard Greek independence as inevitable and therefore desirable.[39]

Talk of money for Greece was thus in the air when three hundred members of the London Greek Committee crowded into a back room of the Crown and Anchor in late February 1824 to meet the two newly arrived delegates. The brief display of mutual support and admiration ended with the delegates handing round copies of the Greek proclamation of independence of two years earlier. The work of organizing the loan had already taken place, led by Bowring. Behaving in a way that was later to prove controversial—he earned the very handsome sum of around £10,000 in commission for the deal—Bowring had agreed with the relatively minor firm of Loughnan and O'Brien that they would act as contractors for a loan of £800,000. Less than a month later the delegates signed an agreement, the loan was advertised in the press, and within a few days it had been oversubscribed.

What the Greeks actually received was a good deal less than the nominal sum of the loan because as usual the lenders got a hefty discount and the starting price was only 59 percent of the face value of the bonds. The lenders also insisted on paying in installments and on appointing British commissioners to oversee the disbursement. Although Orlandos and Louriotis had done their best to downplay Greece's simmering civil strife, reports of factionalism were reaching London, alarming investors and depressing the stock's price. Confidence soon ebbed. News of Byron's death, which reached England some weeks later in May, was another blow. In July, his body lay in state for several days in London—he had been refused a state funeral at Westminster Abbey—before a large crowd watched the bier, accompanied by three coaches, escorted out of the city as it made its way to the remote Nottinghamshire village, near his ancestral home, where he was to find his last resting place. His funeral was scarcely over when the London Greek Committee heard from Colonel

Stanhope. Angry and bitter, Stanhope insisted that Mavrokordatos was untrustworthy and that the loan would do more harm than good. He published an open letter to Bowring warning about the lack of security facing the bondholders, while the price of the Greek bond went further downhill before recovering somewhat later in the year.

At the heart of it all there was Bowring. The architect of the 1824 loan was not a wealthy man but he was in a rush to become one, and his high-mindedness did not prevent him from engaging in some desperate business practices. As an American journalist later recollected:

> Mr. Bowring labored night and day to run up the stock, *bullying* it and the public, through the journals and newspapers, and purchasing to the full extent of all his means, capital and credit which, of course, with the Greek Committee, was not to be questioned, or disparaged: and talking on "Change, by the half-hour, his philhellenism, and prating everywhere about Lord Byron, Colonel Stanhope and Trelawney [*sic*]; and blazing forth at public dinners and meetings in a sort of India-cracker style—fizz, fizz! flash and whirr!—about a free press and the sacrifices due to "that country of gods and godlike men." Meanwhile, he withheld information which, as secretary of the Greek Committee, he was constantly receiving and which, if communicated, would have sent the stock down to zero, if not something lower.[40]

Bowring's role in the bond issue laid him open to accusations of personal profiteering. He had charged the Greeks an enormous sum in commission for having arranged the loan, and the Tory press gleefully publicized his lucrative role in the affair. He also did something clearly disreputable: having reserved an additional £25,000 worth of bonds to himself, and in arrears on the payments, he pressured the Greek delegates to use some of the loan proceeds to keep the bond price up. That was bad enough. But what was worse is that when the maneuver failed, he strong-armed the Greeks to buy his bonds back from him at the original price. Worse still, when the price rose, he asked for them back again. He went on the offensive by getting the London Greek Committee—which in this case basically meant Bowring himself—to complain to the Greek government about the behavior of the two deputies. But as a ruse to get them out of the way it failed, and when the delegates arranged a second loan in early 1825, it was using the firm of J. and S. Ricardo instead. While the first, organized chiefly by Bow-ring, had a nominal value of £800,000; the second was for £2 million. But in each case the real benefit enjoyed by the Greeks was far less: from the first, they received only £312,000 in specie, weapons, and stores, and from the second no more than £291,000 in coin along with perhaps twice as much again that was spent abroad. The precise sums remain controversial—like everything else about the loans—but the basic point is clear: once commissions were set aside, as well as reserved interest payments and money that was spent with merchants on goods in England, only relatively modest sums remained at the disposal of the government. Accusations of corruption, however, dogged the two Greek delegates as well, and for years after. In comparison with the others, Louriotis seems to have behaved properly throughout, and if Orlandos enriched himself this hardly excused Bowring's behavior.

While Bowring was headed to bankruptcy, the London Greek Com-mittee was on the path to extinction. It had certainly made an impact in its few years of existence, spending more than thousands of pounds on equipment ranging from printing presses and surgical equipment to med-icine, maps, weapons and ammunition. It had paid the costs of men traveling out to Greece and found schooling for some Greek boys brought to England. Yet the planned expedition fizzled out without result and the scandal that trailed after the loans fatally damaged popular philhellenism in Britain. George Waddington noted in 1825 in London "such a lifeless indifference to the very cause and name of Greece" that it was "a sympa-thy that appears to be extinct forever." When a proposal came from Geneva philhellenes to raise a third loan through a contact on the com-mittee, the *Morning Post* commented: "The reputation of the Greek Committee cannot have reached Geneva. So gross has been the misman-agement of the two former loans that not one shilling more could be raised in England as long as *any* of its members are known to have a part."[41] The Tory press enjoyed itself in satirical verse:

> Roused by the sound of liberty and scrip
> To arms, to arms the belligerent brokers skip
> Loud rings the cry of freedom far and wide
> Stocks and subscriptions pour in on every side
> Contractors, weeping over Grecian wounds
> Pocket their four-and-sixty thousand pounds.[42]

If we want to follow the money, we should begin in April 1824 when an English brig, the *Florida*, arrived in Zakynthos with the first tranche of the loan. It was accompanied by Blaquiere and by Mavrokordatos's man Polyzoidis, who handed the money over to the bankers on the island as agreed. "All Zakynthos greeted me as a second Messiah," recollected Polyzoidis.[43] The ship then turned around and headed back to England with a reluctant Colonel Stanhope on board, along with Byron's corpse preserved in a vat of rum. Both the poet's death and Stanhope's recall complicated the disbursement of the funds, since they had been appointed commissioners and the argument between the bankers and the government was still continuing when the *Little Sally* docked at the beginning of June with the second installment. The *Florida* returned to Greece for a second trip with the third installment and became the first ship to deliver money directly into the hands of the government. It docked off Nafplion in late September, two days after the arrival of new British commissioners, who had traveled across the Peloponnese to meet it. The remainder of the loan arrived more quickly: the fourth installment in the *Little Sally* left London in November, followed by the *Nimble* the following month, and then the *Lively*, which arrived at Nafplion with £50,000 in April 1825. Over the year in which these six consignments were delivered, Greece moved through a civil war between the two rival governmental authorities to the consolidation of authority in a single executive under the control of the Hydriot magnates. The cause of their triumph was of course the loan.[44]

Given the quarrel between the islanders on the one hand and the Peloponnesians on the other, it was remarkable that British investors had parted with their money at all. Fighter-historian George Finlay wrote later in astonishment about "this display of financial insanity on the London Stock Exchange." The effective result, in his estimation, was that the loan contractors and the committee had between them "placed the absolute control of a sum equal to nearly four years' revenue of the country in the hands of a faction engaged in civil war." Not surprisingly, Kolokotronis told anyone who would listen how much he disliked the idea: he had been outmaneuvered and had foreseen what would happen. So had others. "The government will now be effective and sweep every obstacle before its golden torrent," predicted Trelawny; the kapetans, reported Stanhope, "fear that it will deprive them of power and the means of acquiring wealth."[45]

In Zakynthos, keeping a keen eye on the loan's progress was a well-connected merchant from Epiros called Georgios Tourtouris. He had a low opinion of Kolokotronis whom he once referred to as "that indescribable former butcher from Zakynthos," and he was dismissive of the "passivity, malignancy and disorderly attitude" of the Peloponnesians in general. "My great hope," Tourtouris wrote to his nephew, "is in the loan that the Nation has contracted in England because if that gold comes and the Administration can pay the soldiers, then the fortunes of the rebels will immediately alter."[46] Tourtouris's nephew—Ioannis Kolettis, an increasingly influential government minister from Rumeli—was the key figure in what happened next and the soldiers Tourtouris referred to were the Rumeliot bands that Kolettis planned to bring south to crush the Peloponnesian "rebels." Kolettis had been Ali Pasha's personal physician, amassing significant wealth and contacts over the years before 1821 among the armatoles of western Greece. He had accompanied Mavrokordatos to the first national assembly and he had deputized for him in the first provisional government and served as interior minister. A member of the new Koundouriotis government, Kolettis knew how to best use the loan: they would create a hired army for the island side, paying the Rumeliot and Souliot chieftains out of the London monies to subdue their rivals in the Morea.

Tracking the money became Kolettis's priority. He wrote to Stanhope in that crucial spring of 1824: "Everyone is speaking about the loan. Some say it has arrived at Zakynthos; others at Malta and others somewhere else. However the Administration has no news about it . . . Please, if you have confirmed news about the loan, let me know as quickly as possible." As soon as he had obtained more encouraging information, Kolettis informed the kapetans they should gather information on the numbers and readiness of the men under arms in their areas to give him a sense of the cost, and the leaders of armed bands in both Rumeli and the Peloponnese began to recalibrate their loyalties. The sailors of the shipowning islands too could finally anticipate government pay.[47] "The wages of the ships you manage to put to sea will be paid immediately by the government once the loan arrives from Zakynthos," the executive promised the Spetsiots in June in an effort to get their ships readied. "Another two hundred thousand *thalers* from the loan have come from London to Zakynthos. Additionally the government has learned that a messenger from London arrived in Corfu in only twelve days, who will certainly be carrying new instructions from the lenders to facilitate the unimpeded disbursement of the loan to the government."[48]

By May, as Stanhope wrote, the prospect of a loan had exerted "its wonder-working effect." The Koundouriotis government had already brought over irregulars from central Greece who took Tripolitsa from their rivals and secured the area around Argos. Kolokotronis, who a year earlier had been master of much of the Peloponnese, gave ground before them.[49] From Nafplion, the word spread fast when the first consignments of the loan arrived there. Samuel Sheridan Wilson was a British missionary traversing the Peloponnese when he encountered three armed men. They had only one question for him: "Has the loan arrived?" When they learned that the English brig was in the harbor of Nafplion, they danced in celebration, bade the reverend a cursory farewell, and set off "for the golden fleece."[50]

"The rush to diggings in California and Australia, on the first discovery of gold in those regions, was partial, if not orderly, as compared with the wild and universal rush of the Greeks on Nafplia," Trelawny recalled. "That town was beleaguered by armed legions of robbers, frantically clamoring for their share of the spoil." William (W. H.) Humphreys, a young philhellene who had traveled with Stanhope, left a vivid account of the arrival of the first tranche in Nafplion. The town, he wrote, was "a crowded Babel of vagabonds, in diverse dresses of all nations—a mingled scene of dirty splendor and dirtier wretchedness: and the streets wore the appearance of a sorry masquerade. Half-starved adventurers, candidates for posts and employment in the Government, open-mouthed in expectation of the English Loan, and straining every nerve to have a share, however small, in the general scramble."[51] The Piedmontese Count Palma, one of Restoration Europe's wandering liberals, watched on board the *Florida* as the money was unloaded and "despatched two hours afterwards in different vessels for Hydra, Spessia, Athens and Missolonghi."[52] A spending spree followed as the government doled out funds to its supporters, creating positions for them in the barely existent administration, paying off their disgruntled sailors or subsidizing the armed retinues of their chieftains. "Arrivals of this kind infuse the liveliest joy into the hearts of the Greeks, the greater part of whom do not rightly comprehend the meaning of a 'loan' but very simply conclude it is some European method of making a present," observed James Emerson, who was in Nafplion for the arrival of the

Lively in the spring of 1825 and witnessed the celebratory discharge of pistols, the shouts of "Long Live King George!" and the band playing "God Save the King" in the main square.[53]

The available figures are rudimentary but the conclusion they point to is clear. The proceeds of the loan exponentially but temporarily boosted the resources available to the Koundouriotis government. According to the recent calculations of Simos Bozikis, the main sources of government revenue shot up from around 3 million *grossia* annually in 1822 and 1823 to over 12 million in 1824 and 22.5 million in 1825, before falling back sharply. Although this extraordinary increase was largely because of the loan, revenues also grew from taxes and customs duties. In other words, the boost to the government from the loans allowed it to consolidate its power more broadly and thus to extend its fiscal reach, but the effects lasted only two years.[54]

The Koundouriotis government used this windfall to fund three things: first, the fleet from Hydra, Spetses, and Psara; second, armed bands that would be loyal to the government; and third, new positions for their supporters within the apparatus of the administration. Of these, the navy alone—which meant the ships and crews of Hydra and Spetses above all—consumed over a third of the total, and rather more than that if one includes the significant sums spent on garrisoning the two islands against a possible Ottoman attack—some 5,000 armed men sent to Hydra, 3,500 to Spetses, more than enough to ward off enemies from any direction.[55] The two shipping islands were also able to purchase munitions, fit out new fireships, and prepare to overhaul the damaged ships in their fleets. Large sums were placed at the disposal of Kolettis to pay for his Rumeliot soldiery in the government's war against Kolokotronis and the Peloponnesians. By contrast relatively modest amounts were spent on the provisioning and repair of coastal fortresses and garrisons held by the Greeks and only a tiny sum was reserved for what passed for a regular army unit at the government's disposal.[56]

What can be gleaned from these—the very earliest examples of official statistics in Greece, and unquestionably among the least reliable? First, that the loan's primary purpose was to finance the island-Rumeliot alliance. The Koundouriotis government gave priority to its own in outfitting the fleet, and the sums spent on the shipping of Hydra and Spetses—more than £80,000 (some 4 million *grossia*) in 1824 alone—dwarfed the

753,000 *grossia* the government had managed to dedicate to their fleets in 1822 and the 139,000 in 1823.[57] It is not clear, however, that this spending had much overall impact on the war: the funds came in too late to prevent enemy forces sacking the shipping islands of Psara and Kasos that summer, massacring their inhabitants, and permanently weakening the Greeks' maritime resources. Thus the money did not help the Greeks withstand the well-equipped Egyptian fleet or the revamped imperial Ottoman navy, either then or later. Loan or no loan, the Greek predominance of the seas was a thing of the past.

Money was also wastefully disbursed to Rumeliot chieftains and other kapetans who rallied to the government side in the Morea. Although the government instructed its agents to distribute funds on the basis of the men actually in the field, anecdotal evidence makes it clear that this did not happen: the payments were inflated and the lists drawn up by the chieftains themselves bore little relation to reality. In effect, the government had to pay the usual premium for loyalty. Finlay cites several egregious cases: Dimitrios Makris drew pay and rations for five hundred men when he had only fifty under arms; Alexakis Vlachopoulos mustered fewer than one hundred men but claimed pay for four hundred. Thus money was spent on the wages of soldiers who did not exist instead of improving the fortifications guarding the Peloponnese. Neglecting the ongoing sieges of Patras and Modon, the government allowed hundreds of armed men to flock into Nafplion and enriched their leaders, storing up trouble for the future.[58]

Imperceptibly, however, and more enduringly, the loans also contributed to a kind of shift in the political culture. With the loan came accounting and the lists, tables, controls, and itemization associated with this. That the lists were often fictitious, the accounting mostly imaginative, is not the point here: the mere existence of budgetary statistics, however inaccurate, signaled the beginnings of a new conception of state bureaucracy in Greece. When the first installment of the second loan arrived in March 1825, the hitherto quiescent legislature, alarmed at the lack of accountability for the way the funds were being used, voted to make the executive account for its use of them. Georgios Koundouriotis, the president of the executive, who was not used to being answerable to anyone, began to feel the pressure of fielding questions about the government's spending and took to his bed. This pressure intensified over the following twelve months and made him and his brother Lazaros increasingly defensive and aggrieved. It was the beginning of a new relationship between taxpayers and their political representatives, and also, as Bozikis astutely observes, between soldiers, their pay, and centralized authority. The kapetans and other intermediaries remained powerful figures. But gradually one detects the idea of a new kind of military service emerging—one that used not the old Turkish vocabulary of Ottoman soldiering but the language of military ranks in formalized Greek, with grades and decorations. Everyone was keen to be called "general" (*stratigos*), for instance, which evoked the idea of a national army long before one existed. This language had been in evidence from the start, and the power of the traditional bands remained strong. But the notion of a centralized political authority, one that existed not alongside but above powerful local intermediaries, began to take root. It was after all because the central government was so potentially powerful a means to legitimize wealth extraction that so many people were arguing over who should control it.

Finally, the loans affected the circulation of money itself. Although the government had identified a problem of debased coinage as early as 1822, the existence of new legislation in succeeding years indicated it had not solved the issue; indeed, in July 1824 the death penalty was imposed for forgery. This makes it all the more striking that on both Hydra and Spetses there were mints operating under the control of the major shipowners, which were melting down some of the newly arrived sovereigns and producing fake Ottoman piastres that were then put into circulation around the eastern Mediterranean. The Reverend Wilson paid a visit one day to the mint on Hydra where he found two men at work, one of them a Turkish captive, in a dingy room making Ottoman coins. They explained to him that imperial agents were flooding the Greek lands with debased coinage and hence they were making their own to send to Constantinople, thus using the loan to fund a kind of reciprocal financial warfare with their enemy. Perhaps they were; more likely the resourceful shipowners were finding an ingenious way to stretch the proceeds even further.[59]

The deployment of the loans became a bone of contention throughout the summer of 1824 and eventually contributed to the outbreak of a second round of fighting among Greeks. Andreas Londos was an important notable from the northern shore of the Peloponnese who had taken the government side and been put in charge of the siege of Patras.

In October of that year he complained about how little money had been allotted him. It was in a way the usual grievance of a military leader, complaining about being starved of rations and wages for his soldiers. What was new were the accusations and counteraccusations that swirled around the use of these "national funds." When he was charged with misappropriation and waste, Londos responded by accusing the government of spending the nation's money on mercenaries purely to keep it in power.[60] They were behaving, he insisted angrily, like Ottoman tyrants not members of the Greek nation. He was one of the so-called two Andreases—the other was Andreas Zaimis—who dominated the fertile regions along the northwest littoral of the Morea and their support of the Koundouriotis government had been critical. Now they left it to join their fellow Peloponnesians in opposition.

In early November an anonymous proclamation appeared from "The Patriots" (*oi Patriotai*) to the inhabitants of the Peloponnese: it called on "the peoples of Greece" (*oi laoi tis Ellados*) to oppose the tyranny of the Koundouriotis administration and warned that they were burdening the country with debt that the Moreots would have to mortgage their lands to repay. Government forces sent into Arkadia to control key towns clashed with men from the region commanded by Kolokotronis and Deliyannis. The latter were the self-described "patriots" taking on what they regarded as an illegitimate government, run by a capricious president on Hydra who was abusing his access to the money from London to seize power. "That which we feared, and struggled to extinguish, the flame that is to say of civil war, has begun to grow," wrote another powerful landowner, Panoutsos Notaras, to Londos.[61]

Kolokotronis wrote later: "The loans that had been advanced by Koundouriotis strengthened the government and power made it legitimate."[62] The Rumeliot chiefs organized by Kolettis brought their bands into the Morea, and in under two months, together with the old Etairist Papaflessas and a few other Peloponnesian warlords, they crushed the somewhat half-hearted rebels and despoiled much of the region. Androutsos's former lieutenant Ioannis Gouras defeated the men of the primate Notaras before turning against the strongholds of Zaimis farther west: his men's brutal treatment of the villagers remained long in their memory and caused clashes with some other Rumeliot kapetans. Georgios Karaïskakis, only recently rehabilitated after accusations of dealing with the Ottomans, led his men to plunder Zaimis's home in the mountain village of Kerpini. But it was not just invaders from the north who took the government coin: many Peloponnesian soldiers changed allegiances. When a young *grammatikos* with Kolokotronis returned to his home town of Stemnitsa, he found 1,500 armed men, some of them making merry in his own house. Expecting them to be Rumeliots hired by the government to come into the Morea, he was shocked when it turned out they had been fighting a few months before for Kolokotronis; now they had become government troops, even though they counted themselves the young man's friends and kissed his mother's hand as a sign of respect.[63] Thanks to English gold, the government became strong enough for it to bring the fighting to an end by eventually taking the extraordinary step of arresting Kolokotronis, and other stalwarts of the Peloponnesian opposition, shutting them up in February 1825 in a monastery on Hydra. This was the true cost of the civil war, upon which so much English gold had been spent; it had ended up paying Greeks not to fight the Ottomans but to take up arms against one another.[64]

Among all the warring factions it was perhaps only Mavrokordatos who really believed in the need for a strong centralized administration with its own regular army and navy, and even he had been forced to more or less abandon his constitutional experiment in western Greece and acknowledge the power of the kapetans and armatoles of the region. In the government of 1824–26 the most powerful force remained the Hydriot president Georgios Koundouriotis—or rather his brother Lazaros behind the scenes: their prime concern was to raise the money for their ships and crews that secured their own position on the island. The Hydriot shipowners had no interest in creating a modern navy that would render them redundant, and in fact they resisted proposals made to them by French and English naval men to create such a fleet. Mavrokordatos's other ally Kolettis was comfortable dealing with the Rumeliot kapetans in the ways he had learned at the court of Ali Pasha: he too had little interest in raising a European-style army trained by European officers. Having defeated its internal enemies, the Koundouriotis government thus in effect proposed to wage the ongoing war against the Ottomans with the same forces with which it had begun it—irregular armed bands on land and naval forces from the shipowning islands by sea. These forces had been sufficient both to halt the Ottomans and to prevent the reconquest of the Peloponnese.

But when a new factor emerged on the horizon, the Greeks found themselves fighting against the very kind of army that they lacked and scorned—an army trained by European officers in modern methods. The Greek navy, newly enriched by English sovereigns, turned out to be incapable of preventing an enormous Egyptian fleet landing thousands of troops in the southwest corner of the Peloponnese in early 1825. The arrival of this army—commanded by the son of the pasha of Egypt—changed everything. The Peloponnese, ravaged by two years of fighting against the Ottomans and then further devastated in the civil war, now came under direct attack and it quickly became clear that the old methods were inadequate to ward off an increasingly likely total defeat.

12

MEHMED ALI
INTERVENES

*The only books I ever read are men's faces, and I seldom read
them amiss.*

Mehmed Ali quoted in C. A. Murray, *A Short
Memoir of Mohammed Ali* (London, 1898), 4

*One might say that Mehmed Ali now holds in his hands the fate
of the Ottoman Empire.*

General Pierre Henri Gaston de Livron (Marseille) to
the Minister of Finance (Paris), October 12, 1825 (in
Driault, *L'expédition de Crète et de Morée*, 91)

The visitor to the northern Greek port of Kavala is well advised to leave
the undistinguished harbor and to follow a small stone road that leads
away from the dockside and ascends the headland overlooking the sea.
The noise and bustle of the modern town fades. On the right, after several hundred yards, a long low building with domed lead roofs and a
discreet doorway marks the site of the former Ottoman imaret: this was
a large complex of buildings including a boarding school, shops, baths,
a prayer hall, and the soup kitchen (*imaret*) that provided its name.
Restored in 2004 and converted into a five-star hotel, the complex with
its gardens and courtyards today welcomes visitors with a taste for
understated luxury in historic surroundings. But for many years it was
a ruin, where the tables and chairs of an occasional café could be seen

stacked in its main hall; indeed, the entire complex might well not have survived had it not been for one thing: it belonged to Egypt.[1]

The answer as to why a municipal building in a northern Greek town possesses such an unexpected connection is close at hand, just a few hundred yards farther up the hill where the road eventually peters out in a small tree-lined square. A metal gate in one corner marks the entrance to a beautifully preserved two-story timber-framed house, a fine example of a provincial Ottoman Balkan *konaki*, set in a shady garden above the sea. A sign states that this was the home of Mehmed Ali, the founder of the Egyptian royal family, who was born in Kavala in the Muslim year 1184 (1770/71). While there is some question as to whether he ever lived in that house, there is no doubt about his deep attachment to the town. In Egypt, Mehmed Ali's descendants were chased out by the nationalists in 1953 and the last king, Fuad II, today resides in Switzerland. But in Kavala the traces of their presence remain.

Despite the Egyptian connection, Mehmed Ali was not an Arab and he did not speak Arabic: descended from a modest Turkish family long resident in Kavala, he started out in charge of a local troop detachment, married a prosperous widow with whom he had five children, and was making a fair living in the tobacco trade when the town governor was ordered to send several hundred Albanians to Egypt to help reassert Ottoman authority there after the French invasion. Aged about thirty, Mehmed was one of the officers put in charge of them. He turned out to be an accomplished soldier with a gift for politicking and his rise through what were some of the most turbulent years in Egyptian history was astonishingly rapid: in 1803, backed by his Albanians, whose numbers had swelled to some 4,000 men, he imprisoned and thus made a mortal enemy of the then pasha, Khusrev. In 1805, after a bitter power struggle in Cairo, Mehmed Ali ousted the very Khurshid Pasha who would later defeat Ali Pasha in Jannina in 1822—and took his place as governor of Egypt.[2]

He held this position for the next four decades in the face of formidable challenges. The new pasha began by ignoring his imperial master's orders to leave Egypt for Salonica. Then the British occupied Alexandria in 1807 for several months until he forced their withdrawal. In 1811 he eliminated the country's old ruling elite, the Mamelukes, inviting their leading beys to a celebration in the citadel and then massacring them on their way out, thereby destroying the class that had ruled Egypt for centuries. In the space of a decade the merchant from Kavala thus ascended to the highest level of government in a country he did not know before the age of thirty, having seen off all his rivals and ended a long period of political anarchy. In 1814, after his armies had stamped out a rebellion in the Hijaz to restore Ottoman authority there, he was given the right to collect taxes from the island of Thasos, and the imaret in Kavala became the beneficiary.[3]

But Mehmed Ali's ultimate goal lay beyond the governorship. He wanted to win independence from the sultan in order to create his own family dynasty—it was not for nothing he worshipped the memory of Napoleon—so he supervised the formation of a highly centralized regime that made Egypt the fastest-modernizing part of the Ottoman Empire. Land and tax reforms gave the state—meaning himself—enormous control over the country's economic resources and its foreign trade. Egypt became one of the world's leading producers of cotton, well positioned to reap the advantages of the textiles boom that followed the Napoleonic Wars. Peasant labor was ruthlessly dragooned in corvée for large infrastructural schemes, the workers' obedience ensured by brutal punishments and a breathtaking death toll.

One thing Mehmed Ali valued highly was European know-how. A French doctor, Antoine Clot, known as Clot-Bey, was put in charge of public health while a thirty-year-old architect and engineer, Pascale-Xavier Coste, designed gunpowder and saltpeter works and a new governor's pavilion outside Alexandria. Amid the constant threat of plague and the challenge of managing more than 300,000 conscripted *fellahin* (peasants), many of whom died during the works, Coste completed the Mahmudiyya canal (named in the sultan's honor), which linked Alexandria with the Nile and the rest of Egypt, helping to turn it from an Ottoman backwater into the fastest-growing port in the Mediterranean, its population increasing tenfold in the first half of the nineteenth century. At a time when the telegraph was largely unknown in Europe, Coste even constructed a series of giant brick towers with mechanical signaling equipment to send messages between Alexandria and Cairo: they were capable, he claimed, of transmitting news between the two cities in fifteen minutes.[4]

For more than a decade, Greek merchants and moneylenders, shipbuilders and jewelers, artisans and farmers also established themselves in Egypt—the total Greek-speaking population is estimated to have numbered in the thousands—and the community was of sufficient importance that after Greece became independent, in 1833, it established its first consulates there.[5] The Greeks were the consummate insider-outsiders, bringing the pasha the benefit of their knowledge of both the Ottoman world and Europe. One of Mehmed Ali's closest confidants was a merchant called Michalis Tositsa, who hailed from the town of Metsovon high in the Pindos mountains—his family villa may still be seen there; in the early years of the century, he and his brothers had expanded their father's fur-trading business across the Mediterranean. It is said that when Tositsa arrived in Egypt he was met personally by the pasha, who had formed a close relationship with his family during his Kavala days. What is clear is that it was in the years of the Greek uprising that Tositsa entered the pasha's service. Soon Tositsa was entrusted with the management of Ali's estates, and the pasha's adviser ran the marketing of the country's crops and his relations with European merchants. Suspicious of the Arabs, the pasha surrounded himself with people he trusted: first and foremost his relatives, many of whom he placed in positions of authority, and then Armenians, Turks, and other newcomers to Egypt who understood the Ottoman milieu in which he had grown up. For him, the Greeks too formed part of that world: they were strangers together in an alien land.[6]

The start of the Greek uprising left Mehmed Ali strikingly unbothered. He was inclined to view it much as the sultan himself did, as a scheme cooked up by Ali Pasha in Jannina and of no great consequence in itself. Although his spies reported that the Filiki Etaireia was active in Egypt, he took no measures against its agents and clearly did not regard them as a threat; on the contrary, he actively backed them in raising funds and food. He was happy to let many of his Albanian mercenaries return to their homeland to fight. And when Greek merchants and sea captains sought refuge in Egypt from other parts of the empire, Mehmed Ali welcomed them too. He even gave authorization for 150 Greeks to sail to the Morea, clearly aware they planned to join the insurgency, and is said to have freed a number of Greeks who had been captured by Algerian corsairs so that they could go too.[7]

His reasoning was simple. Whatever kept the sultan busy was to be welcomed, especially as Mehmed Ali had reason to believe Mahmud II was contemplating dividing Egypt into two pashaliks in order to weaken him. But the pasha of Egypt was not a man to place all his eggs in one basket, and in 1822 the sultan gave him his first opportunity to expand his domains at the Greeks' expense. In Crete, Greek insurgents had risen up on learning about what was happening in the Morea. Unlike in the Morea, however, almost half the island's population was Muslim, and relatively well armed. Perhaps for this reason, the Filiki Etaireia had failed to make significant inroads there and bloody clashes throughout the summer of 1821 had ended with Ottoman forces crushing the insurgents and enslaving thousands of Greek captives. But the uprising remained alive in Sfakia, on the southern coast, and in the spring of 1822 a representative of the new national government in the Morea convened a regional assembly for Crete and proclaimed a provisional constitution, momentarily unifying the scattered bands of insurgents under a single leadership. It was at this point that the sultan ordered Mehmed Ali to intervene. It took the Egyptians many months but by the end of 1823 the revolution had largely been suppressed on the island, and the following year the pasha could report that the Sfakiots had been crushed.

For Sultan Mahmud II, the end of the uprising in Crete was a bright spot in an otherwise dismal picture, for by the start of 1824 he had little to show for three years of campaigning. Elsewhere on land, the stalemate continued and his armies had performed so poorly over the preceding twelve months that they had failed even to threaten the Peloponnese. The siege of Mesolonghi fizzled out in early December 1823, testimony to the unreliability of his Albanian troops, and in Istanbul the sultan himself was said to be going around cajoling and threatening ministers to get them to bring the Greek uprising to an end. The prospect of the Greeks raising money in London must have worried him since it indicated they would now be able to field more men, and perhaps more disturbingly still it indicated a shift in British foreign policy. Internationally, there were warning signs that even the Holy Alliance's support for the sultan might be weakening. In January 1824 the Russian foreign minister, Count Nesselrode, circulated a plan among the other Great Powers that proposed giving the Greeks autonomy over a very large area—the opening gambit in a diplomatic to-and-fro that was likely to gather force unless the Porte managed decisively to suppress the insurrection. Heartened by Egyptian successes in Arabia, Sudan, and Crete, in February 1824 the sultan decided to call upon the Egyptians and commanded Mehmed Ali to send in his troops to crush the Greek insurgency in the Morea within the year.[8]

When Mahmud II had asked for the pasha's help against the Persians, Mehmed Ali had managed to refuse.[9] But as the sultan knew, the governorship of the Morea was a prize that Mehmed Ali cherished. The sultan's order praised the pasha, described him as an exterminator of rebels, and offered him the pashalik as the reward for success. Mehmed Ali's advisers urged acceptance: "You are the Napoleon of Egypt," one of his ministers told him, knowing Ali liked to boast that he had been born in the same year as both the emperor and the Duke of Wellington—namely 1769. (In fact, he had probably been born one year later.) A lesser man might have hesitated for not only was Egypt exhausted after years of campaigning and huge ongoing infrastructure projects, but setbacks in the Sudan—where the pasha had sent his troops to round up more conscripts—had even cost him the life of one of his sons. Then, in March 1824, an explosion rocked Cairo after munitions dumps on the citadel caught fire, killing several thousand people. Yet through all this, preparations went ahead and thousands of *fellahin* from Upper Egypt were conscripted for training.[10]

For decades the Ottoman sultans—like other Muslim rulers from Morocco to Qajar Persia—had been aware of the urgent need for military reform. But the institutional impediments remained great—Sultan Mahmud would not be able to eliminate the troublesome and ineffective janissaries until 1826—and the consequences were all too plain in Greece, where the Ottoman troops had been unable to put down what basically amounted to an extended peasant uprising. Mehmed Ali too had been toying for some years with creating regular military units, and since he had already destroyed the main opponents of the idea in Egypt—the Mamelukes—he was able to proceed more quickly than the sultan. Ali placed his eldest son, thirty-five-year-old Ibrahim—a thickset man and a talented soldier with plenty of political and military experience—in command of what would become the first modern army to be organized in the Ottoman lands. In 1817–18, Ibrahim had crushed the Saudi revolt in the Hijaz, showing no mercy as he marched his men through the Arabian desert destroying towns, fortifications, and even the date plantations upon which the inhabitants depended. As commander of the Egyptian expeditionary force, Ibrahim was about to become a figure of decisive importance in the war in the Morea.[11]

Alongside him, he had the organizational mastermind of the new army—a Frenchman called Joseph Anthelme Sève. Surely one of the most remarkable figures in this age of adventurers, Sève was a commanding presence "with a thick head, a large body and blue, piercing eyes"; but what really drew one's attention, wrote a fellow Frenchman, were his "enormous mustaches, which he twirls incessantly":

> He speaks French very well and does not lack that superficial erudition so necessary for this world. However, the tone and manners of a grenadier will never leave him. He has, one might say, a way of speaking all his own: the beautiful, the sacred, the indecent, the abominable, always find a place in his speech, and this way of communicating is one he will never abandon even in the most refined company.[12]

Sève had been born near Lyon and entered the navy as a boy: the Napoleonic Wars had provided his schooling. Cannoneer, infantryman, cavalry instructor, he had seen action everywhere from the Azores to Russia to the Battle of Trafalgar. Twice his horse had been shot from under him; he had been wounded by a lance; he had, to his eternal regret, killed a man in a duel. In 1815 he was a tough, blunt, courageous cavalry lieutenant who fought at the Battle of Waterloo and was devoted to his emperor; five years later, with Napoleon in exile, Sève was yet another struggling former officer with no chance of employment in the armies of Louis XVIII. In debt, and unfitted for a life in commerce, he pondered employment in the Persian army before making his way to Egypt where he met the young Frenchman Coste, who helped him to enter the pasha's service.[13]

Mehmed Ali read the letter of recommendation that Sève brought from the Comte de Ségur, listened to the remarkable tale of his wartime experiences across the battlefields of Europe, and evidently saw in his supplicant a man of energy, ability, and audacity mirroring his own. Both were consummate organizers and men of action; both were conscious of their lack of formal schooling—Mehmed Ali was illiterate for most of his life—and they shared too a passionate admiration for the French emperor whose death in May 1821 they mourned. Mehmed Ali first placed Sève in charge of artillery workshops on the citadel in Cairo and then approved his proposal to create several new army regiments along French lines. Ibrahim, who would become their commanding officer, trained as a recruit, and it is said that his rough treatment by Sève, who was no diplomat, was the source of an enduring tension between them. If so, it scarcely impeded their collaboration. Mehmed

Ali, Ibrahim, and Sève worked closely, harmoniously, and effectively together for twenty years in a series of remarkable campaigns that eventually succeeded in wresting international recognition for Mehmed Ali's dynasty and turning Egypt into a major regional power.[14]

Unusually among the pasha's European advisers, Sève converted to Islam—probably shortly before his departure for the Morea—and was henceforth known as Soliman, rising through the ranks to become a pasha. "Al-Faransawi" ("the Frenchman") became a national figure whose great-granddaughter would marry one of Mehmed Ali's descendants and become queen of Egypt before dying in a Los Angeles suburb. Sève's tomb and a statue of him survive in Cairo to this day. The honors were merited: it was, after all, his six new infantry regiments, levied and trained with merciless brutality from among the *fellahin* of Upper Egypt, that allowed Mehmed Ali to emancipate himself from reliance upon the Albanian irregulars and janissaries who had proved so untrustworthy in the past. A test of the new army came with a large peasant uprising in Upper Egypt in the spring of 1824; it was easily crushed. With that distraction behind them, Sève and Ibrahim began their preparations for the Morea.[15]

Since the expedition required ferrying large numbers of troops over the sea in huge convoys, the Ottomans and Egyptians identified two initial targets for the 1824 season—the seafaring islands of Kasos and Psara in the Aegean—and decided to start off by eliminating the threat posed by their fleets. The Kasos fleet had long bedeviled the Ottomans and the Egyptians. Its sailors were said to throw captives overboard to save on food, and their boats regularly supplied the rebels on Crete and raided Rhodes, Cyprus, and the coast from southern Anatolia to Egypt, carrying off livestock and produce. But despite its mountainous terrain, Kasos was basically defenseless, and the Greek government at Nafplion, preoccupied with fighting its internal enemies, claimed it could not afford to send out ships before the funds arrived from London. "Our common mother [the government] would not be indifferent to wartime needs, and when the loan comes will make preparations accordingly," was its stiff response to the Kasiots' plea for help. "But the warships of Hydra and Spetses do not sail at present for lack of funds in the exchequer to pay the sailors. As soon as funds arrive, and the sailors are paid, they will immediately sail, as they are ready now."[16]

Unopposed, the Egyptian navy made short work of eradicating its target. Led by Hussain Bey, Mehmed Ali's son-in-law and one of his most trusted lieutenants, a force of Christian Albanians landed on longboats and overran Kasos from the rear; Arab soldiers followed. Several hundred islanders were killed and more than 2,000 women and children were captured and consigned to the slave markets of Crete and Egypt. Keen to encourage the island's submission, Hussain Bey terminated the plundering after twenty-four hours—he executed three of his soldiers who disobeyed—and sailed back to Alexandria with twenty-six prize ships and hostages taken from the island's notable families. The loss of Kasos was a crushing blow for the Greeks that brought home how little protection their fleet could offer. When a combined Hydra-Spetses flotilla finally arrived some days later, most of the survivors still on the island preferred to remain under Ottoman rule rather than flee as refugees to the Morea. Indeed, some of them, along with islanders from Karpathos and Simi, had already accepted an offer to serve as sailors in the Egyptian fleet for 50 *grossia* a month—a good wage at the time.[17]

The destruction of the island of Psara farther north was more complete and an even more devastating blow. Strategically located in the eastern Aegean so as to control the passage of Ottoman shipping out of the Dardanelles, it had long been a thorn in the side of the empire. As in the case of Kasos, the impending threat was known weeks in advance to the Greek government, which did nothing. The task of subjugating Psara was entrusted to Mehmed Ali's old enemy, the Kapudan Pasha, Khusrev, who had spent the previous year introducing sweeping reforms into the Ottoman navy. He ordered the islanders to surrender, and when they rejected his terms he led a huge fleet out of Mitylene and arrived the next day. Rocky and almost barren like all the shipping islands, Psara was crowded with refugees and heavily fortified with a garrison that included hundreds of fighters who had fled from Rumeli. There were at least 3,000 men under arms, some 200 cannons—generally poorly positioned—and a large flotilla. The island's inhabitants, having already survived three years of war, were overconfident of their ability to defend themselves. Kanaris, the most experienced and courageous of the Greek captains, tried to warn them and urged the islanders to fight the Ottomans at sea. His advice, however, failed to carry the day and instead, as on Kasos, the attackers were allowed to land unopposed—thanks to effective diversionary tactics at the port—on a remote cove on the other side of the island. In the panic that followed, the inhabitants rushed to the boats, many of them drowning in the effort to get away. Six hundred fighters barricaded themselves in the fortress, together with their wives and children. After a day of heavy fighting, they decided to blow themselves up, and one of the soldiers set fire to the underground powder magazine. The explosion shook the island and left hardly any of the Greeks inside the fortress alive. The catastrophe moved the Ionian poet Dionysios Solomos to write one of his most effective and understated poems: "On the blackened ridge of Psara / Glory wandering alone / Ponders the illustrious young men / And on her brow a crown / From the few tufts of grass /Left on that desolate earth."

The overall death toll on Psara was far higher than on Kasos. More than 3,500 Greeks were estimated to have died, while thousands more were made captive or fled. The island's navy was largely destroyed— with perhaps only one-sixth of its vessels escaping, including Kanaris's own ship. One of the island's most precious icons was saved and taken by refugees to Syros where they settled. In Constantinople there were celebrations when the Ottoman fleet returned carrying its grisly cargo: 200 prisoners, 500 heads, and 1,200 ears, which were displayed along with captured Greek banners outside the palace. Psaran raiders had brought disruption to the Asia Minor coast; now they had been eliminated. But the price was outrage abroad. Two years later, as the British diplomat Stratford Canning, cousin of the foreign secretary, made his way to Constantinople, his ship stopped in at Psara for supplies. The steward went ashore to the seemingly prosperous town for food and was shocked by the "death silence" that greeted him—"not a voice, not a footstep, not an inhabitant; the town a mere shell, plausible to the eye but utterly void of life." Later Canning and his party went ashore as well and stumbled across a pile of bones where entire families had hurled themselves over a cliff rather than give themselves up. They found only two survivors on the island, skeletal beings in tattered rags. It was an experience that reinforced the British diplomat's growing desire for his country to intervene to bring the conflict to an end.[18]

In Alexandria, the summer of 1824 saw preparations proceeding rapidly for the main Egyptian expedition to the Morea. To the north of the town, an army of some 15,000–16,000 infantry and 2,000 cavalry was assembled to supplement the 4,000 soldiers the Egyptians had already stationed in Crete. In the port, a fleet of more than 50 warships and nearly 150 transport vessels, mostly chartered from Austrian and French owners, prepared to take on board the troops, horses, camels, and other pack animals. In July the enormous fleet set sail and made for Rhodes and Bodrum to join up with the Kapudan Pasha before heading for the Peloponnese. The initial plan was to reach Greek shores before the winter, reportedly to move first against Hydra and then on to the Peloponnese. Mehmed Ali was said to be confident of victory, and there were rumors that he was already engaged in secret talks with some of the Greek leaders. However, events were to take an unexpected turn and neither Hydra nor Spetses—which spent large chunks of the proceeds of the London loans on their own protection—would find themselves attacked as Ibrahim instead made directly for the Morea.[19]

With more than seventy armed ships protecting some three hundred transports, the size of the combined Turco-Egyptian flotilla was impressive but it was certainly not invulnerable. It sailed haphazardly, and its ordnance was badly stowed and mounted. The *meltemi*, the powerful northerly wind in the Aegean, was blowing hard that summer, breaking up the fleet and causing damage to the rigging of many ships. The Ottoman navy had some large vessels but the sailors had difficulties handling them. Once the proceeds of the London loan reached Hydra, the Greeks sailed out with around eighty ships of their own, smaller mostly than those of their enemy, but faster and with more skillful crews, and unencumbered by convoy duties. In early September they forced a major confrontation near Kos that was inconclusive. Another followed a few days later. The Greek fireships had a few successes, notably blowing up a Tunisian frigate with hundreds of men on board, and the Ottoman admiral was evidently as frightened of the fireships as his predecessors had been. In early October the Kapudan Pasha gave up campaigning for the season and returned to Constantinople.

For the Greeks, it looked as if they had successfully forestalled the Egyptian plans to reach the Morea that year and like the Ottoman navy, much of the Greek fleet now returned home, assuming the campaign would finish in November as it traditionally did because of the onset of winter. Yet they had reckoned without Ibrahim Pasha, who was waging an entirely new kind of war and felt no need to respect the conventional timetable.[20]

The weeks at sea had depleted his troops through hunger and disease, many of the horses had died, and the contracts for the commercial shipping he had hired had expired. None of these things deterred him, however. He reassembled his fleet and set sail for Crete to pick up more troops, animals, and provisions. He did not remain there long. On February 11, 1825, unchallenged by any Greek ships, he reached the port of Methoni in the southwest Peloponnese. The Maniot chieftains were shocked at the appearance of the Egyptians and made no effort to mount any resistance. Having disembarked 4,000 infantry and 500 horsemen, the Egyptian fleet immediately sailed back to Crete to fetch reinforcements. By the time he had finished, Ibrahim had managed to bring over nearly 20,000 men. It was a remarkable logistical achievement—rivaled perhaps only by Napoleon's seaborne invasion of Egypt twenty-six years earlier when the French had shipped over some 38,000 soldiers in nearly 300 ships. In view of the relative resources available to each country, it would be hard to say which was the greater accomplishment.

The hallmark of Ibrahim's campaign in the Morea was speed, and from the outset he moved faster than the Greeks expected. Within a couple of weeks he had established his main encampment in the fortress of Methoni, which was still in Ottoman hands as the Greeks had never seriously tried to capture it. Ibrahim swiftly brushed aside the initial Greek efforts to confine him to the beachhead, broke the ongoing siege of neighboring Koroni, and returned to Methoni. He was now in control of the entire southwest prong of the Peloponnese and secure in his supply lines to Crete and Egypt. A few miles to the north of Methoni was the Bay of Navarino, the site of ancient Pylos, one of the finest natural harbors in the eastern Mediterranean, protected by the islet of Sfakteria at its mouth. At one end it was guarded by the town's fortress; at the other by a ruined castle, so-called Old Navarino, built on a crag and linked to the mainland by a strip of land. Both fortress and castle were in Greek control, though they had made little effort to improve the defenses of either place, rushing in reinforcements only after the Egyptians had landed.[21]

This desultory attitude reflected the Koundouriotis government's overall complacency in the face of the looming Egyptian threat. The invasion preparations in Alexandria had been common knowledge among the Greeks for months and were even written up in the government newspaper, *O Filos tou Nomou*. On January 16, 1825, for instance, it had reported from Syros that Egyptian troop carriers were being readied in Crete to sail for the Peloponnese.[22] But the Greek government was still fixated on its internal enemy: indeed, it was only a few days before the Egyptian landings that one of Koundouriotis's most trusted men, a Hydriot sea captain called Kyriakos Skourtis, escorted Kolokotronis, two of the Deliyannis brothers, two members of the powerful landowning Notaras family, and the other Peloponnesian "rebels" (*antartes*) on his *goletta* under guard across to Hydra. Flush with funds, and victorious in the civil war, the Koundouriotis government was confident of its ability to defeat any Ottoman force and spoke contemptuously of the Egyptians in particular. *O Filos tou Nomou* declared: "We remain indifferent whether Ibrahim Pasha this year alone commands the enemy's sea forces . . . The one cannot succeed where last year two commanders failed, nor can the son of the so-called king of Egypt turn the sluggish Egyptians from peasants into sailors." A few days later the same paper was confidently predicting the Egyptian forces would be smashed—in the words of the psalm—like "pottery."[23] Thus the government undertook no defensive preparations in the Morea. All it did was bring troops as reinforcements into Hydra and Spetses, an act of evident self-interest but a waste of money as it turned out that neither island was ever attacked. The Spetsiots—ever ready to suspect the worst of their fellow islanders—reproached the government of Koundouriotis for neglecting them and everywhere else: "Each town and island is left to fight the entire force of the Sultan on its own and isolated."[24]

About a month after the initial Egyptian disembarkation, the Greek forces got a taste of the difficulties ahead. Egyptian troops pushing northward and eastward into Messenia from Methoni encountered several hundred experienced fighters from northern Greece at the village of Schoinolakka. Despite the Greeks' defensive advantage, dug in among the houses of the village, the Egyptians had them in difficulties when heavy rain ended the fighting. For the veteran northern Greek commander, Dimitrios Karatasos, the Egyptians' performance in battle was a revelation and a warning, and he lost no time in urging the Koundouriotis government to send reinforcements.[25] It ought to have been well positioned to respond. In fact, it could scarcely have handled things worse. Despite having issued pay to kapetans for a nominal total of about 30,000 soldiers, fewer than 10,000 were actually available. These were still mostly the Rumeliot bands the government had used to crush the rebels; however, they were deeply unpopular with the

Peloponnesians. Moreot troops refused to assemble until their leaders were released from captivity on Hydra, which Koundouriotis refused to do. In fact, he needlessly alienated many of the Greeks' most respected warriors with his strongly anti-Peloponnesian remarks. "I am told you said to my dear mother that the Peloponnesians are unbelievers, myself included," the veteran warrior Nikitaras wrote to Koundouriotis even as the Egyptians were landing. "Excellency! Your words dismayed me greatly."[26]

The scion of Hydra's wealthiest family, Georgios Koundouriotis was simply the wrong man for the moment while his more intelligent brother Lazaros, the real éminence grise, kept out of the limelight. With the support of Mavrokordatos, enriched by English sovereigns, and backed by Ioannis Kolettis's Rumeliots, who appreciated the bountiful funding sent their way, Hydra had emerged victorious in the Greeks' civil wars; but Georgios Koundouriotis was no national leader and he had no basic strategic sense. Indeed, it was some time before he realized the main target that spring would be not Hydra or Patras but instead the Egyptian forces in the southwest. Deciding at that point to head the Greek defense himself, despite his lack of military experience, Koundouriotis departed Nafplion in a magnificent ceremony marked by cannonades from the Palamidi fortress and salutes from ships in the bay, accompanied by bodyguards carrying an enormous sum in coin to pay the troops; the chests had a triple-lock system that required separate keys kept by his aides. Koundouriotis had been reluctant to leave and when he did, the assembled crowds could not but notice that their seafaring president was no horseman. Sore in the saddle, he insisted on frequent stops and took three days to get to Tripolitsa—usually an overnight journey—where he stayed unaccountably for two weeks. In letters to his brother Lazaros from the old Peloponnesian capital, we find a succession of explanations for the delay: "I will leave tomorrow," he promises on March 21. Three days later, the president is still there, held up by heavy rain. Then the horses have problems. Then he has a fever, chills, and a headache. In the end he left for the front only on April 3. It did not help that he was clearly shocked by his first real contact with the soldiers and their leaders, denouncing their apathy, factionalism, and greed. The contrast between Georgios Koundouriotis and Ibrahim Pasha could not have been greater. The Egyptian commander, a battle-hardened leader, lived in the field, prepared well, and led his men from the front.

However, the encounters over the next couple of months were to reveal that problems on the Greek side went much deeper than the question of leadership: the shortcomings of their entire manner of warfare were about to be brutally exposed.[27]

The village of Skala in Messenia was the closest that President Koundouriotis got to the front. Some six or seven thousand fighters had passed through with their chiefs to relieve Navarino: advancing so that they were close to the Egyptian rear, they had halted some miles farther west at the village of Krommidi (today's Kremmidi). Among the Greek leaders were Kitsos Tzavellas and Kostas Botsaris, two highly experienced Souliot chieftains, as well as a large band under the armatole Georgios Karaïskakis. These were some of the Greeks' most accomplished soldiers, yet they had been placed under the command of Koundouriotis's fellow Hydriot, his trusted sea captain Skourtis; nothing could have been better calculated to arouse their scorn and frustration. As the chronicler Ambrosios Frantzis put it sarcastically, it was only during his first battle that Skourtis "realized he was on dry land, commanding troops, and not steering a ship on the sea."[28] Ibrahim did not wait for the Greeks to attack but ordered one of his Arab regiments to charge the Greek lines: obviously outnumbered, they nonetheless affixed their bayonets and made straight for the Souliots. The fighting did not last long before the Greeks turned and fled, pursued by the Egyptian cavalry. It was an indication that the Greeks were now up against a much more intimidating foe; nothing now stopped Ibrahim from concentrating his forces upon Neokastro.

To make matters worse from the Greek point of view, Mehmed Ali's son-in-law Hussein Bey arrived from Crete with a third shipment of troops a few days after the battle. An experienced soldier, Hussein Bey advised Ibrahim to change his approach at Navarino, to halt the bombardment of the town fort, and to focus on capturing the island of Sfakteria from the sea. An Egyptian flotilla carrying troops sailed the few miles up the coast from Methoni while Mavrokordatos, one of the few Greek politicians to show much courage, rushed into Sfakteria to coordinate its defenses. Hydriot sailors helped too, unloading some cannons to try to stop the approaching Egyptian ships. But the Egyptian superiority in numbers was decisive and the Greek positions were overrun. After heavy fighting, 350 Greeks were killed and 200 captured. Among those who died was Anagnostaras, an experienced sixty-five-year-old soldier, locally born, who had been a high-ranking Etairist and minister of war; the Hydriot admiral Anastasios Tsamados; and the Piedmontese philhellene Annibale Santorre di Rossi de Pomarolo, Count of Santa Rosa, a man with a European reputation, who had been living quietly with his wife and ten children in exile in Nottingham before being persuaded to come to Greece. Mavrokordatos was rowed out to the last remaining Hydriot brig in the bay together with its captain, Georgios Sakhtouris, who then guided them skillfully through the crush of Egyptian warships; although their boat was fired at, riddled with holes, and nearly boarded four times, they managed to make their escape, with Mavrokordatos crouched in the hold, pistol in hand.

Four days after the capture of the island of Sfakteria, the castle of Old Navarino surrendered too. It was the first time since the uprising began that Muslim troops had won back such a prize, and it came as a shock to the Greeks. Keen to send the message that surrender was more advantageous than resistance, Ibrahim allowed the defenders to leave unharmed. "This generosity of Ibrahim's will do Greece more harm than if he had cut off a thousand heads," wrote the American philhellene Samuel Howe from nearby Kalamata. The Egyptian commander tried to persuade the Greeks to enter his service—he spent an hour talking with the American philhellene George Jarvis in French to win him over—but they refused and made their way back to Kalamata, their clothing in tatters, their faces scorched from the sun, their lips blackened from thirst. A week later, when the fortress of Neokastro in Navarino town capitulated, Ibrahim let those defenders go free as well. Knowing that his own ranks contained local men who had fled the Greek massacres of 1821 and wanted their revenge, he ensured that as the Greeks left the fortress they were protected by lines of his soldiers. He kept back just two high-profile figures—Beyzadé Georgios Mavromihalis and Panayiotis Yiatrakos from Mistras—as hostages. The British doctor Julius Millingen, who had served under Byron in Mesolonghi before joining the garrison at Navarino, was one of the rare figures to accept Ibrahim Pasha's offer of service; he went on to enjoy a long career as a medical man in Constantinople.[29]

There was really only one moment of Greek success that entire spring when Admiral Miaoulis, with typical bravery, managed to send fireships into the harbor at Methoni while the fighting was continuing up the coast. The explosion of an ammunition store near the harbor lit up the night sky and could be seen for many miles; wreckage was visible in the waters below the castle long after. But while this triumph was hailed by the Greeks as an indication of the Egyptians' vulnerability, and may have reminded Ibrahim of this too, it turned out to be of no real strategic significance. Not even Miaoulis was able to stop the Egyptians taking Neokastro and thus the Bay of Navarino.

Greek supremacy at sea was becoming less assured as their opponents became bolder and more organized. Funded by a new tranche of the loan, a flotilla of thirty-four small brigs sailed out from Hydra some weeks after the loss of Navarino to try to catch the Egyptian fleet as it sailed back to Crete. But changeable winds on the open sea allowed the enemy to make it to Suda Bay unhindered. A Greek plan to send fireships into Suda Bay failed and then a gale scattered their fleet for several days. The culminating misfortune struck when the powder magazine on the Hydriot brig *Nereus* exploded, causing the death of the captain and all but two of the crew, a tragedy unprecedented in the island's experience of the war. When what was left of the fleet tried again to use their fireships off Cape Matapan to intercept the contingent of 4,000 Albanians being sent from Suda, the Turco-Egyptian fleet fought them off and landed those troops at Navarino too.[30]

On Hydra, wartime losses had been relatively modest until the spring of 1825. From lists compiled immediately after, we can see the trend: eleven killed and ten wounded in the two years 1821–22, and only three wounded and one killed in 1823 (which surely indicates the very limited role of the navy that year); seventeen wounded and the same number killed in 1824. These numbers suddenly soared in 1825 when there were sixty-seven wounded and forty-seven killed in encounters with the Ottoman and Egyptian fleets, as well as the thirty-seven killed on the *Nereus* that June.[31] Perhaps the strains of this death toll explain the reaction on the island when the news of the devastating explosion aboard their own ship reached it. A report quickly circulated among the islanders that the explosion had not been accidental but that it had been sabotage by a Muslim slave with a grudge against the ship's captain. The consequences were murderous. There were at this time about 200 Muslims being held on Hydra—many of them captured Egyptian or Ottoman sailors who were employed on the ships or around the town and held in confinement in premises next to the harbormaster's office. Armed with yataghans, a crowd estimated by one eyewitness at several thousand gathered on the street outside calling for revenge for the dead sailors; bringing the Muslims out one by one, they stabbed and beat them to death in the street. Island families were large—the captain who had died on the *Nereus* had dozens of relatives—and extensive blood ties may explain the large numbers of perpetrators involved in the killings. Afterward the mob went on the prowl looking for other victims in private homes or on board ships in the harbor and the killing lasted through the afternoon into the evening. Kanaris, the famous bruloteer, was in a café at the time in the port, in tears at what was happening. A young English visitor was shocked. The killings did not, however, elicit much sign of regret from the townspeople. As for the island's notables, they seem to have concluded there was nothing to be done, and they waited it out. Afterward the episode was common knowledge locally but scarcely spoken or written about. Mavrokordatos warned President Koundouriotis of the anger of the British officers in the region when they had heard the news and told him to make sure Muslim captives were properly protected in future.[32]

After the capture of Navarino, Koundouriotis left Kalamata before the angry Greek soldiers could reach him, fearing the seizure of his war chest, abduction, and perhaps worse. His schooner was waiting for him in the gulf and he sailed off as soon as Mavrokordatos arrived back from Navarino. The president's cowardice disheartened those he left behind and there were angry demonstrations. The Rumeliot chieftains and their men headed north overland for Nafplion; once they had received their pay—another tranche of the English loan on the *Lively* conveniently arrived in time—many of them left the Peloponnese to return to their homelands where the Ottoman spring advance from the north was already under way.

The government might have won the civil war by deploying its Rumeliots throughout the Peloponnese, but most of these fighters had treated the region like an occupied country and were loathed by the inhabitants. With their departure from the scene of battle, the only other available soldiers were the Peloponnesians themselves. Yet they would not obey Koundouriotis but only their own chieftains whom he was keeping under lock and key on Hydra. Since it was now only a matter of time before the Egyptians marched into Tripolitsa itself and conquered the entire province, the government grudgingly proclaimed an amnesty and unwillingly released the Moreot leaders. After a service in the cathedral in Nafplion, men who had spent the past year plotting against one another now proclaimed their friendship and kissed one another in a sign of reconciliation. Among those released were representatives of the great magnate clans of the Peloponnese—the Deliyannis, Notaras, Papatsonis, and Sisinis families, the western Greek armatole Theodorakis Grivas, and several kapetans. The most important prisoner of them all, Kolokotronis, was immediately named commander in chief of the Greek land forces and left for Tripolitsa a few days later.[33]

His former comrade Papaflessas was ahead of him. The remarkable archimandrite, who had played the key role for the Etaireia in laying the groundwork for the uprising in early 1821, was not by this point a popular figure: a Moreot who had allied himself with the government, Papaflessas was mistrusted and disliked, both for his politics and for his notoriously corrupt way of life. He had no real military competence, and many of his men knew this and were thus poorly motivated. He was not afraid of death, however, and he was undeniably brave. Collecting an army of several thousand, of whom perhaps half deserted before the battle, Papaflessas marched down to halt Ibrahim Pasha's advance into Arkadia, digging his men in at the village of Maniaki, in hilly country a few hours' west of the village where he had been born. The local band leaders warned him the spot was badly chosen. Instead of listening he delivered exhortations: they should prove themselves to be heroes and die for their country if necessary. When the Egyptian troops advanced, Papaflessas fought hard and the battle lasted many hours until Ibrahim led a charge and his men stormed the Greek positions. After Papaflessas was killed, his head was brought before Ibrahim who is said to have kissed it as a sign of respect. He then reassembled his forces and with his left flank now secure, marched on the town of Kalamata, which he took without resistance and torched.[34] In only a few months Ibrahim had thus secured his Messenian bridgehead, which gave him communication with Crete and Egypt, as well as the Bay of Navarino and Kalamata with its fertile hinterland. But three months of fighting had also depleted his forces and left him with well under 10,000 men for use in the coming campaign.

Meanwhile, the Greeks were finally organizing their resistance. Released from his island confinement—he is said to have vowed never to leave dry land again—Kolokotronis made his entry into Tripolitsa in triumph. After Kolettis's unpopular Rumeliot bands, the "Old Man" was greeted like a returning hero, and men took up arms and flocked to their chieftains to help him. "The enthusiasm with which he was received is hardly describable," wrote Samuel Howe:

> Men, women and children went out to meet him, and he was welcomed by a shout of joyful voices, ringing musquets and thundering cannon . . . "We do not want Mavrokordatos," say they. "We do not want the Rumeliotes to defend our country, but give us our dear countryman, give us our brave Kolokotrones, and we will follow him to the death."[35]

The truth, however, was that Kolokotronis—so effective at destroying Ottoman positions, both at Tripolitsa and again at Dramali—was not well prepared to preserve the gains that the Greeks had made. His basic strategic conception, he confided to an interlocutor shortly before his release from Hydra, was to destroy all the fortresses in the Morea, thus depriving the enemy of a stronghold, and then to rely on his men's hold over the mountains. It was the classic expression of the virtues of partisan warfare, but it did not explain why the forces under his command had neglected to take Methoni, Koron, and Patras when they could easily have done so, nor how they could win back other towns the Egyptians might take.[36] Over the month that followed, the Old Man's understandable shortcomings were cruelly exposed in the face of a determined, organized, and ruthless enemy.

The Greeks did not take the fight to the Egyptians after Papaflessas's defeat. Instead—in implicit acknowledgment of the respect they had acquired for Ibrahim's troops—they pulled back to defend the passes and prevent their advance up the road to Leondari and Tripolitsa. Kolokotronis was outwitted when the Egyptians unexpectedly focused their main thrust through a smaller pass in the south, at the village of Poliani. Pushing their way northward along narrow tracks through the foothills, the Egyptian infantry, accompanied by field guns they had lugged over the mountain paths, opened the road to Tripolitsa. The 7,000 armed Moreots who had answered Kolokotronis's call abandoned their positions. "Dreadful news," wrote Howe. "All is now confusion, some even fear for Napoli [Nafplion]." Tripolitsa was abandoned and its inhabitants fled the approaching army. A Greek soldier who arrived just ahead of the invaders found a town emptied due to the panic. No one was around, and the place gave him the chills. There were corpses in the streets—he does not explain why but the likeliest explanation is that these were Turkish captives killed by their Greek owners for fear they would help the invaders. In the distance he saw people rushing away carrying their valuables. Entering his own home, he found everyone gone except for an elderly relative, too infirm to have been sent off, even on the back of a mule. His wife had evidently fled in a panic, leaving the table set and the silverware out. He was so upset, he had the presence of mind only to saddle two horses and get out himself.[37]

Kolokotronis had ordered the town's inhabitants to tear down Tripolitsa's walls and gates but these remained standing—a fateful omission. The citadel too was left intact, and it now became Ibrahim Pasha's center of operations: an Egyptian garrison would encamp there for the next three years, beating off all attacks. Displaying extraordinary energy, Ibrahim pushed onward with scarcely 5,000 men, ignoring the logistical difficulties and the summer heat, and forced his troops over the pass and down into Argos. On the afternoon of June 25, the shocked inhabitants of Nafplion caught sight of the Egyptians coming out of the mountains and heading across the plain toward the bay. For a moment, it looked as though they might seize the flour mills at Lerna that provisioned the town, putting Nafplion itself in jeopardy.

While thousands of armed men remained idly in the capital, a few courageous soldiers led by Ioannis Makriyannis, Dimitrios Ypsilantis, and Konstantine Mavromihalis (brother of Petros) took up positions in the orchards and fields around the mills. They were watched from the bay by Captain Gawen Hamilton on board HMS *Cambrian* and by the French admiral Henri de Rigny. Both men thought the entire endeavor doomed but in fact, by the time night fell, the Egyptians had been beaten back in fierce hand-to-hand fighting and to everyone's surprise they did not attack again the next day, leaving the fields strewn with bodies that were stripped and despoiled by the Greeks. "Our escape seems almost miraculous," wrote Howe. As the Egyptians withdrew, they left a trail of destruction behind them. Howe recorded the scene:

> In the afternoon, the enemy set fire to Argos. At first there rose from different parts of this large place distinct columns of thick smoke which soon, uniting into one vast pillar, slowly rolled away, carrying the sad news to all Greece. At night the dreadful picture was heightened; the clouds had passed away, but from the vast bed of living fire shot up a

long, livid blaze, which now flickered, sank down, and then, like lightning, flashed up to the very skies.

Wisely, no doubt, Ibrahim had decided to pull back to Tripolitsa to rest
his exhausted men, who had been fighting and marching continuously
for over a month, and to await supplies from Methoni. The battle at the
Lerna mills was thus no triumph for the Greeks but merely a respite,
and Howe understood what it really meant: if the Greeks could not
prevent Ibrahim's relatively small force advancing to the very gates of
Nafplion, what hope did they have once the expected reinforcements
from Crete and Egypt arrived?

As Howe noted, the Peloponnesian mode of warfare did not lend itself
to planning a drawn-out campaign: "Kolokotrones has with him three to
four thousand men. Next week he may have twelve thousand or only a
hundred. No calculations can be made. No good thing can come out of
such a system. Things must alter or Greece is flat in a few weeks." Kolokotronis's renown managed to bring men in some numbers back up into the
hills around Tripolitsa but there was to be no repeat of 1821. Ibrahim as
usual took the initiative, and before the Greeks could tighten the ring and
mount an assault of their own, they were attacked by the Egyptians and
dispersed. Ibrahim himself led the charge on Trikorfa, the old hilltop
stronghold from which Kolokotronis had masterminded the fall of Tripolitsa in 1821. This time he was lucky to escape. Plapoutas and Kanellos
Deliyannis sent their relatives for safety to Nafplion. Not even the Greek
heartlands were safe: Kolokotronis dispatched a stream of impassioned
letters to Petros Mavromihalis in the Mani begging for help, but the bey
was playing his usual games: in secret communication with Ibrahim, who
had captured his son, Georgios, at Navarino, Mavromihalis seems to
have been hoping to get Georgios released in return for promising the
submission of the Mani. An Egyptian attack on Ypsilantis's headquarters
at Vervena followed. Always on the move, Kolokotronis was worn out
and weary, exhorting, threatening, shouting, trying to keep the men in
the field. But they were trickling away, worried for their families, and
Vervena turned into another rout. At the village of Arachova, the Old
Man tried to get the men from Mistra to halt with so little success that,
in the words of a chieftain with him, "he fell into great anxiety and
decided he would be killed, unable to bear to see those dirty Greeks in
such a wretched situation."[38] After this, the Greeks never again dared to

take on the Egyptians in a pitched battle, reverting to what one band chief called war "in the kleftic style."[39]

The Egyptian answer was a classic anti-guerrilla scorched-earth strategy designed to make peasants think twice before supporting the insurgents. Once Ibrahim was reinforced by the large contingent of Albanian troops landed from Crete, the remorseless pasha led search-and-destroy expeditions that laid waste to the center of the Peloponnese, targeting and burning many of the strongholds that the Greeks had conquered from the Ottomans in the summer of 1821. The villages northwest of Tripolitsa in the mountains up to Vytina were hit first. Ibrahim then turned east beyond Vervena and into Kynouria, finally marching through Sparta and Mistra on his way back to winter at Methoni. The violence, skill, and rapidity of his columns' operations were breathtaking as was the stamina of his men in the summer heat. They torched villages, seized or killed thousands of sheep and goats, and captured hundreds if not thousands of women and children, leading those who escaped to flee higher into the mountains. The Egyptians enslaved those they could and mutilated those they left behind. For years afterward, the peasants would tremble at the name of Ibrahim Pasha. The Greek bands could do little but watch as camel and donkey trains carried the crops into storage at Tripolitsa and sent plunder and slaves southward to the camp at Methoni. A bigger enemy for the Egyptians than the Greeks was the plague that rampaged through Messenia that autumn, but the invaders managed to keep it out of their camp.[40]

In charge of the British squadron in the Aegean, HMS *Cambrian* was a Royal Navy frigate whose captain Gawen Hamilton is a crucially important if undersung figure in the story of the Greek revolution. An experienced naval officer, he had seen service in Egypt, the Caribbean, and the Atlantic, and he had sailed in the convoy that escorted Napoleon to St. Helena in 1815. From the Anglo-Irish gentry and speaking fluent French, Hamilton was popular with his crew and trusted by both the Greeks and the Turks. In the summer of 1825, he was asked by the Greeks to go to the Egyptian camp to obtain the release of Petros Mavromihalis's son, Georgios. The Greeks were offering to exchange two pashas they were holding and one of them, the former pasha of Nafplion, was taken along to the Egyptian camp in the *Cambrian* where he spent the voyage chatting over coffee with Hamilton and his officers. When the pasha of Methoni said the terms of the deal would have to be decided by Ibrahim, who was then in the heartlands of the Peloponnese on campaign, Hamilton sent a party to find him. Among them was the ship's chaplain, the Reverend Charles Swan, whose record of his journey into the heart of the Morea in the midst of the first shock of the Egyptian invasion is one of the most vivid accounts we have of the region at this time.

As he and his companions rode through the foothills of Taygetos, Swan initially saw no signs of the conflict—the orchards were intact, and the fig harvest had already been gathered. Hidden from view, Greek bands manned the heights and their patrols frequently stopped the party to check their purpose. They got to the ruins of Tripolitsa, only to learn that they had just missed Ibrahim who was heading south again. It was as they decended into the valley of the Eurotas that they saw the first signs of the passage of his troops: "a vast number of dead goats, sheep, oxen and horses," some strewn in ditches, others scattered on the ground. Some were roasted and half eaten; others were being consumed by vultures. Mistra was deserted and in flames, Ibrahim's troops having just pulled out. As Swan and his companions approached the sea, they overtook Arab stragglers who were half dead with thirst, while others bringing up the rear were methodically setting fire to the hedgerows. Ibrahim himself turned out to be "a stout, broad, brown-faced man, thirty-five or forty years of age, marked strongly with the small-pox."[41] He greeted his guests and sat them down. He briefly talked about the captives (the swap of notables would in fact take place some weeks later) before he went on to explain to his British visitors precisely the purpose and nature of his campaign:

> He would burn and destroy the whole Morea so that it should neither be profitable to the Greeks nor to him, nor to anyone. What would these infatuated men, the dupes of their own imbecile government, do for provisions in the winter? He knew that his own soldiers would also suffer—that they too must perish. But his father Mehemet Ali was training forty thousand men, and he was in daily expectation of twelve thousand. If these were cut off he would have more; and he would persevere till the Greeks returned to their former state. One of the castles on the plain, he said, had just been carried by the assault, and the garrison all put to the sword; the other was expected to fall immediately. He repeated: "I will not cease till the Morea be a ruin."[42]

In fact, despite Ibrahim Pasha's brave talk, the campaign in the Morea was stretching the Egyptian forces to their limit. The constant reinforcements he was ordering to be sent to the Peloponnese from Crete depleted troop strengths on the island, and the uneasy peace that had emerged there the previous year came under strain. Thus some of the Greeks decided to try to open up another front against the Egyptians by reviving resistance to the Ottoman-Egyptian administration there.

Off the peninsula at the northwestern tip of Crete lies the remote fortress-island of Grabousa, an imposing and almost impregnable rock crowned by Venetian fortifications. "The first sight . . . was splendid," wrote one of the first foreign volunteers to help the Greeks take it over. "A little island, entirely of rocks, rises abruptly from the sea. On its summit is built the fortress. To the west, the rocky wall is two hundred feet perpendicular, and on all the other sides, where nature has not made it inaccessible, art has reared such walls that it is almost impregnable." A Greek merchant who supplied the small Ottoman garrison there had learned there was a monthly rotation of men, and that because incoming troop shipments were often delayed, there was generally a day or two—"before the new moon"—when there were only five or six guards on duty. He passed the information on. That August about 400 Cretan fighters had returned to the island and began attacking Muslim villages in the area. At the critical time in the month, some of them on a Greek brig attacked a Turkish boat, killed the crew, manned it with about thirty Greek fighters dressed as Turks, and sailed for Grabousa.[43]

On the very beach where a century and a half later the newlywed Princess Diana would wander in a yellow bikini while her husband sunbathed, the men disembarked early one morning. On the sands they found a man guarding a tent; he turned out to be a Christian in Ottoman service. He explained that the fortress commandant, seeing ships at sea the previous night and fearing a raid, had sent his wife away from the fort for safety: she was inside the tent and he was her servant. When the Greeks—speaking Turkish—greeted the woman inside the tent, she mistook them for the fresh contingent of men they were expecting and told them the signal: two shots and her husband would come and fetch them.

The commandant was more suspicious when he arrived because he did not recognize the men and so he asked them outright: "Aren't you Greeks (Romaious)?" "'Oh, the blasphemy!' some of them called out in

Turkish: 'You took us for Greeks!'" The historian Trikoupis, who recounts the whole story, tells us they started calling each other "Ali" and "Hasan" to fool him, but the commander was not so easily taken in and demanded that they pray like Muslims: "At which one of them, Androulis the Fat, knowing Turkish well and ready with his words, started to berate him in Turkish for questioning his faith." That was enough to convince the commander who took them across and got his men to let them in. Once the Ottoman soldiers had been disarmed and the fortress was in Greek hands, Grabousa became a bastion from which volunteers planned to retake Crete and reinforcements began to arrive from the mainland.[44]

"There are forty-six brass cannon, water, wheat, corn, dried provisions, etc., enough for many years," wrote Samuel Howe, the young American philhellene. "It is every way a great gain to the Greeks, who may now with confidence call on the islands to rise, since here is a place of refuge in case of need."[45] Only a few days had passed, however, before Howe noticed that the walls and cannons were in poor condition and that food was scarce. Hundreds of Greek volunteers were arriving, but many of them were quarreling with one another and questioning the credentials of their commander. More significantly, they had very mixed success in persuading locals to join them. "It becomes every day more plain to me that the chances of doing anything in Crete are small," Howe wrote after less than a week there. "The inhabitants are divided, a part only wishing a revolution. We are completely shut in from the main island; have neither communication with its inhabitants nor [can] get any of its products." In fact, many Greeks on Crete were actively discouraging the insurgents—two years of revolt had been enough for them. Some weeks after arriving, Howe left again, convinced no larger uprising was going to happen. He was right, although the Greeks were to remain on the fortress another two years, and it would become internationally famous as a nest of pirates—the so-called Pirate Republic of Grabousa. As an effort to weaken the Egyptian venture into the Greek lands, the expedition was a failure.[46]

One last Greek effort against the Egyptians came in the summer of 1825 as they tried to prevent the next large transport convoy from leaving Alexandria for the Morea. Led by Admiral Tombazis's brig, *Themistoklis*, a small group of ships set out from Hydra for the Egyptian port where some 150 ships of all nations were being readied. The three larger Greek ships waited outside the entrance while Kanaris raised the Russian flag on his fireship and made straight for the harbor. Because a local pilot recognized the fireship as he approached it, they were forced to set it alight early, and the wind changed, pushing it off course. As it passed by a French brig, a quick-witted French sailor fired on it, and this raised the alarm. The daring Greeks rowed off under fire and reached the Hydriot vessels, which calmly hoisted the Greek revolutionary flag and headed away while the fireship burned itself out. Twenty-five years later, Kanaris was still ruing that change of wind and the Egyptians' narrow escape.[47]

The pasha, Mehmed Ali, was actually in Alexandria at the time, in the Ras-el-Tin palace overlooking the harbor. The arsenal was nearby, the casualties might have been enormous, and the entire operation in the Morea jeopardized. Beside himself with anger, the pasha took the extraordinary step of heading after the Greek fireships himself in a corvette accompanied by a mere seven ships. Had he found his prey, it is not at all sure he would have had the better of the encounter. To the consternation of his ministers, he was still at sea when the Ottoman fleet under the command of his lifelong rival, the Kapudan Pasha, unexpectedly appeared on the horizon and entered the port; they had run short of provisions after their time off the Greek coast and they were in need of rest. Even though they were allies, and all servants of the sultan, Mehmed Ali's absence was, in the words of the French minister in Alexandria, "un événement très délicat," which threw the pasha's officials into some confusion and they immediately dispatched boats to notify their master and get him to return. No one could forget that the Ottoman admiral Khusrev and Mehmed Ali were sworn enemies, whose rivalry went back nearly two decades to the start of both their careers in Egypt. People even wondered whether Khusrev had come to Egypt on behalf of the sultan to seize the pasha. No one could tell how Khusrev might respond to news of Mehmed Ali's absence, and an infantry regiment was called up from Cairo just in case. In fact, behaving with great propriety, Khusrev requested permission to enter in the usual way, saluted as prescribed with nineteen cannon shots, kept his men on board, and himself refused to set foot on land until the pasha was ready to greet him.[48]

After more than a week, Mehmed Ali reappeared, having scoured the Anatolian coast in vain before learning of the Ottoman fleet's arrival.

He sailed in discreetly at night and made his way straight to his palace. The population had been disturbed by his absence—only the Greeks had, it seems, harbored the secret hope that he might have perished at sea—and the two pashas now put on an impressive show of unity. Receiving the Ottoman admiral the day after his arrival, Mehmed Ali and he held several hours of amicable talks and he gave Khusrev the use of Ibrahim's palace during his stay.

The Greek raid on Alexandria was in the end nothing more than a hiccup, a last gasp of Greek naval resistance, for events were going Mehmed Ali's way. In the late summer and early autumn of 1825, his son Ibrahim reported the pacification of the Morea, with only Nafplion holding out, and the news came from Constantinople that Mehmed Ali himself was to be promoted to grand vizier, above the Kapudan Pasha in rank. Two more regiments of the new Egyptian army finished their training and arrived in Alexandria; more were in progress. Best of all, the large autumn convoy made it to the Morea unscathed. Reports had reached Alexandria that Miaoulis and the Greek fleet—with ten fire-ships prepared—were waiting at Santorini. But when the Egyptian convoy did sail, it had few problems. The Hydriot sailors were as hard to discipline as ever; having struck for higher pay and two months' advance wages, they had sailed home early, alarmed by reports that the Egyptians were heading for their island. With Ibrahim's army rampaging through the Peloponnese more or less unchecked, and more troops coming, the British consul Philip Green had a gloomy prognosis: "the cause of the Greeks is fast declining and . . . it will not be long ere their political existence ceases."[49]

13

MESOLONGHI

Then my guts were in turmoil, and I said my final breath was nigh; and I found myself in a dark and thunderous place tossed around like a grain of corn in a fast-grinding mill, like a bubble in fiercely boiling water. Then I understood that this was Mesolonghi, but I saw no parapet, no encampment, no lagoon, no sea, no earth underfoot, no sky: everything was shrouded entirely in blackness and scalding tar, with flashes and thunder and lightning-bolts . . .

D. Solomos, "Oi eleftheroi poliorkomenoi, Schediasma A," in Solomos, *Apanta ta evriskomena* (Athens, 1901), 172

Sultan Mahmud II had reacted to the unexpectedly durable resistance of the Greeks by making three key appointments. First he brought in the veteran Khusrev Pasha to reform the navy, and then he ordered Mehmed Ali to organize the invasion of the Morea that Ibrahim launched with such success in 1825. Finally, in charge of all the Ottoman land forces in Rumeli, he placed a young protégé of Khusrev's, Mehmed Reshid Pasha, better known as Kütahı Pasha after the Anatolian town he had governed earlier in his career. The forty-five-year-old general, "persistent, tireless, energetic," was the son of a Georgian Orthodox priest. He had been captured when very young, entering Khusrev's household where he converted to Islam and quickly revealed the remarkable abilities that would allow him eventually to rise to the position of grand vizier. Kütahı Pasha worked twenty hours a day and was decisive and fearless in battle—his soldiers called him "Baba" and idolized him. He was ruthless enough to mastermind the empire's reckoning with the

Albanians, massacring dozens of their leaders in cold blood in 1830, and he was politically astute enough to know when leniency might be the better course.[1] This was the man the sultan put in overall command in 1825, instructing him that his principal mission was to eradicate the Greek insurgency in western Rumeli. This meant taking the town of Mesolonghi, which together with Omer Vryonis Pasha he had failed to capture on the first attempt in the winter of 1822, and which had survived the following year's campaign as well: this time, the sultan told him, he had to succeed.

At the start of January 1825, therefore, Kütahı Pasha arrived at the military base of Larissa in Thessaly, and moving quickly across the Pindos mountains via Jannina, his troops descended into western Greece. By the time the Koundouriotis government had instructed the underpaid armatoles of the region to man the passes, the advance guard of the Ottoman army had already got through them, moving south. A young kapetan likened the sight to "a river, which floods and overruns its banks."[2] In early April, thousands of villagers fled to the Ionian island of Kalamos to seek refuge under British protection—their numbers would grow to 17,000, many of them completely destitute—while others made for Mesolonghi itself. By the end of the month, having faced no real opposition, the Ottoman troops were digging themselves in amid the olive groves on the plain outside the walls of the town. At this point, they numbered about 6,000 men. Detachments were sent eastward to seize Salona, which fell in May, temporarily securing the mountains to their rear. Within a month or so, the Ottoman army outside Mesolonghi had grown to some 8,000 soldiers encamped in the plain—Albanians, Bosnians, and Ottoman Turks—along with 4,000 pioneers, mostly Orthodox Christians who had been conscripted to dig trenches and drag equipment, and thousands more servants and slaves, traders, camp followers, and grooms. Few apart from the pasha himself had tents; most slept in the open and lived rough. Units began digging lateral trenches at some distance from the town walls, beginning an elaborate system of traverses and zigzags that came close to Mesolonghi itself.

In the Greek uprising, there were mighty fortresses—places such as Nafplion, Monemvasia, Karystos, and even Grabousa—which remained more or less impregnable behind their solid and towering fortifications. Mesolonghi was not one of them. Indeed, Mavrokordatos had wondered on the eve of the first siege back in 1822 how the town could be held. Since then much hard work had gone into improving its insubstantial fortifications, and the landward wall had been strengthened. Under the supervision of a Chiot engineer, a former Etairist called Mikhail Kokkinis, the townspeople had labored to build a more defensible set of earthworks—more than 6,000 feet long, 10 feet high, and faced with masonry—and gun emplacements that eventually permitted more than forty guns to be stationed at key points. Protecting the fortifications was an enlarged moat, about two and a half meters deep and nine wide, that filled up for most of its length with seawater; on the far side of the moat from the main town wall there was a smaller wall with a path running alongside it that was used to assemble troops for sorties. Under its central section sources of fresh drinking water ran underground and supplied the town. In the spring of 1824, shortly after Byron's death, Kokkinis informed Mavrokordatos that Mesolonghi was now capable of withstanding a substantial enemy assault.

The town's inhabitants were evidently conscious of history in the making. A new fortification on the key islet of Prokopanisto, in the lagoon, was named after Byron. Along the town wall, gun emplacements were named after fighters such as Sachtouris, Miaoulis, and Makris; others immortalized those who had fallen for the cause such as Kyriakoulis Mavromihalis, Markos Botsaris, and philhellenes such as the German general Karl von Normann-Ehrenfels. But it is a reminder of the wide political horizons of the revolutionaries that some of those thus commemorated had little or nothing to do with Greece at all: sections of the wall were also named for Benjamin Franklin, William Tell, William of Orange, and Taddeusz Kościuszko, indicating that the Greeks saw themselves as participants in a single struggle for liberty that extended from the Americas to Poland.

By the spring of 1825, the narrow lanes of the besieged town were crowded with refugees, townspeople, and armed bands under their Souliot and Rumeliot chieftains—a population of around 12,000 of whom perhaps 3,000–4,000 were soldiers. Virtually all supplies had to be brought in by boat and as early as the start of May it was reported that sales of food and drinks had been prohibited; even so, by mid-June there was only enough to last a few weeks. Retaining access to the sea through the lagoon thus became the key to the city's future. In previous sieges, the Ottoman navy had been unable to establish effective control over its shallow reed-covered waters whose sandbanks and winding hidden passages made it treacherous for strangers to navigate. The inhabitants of the town appear to have been confident that the lagoon and the Greek fleet, helped now by the money from the English loan, would protect them once more.[3]

As the summer began, that confidence seemed warranted. An advance flotilla of seven Hydriot vessels landed provisions and supplies, announcing a much larger fleet under Admiral Miaoulis behind them, and heartening the garrison that mounted several sorties. The besieging Ottoman troops tried to end things quickly, getting round the side of the land walls by storming the offshore island of Marmaros, which overlooked the unprotected western shoreline of the town; but they were shot down as they waded through the shallow waters of the lagoon, suffering heavy casualties, and quickly backed off. The following month, however, it was the Ottoman fleet that appeared offshore, forcing the Hydriot brigs to withdraw, and for the first time Kütahı Pasha got the chance to attack from the seaward side. His army now totaled some 20,000 men, and he appeared to have no supply problems.[4] Hoping to end the siege before the main Greek fleet arrived, he offered the town the chance to capitulate. When they rejected his terms, he had several captives beheaded in front of the walls as a warning. A flotilla of fifty shallow boats, carrying nearly 2,000 men, also fired on the town from the water. At the same time the land-based assault was intensified. Although the Ottoman forces lacked adequate firepower and were reduced to using stones as projectiles after they ran out of cannonballs, they also had sappers digging right up to the walls: mostly Christian workmen forced into service for the army, some of them would shout out to the defenders to shoot them and end their misery.[5]

At dawn on August 2, the town was shaken by an immense explosion: the Turks had detonated a mine beneath the Franklin gun emplacement and simultaneously opened up a huge bombardment. Under the cover of heavy musket fire from their lines, which covered the walls in smoke, two hundred Cossacks brought in from settlements in the Danube delta charged the walls; some of them even gained the ramparts and planted their standards before being driven back in hand-to-hand fighting. Fortunately for the Greeks, Miaoulis's flotilla arrived the next day—some thirty-five to forty vessels—and fearlessly challenged the much larger imperial fleet. There was only a brief contest before Miaoulis forced his way into the lagoon. Khusrev Pasha was a good administrator but a timorous admiral and when he saw two Greek fireships headed in his direction, he took the fleet out to sea and off to the safety of Alexandria, where his sudden arrival—as we have seen—caught Mehmed Ali by surprise.

Faced with numerous challenges, Kütahı Pasha now showed his determination. His blockade had collapsed due to the cowardice of the Kapudan Pasha. Behind him Greek bands were assembling in the mountains, threatening to cut off his communications with the north, and beginning to coordinate with the men inside the town. The defenders had perfected the art of nighttime sorties carried out in silence by small groups moving fast in the darkness, using only their yataghans to take the Ottoman soldiers by surprise: many of the pasha's men were killed this way or brought back into the town as prisoners. Albanians were deserting—complaining as usual about their wages—and the army had suffered heavy losses. Undeterred, Kütahı Pasha redoubled his efforts. Focusing on the ravaged area around the Franklin gun emplacement, he ordered his men to build an enormous mound of earth, roughly 100 yards wide, that filled in the ditch and towered over the walls; many lost their lives in the process. In just over a week, it was so high that they were able to fire down on the defenders, killing nine of them. They even hauled up a cannon to threaten the town. Thus began one of the most bitterly fought episodes in the entire siege, the closest Mesolonghi ever came to succumbing to a direct assault. The defenders countered the earth mound by building a second line of defenses behind the walls and peppering the intruders with grapeshot from either side as they advanced. A hellish racket punctuated by explosions, the pitched battle continued for several days, both sides tunneling belowground at the same time as they were firing upon one another—often from a distance of only a few yards. Eventually, after the Greek sappers had tunneled yards underground, they succeeded in blowing up the earthworks that had cost their enemy so many lives to build. "What a horrible sight," recollected one of the Greek fighters. "The ground shook and groaned and from its bowels there erupted to heaven a most gloomy cloud made up of huge lumps of earth, stones and smoke, along with a mass of enemy heads, hands, feet, weapons, and implements of all kinds which then fell almost immediately like hail, some inside the walls, some in the moat and some in the Turkish trenches." After that battle, the Franklin gun emplacement became known to the townspeople as the "Terrible."[6]

The sultan is said to have warned Kütahı Pasha that not merely his career but his life depended on capturing Mesolonghi, but he had also notified Ibrahim that he should provide help if the pasha asked for it. The Greeks' destruction of the earthworks was a turning point. Having congratulated Ibrahim on reconquering the Morea, Kütahı Pasha now requested his assistance "to exterminate with me these sinners of Mesolonghi." "They have become devils," he continued. "I raised before them a mountain which towered above their walls, and they destroyed it thanks to the magic of a certain Kokkinis in their pay . . . Each day the infidels repair the passages which have fallen into ruin, and they dare to insult me from atop their towers. Will you allow me to become the plaything of these *giaours*? The fate of all Greece lies in the walls of Mesolonghi. Come!"[7]

After a siege of nearly six months, it still seemed that the town might survive as it had in the past. The losses among the defenders had been immense yet new reinforcements had arrived, their sea communications were secure, and materiel and foodstuffs were getting through. The garrison now numbered approximately 4,000 men, a figure that at this stage probably outweighed the number of fighting men left on the Ottoman side. Further assaults on the town's defenses were repelled with a heavy loss of life, and the Greeks in the mountain passes attacked the Ottoman supply trains. Karaïskakis led several raids, killing pack animals and camels as well as many soldiers, inducing one of the main Albanian chieftains to take his men back north. As food started to run short, the October rains turned the apartments in front of Mesolonghi into mud, flooding the churned-up ground. Kütahı Pasha withdrew his troops half a mile from the town, prepared new entrenchments, and awaited the Egyptians.

Following a common practice in sieges, the pasha sent a Gheg Albanian chieftain to request admission into the town so that he could gauge the defenders' morale. The visitor was greeted hospitably by a fellow Albanian in the Greek garrison, the elderly Souliot chieftain Notis Botsaris. He asked for some water to drink—to find out if there was a shortage—and was told firmly that the town had no intention of surrendering. When a crowd of fighters gathered round Botsaris's tent to get a glimpse of the new arrival, he looked at them for a minute and is reputed to have said: "Good on you, my brave lads [*palikaria*], keep at it!"[8] A wedding even took place in the town between one of the most powerful of the local chieftains, Dimitrios Makris, and the daughter of a family from the local elite. It was celebrated with much gunfire in the usual fashion; next morning, the Turks on the other side of the walls asked what the shooting had been about, and on being told they congratulated the happy couple.[9]

Greater coordination on the Greek side could probably have forced Kütahı Pasha to withdraw at this point. But under Koundouriotis the Greek government was incapable of providing effective leadership, and the kapetans and armatoles of Rumeli were, as always, internally divided. Indeed, several who had gathered in the southern Pindos to help alleviate the siege took their men back again over the winter to their regional strongholds in Attica and Boeotia. They made no further effort to attack the Ottoman army and precious weeks that could have been used in bringing in a supply of food from the Peloponnese were wasted. The judgment of the knowledgeable George Finlay is unsparing: "Nothing but the irreconcilable jealousies of the Greek chieftains, and their military ignorance, which prevented their executing any combined operations, saved Reshid's army from destruction."[10]

In November 1825 an enormous fleet of 135 ships—carrying another 10,000 troops—landed at Navarino, the fifth and last Egyptian convoy of the year. Ibrahim immediately set out for Mesolonghi, sending on ships to help renew the blockade of the lagoon and leading 4,000 men on foot and horseback up the west coast of the Peloponnese toward Patras. They burned their way through the towns and villages they passed, overriding pockets of resistance, and on November 29 Ibrahim met up in Patras with the Kapudan Pasha, Khusrev, and Kütahı Pasha to coordinate their strategy. Leaving Joseph Sève—now known as Soliman Bey—to run the main camp in Methoni and Navarino, Ibrahim kept another 2,000 men in Tripolitsa and allowed the bulk of his cavalry to graze over the winter in the fields around Patras. Meanwhile he crossed the Gulf of Corinth to the northern side with the rest of his troops and assembled them about ten miles along the coast from Mesolonghi. He readied an infantry division and established gun emplacements, while dozens of flat-bottomed ships were constructed for use on the lagoon. Vast quantities of munitions were carried by his Arab laborers through the mud, rains, and swollen waters of the Evinos river to the camp on the other side; hundreds died of disease or cold in the mudholes that served them for shelter.

On December 12, Egyptian contingents appeared outside the walls of Mesolonghi for the first time. The town's defenders did not seem to have appreciated the scale of the threat now facing them, and they shared the disdainful attitude toward the Arab soldiers that their fellow Greeks had shown for a year or more. Having repelled several Ottoman armies, they did not fear a land attack and they were heartened by the sight of Spetsiot brigs sailing in the Ionian Gulf; armed fighters even slipped through the enemy lines at night. Flour and other provisions from the Ionian Islands were discreetly brought into the town through the reed-covered channels connecting the lagoon with Petala along the coast. In January, Miaoulis and a predominantly Hydriot fleet moored off the island of Vasiladi, fought off Ottoman attacks, and unloaded more supplies for the town.

Yet money was running low, and Mesolonghi did not have stocks to withstand a long siege. In addition to Kütahı Pasha's men, the inhabitants would shortly be facing the 9,000 trained infantry and artillery that Ibrahim was bringing into the attack. The months of heavy fighting had left their mark on the fortifications, now badly dilapidated in places, and the ground had turned to mud where it was not already underwater. Tensions were rising between the kapetans and soldiers defending the garrison, and the townspeople who resented their constant demands for more wages and for rations that were twice what they required.[11] Ibrahim Pasha hoped to solve the situation peacefully, as he had earlier in Messenia, and he asked the Greeks to send emissaries to negotiate the terms of a surrender. Yet they still believed the government in Nafplion would come to their aid—and turned his offer down.

Rumors of Mesolonghi's fall to the Ottomans had been circulating abroad since Ibrahim's men arrived. At the end of December 1825, news of his supposed triumph was celebrated with a cannonade from the fortress at Chania in Crete. Next month it was reported that Mesolonghi had been sacked, 10,000–12,000 inhabitants had been put to the sword, and the Ottoman fleet was sailing round to attack Hydra and blockade Nafplion by sea, while Ibrahim attacked it by land. None of this was correct, but it did suggest that many people believed Mesolonghi's resistance was doomed, and that once it had fallen, there would be little to stop the sultan's forces crushing the last remaining centers of Greek resistance in the Peloponnese. In western Europe, the twists and turns of the siege—along with many embellishments for dramatic effect—were avidly followed and the town's plight became front-page headlines in the newspapers.[12]

When Ibrahim's forces did launch their attack, in the middle of February 1826, it was with a bombardment that exceeded anything the townspeople had experienced before. In three days some 8,000 shells and cannonballs are estimated to have struck Mesolonghi. But although they did a lot of damage to the buildings, the inhabitants were able to find shelter, and relatively few lost their lives. The bigger problem was starvation: by now people were eating pack animals as well as cats and dogs; there were fights over mice and rats. Along the shore of the lagoon they were gathering plants, boiling them over and over again to make them edible: The result was that many people suffered from scurvy, dysentery, and other ailments associated with malnutrition. More and more of them were emaciated, sleep deprived, and desperate. The cemeteries were filled, and with corpses left abandoned—the living being too exhausted to bury them—there were accounts of cannibalism. It was obvious they could not hold out for much longer.[13]

Dawn on February 28 saw the last sustained Turco-Egyptian attack on the town walls. Both Kütahı Pasha and Ibrahim Pasha were there in person urging their men on, risking their own lives amid the musket balls and detonations. Yet astonishingly, the defenders managed to repel them even now, inflicting heavy casualties and capturing several enemy banners. Their courage seems to have led Ibrahim to conclude, as he had at Navarino, that a frontal assault on fortified positions was too costly to continue. He had already crafted a strategy to cut off the town's sources of supply and enforce the blockade. He prepared a small flotilla of rafts and flat-bottomed boats that he armed with 36-pounders and manned with troops who fanned out across the lagoon. On February 26 they stormed the island of Vasiladi and took it after heavy fighting. The leader of the defenders, a veteran Italian philhellene, escaped through the reeds and made his way back to Mesolonghi. Three days later the islet of Dolmas fell to the invaders, followed on March 1 by the surrender of the crucial island stronghold of Anatolikon at the north of the lagoon. Each victory tightened the noose around Mesolonghi and made supplying it more perilous.

The British commissioner of the Ionian Islands tried to mediate but withdrew in the face of the Greek refusal to negotiate a surrender. The pashas attempted one last offer, proposing that the defenders lay down their arms and be given safe conduct out of the town. This offer too was rejected.

The last remaining islet in Greek hands was Kleisova, which guarded the southern flank of Mesolonghi from the lagoon: it was held by a small garrison of around one hundred men, aided by the young Souliot chieftain Kitsos Tzavellas. On March 25, Egyptian rafts and gunboats were sent out to take it while rows of infantry struggled through the waist-high water toward their target. As Kütahı's men fell back under heavy fire from the defenders who were holed up in a tower and could pick men off at will, Ibrahim ordered his brother-in-law, Hussein Bey, to lead the Egyptian troops forward. For hours they persisted until a shot killed Hussein Bey himself. He had been the architect of the pacification of Crete and perhaps Ibrahim's most skilled strategist, so this was a devastating loss for the Egyptian leader. Ibrahim is said to have retired grief-stricken to his tent and did not emerge for several days; when the Egyptians finally withdrew, they left hundreds of corpses floating in the water. But although it had been an extraordinary feat of bravery by the defenders, it was obvious that the town could not hold out much longer. A doctor proposed pickling some of the enemy corpses in brine to be used as a source of meat—everything else had been consumed—but his suggestion was not accepted. The buildings were mostly bombed-out ruins and much of the open ground between them and the walls was underwater.[14]

Admiral Miaoulis made one final appearance offshore on April 1 but his fleet was small and poorly manned: as usual most of the Hydriot sailors had refused to serve without their pay and by this point the government had used up the loan and was bankrupt again. Through one last secret channel in the reeds the townspeople smuggled out a letter to the Hydriot admiral begging for assistance but by the time Miaoulis had prepared a reply, the channel had been cut and the Zantiot sailors caught using it were hanged. There was now no way to get food into the town—the blockade was complete—and the siege was nearing its end.

From outside the position seemed quite hopeless. A British surgeon serving on a warship moored nearby described the view they had of Mesolonghi from the lagoon:

> The town appeared closely encircled by masses of tents, to the distance of two miles or more inland, and the intervening beach and canals were one

line of batteries, gunboats, and armed rafts, on all of which the crimson flag was flying. The town itself presented, at a short distance, a perfect mass of ruins; the houses and walls were apparently knocked to pieces or entirely neglected, and so few people could be seen moving about within the precincts of the place, that it could scarcely be supposed it was the rendezvous of 10,000 living beings, or could be an object for the assembling of such a formidable armament as was now investing it by sea and land.[15]

One of the most inspiring features of the siege was that for all their quarreling and mistrust, the occupants of the town had shown in critical moments a remarkable capacity for collective action. It had been evident in the initial rebuilding of the fortifications, a huge enterprise involving women and children, and in the defenders' successful attempts to repel several direct assaults on the walls. At one point, when the soldiers manning the walls had grown tired, sleep-deprived by the constant bombardment, and angry at not having been fed for several days, the bishop of Mesolonghi encouraged all the townspeople to bring them coffee to help them stay awake. The decision that was now made to end the siege was also a collective one. It began with fears that, as had happened elsewhere, some of the armed bands who were defending the town might simply decide to quit, leaving the inhabitants undefended: this, after all, is what had ended the sieges of Tripolitsa and Corinth. Some of the Greek soldiers were already fleeing, despite the difficulties, making their way at night across the lagoon to the safety of the mountains or the islands. It was understandable, therefore, that mistrust flourished: a man was caught alleged to be carrying letters from Mehmed Ali to one of the town's leading notables, offering him money to change sides.[16]

One of the reasons why the town rejected Ibrahim's offer of surrender, which stipulated that all those leaving should disarm, was the news from the small nearby island-town of Anatolikon, a few miles away in the north of the lagoon, where hundreds of women and children were reported to have been sold into slavery and were enduring "a thousand evils."[17] At a meeting in the church of Ayios Spiridon, the main chieftains in Mesolonghi decided the only option left, once Ibrahim's surrender terms had been rejected, was a final surprise sortie to make for the safety of the mountains by the town's 3,000 fighting men, their families, and those townspeople capable of fleeing. The idea of an organized sortie en masse was not new, nor was it necessarily suicidal: it might well have worked before the Egyptians arrived. Yet it raised the question of the fate of the population that could not fight and run for safety. Eventually, after much discussion, it was decided that those too old, weak, or otherwise unable to leave the town would have to stay behind, and they were encouraged to occupy houses that were packed with explosives so that they could blow themselves up once the Turkish and the Egyptian soldiers came in. There was even talk of killing all the women and children so as to leave the men unencumbered and better able to escape, but this was denounced by the much-respected bishop of the town, Bishop Iosif, and the idea was abandoned. Fewer scruples attended the fate of the many prisoners being held within the town. Their unreliability was a constant concern, and it was decided to put them to death; one source suggests that even Christian captives from the Ottoman forces were killed. Other testimonies pass over the gruesome subject.[18]

Within the town at this time there were perhaps 3,000 soldiers left, many of them wounded or ill, as well as about 1,000 able-bodied townspeople and 5,000 women and children. The plan, which evolved over ten days of discussions before eventually being approved by the bishop, was for those intending to escape to assemble silently at dusk behind the main moat on the southeastern side farthest from the mass of the enemy, and then to flee in three columns: The civilians led by Makris and his men would take the safest path through the plain fringing the lagoon; guarding their left flank and diverting attention, the armed men of the garrison would drive forward through the enemy lines in two columns and aim to head toward the monastery of Ayios Symeon in the foothills of Mount Zygos. The signal for the sortie was to be a fusillade from the hills, a sign that Karaïskakis's government force had arrived to mount an attack on the Egyptian lines from their rear.[19]

On the night in question, April 10, a crucial part of the plan would fail: Karaïskakis, who was prone to bouts of ill-health, was bedridden and his men—not for the first time in the history of the siege—did not give the support the garrison were expecting. But the situation was in fact worse than that: unknown to the defenders, their intentions had become known to the enemy. There is much disagreement as to exactly how this happened: according to one report, which later reached Cairo, the messenger sent to Karaïskakis from the town—a Greek priest who could speak both Arabic and Turkish and was disguised as a Muslim—had been captured. According to another report, the secret was spilled by a Bulgarian deserter. A third blames a Turkish captive who had escaped from the town. The truth is that many Greek escapees from Mesolonghi who made it to the safety of the Ionian Islands also knew about the plan and therefore it would have been impossible to keep such a secret from the enemy. A Habsburg consular official happened to be in Ibrahim's camp on the night of the sortie. When they heard a fusillade from the mountaintop, Ibrahim told him that was the signal and that he knew he would prevail, having prepared his troops across the plain in expectation. Some even suggest the firing itself had come from his men, a trick to trigger the sortie.[20]

Nearly five years earlier, the Muslims of Tripolitsa had contemplated just such a desperate measure; but opting instead to surrender to the forces besieging them, they had been massacred. Now in the spring of 1826 it was the turn of the Greeks of Mesolonghi: unwilling to trust the word of their Ottoman opponents and determined to set a heroic example for their countrymen, they preferred to die with weapons in hand. According to one detailed account, it was around midnight that the fusillade was heard from the mountain. The kapetans met and passed the word around: those fleeing were to assemble by the walls; a few patrols were instructed to remain on the walls and to fire their guns at intervals as usual so as not to arouse suspicion, and those remaining behind were to make for the designated refuges. The sortie would begin in two hours, using four makeshift wooden bridges to cross the moat. They were to cross in silence and then wait facedown in the earth on the other side of the main wall for the signal to attack.

As hundreds of people began to assemble on the open space behind the walls, the four bridges were brought up and in the dead of night the soldiers and their families made their way in silence to where they had been placed. According to one account, it was the noise made by the placing of the bridges, and the inability of some of the children to remain quiet, that alerted the enemy, but we know they were expecting the sortie anyway. Even so, many of the Greeks were able to cross the bridges and gather on the far side of the main ditch, where they were protected by the low wall that lined the second smaller ditch: they lay behind this, faces pressed into the ground, to avoid the enemy bullets. Meanwhile, back in the town, those leaving friends and relatives behind made their farewells. Hundreds of women and children, the elderly and sick, barricaded themselves in houses in the town, many of them in the ammunition store where several hundred barrels of explosives had been left in the charge of the seventy-five-year-old notable Christos Kapsalis.

Now outside the walls, the Greeks were waiting for the sound of firing from the mountains indicating that Karaïskakis's men had begun their attack on the enemy's rear. After the moon appeared, illuminating the plain, those at the front waited impatiently for about an hour, as more and more people pressed behind them, and then quite suddenly someone gave the signal for the charge. With cries of "Forward! Death to the barbarians!" and led by Notis Botsaris's standard-bearer, they ran out against the Egyptians. "Intoxicated with madness," they threw themselves upon the soldiers in the front line, sliding through the muddy earth and fighting across ground pitted with waterlogged trenches. Their charge, which happened virtually on the spur of the moment, came at a time when many of the townspeople were still within the walls making their farewells or sorting out their possessions. Hearing the din, they appear to have thought reinforcements were coming and someone raised a shout that they should retreat and return to the town to wait. As a result, those making the sortie split into two groups—one charging ahead, the other retreating in uncertainty. They would face very different fates.[21]

The two columns of Greek defenders tore through the enemy lines, killing the advance guards near the batteries with their yataghans and knives and pushing onward at a steady pace without pausing across the plain toward the hills. Adept at night fighting, they were a potent force, capable of navigating the confusion of a struggle at very close quarters. With them were a few women dressed in men's clothes, some townspeople, and servants. Armed with a rifle, two pistols, and a sword that Byron had given him, the doctor Petros Stefanitsis was accompanied by his three servants, loaded down with silver coins and valuables. Realizing that the help they had expected was not coming from the hills, the two columns of fighters never separated but remained in a compact mass, warding off the Ottoman cavalry that went round to avoid them. Enemy troops stood off, not daring to engage them in hand-to-hand combat and preferring to let them pass. The bulk of the women and children, meanwhile, who were supposed to be heading along the shore, never made it past the ditches: one of the bridges had broken under the weight, and the trenches were waterlogged death traps. As they ran back to the town, having heard the call to retreat, they were pursued by enemy soldiers who poured in and sacked the place. Many of these women and children were accompanied by brothers, sons, fathers, or husbands who died defending them.[22]

In the dark, fighting across muddy ground pitted with trenches and ditches, the scene must have been one of utter and murderous confusion, punctuated by screams, explosions, yells, and wails, and occasionally illuminated by flashes of musket fire. Sometime later, there was a tremendous explosion as Kapsalis blew up the munitions factory and the plain was lit up; buildings were set ablaze and the fires could be seen from many miles away. On HMS *Chanticleer*, they could hear the screams and see the smoke and flames rising into the sky for hours. Nikolaos Kasomoulis in his memoir writes that from the foothills of Mount Zygos those who had escaped heard "the ferment of women's cries, gunfire, detonations of munitions and mines, one confused and indescribably awful din." Children were separated from their parents; babies were abandoned. Egyptian and Albanian soldiers fought one another, mistaking each other for the enemy or scrapping over spoils: the Arab soldiers are said to have killed at least one hundred of the Albanian irregulars, and doubtless on many occasions they could not tell them apart from the Greeks. The Greek soldiers were fooled too: fighting their way up to the hills, they suffered their greatest losses of the night at the hands of Albanians who were lying in wait for them and tricked them into thinking they were Greeks. Eventually, some of Karaïskakis's men helped to beat them off and the Greek soldiers moved higher up the mountain, waiting only to see who would join them. In fact, few of the townspeople made it that far and many of them died in the plain or in the town where the fighting lasted for nearly two days around houses the Greeks had barricaded. The mill, which was one of the few stone buildings left standing, held out until eventually some of the defenders managed to escape and made their way to safety in the darkness through the lagoon.[23]

Those who died in the town included Bishop Iosif, the Swiss journalist Johan Jacob Mayer, the notable Kapsalis, as well as the genius behind the town's fortifications, the engineer Mikhail Kokkinis; he had been born in Chios, spoke at least four languages, and had fought for the Etaireia in the Danubian Principalities with Ypsilantis before taking charge of Mesolonghi and its defenses. It is impossible to say with any accuracy what the final death toll amounted to. Of the approximately 9,000 inhabitants of Mesolonghi when the sortie took place, perhaps some 1,800 escaped, including 200 women; about 3,000 were killed during the fighting in and around the town, and some 3,000–4,000 women and children were taken as slaves. They had been terribly outnumbered. Confronting the Greeks, Ibrahim had placed two regiments, with another 2,400 soldiers in reserve, 1,000 cavalry, and 2,000 Albanian irregulars. Alongside them there were the forces under Kütahı Pasha: in all, the strength of the Ottoman-Egyptian army had probably amounted to more than 30,000 men. The odds in their favor had been overwhelming and it was astonishing that nearly 2,000 Greeks managed to break through and escape. They were overwhelmingly the fighting men: of the women, children, and the elderly, the vast majority were either killed or sold into slavery.[24]

The morning after the sortie, an Italian doctor serving on Ibrahim's staff made his way across the plain. His horse proceeded tentatively, trampling ground strewn with corpses. The ditches in front of the walls were filled with bodies, so mud-strewn that he could not recognize their age or sex. He was shocked when he reached the walls, which struck him as weak, the guns surprisingly modest. "What an insignificant place! And yet it had been impregnable." Others had the same reaction. Philip Green, the former British consul in Patras and a man reviled by the Greeks for his pro-Ottoman sympathies, was surprised by the fortifications that were "scarcely worth the name" and should have been stormed at any time: it was a lack of courage on the part of the attackers, he thought, along with the poor quality of their artillery fire, that allowed the defenses to hold out. Inside, the town itself was in ruins, and scarcely twenty houses were left standing.[25]

Watching the sortie helplessly that night from a hilltop some thirty miles away was Spiros Milios—known as Spiromilios—a twenty-six-year-old kapetan from a fighting family in the small town of Heimarra, now in southern Albania. A young mountain warrior in most parts of the world in the early nineteenth century would almost certainly have been illiterate and in no position to leave us a record of his experiences. But the Greek language had an extraordinary reach, and from the crags of Heimarra to the centers of European learning was a surprisingly short journey. Following family tradition, Spiromilios had been sent as a boy to Naples, where the Bourbon army had many Greco-Albanians (including his grandfather) in its ranks. There he had learned Latin, Italian, and French as well as soldiering: as a result, although self-taught in written

Greek, Spiromilios was able to pen one of the most remarkable testimonies of the siege that we possess.

A junior commander, critical of the selfishness of the main band leaders, Spiromilios had left Mesolonghi as part of the delegation it sent to the government in Nafplion at the start of 1826 to appeal for help. He bore with him a recommendation from the town's Swiss newspaperman, Johan Jacob Mayer, who described him as "full of commitment and more educated than the rest of the herd of our so-called Generals" (*plein de zèle et plus érudit que le reste de la foule de nos dits Généraux*).[26] The journey took more than two weeks but by the time the Mesolonghi delegates had reached the government capital in Nafplion on February 2, the political discord of the previous year and a half had grown worse than ever. Everything was in suspense ahead of the national assembly scheduled to take place at the start of April to elect a new government. President Koundouriotis seemed incapable of taking any decisive action, now that the loan proceeds had been exhausted. Having spent nearly a year under siege, a time during which, as Spiromilios put it, "we did not speak of anything other than gun emplacements, fortifications and ditches, when we did not hear anything other than the clap of cannon, and muskets, and bomb blasts and explosions," the delegates were shocked by the politicians and their petty quarrels. Yet to those in Nafplion, Spiromilios wrote, the plight of Mesolonghi seemed no closer than events in Peking. People spoke as though its fall were preordained—and had nothing to do with them.[27]

At a specially convened combined session of the legislature and the executive, Spiromilios laid out the defenders' needs. He explained that the enemy had concentrated all its forces on Mesolonghi, regarding the town as the key to the fate of the entire uprising; the Greeks now needed to do the same. The townspeople had given an example of extraordinary endurance and courage, but they could not end the siege without the resources and coordinated strategy that only the national government could provide. They needed funds to provision the fleet to resupply the town, and an army of 7,000–8,000 men on the hills above: the enemy would be forced in this way to engage in a battle to avoid being trapped, and since the town was secure behind its walls, the outcome would likely not only lift the siege but speed the liberation of the rest of the Greek lands.

In his memoir Spiromilios recounts the response. There were fine words for the heroes of the nation, but money was tight and little was done. Some sums were raised by selling off former Ottoman lands to buyers at a discount—notables such as President Koundouriotis himself and the merchant banker Emmanouil Xenos acquired large estates for a song, but not much flowed into the government's coffers. There were futile efforts to raise a loan but they went nowhere. When the delegates met with the Peloponnesian notables, it was made clear that they had no troops to spare.[28] Even Mavrokordatos scarcely reacted when he was informed about the fall of Vasiladi; he and the others were "sunk in their [political] passions and in their internal disagreements."[29] Furious, the delegates from Mesolonghi more or less forced the deputies to hand over some money on the spot, raised money from the town's merchants and shopkeepers, and sent Spiromilios and a few others off with the proceeds to Hydra to try to outfit a fleet. More time was wasted in negotiations among the three shipowning islands over how to share the funds among them; the sailors bargained hard as usual. Spiromilios tells us bitterly that the funds were just enough to spend on two months' wages for the soldiers in Mesolonghi, plus a small flotilla, a shipment of biscuit, and 200 armed men. When they did eventually sail, the fleet was poorly armed and under-crewed, and several of the promised vessels were not there; much more profitable and less risky ventures awaited Greek seamen in the Aegean.

Led by Admiral Miaoulis, this last flotilla arrived at the entrance to the lagoon a few days after Tzavellas's successful defense of the islet of Kleisova. Miaoulis, a figure of unquestioned courage and probity, could see that the Ottoman fleet was far stronger than his own. The Mesolonghi delegates on board proposed fighting their way in, but Miaoulis vetoed the idea and so they made for the island of Petala, up the coast, where thousands of refugees had fled the fighting and were living in terrible conditions. There they heard from recent escapees of the plans for a sortie from Mesolonghi, and they learned that many townspeople had been captured trying to flee. The town had been excited at the sight of the Greek fleet but then plunged into despair when it sailed away again. The bishop had tried to cheer them up: he announced that a girl had seen St. Nikolaos in a dream and that the saint had promised the fleet would return in eight days with food. Spiromilios himself was in despair because two of his brothers were among those trapped in the town and he was unable to do anything. On Petala on the night that the sortie took place, he climbed to the island's highest point from where he could not only hear the battle but actually see the flames. "We understood that the town had fallen, that the Turks had gained the fortifications and that the Greeks had fled to their homes and were holding out for a fighter's death."[30]

The predominant emotion that runs through Spiromilios's memoir of the siege is anger. The townspeople of Mesolonghi had been isolated by the siege but they found themselves isolated in a deeper sense by the apathy and indifference of their fellow Greeks. A trained military man, Spiromilios believed plausibly that the fall of the town could have been averted. It could certainly have been saved before the arrival of the Egyptians and it could even have held out through the spring of 1826 if the delegates had been heeded. Instead, it had been captured because of the Greeks' total lack of strategic awareness or leadership.

It was not as though the Koundouriotis government lacked options. It might have failed to forestall Ibrahim's landing in the Peloponnese, and Kolokotronis, its designated commander in chief, might have failed to stop the Egyptians taking over most of the peninsula; yet in the spring of 1826 the Greeks still had plenty of men under arms. The government had already taken advantage of the presence of a highly experienced French officer, Charles Fabvier, a Napoleonic veteran who had signed the surrender of Paris in 1814, and put him in charge of training new regular detachments. Helped by a new conscription law, by the last tranche of the English loan and some experienced military trainers, this renewal of the old experiment of forging a national army seemed finally to be meeting with some success. Fabvier recruited new infantry companies, drilled them on European lines along with a small quantity of cavalry and artillery, and within two months had raised a force of more than 1,000 men. By the end of 1825 he had over 3,000, including cavalry and artillery. It was the obvious force to have sent to Mesolonghi.[31]

Yet unlike Joseph Sève, his counterpart in Egypt, Colonel Fabvier did not have a Mehmed Ali to back him. Koundouriotis, who had removed himself to his mansion in Hydra, lay ailing on his sickbed, deaf and exhausted, unable or unwilling to respond to state business. For the usual reasons, the armatoles and the military chieftains ensured that the regulars were deployed wherever could do them least harm politically. A proposal to send them to Mesolonghi had been in the air since November but it came to nothing, ostensibly for lack of shipping and money. The result was that in February the government ordered Fabvier's men off in another direction, northeast of Athens, to attack long-held Ottoman positions on the island of Evvia. This expedition turned into a fiasco, the Ottomans remained undefeated, and Fabvier's starving and shoeless troops had to be rescued at the start of April, only a few days before Mesolonghi fell, having accomplished nothing. His men were demoralized, disunited, and rebellious; one group killed their commanding officer. Fabvier was ready to resign and return to France and was only persuaded to stay by his friend Mavrokordatos.[32]

The misuse of manpower went further as armed bands abandoned the national struggle in favor of plunder by sea and on land. Vaso Brajović, known to the Greeks as Vasos the Montenegrin (*Mavrovouniotis*), had been serving in the Ottoman garrison in Athens when he joined the insurgency. He was one of those figures whose fortunes had been made by the war and over three years he had proved himself as a fighter, kapetan, and political operator. Tough and loyal, he was exactly the kind of leader needed at Mesolonghi—a proven fighter, with several hundred men willing to follow him. But because the government could no longer pay him, he went plundering, taking along his blood brother, a chieftain from Evvia called Nikolaos Kriezotis. This was quite normal behavior for men in their position: what made their venture in the spring of 1826 unusual was that it involved crossing the eastern Mediterranean. They had their eyes on the riches of Ottoman-controlled Beirut—wrapped in some implausible scheme for getting the Christians of Mount Lebanon to revolt, which the government may or may not have sanctioned (the sources are ambiguous)—and eventually the two chieftains and their men sailed for Lebanon on about twelve Spetsiot brigs, having first plundered the island of Tzia. The numbers alone give a sense of the vast scale this kind of quasi-piracy was assuming in the Aegean.

Thus around the time Spiromilios was leaving Hydra to return to Mesolonghi, Mavrovouniotis's flotilla reached Beirut. His men scaled the ramparts of the port but were then prevented from going farther by a few harbor guards; despite cannonading the town, they were easily repulsed and within five days they had left. It was worse than a fiasco: the Christian inhabitants were left to the mercy of the Ottoman governor's forces, who killed a few in retaliation. Mavrovouniotis and Kriezotis returned to Attica and helped rescue Fabvier's men from Evvia before resuming their plundering at the expense of peasants from the island of Andros who underwent—in the words of an ardently pro-revolutionary source—"horror" at their hands. It would have been better for the Greek cause if their supporters had all found themselves on the other side of the Pindos fighting the Turco-Egyptian army. But the weakness of the government created too many temptations for the armed bands and the islands in particular suffered immensely. At the end of 1826, the same two chieftains went back to Andros with some 3,000 Rumeliots and plundered it for months, eventually extracting an enormous sum from the desperate inhabitants as the price of their departure.[33]

"[The] so-called secret expedition [to Lebanon] should rather be called a treacherous expedition since, while Mesolonghi has need of every soldier, they sent 500 men to Beirut," fulminated one old Etairist who was trying to drum up support for the town:

> Mesolonghi has need of the navy whose fitting out depends upon funding and its seriousness is frittered away on such idiotic expeditions, just like the one to Karystos. The hour struck for the fleet to sail to the defense of Mesolonghi and the best ships and sailors were off corsairing. The captains look for sailors. The sailors reply to their request: "Let those ones go whom the government sent off corsairing. We won't go to be killed for 60 or 80 grossia a month while they are earning 400 or 500 thalers for no risk." [34]

Even though the government was headed by a Hydriot notable, it was no longer capable of fitting out a fleet to take on the Ottoman forces at sea. Having run out of funds, the Koundouriotis government was encouraging crews to sail by issuing ever larger numbers of privateering licenses, with the result that outright piracy became a plague across the eastern Mediterranean. The rationale for this was purely local—an effort by island notables to placate the mob of unemployed seamen who were always a menace in hard times. On Spetses the sailors rioted, sacking the houses of some notables "in open rebellion"; there were threats against the magnates on Hydra as well. The murderous violence that crowds on Hydra had shown against Egyptian and Turkish captives now seemed a prospect for their own countrymen. Faced not only with mob rule but also a likely attack on the island by the Ottoman and Egyptian forces, some notables left the island; even the Koundouriotis brothers planned to abandon Hydra and were virtually forced to remain by the angry population when this was discovered.[35]

The truth was that everyone spoke of Greece but only a few thought like Greeks and were willing to sacrifice their personal interest for the good of the nation. The Peloponnesian notables and *oplarchigoi*, having suffered at the hands of the Rumeliot chieftains in 1824 and 1825, were now disinclined to send men across the Gulf of Corinth, or even to mount diversionary raids against the Egyptians in the Morea. Their priority was regaining control of the government. As for the Rumeliots, they were no better. In Mesolonghi, what was left of the government in Nafplion ordered Karaïskakis to come to the town's assistance from the rear of the Ottoman army. But it failed to provide him with funds, or to divert many troops, and it told him to collect provisions regionally since none were available in Nafplion and to await the fleet that was about to set sail. None of this could really be taken seriously. The mountain ranges of western Rumeli had been stripped bare by years of war, Karaïskakis's camp was in the process of being dismantled, and at the best of times food stocks in the early months of the year would have been hard to find. Moreover, the instructions specifically exempted the forces of Rangos, Tsongas, and the Souliots from Karaïskakis's authority. Once more the old rivalries of the Rumeliot armatoles were bedeviling the common struggle.[36]

Disunity at the national level contrasted with the way tensions had been managed within Mesolonghi itself. Large numbers of those trapped inside its walls had died of hunger or disease and there had been acrimony for months over rations. Yet for all the factionalism, party politics, and internal dissensions, public order in Mesolonghi had never broken down, and the town's defense had been a remarkable collective action. Military policy had chiefly been made in group meetings of the kapetans. Efforts had been made to develop some kind of care for the wounded; the expertise of engineers, sappers, and doctors was valued. The chief institutions of the Church, the government, and private property still commanded a surprising degree of respect in the circumstances. The town's widely respected Bishop Iosif, who had conducted a final liturgy on the day of the sortie, remained a popular figure and his services continued to be well attended throughout the siege.[37]

The first offer of surrender terms in the spring of 1825 by Kütahı Pasha had discriminated between armatoles, klefts, Souliots, and townspeople: the latter, unlike the others, for example were not to be allowed to leave for wherever they wished. Mesolonghi's response had been that the inhabitants of the town were united, and their struggle would lead either to their death or to their national liberation. This unity was never abandoned. Spiromilios himself was one of the moving spirits in a newly formed municipal society, which quickly numbered 1,000 members, that aimed to root out corruption in the town and preserve respect for the law and the authorities. In such ways, a new political vision was taking shape even amid the pressure of the siege—one that contemplated the prospect of death as a contribution to the forging of a national society.[38]

In resistance and in death this collective spirit had been preserved. For what was so striking about the Mesolonghi sortie was its democratic, anonymous nature. The fighting had taken place at night, amid rain and mud, and had left its thousands of victims mostly unrecognizable and unburied. Who would ever know the names of the dead or their precise fates? Later they would be mourned. But at the time it was the town as a whole whose sacrifice commanded respect. Much of the military leadership and the garrison had managed to cut their way through—even seventy-year-old Notis Botsaris. Yet thousands of ordinary women and children, and elder figures like Bishop Iosif, had been the principal victims, killed or sold into slavery from which many never returned. The bishop himself had gathered around him in an old mill those unable to flee the town; they had held out for two days before detonating explosives and blowing themselves up. What made the sack of Mesolonghi so unusual and compelling was the form of heroism it incarnated—that of an entire society prepared to die for the sake of freedom.

OUTSIDE THE NORMAL
SPHERE OF FEELINGS

Lord Byron's portrait on the wall
And the cast-iron statuette
With folded arms and eyes bent low,
Cocked hat and melancholy brow.

Pushkin, *Eugene Onegin*, canto 7,
verse 17, trans. Henry Spalding

If the catastrophe that followed the fall of Mesolonghi galvanized public opinion in Europe like nothing else in the war, it was because the overwhelming outpouring of feeling that ensued had been some time in the making. Since the spring of 1824, Mesolonghi had become renowned across the continent as the place where Byron had died: the sensational news of his demise had placed the Greek struggle at the center of not only the international struggle for popular liberties but also the burgeoning European culture of Romanticism. When his death was announced, wrote Victor Hugo, "it was as if a part of our future had been snatched away." Heinrich Heine in Germany mourned this "Prometheus" of the spirit. The Italian nationalist activist Giuseppe Mazzini said Byron had typified the "holy alliance of poetry with the cause of the peoples." His ill-fated engagement with the Greeks was a reminder that even after Napoleon's death, glory beckoned: Saint Helena, where Napoleon had died, and Mesolonghi were henceforth mysteriously conjoined. In Pushkin's great poem *Eugene Onegin*, the hero's room is adorned by Byron's portrait and a statuette of the emperor, a sign of the twin influences that loomed not only over Pushkin but an entire literary generation.[1]

In France, which was to become the epicenter of the new philhellenism of the mid-1820s, reports of Byron's death were followed almost immediately by the news that the gouty, obese, sixty-eight-year-old Bourbon king of France, Louis XVIII, distracted by the charms of a mistress thirty years his junior, had dismissed his foreign minister. This would not in itself have been remarkable had the minister in question not been François-René, vicomte de Chateaubriand, a towering, quasi-Byronic figure in his own right. Chateaubriand was a bestselling writer, the figure who more than any other was responsible for glamourizing a new kind of historically conscious Christian conservatism. He also knew and loved Greece and his pioneering Romantic travelogue of 1811, *Itinéraire de Paris à Jerusalem*, contained remarkable passages on his experiences in the Ottoman Morea and was suffused, in the words of a critic, with "the dream of liberation." Removed from power, one of France's most famous authors was now free to devote his considerable energy to preaching a cause that had always remained dear to him: he began popularizing a new defense of the Greeks on the grounds not of revolutionary politics but of Christian solidarity.

His reasons were not solely cultural or spiritual. France, the heartland of revolution, was the weak point of the European Restoration, and Chateaubriand typified the fusion of two causes—Greece and opposition to the Bourbons. Simmering internal discontent only grew when, in the autumn of 1824, Louis XVIII died and was succeeded by his brother, the elderly, conservative Charles X, who installed a government of ultra royalists: it was like a throwback to the days before the Revolution, the country in the hands of men opposed to the constitutional commitments of 1814, seeking to restore the powers of the Catholic Church and the great landed estates. In 1825 and 1826 Mesolonghi's plight became a cause that mobilized a wide coalition of forces opposed to the monarchy and through which French society—in its salons, theaters, poets, galleries, and ateliers—started to criticize the Bourbon Restoration with ever-increasing boldness.

The establishment of the Société philanthropique en faveur des Grecs (widely known as the Comité Grec) in the spring of 1825 signaled this new development. An activist offshoot of an earlier French organization, the Société de la Morale Chrétienne, an all-purpose philanthropic organization that promoted abolitionism, this new body was set up under the patronage of the duc d'Orléans, the king's cousin and the man who would succeed him in 1830, after a brief revolution, as King

Louis-Philippe. Although it would be wrong to see the upsurge in senti-ment for Greece as an Orléanist conspiracy—it was much too widespread for that—it is true that behind the scenes, the Orléans entourage dreamed at one point of getting the Greek throne for one of the duke's sons. The new Comité Grec looked like a high-society affair that included the duc de Choiseul and the marquis de Laborde; a viscount and a royalist as well as an ardent philhellene, Chateaubriand was an active participant. But fellow members also included liberal thinkers such as the writer Benjamin Constant and publisher Firmin Didot, and even Bonapartist officers. Through the Comité, philhellenism became a marker of the Orléanist conception of a forward-looking monarchy, a sign of its contrast with the reactionary Bourbons. The Comité launched subscription drives for funds and its members publicly appealed to the government to abandon its pro-Ottoman policy. "The Greeks are on ev-eryone's mind," wrote the painter Étienne-Jean Delécluze at the end of April 1826, "of those at least who are opposed to the monarchy." "It was an established fact," wrote the comtesse de Boigne of salon life at that time, "that whoever was opposed to the Court was a philhellene."[2]

As the French followed the final stages of the Mesolonghi siege in their newspapers, political agitation merged with philanthropy, and the aristocracy took to the stage in April for an unprecedented charity spec-tacle with a chorus of blue-blooded ladies. "The principal event in the annals of fashion for the past month was the concert for the benefit of the Greeks," Henri Beyle (better known as Stendhal) reported in May 1826 in Paris for the London Magazine. Packed with the beau monde, the evening was a brilliant success, raising a not inconsiderable sum of 30,000 francs: Madame de G** wore white roses in her hair, noted the Journal des dames et des modes, each one adorned with a diamond; the young people were in black, blue, and white in solidarity with the Greeks—and some sported linens in the so-called Missolonghi gray. The glittering show masked a political message for this was the first time in more than two decades that the upper classes had dared show any public opposition to the government. The concert had been the idea of the Duchess of Dalberg and some other ladies who, in Stendhal's words:

. . . trembled lest the massacres of Chios should be renewed at Misso-longhi. The Government opposed the project by a hundred little indiscreet measures. But suddenly a number of *ultra* ladies of rank began to evince symptoms of compassion and in a day or two it became quite the fashion to patronize the concert. An English gentleman paid three hundred francs for a ticket, and the seller immediately presented the sum to the fund for the benefit of the Greeks. This bargain, which was struck on the Exchange, completely established the fashion and the rage rapidly increased.[3]

The maestro of the moment, the Italian Gioachino Rossini, had been instructed by the government not to conduct the concert on the day, but he had shown his sympathies by rehearsing the chorus of aristocratic women who flocked to take part. The success of the occasion had been guaranteed when (incorrect) news arrived that the Turks had been driven away from Mesolonghi—"for the last thirteen days nothing else has been talked of in Paris." The newspapers kept Mesolonghi's plight in the public eye. "Its perils attracted the attention of all Europe," wrote the journalist Jean-Raymond-Auguste Fabre, author of a history of the siege that was published the following year. "All the peoples [of Europe] awaited the outcome as a kind of national event."[4]

When, in this supercharged atmosphere, the news arrived of the dramatic ending to the town's torment, there was unsurprisingly a wave of outrage and an outpouring of odes, cantatas, laments, and elegies: publishers in half a dozen countries advertised sermons, verse dramas, dirges, and even graduation speeches in the following months, which were sold "au profit des Grecs." Philhellenism was becoming a cultural force unifying very diverse swaths of European society, indeed helping to create something we might term a European liberal conscience. In London's Royal Amphitheatre, a historic drama on "The Siege of Missolonghi, or The Massacre of the Greeks" opened on September 4, 1826 and ran for six nights. In Paris, Rossini took the city by storm with an opera entitled *Le Siège de Corinthe*. Despite its title and ostensible subject—the Ottoman capture of the town in the mid-fifteenth century—there was no mistaking what it was really about. His story of a siege involving Greeks and Turks, love and war, ended with a sensational mass suicide that enacted national martyrdom onstage. Performances left the audience screaming in admiration, and there were crowds each night trying to buy tickets. Rossini had tried out two earlier versions over the years, with a different title and different audiences, and each time the opera had flopped. This time—no doubt helped by the addition of its unprecedented mass suicide finale—there were nightly standing ovations, and crowds would follow the composer home.[5]

Rossini's opera even enjoyed the ultimate accolade of a parody. A new play opened at the Théâtre du Vaudeville entitled *Le Dilettante ou Le Siège de l'Opéra*, which lampooned the excitement around the original. From the script of *Le Dilettante*, the royal censor had felt obliged to remove some inflammatory lines:

> Their great cause has awakened the world,
> And our hearts follow their achievements everywhere,
> When around them the storm is already mighty.
> Oh Rossini, may your lyre and voice
> Move the hearts of kings in their favor.
> Support for them comes from all sides
> To sustain their magnificent uprising
> Let these sounds still speak on their behalf.[6]

In both musical and political terms, Rossini was regarded by more old-fashioned writers as an extremist. A nasty critic called his new opera "the Missolonghi of dramatic music" and likened him to Ibrahim Pasha storming the Opéra by force, aided by traitors who did not understand classical values. In music as in art, conservative commentators mistrusted any allusion to contemporary themes. Nor did they appreciate Rossini's love of musical effect—the overpowering sound, the sheer noise that prevented rational contemplation and overwhelmed the mind with passion. Here too they tried to make a connection between supporting Greek revolutionaries and his kind of percussive orchestration. But Rossini understood his market well. He gave audiences what they wanted and he defended his music as what was needed in a particular political moment:

> How else . . . to produce the effect for people and at times where, in the prolonged unfolding of revolutions and bloody wars, spirits turned to political agitation, where qualities outside the normal sphere of feelings and thoughts, in the midst of a clash of States, the reversal of fortunes, the ravages of arbitrary power, the excesses of ambitions, the imposing apparatus of conquest, become completely worn out in the convulsions of such a changeably tormented existence that there is no longer any strength left for ordinary feelings?[7]

In short, the opera was less a musical event than a sentimental catalyst for a European public whose opinion was emerging as a political force for the first time, crystallizing around the Greek cause. Two years after its premiere, *Le Siège de Corinthe* remained as popular as ever and when the tenor Adolphe Nourrit, who starred as the male protagonist, performed five days of concerts in Manchester, they sold out. "As in France," recollected a journalist years later:

> England possessed a mass of passionate advocates defending the cause of the Greeks in the papers, in books, in Parliament, in the clubs, in salons. The British aristocracy associated itself with these expressions of interest in favor of an oppressed people. *Le Siège de Corinthe* was thus a piece of lively current concern. The bourgeoisie, the *monde élégant* flocked to the theater en masse, and despite the high ticket prices, the room was packed with spectators.[8]

The power of stories about the plight of the Greeks to stimulate the feelings and senses could also be seen in the realm of fine art. Théodore Géricault complained that dealers would look at his work only if it reflected the vogue: "The Greek revolution is going strong," his dealer told him, to his annoyance. "Canaris, Collocotronis, Botsaris the Turkophage [*sic*] are doing marvelously well." Romantics understood the power this gave artists: "As if everything were not political today," wrote Victor Hugo. "The brush and the chisel are party tools just as much as the pen." Philhellenism was in vogue but it was also a forcing ground for a new kind of mass politics that used the arenas of bourgeois urban life—the concert hall, the café, the salon, the gallery—to agitate spirits and press for change. It took politics off the page and out of the realm of reasoned argument and made it visible, audible, and visceral for the first time.[9]

For an earlier political masterpiece, *The Raft of the Medusa*, Géricault had conducted painstaking research, seeking out and interviewing survivors of the shipwreck in 1816 off the west coast of Africa that formed his subject. The young Eugène Delacroix had posed for him and admired his boldness in depicting a contemporary disaster involving ordinary men: the painter was, he said admiringly, "extreme in everything." Géricault had been working on Greek themes before he died at thirty-two, but his engagement paled in comparison with that of his friend Delacroix, who was gripped by the Greeks from the start and returned to them again and again over the coming decades. Inspired by the massacres on Chios, Delacroix read extensively—Thomas Hope's *Anastasius*, Savary's *Lettres sur la Grèce et l'Egypte*, several volumes on Turkish costumes—bought engravings, and rented outfits from the region. He even dined with Olivier Voutier, the man who had been present at the discovery of the Venus de Milo and had recently returned from fighting with the Greeks. Voutier's tales, the news of Byron's death in Mesolonghi, a first glimpse of the bold colors of John Constable's landscapes—everything seemed to leave its mark on Delacroix's work. The result was the very opposite of the "reasonable painting" (*peinture raisonnable*) he loathed. When *Scene of the Massacre at Chios* (1824) was displayed in the Paris Salon, Stendhal described it as "Shakespearean" and admired the way it engaged the viewer.[10]

Moved by Mesolonghi's drama, Delacroix intensified his passionate engagement with Greece in the spring of 1826 at Galerie Lebrun in Paris where he participated in a collective exhibition organized by the Comité Grec. By coincidence the opening took place a day or two after news of the sack of Mesolonghi reached Paris and liberal critics hastened to seize the opportunity to castigate the French government's passivity and to praise artists for leading the way:

> History will preserve the memory of the feelings that manifest themselves so vividly in all parts of the civilized world in favor of the poor Greeks; it will not fail to compare the attitude of the peoples with that of the governments, and to point out that whereas in the past the whole of Europe has often risen at the call of its kings and priests in order to march to the rescue of other Christians, this time the thrones and altars have remained silent . . . However the arts, which find their inspiration in the myths and history of Greece, which invoke the Greeks as models and as supports, have refused to stay behind, and the Lebrun gallery has received their brotherly homage.[11]

Delacroix already had some paintings hanging in the exhibition when news arrived of the fall of Mesolonghi, and it had an instant impact on him. Working with record speed on a new canvas, he finished it in time to be shown when the exhibition reopened at Galerie Lebrun that summer. *Greece on the Ruins of Missolonghi* (1826) eschews the panoramic battle scenes of his peers or the static tableau of his Chios picture. Other artists were painting crowded scenes of the town's defenders. Delacroix decided on another approach, distilling the horror and confusion of the sortie into a single stark image of a lone woman amid the debris of the battle. Only two other figures are shown: one, scarcely visible, is the lifeless arm of a dead male defender of the town, crushed under massive stones; the other, standing proudly with banner in hand in the background, is an unmistakably African warrior in Ottoman dress, the victorious representative of Ibrahim's all-conquering army that now dominated European soil. There is a bloodstained slab from a destroyed building in the foreground, and in the background the silhouette of ruined defenses, all shrouded against a dramatic, ominous, blue-black night sky.

It is the woman who compels attention through the light that falls upon her, revealing her dress open to the waist as she half kneels with her arms outstretched in despair. She is alone, unprotected, a survivor calling on the viewer to witness the suffering around her. Despite the virtuoso rendering of the dress, this is essentially allegory, with the pared-down abstraction of a morality tale. The defenseless female, Greece, is also the personification of Liberty, threatened by barbarism, and perhaps too a secularized Virgin Mary threatened with defilement. Among the most thoughtful of artists, Delacroix believed in allegory's power to move the viewer and to provide a reminder of the force of ideals. Four years later his famous painting of Liberty on the barricades would celebrate the overthrow of the monarchy of Charles X in revolution with another such female heroine: in Delacroix's work—and indeed for the liberals of France in life as well—the Greeks of Mesolonghi had led the way. Even those who disliked the genre admired *Greece on the Ruins of Missolonghi*. Victor Hugo conceded its force. Another critic admired the depiction of "a strong spirit which, although shaken by powerful blows, is never crushed." The public was overwhelmed and flocked to see it.[12]

That Greece should be depicted as a defenseless woman, in need of Europe's aid, was nothing new: dozens of eighteenth-century prints can be found with the same motif. What was new was the political context— for a defenseless woman was now a call to arms. But something else was new as well, for this call was answered to an unusual and remarkable degree by women themselves. The wives of the male leaders of the Comité Grec played as prominent a role in drumming up support for the Greek cause as they had in the concert; more important, women and even children, in dozens of small associations formed not only in France but in the United States and elsewhere, collected donations and publicized the cause, often in the face of official disapproval. The widely circulated liberal newspaper *Le Constitutionnel* hailed the prominent role played by aristocratic women on behalf of the Greeks and hoped their example would be emulated "in every department." Sure enough, salons collected funds, or sold pamphlets; follow-up concerts were held in half a dozen or more towns around the country. In Lyon, a Comité Grec des Dames spoke up for the "holy cause of religion and humanity, the cause of the Greeks": they soon raised 2,000 francs. In Chalon-sur-Saône in eastern France, women and children raised 10,000 francs; a similar group in Le Havre in Normandy nearly matched them. By May 1826, "Collections on behalf of the Greeks" had spread outside France into Switzerland, Sweden, and the German lands. The sums involved were considerable: the historian Simos Bozikis, who has studied the public finances of the revolution, has shown that the amount of money raised in private subscription for Greece soared in 1825–26, and that France was far and away the leader of this fundraising effort, the money reaching Greece just as the proceeds of the English loans were drying up.[13]

One might regard this merely as confirming women in their traditional roles as charitable appendages, the expressions of the national religious conscience. Yet that would be to downplay their political impact, because it was not easy for the regime of Charles X to ignore or dismiss them. The police were instructed to check the ladies' committees for evidence of conspiracy; in fact, there was none despite the wilder imaginings of some of their agents who saw the hand of the Carbonari behind everything. Ultra royalists and conservative satirists might mock, but nothing the authorities did could hinder the growing movement of sympathy and support for the Greek cause. Women spread out across towns and cities collecting funds; they sang arias and used their voices for what amounted to a new kind of political expression. The depth of their involvement struck male commentators in Restoration France as something new. In exile in Brussels, the former revolutionary Bertrand Barère remarked that the siege of Mesolonghi had created a political force in France that promised its own kind of revolutionary transformation: "In the midst of the cruel indifference of cabinets and the hypocritical neutrality of kings, women alone have inspired and supported the zeal of nations." Others felt similarly. A dinner was held by the American minister in Paris to celebrate the Fourth of July. It was the fiftieth anniversary of the American Declaration of Independence, the shock at Mesolonghi's fall was at its height, and the April concert was still on people's minds. The elderly Marquis de La Fayette, the symbol of revolutionary international liberalism, who had just returned from the United States, was the guest of honor. "To the lady collectors of the Greek Committee of Paris," was the toast proposed by a young New Yorker, Cornelius Bradford. "Their husbands must be proud to have such wives and if France is asked to show her finest jewels, she will show her daughters!"[14]

Across Europe it was commonplace to equate civilization and moral values with Christendom and to decry Islam as a barbaric faith. But only in France could such apparently uncontentious truisms offer a way to criticize the government. The reason for this was the country's pride in its long and close relationship with the Ottoman sultan. The Bourbon Restoration had exploited the rise of Mehmed Ali to build a new relationship with Egypt and even as the Greeks rose up, French engineers and architects were designing the infrastructure of the pasha's power, and a French soldier was training his army; a military school for Egyptian cadets was established in Paris and a French military mission, approved originally by Louis XVIII, arrived in Alexandria in November 1824. In July 1825 the king had given his permission to allow three vessels to be built for the pasha in the Marseille shipyards, under the supervision of General Pierre Gaston de Livron, head of the French naval mission.[15]

The invasion of Greece by an Egyptian army thus presented the Bourbon government with a huge predicament. The newly crowned Charles X wrapped himself in neo-medieval Christian imagery in an effort to emulate some of the glory of Napoleon's empire. Yet in 1825 and 1826 the fruit of his principal international initiative was an Arab army, staffed by French officers and transported on French-built ships, that was enslaving a Christian people—the Greeks.

Ottoman slavery went back centuries and mostly depended upon the import of trafficked foreigners or war captives from round the Black Sea or from sub-Saharan Africa. The enslavement of domestic subjects as punishment for revolt was not unknown before 1821, but it exploded in magnitude afterward. Compared with the annual average of between 16,000 and 18,000 people imported from Africa, for instance, the 45,000

Greeks enslaved following the massacres on Chios in 1822 represented a shocking increase for a single year, an increase that explains why the price of slaves plummeted; indeed Ottoman markets remained saturated with Greek slaves into the 1830s. Foreign efforts to ransom them were spear-headed by imperial Russia, whose officials felt a special obligation toward their fellow Orthodox Christians; in January 1825 a special commission was set up in the Russian embassy in Constantinople for this purpose and worked hard on individual cases. Nevertheless, even before Mesolonghi's siege ended, they had managed to identify and liberate only a small frac-tion of the total number of enslaved Greeks.[16]

Slavery was the issue that now fused with the drama of Mesolonghi to generate feelings strong enough to transform European politics. Over the previous decades, if there was one cause that had proved capable of mobilizing public opinion on the continent in a way that impacted diplo-macy, it was abolition. To the surprise of almost all statesmen, a highly vocal abolitionist movement had forced the Congress of Vienna to dis-cuss the issue in 1814—making it one of the very first matters ever to be tackled internationally as a result of public pressure. The Congress had concluded with a remarkable if vague declaration calling for the ending of the slave trade as a result of outcry in "all civilized nations," but in the 1820s the outcome was still very much in doubt and considerable work remained to be done.

In the context of Europe's relationship with the Ottoman Empire, abolitionism was a relatively new factor. When European ambassadors in Constantinople protested after the massacres on Chios, the Ottoman response was that enslavement of the Greeks was lawful under Islamic law as a response to rebellion. Preaching religion, the Europeans were simply guilty of hypocrisy where the slave trade was concerned. "The Christian powers of Europe had for ages tolerated it, not because their Messiah commanded it, but because it was a source of gain," a senior Ottoman official reminded Lord Strangford, the British ambassador. "It was true, England had abolished it," Strangford wrote home, summariz-ing their conversation, "but . . . it was only of late years that we had found out that it was wrong—and . . . half of Europe still differed from our opinion on the subject." The Europeans had accepted the Ottoman practice for centuries without protest, the Ottoman official had contin-ued, and the empire's position was straightforward: enslavement was a punishment that the Quran permitted for disloyalty. Moreover, it was a generally agreed principle of international relations to allow each state to act internally according to its own laws and usages. "Why do not the Christian sovereigns interfere to prevent the emperor of Russia sending his subjects into Siberia? Because they know very well what answer they would receive! Thus there is one law of humanity for Turkey and another for Russia!"[17]

It was not only the Ottomans who found something decidedly hypocritical in the fervor that the plight of enslaved Greeks seemed to arouse abroad. Black Americans, too, could not but be struck by the disparity between the ardent sympathy for the Greeks and the general indifference of their fellow countrymen toward their own plight. In *Freedom's Journal*, the first newspaper run by African Americans in the United States, the New York–based editors wondered how one of America's most renowned and effusive philhellenes, the Massachusetts congressman Daniel Webster, could have seriously stated that "the wretched Greeks" suffered a worse oppression than anyone else "in the whole world." "So far as the laws have effect," the newspaper went on, "the black is as absolutely subjected to the caprice of his master, whether actuated by passion or by lust, as the Greek." Was not slavery a crime against the laws of nature, whatever the skin color of the slave or their faith or level of learning? How could supposedly civilized Americans identify themselves with the fight against despotism, tyranny, and the Holy Alliance, and at the same time "believe that God regards slavery here with so favorable an eye?"[18]

The interconnection between unfreedom in the Americas and in the Ottoman lands was especially discussed in France, where the question of Haiti had focused the minds of abolitionists since the revolution of Toussaint Louverture in 1791 and the eventual establishment of the first state in the world to abolish slavery. At the start of 1822, Haiti's president Jean-Pierre Boyer had sent the Greeks a warm letter of support for their cause, hailing an uprising that "cannot leave Haitians indifferent, for we, like the Hellenes, were for a long time subjected to a dishonorable slavery."[19] In 1825, Haitian independence, won through a slave revolt, was finally recognized by France at the price of an enormous indemnity that the French government demanded to compensate out-of-pocket slave owners. The following year, the trade was finally abolished in the French colonies.

As much on people's minds in France as ever, therefore, the topic of slavery was literary dynamite as Mesolonghi's struggle reached its tragic denouement in the spring of 1826. Courtier and philhellene Claire de Duras caused a sensation when she published her remarkable novella *Ourika*, based on a true story about a young Senegalese girl rescued from a slaver and brought to France. For Duras abolitionism and support for the Greeks seemed to be closely associated and she was certainly not the only one to hold this view. How could the French public contemplate the emergence of a new trade in slaves—whose victims would be a Christian people, Europeans, and Greeks no less—even as the old one was being shut down? Royalists were reproached for their passivity. How could France, an ancient crusading nation, stand by and do nothing? In his poem about Mesolonghi written in 1826, *Les têtes du sérail*, Victor Hugo called on "Christian Europe" to save the Greeks, whose warriors had died trying to protect their families, and asked where the new Saint Louis was to come from to provide assistance.[20]

There was an inescapable racial dimension to the outcry as well. It was not only that the Greeks were Christians, nor that they represented a link to the classical past that Europe so prized. It was also that their captors were Muslims and Africans. Delacroix was perhaps the greatest and most deliberate colorist of his time, and his painting of *Greece on the Ruins of Missolonghi* was a virtuoso rendition of dark and light whose overriding feature was the contrast between the almost blinding white of the woman's bare torso and tunic and the night sky in the background where the silhouette of the heavily armed African standard-bearer offsets the darkness of his skin with the slashed orange of his turban. Delacroix had not been the only one to recognize in the fall of Mesolonghi and the enslavement of its survivors by Ibrahim's army the startling triumph of Africa in Europe.

Abolitionism was in this way reinforced by racism, for the idea that not merely Muslim but African soldiers were enslaving white Christian women seemed especially shocking. "We let Greece perish at our door," wrote Chateaubriand in a classic articulation of racist philhellenism, "Abandoning our [sovereignty] in Saint-Domingue for negro liberalism under [President] Boyer. Who knows if we will see one day, under the standard of the crescent and the liberty cap, African legions bringing to us from one side the Koran and from the other the Rights of Man?" Republicanism in Haiti, Islam and Africa victorious in Europe: it was a monarchist's nightmare. Conservatives mocked: "Yesterday it was the issue of the blacks; today the Greeks are the talk of the town; the negrophiles have been transformed into philhellenes."[21] It especially disturbed the French that their own countrymen were complicit. "French officers, run to instruct Negro Muslims in how to massacre Christian whites!" writes Fabre sarcastically in 1827. "Let our shipyards be open to the noble satrap of Egypt, our sailors preserve the conquerors of Psara from the misfortunes of the conqueror of Chios."[22]

Adding to the discomfort was the fact the French and other European officers serving with the Egyptian army were deeply implicated in the slave trade, accumulating their own captives while they were in the field and often justifying this on humanitarian grounds that the women they purchased were better off for their protection. One or two of them felt uneasy and also helped to identify the fates of specific slaves, even redeeming a few. Giovanni Romei, a Piedmontese lieutenant-colonel of engineers in the Egyptian army, was a radical and a Freemason who had secretly been passing on intelligence to Greek contacts since arriving with the Egyptians in the Peloponnese. On the battlefield at Mesolonghi on the night of the sortie, he saved a baby from being killed: afterward, he found a goat to give her milk. He then redeemed two women as well, and had them set free in the Ottoman port of Preveza where he left the baby with one of them and put them in the care of a sea captain returning to the Habsburg lands. He was sorry to see the baby go, he wrote to a contact in Zante: "She can't have been six months old. This unfortunate little orphan girl was always cheerful and smiling, and has given me such true and sweet pleasures that I hardly know how to express it in words."[23]

A fellow Piedmontese who had also been on the battlefield that night had spent a large sum to redeem a "very beautiful" young girl, around thirteen years old, and her mother. On the boat that took them back from Patras to the Egyptian camp at Methoni, the twelve-year-old son of the Genoese captain fell in love with the girl, called Maria. The boy's father and the girl's mother were said to have no objections to their union, so when they got to the camp a contract was drawn up. Signed in the presence of witnesses, all Europeans, including the Austrian vice-consul, this outlined the terms on which the marriage would take place—both parties willing—when the boy reached marriageable age, as well as a dowry the captain would provide his daughter-in-law. Should the marriage not go ahead, the captain promised to keep Maria in his home as if she were his daughter; as for the mother—whom the sapper also "ceded [equally] freely to the captain"—she would receive "all the regard owing to the mother of his future daughter-in-law." Interestingly, the contract itemizes her effects—"clothing, linen, rings, any jewels, silver belts and anything else she has at the time on her person"—an insight into the importance of portable forms of wealth during a crisis.[24]

There is no way of knowing whether Maria and her mother ever made it to the fishing village outside Genoa, which was the captain's home. But they seem to have been relatively fortunate. At the request of the Greeks, Romei tracked down other slaves, probably on behalf of relatives, and mostly the news he provided was grim:

> Signora Anastassena Didachena of Pyrgos died of an illness; the unfortunate Demetrio Salussi, also of Pyrgos, died of plague [*peste*], Mario Panaghioti of Pyrgos together with his second son Demetrio are here, the slaves of a certain Captain Hussein who has said he will free them when the Morea business is over. His first son Caralambo has been sent to Cairo by Ibrahim Pasha together with another 48 young Greek men and 36 girls; as for the entire family of Michele Iconomopulo, I cannot find out anything . . . All the Greek slaves who are to be found in Koron have died of the plague which has desolated this country.

Romei goes on to list others who have died in the epidemic. He was in the process of redeeming a young Souliot girl, the wife of a kapetan who had been enslaved in Mesolonghi, when the plague snatched her away. Another girl, aged sixteen, he bought for 1,750 piastres together with her fifty-five-year-old mother: they were not survivors of the siege but had been caught only weeks earlier by Egyptian soldiers. Was his work humanitarianism or commerce? It is difficult to tell, but what is clear is that Romei evidently disliked the whole business: "the Europeans here, myself included, are the dregs, the absolute dregs."[25]

In October 1826, about the time that the exhibition at the Galerie Lebrun closed its doors, a young French interpreter called Deval, attached to the embassy in Constantinople, was on his way home to France by sea when he decided to visit the Egyptian encampment in the Morea, as much out of curiosity as anything else. Entering Methoni, he was flabbergasted to run into someone he had known at college, now a trader making a good living as an importer of foodstuffs. Prices were high and Ibrahim's army was starving—one can therefore imagine the hunger in the rest of the Morea—and the soldiers were in threadbare uniforms: some were clad in scraps of carpet; others in women's garments they had stolen. It was a grim sight. Deval estimated that of the 24,000 Egyptian soldiers who had been sent to Greece, only 7,000–8,000 had survived. Already there were grumblings of discontent and Arab soldiers were deserting.

But their plight paled when set against that of their Greek captives. In the hills outside the town, Deval passed groups of them, chained and whipped while they gathered firewood for their captors. Because he knew Greek, Deval asked one of them where she was from and learned they had been captured at Mesolonghi. In the town of Methoni itself he visited the slave market at which women, mostly in veils, and young children were being sold. "Captain," a merchant addressed him. "Do you like this young Souliot? A bargain. You'll be happy." By the seashore, Deval almost stumbled on a cluster of human heads—some Greek prisoners had recently been executed, while others were being led off in chains from their quarters, a fetid chamber at the bottom of the fortress washed by the sea.

The following day, the young Frenchman visited the main encampment outside the town. Watching Ibrahim and his officers conducting their regular military drills with the men, he was astonished to find himself "amidst a crowd of compatriots." At least thirty-nine European officers were serving in the Egyptian armies at this time—mostly Frenchmen, Spaniards, Neapolitans, and Piedmontese. The French, veterans of the Napoleonic army, greeted him warmly and toasted together their eventual return to their beloved homeland. A few days later, Deval was able to meet his compatriot, Soliman Bey himself (Joseph Sève), at the house he had requisitioned in Methoni. It was eleven in the morning, and the bey received him in bed, pleading exhaustion. Deval said he was en route to France and offered to assist the bey by sending anything to his family. The bey thanked him courteously and said he planned to write to his friends and in particular to his father in Lyon, adding, after a moment's silence: "I have only ever loved three men, the only three men to do well by me—my father, Napoleon and Mehmed Ali." After this, they smoked and drank coffee together and then moved on to wine, accompanied by several Egyptian officers. With tears in his eyes, Soliman Bey proposed a toast to France and they raised their glasses.

Emboldened by his warm reception as a fellow Frenchman, Deval then made a daring request: he asked whether he might meet Soliman

Bey's harem. After Soliman agreed, the other officers departed and three women entered—Panayiota, eighteen-year-old Chrysoula, and her unnamed sister: all of them were Greek captives who had been with the bey a few months. They had begun to learn Arabic but Deval pleasantly surprised them by speaking with them in Greek and having begun a "very enjoyable conversation," he was delighted when an invitation to dinner allowed them to continue it. It was then that Chrysoula told him their story. They were orphans, who had been living with their aunt—she pointed out an elderly woman seated across the table—outside Tripolitsa when they were captured one day by Arab troops pillaging the area and brought before Soliman who kept them for himself. Their aunt had vanished, sold on for menial labor at a low price, until they saw her one day in Methoni and persuaded Soliman to pay her ransom. "Are you happy with the bey?" Deval asked Chrysoula. "His character is full of sweetness," she replied. "He is steady in his moods and our happiness would be complete were it not that the sight of our unfortunate compatriots, in chains, poisons our pleasure." It turned out that the bey had already given the four women their liberty so that they could stay when he left and they showed Deval their manumission papers. The bey told Deval there were others too: eight Greeks who had fought against him were lodged in his house; he had saved them from being killed. When the evening was interrupted by a child's cries, they were introduced to a baby, seven or eight months old, whom the bey had found under a tree and brought away with him, christening him "Koloko-tronis"—which indicated in what regard the Old Man was held in the Egyptian camp; there was also a little girl, about two, called "Bobolina." It would seem that Soliman Bey's harem probably did remain in Greece as he had promised, because we know that on the voyage back to Alexandria he took with him another Greek woman, Maryam—not a slave, he had met her in Methoni—whom he later married.[26]

There were many differences between the slave experience in the Americas and that in the eastern Mediterranean. However, it is clear that what slavery in the Morea had in common with its transatlantic counterpart was the horrific sundering of families, often forever, and the abuse and exploitation especially of women and young children. Many of the captives from Mesolonghi ended up either in the Albanian lands or in Egypt, but a significant proportion were destined for Ottoman towns in the Balkans or Asia Minor. Alongside those unfortunates from

Mesolonghi, there were thousands more delivered to the Cairo slave market who had been captured by Ibrahim's men in the Morea, also from Crete and the other islands.

The business of redeeming these captives got under way very quickly after the sack of Mesolonghi. As before, the Russians were heavily involved, but for the first time we find the Greek authorities being drawn in. In May 1826 friends of the former garrison commander on the island of Vasiladi sought the government's help to redeem his wife and three young children, two of them infants. The price being asked was 5,000 *grossia*, but he could raise only half that amount and they risked being sent for sale to Egypt. Two men found their wives were in Methoni and approached a local Greek broker there, but they had no money of their own. A year after the Mesolonghi sortie, another man found his wife—he did not know what had happened to his children— in the possession of a Muslim on the mainland opposite Corfu; a former fighter located his family—six women and children—in the Albanian town of Tepenli. One woman and her two daughters had been captured on the night of the sortie: the mother had been bought back in Jannina by Greeks; one of her girls had been sent to Egypt and was redeemed by Christians; the other was still in Methoni, the property of an Egyptian bey, nearly two years later. The virtually bankrupt Greek government received many such petitions, which it mostly passed on to a relief committee in the Ionian Islands that was handling money donated by Swiss philhellenes. When, after independence, the Greeks established their first consulate abroad in Egypt, the tracking down and ransoming of slaves was one of its key concerns.

Occasionally the Greek authorities were asked to arrange exchanges: Alexaina Tzibourakaina requested she be given an Albanian *dervenaga* (keeper of the passes), Ahmed Previstas, so she could hand him over in exchange for her daughter, who was being held by an Albanian bey. Alexaina had spent two years looking for her and had found that her owner was willing to make the swap. Then there was the eighteen-month-old son of the Souliot chieftain Kitsos Tzavellas and his wife Vasiliki: they had lost the infant during the Mesolonghi sortie when his nurse had become separated from them, and the nurse had told the soldiers whose baby it was. A few months later, it was in the possession of an Albanian bey in Preveza, and the negotiations began that eventually reunited the child with its parents. Dealings such as these went on for several years while a trickle of escapees made their way back at great risk across the mountains of the Balkans or by sea to what remained of their homeland. As late as October 1830, Manthi, the wife of Thodori Stravokonstanti, was writing to the Greek government. Her husband had died during the sortie four and a half years earlier. Her two daughters, whom they had sent away earlier by boat to Kalamos, had been captured en route, enslaved, and sent to Alexandria. Their son had also been captured and made to work in the Egyptian fleet and had been killed in the battle of Navarino. Manthi herself had been taken prisoner and sent to Egypt. She had been freed but her two daughters remained slaves there, and when she returned to Mesolonghi she found their home a ruin.[27]

The public outrage abroad at the enslavement of the Greek survivors of Mesolonghi was a decisive factor in the fundamental transformation of European diplomacy that now took place as some leading statesmen began to reconsider the question of intervention. This was something new. At first, sympathy for the Greek cause had been principally a liberal, even radical cause, a minority concern that had died away after 1822. What was different about the engagement that was triggered by the Egyptian invasions was its respectability—or to put it differently, its social breadth. It was not only unemployed army officers and radical philosophers who agitated for urgent assistance to be given to the Greeks but men such as the duc d'Orléans and his circle.

The novel impact of public outrage at Europe's inaction was registered even by Bourbon diplomats, and nowhere perhaps were its diplomatic implications better analyzed than in a prophetic dispatch from London written by the Neapolitan minister there, Guglielmo Costantino Ludolf. His family was a worldly one with a deep and intimate knowledge, acquired over many years, of the Ottoman scene. His master, however, was King Francesco I, the Bourbon ruler of the Two Sicilies, a monarch whose father's throne had been rescued from revolution by Austrian troops. The king was no sympathizer of the Greeks nor of the idea of a popular uprising, and the general impulse of the Neapolitan Crown was to view the revolution with hostility—since its triumph, as another diplomat had written earlier, would probably mean the monarchy's "funeral." Ludolf, who possessed the rare gift of seeing things clearly, had the difficult task of persuading his master, one of the most obtuse European sovereigns, of the way things were moving.[28]

Circumstances had changed since the uprising began, Ludolf noted in his dispatch, and they were bound to change further. When the Greeks had risen up in rebellion in 1821, they and everyone else had assumed they would be supported by the Russians, but that if they were left alone without any help they would be crushed. No one had anticipated that their own powers of resistance would suffice to hold out for years against the might of the Ottoman Empire—nor that they would have established control over most of the Peloponnese and the Aegean for so long, continuing to battle Ottoman authority in central Greece, Evvia, and Crete. This is why the Great Powers had "anathematized, so to say, the war they had declared." Yet their aloofness had been based on a false assumption and the longer the fighting went on, the more public opinion saw in the Greeks not "an act of rebellion" but "an entire people fighting for that which is dearest—their own salvation and their own faith." Even while European governments held fast to the principle of nonintervention, people were starting to demand that "their protection be brought to the aid of their unfortunate brothers in the Orient," which was what they were now calling the Greeks. They were being seen, increasingly, not as insurgents but as fellow Christians, engaged not in revolution but in a war to defend their religious freedom.

European public opinion was itself becoming a factor the diplomats had to take into account, Ludolf advised King Francesco. The desire of the Great Powers to see the Greek revolt brought to a quick end had been a tacit acceptance of the fact that a lengthy resistance would give it legitimacy, and that legitimacy could be conferred by "acts of courage worthy of so just a cause." In the face of Greek stubbornness and valor, the cabinets of Europe were being forced by popular pressure to accept that they could not acquiesce in what appeared to be "the inevitable destruction of an entire nation." Every Greek victory was cheered and every Ottoman massacre was seen as further evidence of the unsustainability of European policy. It was useless any longer to try to reduce things to a question of principle, as if the same approach could be taken to all revolutions in all cases—in Greece as in Spain or America.

The trouble, Ludolf continued, was that all Europe's efforts to get the Greeks and the Turks to lay down their arms—so that the former could return to their homes, and the latter could bestow upon them some version of the regime of autonomy enjoyed in the Danubian Principalities—had failed: the Greeks persisted in fighting to the bitter end, and the sultan refused to consider anything until they submitted. There were no good options anymore: left to their own devices, the Turks would treat all Greeks as they had treated Chios and Psara—to be massacred and enslaved—an argument that gained force as Ibrahim's armies stormed through the Peloponnese. On the other hand, were Greece to become independent, the likeliest outcome would be "civil wars without end." Yet the time was approaching when Europe would have to choose, because the only way of banishing radicalism and returning peace to Europe was for the Great Powers to take control of the situation and act with unanimity. The conclusion—unpalatable for the Neapolitan king to be sure—was clear if unspoken: one outcome led to massacre and mass enslavement and was morally intolerable; the other—independence for the Greeks—presented no more than an inconvenience. Supporting the Greek demands might now be necessary for the tranquility of the continent.[29]

Very similar thoughts were passing through the mind of the British foreign secretary, George Canning. A pragmatist like Ludolf, with an equal dislike of taking universal principles as a guide to policy and a willingness to treat the Greek case on its own terms, he was hesitantly moving in the same direction. Reports of the manner and extent of the Egyptian victories in the Peloponnese had weighed on him. At the start of 1826, even as Ibrahim was establishing his camp outside Mesolonghi, Canning confided in his younger cousin, the newly appointed ambassador to Constantinople, Stratford Canning. He was, the foreign secretary wrote, coming to see that there might be a new reason for the Great Powers to intervene in Greece:

> I mean the manner in which the war is now carried on in the Morea—the character of barbarism and *barbarization* which it has assumed. Butchering of captives we have long witnessed on both sides of the contest . . . But the selling into slavery—the forced conversions—the dispeopling of Christendom—the recruiting from the countries of Islamism—the erection in short of a new Puissance Barbaresque in Europe—these are (not topics merely) but facts new in themselves, new in their principle, new and strange and hitherto inconceivable in their consequences . . .[30]

In this halting way one can detect the brilliant mind of perhaps the most consequential diplomat involved in the entire story contemplating the possibility that Europe was facing a new historical situation—one in which it was moving, not forward toward greater civilization, but backward, under the impact of a resurgent Islam, toward barbarism. Reports from Russia were currently circulating, which eventually found their way into the diplomatic exchanges, that the Egyptians were not merely enslaving thousands of Greeks but actually planning to deport the entire population of the Morea and to resettle it with Arabs. There was almost certainly no truth to these stories, but they were taken seriously enough for Canning to instruct his cousin to demand confirmation from Ibrahim and from the Ottoman authorities that no such plan was contemplated. Four years later, members of the British House of Lords still appeared to believe it was true. Thus even sober and prudent diplomats were susceptible to the kinds of arguments that had erupted into public discourse in England and France over the year that Mesolonghi had been under siege: that the town's fate was a challenge for Europe, that civilization's defense depended on the fate of Greek women, and that therefore Greek weakness rather than Greek strength might turn out to be the issue that would make the Great Powers intervene. This was now a race against time: could the Greeks hold out against the resurgent Ottoman forces long enough to see Europe's policy change and outside help arrive? Or would Kütahı Pasha and Ibrahim between them stamp out the revolution completely before the European powers had time to act?

THE SIEGE OF ATHENS

*While we carry on with our intrigues as if we were in total peace,
and while, rather than marching on our enemy in the Peloponnese with iron and fire, we take aim instead at the breast and
hearth of our very brothers, [meanwhile] in Athens—through
the destitution of the besieged, the lack of firewood, the threat of
plague and the asphyxiating siege—they risk suffering the inevitable, unless we can take action from outside. The government is
doing what it can, but who pays heed to the matter of common
survival?*

Konstantinos Zografos, Aigina, December 26,
1826, in D. Kambouroglou, ed., *Istorikon archeion
Dionysiou Roma*, 2 vols. (Athens, 1901–6), ii, 600

"Greece exists only in name," wrote Colonel Fabvier in February 1826.
"As the campaigning season begins, there are no more provisions, no
soldiers nor money." The sack of Mesolonghi in April confirmed the
sultan's resurgence. "It seems likely that the Morea will not be slow to
be brought under the dominion of the Turks again," wrote an observer
on Zakynthos, "and the cause of the Greeks [brought] to an immediate
and rapid end."[1]

Having taken over all of western Greece, Kütahı Pasha planned to
continue the war without interruption until the final victory, hoping to
end the rebellion in Rumeli and then join his forces to those of Ibrahim in
the Peloponnese. He had been in the field for a year already, but he lost
no time. A few days after his victory at Mesolonghi he had the local Albanian beys write to the armatoles and kapetans of central Greece to tell
them to submit within five days or risk having their villages ransacked.

Karaïskakis refused and made his way to the Peloponnese to consult the government in Nafplion; Makris too remained unpersuaded.[2] But most of the other armatoles bowed to the overwhelming power of the sultan in return for their old positions with advance pay. "In the space of one month after the fall of Mesolonghi," recalled Karaïskakis's secretary, "all the municipalities of continental Greece submitted to Kütahı Pasha without a fight, while he, wishing to calm the agitated spirits of the Greeks, conducted himself with exemplary mildness."[3] As Ibrahim's troops moved back across the Gulf of Corinth to reinforce their positions in the Peloponnese, Kütahı Pasha left a small garrison in Mesolonghi and a much larger one in Salona, then marched eastward toward Athens, which thus became for eastern Greece what Mesolonghi had been in the west: to the Greeks, a stronghold to be defended at all costs; to the sultan, a last impediment to Ottoman victory.

The city that lay at the center of the classical Greek world had shrunk over the years to become a provincial market town of no great economic or strategic significance. The ancient Themistoklean circuit wall had fallen into disrepair and there had been no effective defense perimeter at all for many centuries before a makeshift wall was constructed in 1778 by the people of the town at the orders of the Ottoman *voyvode*, probably to guard against Albanian raids. It took them several months to complete the four-kilometer ring. By 1821, its course enclosed more than thirty neighborhoods along with their gardens and orchards on the north side of the Acropolis. But the poorly built structure was incapable of withstanding a siege of any length and its main purpose was probably to facilitate the policing (and taxing) of goods in and out of its gates.[4]

Quiet, prosperous, and slightly off the beaten track, Ottoman Athens possessed nothing like the strategic or administrative significance of Tripolitsa, Nafplion, or Patras. There were a few mosques, as well as an open-air mihrab in the ruins of the Temple of Olympian Zeus where, we are told, the inhabitants would gather together to pray for rain; the hamams included one on the slopes of the Acropolis where Muslim and Christian women took a bath together at prescribed times. There were two Greek schools and a learned tradition among the local Christian notable families, who successfully retained most of their privileges right up until 1821. A tower in the market housed a mechanical clock given by Lord Elgin, a unique amenity at that time in the Ottoman Empire but a paltry exchange for his vandalism of the Parthenon marbles. A large majority of the town's population—unlikely to have totaled much more than 10,000—was Christian; perhaps another 12,000, the majority of them Christians but Albanian-speaking, were villagers working the olive groves and vineyards in the plain. Muslim inhabitants both of the town and in the Attica region generally were a minority.[5]

While the town as a whole lay relatively defenseless before any serious military assault, its citadel, the Acropolis, was virtually impregnable. It could be bombarded from the hilly ground to the southwest but it was hard to do much damage to its extensive fortifications or to ease the approach up its precipitous flanks. With access protected by a complex sequence of medieval walls and towers—demolished shortly after independence and no longer visible today—hundreds of people could survive for months on the summit once they had passed through the five gates needed to reach it. There amid the ruins was what amounted to a small village with modest houses, barracks for the soldiers, munitions dumps and storehouses, a mill, a mosque (inside the Parthenon), gun emplacements, and a well.

Since the autumn of 1822, Athens had been mostly in the hands of the Rumeliot armatole Odysseus Androutsos, who was nominally the commander in chief of the government forces in eastern Greece but was in reality his own man. In charge of the garrison on the Acropolis, Androutsos had put his longtime lieutenant, Ioannis Gouras, who had fought bravely with him since the battle of Gravia in the first weeks of the uprising. In his new post, Gouras soon accumulated sufficient wealth to consolidate his own position. It was a mark of his status—a classic ascent of the wartime man of arms—that in the spring of 1823 this former shepherd boy from the mountains was able to marry the daughter of a rich notable from the town of Lidoriki. Androutsos was best man and Gouras installed his bride, her sister, and their maid in the former Ottoman commander's haremlik in the basement of the Erechtheion before he proceeded to shake down the town. He and his cousin Ioannis Mamouris seized an Athenian fighter named Nikolaos Sarris and brought him onto the Acropolis, where they tortured him for his money, cut him to pieces, and then threw his body parts down to the horrified townspeople below. Ioannis Makriyannis, never afraid to speak his mind, later told the brutal Gouras to his face: "You are robbing everybody. You and your creature Mamouris tear people's teeth out and chop them to pieces for their money. You murdered Sarris: the fifty thousand grossia that he had on him in cash and jewelery was taken by Mamouris and you shared it between you."[6]

Like Androutsos, Gouras did very little to prepare the district under his control for any eventual fighting. The pier and harbor at Piraeus remained in a miserable condition, choked with sand and mud, and the great olive groves that stretched down to the sea were neglected. The twenty-one-year-old Irish philhellene James Emerson visited Athens in the summer of 1825, describing the town's fortifications as "a low, untenable wall, pierced with loop-holes for musquetry; but in such a state as to be utterly incapable of defense."[7] Unlike Androutsos, however, Gouras was a reliable government man. In 1824–25 English gold bought his agreement to move his men into the Peloponnese to crush the Moreot chieftains in the civil war and his bands quickly became notorious for their brutal treatment of their opponents. They plundered not only defenseless villagers but some of the region's wealthiest men, seizing their property, crops, and livestock. His men ravaged the western Peloponnese, plundering monasteries and torturing monks for their valuables. They even captured the renowned Archbishop Germanos, who had played a prominent role at the very start of the uprising— taking his money, possessions, clothes, and animals, and forcing him to trudge on foot through the snowy mountain paths. Gouras's reward was to be named overall commander of the forces in eastern Greece in place of his former leader who was increasingly mistrusted.[8]

The Ottoman commanders for their part regarded Odysseus Androutsos as "a master of deceit and devilry," but when he approached them once more, they did not reject outright his proposal to run the region on their behalf. Because of his earlier exploits, and his posthumous iconic status, some Greek historians have had difficulty accepting the reality of these negotiations. But the Ottoman archives leave no room for doubt. At the start of 1825, even as Egyptian troops marched into the Peloponnese to the south, Androutsos, who was feeling shunned by the Greek government, reached out to the pasha of Karystos to propose an agreement. In return for an amnesty, the Ottoman authorities would provide him with troops, headquarter him in Thebes, and allow him to march on Athens and other areas that had not yet surrendered. With some misgivings, Kütahı Pasha himself approved the policy. The districts of Livadeia,

Thebes, and Atalanti—inhabited chiefly by Christian Albanians—sent in petitions for amnesty by early April, and villagers around the Isthmus of Corinth requested Androutsos to arrange this on their behalf as well. When fighting broke out between Greek forces and Ottoman cavalry, Androutsos was with the latter. He was captured by Gouras's men and brought back to Athens to face charges of collaborating.[9] Hardened in a tough school, Gouras was not a man to worry about due process. He had his former chief imprisoned in the Frankish tower by the entrance to the Acropolis, and one morning at the start of June, Androutsos's body was discovered lying at the foot of the tower. He was said to have died while falling trying to escape; the postmortem suggested he had been tortured.

Gouras was in the ascendant and in the spring of 1826 he was confirmed as the overall commander of the Greek forces in eastern Greece. Convened at Epidavros as news arrived of the fall of Mesolonghi, a national assembly had chosen as a successor to the presidency of George Koundouriotis an interim government (the so-called directing committee) under the presidency of the Moreot landowner and grandee Andreas Zaimis. The assembly took only two other decisions of consequence. One was to appoint the three military chiefs to their regional commands: Gouras in eastern Rumeli, Kolokotronis in the Morea, and Karaïskakis in western Rumeli. The other, a stark and remarkable indication of the delegates' despair over the worsening military outlook, was to request the British minister in Constantinople, Stratford Canning, to negotiate a truce and peace on their behalf with the Ottoman government. One year earlier Greek deputies would have scorned the idea of settling for something short of full independence. Yet so grim did their prospects now appear that there was virtually no opposition to this idea—even such staunch opponents of foreign support as Kolokotronis accepted the need for help. Disappointed with the Russians, they were opting for British mediation.

News of the fall of Mesolonghi in April made Gouras leave Epidavros and hasten back to Athens. The population—as Captain Hamilton of the *Cambrian* told the Rumeliots at that time—was tired of war, even if the men of arms were not, and villages around the town were contacting Ottoman officials and promising to hand over their weapons. Gouras's instructions were to resist this and to organize the defense of Attica and Boeotia. Regarding these orders as unworkable, he abandoned the region and concentrated on provisioning the citadel for the siege that was coming. In early June an advance force of Ottoman troops arrived from Evvia ahead of the main army and entered the plain, the light cavalry scouting out Piraeus and the walls of Athens. Their rapidity ensured that they, not the Greeks, would control the harvest that year—a critical advantage.

While the national assembly met at Epidavros, the survivors of the Mesolonghi garrison were making their way through the mountains. When, after hours of hard walking, they reached the encampment where Karaïskakis was awaiting them, his men took a roll call. Told how many had survived the siege, he was surprised and exclaimed: "Given that the chieftains all made it out, and 1,500 besides . . . who are the bastards killing?" Not all the soldiers had survived, to be sure, and some had stayed behind and died with their families, but Karaïskakis had a point. A list of sixty-two officers from the town shows that eight died during the siege and only six were killed in the sortie—less than 10 percent of the total officer force. Yet they had suffered nonetheless and they bore the physical imprint of their terrible experiences over the preceding months. "They stood out for their wild expressions and sallow sunken faces," recalled Kasomoulis in his memoir, "for their bloodstained garments, the bullet marks on their clothes, their bloodshot, narrowed, sleep-deprived eyes, their uncombed hair." When on May 16 the survivors of the garrison entered Nafplion, to be showered with gifts and praise by the inhabitants, they were bitter and angry men; they were, wrote the Ionian notable Andreas Metaxas, like "wild beasts," determined to get what they said they were owed or to exact retribution, and the townspeople soon changed their view of them.[10]

A walled town surrounded on three sides by the sea, Nafplion had been the plague-ridden and overcrowded capital of the government since 1823. Unusually, it was dominated by not one but two fortresses: the Its Kalé citadel inside the walls, which loomed over the town, and the Palamidi on the rocky heights above that looked down on both. A massive Venetian fortress, the Palamidi was the key to controlling Nafplion, and although a Souliot chieftain appointed by the previous government was in command, the surviving soldiers of the Mesolonghi garrison took it over. Their desire to dominate the town reflected their fear that with the government now back in the hands of the Peloponnesian notables and with their "homeland" (*patrida*) Rumeli surrendering to Kütahı Pasha, they might easily become the victims of a deal to end the war that would bring freedom for the Peloponnese but leave them homeless for good. This was not an impossible reading of the assembly's decision to approach the British for mediation, but it was also a sign of the suspicions held by Mesolonghi's soldiers: they had been abandoned once and were determined not to let that happen again. The Rumeliots did not only suspect the Peloponnesians and the foreigners; they suspected their Albanian-speaking companions in arms too. Once in the Palamidi, the survivors vowed they would only let themselves be led by a fellow Rumeliot; but they could not agree who that would be because there was little to distinguish one chieftain's status from another. Despite some wrangling, the problem was solved shortly after their arrival in Nafplion when they invited the Rumeliot chieftain Theodorakis Grivas to join them from nearby Spetses.[11]

In the summer of 2020 a well-known actor proposed that all Greek men should celebrate 200 years of independence by growing a mustache: it was certainly due a revival, having fallen out of fashion in the intervening decades, and the mustache far more than the beard or any other facial feature had marked out the fighters from the rest. But none of them, not even Androutsos, could rival Grivas in this department, the splendidly upturned tips to his carefully tended mustache attesting to his warrior credentials. In 1826 Grivas was not yet thirty, ambitious, and battle-hardened. The member of a vast clan, he was the son of a renowned chieftain who had been poisoned by Ali Pasha, and he was linked by marriage or blood to many of the leading armatoles of western Rumeli. He was also newly wed, having just married the wealthy young widow of Kolokotronis's eldest son: George Koundouriotis himself, then president of the government, had been the best man (*koumbaros*) and provided his patronage and protection. Grivas could thus offer the soldiers in the Palamidi the benefits of an alliance with the wealthy Hydriot shipowners; in turn, he could offer the Hydriots the use of some of Greece's toughest soldiers in the event of an attack on their island.

His stature, ties, and family name allowed Grivas to assume command of the Rumeliots in the Palamidi and turned him into a figure of some political importance. Yet with his arrival the presence in Nafplion of the surviving troops from Mesolonghi became not merely a headache for the town but a malign influence on the entire Greek war effort. The hero of many early battles in western Greece, Grivas was undeniably brave. He had fought at Patras and Peta and in February 1826 he had sailed to try to relieve Mesolonghi only to find he could not enter the town. But he was also partisan. His marriage had made him an enemy of Kolokotronis himself and later when he demanded the return of his wife's dowry from her former father-in-law, the personal quarrel between the two men intensified the simmering contest between Rumeliots and Peloponnesians and threatened to reignite the civil war. From their stronghold in the Palamidi, Grivas and the Rumeliots began to treat Nafplion almost like enemy territory, strong-arming its citizens and the government itself. "The entire military force of Rumeli," wrote an eyewitness, "has crowded into Nafplion. Everyone demands some financial support and no one gives way to anyone else. What can the government do? It writes, speaks, issues decrees—and the military element demands money and more money—and always money. This is the situation facing the nation and the government."[12]

The armatole Karaïskakis had also descended from the mountains of Rumeli and arrived in Nafplion to consult with the new government. He was now embarking on the last glorious phase of his military career, a period of months in which he would emerge as a focus of united resistance to the enemy that would culminate in his death on the battlefield outside Athens in April 1827. Karaïskakis was a Rumeliot too and had played his part in the civil war in the Morea two years earlier, but he understood there was a desperate need now to build bridges with the Peloponnesians. With his fellow Rumeliots in the Palamidi, he swore an oath of mutual help, which was cemented by engaging one of his sisters to Grivas's younger brother. But while he understood the Rumeliots' anxiety about their lost homeland and their desire to keep the fortress in their hands, Karaïskakis did not see why this should mean keeping hundreds of experienced fighters idle. When he urged unity with the Zaimis government, however, he met with a hostile reception.[13]

Karaïskakis now sent a messenger to Kolokotronis saying he wanted to meet him. Kolokotronis understood the urgency in his tone and instantly responded, for both men were determined to avoid any repeat of the previous year's civil war. They agreed between them that there would be two campaigns that summer—one led by Kolokotronis against Ibrahim Pasha, the other by Karaïskakis to liberate Rumeli and defend

Athens. They were supported in this plan by Andreas Zaimis, the new president of the government. Only months earlier Karaïskakis's troops had plundered Zaimis's mansion at Kerpini during the civil war in the Morea, but Zaimis was a calm and prudent figure, the epitome of the farsighted Peloponnesian magnate, and he took the long view. Nafplion had become so dangerous that he and the rest of his government had moved from the town to the fortified little islet in the bay called the Bourtzi. Karaïskakis was rowed across so that Zaimis could tell him in person of his appointment as commander of the Greek forces for the whole of continental Greece. Reproached by another of those present for his past conduct, Karaïskakis is said to have replied: "Sometimes I am an angel, and sometimes a devil. In future I am resolved to play the angel."[14]

The government's power might have been dwindling but the rise of Zaimis showed that the great *kodzabashi* landed families of the Peloponnese remained a persistent force in politics. In fact, it was just at this time that another family quarrel—this time involving a nephew of President Zaimis—threw into relief all the ambiguities of their commitment to the national cause. Like the Hydriot shipowner Georgios Koundouriotis, magnates such as Zaimis talked the language of national government; but like him, it was their own local power base that they made sure to secure first. While an Ottoman army moved on Athens, and the Egyptians reassembled in the Peloponnese, the Greeks hemmed into the strategically vital northeastern Peloponnese took to fighting one another yet again over questions of regional power and prestige.

It had all begun with a man of startling good looks, the aristocratic Ioannis Notaras, who was known as "the lord's son" (*archontopoulo*). His connections could not have been better. He was the nephew of Zaimis through his mother, the president's sister. His uncle on his father's side was Panoutsos Notaras, the patriarch of one of the grandest families in the Peloponnese. A quarrel had put Ioannis at odds with a cousin from a lesser branch of the family, Panayiotis Notaras, after two men had fallen in love with the same woman, the beautiful Sofia Rentis. As Makriyannis put it in his usual blunt fashion: "Turks were all over our country, and the citadel of Athens, where lay the hope of Greece, was in danger . . . yet all you could find was lords of the manor with stiff dicks. Forgive me, readers."[15] But what really lay behind the clash of the two cousins was something else: Kolokotronis had ordered them both to levy men under his command, outraging Ioannis who regarded the entire province as his to run. The historian and Etairist, Nikolaos Spiliades, a contemporary, says Ioannis Notaras saw the region as his *timarion*, an old Ottoman term meaning a fiefdom bestowed upon him by the sultan. It is certainly true that Ioannis was disliked because of his domineering ways and his extortionate demands and there was sympathy for his less powerful cousin; the disrespect Ioannis displayed toward him in the matter of Sofia Rentis struck many locally as another example of his "tyranny." Both men started to hire the Rumeliot soldiery from Mesolonghi as reinforcements. "The troops in Nafplion now began to compete who would get a contract first with one of the two Notaras rivals," writes Kasomoulis. "They began at intervals to leave for Corinth and to form two armed camps in the regional Corinthian war." Karaïskakis was enraged with his countrymen's mercenary behavior and began "cursing God and man and the government."[16]

There was another factor as well: this was rich farming country, little touched so far by the war, and both Notaras cousins were demanding to be placed in command of detachments with the right to seize the region's taxable produce. Similar struggles among different factions were taking place in other fertile areas, but the conflict in Corinth with its vineyards and famous currant crop, the source of the Notaras family fortunes, was the sharpest.[17] The situation escalated when Panayiotis captured his rival's father and took him to the small town of Sofikos—an enormous affront to the pride of the principal branch of the family that they were bound to respond to. A letter to the government sent early in August by the headmen of more than sixty villages spelled out what happened next. Ioannis had swept through with his Rumeliots who had behaved like brigands and seized anything the inhabitants had managed to keep hidden from the Turks: their sheep, goats, cows were gone; their crops had been eaten by the Rumeliots' horses. These mercenaries had actually killed one of the headmen and razed Sofikos to the ground, setting the surrounding pine forests ablaze and leaving hundreds of families destitute. They had even gone into the woods and stripped the terrified townspeople who were hiding there of everything they owned. Ioannis Notaras, they protested, had behaved as "a second Ibrahim." His uncle, Zaimis, the president of the government, was also to blame, they declared; they even threatened to appeal for help to Ibrahim or Kütahı Pasha.[18]

President Zaimis was dismissive, saying that his nephew's "justifiable anger" did not merit punishment. When Kolokotronis angrily asked him if he could not have spared a messenger to tell the soldiers to leave the town alone, Zaimis replied that no one had been available. Karaïskakis's man on the spot wrote in despair that he foresaw "the disappearance of our nation." The great landowning families of the Peloponnese were back in charge of the government but their internal feuds and allegiances were destroying crops and villages, and the presence of idle Rumeliot bands in the region had turned toxic. The villagers' threat to turn to the Egyptians for help against their own leaders should have been a warning. They had all of them—the landowners, the chieftains, the great shipping families on the islands—presumed on the endless tolerance of the long-suffering peasantry, but that tolerance might turn out to have its limits.[19]

Kütahı Pasha was meanwhile encamped in the Attica plain, steadily making his preparations for the impending siege of Athens. He was aware of the failure of previous attempts on the town in which his predecessors' inability to muster troops or keep them in the field had betrayed the deep-rooted systemic weaknesses of the Ottoman state. In the summer of 1823, imperial detachments had reached the base of the Acropolis only to disperse because of hunger and thirst; the following year, both janissaries and mercenaries deserted before an adequate force could be assembled. After Mesolonghi, Kütahı Pasha had gathered together 7,000 men, mostly Albanians worn out from the long campaigning, who were chiefly concerned with returning home safely with their loot, and as he was well aware of their unreliability, he moved methodically to secure the necessary crops and livestock.[20] Many of the villagers in the region were glad to see the back of Gouras and his men, and they now made their submission to the pasha, even working as a kind of local auxiliary police to ward off Greek raids. At the same time, a stream of frightened Christians fled for the safety of the town walls of Athens. A mother arrived with her baby, having been forced to leave her two other children behind; another little boy was helped to safety by the defenders and told them he had been taken prisoner at Mesolonghi and bought by an Albanian agha among the pasha's men.[21]

During July, there were desultory skirmishes in the countryside but relatively few casualties. It was only when he learned the Greeks were finally starting to assemble a relief force at Elefsina under Karaïskakis that Kütahı Pasha tightened the siege. At the beginning of August he launched a sustained bombardment, his field guns keeping up a well-aimed continuous fire on the walls of the town for more than twenty-four hours. The following day the Ottoman troops, amply provided with strong alcoholic spirits, attacked the Greeks, quickly broke inside the town and pushed the defenders back onto the Acropolis. It had only been a matter of time: the fortifications were already in disrepair in many areas, and the perimeter was too large to be properly defended. Gouras, his garrison, and the hundreds of townspeople with them on the Acropolis were encircled. From the safety of the great rack, they could look down over the tents and dugouts of the Ottoman lines to the Attica plain and the sea.

Presented with the challenge of relieving the town, Karaïskakis was unfamiliar with the topography of Attica and he was nearly captured scouting out the possibilities of Piraeus as a launching pad for an attack. More distant Elefsina allowed for supply by land as well as sea and offered easier communication with the mountains behind. Gradually, therefore, a substantial force of men was built up there, including nearly 1,000 of Colonel Fabvier's regulars, paid with funds sent from the Greek committee in Paris. The government ordered Karaïskakis and Fabvier to work together, but neither would agree to be subordinate to the other and instead it was settled, somewhat awkwardly, that they would exercise a joint command.

It was the terrain that posed them the greatest challenge, for the plain that surrounded Athens gave the upper hand to cavalry and was not well suited to the Greeks' usual tactics of ambush and raids from hilly ground. The European officers felt in their element. Yet while they understood the topography, they did not understand how much the fighters they were with loathed and feared fighting in the open. When Greek forces moved up and clashed with the Ottoman army, around Haidari, not far from the town, they lasted two days before fleeing back to the safety of Elefsina, harassed by the Ottoman cavalry and leaving behind their field guns and baggage. It was many weeks before the Greeks dared mount another challenge.[22]

A few days after this battle an extraordinary chance encounter took place on the *Sirène*, the frigate of Admiral de Rigny, the French commander of the Levant squadron, which was stationed offshore. Colonel Fabvier had gone on board to pay his respects to de Rigny when he was surprised by the arrival of the two Ottoman pashas, Kütahı and Omer, who had come for the same purpose. All of them were dumbfounded by the arrival of a fourth guest—none other than Karaïskakis himself. Apparently a complete accident, their meeting gave the former armatole and the two pashas the opportunity for a brief conversation. To Kolokotronis a few days later, Karaïskakis wrote simply that after their initial surprise, their meeting had been friendly. According to another account, as recounted later by the Greek commander himself, their exchange had been initiated by Kütahı Pasha and had gone as follows:

"How are you, Karaïskakis? I had hoped you would come to Bitolja to surrender so that I could give you all the provinces [*vilayetia*] from Athens to Arta."

"I surrender? If you are Rumeli Valesi (commander of Rumeli), I too am Rumeli Valesi, and if my government knew that we are talking together they would hang me and the fifteen thousand men with me at Elefsina."

"What do you mean, they would hang you?"

"Can the Sultan not hang you if he wishes? Yes or no?"

"Indeed, because he is my monarch."

"And I too can be hanged, because I have a queen [meaning Greece]."[23]

It was a typical bravura performance with a little disinformation slipped in, for the Greeks had nowhere near the 15,000 men Karaïskakis had boasted of. Despair, rancor, and defeat were leading to desertions on a large scale, and Fabvier unilaterally took his remaining regulars off to Salamis. Karaïskakis faced a dilemma. Although the fighting at Haidari had shown that he lacked the men to confront the Ottoman army and break the siege of Athens directly, the alternative option of moving away to attack the Ottoman supply lines in the hills risked demoralizing the town's defenders, and it was at all costs vital that the garrison not surrender. He made two efforts to send in supplies and reinforcements but neither made it through the ring of besieging troops. But when Gouras himself, the commander of the garrison, was shot while making the rounds and killed on the spot, Karaïskakis ordered the Evvia chieftain Nikolaos Kriezotis to take over. Karaïskakis himself led a diversionary attack on the Ottoman positions, keeping the enemy engaged until the signal came from the Acropolis around four in the morning that Kriezotis and his men had got through and entered the town. With the garrison secure for the time being, Karaïskakis could turn his attention to the enemy rear and "bring revolution to Rumeli," where some of the armatoles were signaling their willingness to return to the Greek cause.[24]

It was thus in the late autumn of 1826 that Karaïskakis marched westward back into the mountains. Moving through a series of upland villages in the direction of Delphi, he and the kapetans under his command learned that a large detachment of experienced Albanians under Kütahı Pasha's lieutenant (*kehayia*), Musta Bey, was heading their way. Musta Bey had already defeated several thousand Greeks on the eastern coast near Atalanta; learning of the new threat posed by Karaïskakis, he led his men round the slopes of the Parnassos range intending to cut the Greeks off at the village of Arachova. He was close by when he and his troops paused for the night outside the hamlet of Dauleia.

Today, a swift stream of air-conditioned coaches carries thousands of tourists a year through Arachova's narrow streets to the ancient site of Delphi just beyond. But in the 1820s the narrow mountain track was easily rendered impassable by rain and snow. Valuable intelligence was passed on to Karaïskakis by the abbot of the monastery where Musta Bey and his Albanian soldiery were spending the night: the bey had been overheard telling his men their destination and the abbot had immediately dispatched his nephew, who slipped past the guards with the news, returning before dawn undetected. Karaïskakis straightaway sent five hundred men on to Arachova so that when the bey and his men entered the village the next morning they were stopped by musket fire and then found their retreat blocked by the rest of Karaïskakis's troops. After heavy fighting, the Greeks forced the 2,000-strong enemy force onto a ridge above the village and kept it pinned down there for six days in the open.

It was now the third week of November and the rains turned to heavy snow. Some of the encircled Albanians were already dying of hypothermia when they eventually attempted to break out on the morning of November 24. It turned into a slaughter as the Greeks hunted them down. It is said that the cold was so great it froze the fighters' guns so that the silence initially led Karaïskakis to think they had managed to get away until he quickly realized from the mounds of bodies that most of them had either perished of cold or been put to death by the sword. His soldiers brought him the ears of the dead, the usual Ottoman practice, and he paid handsomely for the heads of the leading beys, which were sent along with dozens of ears to Nafplion as grim proof of his triumph. A mound of skulls was erected, complete with an inscription recording the victory. It was probably the greatest catastrophe suffered by the Albanian chiefs since the war had begun. Writing after the victory, Karaïskakis called it "the most important victory of Greece" and reckoned they had killed around 1,300 of the enemy; his men had come away with money, valuables, and a thousand horses. "Our fatherland Continental Greece has been liberated," he wrote, with pardonable exaggeration. "In short, the flower of Albania has been lost."[25]

A day or two later, Karaïskakis hailed the "new revolution" (*nea epanastasi*) that had led all continental Greece to take up arms again. This was what he had promised Kolokotronis in the summer as the most effective way to stall Kütahı Pasha's advance southward into the Peloponnese. With extraordinary skill, he had succeeded. He had persisted even though the garrison in Athens was complaining about having to last through the winter. Ordering them to hold out into the New Year, Karaïskakis promised he would descend from the mountains into Attica after Christmas, break the siege, and ensure the men received their pay "to the penny [*eos aspron*]." In the meantime, Colonel Fabvier—keen for his men to share in the glory—reinforced the defenders, leading another force across the enemy lines into the Acropolis, with gunpowder enough to last the winter.[26]

The battle of Arachova was the first major Greek victory over the Ottomans on land in at least three years. It was hailed with joy by the government which proclaimed November 24 the day of the resurrection of continental Greece and it cemented Karaïskakis's legitimacy as commander of the Greek forces there. Fighting went on into the New Year, and by the time Karaïskakis was ready to lead his troops back to the camp at Elefsina, he had shaken off Ottoman rule across much of the entire mountain massif from Mesolonghi, where a small Ottoman garrison lived in constant fear of attack, to the foothills of Thebes and the Attica plain. It was a political and a logistical achievement as well as a military one. He had triumphed not only over an experienced and numerous enemy but also over the rivalries among the chieftains under his command. Something of the internal diplomacy this had required can be gauged from the fact that on the celebratory letter that Karaïska-kis sent to the government announcing the victory, his signature had been followed by more than ninety others, which represented all the chieftains who had fought under his command and who now insisted on being recognized publicly alongside him.

In contrast to the relative unity among the fighters in the mountains, however, the backbiting and infighting among the politicians in Naf-plion were getting worse. Although it had been agreed that the next national assembly should convene by September 1826, there was the usual disagreement about the venue and the politicians were still argu-ing as the year ended. One faction ended up meeting on Aigina while the other, led by Kolokotronis, assembled in the little shipping port of Ermi-oni in the Peloponnese. In January 1827, Karaïskakis wrote the delegates an angry letter from the slopes of Parnassos, accusing them of wasting time and frittering away military success by their quarrels. He addressed head-on the question of unity: "We are all brothers and a single Nation. Let us leave this talk of 'Peloponnesians, Islanders, Rumeliots' but let us all think of ourselves as one, as we are." And he signed himself "Your brother and patriot Karaïskakis."[27]

A couple of years earlier, a British surgeon had spent some time travel-ing with Karaïskakis. Fascinated by him, he had been struck by the Greek warlord's "dark, scintillating eye" with its "fierce glances," the loosely twisted yellow cashmere scarf wrapped around his head that framed the grim expression on his face. "Possessing considerable wit and humor," Karaïskakis entertained his companion, gleefully telling him the shawl had come from a Turkish tax collector he had killed in his days as a kleft, while boasting that the diamond ring on his finger was worth more than 1,500 Spanish dollars. As for Karaïskakis's poli-tics, his companion reckoned that "he had not the most distant idea of the meaning of liberty; confounding it with anarchy. He ridiculed the idea of Greeks aiming at the establishment of a regular government; and invariably spoke of it in the most scurrilous terms."[28]

What makes Karaïskakis such an important and fascinating figure in the story of the emergence of a wartime Greek national consciousness is that, having begun life as the son of a Rumeliot armatole and body-guard to Ali Pasha, a man who had likely been carrying on the usual secret negotiations with the Ottomans as late as 1823, he somehow made the transition—one that others of his background and generation were unable to make—to thinking of himself in national rather than regional or clan terms. Most of the Moreot notables and chieftains conflated patriotism with defense of their village, valley, or region: they spoke the new language of patriotism from time to time, but their actions betrayed their real allegiances. The men in the Palamidi talked about Rumeli as their *patrida* and said they would defend it if necessary even against "the nation" (*ethnos*). The Souliot chieftains remained locked in their allegiance to clan and family. By 1826, Karaïskakis was different from them. As he had told Kolokotronis emphatically, he wanted no part in any future civil wars. He had even left one of his closest aides with Kolokotronis to ensure smooth communications and to prevent others from driving them apart.[29]

In truth, Karaïskakis had always been different. Reputed to be the illegitimate son of the armatole Dimitris Iskos, his most common nickname was "the son of the nun" because his mother, the cousin of another famous armatole, had become a nun after being widowed: Her son had been born out of wedlock. Karaïskakis had never been recognized by his father's family and in a society where parentage was strength, this marked him out. The scion of one of the Rumeliot clans had blustered in the summer of 1826 that he would not take orders from a "bastard"; but Karaïskakis was happy to talk about his unusual parentage and was proud of his illegitimacy: all his life he flouted convention. He was notoriously foulmouthed—his official letters, written for him by well-educated secretaries, give a very misleading impression—and scholarly articles have been devoted to the impressive range of scabrous curses that he lavished on Turks, Albanians, and Greeks alike. Insults were a common feature of fighting men—battles were usually preceded by streams of obscenities hurled from both sides—but Karaïskakis was in a league apart. "Fuck," "prick," "shits," and worse peppered his speech: mortally wounded, he is supposed to have cursed the Turks with one final obscenity. Given his outsider status, not to mention the dark complexion that led people to refer to him as "the gypsy," it is hard not to see his sharp tongue as a mark of defiance.[30]

His constant ill-health—he suffered from tuberculosis—was another feature that distinguished Karaïskakis from most of the chieftains, who liked to project an image of physical indomitability. His fearlessness and physical prowess were not in doubt, but he suffered from frequent illness. And whereas most of the major chieftains strutted around with a large entourage of henchmen, Karaïskakis was often seen alone with Marigo, the young Muslim woman dressed in men's clothing who was his closest attendant, aide, and "nurse," and whom he made sure to remember in his will. He had become estranged from his wife, who lived in the Ionian Islands and died in 1826. He played the same marriage games as other chieftains—notably in the remarkable betrothal of his young daughter to one of the Notaras family—but these ties were reflections of his own achievements. Lacking a name or an ancestral *kastro*, he was, compared with most of the other chieftains, a man without a home or even much of a family. Grivas had dozens of relatives under his command; Kolokotronis's web of in-laws, nephews, and godsons stretched across the Peloponnese. Karaïskakis had no such support. It was perhaps this standing outside the social norms of the time that allowed him to express, as few others in that critical moment, a compelling sense of national solidarity. It was not (as for most Greeks at this time) family but the nation that was the source of his pride, and the reason for this, as he had tried to convey to Kütahı Pasha in their meeting on the French frigate, was that for him more than anyone the nation meant freedom.

Following on the heels of the disaster of Mesolonghi, the sight of Ottoman troops laying siege to Athens drew the attention of Europe and took philhellenic engagement to a new level. Large sums of money were sent to experienced agents to disburse instead of simply handed over to the Greeks. Funds paid for military professionals, of whom Fabvier was the most prominent. In 1826 alone there were ten expeditions, including a small party of Bavarians sent by the ardently philhellenic King Ludwig at the end of the year to scout out the possibility for a larger intervention. This was by far the largest influx of foreign fighters since the first year of the war, the prelude to a final internationalization of the entire Greek struggle.[31]

One of the newcomers was a French-Greek army officer called Constantin Bourbaki, who had unusually close ties to the Bonaparte family: he was the son of an Ionian sea captain who had settled in Marseille, befriended Joseph Bonaparte, Napoleon's brother, and then done important favors at critical times for Napoleon himself. The link between the two families was cemented by trust and favors, and Napoleon himself made sure Constantin was educated at imperial expense at the new military academy of Fontainebleau on the outskirts of Paris. He enjoyed rapid success as an army officer and in 1815 it was Bourbaki who had smuggled word to Napoleon in Elba that it was time to escape. A decade later, Bourbaki volunteered his services to the Comité Grec and he arrived in Nafplion at the end of 1826. He was carrying funds from Paris to carry on the struggle, and in a short space of time he managed to hire fighters to take part in a new operation to liberate Athens.

The Rumeliot chieftain Ioannis Makriyannis, whom the government had entrusted with this task, now found himself surrounded with foreigners. There was Bourbaki, along with men Makriyannis described dismissively as "a thousand carrion-dogs, sweepings from the billiard-tables of Nafplion."[32] There was also the Scottish colonel Thomas Gordon, newly back in Greece and with £14,000 sterling—proceeds of the second Greek loan—that he had been authorized to use. Makriyannis himself had been under siege on the Acropolis and had then broken out and made it across the Ottoman lines, so he knew the situation inside the fortress. He and Gordon agreed to recruit men for the new operation and somehow Makriyannis also managed to persuade the feuding Notaras cousins to stop fighting one another and to help.[33]

The plan was for a double-pronged attack on the besieging Ottoman army. Bourbaki's men, numbering several thousand including irregulars, were to advance to the slopes of Parnitha in the northwest of Athens and dig in. At the same time, the expeditionary force led by Gordon, with around 2,000 men under Makriyannis and Ioannis Notaras, would land with fifteen guns on the beach at Pasalimani and establish a bridgehead on the heights above the sea. This latter part of the operation was a success: arriving on a clear, still night, they managed by dawn to land the men without opposition and to drag the cannon up the slope and dig themselves in along the heights for nearly a mile.

To the north, however, things went badly wrong. Bourbaki's men had advanced with the irregulars as planned and dug in near the village of Menidi. But Bourbaki—a courageous soldier but a stranger to warfare in Greece—then insisted on leading his men downhill to a more advanced position at a village called Kamatero—which was much closer to Athens and more or less indefensible. Coming under attack even before they were dug in, the Greek irregulars fled, leaving Bourbaki's troops exposed. The Ottoman cavalry overran them, advancing all the way to Elefsina and destroying the Greek encampment there, forcing the survivors to flee to the nearby island of Salamis. In the end, more than three hundred Greek fighters died at Kamatero. Colonel Bourbaki was captured and brought before Kütahı Pasha who told him, with what appeared to be genuine regret, that he would be obliged to execute him because of the strength of feeling in Ottoman ranks against the Europeans who were coming to help the Greeks: the most he could do was offer him two days in which to ready himself for his fate. After his death, his head, together with those of two other philhellenes, was paraded before the defenders on the Acropolis and then sent to the sultan.[34]

Left alone to face the brunt of the Ottoman army at the end of January, Makriyannis's force fought off a succession of attacks, and waited for Karaïskakis to arrive. With supplies regularly shipped over from Salamis, and ample artillery to defend them, the 2,500 men on the beachhead suffered principally from lice, the winter rains, and dueling among themselves.[35] One month later Karaïskakis's men descended from the mountains and advanced down the coast. Beating off an Ottoman attack, and reinforced by new detachments from the Peloponnese, they linked up with Makriyannis's men. But Kütahı Pasha was content for them to stay there. Days and weeks went by with no indication that the thousands of men camped out along the Attica shoreline were willing to take on the pasha's army on the plain. It took a further internationalization of the Greek struggle before that changed and when it did, the change led to disaster and confirmed the growing dominance of the Ottoman army.

As February ended, two long-awaited senior British officers arrived among the Greeks, having been invited months earlier by the Greek government to take charge of the overall war effort. Appearing within days of one another were Sir Richard Church, who became generalissimo of the Greek land forces, and the legendary Admiral Thomas Cochrane, who was put in charge of the war at sea. Both were highly experienced and for better or worse Karaïskakis, Kolokotronis—and for that matter, Gordon and Fabvier—were all expected to carry out their orders.

Sir Richard Church was a fiery Bible-reading Irishman with an unusually deep connection to the Greeks. A soldier from the age of sixteen, at twenty-five he had been stationed in the Ionian Islands where he had commanded Kolokotronis and other klefts in the Greek Light Infantry.

In 1822 he had written to his sister about his desire to go to Greece. "I will allow that I am an enthusiast, in loving so dangerous a cause, and in being ready to affront the dangers and difficulties attendant upon it." He was not, however, a wealthy man, and in the spring of 1826, shortly before getting married in England, he asked the Greeks to clarify whether they wished him to come. The result was an official invitation from the Zaimis government, along with one from Kolokotronis hailing his "comrade in arms." There was real affection and respect between the two men, who had fought alongside one another in the past, and when Church arrived he was very warmly greeted. "Our father is come at last," Kolokotronis told his men.[36]

Church had no contract and no specified position. Indeed, he had felt insulted when the Greek deputies in London treated him in a way that suggested they thought he was in it for the money. He felt on the contrary that his destiny was bound up with the emancipation of Greece: it was a place where he felt among friends, and when the war was finally over—he having stayed and fought to the end—he settled in Athens while his wife remained in England. Into the 1860s, by which time he was in his eighties, he could be seen each morning before dawn riding from his house in Plaka, the oldest part of town, down to the sea to take a dip at the spot where, forty years earlier, he had nearly been killed by the Turks.

Even more eagerly awaited by the Greeks, Admiral Sir Thomas Cochrane, 10th Earl of Dundonald, was a brilliant and charismatic sailor, self-assured and capable of astonishing feats of seamanship. But unlike Church, Cochrane had no especial connection with Greece and was obsessed with making money. Reported by a superior officer to be "wrong-headed, violent and proud," he had inherited his father's scientific curiosity and had shocked his contemporaries during the Napoleonic Wars by his willingness to develop fireships and even forms of poison gas for use against the French. After the war, by which time he was also a convicted swindler and dogged by scandal, he sought his fortune in South America where he reaffirmed his reputation for naval brilliance. Having achieved spectacular victories for the Chileans and the Brazilians and having helped bring about the independence of Peru, he had sailed back to Britain in the summer of 1825 to sell his services to the next bidder.

Within the London Greek Committee, there was a long-standing dispute over the relative importance of land and sea power, and exponents of the latter were convinced that Cochrane could single-handedly save Greece. "Within a few weeks Lord Cochrane will be at Constantinople and will burn the Turkish vessels in the port," boasted Edward Ellice MP, who had been entrusted with some of the loan proceeds to commission the construction of a steamship. "You will want neither Napier, nor any other General. Let the whole £150,000 be for the expedition of Lord Cochrane: he will clear Greece of the Turks." Cochrane, who had an equal confidence in his own abilities, drove a hard bargain, insisting the funds be found for a small flotilla of frigates and steam vessels. In August 1825, after much haggling, a provisional contract was drawn up that provided for the construction of six steamships, not to mention the princely sum of £57,000 for his services, of which £20,000 were conditional on Greece being liberated.[37]

In Greece he was awaited "as another Messiah." Yet in the year and a half before Cochrane arrived, his preparations received one setback after another. The original plan to commission eight frigates eventually produced one, admittedly splendid, sixty-four-gun ship, the *Hope* (quickly renamed the *Hellas*), which did not arrive in Greece until the end of 1826 and which Cochrane lacked the funds to crew adequately. Of the six steamships he demanded, in the end only one, the paddle-steamer *Karteria*, saw action. Three arrived after the fighting was over; two were left to rot in the Thames. In Marseille, he watched the French build frigates for Mehmed Ali, while the wealthy Swiss philhellene Jean-Gabriel Eynard fitted out a brig for him. Only when that was ready, in February 1827, did Cochrane finally decide to go. To a member of the London Greek Committee he wrote: "If I do not go I am ruined in one way: and if I proceed I may be disgraced."[38]

Cochrane's nephew, George, who accompanied his uncle, has left a vivid record of their time with the Greeks, starting with the Greek politicians who came to greet them. Mavrokordatos was "a short, stout, well-built man, of very dark complexion, with black eyes, an oval face expressing great intelligence and his hair very long, hanging upon his shoulders." Wearing spectacles, smoking his pipe, and dressed in the European style, he chatted easily with Cochrane in French. Admiral Miaoulis, who accompanied him, a calm figure dressed in the style of his island—a jacket and baggy blue cotton trousers—shook hands with the admiral and spoke with him in broken Spanish. Both had sailed the waters of the western Mediterranean during the Napoleonic Wars—

Cochrane fighting the French, Miaoulis running the British blockade. Now placed in charge of the *Hellas*, Miaoulis briefed the admiral on the naval forces available to the Greeks and offered to serve under his command. Kolokotronis visited Cochrane as well, though not before sending calves, sheep, goats, and poultry on board as a gift. "He is very tall, being about six feet high, has very prominent and marked features, and wears his hair very long," wrote Cochrane who was struck by his dress—"a short, plain, green cloth jacket, and a white cotton fustinello," beneath which he wore drawers down to his calves, black and red cotton leggings, and shoes. Kolokotronis was accompanied by "ferocious-looking" companions, "armed to the very teeth" with pistols and a yataghan tucked into their belts. Cochrane was struck by Kolokotronis's unsmiling expression, his expressive language, and the worry beads that ran through his fingers. Below deck, the Old Man's principal concern was how much money the admiral had brought with him. He could not have been impressed by the answer, which was no more than £8,000 sterling, a trifling sum, and indeed the admiral would soon find that without pay the Hydriot crews were no more willing to serve him than their own captains.[39]

Faced with the bickering of the Greek politicians, Cochrane and Church made a good start, making it clear they would do nothing until the two rival national assemblies that had been squabbling for months had settled their differences. In this way their arrival did have the beneficial effect of forcing a moment of unity. To settle the row over location, Church suggested the two groups simply agree on a *new* place to meet. The assembly was accordingly convened in March outside the small village of Damala in the northeast Peloponnese, in a lemon grove where a large table was laid out for the secretaries and a row of chairs for the dignitaries. The two foreigners were duly voted into office. Wearing an elaborate uniform covered in gold lace, Cochrane was first, making his entrance on horseback. Three days later, Church was voted generalissimo of the land forces. The assembly also made a third appointment as well, however, unquestionably the most important of the three: it voted to offer the presidency of the country to the former Russian foreign minister, Count Capodistrias.

The choice of Capodistrias, a figure so closely aligned with the Russians and with the disappointments of 1821, had not been easy for many of the delegates to accept, and the figure who had swayed the day turned out to be Captain Hamilton of the *Cambrian*. Those opposed to the idea of a Capodistrias presidency had sent Kolokotronis to see him; the British captain had by this point through his long years of involvement, and his combination of firmness, sympathy, and evenhandedness won the respect of the Greeks. When asked for his opinion in the matter, Hamilton ruled out any British or other prince being made available to the Greeks; his blunt advice was to "take Capodistrias or any other devil you like, for you are quite lost."[40] Church helped persuade them too since it was widely believed that he spoke informally for the British cabinet and indeed he was probably aware that the cabinet had concluded Capodistrias was not, despite his background, likely to be subservient to Russian interests. In fact, Capodistrias took his time accepting and—as we shall see—he did not arrive until early in 1828, by which time the entire outlook had changed. But Cochrane and Church were on the spot and facing the same immediate challenge as the Greeks: how to prevent the surrender of Athens.

Karaïskakis was not happy about the new arrivals. The two British officers brought with them authority, money, and the backing of the national assembly. But what they lacked was the kind of knowledge of the terrain and the troops that Karaïskakis had gleaned over many years.[41] The basic choice that confronted them in the defense of Athens was as stark as ever—whether to confront the Ottoman army head-on in battle or attempt to force its withdrawal by cutting off its supply lines. The Greek irregulars had always been reluctant to risk their men in open combat on the Attica plain. Yet efforts to attack Ottoman lines farther north had been mostly unsuccessful. Cochrane was naturally drawn to the idea of continuing to threaten Kütahı's supplies, which gave more importance to sea power, but lacking the ships he scaled back his original plans and left it to a small Greek flotilla, led by Frank Hastings in the steam frigate *Karteria*, to attack Turkish positions up to the Gulf of Volos. Thus the main effort of the Greeks was given over to organizing a major offensive on land, something that they had never managed victoriously in the entire course of the war.

Yet helped by the funds coming in from European backers, the manpower at the Greeks' disposal was as great as it had ever been: there were over 5,000 men with Karaïskakis at Keratsini, another 4,000 round the headland with Gordon and Makriyannis. Together with some

4,000 men recruited by Church and camped at Megara, and additional troops provided by Kolokotronis, the Greek army may have totaled as many as 18,000 men, not including those defending the Acropolis: the largest military force they had mustered for a long time. That still left them outnumbered, however, for opposing them were approximately 30,000 troops under Kütahı Pasha. Aware of the vulnerability of his position against the Ottoman cavalry, Karaïskakis wanted to wait. But Cochrane was impatient to act and set a date of April 25 for the assault. In the meantime, he participated in an attack that successfully connected the Greek beachheads from Keratsini southward. This reinforced the admiral's confidence: "If everybody behaves tomorrow as all, without exception, behaved today the Siege of the Acropolis will be raised and the liberty of Greece assured," he predicted.[42]

A horrible episode now had the effect of pushing the planned offensive forward. The fortified monastery of St. Spiridon—on the same site where its successor now looks over the Piraeus ferry port—commanded the approach from the sea, and its Albanian defenders had successfully held out against heavy Greek bombardment. In order to allow the planned offensive to proceed, Karaïskakis negotiated the surrender of the garrison, supervised its capitulation, and presented himself as a hostage for their safe exit. Unfortunately, while the Ottoman soldiers were making their way out of the safety of the monastery's stone walls, a crowd of Greek irregulars rushed past them into the ruins looking for things to plunder and soon emerged again protesting angrily that nothing remained to be taken. Thomas Gordon and his fellow Scotsman George Finlay were watching from the bay when Finlay suddenly exclaimed: "All those men will be murdered!" Cochrane asked Gordon for his opinion. "My lord," Gordon replied, "I fear it is too true."[43] A tussle to grab one of the defenders' muskets turned quickly into a general slaughter and more than one hundred of the Albanians who had surrendered were killed. Karaïskakis, aware his honor was at stake, begged the survivors for forgiveness, and he and his officers shot some of their own men to restore order.

To the philhellenes watching, it was a shameful sight, and worse, one that placed in jeopardy the lives of the garrison on the Acropolis should their turn come. For their part, Cochrane's Hydriots were outraged that he had prevented them from joining in the search for loot. Gordon, who had been badly shaken by the massacre in Tripolitsa back in 1821, resigned his position and shortly after left Greece for a second time. Equally shocked, Church too resigned, though he was talked out of it afterward by Karaïskakis, who pledged to make up for the crime by immediately advancing on the Acropolis. The massacre thus contributed to the disaster ahead by instilling in the Greek leaders the idea that they needed to take action soon.

Cochrane's lethal streak of impatience now manifested itself. The truth was that Karaïskakis had done well, after Bourbaki's disaster, in expanding the bridgehead along the coast, making use of the hilly ground above the sea, linking up with Makriyannis's men, and inching closer at every step to Athens. His idea was the only sensible one in the circumstances: to infiltrate the large ancient olive groves that ran for miles along the valley of the Kefissus from the sea toward Athens, as these offered cover that would reduce the impact of the Ottoman horsemen. But Cochrane, who was impatient to celebrate victory in the Acropolis, believed a sudden assault from farther down the coast would carry the troops quickly to the walls of Athens; Karaïskakis and Church tried to get him to see that although the distance was a little less, the open ground offered no protection. Because they knew that the Greek garrison had enough supplies to hold out for a long time, they were not swayed by the reports being sent from the town about their desperate plight. None of this counted: Karaïskakis was under Church, who deferred to Cochrane.

On April 22, the Greek chieftains were just about to order the men into their positions when a skirmish along the lines erupted into fierce fighting. It had been going on for about an hour when Karaïskakis rode up: he had been feeling ill but had roused himself to see what was happening and get the men to prepare for the planned assault. Peering through the smoke, he was starting to join in the combat when he was shot and toppled from his horse: one source says Turkish soldiers had recognized him by his distinctive embroidered coat and aimed at him deliberately. He was brought to Church's schooner, where it quickly became clear that the wound was fatal. With time sufficient only to make his farewells and finalize his will, he died within hours. A British lieutenant who had also been wounded in the battle, and was lying in the cabin above dosed with laudanum, was suddenly woken around midnight by piercing shrieks: it was Marigo, his devoted attendant, mourning at Karaïskakis's deathbed.[44]

Karaïskakis's death dealt a huge blow to the Greek soldiers' morale and Cochrane only made matters worse by demanding they go ahead with the planned attack on the Acropolis. The chieftains protested that they needed time to mourn their commander but gave way when Cochrane threatened to leave. Shortly after Karaïskakis's funeral, several thousand troops were embarked and set down around midnight farther down the coast near Faleron. Some of them advanced rapidly toward Athens but by the time dawn broke on April 26, they formed a scattered line four miles long with no overall commander on the ground, no cover, and no trenching tools to dig the earthworks (*tambouria*) that they relied upon for protection. After the advancing Greeks had been seen by lookouts on Philopappou Hill, Ottoman infantry were massed in front of the Temple of Olympian Zeus; the light cavalry were positioned ready to charge. Seeing the danger, a worried Church immediately ordered the Souliot chieftain Kitsos Tzavellas to create a diversion through the valley of the Kefissos, but Tzavellas refused to move and remained calmly smoking his pipe. At a spot called Analatos, today's neighborhood of Neos Kosmos, the Ottoman cavalry charged the Greeks, who fled for the shore and were only saved from being wiped out when the attackers withdrew to celebrate. It was a devastating defeat, one of the worst the Greeks suffered in a war in which they had always tried to avoid pitched battles on open ground. Their casualties included 700 dead and several hundred more captured. Of the 150 men Makriyannis had started out with, only 33 survived. Cochrane and Church were both lucky to escape with their lives. Makriyannis was scathing about Tzavellas's cowardice and that of some of the Peloponnesian troops as well. But the principal reason for the disaster was surely Cochrane's ignorance of the true situation and his impatience, and Church's reluctance to stand up to him.

Characteristically, Cochrane then left the scene. From the nearby island of Poros he informed the Great Powers that the Acropolis could no longer be held, and he warned them that they would need to step in to prevent the garrison from being massacred. The admiral was virtually out of funds and he contributed little more to the Greek cause. His major achievement in the coming weeks at sea was to capture the harem of Kütahı Pasha whom he then gallantly set free without conditions in order, as he put it, to establish a more humane approach to the war. But his efforts to emulate his daring raids of the past did not come off. Like

Kanaris earlier, he tried sending fireships into Alexandria but he was forced to flee without any more damage being done than a series of lengthy and insulting letters he found the time to send to Mehmed Ali: they were empty threats. "Nothing very material has been done by us," he wrote to Church. Cochrane was impatient, a man who wanted quick results. Unable to get them, he left for England at the start of 1828. For him Greece had been a commission not a cause.

Church, however, was cut from a different cloth and the old soldiers really believed in the Greeks. In the immediate aftermath of the defeat, he even managed to persuade his men to remain on the headland. But it was purely an act of short-term defiance, as they had no shelter from the sun, no food, and no money, and eventually Church realized they could not hold out: after two weeks they were ferried over to Salamis. Their departure meant that there was no longer any realistic prospect of relief for the garrison on the Acropolis, and Colonel Fabvier, who had never really wanted to stay there at all and had felt held against his will, arranged for the French admiral de Rigny to negotiate the surrender of the Acropolis with the Ottomans.

The negotiations with Kütahı Pasha lasted three days but the pasha was compliant: he was keen to report to the sultan this second victory, which was even more important diplomatically to the empire than the fall of Mesolonghi. Mindful of the massacre at the St. Spiridon monastery, he kept the Albanians at a distance, guarded by his cavalry, so they could not retaliate against the Greeks. Fabvier along with three of de Rigny's officers headed the column of defenders; de Rigny himself marched at the rear with three Albanian chiefs the Greeks had insisted upon coming along as hostages. Between them were nearly 2,000 people—many of them townspeople—who made their way from the Acropolis down to the sea where they were safely embarked on ships of the French and Austrian Levant squadrons.[45]

It was a far more orderly and peaceful end to a shorter siege than Mesolonghi had endured; there had been much less loss of life to those defending the citadel and less danger of famine. In fact, many on the Greek side thought the garrison had been too quick to surrender. Whatever the scale of the defeat in the plain, they argued, the Acropolis remained impregnable and well supplied. Makriyannis was in Nafplion trying to recover the garrison's back pay when he entered a café and encountered some officers, in lavish uniforms, playing billiards. They began berating him for treachery, saying he had been too quick to abandon the Acropolis. He pointed out that at the time of the surrender he had been in the field, having spent weeks on the beachhead at Piraeus. "A glass of punch for General Makriyannis, who is not one of those traitors!" He drank and left to avoid getting into a fight.[46] Fingers were pointed all around. Some of the Greek chieftains, no doubt on the defensive, publicly blamed Fabvier, and the prickly colonel demanded "public satisfaction" from his accusers. When Church blamed de Rigny for organizing the surrender, the French admiral expressed his puzzlement: "You are free to believe that the forces under your orders were better placed to help the citadel . . . Allow me to think otherwise. I have fulfilled my duty obeying the laws of humanity."[47]

Whoever was really at fault, the loss of Athens was a devastating blow to the Greeks and it left Kütahı Pasha master of almost all the mainland. In the Peloponnese, Ibrahim, after a respite over the winter, renewed his drives across the peninsula in April. Many questioned what benefit the two British officers had brought. The American philhellene Jonathan Miller, the "Yankee Daredevil" from Vermont who had learned Greek and been in the thick of many battles, reflected in February 1828 upon their contribution: "General Sir Richard Church, who arrived in Greece about the same time with Lord Cochrane, has, like him, been able to effect nothing for the good of the country . . . It is decidedly my opinion (and I think I am not alone in it) that if Lord Cochrane and General Church had never seen Greece, Athens would this day have been in the hands of the Greeks and the brave Karaiskaki alive and triumphant in all Attica."[48]

16

THE INEXHAUSTIBLE
PATIENCE OF THE PEOPLE

"Irregularities daily multiply and it is extremely difficult to know whom to trust."
Jonathan Miller, agent for the Executive Greek Committee of
New York, 24 June 1827, in J. P. Miller, *The Condition
of Greece in 1827 and 1828* (New York, 1828), 76

Deprived of the land of our fathers, our fields, our houses, sacrificing parents, children and siblings for the common freedom of Greece, after fifteen months wandering from place to place, unable to find shelter on this safe island for our numerous families, we sold up all we had and built small huts in which we put our parents, children and women.

In the summer of 1827, citizens of Athens who had fled from the Ottoman army to the nearby island of Aigina were in desperate straits—starving, destitute, and suffering in the heat. Their hopes had been lifted when members of the revolution's so-called Vice-Governmental Commission, appointed in Capodistrias's absence, arrived on the island. But then its employees had come and forced them out of their shacks and left them with nowhere to go. How, they asked, could the government itself leave them homeless? Yet what this commission, which in truth was governing in little more than name, could do for them was unclear, for by the summer of 1827 there were tens of thousands of victims of the war in a similar position.[1]

It is scarcely an exaggeration to say that a new collective understanding of the Greek nation emerged out of the wartime refugee experience, for those who had lost their homes, fleeing massacre and upheaval, came from all over the Greek world—Asia Minor, Crete and Cyprus, Chios and Psara, Epirus, Thessaly and Macedonia. The process had begun as early as the summer of 1821 with the flight of thousands from Aivalik on the coast of Asia Minor, or perhaps even earlier—before the insurrection began—in the summer of 1820, when townspeople from Jannina fled the clash between the Ottoman army and Ali Pasha. In the first months and years of the insurrection, the Peloponnese had offered safety, along with the Ionian Islands. But the arrival of the Egyptians in the spring of 1825 made the region the very center of the refugee crisis and many of its villages were emptied as women, children, and the elderly fled the prospect of enslavement or death. These panicked movements were sudden and dramatic and involved large numbers of people. William Black, the British naval surgeon aboard HMS *Chanticleer*, watched the deserted islet of Marathonisi near Gytheion fill up within only a few days with the tents, animals, and belongings of thousands of refugees from the Egyptian advance. Two thousand peasants trekked even farther to reach what is now the secluded tourist retreat of Elafonisos, off the southeastern tip of the Peloponnese, where the beach was strewn with makeshift shelters, around which children and livestock wandered. The Greek bands could do little to prevent their flight, and Kolokotronis's adjutant Fotakos records painful occasions on which he and his men were berated by village women for their inaction. Estimates from 1828 suggest that perhaps as much as one third of the population of the Morea was rendered homeless before the fighting ended, with dozens of villages deserted and thousands of their inhabitants captured. Around Almyros alone, on the edge of the Mani, there were nearly 20,000 starving villagers camped out in the summer of 1827.[2]

The unprecedented disruption to the normal patterns of life in the rural economy caused by the never-ending threat of the Egyptian army, coupled with the political anarchy and breakdown of order in the shrinking territory under Greek control, transformed international affairs by bringing a new subject to the attention of the world: the suffering noncombatant. Although there had been sporadic, small-scale efforts to help Greek refugees over the past six years, philhellenism had previously been mostly martial in its orientation and the first waves of foreign volunteers had been fighters, many of them soldiers. The British philhellenes sent out by the London Greek Committee dreamed of rationalizing government and organizing an expeditionary force to ensure the Greeks triumphed;

the French Comité Grec financed officers and munitions and fantasized about crusades. But the furor over the enslavement of Greek captives following Mesolonghi began to make people newly attentive to the plight of the vulnerable, and as the Greek fighting effort faltered, this international attentiveness to the suffering of civilians increased.

The most decisive and concrete response to the Greek refugee crisis was to be found from a relative newcomer to European affairs. In his classic *Democracy in America*, written a few years later (1835–40), the French thinker Alexis de Tocqueville saw what he called the "spirit of association" as a central feature of the new society that was emerging across the Atlantic in the US. There was perhaps no better illustration of this American tendency to sociability than the numerous committees formed by private individuals in the first months of 1827 to collect money and goods for the Greeks. Donations poured in from schools, colleges, churches, cadets at West Point, and small towns and settlements across much of New England and New York. A charity ball in the Park Theatre in Manhattan raised $1,650; the Stock Exchange Board on Wall Street gave $100. "A Friend to religion and humanity and a friend to the Greeks" donated $50; "a Soldier of the American Revolution" gave $5, a "mechanic" the same amount, which for him was the equivalent of one week's wages. Ten "ladies from Boston" sent a barrel of flour each; "a widow" provided twenty-five chemises. Hats, shoes, blankets, pork, mackerel, medicine, and peas were all packed off. Some $6,000 were raised in New York City in January alone. In under two years the New York committee managed to collect nearly $40,000 dollars, the Philadelphia committee over $25,000.[3]

These were large sums and the organizers were very clear about who they were for and how they were to be disbursed. Unlike the radical, speculative wheeler-dealers in London four years earlier, the sober, serious American merchants in charge in 1827 could not have been more precise about the goal of their philanthropy and the means to make it effective. The funds, they insisted, were not to be used for fighting. In the words of the New York committee, which others followed, they were "intended for the relief of the women, children and old men, non-combatants of Greece." What we have here is the beginning of a modern phenomenon— a policy of organized international relief, one that would be closely identified with America's projection of its power and values abroad for the next two centuries. As in present-day relief efforts, it rested upon a sharp distinction between combatants and noncombatants and also between politics, which lay in the hands of the state, and humanitarian aid, which these outside agencies believed they were best qualified to provide. Nor were they wrong to think this: the Greek government scarcely existed by this time—though what was left of it protested at not being allowed to decide where the relief went—and food was such a valuable commodity that only the most stringent controls on distribution would allow it to go where it was most needed. Young Americans, it turned out, could be trusted to figure this out a lot better than the experienced but self-interested leaders of the Greek revolution.

The approach's success depended on tough, knowledgeable agents with the judgment and experience to handle a volatile situation. Jonathan Miller, the "Yankee Daredevil," was the first: a veteran of the last siege of Mesolonghi, he had fought alongside the Greeks, shaving his head like the Souliots and wrapping himself in a sheepskin cape with his pistols and yataghan in his belt before returning to his home in Vermont. He quickly accepted the terms of the Greek Committee of New York in order to sail back to the Morea with the first shipment of supplies. When he got there, he communicated with Samuel Gridley Howe, the young warrior-surgeon who had been in the country since the start of 1825. Miller's friend, George Jarvis, made a third—an even more formidable figure who had trained Souliots for Byron and fought Ibrahim's men at Navarino. After the death of "our glorious chief Karaisko" and the Greek defeat at Faleron, Jarvis had decided to assist his countrymen. Thanks to their dispatches, we can see the impact of American aid upon a population that few among the leaders of the Greek revolution seemed capable of, or interested in, helping. And we can detect something else, that is, just how deeply the marks of years of war had imprinted themselves upon ordinary Greeks and how exhausted and desperate they were.[4]

The first challenge—which would become the usual one for relief workers in war zones—was to get supplies past the chieftains to where they were needed. At Nafplion, where the initial cargo was unloaded in the late spring of 1827, Kolokotronis and his bitter enemy, the Rumeliot commander of the fortress, Grivas, both swore they would support the young Americans; yet both sent their men to seize the barrels of flour, bread, and other goods in their warehouses. Over time, Howe and Miller worked out how to deal with them, but they came to abhor them and the misery they caused. In July, when Howe returned from distributing aid along the eastern coast of the Peloponnese, he found Nafplion in ruins. Kolokotronis's effort to win back the Palamidi from Grivas had failed, the inhabitants had fled. The streets were strewn with the debris from the shelling and the only signs of life were clusters of trigger-happy soldiers. Howe estimated 20,000 people were living in reed huts outside the town walls because Rumeliots had pillaged their houses and they were too frightened to return. The government was powerless; the secretary of state's own house had been robbed bare. Grivas flaunted the schooner that had formed part of the dowry his wife had brought him from Spetses: moored in the harbor, it was a reminder of his untouchable status.[5]

The arrival of the third shipment at Nafplion in November was placed in charge of another American, Henry Post, who was not as experienced in Greek affairs and it was unfortunate that when he arrived, Miller was away. Grivas did not find it hard to fool the well-meaning newcomer, inviting him ashore and showing him cases of deprivation that—though Post did not know it—Grivas himself had contributed to. It was, Post wrote later in self-defense, "a scene of suffering and distress"; hundreds of emaciated figures, their clothing in tatters, were sheltering in makeshift huts and begged the newcomer for help. "Never were my sympathies so powerfully excited as when I learned that many of these poor sufferers were once among the wealthiest and most respectable inhabitants of Greece, who had fled from the desolation of their lands and the conflagration of their dwellings, and were now struggling to maintain a miserable existence by means which humanity sickens to contemplate." Yet of the 500 barrels of cornmeal that Post ordered to be landed, 430 barrels went to the garrison, and only 70 were given to the poor, as Miller later pointed out.[6]

Undeterred by the warlords, Miller, Howe, and Jarvis took flour, clothing, and shoes by boat and mule into remote corners of the eastern Peloponnese, as well as to the islands of the Argo-Saronic. They were accompanied by soldiers and they themselves carried pistols: trigger-happy men were always trying to muscle in, and a cool head was needed to prevent bloodshed. On Aigina, families were living in caves, not having tasted bread for weeks, surviving on snails and herbs. There were 4,000 refugees there, half of them from Athens. On nearby Angistri, Howe distributed rice, corn, salted fish, bread, and clothes among 3,000 more. Jarvis estimated there were 20,000 destitute villagers across a swath of the northeastern Peloponnese, including Epidavros, Salamis,

Sofiko, and elsewhere. Some of these had escaped the fighting between the Notaras cousins; others had fled Kütahı Pasha's army only to be plundered by the Rumeliot soldiery. The Egyptian troops had left behind a trail of torched buildings and atrocities, and while the town of Leonidion and its secluded valley seemed wonderfully untouched by the war, across the mountains there were devastated villages where abandoned orphans and blind elderly women somehow survived amid the ruins of their former homes. In the hills beyond Nafplion, Miller climbed for three hours to find five hundred women and children on the side of a mountain, living off herbs, grass, and anything else they could find. They were haggard and blistered by the sun, wearing verminous rags: he learned they had not had bread for months. Anticipating that their plight would grow through the winter, he forecast that hundreds if not thousands would die of starvation. Horrified by the cruelties inflicted by Ibrahim's men on Greek women, the Americans were equally appalled to come across Muslim slaves kept by the Greeks, sometimes offered to them for sale, and they redeemed them when they could. Both Miller and Howe were ardent abolitionists who could no more excuse slaveowning among the Greeks than they could among the Turks.

Howe returned to New York in February 1828 in order to publicize Greece's need for further help and wrote on his arrival to the members of the New York Greek Committee. Congratulating them for assisting the country at such a desperate time, he underscored an important conclusion:

> Though the originally small national resources of Greece have been exhausted by a seven-year struggle with their powerful enemy, though the country has been wasted, the crops destroyed, and the villages burned; and, what is worse, broils and civil wars almost continually kept up by the guilty intrigues of her selfish and avaricious chiefs; still the spirit of the people, though bruised is not broken.[7]

Miller and Howe were certainly well placed to gauge the spirit of the Greek people. Both men had fought alongside them, spoke their language, loved the country, and seen the plight of the civilian population. But although Howe did not dwell on the point in his letter, it was not a foregone conclusion that in the face of such suffering "the spirit of the people" would remain unbroken, and he could, in the circumstances, have been forgiven for exaggerating. For there were in fact signs that even in the Peloponnese, popular resolve to hold out was starting to give way. The fall of Athens had been a crushing blow and many Greeks were coming to believe that between the defeats their armies had suffered and the destructive and quarrelsome behavior of their own leaders, their cause was doomed. Miller was at sea when he and his shipmates learned from a passing sea captain from Poros that the garrison on the Acropolis had capitulated. "Alas," exclaimed one of the passengers, "my country must be lost then."

Things had become very grim for the Greeks. Ibrahim had rested his army over the winter of 1826–27. But he was on the move again in the spring, leaving a new trail of devastation across the Peloponnese and terrifying an already disoriented and destitute rural population. With Rumeli in Ottoman hands, it remained to complete the conquest of the Morea. However, his own men were worn out, hungry, and increasingly sick, as well as being far from home. As Ibrahim had realized the previous year, he also lacked the numbers to occupy the entire region. Kolokotronis's bands could not inflict serious damage on his men, but they remained a nuisance and a threat. That winter an Ottoman supply train had been attacked on its way from Methoni to Tripolitsa, leaving many of Ibrahim's men dead and allowing the Greeks to carry off the biscuit, rice, coffee, butter, rum, clothes, and shoes that had been destined for Soliman Bey.[8] If Ibrahim could not wipe out the Greek bands, what he could do was defeat them in the war of morale. His punishment raids thus served a triple purpose: they secured the land's resources for his own men; they kept the crops out of the hands of the Greek commanders, thus affecting their ability to maintain their own bands in the field; and, above all, they could make the civilian population reassess the wisdom of holding out.[9] To many of the terrified rural inhabitants of the Peloponnese, the coming of the Egyptians must have seemed like the latest chapter in a long history of tribulation. The traditional structures of authority in the countryside had already been badly battered by the Albanian raids of the late eighteenth century, and then later by the kleftic bands and by Ali Pasha's henchmen in the years before the uprising. Even in times of relative stability, the population had lived under the overweening power not only of the local bey, agha, and voivode, but of Greek landed magnates and their kapos, or toughs: their own village headmen were always a weak defense against armed outsiders. Coming on top of all this, and in the absence of the sultan and the entire system of power he headed, the fighting of the war years produced a real crisis of moral authority in some regions. Between the civil war that raged across Achaia in the northern Peloponnese in 1825 and the coming of the Egyptians later that year, a vacuum of power and leadership opened up that was filled in unexpected ways.

A holy man known as "Holy Father" (Ayios Pateras), Evgenios, or more colloquially by the country folk as the "Little Priest" (Papoulakis, or in some versions Papoulakos) had been wandering the area between Patras and Vostitsa before ending up in 1825 in a remote hilly region, green and fertile, amid the ruins of ancient Psofis in the northwest of the Peloponnese. There, he won a reputation for seeing into the future and performing miracles, while a "nun" who accompanied him reportedly conversed with the Virgin.

Papoulakis preached a fiery message of abstinence, repentance, and devotional dedication. He told ever-larger audiences of village people from the area that the sins of the Greeks would catch up with them and that those who had looted things from the Muslims should give them up or burn them—or be taken prisoner themselves. The peasants flocked to hear him, brought gifts, and helped build him a monastery. He ordered them to fast, give up meat, and abandon their weapons, promising that when the time came, he would lead them against the Egyptians unarmed and that Ibrahim would be annihilated. Fire would purge them of their sins; rain would fall and they would become pure again and invincible.[10]

In the summer of 1825, worried by Papoulakis's popularity, an educated visitor went to see what was happening. Papoulakis, he reported to the Greek revolutionary authorities, began his sermon with some simple injunctions: he who did not return what he had stolen would be unforgiven; he who killed a Christian, Jew, Armenian, or Turk would be always unforgiven. Asked whether this was true even in war, Papoulakis replied that it was since "the Turks are men too."[11] A few months later, a fellow priest was sent in to spy on him for the government in Nafplion, and this report gives us a verbatim account of Papoulakis's preaching:

"I told you: get rid of this Turkish stuff and give back what you've taken from Christians, fast until Easter, no oil every day, nor wine, only bread and nothing else and then a light rain will fall and the enemy will be defeated. But you do not listen . . . You don't fast. You keep your Turkish women and men; you steal from Christians; you take their clothes off their backs; you take their dignity, you kill them, you have no piety, no fear of God. You trample on the laws and you are worse than the Turks, and that is why now your sins have come to life and they have found this hellish and contemptible Arab . . . and they have come to make slaves of you, to ruin you, not only the sinner but the virtuous as well."[12]

When someone asked Papoulakis about the Greek leaders, he was told to focus on himself and not to worry—God had punishment in store for their "atheist" superiors. His basic message was that the Greeks had fallen into sin through the war and their leaders had led them astray. They fornicated with Turkish women, with Christian women, with boys—an allusion perhaps to widespread rumors in the region about the unbridled behavior of some local *kodzabashis*. He went on to attack the kapetans and chieftains as well: as if what they had done to the Turks was not enough, they had despoiled fellow Christians and killed them— this was only months after the civil war—and done them such wrongs as not even the Turks had done. The result was that they had become slaves to their passions and ended up falling upon one another. Rapt crowds listened to the preacher and gifts piled up: "horses, oxen, cows, sheep, goats, silverware, coin, bread, raki, olives, oil, and wine."[13] Papou- lakis conveyed warnings through parables: a man had stolen a sheep and hidden it, only to find when he went to collect it that it had turned into a snake, which bit and killed him. There were others. As his reputa- tion spread "among the simple folk" throughout the Peloponnese, more and more people joined the crowds at the monastery, even some band leaders. When one of the Notaras clan sent in some armed men to try to seize the monastery's loot, Papoulakis met them outside, told them why they had come and what their names were. Astonished, they repented on the spot, and handed over their valuable silver-engraved pistols; a kapetan from Epiros is said to have given up fighting to become a monk in the monastery where he is reported to have been living some three decades later. Things got to the point where the population of the area turned their back on the war, and no one dared speak against the preacher. Even the brigands temporarily desisted.

What is striking is to see the way Papoulakis emerged as a figure of defiance to the Greek revolutionary authorities in the region and to the armed chieftains in particular. The Greek Etairist (and cleric) Frantzis, who obviously regarded him as a dangerous charlatan, tells us the ordinary people viewed him "as sent from God and another Moses and Ilias [Elijah]." Nikitaras the "Turk-eater," the renowned fighter who passed through the area, cannot have anticipated that the monk would publicly berate him for impiety and vice. Remaining silent, Nikitaras told his uncle Kolokotronis what had happened. Kolokotronis was worried that Papoulakis was undermining the morale of the villagers in the region and conferred with the notable Andreas Zaimis about how to cut what he called the "Gordian knot." Kolokotronis wrote suggesting Papoulakis come into battle with him, but he got nowhere. Zaimis actually went and was made to stand for hours bareheaded in the blazing sun listening to the monk preach, afraid to object in case the crowd turned on him. When the landowner and memoirist Kanellos Deliyannis arrived with his soldiers, he was dismayed when they laid down their weapons and rushed to kiss Papoulakis's hand as if he were a notable or a bishop. When Deliyannis upbraided his men, an enraged Papoulakis accused him of impiety and loving Turks, and reminded everyone that Deliyannis was nicknamed "Ali Farmakis," because of his resemblance to the famous Muslim agha of the area.

It must have been to the great relief of most of the leading figures of the revolution in the region when in September 1826 Arab troops arrived at the village, burst into the monastery, killed Papoulakis, and took the nun as a slave. The loot was immense and was divided up among the soldiers. The invaders and Kolokotronis could agree on one thing: the war should go on. But many of those anonymous villagers who had flocked to Papoulakis were starting to disagree and wondering how to save themselves.[14]

Submission was the Ottoman endgame. For the Greeks, the goal had always been to drive the Ottomans out of their lands—not only the soldiers but the long-settled Muslim civilians as well—in such a fashion as to create a situation in which, in Kolokotronis's uncompromising words, "it is impossible for Greek and Turk to live together."[15] For the sultan, on the other hand, the goal was the preservation of his empire, and ultimately this meant not eliminating Greeks but getting them to surrender. If mass violence against Christians aroused anger in Europe, public professions of their loyalty to the sultan undermined the Greek case abroad and strengthened the Ottoman position. This was well understood by the Greeks themselves: as early as 1822, one of Androutsos's advisers had warned him against signing a formal document of submission even as a way of buying time, lest it become known to the European diplomats at the Congress of Verona and leave an adverse impression upon them. Two years later, an assembly in Salona forbade such arrangements, which had until then been typical of the armatoles, for similar reasons.[16]

Moreover, there were demographic as well as diplomatic reasons why the Ottomans preferred getting the Greeks to surrender. Although there was always the threat of extermination in response to rebellion, whatever it might have looked like in the aftermath of the massacres at Aivalik, Naoussa, and Chios, driving the Greeks out forever was essentially inconsistent with the long-term needs of a multinational empire, not least because in Rumeli, Muslims were and had always been in the minority while large Christian Orthodox populations continued to live—with some degree of normality—in Anatolia, around the Black Sea, and in the Balkans. This imperial policy had proven to work and collective professions of loyalty by Greek communities and their leaders had followed the crushing of the uprisings in central and eastern Rumeli. In western Rumeli, too, as we have seen, the Ottoman reconquest brought armatoles such as Varnakiotis around to supporting the sultan, and after Mesolonghi others followed Varnakiotis's lead. But the Morea had remained proudly free from this trend until Ibrahim's all-out war on rural society—in which thousands of villagers, mostly women and children, were enslaved—led more and more villagers there to consider surrendering.[17]

What had worried Kolokotronis about Papoulakis in the summer of 1825 was that he might be sapping the will of the local population to resist the Egyptians. And indeed a wave of submissions started in the Peloponnese on a small scale in late 1825 seems to have paused during Ibrahim's absence for the siege of Mesolonghi and accelerated during the spring of 1827. The phenomenon betrayed the enormous strains that the peasants of the Morea had been living under for years and posed an existential threat to the continuation of the Greek struggle. Never, Kolokotronis recollected later, had he been so worried. The deterrents to submission that the revolutionary leaders had imposed on peasants in the Morea in the spring of 1821, so as to force them into the struggle, were finally wearing off. "During the time when they were submitting all round I feared for my country, but only then," Kolokotronis remembered. "The whole of Rumeli had submitted, Athens had fallen, the Rumeliot army had dispersed, and only the Peloponnese and the two islands were left to us . . . If I had not exerted myself against the submission which was being carried on, the Peloponnese would also have submitted, and then what could Hydra and Spetsai have done?"[18]

Some brave individuals never wavered, their courage later memorialized in folk songs. Even at the beginning of the twentieth century, villagers in Arkadia still remembered the old brigand chief Mitropetrova—one of the few to have actually fought back in 1770 as well—who had attacked some of Ibrahim's men to free the women of Garantza. Another kleft, the semimythical "Wild Yianni" (Agrioyianni)—"stocky, dark-skinned, with deep black eyes, long hair, a long beard and mustache, a pock-marked face and an unruly character"—left behind him a trail of oral ballads that commemorated his defiantly heroic death in various settings dating from 1804 to the moment in 1826 when he had supposedly been hunted down by Ibrahim's men.[19] But those holding out were fighting against a growing trend among the Greeks of the Peloponnese.

The submissions began in villages in the northwest of the peninsula, a region that had not only suffered acutely at the hands of the Rumeliots in the civil war but was especially exposed to the Egyptian threat. This was because the fortress of Patras, long under siege by the Greeks, had never fallen, and once Ibrahim arrived in the Morea it became a base for punitive raids across the region. During the Egyptian raids into the hills and mountains behind the town over three campaigning seasons, hundreds of villagers were enslaved and brought into Patras to be sent, as the local Greeks told it, into "Arabia"; the final raid, in May 1827, ended with no fewer than 2,000 villagers being taken.

Among the minor chieftains of the region was a man called Dimitrios Nenekos, who came from an impoverished upland village in an area of Albanian-speaking Christians a few hours away. He had formerly been in the service of one of the wealthiest notables of Patras, had fought bravely with Zaimis, Andreas Londos, and Kolokotronis, and had acquired a following of his own. Reaching an understanding with Ibrahim, Nenekos managed to get 1,000 of the captives freed that spring in return for providing a pledge of loyalty. At the same time, villagers from the nearby hills began resuming contact with the town again, bringing their produce to the Patras garrison and selling poultry, milk, eggs, and wood at the inflated prices the soldiers were prepared to pay. The Ottoman commander allowed them to bring down their sheep to graze—instructing his soldiers they were not to be touched—and made the fields outside the town available for planting. Among those defending the fortress for the Ottomans were many local Muslim Albanians who had been driven out of the area of Lala, not far away, in the spring and summer of 1821; and as they were not strangers, and for many of them Albanian was a common tongue, communication between them and the Christian peasants was easy and familiar.[20]

After negotiations with the Ottoman commander in Patras, Deli Ahmed, Nenekos went even further, levying local men to form a unit to fight alongside the Ottomans, and using them to target Greek villagers who would not go over to the Ottoman side. To force Greeks to submit, he would kill their friends and relatives, chop off men's hands, steal their sheep and clothes, and even force young women into undesirable marriages to shame their families. In a short space of time he became wealthy, earning the trust and respect of Ibrahim himself. Proof of his new status as a valued auxiliary in Ottoman eyes came after a misadventure in which Ibrahim became separated from his entourage. Losing his way in the forested mountain valleys one morning, the Egyptian pasha found himself alone with only a single bodyguard to protect him, some eight hours from the nearest town, when he stumbled upon Nenekos and his men who guarded him faithfully. It is said that Ibrahim felt so safe that he fell asleep in the heat of the day under a tree before waking up and pursuing his journey. Sleep was always a moment of great vulnerability for commanders on both sides, and this was a mark of trust and confidence. When Nenekos brought him to the safety of his own camp, Ibrahim not only punished his bodyguards, he also recommended that Nenekos be given the title of bey, which was henceforth how he was known. Nenekos subsequently got much of the poor hilly country behind Patras to come over to the Turkish side.

Kolokotronis is said to have been so angered by the news of Nenekos's behavior that—very unusually—he ordered him to be killed, entrusting the deed to another man from his village, a kapetan called Athanasios Sayias. In fact, the assassin had good reasons to hesitate and did not carry out the killing until some months after the fighting had stopped and Capodistrias had proclaimed an amnesty for those villagers who had gone over to the Ottoman side. Afterward, the assassination of a bey, albeit a Christian one, is said to have elicited protests from Constantinople while Nenekos's relatives came after Sayias, his family, property, and associates, and their vendetta eventually forced him out of his village.

Nenekos's name has come down in modern Greek as a synonym for a turncoat or collaborator. It is a mark of the shift in sensibilities over the course of the war that what was originally regarded as customary behavior among the armatoles of western Greece—a constant shifting from one side to another—was by this point seen under the sign of nationalism as an unpardonable sin and the mark of a traitor. To be sure, Nenekos had never enjoyed the kind of regional power of an armatole and had always been dependent upon his Ottoman backers. It was precisely the precariousness of his power locally that explained the violence that made him so hated. Subsequent historians, when they have not passed silently over this episode, have explained it either in ethnic terms—Nenekos came from an Albanian-speaking village, so what else could one expect?—or else as a divine intervention that eased the mind of the sultan and prevented him from sending Kütahı Pasha's army into the Morea as well.[21]

The simpler explanation is socioeconomic: submission was a way for the farming populations furthest removed from the reach of the Greek warlords to gain a measure of security in a terrifying situation. They could thereby ensure that Ottoman or Egyptian soldiers did not come and enslave their families, and they could continue to cultivate their crops and pasture their herds. Some resisted the option and moved away but they tended to be those with the resources to do so. Skeptics questioned whether the Ottoman side could be trusted to honor the terms of submission, remembering how the Greeks had treated the Muslims back in the first year of the uprising and fearing revenge. But that threat of betrayal—the glimmering perhaps of an uneasy conscience—seemed much less pressing to many villagers than the fear of immediate retribution if they did not give in.

Viewed from the peasants' perspective—especially those in the defenseless farming lowlands along the shoreline—submission also offered release from the endless infighting of the Greek chieftains. This fighting had been at their expense, after all, because the taxes that the Greeks levied on their crops were effectively the only revenues available in the Morea to the government and its forces. In fact, these revenues were so precious they were being demanded twice. In the early spring, the government would auction off the tax-farming rights, collecting money from the magnate families who paid for them. Come harvesttime, however, Kolokotronis's men would ignore these arrangements and help themselves. Kolokotronis could claim his troops "protected the people from plundering and raids," but his soldiers were often perceived to be among the plunderers. So too were the notables. Kanellos Deliyannis warned the villagers in his district at one point to hand over the crops to his "representatives": "Don't make the least resistance," he threatened them in a letter, or they should be prepared to bear the consequences. But his letter then continued almost plaintively: "I hope that you feel that we are fellow countrymen and neighbors, and we are not Americans or Chinese!" It is in such throwaway remarks that we discern the enormous gulf that had opened up between the landowners and the peasants, and the alienation and resentment Greek villagers felt after six years of war toward those who were their supposed leaders. It had flared up once—on Dimitrios Ypsilantis's arrival in the Peloponnese back in the summer of 1821; now, six years later, it was flaring up again, and this time it was leading them to surrender to Ibrahim Pasha.[22]

Kolokotronis and his chieftains were deeply worried at this unprecedented situation and not sure how to respond. In the mountains of northwestern Peloponnese, they reported, "the people have reached a state of the utmost despair." With the Egyptians threatening Kalavryta, even monks in the monastery of Mega Spilaio were thinking of going over to the Ottomans. Villages from Patras to Vostitsa along the coast "had submitted shamefully to the enemy" and more threatened to follow: "The Peloponnese, brothers, runs the most extreme and shameful danger, and I do not see how once that goes there will be a Greece any longer." But from the government, or what was left of it, no help was forthcoming. In Nafplion the fighting with Grivas had worsened and the government's power anyway no longer extended much beyond the safety of the islet of the Bourtzi, from where it helplessly watched the disarray in the town.[23]

Kolokotronis tried sending an ultimatum to the villages that had gone over to the Porte, threatening force if they persisted, and claiming he had some 5,000 men up in the mountains. It changed nothing: the Egyptians were a greater threat than he was. The wave of submissions started to spread down the west coast, accelerating after Ibrahim released captives and offered to free villages, if they surrendered, from the forcible conscription he was proposing to introduce. When Kolokotronis's men passed through the areas they wanted to reclaim, they were met with a wall of suspicion. "There is no longer any trust," wrote the Kalavryta chieftain, Vasilios Petimezas. "They tell us one thing and think another . . . What's the point when we don't know who is loyal [to us] and who are pro-Turk?" He wanted Kolokotronis to come quickly so they could begin the work of persuasion "with fire and sword."[24]

By July, Kolokotronis realized it was actually becoming dangerous for him to remain in the northwest. He brought in some reliable men from his own region of Karytaina, made a couple of arrests for dealing with the enemy, and even went so far as to hang a fellow Greek suspected of spying on his movements for Ibrahim; the dead man was left with a placard around his neck as a warning and only later buried by the Egyptians. Kolokotronis sent two other Greek suspects to the monks of the Mega Spilaio with orders that they too were to be hanged—evidently in an effort to compromise them in the eyes of the Egyptians—but the monks successfully pleaded not to be forced to do this. These events indicated the depth of the social and political crisis facing the region, for most Greeks in the war generally hesitated to take the lives of other Greeks, however extreme the circumstances. Beatings, torture, imprisonment were common but killing in cold blood was not, and those who killed readily—such as Grivas and Gouras—were not only feared but despised. Assassinations were not unknown but they were fairly rare and it was no mark of honor to have ordered one. So Kolokotronis's very public execution of a fellow Greek and his order to kill Nenekos marked how precarious the situation had come to seem.[25]

Lack of funds had always made it difficult for the Greek commanders to keep men in the field: they would leave when they felt they needed to protect their families, and chiefs could never be sure how many would stay and fight. As Kolokotronis's men slipped away from him, the force assembled by Deli Ahmed in Patras, supplemented by Nenekos's bands, moved round the coast of the Gulf of Corinth to the town of Vostitsa to guard the currant harvest. The Greek government irregulars advanced to the heights above the vineyards but they were powerless against the Egyptian cavalry and feared to descend. Another major source of food and income had now been cut off from them. When the submissions spread down into Messenia in the south, Kolokotronis decided to move there to try to make contact with the Mani, keep an eye on the Egyptian army, and above all boost the morale of the peasantry.

The Mani peninsula was the only place where the Egyptians had been checked. Ibrahim had mounted two expeditions to conquer it but was forced back each time without getting very far. He had tried negotiating with Petros Mavromihalis but so far the bey had managed to hold out. He had also tried to employ a rival chieftain to persuade the Maniots to surrender to him; but the traitor was killed and the Mani remained, along with the Argolid, the only area of the Peloponnese not under his sway. In October 1826 its chieftains sent a triumphant letter to the government in Nafplion, vaunting the success of "the Spartans"—as they called themselves—in holding off the Egyptian army.[26] That done, the Maniots reverted to their predatory ways, beginning their own summer raids again in 1827 into the vineyards, olive groves, and fig trees of the lowlands. A camp above the Messenian plain had been set up on the instructions of Kolokotronis, and his nephew, Nikitaras—one of the most experienced chieftains of the uprising—reported from there that the villagers needed protection from the Maniot threat whose unruly violence might end up driving them into the hands of the Egyptians.

But Ibrahim was on his way to the Mani too, and contemplating a new and highly disturbing means of persuasion. On August 13 the first reports reached Kolokotronis that Ibrahim planned to force the peasants of Messenia to pledge loyalty to him by threatening to burn or uproot their orchards. Some Greek prisoners who had escaped from the Egyptian camp told Nikitaras's men that a large quantity of axes had arrived, with which Ibrahim's soldiers were planning to fell all the trees in the Gulf of Messenia. The pasha was clearly in a hurry to crush the region so that he could get on with embarking his troops for his long-deferred attack on Hydra and Spetses, the operation that would likely end the war completely before the end of autumn.[27]

Arriving at Nikitaras's encampment, near the ruins of ancient Thouria, Kolokotronis was shocked to find things "in a state of extreme paralysis." It was not the men's fault: the so-called government, which no longer bothered to reply to his letters, had left them bereft. The peasants were in a state of despair, he wrote, and reduced to eating grass; he would not have believed it unless he had seen it himself. Watching the Egyptians plundering their harvest, the peasants were fearful of what was to come, and only the presence of Nikitaras prevented them from giving up the struggle completely. Kolokotronis himself was beset by worries, of the civilian population giving in, the government giving up, and perhaps worst of all, the prospect—reliably reported to him by escapees from the Egyptians and backed up by intelligence from Alexandria—of the coming attack on Hydra and Nafplion. For as he and everyone else knew, the Greeks could no longer stop the enemy: the government had run out of money, while the Rumeliot bands were about to head north and would not reinforce the islands. What guarantee was there that Kolokotronis's detested rival, Grivas, would not come to some arrangement and hand the Palamidi at Nafplion over to Ibrahim and end the struggle once and for all? At that point all would be lost—as it had been back in 1770.[28]

On September 22, the Egyptian commander, who was stationed only a few miles away from the Greek camp in the Messenian plain, issued a warning to the village headmen there. He had been sent by Ibrahim, he proclaimed, to "cut down, burn and make disappear all your trees that are useful to you and necessary for your sustenance." The only remedy for the "poor people" to avoid this destruction was "to resign from this nonsense of a rebellion" and, as others had done, to declare their willingness to submit to the pasha. A counter-proclamation from "the Inhabitants of the Districts of Messenia" breathed defiance, but it is not clear who wrote it, still less whether anyone in the region saw it.[29] One suspects that the document was primarily for foreign consumption.

Admiral Codrington of the British navy had sailed into the region as part of a growing international presence, and Kolokotronis contacted him in order to tell him about the Egyptian threat and the Messenians' response. But the Egyptians were already chopping down trees and setting fire to what was left, and the smoke was rising above the olive groves and figs around Kalamata. A year later, a French officer made his way through the devastated fields: "One saw nothing but the charred roots of olive trees; all the trees had been set on fire; not even the shrubs and bushes had been spared. We could not take a single step without the bottom of our trousers being dirtied." There were still "layers of ash and the burned olive trees" along the road out of Methoni.[30] Kolokotronis was not easily shocked but he was taken aback by a crime that no previous invader had ever stooped to: all of them, he protested, had respected the fruit groves as "holy." His government said nothing; only the British signaled their concern.

A mark of that concern was the arrival of the familiar figure of

Captain Hamilton, who anchored HMS *Cambrian* in the Gulf of Messenia. Hamilton wanted to see for himself what was happening but he also had important new information that he wanted to pass on to the Greeks. A Russian fleet had recently arrived off Navarino to join Codrington's force, and they were expecting the return of a French squadron any day as well. The three fleets had apparently received instructions from their capitals to end the Egyptian campaign in the Morea for good. Kolokotronis must have been still contemplating the implications of this remarkable news when five days later, on October 9, an even more extraordinary message reached him from his nephew Nikitaras, who was with the Maniot chieftains at Almyros along the coast. Having heard powerful and sustained gunfire the previous day, October 8 (October 20, NS), they had received reports of a tremendous battle between the allied fleet and the Ottomans. The din was so great it had carried some thirty miles and it had been so fierce "that the mind of man cannot measure the cannonades, neither measure it nor figure out how many cannon were firing each minute." From what Nikitaras had heard, the enemy fleet had been destroyed. "Rejoice," he wrote to Kolokotronis. "For today our much-suffering beloved fatherland Greece has risen and its unbearable woes are at an end." It was scarcely believable but it was true. An allied fleet had sailed into the Bay of Navarino, a fierce battle had taken place, and in the space of a single afternoon the Ottoman and Egyptian fleets had been annihilated.[31]

NAVARINO:
THE FORCE OF THINGS

*Are we to surrender the pleasing hopes of seeing improvement in
the moral and intellectual condition of Man? The events in
Naples and Piedmont cast a gloomy cloud over that hope: and
Spain and Portugal are not beyond jeopardy. And what are we to
think of the Northern triumvirate, arming their nations to dictate despotisms to the rest of the world? . . . And what of the
poor Greeks, and their small chance of amelioration even if the
hypocritical Autocrat should take them under the iron cover of
his Ukazes. Would this be lighter or safer than that of the Turks?
These, my dear friend, are speculations for the new generation . . .
Yet I will not die without a hope that light and liberty are on
steady advance . . . The flames kindled on 4th of July 1776 have
spread over too much of the globe to be extinguished by the
feeble engines of despotism.*

> Thomas Jefferson to John Quincy
> Adams, September 12, 1821[1]

*[Non-intervention] is a metaphysical word, and a political one,
meaning more or less the same thing as intervention.*

> Charles Maurice de Talleyrand-Périgord, 1832[2]

Early in the Greek uprising, a British diplomat had hazarded a prediction:
the Russians would come in, Ali Pasha would triumph, and "the Turkish
power in every part of Greece will be annihilated." After all that, he went
on, looking further ahead, Greece would end up as an independent state

under the guarantee of "all the Powers of Europe," with the Russian foreign minister Count Capodistrias at the helm.[3] Six years later, he appeared to have been wrong on all counts. The Russians had not declared war, Ali Pasha was dead, and Sultan Mahmud II's troops had not only retained control of the Balkans as far south as Athens and the Gulf of Corinth but had virtually reconquered the Peloponnese.

As for Capodistrias, who had rebuffed the emissaries of the Etaireia when they had come knocking, his efforts to reconcile his private devotion to his homeland with total loyalty to the czar, his master, had failed. The Greek uprising had undermined his position and he had fallen victim to the enmity of Prince Metternich. He left St. Petersburg in 1822, beset by the anxiety that the czar no longer confided in him, and for many months he tried in vain to clarify where he stood in his master's estimation. A cosmopolitan man and a believer in enlightened reform, sensitive, pious and thwarted in love, he went into semi-retirement in Geneva. There he lived on a strict budget in rented rooms with a single servant, working behind the scenes to support victims of the war. Occasionally, he would be seen in salon society, his conversation polished and serious as befitted a man of wide reading, enchanting ambassadors and savants, enjoying the company of the great German polymath Alexander von Humboldt or the young French poetess of the Restoration, Delphine Gay.[4]

Yet the former Russian foreign minister remained confident in the ultimate triumph of the Greek cause. In 1826 Capodistrias was in Paris to see his doctor when the news arrived that Mesolonghi had fallen. He had just settled into his hotel, the fashionable Hotel de Douvres on the rue de la Paix, when he was notified that he had a visitor; to his astonishment, it was none other than the French foreign minister. He had met the Baron de Damas only once, more than a decade earlier when the baron had been in the Russian service fighting Napoleon. Since then he had married and put on weight, and Capodistrias, slim and ascetic, did not recognize him. When the foreign minister said he wanted to talk about Greece, Capodistrias protested: he was out of touch, he had no idea what European statesmen were currently thinking, and he could do no more than "improvise a nice story about politics" (*improviser un roman politique*). "Yes," rejoined the baron, "but you know more about Greece than anyone else . . . Your views on the actual state of Greece and how to save it from misery would be useful." So Capodistrias consented, in his words, to "improvise":

> The *Cabinets* want above all to preserve general peace and the European
> Alliance, hence they are unanimous in their determination not to inter-
> vene save by negotiation to save Christians from destruction or apostasy,
> to procure some years of life to the Ottoman Empire, to remain united
> against revolution and disturbance. Admitting all this, the facts show, as
> I said in 1821: *either* the Turks triumph, *or* the Greeks win, *or* disorder is
> prolonged. In *each* case, the progressive decadence and perhaps the col-
> lapse of the Ottoman Empire is to be expected. Conciliation between
> Turks and Greeks is no longer possible—the infection will spread to
> Dacia, Serbia and other Slav populations. The *only possible* assumption
> is that they cannot now live together.[5]

He left the minister to draw his own conclusions, but with another visitor
a few days later he was more explicit: the European powers should declare
Greece to be separated de facto from the Ottoman Empire and accept that
granting independence to the Greeks was now the only means by which
to bring peace to the entire region. Europe's cabinets, he told another
official at about the same time, might reject this idea, but "the force of
things" (*la force des choses*) would lead it to prevail. He was, in effect,
suggesting that the European powers would be obliged to intervene, just
as a year and a half later—at the battle of Navarino—they did. But for
that to happen, a sea change had first to take place in one of the most
basic assumptions of the continent's diplomacy: that the intervention of
the Great Powers was needed, not to suppress revolution but to support it.[6]

Near the end of the twentieth century, the so-called right to intervene
(later recast as the responsibility to protect) emerged in international
diplomacy in connection with humanitarian relief. But it had started
out, in the years after 1815, as an instrument of counterrevolution that
the representatives of Austria, Russia, and Prussia agreed might be
needed to preserve the peace. "All our faculties should be directed,"
Czar Alexander had confided to a British observer at the Congress of
Troppau in October 1820, "to counteract and oppose that fatal spirit
which was making such rapid progress in Europe, and to settle upon
some principle of common action and conduct with regard to it, so that

military revolution and the machinations of occult sects and incendiaries should be arrested and paralyzed."[7] To nervous defenders of the Restoration trouble was brewing everywhere, although in the face of overwhelming force most uprisings were suppressed quickly and without great difficulty. In March 1821, the Austrians quelled a constitutionalist rebellion in Piedmont and suppressed the more serious revolt in the Kingdom of the Two Sicilies as well, restoring the Bourbon king Ferdinand to his throne in Naples. Ottoman forces had defeated Alexandros Ypsilantis and his men in Moldavia by the end of June that year, the Great Powers standing back to allow the sultan to reclaim his territories. After the summer of 1821, only the constitutionalists in Spain—alongside the rebels in Greece—were left to trouble the Holy Alliance in Europe.

The ongoing fighting of independence movements in Spanish America raised the question of whether the Holy Alliance should intervene there too.[8] The alternative—doing nothing—seemed inadequate: the Spanish ambassador in London warned in 1822 that granting international recognition to the new republics of the western hemisphere would mean the unveiling of "a great truth: there would appear in the future an *American* interest absolutely divergent from the *European* interest—an interest which would begin to ignore openly the principles of public law and even certain rules of convenience and decorum which have hitherto been respected by all civilized nations."[9] The ambassador's French colleague, none other at this time than the man of letters François-René de Chateaubriand, echoed the thought: "If the New World ever becomes entirely republican, the monarchies of the Old World will perish."[10] Could armed action by the Holy Alliance avert this frightful possibility? Chateaubriand was determined to try. Appointed minister of foreign affairs in Paris at the end of 1822, he engineered a successful French military intervention into the Iberian peninsula on behalf of the Bourbon monarchy. At the same time, he plotted a naval expedition that would place Bourbon princelings upon the thrones of the new states of South America to ward off the spread of republicanism.

To the Americans in the north, already in possession of their own independent republic, such conservative interventionism was deeply worrying. Washington's negotiations with Spain for Florida and the Texas borderlands, its fear of a Russian push southward from Alaska toward California, and above all the very real prospect of an invasion of the Spanish colonies by the Holy Alliance, all prompted President Monroe to inform Congress in the spring of 1822 that it was time to grant recognition to the new states of South America: the United States should preserve "perfect neutrality" in the dispute between them and their mother country, Spain, while accepting that they now existed "in the full enjoyment of their independence."[11] At the end of 1823, some months after the French invasion of Spain, Monroe famously warned Europe that the independence won by the free states of the Americas was not to be reversed by any future colonization. But this strong liberal endorsement of the principle of *nonintervention* was made amid the powerfully philhellenic climate of the eastern seaboard, which obliged the president to say something about the reciprocal question of a possible American *intervention* in the conflict in Ottoman Europe as well. Juxtaposed with Monroe's comments on principle was thus a much more specific statement on Greece:

> A strong hope has been long entertained, founded on the heroic struggle of the Greeks, that they would succeed in their contest and resume their equal station among the nations of the earth. It is believed that the whole civilized world takes a deep interest in their welfare. Although no power has declared in their favor, yet none according to our information has taken part against them. Their cause and their name have protected them from dangers which might ere this have overwhelmed any other people. The ordinary calculations of interest and of acquisition with a view to aggrandizement, which mingle so much in the transactions of nations, seem to have had no effect in regard to them. From the facts which have come to our knowledge there is good cause to believe that their enemy has lost forever all dominion over them; that Greece will become again an independent nation. That she may obtain that rank is the object of our most ardent wishes.

This is the often forgotten Greek dimension of the Monroe Doctrine—a justification as much as a warning. It was a formulation that carefully trod a middle path between Secretary of State John Adams's desire to keep out of Greece and Monroe's own more activist inclinations; yet nothing could hide its renunciation of American intervention in Europe. As Monroe said, quite explicitly: "In the wars of the European powers in matters relating to themselves we have never taken any part, nor does it comport with our policy to do so." It was a statement to keep the philhellenes at bay.

The Monroe Doctrine served to set an imaginary line between Europe and the Americas; it stated that the political norms applicable in one hemisphere were inapplicable in the other. Some commentators disagreed, however, because they thought the cause of freedom was universal and demanded international action in both. The Abbé de Pradt was a widely read and prolific French pamphleteer for whom (in the barbed words of a critic) "rest was exhausting and obscurity a torment." He had reinvented himself as a foreign-policy pundit after a checkered career under Napoleon and the Bourbons, and he was increasingly ardent in his support for the Greeks.[12] In his 1825 *Vrai Système de l'Europe, relativement à l'Amérique et à la Grèce,* he argued that the Americas were paving the way for a republican future globally, while the Greeks were fighting for the principle to triumph in Europe. The latter struggle was thus a continuation of the one in South America but harder because the Greeks enjoyed none of the compensations of distance from Europe that the American revolutions had enjoyed.[13] De Pradt's works circulated widely; Jefferson and Monroe were among those reading him. But in Europe his was not the voice the Greeks needed. His republicanism might appeal to Americans, but it was an irrelevance to the Greeks themselves. Worse, it made him dangerously radical in conservative eyes and was therefore a poor instrument for changing the direction of the continent's diplomacy.

A very different, and more potent, kind of argument for intervention on the Greeks' behalf was being made at the same time by a far more prominent figure—none other than Chateaubriand himself. Having served Louis XVIII as minister of foreign affairs between 1822 and 1824, Chateaubriand had been suddenly dismissed and—as we saw earlier—he had then gone into the opposition, identifying himself with the Greek cause. Like de Pradt, he took the Americas very seriously: he was, after all, the author of that phenomenal bestseller of early Romanticism, the novel *Atala*—subtitled "the loves of two savages in the desert"—that was set in the Southern states and very loosely based on his own experiences when he had traveled through the United States as a young man. Unlike de Pradt, however, Chateaubriand was a confirmed monarchist. Unlike him, too, he was knowledgeable about Greece, having crossed the Peloponnese in 1806 and been appalled by the contemptuous way the Turkish beys treated the Greek peasantry and by the ruined state of the country. "Around me there were tombs, silence, destruction, death," he had written in his famous *Itinéraire*, "where some Greek sailors slept without cares or dreams on the ruins of Greece." His remarkable travelogue, a reverie of Romantic melancholia, had inspired Byron to make his own journey to the region; two decades later, Byron's death contributed to awakening Chateaubriand's slumbering philhellenism. He was by temperament a man of action and the same energy he had devoted to getting France to march into Spain he now dedicated to sending it into war for the Greeks. In his *Note sur la Grèce*—perhaps the most fascinating political text published by any philhellene in those years—Chateaubriand made the interventionist case for conservatives.[14]

A monarchist but not an unthinking one, Chateaubriand started out with a statement of the challenge facing royalty across the continent after the French Revolution. Europe's task, he wrote, was to respond to what he called "the greatest political discovery of the last century," namely the emergence of the "representative republic" in the United States. "The formation of this republic has resolved a problem previously thought insoluble": the possibility for several million people to exist in society under popular institutions. For Chateaubriand, this required European monarchy to prove it could adapt to the new age of representative government. "If one tries to return to the past, then perhaps after a century all Europe will be republican or else have fallen into military despotism." His reflections on the future of an imminently independent Greece merged here with his opposition to Louis XVIII. For Chateaubriand, if a republican world was to be avoided it was more important than ever to turn despotisms into properly functioning modern monarchies.[15]

The problem in Greece, the *Note* argues, is precisely that it was impossible for the Ottoman sultan to make this transformation. First, he recognized no principle of sovereignty as it would be understood by Europeans; second, he refused to give his Christian subjects their rights. Thus he lay outside what contemporaries called "the political system of Europe." In Naples and Spain, Chateaubriand argued, men had risen against their legitimate rulers and so the Holy Alliance had been justified in acting against the insurgents. The Greek cause was quite different because it was not really revolutionary at all but the "legitimate" bid of a people against a thoroughgoing despotism. In short, Chateaubriand was adopting and popularizing a political argument that had long been promoted by the less radical elements in and around the Etaireia—men like Archbishop Ignatios and the Mavrokordatos circle. Such men understood that after Napoleon's defeat, the Holy Alliance had emerged around the principle of legitimacy and that in stigmatizing revolution, the alliance's defenders rooted their interventionism in the idea of a right to rule. But the right to rule rested on more than mere authority: legitimacy had to be sanctioned, as one Russian diplomat put it, "by the exercise of power." A monarchy sensitive to the needs of its subjects was for many of them the best form of polity, whereas a despotism by its nature could never be legitimate. Capodistrias and his secretary, the Greek-Russian diplomat Alexander Stourdza, had been arguing since 1821 that because the sultan governed his Christian subjects tyrannically and failed to secure their rights to life and property, he had forfeited his own right to be considered their legitimate ruler. And as they well knew, a despotism that trampled on the rights of Christians posed a specific problem for the rulers of the Holy Alliance, with its avowed if vague Christian penumbra.[16]

This way of conceptualizing what was at stake in the eastern Mediterranean weakened conservative opposition to intervening. Chateaubriand's "Christianism" allowed monarchists and republicans to coalesce around a culturalist argument, based on an attitude of Christian solidarity, a mythical yearning for the spirit of the Crusades, and a critique of the supposed civilizational deficiencies of the Ottoman polity that had deep roots in European attitudes to Islam. It took the principle of legitimacy that conservatives had relied upon to defend the Restoration of the Bourbons after Napoleon and turned it around into an attack on the Ottoman polity.

Chateaubriand's *Note* was an important intervention in an unprecedentedly public discussion. Liberals deserved the credit for weaponizing the power of opinion. "There is *one empire* which they can never hope to subdue—THE EMPIRE OF OPINION," proclaimed a British philhellene in an open letter in 1823. De Pradt too recognized "*publicité*" as the new force in international affairs. But what Chateaubriand's involvement showed was that support for intervention on the side of the Greeks was growing across the political spectrum, bringing together radicals calling for republicanism, liberals demanding constitutions, and voices such as Chateaubriand's demanding solidarity with Christians threatened by non-European despots. It comes as no surprise that the British foreign secretary George Canning worried that the next war in Europe would be one "not of armies but of opinions." Canning likened the handling of British foreign policy to someone being forced to make their way down a raging torrent, sometimes compelled to jump one way across the stream, sometimes the other. The implication was that the evocation of principle was unhelpful: sometimes Britain's interest might dictate following one principle, sometimes another.[17]

Canning, who had become foreign secretary in September 1822, was at the heart of the reorientation of European diplomacy that was about to take place, but he was not the man to make a theoretical case on first principles for anything. When, in March 1823, Britain became the first Great Power to recognize the Greeks as belligerents and Metternich protested, Canning played down the implications: belligerency, he remarked, "was not so much a principle as a fact." But Canning's mistrust of principles did not mean he lacked a purpose. His own ultimate goal was understated but clear—the breakup of the Holy Alliance—and the Greek cause was a means to achieve that. What he believed was that ending the alliance as a force in politics could not be done quickly nor in a way that ended up strengthening Russia, Britain's enemy in the eyes of many of his colleagues in government. In 1824 Canning declared publicly his willingness to offer British mediation to settle the Greek conflict if the other European powers approved. But although there were signs earlier that privately he had some sympathy for the Greeks, Canning was resolved to avoid the use of force and he was not prepared to sacrifice British interests or prestige for a hopeless cause.[18]

The key figure in all this was the czar, whose creation the Holy Alliance was and whose support underpinned it. Yet at the same time it was Russia that was the power most likely to go to war with the Ottoman Empire, and without it no intervention on the Greek side was conceivable. Allowing a unilateral Russian intervention on behalf of the Greeks was a nonstarter for the rest of Europe since its likely outcome—an extension of Russian rule into the Danubian Principalities and of its influence down into the Morea—would have represented a profound threat to the balance of power. Fortunately for the noninterventionists, Czar Alexander's conservatism had remained uppermost in 1821. "Nothing," he told Chateaubriand at the Congress of Verona in October 1822, "would have appeared more in my interest, in that of my people, in the opinion of my country, than a religious war against Turkey; but I believed I saw, in the troubles in the Peloponnese, the mark of revolution and so I held back."[19] But by 1823 the czar was privately wavering. In 1824 he tried to satisfy both principles—conservatism and Christian solidarity—by proposing to the other powers that they urge the sultan to carve out of the Greek lands three huge autonomous principalities, which would remain under Ottoman rule and be guaranteed by the European powers. No one liked the idea. The other Europeans suspected an arrangement that might give the Russians even more influence in the Balkans than they already possessed. The Ottoman Empire was appalled at the idea of giving autonomy to a territory much larger than the one the Greek insurgents actually controlled. The Greeks themselves were disappointed that the czar would be content with an arrangement short of independence, and for the first time they began to wonder whether Russia was really destined to be their European protector. More out of mischief than anything else, it was Metternich who suggested the alternative of creating a small sovereign and independent Greek state—the first time that any European statesman had openly come out in favor of such a solution. Although Metternich cannot have meant it to be taken seriously, it presaged further changes ahead and it marked, if only formally, the first time the Holy Alliance had countenanced such a radical break with their precious principle of legitimacy. None of these suggestions went anywhere because none envisaged any kind of intervention to back them up and without the threat of force, Sultan Mahmud was never going to make concessions. Only the czar was willing to contemplate war, a prospect that terrified his partners.

Then in 1825 the Egyptians had invaded the Morea. Terrified by the speed of Ibrahim's advance, the Greek chieftains in the Peloponnese appealed to London to mediate with the sultan for them: George Canning had the opening he sought and sent his cousin, Stratford Canning, to Constantinople as ambassador. On his way to the Ottoman capital at the start of 1826, Canning moored off Hydra in order to meet with Mavrokordatos, who came aboard his ship for a conversation in which they discussed the idea of turning the Morea and the islands into a single tributary state of the empire, a goal that fell far short of independence. Their informal exchange turned out to be highly consequential: not only did it signal the Greeks' growing orientation toward the British, an orientation already anticipated by the two loans, but without the conversation between the two men, the Holy Alliance might have remained intact and there would have been no Anglo-Russian negotiations, no Protocol of St. Petersburg that spring, no Treaty of London, and no battle of Navarino. It was immediately after this meeting that Stratford Canning sailed on to the depopulated island of Psara and came face-to-face, as he wrote in his memoirs, with the "cruel evidence of what war is when kindled by the antipathies of race and creed."[20]

In taking this initiative, George Canning had been prompted by secret intelligence of a radical change of heart on the part of the czar in St. Petersburg—intelligence that came from an unimpeachable source: the czar himself. For some time Alexander had been growing impatient with Metternich's endless reasons for doing nothing, and the news that the Greeks had appealed directly to the British must have come as an unwelcome surprise to him: it was essential to his prestige that Russia should be involved in any discussions about Greece's future. In the summer of 1825, therefore, he quietly resolved to accept Canning's invitation of a joint Anglo-Russian mediation on behalf of the Greeks.

Any shift in Russian diplomacy away from the Austrians—after a decade of the closest cooperation—was a matter of such delicacy and secrecy, however, that the czar decided it had to be handled in a very special way. Haughty and smart, witty and extremely discreet, Dorothea Lieven was the wife of Count Christoph von Lieven, the long-serving Russian minister in London. She had been one of the Lady Patronesses of the most exclusive club in Regency high society, Almack's, where she had supposedly introduced the waltz into England; she had been romantically involved with Metternich, and she was a confidante of Lord Castlereagh and Earl Grey. It was to this remarkable woman and not her husband that the czar now confided "the great secret." She had been visiting Russia and was about to return to England when the foreign minister Count Nesselrode told her he had an urgent message to deliver to her before she left. When she called on him on the morning of her departure, he gave her "as minister to minister" a verbatim account of a conversation he had had the previous evening with the czar. The gist of it was that if the British wished to propose a partnership with Russia for the purpose of "establishing in the East an order of things conformable to the interest of Europe and to the laws of religion and humanity," it would be listened to sympathetically. Why had the czar chosen her?

Lieven asked. "A woman," Nesselrode went on, "knows how to make people speak and this is precisely why the Emperor considers you have an opportunity." When she requested instructions in writing, Nesselrode went to his desk and handed her a note that read simply: "Believe all the bearer tells you."[21] Back in England, she delivered the message, while her husband showed Canning dispatches that illuminated the tension between Czar Alexander and Metternich. He also confided to Canning that Russian intelligence indicated Ibrahim Pasha planned not only to defeat the Greeks but to deport them en masse into slavery in Egypt and replace the entire population with Muslims. This was the "Barbarization" project that preyed on Canning's mind and that he mentioned to his cousin some months later.[22]

Czar Alexander's sudden death from typhus in December 1825 did nothing to slow the emerging partnership between Britain and Russia. His successor, Nicholas I, was supportive and the following April the two powers signed the Protocol of St. Petersburg, which has been described as the first formal step toward the establishment of an independent Greece: this empowered Britain, with Russian backing, to suggest to the Porte a settlement in which Greece would become an autonomous but vassal state of the empire. Metternich was appalled and wondered whether this meant the British would now accept mediation in Ireland. But a new lineup of interventionist powers was emerging. For the Russians, this partnership had the merit of allowing them to act on behalf of Orthodoxy; for the British, it separated Russia off from the Holy Alliance; and for the French, who joined later in the year, it raised the prospect of the kind of adventure abroad that its monarchy craved. The main problem with the protocol, as the Russians themselves pointed out, was that it contained no enforcement mechanism. Mediation was all very well as an idea, but what if it was rejected by the Porte? The British and French already had squadrons in the Levant, and thus in September 1826 they came around to the idea of a naval deterrent, establishing a joint fleet that would be powerful enough to cut Ibrahim's army off from Egypt if necessary. The British sent Admiral Sir Edward Codrington into the Mediterranean; the French admiral Henri de Rigny was already there and the Russians prepared their fleet to sail. An early experiment in the politics of deterrence was about to begin.

Capodistrias was also increasingly involved and being drawn out of his reluctant retirement. He had attended a funeral service for

Alexander I and was on his way to meet his successor, Czar Nicholas I, in Russia in the spring of 1827 when he learned that the national assembly at Troezen had invited him to become president of Greece. The invitation transformed the nature of his trip entirely and at the same time galvanized the Russians, who could now anticipate their former foreign minister being placed in charge of Greece's fortunes. Shortly afterward came the news that the two powers who had signed the Procotol of St. Petersburg had been joined by the French and agreed to a more binding commitment: under the Treaty of London, signed in the summer of 1827, Britain, France, and Russia pledged to obtain the autonomy of Greece under the sultan's suzerainty, without going to war. They would ask both sides to consent to an armistice and negotiations that would then take place in Constantinople; one important change from the protocol was the stipulation that these negotiations would take place not with the Ottoman side alone but with the Greeks in attendance as well, something that greatly lessened the chances of the sultan's acceptance. The treaty stipulated too that if the Turks refused mediation—the assumption was that the Greeks would accept, since they had already requested British mediation on such terms—the navies of the three powers would intervene and prevent them continuing to wage war on the Greeks by measures short of hostilities. It was the inevitable diplomatic fudge—designed to satisfy both the British and French, who were determined to avoid a war, and the Russians, who insisted on some kind of credible threat. Like most such arrangements, the treaty left it to the future—and to others—to clarify what it would all mean in practice.

Capodistrias was distressed that the Treaty of London envisaged Greece as nothing more than an autonomous part of the Ottoman Empire. On the other hand, most observers saw this as a technicality: independence was surely the inevitable outcome and in the course of long conversations with the new czar, Capodistrias came around to this view too. Czar Nicholas was a different man from his more mystical predecessor, less committed to the old alliances in Europe and keener on war; indeed, he told Capodistrias that he regarded it as inescapable. Well satisfied by his visit, Capodistrias left St. Petersburg to make the rounds of the other European capitals for support and funds, while the Russians dispatched a naval force from the Baltic base of Kronstadt. Rousing words from the czar made it unmistakably clear to the sailors that war was in the offing. What most of them did not know was where they would be going: were they sailing across the Atlantic to help regain the South American colonies for Spain or into the Mediterranean to fight the Turks? When they reached Portsmouth in England, they realized it was the latter. In the following months, while Capodistrias pursued his diplomatic offensive in Europe, his fate and that of the small country he had been chosen to lead were determined at sea.

In Constantinople, the three ambassadors duly asked the Porte if the Ottomans would respect the proposed armistice, and the sultan predictably refused to admit even their right to become involved in his affairs. When a similar demand was made of the Greek government a few days later, it was equally predictably accepted. The situation envisaged in the treaty had thus come about and it fell to the admirals of the British, French, and Russian squadrons to enforce compliance upon the Ottoman side. The architect of this new situation, George Canning, died unexpectedly at only fifty-seven—after the shortest term in office of any British prime minister (119 days)—on August 8, 1827. Yet it made little difference: the revolution in European diplomacy, which this brilliant man had made it his mission to accomplish since becoming foreign secretary nearly five years earlier, reached its culmination after his death in the shape of the allied fleets now sailing into the eastern Mediterranean.

The three naval commanders enjoyed a good working relationship. The Frenchman, Henri de Rigny, the most familiar with the Levant, had fought on land and sea under Napoleon and had been in command of the French squadron in the Aegean since 1822. The Russian admiral— Lodewijk Sigismund Vincent Gustaaf Reichsgraf van Heiden—was in fact an affable Dutchman who had been born in the poor landlocked province of Drenthe and served the czars at sea for over thirty years. Sir Edward Codrington was the most senior of the three—he had entered the Royal Navy more than forty years earlier—and he was also a kind of intermediary, as the French and Russians had been on uneasy terms ever since the end of the Napoleonic Wars and the relationship of their two commanders was a delicate one. Thus they agreed Codrington should be in overall command: his sociable personality combined with the respect he enjoyed and expressed for his colleagues would make for surprisingly unified operations. Codrington liked de Rigny but found him wanting in patience; the Russian count Heiden, on the other hand, Codrington regarded as "a straightforward sort of fellow."[23]

Their instructions from the diplomats were anything but clear. The initial guidance was to treat the Greeks as friends in the event of an Ottoman refusal to negotiate and to intercept supplies from Egypt and the Dardanelles. Yet the naval commanders had also been told to make sure such operations did not turn into outright conflict and to avoid the use of force. Policies of deterrence necessarily involve wishful thinking: the diplomats had left it to the admirals to determine when and if that wishful thinking should be replaced by action. And they had done so with sufficient ambiguity that any hostilities that followed could be disavowed afterward if need be.

When he learned about the signing of the Treaty of London, Admiral Codrington's immediate concern was trying to end fighting among the Greeks so that some plausible provisional government survived for him and the diplomats to deal with. At the end of August 1827, however, he heard that the sultan had rejected the idea of an armistice and, a week later, that the Greek side had accepted it. The question now became how to enforce its provisions, above all upon Ibrahim and the Egyptian army in the Morea, which was about to be reinforced by another large convoy. When news of the treaty reached Mehmed Ali in Egypt, the pasha had instantly understood two things. The first was that its provisions were extremely unclear, and the second was that the sultan was most unlikely to accept an armistice. As Mehmed Ali tried to explain to the British and French consuls, this meant conflict was likely since his son Ibrahim, as he told them, would faithfully carry out whatever the sultan ordered. Mehmed Ali was to spend the next months trying, subtly and in vain, to persuade the sultan that the Europeans were serious, but the Porte's line never changed, nor did its instructions to Ibrahim: to continue with his operations and to prepare his troops for the attack on Hydra that would end the war.[24]

The Egyptian troop convoy arrived in Methoni just as Codrington received his orders to "enforce the maintenance of an armistice by sea," and he determined to prevent further naval movements in or out of Ibrahim's camp. He told his captains they should "enter into friendly relations with the Greeks" and "intercept every supply of men, arms, etc., destined against Greece." This was to be done without fighting if possible, but "when all other means are exhausted, by cannon shot." Yet at this point, Codrington had only five vessels under his command and was not even sure where the French and Russian squadrons were. As for Ibrahim, he also knew about the treaty but in accordance with his own instructions, he was hoping to attack Hydra before he could be prevented. He nearly managed it. The Egyptian soldiers were mostly embarked from Methoni, and had just set off, when the arrival of de Rigny and the French forced them back to port.

Four days later, Ibrahim, Codrington, and de Rigny met at Navarino for talks in the pasha's tent overlooking the bay. After long, gem-studded *chibouks* (tobacco pipes) had been passed around, and cups of sweet coffee drunk, a lengthy conversation ensued, Codrington speaking mostly in French with Ibrahim's translator hard at work. It was courteous but to the point and it was Ibrahim who eventually gave ground, when he agreed to request new instructions from the sultan in Constantinople and his father in Alexandria. That would take some weeks, however, and in the meantime he committed to suspending his land and sea operations. Henry Codrington, who was serving on his father's flagship, has left a vivid account of this meeting. When Ibrahim started mocking the Greeks—saying "there never was a Greek worth anything"—Codrington retorted that he should not undervalue men he had gone to such lengths to conquer nor indeed his officers who had undertaken several campaigns against the Greeks without achieving their object. Ibrahim gave as good as he got, reminding his guests that although the European newspapers were always advertising his massacres, he had several hundred villages under his command in the Morea, "now very quiet and . . . fed and provided by him."[25]

Lord Cochrane and his tiny Greek fleet were still conducting operations up the west coast of Greece, however, and Ibrahim was keen to confront it and did not see why he should be prevented. In the interval, while everyone waited for word from the sultan, the allied blockading force temporarily dispersed and some of the British ships returned to Malta for supplies. Taking advantage of their absence, the Ottoman fleet sailed north in order to take on Cochrane. Codrington was furious at what he regarded as Ibrahim's breach of promise. He therefore chased the fleet down and insisted that it return to Navarino. Despite having only four ships against more than fifty, his threat to attack them had its effect and the fleet turned around. Codrington was delighted and seems to have concluded that a show of force had been enough to avert further conflict. Viscount Dudley, the British foreign secretary, sent him a private letter of congratulation. The Ottoman forces could justly have felt aggrieved that Codrington did not prevent the Greeks from attacking and destroying several of their vessels, yet from this moment onward the British admiral felt he could no longer trust Ibrahim. Codrington's thinking may have been influenced by the British high commissioner in the Ionian Islands, Sir Frederick Adam, a veteran of Waterloo, who wrote to him with some thought-provoking observations. It was fairly certain, wrote Adam, that the sultan intended to carry on the war by land against the Greeks. What use was a naval blockade if the coming months led the Greeks to be "exterminated," thereby negating the purpose of the treaty?[26]

After a four-month voyage, the Russian squadron joined up with Codrington off Zante on October 1, and the combined allied fleet assembled off Navarino. Codrington was clearly worried not only about communications with the Egyptian army but about their "laying waste to the country." He regarded the Egyptian advance into the plain of Kalamata as a further contravention of Ibrahim's commitment to him made the previous month. He sent Captain Hamilton off in the *Cambrian* to see if the destruction was continuing and he dispatched the *Dartmouth* into Navarino to deliver a stern letter to Ibrahim signed by the three admirals. They protested that his troops were marching through the Morea with "excessive violence . . . hastening to turn this country into a veritable desert." This, they insisted, was against the terms of their agreement to which he had pledged his word of honor. They warned Ibrahim that they no longer considered him covered by "the law of nations," and demanded an instant answer to the question of whether he would observe the terms of the treaty. The next day, Ibrahim's interpreter told them that as the pasha's movements "had been kept a profound secret," they could not forward the letter to him: Codrington naturally regarded this as a further lie. What he did not know but may have suspected was that the Porte had in fact ordered Ibrahim to ignore the allies.[27]

As Codrington was digesting this scarcely civil response, he received a dramatic report from Hamilton on the *Cambrian* who had just returned from meeting Kolokotronis's men. Hamilton told Codrington that he had no sooner entered the Gulf of Messenia than he had seen the "clouds of fire and smoke" that indicated the Egyptians' "work of devastation" was continuing. Entering the Greek camp, he had been shocked by the sight of the women and children who had fled the Egyptian onslaught, "dying every moment of absolute starvation and hardly any

having better food than boiled grass." Hamilton reckoned that if Ibrahim remained in Greece, "more than a third of its inhabitants will die of
absolute starvation."[28] As Hamilton was a level-headed officer who had
been in the Levant for some six years, and probably had greater insight
into the situation at this point than any other man in the allied fleet, his
views were taken very seriously by the admiral. Neither Hamilton nor
Codrington had entered the Aegean as philhellenes; but both, on the
evidence of what they saw, were gradually being brought around to an
interventionist position.

On that same day, October 6, the three admirals took the bold step
of deciding to enter the bay at Navarino with their entire fleet in order
to force Ibrahim to end his operations. It may have been de Rigny who
had the original idea but all three quickly agreed it was their best option.
They had, they considered, three choices before them: one was to try to
maintain the naval blockade of the Morea through the winter, which
would have been difficult since any storm might disperse their ships and
allow the Egyptians the chance to return to sea. Another was to keep the
fleet off Navarino, but this would still allow for Egyptian operations on
land, and since there was no good mooring along the coast the currents
and winds would constantly blow them off course. Third, they could
enter the bay itself, a course of action that might "without hostilities but
simply by the imposing presence of the squadrons, produce . . . the
desired object." Codrington believed and hoped that the mere sight of
the allied fleet would overawe Ibrahim.

The combined Ottoman-Egyptian fleet was already arrayed in the
bay when Codrington drew up the line of battle. He ordered the ships
in his fleet to open fire only when fired upon and having reminded everyone of Nelson's words—that in a battle one could not go wrong by placing one's ship right alongside the enemy—he then wrote a letter to his
wife. The wind had been too weak to carry them in, he told her, so they
had spent the day outside the bay. Their preparations had been made;
the ships were in fine condition and they would enter on the morrow.
How strange it would be, he wrote, if, as he expected, it all ended without any real action. On HMS *Genoa*, the men had been instructed on
October 6 to clear their decks for battle and had spent the next day
fishing and waiting for a wind. A Scottish seaman on board, Charles
McPherson, helped a fellow sailor draft a letter home, warning his family they were about to go into the bay "*to beat the Turks* so whether I'll

be sent to Davy or not I cannot tell." The next morning, October 8, their officers gave them a rousing talk and prepared them for action. McPherson's ship was second in line, right behind Codrington's flagship, the *Asia*. The three squadrons assembled in formation and at two o'clock in the afternoon under a gentle breeze they began to enter the Bay of Navarino through the narrows beneath the fortress.

For several days the Ottoman and Egyptian ships had been readied at their stations, and young McPherson saw them now forming a huge horseshoe around the bay with fireships at either tip less than a mile apart; as the allied fleet entered, they were thus almost entirely surrounded. Codrington could have sailed his vessels through their line but this would have suggested hostile intent, so he took the more perilous course of lining up his ships along the inside of the horseshoe. On paper, the allied fleet was outnumbered: they had some 1,300 guns compared with over 2,100 in the Ottoman-Egyptian fleet and certainly fewer vessels—twenty-seven versus sixty-five—and fewer sailors, 17,500 versus 20,000. On the other hand, in larger ships they were relatively evenly matched and the allied fleet was vastly superior in preparation, experience, and gunmanship. As Codrington's flagship sailed under the batteries of the fort, a boat rowed out with a message saying they had not been given permission to enter and should leave immediately. Codrington replied he had come to give orders, not to receive them, and that the first gun that fired at them would prompt the destruction of their fleet: his ships continued to pass into the bay unimpeded. As the lead ships took up their stations, and furled their sails, a band was playing on board the *Asia* and—at least in the memory of one young cadet—"things really appeared rather dull and peaceful."[29]

Many of the ships had yet to enter the bay when the firing began almost by accident. Captain Fellowes of the *Dartmouth* had been instructed by Codrington to remove any enemy fireships from dangerous positions, so when Fellowes noticed the crew of one of them ready to set it alight, he sent a boat to demand its removal. Their response was to attack his men and then light the fireship, and when Fellowes sent another boat to tow it aside, the lieutenant in charge was killed by musket fire. The *Dartmouth* responded, supported by the French flagship, de Rigny's *Sirène*, and once one of the Ottoman corvettes opened up with its cannons at both of them, the firing became general down the line. The signal was hoisted on the *Asia* to engage and "the British ships commenced to blaze away at their nearest enemy." Shortly after 3 p.m., as the last of the Russian ships reached their station in the bay, so many vessels were involved that they had to make their way through great clouds of smoke. Codrington had sent his Greek pilot to tell the Egyptian commander he wished to avoid bloodshed, but when the pilot too was shot, Codrington's gunners disabled the Egyptian flagship, killing dozens if not hundreds of sailors. Such thick smoke obscured the scene that the *Asia*'s gunners had to aim by guesswork and for a long time the others could not see whether the *Asia* itself was still afloat; Codrington was forced to cease running up signals because they were useless. Elsewhere, the allied and enemy ships were so close that the gunners could see one another loading and reloading; they risked being shot by musket fire from the deck opposite, or being hit by flying splinters or grapeshot. Enormous marble-shot, some weighing more than 100 pounds, flew overhead; when one ball hit the *Genoa*'s main deck, the crash was so loud it sounded as though another ship had collided with it. The Russian flagship, the *Azov*, was said to have had at least five enemy ships targeting her. "All hell seemed to have opened before us!" a Russian officer recalled later. The *Albion*'s rigging became entangled with a sixty-gun Turkish frigate, which was briefly boarded before the frigate was cut adrift, on fire: eventually her magazine exploded with the loss of hundreds of lives. Other ships sank or ran aground.[30]

On these ships, there were boys serving as young as ten and twelve years old, and on the *Genoa* there were also women, wives of the petty officers, who helped the ship's surgeon tend to the wounded. Working amid the groans of the men in agony, this was one of the worst jobs of all and some of the boys and women were too overcome by the stench and the screams to help—an understandable reaction when one realizes that below deck filled up quickly with mangled corpses, amputated limbs, and blood: indeed, orders were given in some cases that sailors should not go below to spare them the sight. In the water, sailors from the Ottoman ships clung to masts and yardarms. Some were picked up by allied sailors; others were left to drown or were shot; some of the Greeks who had been taken on as pilots on the British ships were standing on deck with the marines firing at the enemy with their muskets. A number of Greeks had been forced into Ottoman service too—including some survivors of Mesolonghi—and there were even a handful of

Englishmen and Americans as well. During and after the battle, dozens of them somehow got over to the allied ships, some with shackles still around their legs.

By five in the afternoon, the superior firepower of the allied fleet had all but annihilated the main Ottoman and Egyptian ships, and it was the turn of the smaller vessels behind them to be targeted. Only in the evening, after hours of continuous cannonades, explosions, and gunfire, did the fighting subside and the smoke clear. The moon rose to reveal the *Albion* with its rigging damaged, its masts cut away. An Ottoman corvette had run ashore, its deck strewn with bodies and human remains. On the *Genoa*, barely afloat, the sailors gathered together and congratulated one another on having survived the day. Their faces blackened, scratched, bloodied, and wounded by splinters, handkerchiefs around their heads and armed with pistols and cutlasses, they drank in honor of their captain who was dying below deck.

Nightfall brought new terrors and a Russian officer recalled later that these hours were "worse than the battle itself." Anticipating new attacks, he and his men remained at their station and around midnight they were alarmed to see a large warship bearing down on them: only prompt action by some of the Russian sailors, who boarded it and killed its crew, prevented it being set alight as a fireship. Because ships remained close together, many collided in the darkness or were fouled by cables. Across the bay damaged ships were blown up by their Ottoman officers, often with slaves and the wounded still on board, to stop the vessels falling into hostile hands, while others were holed by the allies as they drifted in flames on the waters. On the surface of the water, thousands of corpses floated amid the debris: "Out of the large and majestic Turkish fleet that had that day been stretched in the form of a crescent round the bay, only 15 small vessels were to be seen close to the shore; the remainder being either sunk, burned or mere wrecks."

Later that night, the sailor McPherson eventually lay down on deck and slept briefly:

> A slumbering drowsiness came over me, but I could not call it sleep. Visions of the conflict flitted before my eyes, and hideous phantasms, full of terrible combats and strifes, conflagrations and uproar, mingled with dismal apparitions of gory bodies, among them I could see my messmate Morfiet covered with blood and casting his dying glance at me.

At one point he was woken by the sound of two drowning Ottoman sailors shouting for help; but allied sailors had been ordered not to allow the enemy on board and exhausted, McPherson fell back asleep. The next morning the crew were mustered on the quarterdeck for the roll call. The silence that followed was punctuated only by the words "Here!," "Killed," and "Wounded," with the occasional loud blast as more enemy ships were blown up. McPherson wrapped the body of his companion in his spare hammock, keeping only his thimble as a keepsake, threaded the hammock with twine, and loaded two thirty-two-pound shot around the feet; then, while a messmate read from the prayer book, they tipped the body overboard:

> It now struck me for the first time that this was Sabbath morning—a Sabbath morning, how different from those I had been used to at home! Instead of bells tolling to church, random guns still rang in our ears and loud explosions of vessels rent the air; and instead of well-dressed people going quietly along to worship, were to be seen some hundreds of men with faces blackened by gunpowder, and clothes stained with blood, swearing, whistling and working, as if no such day were in their calendar.[31]

Codrington's first thought had been for the dying captain of the *Genoa*, Walter Bathurst. The admiral was rowed over to bid him farewell and on his return, he penned another note to his wife: "Well, my dear," he wrote, "the Turks have fought, and fought well too; and we have annihilated their fleet."[32] Codrington had remained on his poop deck throughout: only near the end of the battle did he go below to check whether his son Henry, a midshipman, was dead or alive. It turned out the boy had been seriously wounded in the leg but survived; later he too become an admiral. Codrington himself had escaped with nothing more than bullet holes in his hat and sleeves and a dented watch. He had led a charmed life: Ottoman riflemen had been ordered to shoot at him, and the *Asia*'s mizzen mast had come down on the spot where he was standing just moments after he had moved away. The boatswain had been shot dead when in conversation with him, and so had the ship's master. The captain of marines had been killed close by.

The allied casualties were around 180 killed and nearly 500 wounded, a disproportionate number of whom had served on the three flagships. Almost miraculously, not a single vessel from the allied squadrons was lost, though many suffered extensive damage and the Russian *Azov* alone suffered 153 hits. The losses on the Ottoman side were far greater: several thousand men perished, and while it was an exaggeration to say that the entire fleet was destroyed, it is clear that the vast majority of its first-line ships were either sunk or destroyed beyond repair and that as a naval force it was henceforth useless.[33] This was the last great naval battle of the age of sail—an epilogue to the legendary encounters of the Napoleonic Wars. But this did not exhaust Navarino's historical significance, for it was immediately clear to the world that it was a decisive moment in the Greek revolution and indeed—by underlining the weakness of the Ottoman Empire—in European history as a whole. After six and a half years of inconclusive hostilities, the war between the sultan and the Greeks had been ended with the most extraordinary and unexpected suddenness.

Of the great powers involved, there was only one country in which the reaction was one of unmitigated delight—and that was Russia. Many there saw the battle as a victory of faith and a story spread that after the Russian *Gangout* knocked an Ottoman fireship out of action and sank it, an image of the Virgin Mary was seen floating on the surface of the sea—a divine sign of the victory of the true believers over the infidel. The new czar was thrilled and was not upset that the dramatic outcome to the battle led relations between the Porte and the three great powers to deteriorate. Indeed, the Russians now took the opportunity to embark upon the larger war that he wanted. Twelve months before the battle of Navarino, the Russians and Ottomans had signed the Treaty of Akkerman, which gave Russia a new say in the governance of the Danubian Principalities, obliging the Ottoman army to withdraw once more, and also providing autonomy to the Serbs. Angered by the news from Navarino, the sultan denounced the treaty and declared jihad, and thus in April 1828 the Russo-Turkish war broke out that the other European powers had hoped to avert, the first major hostilities on the continent since the defeat of Napoleon. Russian victory took longer than anyone had expected, but it came in 1829 with further gains at Ottoman expense. The following year Admiral Codrington was invited to St. Petersburg, where the czar went out of his way to treat him with exceptional friendliness, virtually dragging him by the hand around the palace, seating the admiral in the place of honor at banquets, and happily watching him dance the evening away with the royal family.[34]

It all made for a poignant contrast with Codrington's far more ambiguous reception at home. For a moment he was a popular hero. But so far as the British and the French governments were concerned, the purpose of unifying their forces with the Russians had been to avoid hostilities and preserve Ottoman power: for them, therefore, Navarino was the most controversial and unwanted of triumphs. George Canning's death had left the government in London in the hands of men who were strongly anti-Russian and pro-Turkish; and they were unnerved by the possible consequences of what George IV in the King's Speech of 1828 infamously called "the untoward event." The ardently anti-Russian new prime minister, the Duke of Wellington, believed Codrington had exceeded his instructions and pushed the country to the brink of war with an ally, weakening the sultan in a way that had never been intended.

In France, news of the battle arrived on the eve of elections that saw the ultra-royalists and the cause of Charles X suffer. The philhellenes rejoiced and took Navarino as a sign of future victories to come against the Bourbon dynasty in France. "Greece is saved!" proclaimed the *Journal des Débats* on November 9. *Le Constitutionnel* declared that "no naval battle has ever produced so complete a destruction." Meanwhile pro-government newspapers adopted the language of Chateaubriand and tried to claim the victory for the government. The *Moniteur universel* looked forward to an end to the war in the east: "In one blow, the terrible struggle which for four years has saddened humanity, has been ended; in one blow peace is restored to the world." Later it went further: the success at Navarino was "entirely French and entirely royalist." The crusading spirit that had been unleashed against Ibrahim and that promised to give the monarchy in France a new lease of life would soon find another outlet; already the French navy was blockading the coast of Algiers, a prelude to the invasion two years later that would lead to the bloody conquest of Algeria, which ended three centuries of Ottoman rule there as well.[35]

The truth was that allied diplomacy had rested on a deliberate ambiguity over how the proposed armistice was to be enforced. The admirals' instructions did indeed countenance the use of force in the event that Sultan Mahmud II rejected mediation. Moreover, that was bound to happen because the sultan had consistently refused to recognize the right of the allies to intervene and had been prepared for a clash if necessary. He seems to have believed they were bluffing and ignored Mehmed Ali's warning that if they were not, the Ottoman-Egyptian navy would be no match for the technically superior allies. Thus the battle followed from the Porte's orders to Ibrahim to ignore the demands being made on him by Codrington and to continue his war on the Greeks.

Codrington certainly believed Ibrahim had been ready to do battle: the Ottoman-Egyptian fleet had already, two days beforehand, taken up a hostile attitude; the deliberate preparing of the fireship had reinforced that impression on the day itself. Once things were under way, the allied admirals had given the Ottoman and Egyptian counterparts at least two opportunities to stop firing, and it was only after the second of these had ended with the shooting of the pilot of the *Asia* that the firing became general. Afterward Codrington learned that the fireships had been intended for use against his fleet once they were all in the bay; this was why his decision to make them inoperative at the start had precipitated the encounter. By sailing his ships so close to the enemy line, he had foiled the Ottoman plan, which was to force the allied fleet to cluster together in the center of the bay and so make it an easier target.[36]

A more difficult question for Codrington might have been whether the immediate motive for his action—the continuation of Egyptian land operations in the Morea, the nature of those operations, and in particular their use of what the admirals had termed "excessive violence"—was the sort of issue that the diplomats had envisaged as a reason to use force. For it was this campaign and not the continued supply of the Egyptian troops by sea that was the last straw for the three admirals. On the one hand, the ostensible purpose of the conference that he and de Rigny had held with Ibrahim had been to stop Ibrahim sailing on Hydra and interdicting his movements by sea. At the same time, the admirals clearly believed that Ibrahim had committed to suspending all land operations and according to the British minutes at least, he had given such a commitment. At the most fundamental level, they had decided not to let the Egyptians triumph in the Morea because they had come to believe they were waging what the Treaty of London itself called a "war of extermination." Codrington saw that continuing. The proof for him seems to have been not only the destruction of homes, and the enslavement of villagers, but crucially perhaps, the intent to

deliberately make the land infertile by uprooting trees and vines—
turning it, in Codrington's words, into "a desert." It was, after all, only
a few years earlier that Ibrahim and his army had pursued very similar
tactics in the Hijaz, systematically destroying date plantations there to
end the Saudi revolt. Blocking the Egyptian maritime communications
was therefore a means to an end, not the raison d'être for European
diplomacy. In this sense, Codrington's actions were consistent with the
treaty's goals.[37]

The two main ostensible victims of the defeat—Sultan Mahmud II
and Mehmed Ali Pasha in Egypt—had both anticipated a possible clash.
Yet their reactions could scarcely have been more different. The sultan
and his ministers had been sanguine about the outcome and were
shocked by the humiliation. When the news of the total destruction of
his fleet arrived in Constantinople, Mahmud was furious at what he
regarded as an unwarranted intervention in his domestic affairs at the
very moment when he seemed about to crush the Greek revolt once and
for all. In contrast, Mehmed Ali received the news with exemplary calm.
Although he knew that challenging the Europeans meant uselessly risking the lives of thousands of men, Mehmed Ali's position required him
and his son Ibrahim to demonstrate their obedience to the sultan. Yet
what Mehmed Ali surely understood above all was that disaster for the
sultan must in the long run favor him. Calling in a French naval commander, Comte d'Oysonville, who had not yet heard the news, Mehmed
Ali conveyed the outcome of the battle to him "with the greatest calm."
British and French diplomats were astonished at his equanimity. But
Mehmed Ali, nothing if not farsighted, had already realized that Navarino would create new opportunities for him. And indeed, the sultan's
war with the Russians in 1828–29 was followed in 1831 by one with
the Egyptians themselves. The Ottoman dynasty, whose military reforms
lagged behind Mehmed Ali's by some years, was fortunate to survive as
Ibrahim's army marched into Syria, and then into Asia Minor, directly
threatening the Ottoman heartlands. At Konya, Ibrahim and the all-
conquering Egyptians triumphed over a force twice their size, capturing
the grand vizier, who was none other than Kütahı Pasha, Ibrahim's former rival and partner at Mesolonghi. The outcome, after a decade of
hard bargaining and European mediation, was that the sultan had to
grant Mehmed Ali and his family hereditary rule over Egypt and Sudan.
It was an unprecedented achievement: in effect, Mehmed Ali had

succeeded where Ali Pasha of Jannina failed, and he had used the Greek revolt to further his own ambitions.[38]

Capodistrias himself was slowly making his way all this time through the chief capitals of Europe to garner support for his presidency. Such diplomatic backing had been a precondition, he told the Greeks, for his accepting their offer and was needed to establish his authority. Unfortunately, he reached London a week after George Canning's untimely death and Canning's undistinguished successor, Lord Goderich—described by George IV as a "damned sniveling, blubbering blockhead"—was friendly but did not carry the same weight. The king received Capodistrias at Windsor and was barely civil; the foreign secretary was courteous but reserved. Many in the British government suspected that Capodistrias was nothing more than a Russian agent. In fairness, it must be said that he was no great fan of the British governing class either, disliking their snobbery and philistinism. In Paris, Charles X was even more hostile than the British king had been, writing to his prime minister that he regarded Capodistrias as "a rogue and a real revolutionary." Capodistrias had not yet formally accepted the Greek government's offer of the presidency and intended to wait until he had had the chance to discuss the terms on the spot. What was clear to him was that he would need both funds and troops and he urged the European powers to allow him to raise a Swiss battalion. He also embarked upon a lengthy negotiation over the Greek borders that would last until well after his arrival—and indeed not be resolved until after his death.[39]

News of the outcome of Navarino reached Capodistrias in Turin in the second week of November, and his reaction was characteristic: in a letter to his friend, the Prussian reformer Baron vom Stein, he wrote that the victory "opens one more chance for the future which God seems to reserve for this Greece of ours, for which he performs so many miracles."[40] Capodistrias was driven by a belief in Providence and the long-term view this gave him contrasted strikingly with the anxiety of the Greeks who were calling on him to return at once. He was in no hurry. His basic assumption seems to have been, as it always had been, that Greek independence would be achieved sooner or later, and that what was important was to remain clear of internal quarrels and factions and prepare the ground for the kind of autocratic good government that practical pious men like him could provide, a form of government that would render party politicking a thing of the past.

By late November he was in Ancona on the Italian coast from where Codrington had been ordered to send a ship to fetch him. It took six weeks to arrive—all the ships in the British squadron had needed repairs after Navarino—and Capodistrias found the wait frustrating. He lived as modestly as always in a small hotel suite, accompanied by a couple of servants, and he spent most of his time dictating letters, sometimes several simultaneously, taking afternoon walks, and whiling away the evenings playing chess. This was his habitual way of life, and it was one he continued, interrupted only by prayer and by meetings with potential benefactors and supporters. His patience was further tested by the news that he would not be allowed to dock at Corfu—the high commissioner was worried about disturbances on the island if he appeared there—but would travel instead directly to see Codrington in Malta.

When Capodistrias arrived there on December 28, he and Codrington found they got on well and enjoyed one another's company. At dinner on his first evening, Capodistrias charmed the admiral's large family with stories of his diplomatic experiences and the next morning the two men got down to business. Codrington made it clear to the Greek where he stood: "I am no philanthropist nor am I the least of a Philhellenist; I set no particular value upon either Greeks or Turks and have no personal feeling toward either. I am guided solely by my duty as an English officer and my duty in this case is pointed out by the Treaty of London and my instructions emanating from it." Capodistrias assured him that he too desired to fulfill the objectives of the treaty and the two of them henceforth worked closely together. Codrington found Capodistrias's conversation "fascinating" and felt he could trust him. Although he received numerous warnings to be careful of the count's pro-Russian sympathies, Codrington rightly disregarded such advice. Capodistrias's view of the British also improved and he felt more optimistic about working with them. In a mark of favor, the governor of Malta released about one hundred convicted Greek pirates so that they could be repatriated.

On January 2, 1828, Capodistrias left Malta on HMS *Warspite*, rounding the Peloponnese in gale-force winds, which prevented it from making directly for Aigina as planned and forcing it to anchor in the

bay of Nafplion instead. The British warship was accompanied at Capodistrias's request by Russian and French ships, both of which had
fought at Navarino, in order to make it clear that he had come with the
backing of the three allied powers. He had after all reached his destination not only without the abortive Swiss battalion but without even a
bodyguard: Capodistrias was not lacking in courage and he must have
wanted to make a statement about the nature of his power.[41] They
anchored at a moment when the warlord Grivas was poised to pillage
Nafplion once more, so it is not surprising that Capodistrias's arrival
was regarded by the townspeople as the coming of the Messiah. Grivas
sent an intermediary down to meet him and was told to present himself
in person. After Grivas came aboard HMS *Warspite*, Capodistrias made
him and his rivals promise to stop fighting, to release their prisoners,
and to hand over the forts: Grivas did indeed relinquish the Palamidi, as
he had pledged.[42]

When Capodistrias disembarked in the town to attend Sunday Mass
on January 8, a large crowd gathered and cheered his arrival. But he
told everyone that he still regarded himself as a mere private traveler
and would have no official standing until he had conferred with the
Greek government on Aigina on the terms of his appointment. Setting
sail, he left behind a mysterious and remarkable figure, a talented French
military officer of Corfiot origin called Stamati Boulgari who had come
from Ancona with him and whom he now put in charge of charting the
war damage, repairing the town, and establishing the needs of the refugees. In this fashion, the first steps toward the postwar reconstruction of
the country began.[43]

Arriving on Aigina on January 11, Capodistrias asked the state secretaries to report on the condition of the government, and their responses
made grim reading. The national navy comprised a mere ten or eleven
ships including an Egyptian corvette captured by Cochrane; all the rest
were privately owned, as they had been from the start. Most of the
armed bands were fighting one another or had been dissolved: there was
no mention of any regular formations at all. Customs duties and revenues from tax-farming in the Peloponnese had fallen away to almost
nothing; little came out of the islands, and nothing from continental
Greece. As for justice, there was only a commercial court established in
Syros; a criminal court set up in Nafplion in 1826 had been dissolved.
The secretary of the interior, Anastasios Lodtos, summed things up:

As regards commerce, crafts, industry, and agriculture, I can say that there is none of these, neither commerce, nor handicrafts, nor industry. Farming is at a minimum, because the farmers are not sowing seed anymore, since they do not have security to harvest it, and if it ripens they do not know if they can collect the harvest and keep it from being seized by soldiers. The merchant is not safe in the towns, trembling for fear of pirates . . . And the craftsman, poor man, is never sure if he will be paid, because only the right of the stronger prevails, the social ties have been dissolved, and the citizen is bereft of the law's protection. Only the inexhaustible patience of the people puts off the further deterioration of things.[44]

Capodistrias made it clear that he was not willing to accept the position of governor (*kyvernitis*) on the terms implied by the Troezen constitution of the previous year. He was in a strong position because of the sense that he was backed by the three great powers and although this backing was chiefly symbolic, few wanted to test whether their support would last if he refused to serve. As a result, the provisional government resigned and at the end of the month the legislature, meeting in secret session, agreed to his demand to grant him full powers. The constitution of Troezen, which had been drawn up with the intention of restricting just such sweeping authority for the executive as he now demanded, went into abeyance. In place of the parliamentary legislative body it envisaged as one of the three coequal branches of administration, Capodistrias created an advisory Panhellenion of twenty-seven leading figures of the revolution, whose influence was thus acknowledged but effectively nullified.

Capodistrias has been criticized for not simply reconvening the national assembly and for asking it instead to revise the constitutional basis for his appointment, and it is true he was not, by background, temperament, or experience, a democrat. An exponent of enlightened paternalism, shaped by his early medical studies as well as his experiences of political life in the highly stratified world of the Ionian Islands and in czarist Russia, Capodistrias believed in the rule of law in the hands of an educated elite. On the other hand, it must be admitted that previous constitutional experiments had done nothing to produce effective government during the revolution. The Troezen constitution was—like its predecessors—an elaborate and rhetorical idealization of a situation that did not yet exist. How, for instance, could the governor take an oath—as it said he should—to "defend and preserve the independence of Greece" when that independence had not been achieved? Capodistrias wrote his own oath of office instead, swearing by the Holy Trinity to work for the "national and political restoration of Greece," so that it could enjoy "the important benefits promised to it by the Treaty of London of 6 July 1827."[45]

That these benefits did not as yet include either independence or an agreed-upon set of international borders shows just how far Greece still was from enjoying the rights of a sovereign state. Patras and other forts in the Peloponnese remained in Ottoman hands, as did Mesolonghi and Athens. Thousands of Egyptian troops were still in Messenia, and in Constantinople the sultan was vowing not to capitulate to European pressure and even sending emissaries from the patriarchate to Aigina to persuade the Greeks to submit to his authority. To negotiate the terms upon which Greece's new international existence could begin, to wrest back control from its enemies, and to determine what its boundaries would be, were Capodistrias's chief tasks. Internally, the challenges were perhaps even greater. None of this changed the fundamental fact that the country he governed was now in effect protected by three European great powers. The old taboo against intervention had been broken and it was inconceivable that Europe would ever again allow the Greeks of the Morea and the islands to fall under the sway of the sultan.

LOVE, CONCORD, BROTHERHOOD, 1828–33

*I pondered all these things, and how men fight and lose the bat-
tle, and the thing that they fought for comes about in spite of
their defeat, and when it comes turns out not to be what they
meant . . .*

William Morris, *A Dream of John Ball*, 1886

*"Come Napoleon," said [Czar] Alexander: "Let us go and see
the ancient Greeks in the place where they dwell and find old
master Socrates and Plato and Themistokles and the gallant
Leonidas, and tell them the thrilling news that their descendants, who had been lost and wiped out from the list of mankind,
stand on their feet once more . . . The poor Greeks, few and
untrained, have beaten the Grand Signior."*

Makriyannis, *Memoirs*, 147

The 1827 Treaty of London had been signed not to make Greece independent but to establish peace in the region—to restore "the tranquility
of Europe." Thus the destruction of the Ottoman fleet at Navarino did
not mean the Greeks could count upon the support of the great powers
to press their claim for complete independence—which the sultan still
firmly rejected—nor even to let them go on fighting. On the contrary,
the allied admirals were under orders to prevent, so far as they could,
all "collision" between the two sides. When Cochrane and Fabvier set
out on an expedition to conquer Chios, for example, Admiral Codrington warned this would not be tolerated, and it fizzled out. Fighting

continued on Crete even after Capodistrias made it clear it lacked his support but subsided in 1830 once it became evident the island would not be included within the proposed boundaries of the new Greek state. Like Samos, which eventually became an autonomous tributary of the Ottoman Empire, Chios and Crete were joined with Greece only in 1913.

"The tranquility of Europe" meant not only eradicating fighting on land. It meant above all using European naval power to reestablish the security of international commerce by stamping out piracy. This problem had exploded in the Aegean in the months before the battle of Navarino, reaching unprecedented levels. In May 1827, for example, Greek raiders off Serifos had attacked the *Robert*, a British schooner temporarily becalmed on its way back from Smyrna to Liverpool. They transferred its cargo of dry goods, sugar, and hops to their boats, not to mention the crews' shoes and shirts, the cabin furniture and equipment, leaving the decks "in a most confused state." There were dozens of such raids in these months, which pushed up the costs of shipping and drove European merchants into bankruptcy. Even sailing in convoy failed to stop the often murderous attacks. But it was not only foreign merchants who were targeted; in some ways Greek islanders suffered more. From Karpathos, islanders begged for protection from hundreds of pirates who had settled there; the pirates were stealing their livestock and clothing, emptying their homes, levying "fines," and even abducting girls. In 1827, according to a report from Serifos, men from Crete and Hydra had stolen their grain, ransacked their houses, seized livestock, and made the islanders pay for protesting. On Naxos a domineering Cretan kapetan forced the local people to fit out a ship so that his band could plunder commercial traffic to and from Egypt. Around him sprang up an entire network of merchants, fences, and brokers who toured the smaller local people selling off looted metal ingots, brushes, inkpots, and locks.[1]

Some pirate enterprises consisted of bands that had ceased operations against the Ottomans and made the switch from fighting Turks on land to plundering Greeks and foreigners at sea. Kapetans from the north, from the slopes of Olympos to the Chalkidiki peninsula, plagued the islands from Trikkeri to Evvia with their raids and requisitions, sometimes in fleets of a dozen or more ships at a time. They were joined by unemployed crews from the shipping islands, for whom piracy was the most lucrative work available. What exacerbated the problem was that Greek administrations had been handing out numerous privateering licenses.[2] In theory, privateers were supposed to abide by certain rules; in practice, they were often little different from pirates. Some of them operated on their own account, but many more were financed and backed by kapetans, wartime chieftains, and even by well-known shipowners and political figures at the highest levels. Some of the Hydriot notables were heavily involved; so was the Mavromihalis clan in the Mani.[3]

Off Navarino, in the midst of his negotiations with the Egyptians, Codrington wrote to "the persons exercising the functions of Government in Greece" that "the world knows no equal to the villainy which is now being practiced under the Greek flag"; he warned that if they did not curb the problem, he would "consider Greece as without a government." Two days before the battle of Navarino, he wrote again demanding to know why they protected ships "committing piracy upon the commerce of the three Allied Powers which are making such enormous sacrifices for them?" The next day, on the eve of entering the bay, Codrington wrote to the legislature: "Judge Gentlemen, under these circumstances, what are my feelings that in the meantime the boasting Hydriotes, Spezziots, Ipsariotes &c., have been plundering the ships of all nations, even at the distance of Malta and Maritimo; and . . . judge of my indignation at finding their so-called cruising has been under the sanction of your Provisional Government." After the battle, the three allied admirals issued a final stark warning to the Greeks: "The [Turkish fleet] exists no more. Take care of yours, for we will also destroy it, if need be, to put a stop to a system of robbery on the high seas, which would end in your exclusion from the law of nations."[4]

What followed was a coordinated anti-piracy campaign—an early example of the new internationalism of the Restoration decades—that brought in other countries beside the three allied powers. Austrian ships bombarded Naxos, seized suspected pirate vessels in Tinos, and fined villagers on Mykonos for their involvement; the Americans—present in force in the eastern Mediterranean for the first time—sent seven warships that ran convoys, fought pirates, and landed marines to recover stolen goods.

The Greek raiders operated out of the Cyclades where some bands had taken over entire islands, but also utilized the numerous small bays and coves along the coast of the southern Peloponnese and up the coast of Evvia to the Sporades and the Gulf of Volos. By far their most important base, however, was the fortress-islet of Grabousa off the northwest tip of Crete, the so-called pirate republic, which had been transformed since the summer of 1825 from a springboard for Cretan resistance to the Turks into a center of the piracy whose inhabitants had seized some five hundred merchantmen. Grabousa became Codrington's target and on January 19, 1828, five British naval vessels along with two French corvettes sailed into the shadow of the great rock.

They quickly sank or burned the schooners and brigs they found in the port and then turned their attention to the huge fortress where no fewer than 6,000 hungry people, armed with more than 3,000 muskets, were living in miserable conditions out in the open. Not all of them had been involved in piracy and many were refugees; nevertheless it took several weeks of tense negotiations and on-the-spot assistance from Alexandros Mavrokordatos before 130 British marines made the inhabitants leave and arrested several suspected corsairs. The golden age of Aegean piracy thus came to a close. In the course of these maneuvers, HMS *Cambrian* foundered on rocks beneath the fortress and had to be abandoned. It was an unfortunate end to a vessel that had done such good, from spiriting Muslims away from danger after the surrender of Nafplion in 1822, to reporting on the plight of the Greeks to Codrington just before the battle of Navarino. Captain Hamilton was cleared of any wrongdoing at the subsequent inquiry but he appears never to have recovered from his ship's loss.[5]

After Navarino, Sultan Mahmud II remained defiant. He regarded talk of a Greek government as nonsense, offered the Greeks a pardon if they returned as loyal subjects, and rejected calls to grant them some form of tributary autonomy, as the Treaty of London had proposed. But the foundations of his power over them were crumbling, and Ibrahim and his father Mehmed Ali were by now clearly looking for a way to extricate their starving and disease-ridden troops from the Peloponnese. A new government in France, thirsting for glory, prepared an expeditionary force of 14,000 men under the command of General Nicolas Maison to supervise the Egyptians' departure, but by the time it landed west of Kalamata in the summer of 1828, Codrington had already agreed to an evacuation plan with Mehmed Ali. Between September and October, most of the Egyptians left for home and those men who had stayed to guard the forts of the Peloponnese followed soon after. A brief French bombardment obtained the surrender of the Castle of the Morea, guarding the entrance to the Gulf of Corinth, but the others gave in peacefully. The frustrated General Maison, an experienced officer already decorated both by Napoleon and his Bourbon successor, dreamed of attacking the Turks in the Acropolis for one last stab at glory but he was not allowed the chance: the approximately 1,500 casualties his men suffered were mostly from malaria.[6]

Although the so-called *Armée de la Morée*—a precursor to the larger, more violent, and consequential force the French would send a few years later into Algiers—did not see much fighting, it was neither idle nor useless. While some troops stayed on for what we would now call peacekeeping duties, French military engineers arranged the first systematic topographical surveys of the Morea, built bridges and roads, and redesigned the towns of Methoni and Pylos. Colonel Stamati Bolgari, the Franco-Greek officer whom Capodistrias had installed in Nafplion, mapped Argos and suggested improvements in its layout before moving on to Tripolitsa and Patras. In this way, the French inaugurated the technical infrastructure of the contemporary Peloponnese and prepared the beginnings of a national network of roads that would facilitate the expansion of the modern state.[7]

Inspired by the Napoleonic mission to Egypt, a scientific commission accompanying the *Armée* brought geologists, geographers, statisticians, epidemiologists, and other Parisian savants. Their expedition left a lasting memorial in two lavishly illustrated collaborative works of staggering bibliographic beauty—Abel Blouet's three folios of archaeological and architectural studies, and Bory de Saint-Vincent's six volumes on their scientific inquiries. Never before had the Peloponnese and its past received such detailed attention in print. To the French scholars, the long-term effects of the fighting were inescapable. The "incredible sparseness of the population" struck one of the team, the young painter Eugène Amaury-Duval, who was away from France for the first time. "Sometimes we would walk for whole days at a time without meeting a living soul." The survivors they encountered terrified them with their stories and also their appearance. Having been excited at the idea of setting foot in Greece, Duval was brought painfully down to earth on his first day when he stumbled across:

> . . . the worst sight I have ever seen in my life. Amidst some wooden shacks, built along the shore outside the town . . . there circulated

haggard and ragged men, women and children who scarcely looked human; some lacked a nose, others ears, all more or less covered in scars, but what left us completely distraught was the sight of a small child of four or five whose brother held him by the hand: I came close. His eyes were empty sockets. The Egyptians and Turks had spared no one in that war.[8]

This was, as Duval recalled, not only a reminder of what the country had been through but an almost incomprehensible contrast to the beauties of the natural world and the ancient remains they were there to document.

On top of this legacy of atrocities, the Greek authorities had to deal with an outbreak of bubonic plague that had occurred in the spring of 1828 on a ship, the *Afroditi*, which had brought freed slaves from the Egyptian camp to the Capodistrias government's headquarters on the island of Aigina. From there it spread into Hydra, Spetses, and Poros before crossing over into the Peloponnese again. The *Afroditi*'s captain and three crew perished before reaching home; more died on board as the ship tacked for days between Hydra and the mainland, unable to land. On Aigina, a medical team fumigated houses and built a lazaretto on the headland near the port. Turkish prisoners buried the dead; cafés, churches, and cabarets were closed. "We live in a small isolated country place by the sea about a league from town," Capodistrias's hardworking Swiss secretary Élie-Ami Bétant wrote to his parents. "I have my own tent in the middle of a garden, under the orange trees. We don't mix with anyone, we have a guard around the house and for my part I am not in discomfort."[9]

Hydra and Spetses were placed under quarantine, commerce with the mainland was suspended, and special markets under government guard were established on the shore opposite so that the islanders could purchase food. These measures stopped the plague on the islands within a couple of months, though in the Peloponnese it died away only in the spring of 1829. By the time it was over, the fearless Swiss doctor Louis-André Gosse had tracked nearly eight hundred deaths. Fatality rates were high, especially among the malnourished refugees, but could have been far higher without the isolation of both individuals and families. In contrast to the wartime years in which plagues and other epidemics had been allowed to rage then flicker out by themselves, the fledgling

Capodistrian state had shown its capacity to deploy European scientific expertise, a taste of its technocratic approach to governance more generally.[10]

The spring of 1828 was also the time when relations between the Porte and Russia finally broke down. With a new, more belligerent czar at the helm, a Russian army of 100,000 men invaded Moldavia and Wallachia before crossing the Danube and heading for the imperial capital. Ottoman resistance was initially surprisingly effective, but the war, which lasted a year and a half, ended in an emphatic Russian victory. It not only revealed the continued limitations of the Ottoman army, which the sultan was in the midst of dramatically modernizing along Egyptian lines; it also undermined the bargaining position of the Ottoman state vis-à-vis the Greeks and thus decisively shaped the last phase of the discussions around the new country's future. In particular, it gave the Greeks another chance to win territory either side of the Pindos ahead of the international delineation of the country's border. The Greeks seized the opportunity that had been presented to them: in the west, Greek forces under Richard Church captured the key town of Vonitsa early in 1829, while later that spring Mesolonghi was recaptured too. Across the mountains, Dimitrios Ypsilantis—fighting to the last— defeated a much larger, 7,000-strong Albanian force that September as it headed north to the Russian front. This was the battle of Petra, which ended with the Ottoman troops being allowed to continue their journey in return for clearing out from much of eastern Greece. It turned out to be the last battle of the war. The country's fate—and its frontier—now depended not upon the battlefield but upon the three great powers and their choice of ruler: for it was with the new future king and not with Capodistrias that they would eventually reach an agreement.[11]

One of the striking features of the entire revolution was the distinct lack of concern among most Greeks about the constitutional question. In the twentieth century, the country would tear itself apart over the so-called national schism between republicans and royalists. But in the 1820s outright republicans were a small minority and the vast majority of Greeks accepted the inevitable arrival of a foreign king. Some understood this was the price of European protection, but for many it was simply the way of the world and entirely consistent with the prophetic traditions of a national resurrection. The question was: from where would this king come?[12] There were at least half a dozen candidates for the Greek throne among Europe's minor royalty, but once the unacceptable and the uninterested had been weeded out, the Greeks were left by a process of elimination with Leopold of Saxe-Coburg, with whom Capodistrias had been intermittently in touch for several years. In February 1830 the three great powers met in London and agreed to offer Leopold the throne of Greece as a fully independent state. Henceforth, while almost everything else remained to be settled—borders, compensation, property and citizenship rights, even the precise title of the new ruler—the fundamental point that the new country would not be under the rule of the sultan in any way was settled. Yet this was in effect an agreement among monarchs, one in which neither the Greek people nor their chosen representatives had any diplomatic standing. And there was a wrinkle: the new frontier proposed to Leopold actually reduced the size of the future Greek state compared with the line agreed by the powers the previous year, leaving out most of the territory that Church had just won in western Rumeli. Unable to get this changed, and perhaps already having second thoughts, Leopold announced he was withdrawing his candidature: he ended up on the throne of Belgium the following year.

Capodistrias was alarmed when Leopold pulled out: the subsequent charges made by his enemies that he aspired to sole rule could not have been further from the truth and he was dismayed that the great powers could not quickly find a replacement. But a revolution in France, which replaced Charles X with the duc d'Orléans, kept them occupied, and after that there were revolts in Belgium, Poland, and Brazil. It was not until early 1831 that the philhellenic King Ludwig of Bavaria came into the picture and another year before his seventeen-year-old son Prince Otto von Wittelsbach—whom the European powers had previously regarded as too young—was formally offered the crown. Thanks to some hard bargaining by his father, the Greeks ended up with a much more favorable frontier in the north closer to the line agreed in 1829, but by that time Capodistrias was not around to share in the credit.

The "Governor," to give Capodistrias his formal title, had been working flat out: there was the public health emergency, the perennial search for another foreign loan, the construction of a new road and harbor in Aigina, the purchase of presses from the Knights of Malta to mint the first coin of the independent state. No detail was too small: he ordered mulberry trees from the Peloponnese for roadside shade, potato seeds for planting, farm tools for distribution to the refugees. At the end of 1830, in a letter to his former secretary, he added up what had been done: an orphanage and two *écoles normales* set up on Aigina, a printing press for their books; a military academy in Nafplion; a seminary on Poros; a model farm near Tiryns; and the first proper road traced out from Nafplion to Argos, which could now be reached in only three-quarters of an hour by carriage. The inhabitants of Greece, Capodistrias told his former secretary Bétant, enjoyed "perfect tranquility."[13]

If only it had been true. In reality, opposition to Capodistrias was coalescing, and his authority was increasingly fragile: he trusted few Greeks, relied on foreigners, and gave too much power to his two brothers whose police persecuted opponents with threats of imprisonment or exile. For the first time, Dimitrios Ypsilantis, Mavrokordatos, the Koundouriotis brothers, Church, and others found a common purpose in standing against what they regarded as incipient tyranny. The unity among the great powers evident under Admiral Codrington had been replaced by politicking, and only the Russian squadron and a few chieftains offered Capodistrias much support. Charged with nepotism and unconstitutional rule, he unwisely muzzled criticism and banned newspapers.

From the very start of the war, the fundamental tension on the Greek side had been between the desire for freedom and the need for centralized government. Alarmed by the administrative vacuum that had greeted him on his arrival, Capodistrias had followed his instincts, which were those of a centralizer. Thus some kind of clash was more or less inevitable, especially as Greece's revolutionary rulers had basically been regional power brokers who were now having to come to terms with the disappearance of many of their wartime sources of income and influence. The clash could be seen in Capodistrias's efforts to establish reliable statistics for the formerly Muslim-owned national lands, a vital element in his plan to create a republic of small, economically independent, politically free landowning citizens from among the refugees, to counter the influence of the traditional landowning notables. The collection of essential information was blocked within months by local opponents, a fateful check that undermined his efforts at fiscal modernization.[14]

Hydra's position, once preeminent, had become especially precarious. It had been affected by the anti-piracy crusade, it had lost the business of converting its ships for government use, and its shipowners—

awaiting payment for many of their wartime expenditures—lacked the funds to repair their fleet and compete with the Europeans. The end of the fighting meant a sudden fall in the island's influence and power: ships lay idle in the harbor, and unemployment among its sailors soared. With other sources of income draining away, Hydra's notables tried to keep their control over the lucrative customs revenues of Syros—now emerging as the peacetime center of Greece's maritime economy—and resisted Capodistrias's efforts to assert the rights of the central government over them. Like everyone else, they also submitted a huge bill for compensation for their wartime expenses, which the government was in no position to meet. Discontent turned into outright rebellion as the Hydriot admiral Miaoulis sailed to Poros, seized several government ships and, when challenged, sank them.[15]

In the Peloponnese, too, the notables seethed at Capodistrias's efforts to rein in their power and were actively blocking or bribing his civil servants to prevent them from carrying out their work. For families that had lived off the war, things were desperate. The clearest case was that of Petros Mavromihalis in the Mani, for whom the end of the fighting meant a kind of existential crisis since he could no longer rely on his old sources of revenue to keep his vast household. Notorious for his extravagance and his endless demands for money, Mavromihalis regarded Greece "as his field" in the acerbic words of Georgios Stavros, the chief financier of the new state. But the Capodistrian state insisted on collecting its own customs revenues and would not give Mavromihalis the resources to which he was accustomed. To make matters worse, the other clans of the Mani—longtime rivals he had once supplanted—no longer recognized his Ottoman status as bey and regional leader. His son, the *beyzadé* Georgios, became engaged to one of the Notaras women, thus accessing the wealth of the northern Peloponnese currant trade, but the wedding had to be deferred because of the *beyzadé*'s extravagant expectations for the event. The truth was that the Mavromihalis family was massively in debt. Even piracy, one of their traditional income streams, was increasingly costly. After repeated run-ins with the British navy for sheltering pirates, senior family members were again in the spotlight accused of having plundered a Sardinian vessel that had been carrying merchandise for the French consul in Crete, while two were also in court charged with the attempted murder of a cousin from a rival branch of the family. By 1829 they had either been found guilty of these crimes or were still detained pending further investigation.[16]

Capodistrias had behaved toward the Mavromihalis clan with remarkable moderation in the circumstances, but once they began fomenting armed revolt—the traditional means of demonstrating their power—he clamped down. He imprisoned Petros Mavromihalis and used his son as the unwitting means to persuade Petros's older brother, Ioannis Mavromihalis, to come to Nafplion, where he too was promptly arrested and detained. Almost every member of the family was removed from public office and placed under police surveillance or confinement. These were extreme measures and unforgivable insults to men of standing from a region known for the fierceness of its vendettas. Petros Mavromihalis's much younger brother Konstantinos and his son Georgios resolved to avenge the family honor—by assassinating Capodistrias in Nafplion.

Having purchased several pairs of pistols and made their preparations, uncle and nephew decided to kill the president when he attended church. After they had twice waited in vain, they tried a third time on Sunday, September 27, 1831. Shortly before six o'clock in the morning they took up positions on either side of the door so that anyone going in had to pass between them. With them were two men employed by the municipal police who were supposed to be keeping an eye on them but who, to judge from their subsequent behavior, seem to have been in on the plot. Coming down the lane along the side of the church of Saint Spyridon, Capodistrias approached the narrow marble doorway and noticed the two Mavromihalis men; as he passed them to go inside, they reached inside their capes and fired several shots at point-blank range. Then one of them stabbed him with a small knife; he fell without uttering a word, hit his head on the ground, and died almost at once. A popular depiction of the scene shows Capodistrias in a frock coat, waistcoat, and white trousers, his cane and top hat fallen to the ground before the eyes of the horrified churchgoers, with the assassins in their Maniot garb finishing him off.[17]

All four men ran away. Konstantinos Mavromihalis was fired at and wounded but made it to a house nearby before he was dragged out by a mob, killed, and hung up by the feet from a tree in the street. Around four o'clock in the afternoon his bloodied corpse was tossed into the sea. Georgios, followed by his two police guards (whose ambiguous role in the affair was never fully clarified), ran first into one house and then into the garden of the French resident Baron Rouen, where they gave themselves up. Claiming it had been a political crime, motivated by the need to rid the country of a tyrant, Georgios was instead arraigned before a military tribunal and sentenced to death.[18]

Petros Mavromihalis was being held in a cell from which he could see the place of execution as well as the enormous crowd that gathered to watch as his son was brought down. Offered the chance to speak, Georgios Mavromihalis is said to have uttered only three words: "Love, concord, brotherhood." With that old Etairist slogan he saluted his father, dropped to his knees, and gave the signal to the firing squad.[19] One of his police guards, Ioannis Karayannis, also condemned to death, had waited till the day of his execution to divulge new details of the supposed plot behind the assassination; six months later he was quietly allowed to go free. Conspiracy theories were rampant then and later, and the investigators interviewed dozens of people. It is clear that the guards had somehow become complicit, and some people pointed the finger of suspicion at their superiors or at notables of the Peloponnese who were not sorry to see the president out of the way. As recently as 1977 a serious scholar suggested French military officers in the town were behind the killing; the evidence for any of these theories, however, remains circumstantial at best. And the Mavromihalis clan were quite capable of having acted alone.[20] Capodistrias's brother Agostino tried to take over the reins of government but he lasted only until the following April when he fled the country, taking his brother's body with him. Today it lies in the Platytera monastery on their native Corfu, a simple slab under a miniature neoclassical pediment with the stark inscription: "Governor of Greece" (*Kyvernitis tis Ellados*). To his followers, Capodistrias was a martyr; to his enemies, a tyrant. His death could not heal their divisions and over the next fifteen months anarchy ruled in the Peloponnese.[21]

In the spring of 1832, the Greek monarchy was finally established after the three great powers—England, France, and Russia—agreed to terms with the Bavarians. King Ludwig was a relatively liberal ruler and an ardent classicist who was keen on the Greeks both ancient and modern. It was agreed that his son, the seventeen-year-old Otto von Wittelsbach, would be given the title "King of Greece" and his throne would be hereditary, but that until he came of age his rights would be exercised by a regency of three figures chosen by his father. Otto was a devout Catholic and the Greeks would have preferred an Orthodox ruler, but none of the European powers was much worried what they thought and the issue was not as seriously regarded then as it would later become. Under the presidency of eighty-year-old Panoutsos Notaras, a short-lived national assembly met to approve Otto's selection: it was more than a decade before a successor was convened. The Bavarians contributed an army of 3,500 men to replace the French and a loan was pledged to cover some of the costs. In July 1832, Sultan Mahmud II recognized the new kingdom with a northern frontier running from the Gulf of Arta in the west to the Gulf of Volos in the east, which is where it would remain for nearly half a century.

The frontier itself was mapped out with some difficulty by British and French military surveyors who trudged on foot over the previously uncharted mountains of the Pindos. They marked the line every couple of miles by boundary stones that were periodically uprooted by Ottoman officials and then had to be replaced, an apt illustration of the tussle over borders that was to characterize Greco-Turkish relations thereafter. The very existence of an international frontier, however, marked a definitive break with centuries of social organization in the region and inaugurated new forms of political power and new challenges for local power brokers. The border became something to defend, violate, shelter behind, and argue over. To the shepherds of the mountains, moving their vast flocks over many miles each year, it was something to ignore; to patriots it was a provocation to further conquest. The border seemed to fix the meaning of "Greece" for the first time, except that of course for many involved in the fighting it was not where it was supposed to be, and they devoted themselves, as several generations did after them, to the task of redrawing the map and increasing the size of the country.[22]

On the other side of the line, the Ottoman state reasserted itself in Rumeli. Kütahı Pasha, now promoted to grand vizier, embarked upon his long-deferred reckoning with the Albanians, slaughtering dozens of their leading beys in cold blood in the town of Bitolj, and following the massacre up with a surprise assault on the Greek armatoles. Those who survived the pasha's onslaught fled across the border into Greece, where they contributed to the mayhem that followed Capodistrias's assassination and took the chance to refurbish their rather tarnished patriotic credentials. In the Indian summer of the wartime chieftains, 8,000

Rumeliot irregulars led by some familiar names fought their way into Argos and entered Nafplion, where Grivas and his men proceeded to act with a brutality that brought to mind the worst days of the past.[23]

Farther to the south, the miserable peasants of Messenia were being plundered as usual both by Kolokotronis's bands and by the Maniots. It seemed somehow symbolic when Dimitrios Ypsilantis—one of the few heroes of the war to have managed mostly to steer clear of politics—died, not yet forty. Despite poor health, he had fought on the battlefield from beginning to end and his disinterested patriotism was as rare as his courage. His family was one of those which had sacrificed its fortune for the Greek cause, and he had never tried to replenish it as others had done by laying waste to the country. In January 1833, on the eve of the Bavarians' arrival, one last serious clash took place in Argos between Greek irregulars and French troops. It ended with 160 Greeks and about 20 French dead, a shocking reminder to the chieftains of the firepower that could now be arrayed against them.[24]

A few days later, an international flotilla assembled in the bay of Nafplion to herald the coming of Greece's young Bavarian king, and when Otto arrived on HMS *Madagascar* on January 18 the French and Russian admirals went aboard to pay their respects. With Otto were three representatives of the Greeks who had gone to Munich to join his entourage: Admiral Miaoulis, the Souliot Kitsos Botsaris, and the Peloponnesian chieftain Plapoutas—the same man who had once worked as a kapo for the great Deliyannis family. Sicilian and Austrian warships were there, bedecked with flags; a steamship brought the British governor of Malta. Huge crowds gathered to watch from the hills and beaches around the bay—the German philhellene Ludwig Ross estimated their size at around 50,000, which would have likely made it the largest gathering ever seen in the country—as the impressively disciplined Bavarian troops disembarked. Finally, on January 25, 1833, with the morning's warmth presaging spring, the sun glinting in the waters and the bay resounding with cannonades, Otto stepped ashore at a garlanded landing stage two miles outside Nafplion. Kolokotronis was in the throng, recognizable by his crested helmet, the memento of his service in Richard Church's light infantry, and near him Mavrokordatos, neatly dressed in the French style and wearing gold-rimmed glasses. Eyewitnesses claim the king slipped as he took his first step onto Greek soil—an omen perhaps of his later misfortunes. But for the moment all political animosities were forgotten as the highly choreographed royal procession made its way, led by Otto on horseback, through the massed and euphoric crowds, flanked by Bavarian soldiers in their pale blue uniforms.[25]

Beneath a triumphal arch in front of Nafplion's main gate, the French commandant of the town handed the king the keys. "Hellenes!" Otto declared in his first proclamation:

> Called to you by the wishes of the High Mediating Powers to whose protection you owe the possibility of gloriously terminating a long and destructive war, called equally by your free votes, I ascend the throne of Greece.

The Greeks, he went on, had acquired "a political existence" and independence, and they had done so showing themselves worthy of their glorious ancestors. But despotism had been succeeded by anarchy and the countryside languished, manufacturing was in its infancy, and the arts and sciences had still not returned "to their ancient homeland." It was time to end an all-consuming civil war and focus on one goal: "prosperity, the happiness and glory of your fatherland which has now become mine." The proclamation was signed by three regents—Count Josef Armansperg, Georg Ludwig Maurer, and Carl von Heideck—as the king was still underage.[26]

Less than three months later, at nine o'clock one spring morning at the beginning of April 1833, a detachment of Bavarian troops approached the slopes of the Acropolis and clambered "with some difficulty up the steep narrow path filled with stones and ruins." "When we arrived at the entrance," Lieutenant Christopher Neezer wrote later, "we were met by the two hundred and fifty or so men of the Ottoman garrison who looked more like a band of robbers than the unit of a regular army, many in tatters and the soles of their shoes worn through, though their weapons were clean and gleaming, long Spanish muskets, pistols, knives and scimitars, an entire armory in their belts." Silent and sullen, they marched past the Bavarians without saluting, emerging on the open ground below in groups of ten to twelve men. Looking on, George Finlay noted their "dirty ragged clothes, 2 richly caparisoned horses, a mule and a man pulling a ram by the horns." Their commander, Osman Efendi, formally handed over the fortress to the Bavarians; with him departed the last vestige of the sultan's authority in Greece.[27]

Neezer spent the first night with his men under the columns of the Parthenon, overwhelmed by the significance of the moment. He watched the sun set over the mountains of the Peloponnese and as the moon rose he saw before him, in a kind of reverie, the ghosts of Perikles, Socrates, Euripides, and Demosthenes. The next morning he was startled awake by the appearance of a stocky elderly Chiot sailor who introduced himself as kapetan Dimitris and said that he had come up from Piraeus with his son. In broken Italian, the son explained that his father had brought a Greek flag with him. Neezer and his soldiers stood at attention and saluted with their swords as the old man raised it high amid a great shout of "Long live Greece, long live the king!" Then their work began: among the fragments of ancient masonry and huge broken marble columns, the ground of the Acropolis was still strewn with cannonballs, shrapnel, and human remains. Skulls and bones lay thickly around the caryatids on the half-destroyed Erechtheion. Neezer's men started to gather them up and found a basement storeroom in which to put them.

These soldiers were a detachment of the troops who had landed in Nafplion with Otto a few months earlier. The Peloponnesian port itself was disease-ridden and overcrowded, and Otto and his advisers had quickly decided that the kingdom needed a new permanent capital: after some discussion they opted for Athens. The renowned Prussian architect Karl Friedrich Schinkel liked the idea of using the Acropolis for the site of the new royal palace, a low neoclassical complex—at least in his drawings—with a sunken hippodrome and a giant bronze reconstruction of the statue of Athena, spear in hand, towering over the town. But the king's advisers damned this as "a charming *Midsummer Night's Dream*" and chose to build instead looking over to the Acropolis from the hillock of Boubounistra where the palace—an uncompromisingly stark rectangle with a classical facade tacked on as an afterthought—survives to this day as the home of the Greek parliament.[28]

The Bavarian garrison continued to be lodged on the Acropolis until the following year. After it was decided to establish the entire area as an archaeological site, Otto's chief architect, Leo von Klenze, staged a ceremony to mark the moment. Inside the Parthenon, the young king sat on a throne decorated with laurel, olive, and myrtle branches, while von

Klenze hailed the start of a new era. "Your Majesty's foot has today trod for the first time, after many centuries of barbarism, on this sacred rock . . . The traces of a barbaric period, ruins and formless rubble, will be effaced here, as everywhere in Greece, and the remains of the glorious past will be restored with a new brilliance." In a process that was to take years and indeed decades, the Ottoman garrison village on the Acropolis was demolished, the Frankish tower from where Androutsos had fallen was torn down, and the entire complex of bastions, gates, and flanking walls that had protected the entrance through the war gradually vanished. Mounds of rubble were tipped over the walls onto the slopes below. The restoration of the architectural glories of the Classical age, as von Klenze had made clear, meant the destruction of any physical obstacle from the intervening centuries that could come between the modern imagination and the ancient glories. An archaeological service was established, war veterans were appointed as guards, and the first tickets were issued to visitors in the spring of 1835. The Acropolis ceased to become an integral part of the military administration of the town of Athens, which had been its historic role, and was transformed into a symbol of Greece's resurrection.[29]

Otto arrived by boat from Nafplion in December 1834, to take up residence in his new capital. Besides the old Turkish customs house, a palm tree, horses, donkeys, and a few camels, there was almost nothing standing on the Piraeus shoreline where fierce fighting had taken place seven years earlier. The Bavarian regents and their Greek ministers met the young monarch at the waterfront, and the cavalcade made its way through the miles of olive groves that led into the town. Near the Theseion, several thousand Athenians had gathered to welcome their new king. They were said to have been disappointed by the lack of pomp and amazed by the extraordinary amount of royal baggage. The city had been ravaged by the war and struck one visitor as a "disgusting and filthy place." Two years after work on Otto's palace had started, a French reporter scoffed: "[New Athens] is a town which does not yet have a road, but where they started by building a palace—a sufficiently correct image of a country where they first made a king before they were assured that there was a nation."[30]

One of the most immediate and urgent legacies of the war was financial. Capodistrias had warned Leopold of Saxe-Coburg that "there is not a single Greek who has not suffered considerable losses; there is not one who does not expect compensation."[31] The language of promissory notes, forced loans, and government bonds had spread during the revolution, and the archives are full of an astonishing number of bills and invoices, some of them dating back to 1821, from carters and ostlers to princes, landowners, shipowners, and admirals. There were townspeople whose houses had been destroyed; farmers whose barns had been plundered; tax farmers who had never received their crops; and of course innumerable wage bills for ships and the soldiery, some genuine, some fictitious. There was a veritable industry in affidavits testifying to wartime service. Provisional governments during the uprising had been short of money but lavish with promises, and among the groups to whom they specifically pledged compensation were members of the garrison at Mesolonghi, units commanded by Karaïskakis and various Moreot leaders, and the widows and orphans of fallen fighters. It seemed as though the whole of society now looked to the new state for assistance and funding. A committee was set up to scrutinize these claims, which took into the 1850s to sort out. Gifts of property, positions, and honors allowed many of those who had fought—as well as plenty who had not—to orient themselves toward the new center of power. Yet those who gained the most from Bavarian patronage tended to be those who for one reason or another could be useful to them, and this left many veterans of the war empty-handed.

The men who had started the uprising—the leaders of the Etaireia—did not, on the whole, profit from the new dispensation and many of them died penniless. Emmanouil Xanthos moved back to Greece in 1837 and lived in acute poverty until his death in 1852. Had he not penned his own memoir, angered by reading misleading accounts of how it all began, his key role in the Etaireia's establishment would have been entirely overlooked. Panayiotis Anagnostopoulos, who escorted Dimitrios Ypsilantis to Trieste and Hydra in the spring of 1821, died a poor man. Panayiotis Sekeris, who had expended his fortune for the cause, was a customs official when he passed away in Nafplion in 1846, leaving behind an invaluable collection of papers. The many Etairists who did populate the new state apparatus—becoming mayors, prefects, teachers, writers, and lawyers—tended to be the younger and more highly educated ones who had been active in the wartime politicking of the revolution.

The Etaireia itself had been too radical, too conspiratorial, and too Russian in its orientation for the comfort of the Bavarian regency. In 1837 a wealthy Greek benefactor called Baron Constantine Bellios visited Athens where he helped establish the new archaeological society. The baron was based in Vienna and had been ennobled by the Austrian emperor Francis I. At the same time, he had close ties with the Danubian Principalities and he was an ardent patriot. One day he mentioned in conversation that while in Athens he planned to attend a meeting of the local society (Etaireia) for natural history and he was instantly rebuked for using the word "etaireia." "Why not, sir?" he responded in irritation. "You should not be bothered by a little word so worthy of our respect, since that fortunate word brought you and everyone else together here." That was not the monarchy's view, however, and when the following year the beginning of the struggle for independence was officially celebrated for the first time, the government ignored the date of Alexandros Ypsilantis's crossing of the Pruth—February 22—and opted instead to mark the start of the uprising in the Peloponnese one month later.[32]

On the other hand, many of the Phanariot nobility—if they escaped the sultan's wrath—ended their days in the new Greece in positions of rank and power. Sacrificing deference for security, Ioannis Karatzas, once the all-powerful *hospodar* of Wallachia, found that in Greece, as Baron Bellios poignantly noted, he was no longer addressed as prince or master but merely as mister (*kyrios*): his granddaughter would marry into the Kolokotronis family. Karatzas's nephew, the former *hospodar* of Moldavia, Mihail Soutzos, served Greece as a diplomat—his ten languages coming in useful—before retiring to Athens where he was buried in the First Cemetery amid great pomp one scorching summer day in July 1864, near the tombs of Petros Mavromihalis, Kolokotronis, and Zaimis. The man who had been his secretary, Iakovaky Neroulos, became foreign minister, ambassador, and a founder of both the national university and the archaeological society. Mary Shelley's friend Alexandros Mavrokordatos became prime minister in 1833—the first of his four terms holding the office over the next two decades. Prince Alexandros Kantakuzinos, who had helped Dimitrios Ypsilantis escape Trieste, invested cannily in buying up the estates of Ottoman notables around the capital.

Most of the great landed families of the Peloponnese adjusted even more smoothly to the new regime: once the Greek parliament was established in 1844, this became the new guarantor of their grip on their respective regions. Kanellos Deliyannis's nephew, Theodoros, who had been born in the family stronghold of Langadia in the middle of the war, became one of the most prominent politicians of the nineteenth century, five times prime minister; all told, the family sent more than a dozen deputies to parliament. Andreas Notaras, who married Karaïskakis's daughter, was deputy for Corinth between 1844 and 1879; their son continued in what had become a family appanage until 1905, his great-nephew until 1915. The Zaimis and Koundouriotis clans featured prominently in Greece's political life for decades. Descendants of Athanasios Kanakaris, the last delegate (*vekil*) of the Peloponnese to the Porte before the revolution, represented his hometown of Patras as mayors and deputies deep into the twentieth century.

Participation in the revolution was more or less a prerequisite for a political career and most of the country's early prime ministers were former protagonists of the struggle. Spiridon Trikoupis and his brother-in-law Alexandros Mavrokordatos served as Otto's first two prime ministers as the Bavarian regime established itself. All but one of the eleven individuals who served as prime minister under Otto—excluding the years in which he or his regents took the position—had been prominent in the war, and the influence of that generation lingered until the last of them, the Psaran fireship virtuoso, Konstantine Kanaris, admired as much for his modest lifestyle as for his courage, died in office at the age of eighty-four in 1877.

The relationship of many of the military chieftains with the new Bavarian regime, however, was thorny from the outset. Men such as Kolokotronis who had battled the sultan were not likely to lie down before the Bavarians or accept the regents' constant deferral of representative government, especially those among them who had been supporters of Capodistrias and still saw Orthodox Russia as their natural protector. In the spring of 1834, the government foolishly tried Kolokotronis and Plapoutas for treason on the grounds that they had been conspiring with the Russians against the regency. An extraordinary court was convened in the former mosque in Nafplion, and the prosecution was led by a Scottish philhellene called Edward Masson, a hard-line anti-Russian who spoke perfect Greek. Although the accused were sentenced to death, two of the judges objected and the sentences were commuted. Plapoutas expressed outrage that he had been accused of consorting with robbers and anarchists: the former kapo was keen now to assert his credentials as one of the dignitaries of the state. Kolokotronis's response was different: famously identifying himself as "a soldier, musket in hand, a fighter for the fatherland," he listened impassively to the proceedings, playing with his worry beads and presenting himself as a simple countryman who had been happy that the arrival of the king would allow him to retire quietly and hang up his cap.[33]

The "Old Man" knew exactly what he was doing in crafting this image. A series of uprisings and disorders across the southern Peloponnese reminded the Bavarians of his continued influence and a year after their death sentence, Kolokotronis and Plapoutas were released from prison and quickly brought into royal favor along with many other of the wartime chieftains.[34] Kolokotronis's son, Gennaios, became an aide to the king. So did Vasos Mavrovouniotis, the Montenegrin plunderer of Beirut and Evvia, and Petros Mavromihalis's nephew Katsakos; Petros himself was made a state counselor and given access to large lands in Lakonia in a futile effort to stop his endless claims for financial support. Otto bestowed a large area of forest near Mesolonghi upon another aide, Kitsos Tzavellas, while the Grivas brothers got vast estates around Vonitsa. The Bavarians also associated the monarchy with the revolution's dead heroes: they provided the dowry for Karaïskakis's daughter and sent Odysseus Androutsos's son, Leonidas, to the court in Munich. On royal occasions, many of the old warriors were fixtures. When a ball was held in honor of King Ludwig of Bavaria, who was visiting his son in Athens, the young couples whirled round to the waltz, polonaise, and quadrille until, for one extraordinary moment, at Ludwig's request, the orchestra stopped. Kolokotronis, Grivas, Vasos, and a few others then formed a line and began to dance the *syrtos* with Makriyannis in the lead, "as active as a youth of sixteen," crouching down and jumping into the air.[35]

The chieftains remained very much their own men, willing to remind the Bavarians of their independence and starting to fashion themselves into the figures that later generations would venerate—plain-speaking, courageous, and unpolitical men of the people, fighting a new foreign occupier and holding out for freedom. In 1838 Kolokotronis made a famous speech on the Pnyx in Athens that called for continued opposition to the Bavarian regime. "When we decided to make the Revolution," he told his audience of astonished students, "we did not weigh up how many we were, nor how many arms we had . . . but, like a rain, there fell over us all the desire for our freedom, and all of us—the clergy, the notables, the kapetans, the educated ones, the merchants, big and small, we all agreed on this goal and made the Revolution."[36]

The call for constitutional government became sharper with time, and demands grew for the "Bavarocracy" (*Bavarokratia*) to go the way of the Turks (*Tourkokratia*). In 1843, only a few months after Koloko-tronis's death at the age of seventy-two, Makriyannis, Andreas Londos, and other veterans led a peaceful rebellion that eventually produced Greece's first postindependence constitution, one of the most demo-cratic in Europe. Finally, independent Greece acquired a parliament and it was then that the square in front of the royal palace was renamed Constitution Square, a permanent reminder to the monarchy. Enmeshed in these events, the Russian minister in Athens at the time, Gavriil Katakazis, was the same man who more than two decades earlier had been the Etairist apostle for Russia and who had recruited the Ypsilantis brothers for the cause: despite the Bavarians' best efforts, the spirit of the Etaireia was not completely dead. Indeed, in its combination of con-stitutionalist and religious impulses—the primary driver for Katakazis, as for many in the Russian faction in Greece, was above all the desire to strengthen Orthodoxy—the rebellion of 1843 was driven by much the same mix of impulses that had fueled the Etaireia.[37]

This sense of unfinished business—the work of the *romeïko* that remained to be completed—was equally visible in the growing power of a restless lobby that did not regard the 1832 boundaries with the Otto-man state as anything more than a temporary compromise in a larger struggle to bring the Greeks of the empire together. There were perhaps three times as many Greek speakers outside the new kingdom of Greece as there were within it and redeeming the so-called unredeemed breth-ren became the core of the "Great Idea" of a larger Greece, an irredentist passion that lasted for the best part of a century. Its primary adherents were the Rumeliot kapetans and their armed clienteles in the northern borderlands, sometimes serving as gendarmes against the bands of rob-bers and brigands that plagued the mountains, and sometimes mounting incursions of their own into Ottoman territory. In 1844 Grivas was still preaching war and marching through the streets of Athens with a large armed retinue. During the Crimean War, after the czar appealed to the Christians of the Balkans to act in his support, Grivas led a raid to "liberate" Epirus and Thessaly, and some familiar names—Kitsos Tsavellas, a young Karaïskakis—joined him in a mission that produced large quantities of plunder for the returning heroes but defeat at the hands of the Ottoman army.[38]

The three signatory powers of the Treaty of London exercised enormous influence over the country and it was not only the Russian minister in Athens who meddled deeply in domestic Greek politics—his English and French colleagues did so too. It was always tempting to regard them as another form of tyranny, one that independence had created not ended. But they did not prevent the establishment of a rational assembly in 1843 nor did they interfere later, in 1862, when Otto, who had neither produced an heir nor observed the constitution, fled the country on a British warship after another popular uprising. Back in Bavaria, the former king wore the fustanella around the bishop's palace in Bamberg, continued to practice his spoken Greek, and died a few years later with the word "Greece" supposedly on his lips. The search for his replacement ran through Prince Alfred of England and Duke Ernest of Saxe-Coburg-Gotha, and sounded out the interest of the Habsburg Archduke Maximilian who is said to have remarked that having visited Greece and studied it, "he was astonished . . . that [King Otto] was not thankful to have left the country for ever." Maximilian opted instead for Mexico where he lasted three years as emperor before being executed by a republican firing squad.[39] Eventually Otto was succeeded—to almost everyone's satisfaction—by Denmark's Prince William of Schleswig-Holstein-Sonderburg-Glücksburg, who (as King George) established a dynasty that ruled the country for much of the following century. It may be worth pointing out that no king of Greece died quietly in office before 1947: Otto was driven out, George I was assassinated in 1913, Constantine was exiled twice, and Alexander's brief reign ended with a monkey bite. George II, who managed it, is said to have remarked that "the most important tool for a king of Greece is a suitcase."

By the 1850s, the memory of the revolution was beginning to enter the realm of legend. The transcriber of Kolokotronis's memoirs, Georgios Tertsetis, paid homage to him after his death by imagining him as the old Oedipus questioning a young Antigone on his entry into Attica: "The labors of the struggle, where did they lead us? Which city of men have we built? What society have we shaped?" The fighters were being heroized, almost deified, and their stories seemed to belong to another time entirely. Visitors queued up to see the "old Pallikars with their iron hands and their torsos all covered in wounds." When two French travelers—Maxime Du Camp and his friend Gustave Flaubert—met Kanaris in Athens, they found it impossible to equate the famous hero of the fireships, the warrior "who had put the Turkish fleets to flight and before whom Alexandria wept in fear," with the man "dressed in a bourgeois frock coat, his white hair neatly trimmed, heavy mustache, kindly glance . . . now a political personality, a little lost in the role."[40]

Aging heroes were everywhere. In the Hotel d'Angleterre a certain Colonel Touret in a sky-blue uniform marched up to Du Camp and Flaubert and saluted them, announcing himself as a fellow countryman. He recounted his adventures from the last days of the empire through to his combat experiences in Chios, Corinth, and the siege of Athens. As he spoke, "we rediscovered in his tales the echo of the preoccupations which our infancy had witnessed. We had been rocked in the cradle to the sound of Albanian legends . . . we had thrilled to the sound of the artillery announcing the victory at Navarino." They felt an affection for the old colonel, who regaled them so happily with his memories; they felt moved by the settings, for "the immortality of the places adds to their grandeur and those who fought against the Turks are reminded no doubt of those who fought against the Persians." Even their guide on the road to the steamboat at Patras had amazing stories to tell: a fighter, he had been wounded, imprisoned, escaped, shipwrecked, retaken by the Turks, converted, enslaved in Egypt, and sent to Constantinople by a pasha before abducting his master's wife and returning to Greece. It was becoming hard to distinguish truth from myth.[41]

Children's memories lasted longest. One Friday afternoon in the 1870s during a ride in the park, Mrs. Rallis, an ardent anglophile and a member of London's prosperous Anglo-Greek community, surprised her upper-class companion with the story of her dramatic escape from Chios half a century before. Born Maria Argenti, the daughter of a prosperous merchant, she could have been only four or five years old at the time of the massacres. She remembered having to take off her clothes (so as not to reveal her family's status) and running naked between her mother and aunt over the sharp stones; she remembered "being with a great number of people on a high mountain, but for how many days I do not know."[42]

A few of the stories from Chios were less of trauma than of staggering transformation. The grand vizier of the Ottoman Empire during the Near Eastern crisis of 1877–78, Ibrahim Edhem Pasha, had been about three years old when the Turks carried him off from Chios: he had been adopted by Husrev Pasha, Mehmed Ali's great rival, and raised in his household. Isma'il ibn Ahmad ibn Hassan bani Yani—better known simply as Raghib Pasha—was another enslaved Chiot boy who went on to become prime minister of Egypt. Perhaps most remarkable of all was the story of five-year-old Georgios Stravelakis. Sent by a slave dealer with his brother to the bey of Tunis, he converted to Islam, married a princess, and rose to become the grand vizier for more than thirty years: under his assumed name of Mustafa Khaznadar he is remembered today as one of the most important figures in nineteenth-century Tunisian history. These men testified to the final decades of a centuries-old practice in Muslim polities of staffing the highest levels of imperial governance with slave recruits.[43]

If such stories have come down to us, it is because of their subjects' prominence and also because they were male, which meant the possibility for at least a fortunate few to advance into some kind of public life. We know much less about enslaved Greek girls and women. The dragoman at the British consulate regularly took travelers to the Egyptian capital to see the Cairo slave market and he even made purchases on behalf of his guests. Two of them ended up marrying their acquisitions, which is how we know about them. Robert Hay of Linplum, a Scottish country gentleman and a serious amateur Egyptologist, ransomed several girls and married one of them, Kalitsa Psaraki, the daughter of a Cretan notable, who had been abducted together with her brothers and sisters by Egyptian soldiers during a raid: thanks to her husband, she seems to have been able to return to see her parents, the only one of her siblings to do so. Hay's assistant and friend Edward Lane, who was to become one of the foremost Arabists of the century, was so upset by the sight of a seven-year-old slave girl called Nafeeseh that he purchased her and left her in the care of his mother while he got on with writing his *Description of Egypt.* When she turned twenty he married her under her real name, Anastasoula Georgiou.[44]

Thousands of orphans had been created by the war, but unlike the business of slave redemption, which was the focus of immense public and private engagement in the decade after the conflict ended, the plight of the orphans remaining inside Greece was relatively neglected and underfunded. Their care had been explicitly mentioned as a duty of government in the 1827 Troezen constitution and Capodistrias was one of the few national leaders for whom it was a priority. With his support, the American Samuel Howe constructed an orphanage in Aigina; another was established on Andros. Several orphans also ended up being sent across the Atlantic. Working for the New York Greek Committee, Jonathan Miller adopted a boy whom he named Lukas Miltiades Miller, who eventually entered Congress as a Democrat from Wisconsin in 1891.[45] A girl called Garafilia Mihalbey was rescued from captivity in Smyrna by an American merchant and brought to Boston. She died at the age of thirteen of tuberculosis, but after her death she became the subject of a famous engraving and her story was invoked by Harriet Beecher Stowe, the author of *Uncle Tom's Cabin*.

The arriving orphans, living testimony to the struggle for freedom, were caught up in the intensifying drama of American unfreedom. One of the most striking cases was that of John Zachos, a Greek orphan brought to the United States by his foster father Samuel Howe. Zachos became an ardent abolitionist and educator who devised literacy programs for former slaves and later helped establish Cooper Union in New York as a place of free education. What was obvious to Zachos was by no means clear to many American philhellenes who continued to tolerate slavery at home. African American abolitionists were especially conscious of the double standard: in his 1829 *Appeal to the Coloured Citizens of the World*, David Walker described a South Carolina newspaper that juxtaposed an article on Turkish barbarism with an advertisement for the sale of "eight well-built Virginia and Maryland Negro fellows and four wenches." The leading abolitionist, William Lloyd Garrison, had nearly gone off to join the Greeks as a young man and he openly criticized contemporaries for supporting a tyranny that, as he put it, was "much more inexcusable than Turkish [slavery]." As time went on, the force of this comparison became more marked: with the astonishing furor around the display of Hiram Powers's famously shocking marble sculpture, a female nude entitled *The Greek Slave*, which toured America in the late 1840s, the Greek cause became a vehicle for abolitionism.[46]

Many of those who had taken up the cause of Greece, or suffered for it, saw the struggle for liberty as universal. This is why some philhellenes had fought previously in Piedmont, Naples, Spain, or South America, and it is what also made them sensitive not only to questions of slavery but to the claims of fellow nationalists as well. A few went on to fight for the Poles in the uprising of 1830; others returned to Italy to fight there. Deep and enduring connections bound the Greeks to Italian nationalists as well as to Saint-Simonians like Gustav d'Eichthal, a supporter of European unity. The itinerant German-Danish philhellene Paul Harro Harring, part of an international circle of republicans for whom expulsion was a way of life, plotted a revolt against czarist rule in Poland, got himself banned from France, Switzerland, Bavaria, and Saxony, and was mixed up in numerous uprisings and attempted rebellions. In 1848, the year of revolutions across Europe, he was one of many activists who had once fought for the Greeks. Indeed, Greece itself became a kind of sanctuary for freedom fighters from across Europe until the government came under pressure from Russia and Austria to clamp down and poverty forced them to immigrate to Britain or the United States.[47]

The memory of the Greek struggle lingered long into the nineteenth century and left its mark. The German philhellene Francis Lieber eventually immigrated to the United States and became a university professor: shaped by his own bitter experiences in Greece, the guidance he drafted during the American Civil War for the Union side on how soldiers should behave in the field has come to be regarded as a foundational document in the international law of war. As for the most influential and durable liberal statesman of nineteenth-century Europe, British Prime Minister William Gladstone, he never forgot youthful conversations he had had with George Canning, nor his own father's philhellenic speeches. In 1824, as a fifteen-year-old at Eton, fired up by Byron and "an ardent Canningite," Gladstone had dressed up in "all the glories of the costume of a Greek patriot," an embrace of the Hellenic cause that prefigured his long commitment to national struggles across the continent.[48] Men like Gladstone and Lieber traversed an arc from youthful militancy to professional intervention at home and abroad for the sake of peace and social justice; it was an arc of commitment that had started with the Greeks and that mapped liberalism's trajectory across the century.

A sole photograph survives of Alexandros Mavrokordatos, taken in 1863, two years before his death. It shows the four-time prime minister seated with his walking stick, sick and nearly blind, listening to the national assembly debate a new constitution, a product of the European-style political system he had envisaged in Pisa forty years before. He lived just long enough to see Britain hand over the Ionian Islands, Greece's first major acquisition of territory since independence. His generation, the wartime generation, was dying out. The last of the armatoles, Ioannis Rangos, passed away in 1870. Sir Richard Church, who had settled in Athens, died in 1873, followed soon after by his friend and landlord, George Finlay. Fotakos, Kolokotronis's adjutant, died at the end of the decade having authored one of the finest memoirs of the entire war.

Some of the women of the revolution lasted longer, though they were neglected by historians, and the stories they could have told have vanished. There was general astonishment in 1879 when it turned out that Androutsos's wife, Eleni, had been living quietly in Athens all the time: somehow the great chieftain heroes were never imagined with wives. Vasiliki Tzavellas was the widow of the Souliot chieftain Kitsos Tzavellas: she had fought her way out of Mesolonghi alongside him, later miraculously redeeming their infant who had been captured during the exodus. She died in her small cottage in the Athens suburb of Kefissia, much admired for her charitable deeds. As for the philhellenes, Byron's friend Edward Trelawny, the adventurer who had consigned Shelley's body to the pyre and numbered the half sister of Odysseus Androutsos among his three wives, died in 1881. After him, not many were left. Perhaps the last of them was Maxime Raybaud, who died in 1894 in his native France, more than seventy years after he had stepped off the boat in Mesolonghi with Mavrokordatos.

As the nineteenth century ended, a short, slim, upright old man was still to be seen taking his daily walk through the streets of Athens, assured in his movements and entirely lucid with the journalists who flocked to his door. Apostolos Mavroyeni was the last Greek fighter of the war, a survivor from a vanished world. Born in or around 1792, he had studied medicine in Pisa before fighting against Ibrahim's troops in the Morea. In 1854 he followed the aging warlord Grivas on a foray into Ottoman Epiros. Almost half a century later, Mavroyeni attended the ceremony at which King George unveiled a statue to Kolokotronis in Nafplion. This was the first monumental statue of a hero on horse-back to be erected in Greece, and it had been cast in bronze supposedly melted down from cannons on the Palamidi. After chatting familiarly with the king—it was noted that they used the second-person singular with one another—Mavroyeni placed a wreath "to the memory of the glorious chief, of the fighter who was my personal friend."[49]

"The last surviving holy relic of the Struggle," Mavroyeni died, in November 1906, at a wondrous age. He had been a veteran of about forty when King Otto rode into Athens to set up court amid the ruins of a small Ottoman town. By the time Mavroyeni passed away, the Greek capital's population exceeded 100,000, and there was a railway down to Piraeus, one of several entirely new towns that had sprung up after independence. The country's population had more than doubled, even as some of the heartlands of the revolution—Hydra, Spetses, the Mani—became depopulated and a wave of emigrants crossed the Atlantic. There were banks, hotels, brothels, and university students; telegraph cables had accelerated communications and paved roads snaked across the country. None of these things had existed in the old days. Neither had streets with names nor steamships on schedules: the connection to Trieste that had once taken weeks now took three days through the new Corinth Canal. Virginia Woolf, Sigmund Freud, and the young Swiss architect Charles-Édouard Jeanneret—later known as Le Corbusier—were among the tourists who visited the Acropolis that Androutsos, Gouras, and the Ottomans had fought over. The skulls and human remains had long been cleared away. Amid the blinding splendor of the ancient past the ghosts of 1821 wandered unseen.

EPILOGUE: THE ECONOMY
OF THE MIRACLE

I remember that when today's Kingdom of Greece was estab-
lished, the inhabitants said: "Look, the romeïko *has come about."*
I. Isidore Skylissis, 1871[1]

Hugging the side of the Kechrovouni mountain high above the port of
Tinos is a fortified convent about a millennium old. Surrounded by terraced fields and pine woods, its great whitewashed walls protect the
quiet labyrinth of cells and chapels within. On the steps outside the
main gate villagers sell oregano and honey to tourists who come and
admire the breathtaking panorama across the Aegean that can reveal a
dozen islands on a clear day. But the convent's main attraction lies
inside, drawing busloads of pilgrims to the place where an elderly nun
had a vision in the middle of the war that led to the discovery of what
is today Greece's most famous miracle-working icon.

In 1821 the conflict must have seemed very close to the eighty or so
nuns who were living there. From their vantage point, they could see the
first ships of the revolution arriving from Spetses and Hydra, the boats
bringing refugees from Asia Minor, and later the vast fleet of the
Kapudan Pasha sailing to and from the Peloponnese. Watching the
French philhellene Maxime Raybaud test explosives in a nearby field,
some of them asked him if he knew a way they could blow themselves
up in case the Turks attacked.[2]

Seventy-year-old Pelagia had been a nun for more than half a century
and was respected for her piety. Her father had been a priest in a nearby
village. Born when the island was still under the rule of Venice, he had
raised his family in a stone cottage with a few livestock, poultry, and

their crops for sustenance. But he had died when Pelagia was young and so she entered the monastery where an aunt of hers already resided. She gave a plot of land she inherited to an older sister for her dowry, keeping in her possession a tiny country chapel dedicated to the Virgin and enough money to pay for the construction of the modest stone dwelling that became her new home inside the monastery walls. The nuns would gather firewood, till the fields on the adjacent hillside, and trudge to nearby chapels on saints' days. Their time was governed by the rhythms of the liturgy and the holy calendar. Pelagia spent evenings in prayer before icons illuminated by flickering candlelight. On several occasions she is said to have communed with saints.[3]

One Sunday night in July 1822, shortly before dawn, a woman of queenly beauty and luster came to Pelagia in her sleep and told the nun she wanted the islanders to dig near the town and build a magnificent dwelling. She specified the name of the man she wanted to get the work done and the particular field they were to dig up. On waking, Pelagia concluded it was either her imagination or the devil at work and so she said nothing. Seven days later, at precisely the same time, the same thing happened. On a third occasion, the woman identified herself as the Virgin Mary and threatened punishment if she was not obeyed. So Pelagia notified the abbess, who told her to find the man the Virgin had named. Stamatelos Kagkadis was an island notable and a member of the supervising committee of the convent, and he in turn went to see the archbishop. Archbishop Gabriel knew Pelagia and realized this was not a "dark dream," so he ordered digging to begin. But the field the Virgin had specified, on a bluff above the town, was owned by a Tiniot away in Constantinople on business and his wife's reluctance to allow the excavations in his absence delayed things. The initial digging revealed the ruins of an early Christian church, as well as a spring, before the organizers become discouraged. These were tense and dangerous months on the island. A ship from Constantinople had brought the plague, which was spreading rapidly, especially among the thousands of refugees who had come from Chios and Asia Minor. Regarding the epidemic as a sign of the Virgin's anger, the islanders resumed their excavation and at the end of January 1823, on the feast day of the Three Holy Hierarchs, a workman's shovel scraped against something.

A decade later, by which time the site was already famous, a pamphlet told of how the object had turned out to be an ancient icon buried centuries before, how crowds had thronged to the field on hearing the news, how astonishingly the plague did not spread among them, and how many of those already afflicted were saved. Among them was the son of one of the monastery supervisors. The boy had been struck down some days earlier and his family had been obliged to leave him alone with attendants. But then his weeping father took a handful of the earth where the icon had been found, sprinkled it with the holy water, and gave it to the nurses to apply to the swellings under his son's armpits. The next morning, the boy was cured.[4]

The plague had subsided and other miracles had followed. The early beneficiaries of the Virgin's grace included local members of the far-flung and immensely powerful Mavroyeni family, a sailor aboard Hastings's steam frigate who was brought to the island in a coma, a young man from Mitylene, a blind man from Athens, and a Catholic from the island suffering from dropsy. The Virgin was ecumenical in her favors, bringing together rich and poor, from all the corners of the Greek world and extending her blessings beyond the Orthodox. Her fame spread, and as pilgrims flocked to the island they provided the funds to continue the construction. Thus, in the midst of the war, a remarkable marble building arose on the hill above the town and a wide avenue was built up to it from the port. Reverend Charles Swan recorded the building of "a monastery of considerable magnitude . . . now two years in progress" when HMS *Cambrian* passed that way in 1825. Three years later, an agent of the New York Greek Committee was struck by the new church's size and unusual proportions—"probably the finest modern building in Greece"; in 1833 it was visited by the newly arrived King Otto of Greece, on board the first steam cruiser to tour the eastern Mediterranean. When Prince Pückler-Muskau visited at the end of the 1830s, he described the church as "without doubt the most beautiful and one of the largest I have yet seen in the Kingdom of Greece." By 1840 it was attracting visitors from "all the islands of the Archipelago, all corners of Greece and Asia Minor," and approximately 45,000 pilgrims came each year as the century drew to a close.[5]

When Pelagia died in the spring of 1834, the old Ottoman world of her birth had been wrenched asunder. So far as we know she had never left the island of Tinos but the war and its aftereffects had been visible to her nonetheless. The island's dozens of churches and hundreds of chapels survived mostly intact, yet the number of priests had dropped by half.[6] At the same time, her visions and the miraculous discovery of the icon had brought prosperity to the monastery and the island and turned Tinos into a spiritual center of the new state. The king himself had come to pay homage and Pelagia's homeland was now part of an independent Greece in which Orthodoxy was the regnant faith.

The war against the sultan had been a struggle for land, and none knew its value better than those who toiled it. The parched earth of the eastern Mediterranean hid treasures that could effect miracles. It might disgorge ancient remains of great value; it might reveal the sources of water that made life possible. And as the events of 1822–23 demonstrated, it might also preserve traces of the Greeks' long and faithful connection with their God. It took the war to bring those traces to the surface. A decade later, peasants on the nearby island of Naxos also began dreaming about buried icons and eventually discovered some. The authorities' response was to put the humble visionaries on trial and to confiscate the icons. Their clampdown was revealing. By the 1830s there was a Holy Synod to regulate claims of miracles and there was an archaeological service backed by legislation that governed the fate of any antiquity found in the soil. A functioning Greek state based in Athens claimed its own power over the land and the treasures within.[7]

In the 1820s, this power had not yet emerged and there was no effective Greek state. The ecclesiastical hierarchy of Orthodoxy had collapsed, and the patriarch in Constantinople was telling the islands to remain loyal to the sultan. Even the archbishop on the island, Gabriel, had been uncertain what to do. In the resultant vacuum of authority, the initiative had been taken by local notables on Tinos waging a canny battle to preserve their traditional influence. This influence was threatened not so much by the Turks as it was by the strangers who arrived after 1821 to rule the island in the name of the revolution. There was little love lost between the islanders and the Hydriot sailors: when they came ashore, knife fights and brawls were common and shootings not unknown. Even neighboring villages were locked in conflict and there were 16,000 refugees to feed and house. "The whole island is at war," wrote the government commissioners in October 1822. Amid this tubulence, it was the Kagkadis brothers and their fellow notables who supported the excavations and who later publicized the icon and its miracles in books and pamphlets. By the time Greece became independent, the site had become so popular it was beyond challenge. Stamatelos Kagkadis became the first mayor of the island, a position he held for a decade. The war itself thus made the miracles possible, allowing a local vision of the national past to reveal itself that, as the unfortunate peasants on Naxos discovered, could only have emerged in the interregnum between the death of one secular power and the birth of its successor.[8]

That interregnum had been a time of perils, however. The Ottoman fleet regularly passed by the island on its way back to Constantinople, and on at least one occasion came so close that a Tiniot bastion on a headland fired its cannons at an imperial frigate. Even as the church was under construction, Stamatelos's own brother, Iakovos Kagkadis, was being tipped off by a Muslim acquaintance from Constantinople that the Egyptian fleet was sailing into the area; his friend offered to negotiate if Tinos wanted to submit to the sultan. In the face of such fears and temptations, the Virgin Mary reminded the islanders of their past sufferings—in the form of an icon half destroyed during the Saracen raids hundreds of years earlier—and of their ability to survive through centuries of tribulations. A time of deep uncertainty was the time for faith. She had offered them protection from the plague and she had shown them that if they worked together they could build a future for the island in the midst of the war.[9]

And a future for the country too—for the greatest miracle of all was surely the outcome of the war itself. At the Etaireia's critical meeting at Ismail in October 1820 when it was resolved to launch the uprising, the majority had set aside warnings that it was too soon with a simple argument: they would "leave the rest to God." It was in this specific sense that they regarded theirs as a holy struggle and enlisted divine help. When Kolokotronis gathered three hundred men outside Kalamata, the first thing they did was to paint the cross on their banners. Priests participated in the revolution's fighting and archbishops in its assemblies. Their enemy invoked faith too to be sure, and in the spring of 1821 the sultan had declared the war against the rebels to be a holy war. It was thus a religious struggle for both sides. But whereas the sultan sought God's help for a quick return to the normal order of things, the Greeks saw the decision to rise up as a test of their faith for two quite different reasons: first, because there was nothing normal about the resurrection of a nation; and second, because the odds against them were so steep. Intelligent men like Capodistrias, Korais, Mavrokordatos, and Ignatios all opposed the Etaireia's plans, believing them to be a recipe for disaster: once the war started, they too were forced to hope. Yet the odds continued to deteriorate until hope was in short supply. From 1825, the Greek chieftains could do nothing against Ibrahim's well-organized armies and even the "inexhaustible patience" of village society was showing signs of reaching its limits. The dream of Greek independence in the summer of 1826 had struck Sir Stratford Canning, newly arrived in Constantinople, as "a simple impossibility."[10]

Who could have guessed, after Karaïskakis was killed and Athens capitulated, as one district after another surrendered in the Peloponnese, that George Canning would remain alive just long enough to ensure the signing of the Treaty of London, or that Admiral Codrington's fleet would be reinforced in the nick of time to prevent the impending attack on Hydra and Spetses that would have finished off the Greeks? Who could have predicted the miscalculations by Sultan Mahmud II—starting with the death of Khurshid Pasha in 1822 and continuing right up until his intemperate reaction to Navarino—that eventually gave the Russians the opening they were looking for to go to war, leaving the Ottoman Empire permanently weakened and allowing Greece to emerge on the international stage. "God alone saved Greece by miracles," was the verdict of Petros Mavromihalis's bodyguard, the Maniot warrior Ilias Salafatinos, a man who fought through the struggle from start to finish.[11] So it was that on the very edge of Europe, and against all the odds, the first successful revolution took place in which a people claimed liberty for themselves and took on the might of an entire empire to attain it, transforming diplomatic norms and the direction of world politics in the process.

"Let us be inwardly persuaded that He does not work his miracles in vain," Capodistrias had said. But bearing the burden of divine grace was a heavy load and almost as soon as independence was gained, it became commonplace to criticize the result: foreigners complained the Greeks had failed to live up to their ancient forebears; the veterans of the struggle muttered that the young had failed to measure up to them. The great powers complained the Greeks were unreliable and profligate; the Greeks complained that their independence was illusory. Irredentists insisted that the romeïko was not over until the country liberated Constantinople; radicals complained the revolution was incomplete until justice went deeper.[12] This litany of all-round dissatisfaction became a trope that endures to this day. It is as if hidden inside the secular belief in national resurrection was an implicit eschatology—the residue of an earlier expectation that with the throwing off of the sultan's rule marking God's favor for the Greeks, they would henceforth be emancipated from the historical process itself. Disappointment resulted when this turned out not to be true. "Greece when cultivated will be a true paradise, but it will take time, we will grow old, our children will grow old and likely neither they nor we will see the golden age," the Swiss doctor Louis-André Gosse had written on his departure from the country in 1828.[13] The truth is that what the Greeks had won in defeating the Turks was not an exit from our fallen world into the Kingdom of God but something else, mundane but no less precious: the freedom to shape their future in a state of their own within an international system of states. With the success of their struggle, one story ends and another begins.

Guide to Further Reading

There is no event in modern history calculated to impart such unmingled delight to the mind as the Greek Revolution.
Edward Blaquière, "The Greek Revolution,"
Westminster Review (June 1824), 714

The Greek uprising was scarcely a year old when Claude-Denis Raffenel published the first volume of his *Histoire des événemens de la Grèce*, perhaps the first history of the conflict and a book that remains well worth reading. "There are famous epochs which seem marked out by Providence," he writes. "Such were the centuries of Sésostris, Priam, Alexander, Caesar, Mohammed and Louis XIV, and such, too, is our own." Conscious that they were living amid historic times and events, participants and observers produced a rich stream of reflections and records. Some of the finest early histories were written by foreign participants, notably Thomas Gordon and George Finlay, whose masterly works have lasted well.

It is, however, one of the most precious and unusual aspects of 1821 that we can also read about it in the words of the Greek fighters themselves. The vast bulk of Ottoman Christian society was illiterate, yet compared with their counterparts in Spain or much of eastern Europe, Greek peasants were never very far from the written word, and thanks to the Church and a network of village schools and enterprising merchants, a surprising number of bright young village boys learned to read and write. (For girls it was far rarer.) Some served as secretaries to the chieftains; some kapetans taught themselves to write as well. The result is a remarkably rich and entertaining body of eye-opening accounts by protagonists from all walks of life that take us from mountain shepherds' huts to the palaces and serails of the revolution. The infighting that plagued the Greeks during the war itself was if anything dwarfed by the speed and acrimony with which the veterans charged into print to do battle with one another in memoirs that make up for in vivid anecdote and revealing detail what they occasionally lack in accuracy. Two of the standout texts—by Kolokotronis and Makriyannis—have been translated in dated but still highly readable abridgments: both get the reader closer to the rough voices and values of the uprising than anything composed by more polite and polished scholars. Three other extraordinarily rich memoirs—by Deliyannis, Fotakos, and Kasomoulis—have yet to be translated. There are some eyewitness accounts originally published in English—Castanis's *The Greek Exile*, Mengous's *Narrative of a Greek Soldier*, and Stephanini's *Narrative*—that can easily be found online and illuminate life in Turkish captivity and many other dimensions of daily life during the war.

The best account of the philhellenes is the still superb *That Greece Might Still Be Free* by William St. Clair. But the philhellenes left a good deal of their own writing behind them. One place to start is the little-known series of anonymous articles published in the *London Magazine* in 1826–27 under the title "Adventures of a Foreigner in Greece"; likely written by the Italian philhellene Brengeri, it provides an unsparing account of the war. Julius Millingen's *Memoirs of the Affairs of Greece* is an excellent introduction to the wartime scene in western Greece by a young British surgeon who attended Byron and may have unwittingly hastened his demise. *Life on Board a Man-of-War: Including a Full Account of the Battle of Navarino by a British Seaman*, written by a Scottish seaman, Charles MacPherson, gives a unique description of what it had been like to go through the last great naval battle of the age of sail.

For those who read French, Raybaud's two volumes of *Mémoires sur la Grèce* are superbly written and generally reliable, a lot more so than the tall tales of his rival Voutier—Delacroix's dining companion—which so outraged Raybaud that he fought a duel with Voutier over them. Miller's *The Condition of Greece in 1827 and 1828* and Howe's *Letters* are remarkable for their attentiveness to the plight of ordinary Greeks. What we can but glimpse is the view of the war from the Ottoman side, partly because Muslim participants did not rush to write up their impressions, still less put them in print, and partly because the scholarship on the subject is in its infancy. For now, we have two remarkable accounts available in English. One is from the Morea by Yusuf el-Moravi, a high-ranking military official; the other, a memoir by a freelance Ottoman cavalryman who operated in Evvia and central Greece, Kabudli Vasfi Efendi, translated by Schmidt. The view from Alexandria may be glimpsed in works by Douin and Driault.

Of recent scholarship, Beaton's *Byron's War* and Mazurel's *Vertiges de la Guerre* are both about much more than Byron, massively important though he is. Barau's *La Cause des Grecs* is encyclopedic. There is little in English on the Russian angle, though the works of Prousis are a good start. On the Phanariots, the best study remains Blancard's *Les Mavroyéni*, now well over a century old, though Hope's *Anastasius* is more entertaining and remains a lively and often mind-boggling read. The best scholarship these days is unquestionably from Greece where the range and quality of professional history is, for the size of the country, second to none; some idea may be glimpsed from two collections of essays in English, *The Greek Revolution of 1821: A European Event* and *Ottoman Rule and the Balkans, 1760–1850*. John Koliopoulos's *Brigands with a Cause*, which extends well beyond the 1820s, is deservedly a classic. On the language of the revolution, Nikos Sarantakos's *To zorbaliki tou rayiadon* (Athens, 2020), based on the author's blog, is insightful. The best guide to the current state of research is the recent collective volume *The Greek Revolution: A Critical Dictionary*, edited by two distinguished scholars, Paschalis Kitromilides and Constantinos Tsoukalas. But the first port of call for anyone interested in going further into this subject should be the online bilingual *1821 Digital Archive*, accessible at https://1821.digitalarchive.gr/. This makes available an astonishing array of archives, publications, and exhibits and is now the single most important library in existence on the Greek revolution.

Bibliography

PRIMARY SOURCES
Greek

Agapitos, A., *Oi endoxoi Ellines tou 1821, i oi Protagonistai tis Ellados* (Patras, 1877).

Ainian, D., *Apomnimonevmata, kai viografia tou stratigou Georgiou Karaïskaki* (Athens, 2011).

[Ali Pasha], V. Panayiotopoulos et al., eds., *Archeio Ali Pasa, syllogis I. Xhotzi*, 3 vols. (Athens, 2007).

Anon., "Cheirografon tou 1821 etous," *Pandora* (July 15, 1863), 199–206.

Anon., "Ellinikai Efimerides," *Pandora*, 443 (Sept. 1, 1868), 212–16.

Anon., *Evresis tis panseptou eikonos tou evangelismou tis theotokou kai oikodomi tou ierou naou tis Evangelistrias eis tin nison Tinon* (Venice, 1833).

Anon., *Politikon systima tis Ellados* (Troezen, 1827).

Anon., "Schimatismos tou protou en Elladi taktikou stratou," *Estia* (Jan.–June 1877), iii, 180–84.

Archeia tis Ellinikis Palingenesias, 1821–1832 (Athens, 1971–2012), 23 vols.

Archeio Stefanou, Elliniko Laografiko kai Istoriko Archeio, Athens.

Arsh, G., ed., *I Russia kai ta pasalikia Alvarias kai Ipeirou, 1759–1831* (Athens, 2007).

Asimakopoulos, N., ed., *Anagnosti Kontaki apomnimonevmata* (Athens, 2009).

[Capodistrias], *Archeion Ioannou Kapodistrias*, 9 vols. (Kerkyra, 1976–87).

Chrysanthopoulos, F., *Apomnimonevmata peri tis Ellinikis Epanastaseos*, 2 vols. (Athens, 2019: reprint of 1899 ed.).

——*Vioi Peloponnision andron kai ton exothen eis tin Peloponnonison elthonton klirikon, stratiotikon kai politikon ton agonismenon ton agona tis epanastaseos* (Athens, 1888).

——*Vios tou papa Flessas* (Athens, 1868).

Daskalakis, A., *Keimena-pigai tis istorias tis ellinikis epanastaseos*, 3 vols. (Athens, 1966–88).

———"Ta topika politevmata kata tin epanastasin tou 1821," *Epistimoniki Epetiris tis Filosofikis Scholis tou Panepistimiou Athinon,* 15 (1964–65), 161–270.

Deliyannis, K. [E. Protopsaltis, ed.], *Kanellos Deliyannis: apomnimonevmata,* 3 vols. (Athens, 1957).

[Deliyannis], Liata, E., ed., *Archeion Kanellou Deliyanni: ta engrafa, 1779–1827* (Athens, 1993).

Diamantis, K. A., *Athinaikon Archeion* (Athens, 1971).

Dimitriadis, M., ed., *"Archeio Agonos": 1806–1832: apo ta istorika archeia tou Mouseiou Benaki,* 2 vols. (Athens, 2011).

Dimos, Tselios J., "Diigisi Dimou Tseliou," in N. Konomos, ed., *O Georgios Tertsetis,* 805–6.

Doukas, P., *I Sparti dia mesou ton aionon* (New York, 1922).

Dragoumis, N., *Istorikai anamniseis* (Athens, 1874).

Drakakis, A., *Istoria tou oikismou tis Ermoupoleos (Syros),* 2 vols. (Athens, 1979).

[Elster], C. Oikonomos, ed., *To tagma ton filellinon apo to imerologio tou Johanna Daniel Elster* (Athens, 2010).

Eumorfopoulos, D. [E. Protopsaltis, ed.], *Dionysiou Eumorfopoulou apomnimonevmata* (Athens, 1957).

Filos tou Nomou, 1825–26.

[Flogaïtou], "Avtoviografia Nikolaou Flogaïtou," *Ellinismos,* 1–2 (1898), 463–64.

Fotakos, *see* Chrysanthopoulos.

Foteinos, I., *Oi Athloi tis en Vlachia ellinikis epanastaseos to 1821 etos syggraphentes para Ilia Photeinou* (Leipzig, 1846).

[Fousekis-Farmakis], I. M. Hatzifotis, "To polemiko imerologio tou oplarchigou Ioannou Fouseki-Farmaki," *Parnassos* (July–Sept. 1972), 420–32.

Frantzis, A., *Epitomi tis istorias tis anagennitheisis Ellados archomeni apo tou etous 1715 kai ligousa to 1835,* 4 vols. (Athens, 1839–41).

Fysentzidis, N., *Anekdotoi avtografoi epistolai ton episimoteron ellinon oplarchigon kai diafora pros avtous engrafa tis dioikiseos meth'istorikon simeioseon* (Alexandria, 1893).

Gazis, G., *Viografia ton iroon Markou Botsari kai Karaïskaki* (Aigina, 1828).

Germanos Palaion Patron, *Apomnimonevmata* (Athens, 1900).

Goudas, A., *Vioi paralliloi ton epi tis anagenniseos tis Ellados diaprepsanton andron,* 8 vols. (Athens, 1872–76).

Hadzianargyrou, A. A., *Ta spetsiotika, itoi syllogi istorikon engrafon kai ypomnimaton aforonton ta kata tin ellinikin Epanastasin tou 1821 aristheisa ek ton archeion tis nisou Spetson,* 3 vols. (Athens, 1861).

[The Hague], G. Zoras, ed., *Engrafa tou archeiou Hagis peri tis ellinikis epanastaseos* (Athens, 1991).

[Ignatios], E. Protopsaltis, ed., *Ignatios Mitropolitis Oungrovlachias (1766–1828),* 2 vols. (Athens, 1959–61).

Ioannou, N., *Evvoïka, itoi istoria, periexousa tessaron eton polemous, tis nisou Evvoias* (Ermoupolis, 1857).

[Karaïskakis], "Archeion Georgiou Karaïskaki (1826–1827)," *Navtiki epitheorisis*, 11:45 (July–Aug. 1924), 385–435.

———G. Charitos, ed., *Archeion stratigou Georgiou Karaïskaki (1821–1835)* (Athens, 2009).

Kasomoulis, N. [G. Vlachoyannis, ed.], *Enthymimata stratiotika tis epanastaseos ton Ellinon, 1821–1833*, 3 vols. (Athens, 1939).

[Koletti], B. Playainakou-Bekiaris and A. Stergellis, eds., *Archeion Ioanni Koletti*, 2 vols. (Athens, 1996–2002).

Kolokotronis, Th., *Diigisis symvanton tis ellinikis fylis apo ta 1770 eos ta 1836* (Nafplion, 1846).

Kolokotronis, I., *Ellinika ypomnimata, itoi epistolai kai diafora engrafa aforonta tin ellinikin Epanastasin* (Athens, 1856).

[Kolokotronis, Th.], *O logos tou Theodorou Kolokotroni stin Pnyka* (Athens, 2008).

———T. Gritsopoulos, ed., *Theodorou Kolokotroni diigisi symvanton tis ellinikis fylis apo ta 1770 eos ta 1836* (Athens, 1981).

Konomos, N., ed., *O Georgios Tertsetis kai ta evriskomena erga tou* (Athens, 1984).

Konstas, K. S., "Istorika engrafa Mesologgiton tis 'exodou,' 1826–1833," *Epetiris Etaireias Stereoelladikon Meleton*, i (1968), 101–28.

Kontakis, A. [N. Asimakopoulos, ed.], *Apomnimonevmata* (Athens, 2009).

[Koudouriotis], A. Lignos, ed., *Archeia Lazarou kai Georgiou Koundouriotou, 1821–1832*, vols. 1–5 (Athens, 1920–27).

———K. Diamantis and E. Protopsaltis, eds., *Archeia Lazarou kai Georgiou Koundouriotou, 1821–1832*, vols. 6–10 (Athens, 1966–69).

Koutsalexis, A., *Diaferonta kai perierga tina istorimata* (Athens, 1882).

Kriezis, D. I., *Epanorthosis esfalmenon tinon ek ton apomnimonevmaton peri tis ellinikis epanastaseos tou Fotakou* (Athens, 1874).

Laios, G., ed., *Anekdotes epistoles kai engrafa tou 1821* (Athens, 1958).

[Lidorikis], T. Lappas, ed., *Athanasiou Lidoriki apomnimonevmata* (Jannina, 1955).

Lignos, A., ed., *Archeion tis koinotitos Hydras, 1778–1832*, 16 vols. (Piraeus, 1921–31).

[Londos], *Istorikon archeion tou stratigou Andreou Londou (1789–1847)*, 2 vols. (Athens, 1914–16).

[Makriyannis], G. Vlachoyannis, ed., *Stratigou Makriyanni Apomnimonevmata* (Athens, 1947), vol. i.

———S. Adrachas, ed., *Makriyanni apomnimonevmata* (Athens, 1957).

Malandrakis, M., *Sympliromatikai selides tis istorias tis Ellinikis Epanastaseos* (Athens, 1929).

Mamoukas, A. Z., ed., *Ta kata thn anagennisin tis Ellados itoi syllogi ton peri tin anagennomenin Ellada sintachthenton politevmaton, vomon kai allon episimon praxeon apo tou 1821 mechri tou telous tou 1832*, 3 vols. (Piraeus, 1839).

[Mavrokordatos], E. Protopsaltis, ed., *Istorikon archeion Alexandrou Mavrokordatou*, 6 vols. (Athens, 1963–86).

[Mavromihalis], Anon., *Oi Mavromihalai: syllogi ton peri avton grafenton* (Athens, 1903).

Metaxas, K., *Istorika apomnimonevmata ek tis ellinikis epanastaseos* (Athens, 1956).

Mexas, V., *Oi Filikoi: katalogos ton melon tis Filikis Etaireias ek tou archeiou Sekeri* (Athens, 1937).

[Michos, A.], M. Efthymiou and V. Sarafis, eds., *Apomnimonevmata tis defteris poliorkias tou Mesolonghiou (1825–1826) kai tines allai simeioseis eis tin istorian tou megalou agonos anagenomenai* (Athens, 2019).

Neezer, C., *Apomnimonevmata ton proton eton tis idryseos tou Ellinikou Vasileiou* (Istanbul, 1911).

Nikodimos, K., *Ypomnima tis nisou Psaron* (Athens, 1862).

Oikonomou, M., *Istorika tis ellinikis palingenesias* (Athens, 1873).

Omiridis, P. S., *Synoptiki istoria ton trion naftikon nison Ydras, Petson kai Psaron* (Nafplion, 1831).

Orlandos, A., *Navtika, itoi istoria ton kata ton yper anexartisias tis Ellados agona pepragmenon ypo ton trion navtikon nison, idios de ton Spetson*, 2 vols. (Athens, 1869).

Papadopoulos, K., *Anaskevi ton eis tin istorian ton Athinon anaferomenon peri tou stratigou Odysseos Androutzou* (Athens, 1837).

———*Ta kata G. Varnakiotin kai anaktisis tou Mesolongiou* (Mesolonghi, 1861).

[Papatsonis], E. Protopsaltis, ed., *Panayiotou Papatsoni apomnimonevmata* (Athens, 1960).

Perraivos, Ch., *Apomnimonevmata polemika*, 2 vols. (Athens, 1836).

Pispiringkou, F., ed., *To imerologio tou "Kimonos"* (Athens, 2012).

Pissas, E., *Apomnimonevmata 1821* (Athens, 2017).

Politis, N., *Eklogai apo ta tragoudia tou ellinikou laou* (Athens, 1914).

Protopsaltis, E., *Apomnimonevmata Athinaion agoniston* (Athens, 1957).

[Psara], V. Sfyroeras, ed., *Archeion Psaron, 1821–1827* (Athens, 1974).

Pylia, M., ed., *Apo to 1821 sto 2012* (Athens, 2012).

Reppas, C., *Ypotheseis kataskopias kata tin epanastasi tou 1821: archeiaka keimena* (Athens, 2012).

Rigopoulos, T., "Anekdoton imerologion tou Agonos," in I. Theofanidis, ed., *Istorikon Archeion (1770–1836)*, 3 vols. (Athens, n.d.).

———[A. Fotopoulos, ed.], *Apomnimonevmata apo ton archon tis Epanastaseos mechri tou etous 1881* (Athens, 1979).

[Romas], D. Kambouroglou, ed., *Istorikon archeion Dionysiou Roma*, 2 vols. (Athens, 1901–6).

[Safakas], D. Loukopoulos, ed., *O Roumeliotis kapetanios tou 1821 Andritsos Safakas kai to archeio tou* (Athens, 1931).

Salafatinos, I., *Syntomoi paratiriseis epi tinon peristatikon anaferomenon eis ta legomena apomnimonevmata tou K. N. Spiliadou* (Athens, 1853).

Solomos, D., *Apanta ta evriskomena* (Athens, 1901).

Soutsos, A., *Elliniki Plastigx* (Athens, 1836).

Spiliades, N., *Apomnimonevmata* (Athens, 1851–57), 4 vols.

Spiromilios, *Apomnimonevmata tis defteris poliorkias tou Mesolongiou* (Athens, 1926).

[Spiromilios], ed. G. Vlachoyannis, *Chroniko tou Mesolongiou, 1825–1826* (Athens, 1969).

Stamatiadis, E., ed., *Samiaka, itoi istoria tis nisou Samou*, 2 vols. (Samos, 1881).

[Stavrianos, L.], E. Angelomatis-Tsougkarakis, ed., *Pragmateia ton peripeteion tou viou mou* (Athens, 1982).

[Stefanitsis], T. Sklavenitis, ed., *Petros D. Stefanitsis: Apomnimonevmata (1821–1839)* (Athens, 2019).

Stefanopoulos, S., *Apomnimonevmata tina tis epanastaseos tou 1821* (Tripolis, 1864).

Tertsetis, G., *Exakolouthisis ton Prolegomenon eis ta ypomnimata tou Theodorou Kolokotroni* (Athens, 1852).

——*Logos ekfonitheis en to anagnostorio tis Ellinikis Voulis* (Zakinthos, 1856).

——[N. Konomos, ed.], *Anekdota keimena* (Athens, 1959).

Tsamados, A., *Istorika imerologia ton ellinikon navmachion tou 1821* (Athens, 1886).

[Varnakiotis], K. Papadopoulos, *Ta kata G. Varnakiotin kai anaktisis tou Mesolongiou* (Mesolonghi, 1861).

[Vatican], G. Zoras, ed., *Engrafa tou archeiou Vatikanou peri tis ellinikis epanastaseos*, 2 vols. (Athens, 1979–86).

Vios, S., *I sfagi tou Chiou eis to stoma tou Chiakou laou* (Chios, 1922).

Vlachoyannis, G., *Chiakon archeion*, 2 vols. (Athens, 1924).

Vyzantios, C., *Istoria tou taktikou stratou tis Ellados* (Athens, 1837).

Xanthos, E., *Apomnimonevmata peri tis Philikis Etaireias* (Athens, 1845).

[Ypsilantis] Moraitinis-Patriarcheas, E., ed., *Apomnimonevmata tou prinkipos Nikolaou Ypsilanti* (Athens, 1986).

Zafeiropoulos, I., *Oi archiereis kai oi prouchontes entos tis en Tripolei fylakis en etei 1821* (Athens, 1852).

Non-Greek

Alexander, John C., "Yusuf bey al-Moravi on the siege and capture of Tripolitsa in 1821," in K. Lappas et al., *Mnimi Penelopis Stathis meletes istorias kai filologias* (Rethymnon, 2010), 139–57.

Amaury-Duval, E., *Souvenirs (1829–1830)* (Paris, 1885).

Andonov-Poljanski, Ch., ed., *British Documents on the History of the Macedonian People* (Skopje, 1968).

Anon., *Life on Board a Man-of-War including a Full Account of the Battle of Navarino by a British Seaman* (Glasgow, 1829).

Anon., *The Notebooks of a Spinster Lady, 1878–1903* (London, 1919).

Anon., "People of colour," *Freedom's Journal*, 1:4 (Friday, April 6, 1827).

Anon., *Précis des opérations de la flotte grecque durant la révolution de 1821 et 1822 écrit par un grec* (Paris, 1822).

Archives de la Ministère des Affaires Étrangères [France]: Smyrne 36 [Nantes, France].

Archives of the Catholic Archbishopric of Tinos [Xynara, Tinos].

Argenti, P., ed., *The Massacres of Chios, described by contemporary diplomatic reports* (London, 1932).

Arsh, G., *I Rossia kai ta pasalakia Alvanias kai Iperou, 1759–1831: engrafa rosikon archeion* (Athens, 2007).

Baker, Lt.-Col., "Memoir on the northern frontier of Greece," *Journal of the Royal Geographical Society*, 7 (1837), 81–94.

Belloc, L. S., *Bonaparte et les Grecs* (Paris, 1826).

[Bentham], L. O'Sullivan and C. Fuller, eds., *The Correspondence of Jeremy Bentham*, 12 (Oxford, 2006).

Berchet, J.-C., ed., *Mémoires de la comtesse de Boigne*, ii (*De 1820 à 1848*) (Paris, 1971).

Bétant, E., ed., *Correspondance du Comte J. Capodistrias, Président de la Grèce* (Geneva, 1839).

Black, W., *Narrative of Cruises in the Mediterranean in HMS "Euryalus" and "Chanticleer" during the Greek War of Independence (1822–1826)* (Edinburgh, 1900).

Blaquiere, E., *Report on the Present State of the Greek Confederation, and on its Claims to the Support of the Christian World, read to the Greek Committee on Saturday, September 13, 1823* (London, 1823).

——*Additional Facts, submitted to the Greek Committee by Mr. Blaquiere, on the Actual State of Affairs in the Morea and other points of the Confederation, read on Saturday, September 20th, 1823* (London, 1823).

——"Mr. Blaquiere's Report on Greece," *Blackwood's Edinburgh Magazine*, 14:82 (Oct. 1823).

Bollmann, L. de, *Remarques sur l'État moral, politique et militaire de la Grèce* (Marseille, 1822).

Bowring, L. B., ed., *John Bowring: Autobiographical Recollections* (London, 1877).

[Brengeri], "Adventures of a foreigner in Greece," *London Magazine*, 6:24 (Dec. 1826), 536–38.

Bulwer, H. Lytton, *An Autumn in Greece* (London, 1826).

Camp, Maxime Du, *Souvenirs littéraires*, 2 vols. (Paris, 1893).

Candolle, A.-P. de, *Mémoires et souvenirs de Augustin-Pyramus de Candolle écrit par lui-même publiés par son fils* (Geneva, 1862).

Capodistrias, I., "Aperçu de ma carrière publique, depuis 1798 jusqu'à 1822," *Sbornik imperatorskogo russkogo istoricheskogo obshchestva*, iii (1868), 163–292.

[Capodistrias], C. W. Crawley, *John Capodistrias: Some Unpublished Documents* (Thessaloniki, 1970).

Carte segrete e atti ufficiali della polizia Austriaca in Italia dal 4 giugno 1814 al 22 marzo 1848, 2 vols. (Capolago, 1852).

Castanis, C., *The Greek Captive, or a Narrative of the Captivity and Escape of Christophorus Plato Castanis* (Worcester, MA, 1845).

Cavaignac, E., "Expedition de Morée (1828–1829), Lettres," *Revue des Deux Mondes*, 141 (1897), 47–70.

Chapuisat, E., *Élie-Ami Bétant, Secrétaire de Capodistria et ses Lettres inédites (1827–1829)* (Le Puy, 1926).

Chateaubriand, F.-M., *Congrès de Vérone* (Brussels, 1852).

"Citoyen Grec" (M.G.A.M.), *Resumé géographique de la Grèce et de la Turquie d'Europe* (Paris, 1826).

Clarke, E. D., *Travels in Various Countries of Europe, Asia and Africa* (London, 1814), iii.

Cochrane, G., *Wanderings in Greece*, 2 vols. (London, 1837).

[Codrington], J. Bourchier, ed., *Memoir of the Life of Admiral Sir Edward Codrington: with selections from his public and private correspondence*, 2 vols. (London, 1873).

Coste, P.-X., *Mémoires d'un artiste: notes et souvenirs de voyages (1817–1877)*, 2 vols. (Paris, 1878).

Dakin, D., *British Intelligence of Events in Greece, 1824–1827: A Documentary Collection* (Athens, 1959).

Debidour, A., *Le Général Fabvier: sa vie militaire et politique* (Paris, 1904).

[Delacroix], M. Hannoosh, ed., *Eugène Delacroix: Journal*, 2 vols. (Paris, 2009).

De Pradt, Abbé, *De l'intervention armée pour la pacification de la Grèce* (Paris, 1828).

[Deval], C[harles] D[eval], *Deux années à Constantinople et en Morée (1825–1826)* (Paris, 1828).

De Voulx, A., "Recherches sur la coopération de la Régence d'Alger à la guerre de l'indépendance grecque," *Revue africaine*, 2 (1857), 129–55.

Dodwell, E., *A Classical and Topographical Tour through Greece during the Years 1801, 1805 and 1806*, 2 vols. (London, 1819).

Driault, E., *L'expédition de Crète et de Morée (1823–1828)* (Cairo, 1930).

Eliot, C. W. J., *Campaign of the Falieri and Piraeus in the Year 1827* (Princeton, NJ, 1992).

Emerson, J., G. Pecchio, and W. Humphreys, *A Picture of Greece in 1825*, 2 vols. (London, 1826).

Fabre, A., *Histoire du siège de Missolonghi* (Paris, 1827).

Felton, C. C., *Greece, Ancient and Modern* (Boston, MA, 1867).

[Finlay], "An adventure during the Greek revolution," *Blackwood's Edinburgh Magazine* (Nov. 1842), 669–70.

———J. M. Hussey, ed., *The Journals and Letters of George Finlay, i: The Journals* (Camberley, Surrey, 1995).

Garston, E., *Greece Revisited, and Sketches in Lower Egypt in 1840, with Thirty-Six Hours of a Campaign in Greece in 1825*, 2 vols. (London, 1842).

Giffard, E., *A Short Visit to the Ionian Islands* (London, 1837).

Gordon, T., *History of the Greek Revolution*, 2 vols. (London, 1832).

[Gordon], Thomas Gordon papers, University of Aberdeen.

Green, P., *Sketches of the War in Greece* (London, 1827).

Hamilton-Browne, J., "Narrative of a Visit, in 1823, to the Seat of War in Greece," *Blackwood's Edinburgh Magazine*, 36:226 (Sept. 1834).

Holland, H., *Travels in the Ionian Isles, Albania, Thessaly, Macedonia etc., during the Years 1812 and 1813* (London, 1815).

Hugo, V., "Sur George Gordon, Lord Byron," *La Muse française* (June 15, 1824), 327–39.

[Jarvis], G. G. Arnakis, ed., *George Jarvis: His Journal and Related Documents* (Thessaloniki, 1965).

Jourdain, P.-J., *Mémoires historiques et militaires sur les événements de la Grèce*, 2 vols. (Paris, 1828).

Kambouroglou, D. G., ed., *Mémoires du Prince Nicolas Ypsilanti* (Athens and Paris, n.d.).

Laiou, S., "The Greek revolution in the Morea according to the description of an Ottoman official," in P. Pizanias, ed., *The Greek Revolution of 1821: A European Event* (Istanbul, 2011), 241–55.

Leopardi, M., *Catechismo filosofico per uso delle scuole inferiori* (Rome, 1837).

Lessen, F. A., *Schilderung einer enthusiasmirten Reise nach Griechenland im Jahr 1822* (Görlitz, 1823).

Lieber, F., *Reminiscences of an Intercourse with Mr. Niebuhr the Historian* (Philadelphia, PA, 1835).

[Lieber], T. S. Perry, ed., *The Life and Letters of Francis Lieber* (Boston, MA, 1882).

Linner, S., ed., *W. H. Humphreys "First Journal of the Greek War of Independence" (July 1821–February 1822)* (Stockholm, 1967).

Liprandi, I., "Iz dnevnika i vospominanii I. P. Liprandi," *Russki Arkhiv*, iv (1866), 1408–11.

Madden, R. R., *Travels in Turkey, Egypt, Nubia and Palestine in 1824, 1825, 1826 and 1827*, 2 vols. (London, 1829).

[Makriyannis], H. Lidderdale, ed., *The Memoirs of General Makriyannis, 1797–1864* (London, 1966).

Mangeart, J., *Souvenirs de la Morée. Recueillis pendant le séjour français dans le Péloponèse* (Paris, 1830).

Mauro, A. N., *La ruine de Missolonghi* (Paris, 1836).

Mengous, P., *Narrative of a Greek Soldier, Containing Anecdotes and Occurrences illustrating the Character and Manners of the Greeks and Turks in Asia Minor, and detailing Events of the Late War in Greece* (New York, 1830).

Metaxas, K., *Souvenirs de la Guerre de l'Indépendance de la Grèce* (Paris, 1888).

Metternich, R., ed., *Memoirs of Prince Metternich*, 5 vols. (London, 1880).

Miller, J. P., *The Condition of Greece in 1827 and 1828* (New York, 1828).

Millingen, J., *Memoirs of the Affairs of Greece* (London, 1831).

Montgomery, R., *The Age Reviewed: A Satire in Two Parts* (London, 1828).

Moore, John, *A Journey from London to Odessa, with Notices of New Russia* (Paris, 1833).

Müller, C., *Journey through Greece and the Ionian Islands in June, July and August 1821* (London, 1822).

[Nakhimov], L. I. Spiridonova, ed., *P. S. Nakhimov: dokumenti i materialy*, 2 vols. (St. Petersburg, 2003).

Neal, J., *Wandering Recollections of a Somewhat Busy Life* (Boston, MA, 1869).

Nuzzo, A., *La rivoluzione greca e la questione d'oriente, nella corrispondenza dei diplomatici napoletani (1820–1830)* (Salerno, 1934).

Ommanney, E., "Memories of Navarino," *World Wide Magazine*, i (1898), 48–52.

Palma, A., *Greece Vindicated* (London, 1826).

Papadopoulos-Vretos, A., *Mémoires biographiques-historiques sur le président de la Grèce comte Jean Capodistrias* (Paris, 1837).

Parry, W., *The Last Days of Byron* (London, 1825).

[Parry], "Parry's Last Days of Byron," *Blackwood's Edinburgh Magazine*, 18:103 (August 1825).

Pellion, J., *La Grèce et les Capodistrias pendant l'Occupation française de 1828 à 1834* (Paris, 1855).

[Persat], G. Schlumberger, ed., *Mémoires de Commandant Persat, 1806 à 1844* (Paris, 1910).

Pitcairn Jones, C. G., ed., *Piracy in the Levant, 1827–28, selected from the Papers of Admiral Sir Edward Codrington KCB* (London, 1934).

Post, H. A., *A Visit to Greece and Istanbul in the Year 1827–1828* (New York, 1830).

Prevelakis, E. and K. Kalliatakis Merticopoulou, eds., *Epirus, Ali Pasha and the Greek Revolution: Consular Reports of William Meyer from Preveza*, 2 vols. (Athens, 1996).

Prokesch-Osten, A. von, *Geschichte des Abfalls der Griechen vom Türkischen Reiche im Jahre 1821* (Vienna, 1867), vol. 3: Beilagen 1.

Prousis, T., *Lord Strangford at the Sublime Porte (1822)* (Istanbul, 2012).

———*Lord Strangford at the Sublime Porte (1823)* (Istanbul, 2014).

———*Lord Strangford at the Sublime Porte (1824)* (Istanbul, 2017).

———"British embassy reports on the Greek uprising in 1821–22: war of independence or war of religion?," *Archivum Ottomanicum*, 28 (2011), 171–232.

———"Smyrna in 1821: A Russian view," *Modern Greek Studies Yearbook*, 27 (1992), 145–68.

Psatelis, D., *A Sketch of the Causes of the Revolution in Greece* (Oxford, 1823).

Puckler-Muskau, H., *Entre l'Europe et l'Asie: Voyage dans l'Archipel* (Brussels, 1840).

Quincy, Q. de, *An Essay on the Nature, End and the Means of Imitation in the Fine Arts* (London, 1837).

Quinet, E., *De la Grèce moderne et de ses rapports avec l'antiquité* (Paris, 1830).

"R," "A Panhellenic festival of today," *Macmillan's Magazine*, 48 (1883–84), 474–77.

Raffenel, C. D., *Histoire des événemens de la Grèce, depuis les premiers troubles jusqu'à ce jour* (Paris, 1822).

Raikes, T., *A Portion of the Journal kept by T. Raikes, Esq. from 1831 to 1847*, 3 vols. (London, 1858).

Raybaud, M., *Mémoires sur la Grèce pour servir à l'histoire de la guerre de l'indépendance*, 2 vols. (Paris, 1824).

R[edordon], F., *Lettres sur la Valachie, ou Observations sur cette Province et ses Habitans, écrites de 1815 à 1821* (Paris, 1822).

Richards, L., ed., *Letters and Journals of Samuel Gridley Howe* (Boston, MA, 1906).

Rizos Neroulos, I., *Précis de l'histoire moderne de la Grèce* (Geneva, 1828).

Ross, L., *Erinnerungen und Mitteilungen aus Griechenland* (Berlin, 1863).

Rothpletz, E., ed., *Lettres du Genevois Louis-André Gosse à sa mère pendant son séjour en Grèce (1826–1830)* (Paris, 1920).

Roux, G., *Histoire médicale de l'Armée Française en Morée pendant la campagne de 1828* (Paris, 1829).

Sadlier, G. F., "Account of a journey from Katif on the Red Sea to Tamboo on the Persian Gulf by Capt. G. F. Sadlier," *Transactions of the Literary Society of Bombay*, iii (London, 1823), 449–93.

Schack, F.-R., *Campagne d'un jeune Français en Grèce* (Paris, 1827).

Schmidt, J., "The adventures of an Ottoman horseman: the autobiography of Kabudli Vasfı Efendi, 1800–1825," in *The Joys of Philology*, i (Istanbul, 2002), 165–286.

Sideris, E. G., and A. A. Konsta, "A letter from Jean-Pierre Boyer to Greek revolutionaries," *Journal of Haitian Studies*, 11:1 (Spring 2005), 167–71.

Stanhope, L., *Greece in 1823 and 1824* (London, 1824).

[Stendhal], K. G. McWatters, ed., *Chroniques pour l'Angleterre: contributions à la presse britannique*, 6 vols. (Grenoble, 1991).

[Stephanini], *The Narrative of J. Stephanini, a native of Arta in Greece* (Charleston, SC, 1829).

[Stourdza], *Mémoires de la Comtesse Edling (née Stourdza)* (Moscow, 1888).

Swan, C., *Journal of a Voyage up the Mediterranean, principally among the Islands of the Archipelago and in Asia Minor, including Many Interesting Particulars relative to the Greek Revolution, especially a Journey through Maina to the camp of Ibrahim Pasha*, 2 vols. (London, 1826).

Tennant, C., *A Tour through Parts of the Netherlands, Holland, Germany, Switzerland, Savoy and France in the Years 1821–22* (London, 1824).

Trelawny, E. J., *Records of Shelley, Byron and the Author* (New York, 2000).

Urquhart, D., *The Spirit of the East*, 2 vols. (London, 1838).

Valon, A. de, *Une année dans le Levant* (Paris, 1846).

Vaulabelle, A. de, *Histoire scientifique et militaire de l'Éxpédition française en Égypte* (Paris, 1830–36).

Waddington, G., *A Visit to Greece in 1823 and 1824* (London, 1825).

Walsh, R., *A Residence at Constantinople during the Greek and Turkish Revolutions*, 2 vols. (London, 1836).

Webster, C. K., *Britain and the Independence of Latin America, 1812–1830: Selected Documents from the Foreign Office Archives* (London, 1938).

Weil, M.-H., ed., *Les dessous du Congrès de Vienne*, 2 vols. (Paris, 1917).

Wilson, S. S., *A Narrative of the Greek Mission, or Sixteen Years in Malta and Greece* (London, 1839).

SECONDARY SOURCES

About, E., *La Grèce contemporaine* (Paris, 1854).

Alexiou, M., *The Ritual Lament in Greek Tradition* (Cambridge, MA, 1974).

Aliprantis, C., "Lives in exile: foreign political refugees in early independent Greece (1830–1853)," *Byzantine an Modern Greek Studies*, 43:2 (2019), 243–61.

Alivizatos, N., *To syntagma kai oi echthroi tou stin neoelliniki istoria, 1800–2010* (Athens, 2011).

Anastasopoulos, A., and Kolovos, E., eds., *Ottoman Rule and the Balkans, 1760–1850: Conflict, Transformation, Adaptation* (Rethymnon, 2007).

Anderson, R. C., *Naval Wars in the Levant, 1559–1853* (Liverpool, 1952).

Andreades, A., "L'administration financière de la Grèce sous la domination turque," *Revue des Études Grecques* (1910), 131–83.

Angelomatis-Tsougarakis, H., "Women in the Greek War of Independence," in M. Mazower, ed., *Networks of Power: Essays in Honour of John Campbell* (New York, 2008), 45–69.

Anon., *Great Moments in Greek Archaeology* (Athens, 2007).

Aravantinos, S., *Istoria Ali Pasa tou Tepelenli* (Athens, 1895).

Ardeleanu, C., "Military aspects of the Greek War of Independence in the Romanian principalities: the Battle of Galati (1821)," in G. Harlaftis and R. Păun, eds., *Greeks in Romania in the Nineteenth Century* (Athens, 2013), 141–66.

Armitage, D. and Subrahmanyam, S., eds., *The Age of Revolutions in Global Context, c. 1760–1840* (London, 2010).

Arsh, G., "On the life in Russia of the Greek patriotic family Ypsilanti," *Balkan Studies,* 26 (1985), 73–90.

Asdrachas, S., *Protogoni epanastasi: armatoloi kai kleftes (180s–190s aiones)* (Athens, 2019).

Athanassoglou-Kallmyer, N., *French Images from the Greek War of Independence, 1821–1830* (New Haven, CT, 1989).

Azevado, A., *G. Rossini: sa vie et ses oeuvres* (Paris, 1864).

Balanikas, A., et al., "Medical care in free-besieged Messolonghi (1822–1826)," *Acta Med. Hist. Adriat.,* 14:1 (2016), 95–106.

Baldassare, A., "The politics of images," in H. Blume, ed., *Narrated Communities, Narrated Realities* (Leiden, 2015).

Barau, D., *La cause des Grecs: une histoire du mouvement philhellène, 1821–1829* (Paris, 2009).

Bartle, G. F., "Jeremy Bentham and John Bowring: a study in the relationship between Bentham and the editor of his *Collected Works,*" *Bulletin of the Institute of Historical Research* (Oct. 1963), 27–35.

———"Bowring and the Greek loans of 1824 and 1825," *Balkan Studies,* 3:1 (1964), 61–74.

Bartzis, D., "Ta palatia tou Kiamil Bey stin Korintho," https://argovivliothiki.gr/tag/kiamel-beys-palaces-at-corinth.

Beaton, R., *Byron's War: Romantic Rebellion, Greek Revolution* (Cambridge, 2013).

———"Antique nation? 'Hellenes' on the eve of Greek independence and in twelfth-century Byzantium," *BMGS,* 31:1 (2007), 76–96.

———and D. Ricks, eds., *The Making of Modern Greece: Nationalism, Romanticism and the Uses of the Past (1797–1896)* (Ashgate, 2009).

Belsis, K. P., *Apo tin othomaniki nomimotita sto ethniko kratos: Lykourgos Logothetis, politiki viografia* (Athens, 2014).

Berchet, J.-C., *Chateaubriand* (Paris, 2012).

Bitis, A., *Russia and the Eastern Question: Army, Government, and Society, 1818–1833* (Oxford, 2006).

Black, L., *Russians in Alaska, 1732–1867* (Fairbanks, AK, 2004).

Blancard, T., *Les Mavroyéni,* 2 vols. (Paris, 1909).

Blaufarb, R., "The western question: the geopolitics of Latin American independence," *AHR,* 112:3 (June 2007), 742–63.

Bogdanovich, E. V., *Navarin, 1827–1877* (Moscow, 1877).

Bornholdt, L., "The Abbé de Pradt and the Monroe Doctrine," *Hispanic American Historical Review,* 24:2 (May 1944), 201–21.

Boukalas, P., ed., *The Klephtic Ballads: An Anthology of 19th-Century Greek Popular Songs* (Athens, 2020).

Bourguet, M.-N., et al., eds., *Enquêtes en Méditerranée: les expéditions françaises de Égypte, de Morée et d'Algérie* (Athens, 1999).

Bouvier-Bron, M., "La mission médicale de Louis-André Gosse pendant son séjour en Grèce (1827–1829)," *Gesnerus: Swiss Journal of the History of Medicine and Sciences*, 48:3–4 (1991), 343–57.

Bouyssy, M., "Women in philhellenism," in C. Fauré et al., eds., *Political and Historical Encyclopaedia of Women* (London, 2004).

Bowring, P., *Free Trade's First Missionary: Sir John Bowring in Europe and Asia* (Hong Kong, 2014).

Bozikis, S., *Elliniki epanastasi kai dimosia oikonomia: I synkrotisi tou ellinikou ethnikou kratous (1821–1832)* (Athens, 2020).

———"Dynamikes kai adraneies sti forologia kai sto forologiko mechanismo kata tin Epanastasi tou 1821," *Mnimon*, 31 (2010), 31–68.

Brewer, D., *The Greek War of Independence: The Struggle for Freedom from Ottoman Oppression and the Birth of the Modern Greek Nation* (Woodstock, NY, 2003).

Burgi-Kyriazi, M., *Demetrios Galanos—énigme de la Renaissance orientale* (Paris, 1984).

Capaitzis, D. G., "'Karteria': the first steam warship in war (1826)," *Historic Ships* (2009).

Cappon, L., ed., *The Adams-Jefferson Letters*, 2 vols. (Chapel Hill, NC, 1959).

Carter, R., "Karl Friedrich Schinkel's project for a royal palace on the Acropolis," *Journal of the Society of Architectural Historians*, 38:1 (March 1979), 34–46.

Castignino-Berlinghieri, U., "Balance of power and legitimacy at the Congress of Vienna: the case study of the Order of Malta," in W. Telesko et al., eds., *Der Wiener Kongress 1814/15* (Vienna, 2019), i, 179–86.

Chaldeos, A., "The Greek community in Tunis between 1805 and 1881: aspects of its demographics and its role in the local economic and political context," *Journal of North African Studies*, 24:6 (2019), 887–95.

Charitakis, G., *I ekatonaetiris tis epanastaseos* (Athens, 1921).

Church, E. M., *Chapters in an Adventurous Life: Sir Richard Church in Italy and Greece* (London, 1895).

Clayer, N., *Mystiques, état et société: les Halvetis dans l'aire balkanique de la fin du XVe siècle à nos jours* (Paris, 1994).

Clogg, R., ed., *The Struggle for Greek Independence* (London, 1973).

———*Balkan Society in the Age of Greek Independence* (London, 1981).

Connelly, M. J., "Rethinking the Cold War and decolonisation: the grand strategy of the Algerian war of independence," *International Journal of Middle Eastern Studies*, 33 (2001), 221–45.

Crawley, C., *The Question of Greek Independence* (Cambridge, 1930).

———"A forgotten prophecy (Greece 1820–21)," *Cambridge Historical Journal*, 1:2 (1924), 209–13.

Cresson, W. P., "Chateaubriand and the Monroe Doctrine," *North American Review*, 217:809 (April 1923), 475–87.

Dakin, D., *British and American Philhellenes during the War of Greek Independence, 1821–1833* (Thessaloniki, 1955).

Daskalakis, A., *Oi topikoi organismoi tou 1821* (Athens, 1966).

———"I enarchis tou agonos tis eleftherias: thrylos kai pragmatitokis," *Epistimoniki Epetiris tis Filosofikis Scholis tou Panepistimiou Athinon*, 12 (1961), 9–138.

Daupeyroux, Colonel, "La curieuse vie de l'Abbé de Pradt," *Revue des études historiques*, 90 (1929), 279–312.

Dawson, D., "The archduke Ferdinand Maximilian and the crown of Greece, 1863," *English Historical Review*, 37:145 (Jan. 1922).

Dawson, F. Griffith, *The First Latin American Debt Crisis* (New Haven, CT, 1990).

Delis, A., "A hub of piracy in the Aegean: Syros during the Greek war of independence," in D. Dimitropoulos, G. Harlaftis, and D. J. Starkey, eds., *Corsairs and Pirates in the Eastern Mediterranean, Fifteenth–Nineteenth Centuries* (Athens, 2016), 41–54.

Diakakis, A., *To Mesolonghi sto 1821: polemos, oikonomia, politiki, kathimerini zoi* (Athens, 2019).

Diamandouros, N., et al., eds., *Hellenism and the First Greek War of Liberation (1821–1830)* (Thessaloniki, 1976).

Dimakis, J., *La presse française face à la chute de Missolonghi et à la Bataille navale de Navarin* (Thessaloniki, 1976).

———*Filellinika* (Athens, 1992).

———"La 'Societé de la Morale Chrétienne' de Paris et son action en faveur des Grecs lors l'insurrection de 1821," *Balkan Studies*, 7:1 (1966), 27–47.

Dimitropoulos, D., *Martyries yia ton plythismo ton nision tou Aigaiou, 15os–arches 19ou aiona* (Athens, 2004).

———*Treis Filikoi, eparchoi stin Andro* (Athens, 2020).

———"O 'geros tou Moria': ktizontas mia patriki figoura tou ethnous," in D. Dimitropoulos and K. Dede, eds., *"I matia ton allon": proslipseis prosopon pou sfragisan treis aiones (18os–20os aiones)* (Athens, 2012), 69–90.

———"Tiniakoi metanastes, thymata peiraton sta chronia tis Epanastasis. Oikonomia tis agoras kai oikonomias tis vias," in K. Danousis and K. Tsiknakis, eds., *Ministerium Historiae: timi ston pater Marko Foskolo* (Tinos, 2017),153–75.

Dimitropoulos, D., et al., eds., *I epanastasi tou 1821: meletes sti mnimi tis despoinas Themeli-Katifori* (Athens, 2018).

———*Opseis tis epanastasis tou 1821* (Athens, 2018).

———*1821 kai apomnimonevma: istoriki chrisi kai istoriografiki gnosi* (Athens, 2020).

Dontas, D., *The Last Phase of the War of Independence in Western Greece (December 1827 to May 1829)* (Thessaloniki, 1966).

Dorizas, G., *I Tinos epi Tourkratias kai kata ton Agona tou 1821* (Athens, 1978).

———*Viografia tis Ayias Monachis Pelagias tis Tinou* (Athens, 1978).

———*Oi ekklesies kai ta proskynimata tis Tinou* (Athens, n.d.).

Douin, G., *Une mission militaire française auprès de Mohammed Aly* (Cairo, 1923).

——*Les premières frégates de Mohammed Aly (1824–1827)* (Cairo, 1926).

——*Navarin, 6 juillet–20 octobre 1827* (Cairo, 1927).

Doxiadis, E., "Legal trickery: men, women and justice in late Ottoman Greece," *Past and Present*, 210 (Feb. 2011), 129–53.

——*State, Nationalism, and the Jewish Communities of Modern Greece* (London, 2018).

Droulia, L., *Philhellenisme: ouvrages inspirés par la guerre de l'indépendance grecque, 1821–1833* (Athens, 1974).

——"Towards modern Greek consciousness," *Historical Review*, i (2004), 51–67.

Dumas, A., *The Count of Monte-Cristo*, 2 vols. (London, 1846).

Dunn, J. P., "Missions or mercenaries? European military advisors in Mehmed Ali's Egypt, 1815–1848," in D. Stoker, ed., *Military Advising and Assistance* (London, 2007), 11–25.

Dursteler, E., "Speaking in tongues: language and communication in the early modern Mediterranean," *Past and Present* (Nov. 2012), 47–77.

Échinard, P., *Grecs et philhellènes à Marseille de la Révolution française à l'indépendance de la Grèce* (Marseille, 1973).

Efthymiou, M., "Cursing with a message: the case of Georgios Karaïskakis," *Istorein* (2000), 173–82.

Eisler, B., *Byron, Child of Passion, Fool of Fame* (New York, 1999).

Ellgood, R., *The Arms of Greece and her Balkan Neighbors in the Ottoman Period* (London, 2009).

Enepekidis, P., *Alexandros Ypsilantis: I aixmalosia tou eis tin Austrian, 1821–1828* (Athens, 1969).

Erdem, H., "'Do not think of the Greeks as agricultural labourers': Ottoman responses to the Greek war of independence," in F. Birtek and T. Dragonas, eds., *Citizenship and the Nation-State in Greece and Turkey* (London, 2005), 67–84.

——"'Perfidious Albanians' and 'zealous governors': Ottomans, Albanians and Turks in the Greek War of Independence," in A. Anastasopoulou and E. Kolovos, eds., *Ottoman Rule and the Balkans, 1760–1850: Conflict, Transformation, Adaptation* (Rethymnon, 2007), 61–72.

Erdem, Y. H., "The Greek revolt and the end of the old Ottoman order," in P. Pizanias, ed., *I elliniki epanastasi tou 1821* (Athens, 2009), 281–89.

Esse, M., "Rossini's noisy bodies," *Cambridge Opera Journal*, 21:1 (March 2009), 27–64.

Fahmy, K., *Mehmed Ali: From Ottoman Governor to Ruler of Egypt* (Oxford, 2009).

——"Mutiny in Mehmed Ali's new nizam army, April–May 1824," in J. Hathaway, ed., *Mutiny and Rebellion in the Ottoman Empire* (Madison, WI, 2002), 129–39.

Farsolas, D., "Alexander Pushkin: his attitude towards the Greek revolution, 1821–1829," *Balkan Studies*, 12:1 (1971), 57–80.

Fauriel, C., *Chants populaires de la Grèce moderne* (Paris, 1824).

Felton, C. C., *Greece Ancient and Modern* (Boston, MA, 1867).

Filemon, I., *Dokimion istorikon peri tis Filikis Etaireias* (Nafplion, 1834).

———*Dokimion istorikon peri tis ellinikis epanastaseos*, 4 vols. (Athens, 1859–61).

Finlay, G., *History of the Greek Revolution*, 2 vols. (Edinburgh, 1860).

Flandreau, M., and Flores, J., "Bonds and brands: foundations of sovereign debt markets, 1820–1830," *Journal of Economic History*, 69:3 (Sept. 2009), 646–84.

Fleming, K., *The Muslim Bonaparte: Diplomacy and Orientalism in Ali Pasha's Greece* (Princeton, NJ, 1999).

Fotopoulos, A., *Oi kotzabasides tis Peloponnisou kata ti defteri Tourkokratia (1715–1821)* (Athens, 2005).

Frary, L., and M. Kozelsky, eds., *Russian-Ottoman Borderlands: The Eastern Question Reconsidered* (Madison, WI, 2014).

Gaffarel, P., "Marseille et les Philhellènes en 1821 et 1822," *Revue historique*, 129:2 (1918), 244–76.

Gardikas, K., "O Anastasios Polyzoidis kai elliniki epanastasi," *Mnimon*, 1 (1971), 23–52.

Georgis, G., ed., *O Kyvernitis Ioannis Kapodistrias* (Athens, 2015), 88–107.

Georgopoulou, M., and K. Thanasakis, eds., *Ottoman Athens: Topography, Archaeology, History* (Athens, 2019).

Ghekas, S., *Xenocracy: State, Class and Colonialism in the Ionian Islands, 1814–1864* (London, 2016).

Ghekos, G., *I epistrofi: agonistes tou Alexandrou Ipsilanti ston dromo yia tin Ellada, 1822–1823* (Athens, 2019).

Ghervas, S., *Réinventer la tradition: Alexandre Stourdza et l'Europe de la Sainte Alliance* (Paris, 2009).

———"Le philhellénisme en Europe et en Russie," in *Peuples, états et nations dans le sud-est de l'Europe: Contributions roumaines* (Bucharest, 2004).

———"A 'Goodwill Ambassador' in the post-Napoleonic era: Roxandra Edling-Sturdza on the European scene," in G. Sluga and C. James, eds., *Women, Diplomacy and International Politics since 1500* (London, 2015), 151–66.

Gkinis, D., "O Dimitris Ypsilantis katevainei stin Ellada," *Eranistis*, 2 (1964), 187–89.

Gordon, T., *History of the Greek Revolution*, 2 vols. (London, 1832).

Gouin, E., *L'Egypte au XIX siècle* (Paris, 1847).

Gounaris, B. C., "Blood brothers in despair: Greek brigands, Albanian rebels and the Greek-Ottoman frontier, 1829–1831," *Cahiers balkaniques*, 45 (2018), 1–24.

Gounaris, V., *"Den ein'o persinos kairos . . .": ellines kleftarmatoloi kai alvanoi stasiastes (1829–1831)* (Athens, 2020).

Grimsted, P. K., "Capodistrias and a 'New Order' for Restoration Europe: the 'Liberal' ideas of a Russian foreign minister, 1814–1822," *Journal of Modern History*, 40 (1968), 166–92.

Grigsby, D. G., *Extremities: Painting Empire in Post-Revolutionary France* (New Haven, CT, 2002).

[Grivas], anon., *Theodoros Grivas: viografikon schediasma* (Athens, 1896).

Hadjianastasis, M., ed., *Frontiers of the Ottoman Imagination: Studies in Honour of Rhoads Murphey* (Leiden, 2015).

Halbertsma, R. B., *Scholars, Travellers and Trade: The Pioneer Years of the National Museum of Antiquities in Leiden, 1818–1840* (London, 2003).

Harlaftis, G., and K. Galanis, eds., *O emporikos kai polemikos stolos kata tin elliniki epanastasi, 1821–1831* (Rethymnon, 2021).

Harlaftis, G., and K. Papakonstantinou, eds., *Navtilia ton Ellinon, 1700–1821* (Athens, 2013).

Harlaftis, G., and R. Pāun, eds., *Greeks in Romania in the Nineteenth Century* (Athens, 2013).

Harris, J., "Bernardino Rivadavia and Benthamite 'discipleship,'" *Latin American Research Review*, 33:1 (1998), 129–49.

Hatzis, A., "Establishing a revolutionary newspaper: transplanting liberalism in a pre-modern society," in L. Kiousopoulou et al., eds., *Human Rights in a Time of Illiberal Democracies* (Athens, 2020).

Hatzopoulos, M., "Eighteenth-century Greek prophetic literature," in D. Thomas and J. Chesworth (eds), *Christian-Muslim Relations: A Bibliographical History, 14: Central and Eastern Europe (1700–1800)* (Leiden, 2020), 382–402.

———"Saints in revolt: the Anti-Ottoman vision of *Kyr Daniel*," in L. Laborie and A. Hessayon, eds., *Early Modern Prophecies in Transnational, National and Regional Contexts, ii: The Mediterranean World* (Leiden, 2020), 246–76.

Hazareesingh, S., "Memory and political imagination: the legend of Napoleon revisited," *French History*, 18:4 (2004), 463–83.

Hazlitt, W., "Jeremy Bentham," in *The Spirit of the Age* (London, 1825).

Herlihy, P., "Greek merchants in Odessa in the nineteenth century," *Harvard Ukrainian Studies* (1978–79), 399–420.

Holt, E. Gilmore, *From the Classicists to the Impressionists: Art and Architecture in the 19th Century* (New Haven, CT, 1966, 1978).

Ilicak, H. S., "Revolutionary Athens through Ottoman eyes," in M. Georgopoulou and K. Thanasakis, eds., *Ottoman Athens: Topography, Archaeology, History* (Athens, 2019).

Inalcik, H., and D. Quataert, eds., *An Economic and Social History of the Ottoman Empire, 1300–1914* (Cambridge, 1994).

Innes, J., and Philp, M., eds., *Re-Imagining Democracy in the Mediterranean, 1780–1860* (Oxford, 2018).

Institute of Balkan Studies, *Les relations gréco-russes pendant la domination turque et la guerre d'indépendance grecque* (Thessaloniki, 1983).

Jarrett, M., "No sleepwalkers: the men of 1814–15: bicentennial reflections on the Congress of Vienna and its legacy," *Journal of Modern European History*, 13:4 (2015), 429–38.

Jelavich, B., *Russia's Balkan entanglements, 1806–1914* (Cambridge, 1991).

Jewsbury, G., "The Greek question: the view from Odessa, 1815–1822," *Cahiers du monde russe*, 40:4 (1999), 751–62.

Jurien de la Gravière, E., "Les missions extérieures de la marine: III. La station du Levant," *Revue des Deux Mondes*, 103:4 (Feb. 15, 1873), 763–89.

Kaltchas, N., *An Introduction to the Constitutional History of Modern Greece* (New York, 1940).

Kandiloros, T., *Istoria tis Gortynias* (Patras, 1899).

———*O armatolismos tis Peloponnisou, 1500–1821* (Athens, 1924).

Kargakos, S., *Dimitrios Galanos o Athinaios (1760–1833)* (Athens, 1994).

Karaman, K., and S. Pamuk, "Ottoman state finances in European perspective, 1500–1914," *Journal of Economic History*, 70:3 (Sept. 2010), 593–629.

Katifori, D., "Katadromi kai peirateia kata tin epanastasi tou 1821," *Parousia*, 5 (1987), 239–54.

Katsardis-Hering, O., ed., *Oi poleis ton Filikon* (Athens, 2018).

Kiel, M., "Corinth in the Ottoman period: (1458–1687) and (1715–1821)," *Shedet*, 3 (2016), 45–71.

Kiousopoulou, L., ed., *Human Rights in a Time of Illiberal Democracies* (Athens, 2020).

Kissinger, H., *A World Transformed: Metternich, Castlereagh and the Problems of Peace* (New York, 1957).

Kitromilides, P., and K. Tsoukalas, eds., *The Greek Revolution: A Critical Dictionary* (Cambridge, MA, 2021).

———and H. Sukru Ilicak, *1821: I gennisi enos ethnous-kratous* (Athens, 2010).

Knapton, E. J., "The origins of the Treaty of Holy Alliance," *History*, 26:102 (Sept. 1941), 132–40.

Kokkonas, G., *O politis Petros Skylitzis Omiridis, 1784–1872* (Athens, 2003).

Koliopoulos, J., *Brigands with a Cause* (Oxford, 1984).

Konrad, F., "Religion, political loyalty and identity: French and Egyptian perceptions of Suläyman Pasha Sève," in S. Jobs and G. Mackenthun, eds., *Agents of Transculturation* (Munich, 2013), 89–115.

Konstantaras, D., "Christian elites of the Peloponnese and the Ottoman state, 1715–1821," *European History Quarterly*, 43:4 (2013), 627–56.

Konstantinidis, T., *Karavia, kapetanoi kai syntrofonavtai, 1800–1830* (Athens, 1954).

Kontoyiannis, P., *Ethnikoi evergetai* (Athens, 1908).

Kotsonis, K., *O Ibraim stin Peloponniso* (Athens, 1999).

Koulikourdis, G., *Aigina*, I (Athens, 1990).

Koulouri, C., and C. Loukos, *Ta prosopa tou Kapodistria: o protos kyvernitis tis Elladas kai i neoelliniki ideologia (1831–1996)* (Athens, 1996).

Koulouris, C., "Yiortazontas to ethnos: ethnikes epeteioi stin Ellada ton 19° aiona," in *Atheates opseis tis istorias: keimena afieromena ston Yianni Yiannoulopoulo* (Athens, 2012).

———"O Kapodistrias os ethnikos iroas: oi antifaseis tis mnimis kai tis istorias," in G. Georgis, ed., *O Kyvernitis Ioannis Kapodistrias* (Athens, 2015), 88–107.

Kremmydas, V., "I dolofonia tou Kyberniti Ioanni Kapodistria," *Eranistis*, 14 (1977), 217–81.

Kyrkini-Koutoula, A., *I othomaniki dioikisi stin Elladai periptosi tis Peloponnisou* (1715–1821) (Athens, 1996).

Laiou, S., "Entre les insurgés reaya et les indisciplinés ayan: la révolution grecque," in M. Hadjianastasis, ed., *Frontiers of the Ottoman Imagination: Studies in Honour of Rhoads Murphey* (Leiden, 2015), 213–28.

———"Patronage networks in the Aegean Sea, end of the 18th–beginning of the 19th century," in M. Sariyannis, ed., *New Trends in Ottoman Studies* (Rethymnon, 2014), 413–23.

Lampridis, I., *Epirotika meletimata* (Athens, 1887).

Lane-Poole, S., *The Life of the Right Honorable Stratford Canning*, 2 vols. (London, 1888).

———*Sir Richard Church* (London, 1890).

Lappas, T., "Foresia kai armata stin Epanastasi tou 1821," *Nea Estia*, 546 (April 1950).

Lelekos, M. S., ed., *Dimotiki anthologia* (Athens, 1868).

Lemaitre, A., *Musulmans et chrétiens: notes sur la guerre de l'indépendance grecque* (Paris, 1897).

Liata, E., *"Ek tou ysterimatos armatosan": I fregata "Timoleon" stin epanastasi tou 1821* (Athens, 2020).

———"Oi anavathmoi tis apomnimonevsis kai oi politikes stratigikes mias oikoyeneias," *Eranistis*, 20 (1995), 163–223.

Lieber, Francis, *The Miscellaneous Writings of Francis Lieber*, ii (London, 1881).

Lignadis, A., *To proton daneion tis anexartesias* (Athens, 1970).

Lignos, A., *Istoria tis nisou Ydras*, 2 vols. (Athens, 1953).

Loukatos, S., "Tourko-Albanikou filellenismou eranisma kata tin ellinikin ethnoegersian," *Athina* (1973), 43–63.

———"La philhellénisme balkanique pendant la lutte pour l'indépendance Hellénique," *Balkan Studies*, 19:2 (1978), 249–83.

———"Les Arabes et les Turcs philhellènes pendant l'insurrection pour l'indépendance de la Grèce," *Balkan Studies*, 21:2 (1980), 233–73.

Loukos, C., "O kyvernitis I. Kapodistrias kai oi Mavromihalaioi," *Mnimon*, 4 (1974), 1–110.

———"I ensomatosi mias paradosiakis archontikis oikoyeneias ston neo elliniko kratos: i periptosi ton Mavromihalaion," *Ta Istorika*, 1:2 (Dec. 1984), 283–97.

———"I epanastasi tou 1821. Apo kyriarcho antikeimeno erevnas kai didaskalias stin ypovathmisi kai siopi," in P. Kitromilides and T. Sklavenitis, eds., *Historiografia tis neoteris kai synchronis Elladas, 1833–2002*, 2 vols. (Athens, 2004), 1: 579–93.

Lowry, H., *Ottoman Architecture in Greece: A Review Article with Addendum and Corrigendum* (Istanbul, 2009).

———and I. Erünsal, *Remembering One's Roots: Mehmed Ali Pasha of Egypt's Links to the Macedonian Town of Kavala: Architectural Monuments, Inscriptions and Documents* (Istanbul, 2011).

Malakis, E., "Chateaubriand's contribution to French philhellenism," *Modern Philology*, 26:1 (August 1928), 91–106.

Malavetas, T., "O tafos tou Hoursid Pasas," *Thessalika grammata*, ii (Feb. 1935), 13–14.

Mallouchou-Tufano, F., "The vicissitudes of the Athenian Acropolis in the 19th century," in [n.a.], *Great Moments in Greek Archaeology* (Athens, 2007).

Manolopoulos, K., *Antimetopisis polemikon dapanon kata tin ethnergesian tou 1821* (Athens, 1973).

Martinez, J., *The Slave Trade and the Origins of International Human Rights Law* (Oxford, 2012).

Massé, A., "French consuls and philhellenism in the 1820s: official positions and personal sentiments," *Byzantine and Modern Greek Studies*, 41:1 (April 2017), 103–18.

Mazarakis-Aincan, J. C., and L. Navari, trans., *Greek Printing Presses and the Struggle for Independence* (Athens, 2020).

Mazurel, H., *Vertiges de la guerre: Byron, les philhellenes et le mirage grec* (Paris, 2013).

McGrew, W., *Land and Revolution in Modern Greece, 1800–1881: The Transition in the Tenure and Exploitation of Land from Ottoman Rule to Independence* (Kent, OH, 1985).

Mébul, L., "L'aumòne d'un grand artiste," *Le guide musical* (Aug. 18–25, 1859).

Meletopoulos, I. A., *I istoria tis neoteras Elladas eis tin laikin eikongrafian* (Athens, 1968).

Miaoulis, A., *Istoria tis Nisou Hydras* (Athens, 1874).

Moschopoulos, N., *Istoria tis ellinikis epanastaseos (Ti egrapsan oi Tourkoi istoriografoi)* (Athens, 2003).

Moutzouris, I., *I armosteia ton nison tou aigaiou pelagous sta chronia tis ellinikis epanastaseos* (Athens, 1984).

Murat, L., *L'homme qui se prenait pour Napoléon* (Paris, 2011).

Narotschnitzki, A. L., "La diplomatie russe et la préparation de la Conference de St. Petersbourg," Institute for Balkan Studies, *Les relations gréco-russes pendant la domination turque et la guerre d'indépendance grecque* (Thessaloniki, 1983).

Neal, L., and L. Davis, "The evolution of the structure and the performance of the London Stock Exchange in the first global financial market, 1812–1914," *European Review of Economic History*, 10:3 (Dec. 2006), 279–300.

Negroponte, J., *Le tsar Alexandre 1er et les grecs* (Paris, 1893).

Nicolopoulos, J., "From Agathangelos to the Megale Idea: Russia and the emergence of modern Greek nationalism," *Balkan Studies*, 26:2 (1985), 41–56.

Notopoulos, J., "New sources on Lord Byron at Missolonghi," *Keats-Shelley Journal*, 4 (Winter 1955), 31–45.

Oeconomous, L., *Essai sur la vie du Comte Capodistrias depuis son départ de Russie en août 1822 jusqu'à son arrivée en Grèce en janvier 1828* (Paris and Toulouse, 1926).

Oikonomous, I., *O theos kai to 1821* (Athens, 2018).

Oikonomou, M., *Istorika tis ellinikis palingenesias* (Athens, 1873).

Otetea, A., "L'Hétairie d'il y a cent cinquante ans," *Balkan Studies*, 6:2 (1965), 249–64.

Oxford Dictionary of National Biography (online).

Pakkanen, P., *August Myhrberg and North European Philhellenism* (Athens, 2006).

Palairet, M., *The Balkan Economies, c. 1800–1914* (Cambridge, 1997).

Paliyenko, A., *Genius Envy: Women Shaping French Poetic History, 1801–1900* (Philadelphia, PA, 2016).

Pamuk, S., "The end of financial institutions in the Ottoman empire, 1600–1914," *Financial History Review*, 15:1 (2004), 7–32.

Panagopoulos, E., "The background of the Greek settlers in the New Smyrna colony," *Florida Historical Quarterly*, 35:2 (Oct. 1956), 95–115.

Panayiotopoulos, V., *Dyo prinkipes stin elliniki epanastasi* (Athens, 2015).

——*Konstantinos Kantiotis, Kerkyraios: elasson Filikos, agonistis tis ellinikis epanastasis* (Athens, 2019).

——"Apo to Navplion stin Tripolitsa: i simasia tis metaforas mias periferiakis protevousas ton 18o aiona," *Eranistis*, 11 (1974), 41–56.

——"Kati egine stin Piza to 1821," *Ta istorika*, 3:5 (June 1986), 177–82.

——"I Filiki Etaireia: organotikes proypotheseis tis ethnikis epanastasis," *Istoria Neou Ellinismou* (Athens, 2003), iii, 9–32.

Papageorgiou, S., "Vasos Mavrovouniotis, a Montenegrin chieftain on the threshold of modernity," *Mediterranea: ricerche storiche*, 32 (Dec. 2014), 463–81.

Papageorgis, K., *Ta kapakia: Varnakiotis, Karaïskakis, Androutsos* (Athens, 2003).

Papalas, A., *Rebels and Radicals: Icaria 1600–2000* (Wauconda, IL, 2005).

Papamichalopoulos, K., *Poliorkia kai alosis tis Monemvasias ypon ton ellinon toi 1821* (Athens, 1874).

Papanikolaou, L., *I kathimerini istoria tou eikosiena* (Athens, 2007).

Paparrigopoulos, K., *Georgios Karaïskakis* (Athens, 1867).

Papoulidis, C., "Un document characteristique de Gabriel Catacazé tiré des archives de la Politique Extérieure de la Russie," *Balkan Studies*, 23:2 (1982), 1–7.

——"Les grecs de Russie au 19e siècle et au début du 20e," *Balkan Studies*, 32 (1991), 235–70.

——"A propos de l'oeuvre des employés grecs du Ministère des Affaires Étrangères de la Russie impériale aux XVIIIème, XIXème et XXème siècles," *Balkan Studies*, 35 (1994), 5–14.

Parolin, C., *Radical Spaces: Venues of Popular Politics in London, 1790–c. 1845* (Canberra, 2010).

Patrinellis, C. G., "The Phanariots before 1821," *Balkan Studies* (2001), 177–98.

Penn, V., "Philhellenism in England. II," *Slavonic and East European Review*, 14:42 (April 1936), 647–60.

Pesenson, M., "Napoleon Bonaparte and apocalyptic discourse in nineteenth-century Russia," *Russian Review*, 65 (July 2006), 373–92.

Petropoulos, J., *Politics and Statecraft in the Kingdom of Greece* (Princeton, NJ, 1968).

Pizanias, P., *The Greek Revolution of 1821: A European Event* (Istanbul, 2011).

——*The Making of the Modern Greeks, 1400–1820* (Newcastle, 2020).

Ploumidis, S., "I ennoia tou 'thanatou' stin elliniki epanastasi (1821–1832): ideologikes proslipseis kai politiki praktiki," *Mnimon*, 32 (2011–12), 59–86.

Polemis, D., *History of Andros* (Andros, 2016).

Politis, A., *L'Hellenisme et l'Egypte moderne*, 2 vols. (Paris, 1929–30).

Politis, N., *Ellines i Romioi?* (Athens, 1901).

Prokopios, G., *To archontiko tou G. Voulgari stin Hydra* (Athens, 2001).

Prousis, T., "Bedlam in Beirut: a British perspective in 1826," *Chronos: Revue d'Histoire de l'Université de Balamand*, 15 (Lebanon, 2007), 89–106.

Prousis, T. C., *Russian Society and the Greek Revolution* (DeKalb, IL, 1994).

Pylia, M., "Leitourgies kai avtonomia ton koinotiton tis Peloponnisou kata ti defteri Tourkokratia (1715–1821)," *Mnimon*, 23 (2001), 67–98.

——"Conflits politiques et comportements des primats chrétiens en Morée, avant la guerre de l'indépendance," in A. Anastasopoulos and E. Kolovos, eds., *Ottoman Rule and the Balkans, 1760–1850: Conflict, Transformation, Adaptation* (Rethymnon, 2007), 137–49.

Quemeneur, P., "Chateaubriand et la Grèce," *Balkan Studies*, 3:1 (1962), 119–32.

Robertson, W. S., *France and Latin American Independence* (Baltimore, MD, 1939).

——"The United States and Spain in 1822," *AHR*, 20:4 (July 1915), 781–800.

Rotzokos, N., *Epanastasi kai emfylios sto eikosiena* (Athens, 1997).

Sabry, M., *L'empire égyptien sous Mohamed-Ali et la question d'Orient (1811–1849)* (Paris, 1930).

Sachs, H., *The Ninth: Beethoven and the World in 1824* (New York, 2010).

Sainte-Beuve, C., "La Grèce en 1863," *Nouveaux lundis*, v (Paris, 1884, revised ed.), 308–30.

Sakellariou, S., *I Filiki Etaireia* (Odessa, 1909).

Sarantakes, N., *To zorbaliki ton rayiadon* (Athens, 2020).

Schellenberg, T. R., "Jeffersonian origins of the Monroe Doctrine," *Hispanic Atlantic Historical Review*, 14:1 (Feb. 1934), 1–31.

Sfoini, A., "'Epanastasi': chriseis kai simasies tis lexis sta keimena tou '21," in D. Dimitropoulos et al., eds., *Opseis*, 307–40.

Sfyroeras, V., *Ta ellinika pliromata tou tourkikou stolou* (Athens, 1968).

Sifneos, E., "Preparing the Greek revolution in Odessa in the 1820s: tastes, markets and political liberalism," *Historical Review* (Athens), 11 (2014), 139–70.

Simmons, C., "The claim of blood: Gladstone as king of Greece," *Nineteenth Century Contexts*, 13:2 (1989), 227–37.

Sinclair, D., *The Land That Never Was: Sir Gregor MacGregor and the Most Audacious Fraud in History* (Boston, MA, 2003).

Skylissis, I., *Molierou arista erga* (Trieste, 1871).

Smiley, W., *From Slaves to Prisoners of War: The Ottoman Empire, Russia and International Law* (Oxford, 2018).

Sofianos, D., "Enkyklioi (Avg. 1821–Ian. 1822) tou Oikoumenikou Patriarchou Evgeniou B' peri doulikis ypotagis ton Ellinon ston Othomano kataktiti," *Deltion tou Kentrou Erevnas tis Istorias tou Neoterou Ellinismou* (2000), ii, 19–41.

St. Clair, W., *That Greece Might Still Be Free: The Philhellenes in the War of Independence* (Oxford, 1972).

Stamatopoulos, D., "Constantinople in the Peloponnese: the case of the Dragoman of the Morea Georgios Wallerianos and some aspects of the revolutionary process," in A. Anastasopoulos and E. Kolovos, eds., *Ottoman Rule and the Balkans*, 149–67.

Stamatopoulos, T., *Oi tourkoproskynimenoi kai o Kolokotronis* (Athens, 1974).

Stasinopoulos, E., *I Athina tou perasmenou aiona (1830–1900)* (Athens, 1963).

Stathis, P. "From klephts and *armatoloi* to revolutionaries," in A. Anastasopoulos and E. Kolovos.,eds., *Ottoman Rule and the Balkans*, 167–79.

Stewart, C., *Dreaming and Historical Consciousness in Island Greece* (Oxford, 2012).

Stites, R., *The Four Horsemen: Riding to Liberty in Post-Napoleonic Europe* (Oxford, 2014).

Stourdza, A. C., *L'Europe orientale et le rôle historique des Maurocordato, 1660–1830* (Paris, 1913).

Syriana Grammata [Afieroma: I Syra stin Epanastasi tou 1821], 6:2 (Dec. 2019).

Telalis, A., ed., *Plapoutas* (Athens, 1952).

Temperley, H., *The Foreign Policy of Canning, 1822–1827: England, the Neo-Holy Alliance and the New World* (London, 1925).

Theocharakis, A. M., "The ancient circuit wall of Athens: its changing course and the phases of construction," *Hesperia*, 80:1 (Jan.–March 2011), 71–156.

Theodoridis, G., *Alexandros Mavrokordatos: enas phileleftheros sta chronia tou Eikosiena* (Athens, 2012).

Theotokas, N., and N. Kotarides, *I oikonomia tis vias: paradosiakes kai neoterikes exousies stin Ellada tou 19ou aiona* (Athens, 2006).

Thiersch, F., *De l'état actuel de la Grèce et des moyens d'arriver à sa restauration*, 2 vols. (Leipzig, 1833).

Thompson, J., "Osman Effendi: a Scottish convert to Islam in early nineteenth-century Egypt," *Journal of World History*, 5:1 (Spring 1994), 99–123.

Tolias, G., "Antiquarianism, patriotism and empire: transfer of the cartography of the Travels of the Anacharsis the Younger, 1788–1811," *Perimetron*, 3:3 (2008), 101–19.

Tricha, L., *Spyridon: o allos Trikoupis, 1788–1873* (Athens, 2019).

Trikoupis, S., *Istoria tis ellinikis epanastaseos*, 4 vols. (London, 1853–57).

Troelenberg, E.-M., "Drawing knowledge, [re-]constructing history: Pascale Coste in Egypt," *International Journal of Islamic Architecture*, 4:2 (2015), 287–313.

Tsiamalos, D., *Oi armatoloi tis Roumelis* (Athens, 2009).

Tsitselikis, K., *Old and New Islam in Greece: From Historical Minorities to Immigrant Newcomers* (Leiden, 2012).

Turner, M. J., "'Arraying Minds against Bodies': Benthamite radicals and revolutionary Europe during the 1820s and 1830s," *History*, 90:2 (April 2005), 236–61.

Tzakis, D., "Apo tin Odysso sti Vostitsa" in Katsardis-Hering, O., ed., *Oi poleis ton Filikon* (Athens, 2018).

——— "Polemos kai scheseis exousias stin epanastasi tou 1821," in D. Dimitropoulos et al., eds., *Opseis tis epanastasis tou 1821* (Athens, 2018), 154–74.

Tzourmana, G., *Vretanoi Rizospastes metarrythmistes* (Athens, 2015).

Vakalopoulos, A., *Aichmalotoi ellinon kata tin epanastasin tou 1821* (Thessaloniki, 1941).

Vauthier, G., "Un projet de démembrement de la Turquie en 1808," *Annales révolutionnaires*, 8:5 (Oct.–Dec. 1916), 713–19.

Veis, N., "Arkadika glossika mnimeia," in *Deltion Istorikis kai Ethnologikis Etaireias tis Ellados*, 6:22 (Aug. 1903), 211–75.

Veremis, I., and H. Sükrü Ilicak, *1821: i gennisi enes ethnous-kratous* (Athens, 2010).

Vick, B., *The Congress of Vienna: Power and Politics after Napoleon* (Cambridge, MA, 2014).

Vingtrinier, A., *Soliman-pacha, colonel Sève, généralissime des armées egyptiennes* (Paris, 1886).

Vios, S., *I sfagi tou Xiou eia to stoma tou Chiakou laou* (Chios, 1922).

Vitali, F., "O Tinou Gavriil Sylivos kai i symvoli tou eis tin ethnegersian tou 1821," *Epetiris Etaireia Kykladikon Meleton* (1971–73), 137–55.

Voglis, E., *Erga kai imerai ellinikon oikogeneion, 1750–1940* (Athens, 2005).

Vreto, M. P., "'Othon A': Vasileus tis Ellados," *Ethnikon Imerologion tou etous 1869* (Leipzig, 1869), 242–84.

Vryonis, S., "The ghost of Athens in Byzantine and Ottoman times," *Balkan Studies*, 43:1 (2002), 5–115.

Vyzantios, C., *Istoria tou taktikou stratou tis Ellados* (Athens, 1837).

Walker, W. L., "Recognition of belligerency and grant of belligerent rights," *Transactions of the Grotius Society*, 23 (1937), 177–210.

Walton, B., *Rossini in Restoration Paris: The Sound of Modern Life* (Cambridge, 2007).

Webster, C., *The Foreign Policy of Castlereagh, 1812–1815* (London, 1931).

———*Britain and the Independence of Latin America, 1812–1830: Selected Documents from the Foreign Office Archives* (London, 1938).

Witt, J. F., *Lincoln's Code: The Laws of War in American History* (New York, 2012).

Woodhouse, C. M., *Capodistrias: The Founder of Greek Independence* (Oxford, 1973).

Yakovaki, N., "The Philiki Etaireia revisited: in search of contexts, national and international," *Historical Review* (Athens), 11 (2014).

Zanou, K., *Transnational Patriotism in the Mediterranean, 1800–1850: Stammering the Nation* (Oxford, 2018).

Zei, E., *O agonas sti thalassa* (Athens, 2010).

Zorin, A., *By Fables Alone: Literature and State Ideology in Late Eighteenth-Century and Early Nineteenth-Century Russia* (Boston, MA, 2014).

Theses

Andriakaina, E., " 'To noima tou 21' sta apomnimonevmata tou Fotakou," PhD, Panteion University (1999).

Bitis, A., "The Russian army and the eastern question, 1821–34," PhD, London School of Economics (2000).

Bozikis, S., "Dimosia oikonomia kai synkrotisi ethnikou kratous kata tin Elliniki Epanastasi tou 1821," PhD, Ionian University (2018).

Diakakis, A., "I poli tou Mesolongiou kata tin epanastasi tou 1821: polemos, oikonomia, politiki, kathimerini zoi," PhD, University of Crete (2017).

Dimitropoulous, M., "Pyrgospito Kiamil bey stin Sykia Korinthias," Patras University (2011).

Fotopoulos, A., "Oi kotzabasides tis Peloponnisou kata tin defteri Tourkokratia (1715–1821)," PhD, National Capodistrian University, Athens (1995).

Frangos, G., "The Philike Etaireia, 1814–1821: a social and historical analysis," DPhil, Columbia University (1971).

Glavanis, P. M., "Aspects of the economic and social history of the Greek community in Alexandria during the nineteenth century," PhD, University of Hull (1989).

Grenet, M., "La fabrique communautaire: les grecs à Venise, Livourne et Marseille, c. 1770–c. 1830," PhD, European University Institute, Florence (2010).

Hadziiosif, C., "La colonie grecque en Egypte," PhD, Sorbonne: Université de Paris IV (1980).

Hill, K. M., "Pascale-Xavier Coste: a French architect in Egypt," PhD, Massachusetts Institute of Technology (1992).

Kalpadakis, G., "Technocratic efforts in institution-building in the early modern Greek state," unpublished paper.

Nikolaou, G., "Islamisations et Christianisations dans le Peloponnése (1715–c. 1832)," thèse du doctorat, Université de Strasbourg (1997).

Stavroulaki, E., "O Anthimos Gazis (1758–1828)," PhD, National Capodistrian University, Athens (2001).

Themelis-Katiforis, D., "I dioxis tis peirateias kai to Thalassion Dikastirion, 1828–1829," PhD, National Capodistrian University, Athens (1973).

Tzakis, D., "Armatolismos, syngenika diktya kai ethniko kratos. Oi oreines eparchies tis Artas sto proto imisi tou 19ou aiona," PhD, Panteion University, Athens (1997).

Vlachopoulos, Ch., "Dionysios Romas kai i epitropi Zakynthou ston dromo yia tin ethniki synkrotisi," PhD, National Capodistrian University, Athens (2015).

Wombwell, J. A., "The long war against piracy: historical trends," Occasional Paper, no. 32, Fort Leavensworth, Kansas (2010).

Zarakostas, E., "From observatory to dominion: geopolitics, colonial knowledge and the origins of the British Protectorate of the Ionian Islands, 1797–1822," PhD, University of Bristol (2018).

Notes

INTRODUCTION

1. G. Tertsetis, *Logos ekfonitheis en to anagnostirio tis Ellinikis Voulis* (Zakynthos, 1856), 11–12.

2. Laura Richards, ed., *Letters and Journals of Samuel Gridley Howe* (Boston, MA, 1906), i, 188; Dimitris Dimitropoulos, *Martyries yia ton plythismo ton nision tou Aigaiou, 15os–arches 19ou aiona* (Athens, 2004), 227–29; D. G. Capaitzis, "'Karteria': the first steam warship in war (1826)," *Historic Ships* (2009).

3. D. Armitage and S. Subrahmanyam, eds., *The Age of Revolutions in Global Context, c. 1760–1840* (London, 2010).

4. J. E. Acton, "Nationality," *Home and Foreign Review*, i (1862), 1–15, here 12–13; A. Andreades, "L'administration financière de la Grèce sous la domination turque," *Revue des Études Grecques* (1910), 131–83, here 170.

5. L. Woolf, *International Government: Two Reports* (London, 1916), 30.

6. See now *Afieroma: i Syra stin Epanastasi tou 1821*, a special issue of *Syriana grammata*, 6:2 (Dec. 2019).

7. D. Dimitropoulos, "O 'geros tou Moria': ktizontas mia patriki figoura tou ethnous," in D. Dimitropoulos and K. Dede, eds., *"I matia ton allon": proslipseis prosopon pou sfragisan treis aiones (18os–20os aiones)* (Athens, 2012), 69–90.

8. C. Koulouri, "O Kapodistrias os ethnikos iroas: oi antifaseis tis mnimis kai tis istorias," in G. Georgis, ed., *O Kyvernitis Ioannis Kapodistrias* (Athens, 2015), 88–107.

9. Anon., "Ellinikai efimerides," *Pandora*, 443 (1 Sept. 1868), 215, using the unpublished memoirs of Haralambis Papapolitis.

10. Quotation from E. Panagopoulos, "The background of the Greek settlers in the New Smyrna colony," *Florida Historical Quarterly*, 35:2 (Oct. 1956), 95–115 (here 100); on Russian Alaska and Evstrat Delarov, see L. Black, *Russians in Alaska, 1732–1867* (Fairbanks, Alaska, 2004), 108.

11. E. Garston, *Greece Revisited, and Sketches in Lower Egypt in 1840, with Thirty-Six Hours of a Campaign in Greece in 1825*, 2 vols. (London, 1842), ii, 312–13.

12. Metternich on Hope in C. M. Woodhouse, *Capodistrias: The Founder of Greek Independence* (Oxford, 1973), 249; M.G.A.M., "Citoyen Grec" (George Manos), *Résumé géographique de la Grèce et de la Turquie d'Europe* (Paris, 1826), 11–12.

13. Ibid., 4, 218–19; G. Tolias, "Antiquarianism, patriotism and empire," *Perimetron*, 3:3 (2008), 101–19; "Eleftherian eis tin klassikin gin ths Ellados" is the call by Ypsilantis, cited in A. Sfoini, "'Epanastasi': chriseis kai simasies tis lexis sta keimena tou '21," in D. Dimitropoulos et al., eds., *Opseis*, 307–40.

14. M. S. Lelekos, ed., *Dimotiki anthologia* (Athens, 1868), 54; "Ellinikai efimerides," *Pandora*, 443 (1868), 215; S. Asdrachas, "To pothoumeno," in his *Protogoni epanastasi: armatoloi kai kleftes (180s–190s aiones)* (Athens, 2019), 297–307, and M. Hatzopoulos, "Eighteenth-century Greek prophetic literature," in D. Thomas and J. Chesworth (eds.), *Christian-Muslim Relations: A Bibliographical History, 14: Central and Eastern Europe (1700–1800)* (Leiden, 2020), 382–402. My thanks to Dr. Hatzopoulos for his generous help with this subject.

15. On "Hellene," "Graikos" and "Romaios," see R. Beaton, "Antique nation? 'Hellenes' on the eve of Greek independence and in twelfth-century Byzantium," *BMGS*, 31:1 (2007), 76–96. An entry into a fierce debate about the relative merits of the two terms is N. Politis, *Ellines i Romioi?* (Athens, 1901); Ali Pasha in L. Droulia, "Towards modern Greek consciousness," *Historical Review*, 1 (2004), 51–67, citing D. G. Fokas, *O ploiarchos Leonidas Palaskas* (Athens, 1940), 4.

16. S. Laiou, "The Greek revolution in the Morea according to the description of an Ottoman official," in P. Pizanias, ed., *The Greek Revolution of 1821: A European Event* (Istanbul, 2011), 244–45; G. Gazis, *Viografia ton iroon Markou Botsari kai Karaïskaki* (Aigina, 1828), 32–33.

17. Y. H. Erdem, "The Greek revolt and the end of the old Ottoman order," in P. Pizanias, ed., *I elliniki epanastasi tou 1821* (Athens, 2009), 281–89; F. Chrysanthopoulos, *Apomnimonevmata peri tis Ellinikis Epanastaseos*, 2 vols. (Athens, 1899), i, 294 (cited hereafter as Fotakos, *Apomnimonevmata*); E. Protopsaltis, ed., *Istorikon archeion Alexandrou Mavrokordatou*, 6 vols. (Athens, 1963–86), ii (cited hereafter as IAAM); "den ito Haldoupis" in Koutsalexi, *Diaferonta kai perierga tina istorimata*, 24; cf. https://sarantakos .wordpress.com/2020/10/02/halldup.

18. H. S. Ilicak, "Revolutionary Athens through Ottoman eyes," in M. Georgopoulou and K. Thanasakis, eds., *Ottoman Athens: Topography, Archaeology, History* (Athens, 2019), 252; H. Erdem, "'Perfidious Albanians' and 'Zealous Governors': Ottomans, Albanians and Turks in the Greek War of Independence," A. Anastasopoulos and E. Kolovos, eds., *Ottoman Rule and the Balkans, 1760–1850: Conflict, Transformation, Adaptation* (Rethymnon, 2007), 222.

19. For one example, K. Gardikas, "O Anastasios Polyzoidis kai i elliniki epanastasi," *Mnimon*, 1 (1971), 35.

20. See the useful glossaries compiled by Protopsaltis at the end of the initial volumes of IAAM. Also in T. Konstantinidis, *Karavia, kapetanoi kai syntrofonavtai, 1800–1830* (Athens, 1954), 551–72; as an introduction to a vast literature on the lingua franca of the early modern Mediterranean, see E. Dursteler, "Speaking in tongues: language and communication in the early modern Mediterranean," *Past and Present*, (Nov. 2012), 47–77.

21. Question 2 in the 2019 poll, whose results are given in https://s.kathimerini.gr/resources/article-files/pws-vlepoyn-oi-ellhnes-thn-epanastash-toy-1821-kefim-analytikh-ek8esh-apotelesmatwn.pdf.

22. Office of the Prime Minister, "Anakoinosi grafeiou typou prothypourgou yia tin Gianna Angelopoulou," July 31, 2019; https://www.ant1news.gr/eidiseis/article/542839/gianna-aggelopoyloy-oristike-proedros-tis-epitropis-ellada-2021-eikones.

23. G. Charitakis, *I ekatonaetiris tis epanastaseos* (Athens, 1921).

24. On Greek endurance, see P. Kitromilides and H. Sükrü Ilicak, *1821: i gennisi enos ethnous-kratous* (Athens, 2010), 84; [Makriyannis], S. Adrachas, ed., *Makriyanni apomnimonevmata* (Athens, 1957), 547.

CHAPTER 1: OUT OF RUSSIA

1. T. Gritsopoulos, ed., *Theodorou Kolokotroni diigisi symvanton tis ellinikis fylis apo ta 1770 eos ta 1836* (Athens, 1981), 49; A. Lignos, ed., *Archeia Lazarou kai Georgiou Koundouriotou, 1821–1832, i: 1821–1823* (Athens, 1920), 4; I. Filemon, *Dokimion istorikon peri tis Filikis Etaireias* (Nafplion, 1834), 143.

2. *Mémoires de la Comtesse Edling (née Stourdza)* (Moscow, 1888), 144–45; on the remarkable Roxandra Stourdza, see S. Ghervas, "A 'Goodwill Ambassador' in the post-Napoleonic era: Roxandra Edling-Sturdza on the European scene," in G. Sluga and C. James, eds., *Women, Diplomacy and International Politics since 1500* (London, 2015), 151–66.

3. Cited in M. Jarrett, "No sleepwalkers: the men of 1814/15: bicentennial reflections on the Congress of Vienna and its legacy," *Journal of Modern European History*, 13:4 (2015), 429–38.

4. Woodhouse, *Capodistrias*, 53; M. Pesenson, "Napoleon Bonaparte and apocalyptic discourse in early nineteenth-century Russia," *Russian Review*, 65 (July 2006), 373–92; E. J. Knapton, "The origins of the Treaty of Holy Alliance," *History*, 26:102 (Sept. 1941), 132–40; S. Ghervas, *Réinventer la tradition: Alexandre Stourdza et l'Europe de la Sainte-Alliance* (Paris, 2009).

5. H. Kissinger, *A World Transformed: Metternich, Castlereagh and the Problems of Peace* (New York, 1957), 292; P. K. Grimsted, "Capodistrias and a 'New Order' for Restoration Europe: the 'Liberal' ideas of a Russian foreign minister, 1814–1822," *Journal of Modern History*, 40 (1968), 166–92.

6. M.-H. Weil, ed., *Les dessous du Congrès de Vienne* (Paris, 1917), 276.

7. I. Capodistrias, "Aperçu de ma carrière publique, depuis 1798 jusqu'à 1822," *Sbornik imperatorskogo russkogo istoricheskogo obshchestva* iii (1868), 163–292, here 203.

8. C. Webster, *The Foreign Policy of Castlereagh, 1812–1815* (London, 1931), 427–30.

9. Weil, *Les dessous*, 186; B. Vick, *The Congress of Vienna: Power and Politics after Napoleon* (Cambridge, MA, 2014), 225.

10. A. de la Garde-Chambonas, *Anecdotal Recollections of the Congress of Vienna* (London, 1902), 1–2; J. Negroponte, *Le tsar Alexandre Ier et les grecs* (Paris, 1893), 21.

11. "Quelques Grecs, d'une classe fort obscure," in D. G. Kambouroglou, ed., *Mémoires du Prince Nicolas Ypsilanti* (Athens and Paris, n.d.), 4; on the building and neighborhood, see E. Sifneos, "Preparing the Greek revolution in Odessa in the 1820s: tastes, markets and political liberalism," *Historical Review* (Athens), 11 (2014), 144–46.

12. G. Frangos, "The Philike Etaireia, 1814–1821: a social and historical analysis," DPhil, Columbia University (1971); E. Xanthos, *Apomnimonevmata peri tis Philikis Etaireias* (Athens, 1845), 11–12.

13. A. Zorin, *By Fables Alone: Literature and State Ideology in Late Eighteenth-Century and Early Nineteenth-Century Russia* (Boston, MA, 2014), 24–28.

14. P. Herlihy, "Greek merchants in Odessa in the nineteenth century," *Harvard Ukrainian Studies* (1978–79), 399–420, esp. 400–401; John Moore, *A Journey from London to Odessa, with Notices of New Russia* (Paris, 1833), 149; V. Karidis, "A Greek mercantile *paroikia*: Odessa 1774–1829," in R. Clogg, ed., *Balkan Society in the Age of Greek Independence* (London, 1981), 47–48; Sifneos, "Preparing the Greek revolution," 139–70; Pushkin cited in H. Sachs, *The Ninth: Beethoven and the World in 1824* (New York, 2010), 21.

15. C. Papoulidis, "Les grecs de Russie au 19e siècle et au début du 20e," *Balkan Studies*, 32 (1991), 235–70; quotation from Papoulidis, "À propos de l'oeuvre des employés grecs du Ministère des Affaires Étrangères de la Russie impériale aux XVIIIème, XIXème et XXème siècles," *Balkan Studies*, 35 (1994), 5–14 (here p. 5).

16. Under his revolutionary name, Fotakos, he would write one of the key memoirs to come out of the conflict.

17. Moore, *A Journey from London to Odessa*, 154–55, cited by Herlihy, "Greek Merchants in Odessa in the Nineteenth Century," 399–420, p. 416; Sifneos, "Preparing the Greek revolution".

18. Xanthos, "Antigrafa epistolon," in Xanthos, *Apomnimonevmata*, 130; ibid., 48 (for the code names); V. Mexas, *Oi Filikoi: katalogos ton melon tis Filikis Etaireias ek tou archeiou Sekeri* (Athens, 1937), 58, n.2.

19. Frangos, "The Philike Etaireia," 75.

20. "Aposmasma ex anekdotou cheirografou tou Stamati Koumbari," in S. Sakellariou, *I Filiki Etaireia* (Odessa, 1909), 63.

21. *Carte segrete e atti ufficiali della polizia Austriaca in Italia dal 4 giugno 1814 al 22 marzo 1848*, i (Capolago, 1852), 186–204.

22. N. Yakovaki, "The Philiki Etaireia revisited: in search of contexts, national and international," *Historical Review* (Athens), 11 (2014), 178.

23. On Galanos: M. Burgi-Kyriazi, *Demetrios Galanos—énigme de la Reniassance orientale* (Paris, 1984); S. Kargakos, *Dimitrios Galanos o Athinaios (1760–1833)* (Athens, 1994); E. Stavroulaki, "O Anthimos Gazis (1758–1828," PhD, National Capodistrian University of Athens (2001); I. Filemon, *Dokimion istorikon peri tis Filikis Etaireias* (Nafplion, 1834), 186.

24. G. Kokkonas, *O politis Petros Skylitzis Omiridis, 1784–1872* (Athens, 2003), 95; on eschatological traditions, see M. Hatzopoulos, "Saints in Revolt: the Anti-Ottoman vision of *Kyr Daniel*," L. Laborie and A. Hessayon, eds., *Early Modern Prophecies in Transnational, National and Regional Contexts*, ii: *The Mediterranean World* (Leiden, 2020), 246–76.

25. Kokkonas, *O politis Petros Skylitzis Omiridis*, 95–96.

26. Frangos, "The Philike Etaireia," 47–50.

27. Cited by Woodhouse, *Capodistria*, 163.

28. Ibid., 165.

29. Cited by Vasilis Panagiotopoulos, "The Filiki Etaireia: organisational preconditions of the national war of independence," in P. Pizanias, *The Greek Revolution of 1821: A European Event* (Istanbul, 2011), 101–29, here at p. 113. A good discussion of Galatis' contacts with the Phanariot circles in the Principalities in G. Theodoridis, *Alexandros Mavrokordatos: enas phileleftheros sta chronia tou Eikosiena* (Athens, 2012), 84–91: March 1817 expelled from Kishinev to Jassy; June: Bucharest then back to Jassy, Sept. 1817; summer 1818 Bucharest; autumn 1818 Constantinople and thence to Peloponnese and assassinated Jan./Feb. 1819.

30. Capodistrias, "Aperçu de ma carrière publique," 220.

31. Filemon, *Dokimion istorikon peri tis Filikis Etaireias*, 227–30.

32. See the excellent remarks by N. Yiakovaki, "Odyssos, Konstantinoupoli, Ismaili: treis organotikoi stathmoi enos achartografitou dromologiou," in O. Katsardis-Hering, ed., *Oi poleis ton Filikon* (Athens, 2018), 173–201.

33. The membership list may be found in Mexas, *Oi Filikoi*; Sakellariou, *I Filiki etaireia*, 70.

34. See the meticulous reconstruction in V. Panayiotopoulos, *Konstantinos Kantiotis, Kerkyraios: elasson Filikos, agonistis tis ellinikis epanastasis* (Athens, 2019).

35. Capodistrias, "Aperçu de ma carrière publique," 225.

36. G. Arsh, "On the life in Russia of the Greek patriotic family Ypsilanti," *Balkan Studies*, 26 (1985), 73–90.

37. Xanthos, *Apomnimonevmata*, 17; E. Moraitinis-Patriarcheas, ed., *Apomnimonevmata tou prinkipos Nikolaou Ipsilanti* (Athens, 1986), 160–65.

38. Woodhouse, *Capodistria*, 224, 229; cf. Ypsilantis' own account in P. Enepekidis, *Alexandros Ypsilantis: i aixmalosia tou eis tin Austrian 1821–1828*

(Athens, 1969), 176–82. Another account is in the memoirs of Nikolaos Ypsilantis.

39. F(rançois) R(édordon), *Lettres sur la Valachie, ou Observations sur cette province et ses Habitans, écrites de 1815 à 1821* (Paris, 1822), 141; Liprandi cited in E. Tappe, "The 1821 revolution in the Romanian Principalities," in R. Clogg, ed., *The Struggle for Greek Independence* (London, 1973), 135–56, here 153; A. Stourdza, "Notice biographique sur la Comte J. Capodistrias, Président de la Grèce," in E. Bétant, ed., *Correspondance du Comte J. Capodistrias, Président de la Grèce,* i (Geneva, 1839), 62–63.

40. Vasilis Panayiotopoulos, *Dyo prinkipes stin elliniki epanastasi* (Athens, 2015), 190; Frangos, "The Philike Etaireia," 266–67.

41. I. Rizos Neroulos, *Précis de l'histoire moderne de la Grèce* (Geneva, 1828), 282–83.

42. Filemon, *Dokimion istorikon peri tis Filikis Etaireias,* i, 76; M. Efthymiou, "To 'mega schedion' i pos Filikoi upelavon dynata ta adynata," in Katsardis-Hering, *Oi poleis ton Filikon,* 45–57. On the war against Ali Pasha, see next chapter.

43. V. Panayiotopoulos, *Dyo prinkipes stin elliniki epanastasi* (Athens, 2015), 67–68. My only disagreement with this is the assertion that the spring of 1821 was set then, rather than later on; cf. the very useful and reliable summary in E. Protopsaltis, *I Filiki Etaireia: amamnistikon tevchos epi ti 150 etiridi* (Athens, 1964), 71–83, which gives the end of the year as the initial date; Xanthos, *Apomnimonevmata,* 124; Efthymiou in Katsardis-Hering, *Oi poleis ton Filikon.*

44. Filemon, *Dokimion istorikon peri tis ellinikis epanastaseos,* 266–67; F. Chrysanthopoulos, *Apomnimonevmata peri tis ellinikis epanastaseos,* 2 vols. (Athens, 1899), i, 49–50.

45. E. Protopsaltis, ed., *Dionysiou Eumorfopoulou apomnimonevmata* (Athens, 1957), 5, 9–10; M. Oikonomous, *Istorika tis ellinikis palingenesias* (Athens, 1873), 74–75; N. Spiliades, *Apomnimonevmata,* 4 vols. (Athens, 1851–57), i, 9–10; Filemon, *Dokimion istorikon peri tis Filikis Etaireias,* 231, is strikingly insistent that the order to kill Kamarinos came from Ypsilantis and not the collective Etaireia leadership. Three letters in Xanthos, *Apomnimonevmata,* 102–4, October 19 and 21, seem to refer to the killing and the papers that had been seized from Kamarinos to be passed onto Ypsilantis.

46. I. Filemon, *Dokimion istorikon peri tis ellinikis epanastaseos,* 4 vols. (Athens, 1859–61), i, 234–38.

47. Ibid., 88–94.

48. A. Bitis, "The Russian army and the eastern question, 1821–34," PhD, LSE (2000), 59–60; *Avtoviografia Nik. Ipsilantou,* 169; Filemon, *Dokimion istorikon peri tis ellinikis epanastaseos,* i, ch. 3.

49. D. Farsolas, "Alexander Pushkin: his attitude towards the Greek revolution, 1821–1829," *Balkan Studies,* 12:1 (1971), 57–80.

50. Rizos Neroulos, *Précis de l'histoire moderne de la Grèce,* 278–79.

51. Filemon, *Dokimion istorikon peri tis ellinikis epanastaseos*, i, 292.

52. Frangos, "The Philike Etaireia," 276; A. Daskalakis, "I enarchis tou agona tis eleftherias: thrylos kai pragmatikotiis," *Epistimoniki Epetiris tis Filosofikis Scholis tou Panepistimiou Athinon*, 12 (1961), 14–15; Filemon, *Dokimion istorikon peri tis ellinikis epanastaseos*, i, 323.

53. "Sudden resolution," in Rizos Neroulos, *Précis de l'histoire moderne de la Grèce*, 286; Filemon, *Dokimion istorikon peri tis ellinikis epanastaseos*, i, 125; Filemon, *Dokimion istorikon peri tis Filikis Etaireias*, 301–3.

54. The best general account is Constantin Ardeleanu, "Military aspects of the Greek War of Independence in the Romanian principalities: the Battle of Galati (1821)," in G. Harlaftis and R. Păun, eds., *Greeks in Romania in the Nineteenth Century* (Athens, 2013), 141–66; *Apomnimonevmata peri tis Philikis Etaireias ypo Emmanouil Xanthou* (Athens, 1845), 113–14, 145, 156; G. Laios, ed., *Anekdotes epistoles kai engrafa tou 1821* (Athens, 1958), 49; a more or less contemporary account is I. Foteinos, *Oi Athloi tis en Vlachia ellinikis epanastaseos to 1821 etos syggraphentes para Ilia Photeinou* (Leipzig, 1846), 29–30; R. Stites, *The Four Horsemen: Riding to Liberty in Post-Napoleonic Europe* (Oxford, 2014), 201–2.

55. Filemon, *Dokimion istorikon peri tis ellinikis epanastaseos*, i, 323–25; on the situations in Jassy, Filemon, *Dokimion istorikon peri tis Filikis Etaireias*, 301–7; Stites, *The Four Horsemen*, 200.

56. A. Otetea, "L'Hetairie d'il y a cent cinquante ans," *Balkan Studies*, 6:2 (1965), 249–64, here 260–61; Filemon, *Dokimion istorikon peri tis Filikis Etaireias*, 304; Laios, *Anekdotes epistoles*, 60–61.

57. Farsolas, "Pushkin," 64; Laios, *Anekdotes epistoles*, 50–51.

58. A. Daskalakis, *Keimena-pigai tis istorias tis ellinikis epanastaseos*, 3 vols. (Athens, 1966–68), i, 118–19; Spiliades, *Apomnimonevmata*, 38–40.

59. Frangos, "The Philike Etaireia," 283–85: "andres Grekoi, osoi evriskesthe eis Moldavian kai Blachian.".

60. Panayiotopoulos, *Dyo prinkipes*, 262–64; boyars' appeals in Laios, *Anekdotes epistoles*, 41, 43.

61. "Imerologion ton kata tin Vlachian," in Filemon, *Dokimion istorikon peri tis ellinikis epanastaseos*, ii, 356.

62. Stites, *The Four Horsemen*, 202–4.

63. Frangos, "The Philike Etaireia," 285; Panayiotopoulos, *Dyo prinkipes*, 263–65.

64. Both letters in A. von Prokesch-Osten, *Geschichte des Abfalls der Griechen vom Türkischen Reiche im Jahre 1821* (Vienna, 1867), vol. 3: Beilagen, 1: 61–63.

65. B. Jelavich, *Russia's Balkan Entanglements, 1806–1914* (Cambridge, 1991), 54; text in Prokesch-Osten, *Geschichte*, 67.

66. Enepekidis, *Alexandros Ypsilantis*, 15–25; Farsolas, "Pushkin," 72; I. Laprandi, "Iz dnevnika i vospominanii I. P. Liprandi," *Russki arkhiv*, iv (1866), 1,408–11;

S. Ghekos, *I epistrofi: agonistes tou A. Ypsilanti ston dromo yia tin Ellada, 1822–1823* (Athens, 2019), passim.

67. Otetea, "L'Hétairie d'il y a cent cinquante ans," 261–62.

68. For a timeline of when information reached the Ottoman capital, see Prokesch-Osten, *Geschichte*, vol. 3: Beilagen 1, 104–16.

69. Prokesch-Osten, *Geschichte*, 107–8.

70. H. Sükrü Ilicak, "The revolt of Alexandros Ypsilantis and the fate of the Fanariots in Ottoman documents," in Pizanias, *The Greek Revolution of 1821*, 225, 234–35.

71. R. Walsh, *A Residence at Constantinople during the Greek and Turkish Revolutions*, 2 vols. (London, 1836), 306–7; S. Trikoupis, *Istoria tis ellinikis epanastaseos*, i (London, 1853), 100–105; S. Zipperstein, *The Jews of Odessa: A Cultural History, 1784–1881* (Stanford, CA, 1987), 119–20.

72. "Cheirografon tou 1821 etous," *Pandora* (July 15, 1863), 199–206; N. Moschopoulos, *Istoria tis ellinikis epanastaseos (Ti egrapsan oi Tourkoi istoriographoi)* (Athens, 2003), 136–82.

73. Cited in T. Prousis, "British embassy reports on the Greek uprising in 1821–22: war of independence or war of religion?," *Archivum Ottomanicum*, 28 (2011), 187.

74. Veremis and Ilicak, *1821*, 84–137.

75. Walsh, *A Residence at Constantinople*, i, 314–16; Prousis, "British embassy reports," 190–96.

76. Ghervas, "Le philhellenisme en Europe et en Russie," in *Peuples, états et nations dans le sud-est de l'Europe: Contributions roumaines* (Bucharest, 2004), 107.

77. R. Metternich, ed., *Memoirs of Prince Metternich*, 5 vols. (London, 1880), iii, 495; C. Crawley, *The Question of Greek Independence* (Cambridge, 1930), 18–19; Woodhouse, *Capodistrias*, 263–68.

78. Laios, *Anekdotes epistoles*, 88.

CHAPTER 2: ALI PASHA'S ANCIEN RÉGIME

1. H. Holland, *Travels in the Ionian Isles, Albania, Thessaly, Macedonia, etc. during the years 1812 and 1813* (London, 1815), 98; K. Fleming, *The Muslim Bonaparte: Diplomacy and Orientalism in Ali Pasha's Greece* (Princeton, NJ, 2014); A. Dumas, *The Count of Monte-Cristo*, 2 vols. (London, 1846), ii, 463.

2. T. Lappsa, ed., *Athanasiou Lidoriki apomnimonevmata* (Jannina, 1955), 19.

3. E. Prevelakis, K. Kalliatakis Merticopoulou, eds., *Epirus, Ali Pasha and the Greek Revolution: Consular Reports of William Meyer from Preveza*, vol. 1 (1819–21) (Athens, 1996) [henceforth abbreviated to Meyer], 47–49, 58–59.

4. Meyer, 49; G. Zoras, ed., *Engrafa tou archeiou Vatikanou peri tis ellinikis epanastaseos*, 2 vols. (Athens, 1979–86), i, *1820–1826* (Athens, 1979) [henceforth abbreviated to *Vatican*], 116–17; Ahmet Uzun, "O Ali Pasas o Tepelenlis kai i perousia tou," 12, downloaded from http://www.eie.gr/nhrf /institutes/inr/instr-studiorumbalk/tepelenlis.pdf.

5. Meyer, 120.

6. Meyer, 122, 134; A. Marou, "I Filiki Etaireia kai i avli tou Ali Pasha: voli-doskopiseis, epiloges kai diktyoseis," 179–215; G. Arsh, ed., *I Rossia kai ta pasalakia Alvanias kai Ipirou, 1759–1831: engrafa rosikon archeion* (Athens, 2007), 265–83; D. Dimitropoulos, "Yianniotes sti Filiki Etaireia. Oi diadromes tis myisis," Katsiardi-Hering, *Oi poleis*, 109–25.

7. Text in *Vat.*, 125–26.

8. Meyer, 219.

9. Koutsalexis, *Diaferonta kai perierga tina istorimata*, 28–29; Arsh, *I Rossia*, 291.

10. Meyer, 255.

11. I. Kolokotronis, *Ellinika ypomnimata, itoi epistolai kai diafora engrafa aforonta tin Ellinikin Epanastasin* (Athens, 1856), 6–7.

12. Meyer, 385; Ch. Perraivos, *Apomnimonevmata polemika*, 2 vols. (Athens, 1836), 3.

13. Perraivos, *Apomnimonevmata polemika*, 14–15; Arsh, *I Rossia*, 307.

14. H. Lidderdale, ed., *The Memoirs of General Makriyannis, 1797–1864* (London, 1966), 12–14; original in G. Vlachoyanni, ed., *Stratigou Makriyanni Apomnimonevmata*, i (Athens, 1947), 116–17.

15. Perraivos, *Apomnimonevmata polemika*, 23–24; D. Skiotis, "The Greek revolution: Ali Pasha's last gamble," in N. Diamandouros et al., eds., *Hellenism and the First Greek War of Liberation (1821–1830)* (Thessaloniki, 1976), 97–109.

16. Koutsalexis, *Diaferonta kai perierga*, 33; Meyer, 319–20.

CHAPTER 3: THE LAST DAYS
OF THE OTTOMAN MOREA

1. [na], *Ethnika Asmata tis Ellados, 1453–1821* (Athens, 1896), 90–91. Note: *reaya* were the lower class of Ottoman taxpaying subjects, often equated with non-Muslims; *kodzabashis* were the Greek landowners; *klefts* were brigands.

2. B. Panayiotopoulos, "Apo to Navplion stin Tripolitsa: i simasia tis metaforas mias periferiakis protevousas ton 18o aiona," *Eranistis*, 11 (1974), 41–56.

3. On the demography, see G. Nikolaou, "Islamisations et Christianisations dans le Peloponnèse (1715–c. 1832)," thèse du doctorat, Strasbourg (1997), 113–62; also Kandiloros, *O armatolismos*, 420, and Filemon, *Dokimion istorikon*, i, 373, for manpower estimates.

4. Estimates of armed manpower in Filemon, *Dokimion istorikon*, i, 211–15.

5. D. Konstantaras, "Christian elites of the Peloponnese and the Ottoman state, 1715–1821," *European History Quarterly*, 43:4 (2013), 627–56; A. Fotopoulos, "Oi kotzabasides tis Peloponnisou kata tin defteri Tourkokratia (1715–1821)," PhD, Athens (1995); M. Pylia, "Leitourgies kai avtonomia ton koinotiton tis Peloponnisou kata ti defteri Tourkokratia (1715–1821)," *Mnimon*, 23 (2001), 67–98; A. Kyrkini-Koutoula, *I othomaniki dioikisi stin Ellada: i periptosi tis Peloponnisou* (1715–1821) (Athens, 1996), 198–99.

6. P. Pizanias, *The Making of the Modern Greeks, 1400–1820* (Newcastle, 2020), 390–93; M. Pylia, "Koinonikos apokleismos kai epanastasi," in Pylia, ed., *Apo to 1821 sto 2012* (Athens, 2012), 19–29.

7. Pylia, "Leitourgies kai avtonomia," 98; the chief work is Fotopoulos, "Oi kodzabasides tis Peloponnisou".

8. I. Salafatinos, *Syntomoi paratiriseis epi tinon peristatikon anaferomenon eis ta legomena apomnimonevmata tou K. N. Spiliadou* (Athens, 1853), 11.

9. Pylia, "Leitourgies kai avtonomia," 90.

10. Ibid.; and Pylia in A. Anastasopoulos and E. Kolovos, eds., *Ottoman Rule and the Balkans, 1760–1850: Conflict, Transformation, Adaptation* (Rethymnon, 2007); on conversions, see the brilliant dissertation by Nikolaou, "Islamisations," esp. 161–72, 241–89, 300.

11. Fotakos, *Apomnimonevmata*, 33–34.

12. K. Papamichalopoulos, *Poliorkia kai alosis tis Monemvasias ypon ton ellinon toi 1821* (Athens, 1874), 58–60; J. Bouchard, "Agnosti epistoli tou G. Tertseti," *Eranistis*, 26 (1967), 33–39.

13. A. Goudas, *Vioi paralliloi ton epi tis anagenniseos tis Ellados diaprepsanton andron* (Athens, 1874), vi, 121–25, has Sukur Bey Petrobey's brother. Cf. (L. Stavrianos), E. Angelomatis-Tsougkarakis, ed., *Pragmateia ton peripeteion tou viou mou* (Athens, 1982), 155, note 25; Gritsopoulos, ed., *Theodorou Kolokotroni diigisis*, 8; T. Rigopoulos, [A. Fotopoulos, ed.], *Apomnimonevmata apo ton archon tis Epanastaseos mechri tou etous 1881* (Athens, 1979), 12–16, 57–59.

14. T. Kolokotronis (trans. and intro. by Elizabeth M. Edmonds), *Theodoros Kolokotrones: "the Old Man of the Morea"* (Brookline, MA, 1984), 113.

15. D. Psatelis, *A Sketch of the Causes of the Revolution in Greece* (Oxford, 1823), 23; Fotakos, *Apomnimonevmata*, I, 424–26.

16. Cited in Nikolaou, "Islamisations," 147–211.

17. A. Frantzis, *Epitomi tis istorias tis anagennitheisis Ellados archomeni apo tou etous 1715 kai ligousa to 1835*, 4 vols. (Athens, 1839–41), i, 365–66.

18. T. Kandiloros, *O armatolismos tis Peloponnisou, 1500–1821* (Athens, 1924).

19. "Tou Zacharia," in C. Fauriel, *Chants populaires de la Grèce moderne* (Paris, 1824), i, 76: the "bride" is a daughter-in-law.

20. N. Asimakopoulos, ed., *Anagnosti Kontaki apomnimonevmata* (Athens, 2009), 18–21; P. Doukas, *I Sparti dia mesou ton aionon* (New York, 1922), 724–54, is more hagiographic.

21. Kandiloros, *O armatolismos*, 280–321.
22. Kyrkini-Koutoula, *I othomaniki dioikisi*, ch. 5; on the 1808 initiative, see Konstantaras, "Christian elites of the Peloponnese," 637–38; G. Vauthier, "Un projet de démembrement de la Turquie en 1808," *Annales révolutionnaires*, 8:5 (Oct–Dec. 1916), 713–19.
23. P. Stathis, "From klephts and *armatoloi* to revolutionaries," in A. Anastasopoulos and E. Kolovos, eds., *Ottoman Rule and the Balkans*, 173–75; see also A. Politis, "The klephts and their songs," in P. Boukalas, ed., *The Klephtic Ballads: An Anthology of 19th-Century Greek Popular Songs* (Athens, 2020), 11; an account of Kolokotronis on Zakynthos in Kandiloros, *Armatolismos*, 435–37.
24. Based on the following sources: K. Deliyannis, *Apomnimonevmata*, i (Athens, 1957), 84–88; S. Stefanopoulos, *Apomnimonevmata tina tis epanastaseos tou 1821* (Tripolis, 1864), 16–19; A. Telalis, *Plapoutas* (Athens, 1952), 129–37.
25. T. Kandiloros, *Istoria tis Gortynias* (Patras, 1899), 217–19, places the episode in 1819 and recounts that the tombs of the two murdered villagers were still visible outside their village at the time of writing.
26. Deliyannis, *Apomnimonevmata*, 80.
27. Konstantaras, "Christian elites," 642–43; cf. Tsakis, "Apo tin Odysso sti Vostitsa," in Katsardis-Hering, *Oi poleis*, 125–49.
28. A. Goudas, *Vioi paralliloi* (Athens, 1872), 148.
29. Fotakes, *Vios tou Papa Flessa*, 8–10.
30. Oikonomou, *Istorika tis ellinikis palingenesias*, 79; Filemon, *Dokimion istorikon*, 351–52.
31. Fotakos, *Papa Flessa*, 13–22.
32. Daskalakis, "I enarchis tou agona," 9–138; Panayiotopoulos, *Dyo prinkipes*, 67–75.
33. Stefanopoulos, *Apomnimonevmata*, 29–31.
34. Daskalakis, "I enarchis tou agona," 34, n. 1.
35. Fotakos, *Papa Flessa*, 23.
36. Perraivos, *Apomnimonevmata polemika*, 3.
37. Stefanopoulos, *Apomnimonevmata*, 24; cf. T. Gordon, *History of the Greek Revolution*, 2 vols. (London, 1832), i, 144.
38. Stefanopoulos, *Apomnimonevmata*, 15.
39. I. Zafeiropoulos, *Oi archiereis kai oi proychountes entos tis en Tripolei fylakis en etei 1821* (Athens, 1890), 8–10; Daskalakis, "I enarchis tou agona tis eleftherias," 39.

CHAPTER 4: ON OR AROUND MARCH 25, 1821

1. Trikoupis, *Istoria*, i, 389.
2. C. Koulouris, "Yiortazontas to ethnos: ethnikes epeteioi stin Ellada ton 19° aiona," in *Atheates opseis tis istorias: keimena afieromena ston Yianni*

Yiannoulopoulo (Athens, 2012), 181–210; Daskalakis, "I enarchis tou agonos tis eleftherias," 1.

3. Daskalakis, "I enarchis tou agonos tis eleftherias," passim, esp. 71.

4. E. Liata, "Oi anavathmoi tis apomnimonevsis kai oi politikes stratigikes mias oikoyeneias," *Eranistis*, 20 (1995), 208; also Fotakos, *Apomnimonevmata*, 68–9; Deliyannis, *Apomnimonevmata*, i, 141–42.

5. See the important insights of D. Tzakis, "Polemos kai scheseis exousias stin epanastasi tou 1821," in D. Dimitropoulos et al., eds., *Opseis tis epanastasis tou 1821* (Athens, 2018), 154–74.

6. Frantzis, *Epitomi tis istorias*, i, 371.

7. Ibid., 374.

8. Anon., "Ellinikai Efimerides," *Pandora* (Sept. 1, 1868), 212–16.

9. Xanthos, *Apomnimonevmata*, 41; D. Tzakis, "Apo tin Odysso sti Vostitsa," in Katsardis-Hering, O., ed., *Oi poleis ton Filikon* (Athens, 2018), 144–45.

10. Kontakis, *Apomnimonevmata*, 35; Fotakos, *Apomnimonevmata*, i, 70.

11. Stefanopoulos, *Apomnimonevmata*, 35–36; Kontakis, *Apomnimonevmata*, 35.

12. Trikoupis, *Istoria*, i, 389.

13. Orlandos, *Nautika*, 119, 121–22; Kolokotronis, *Ellinika ypomnimata*, 65; Fotakos, *Apomnimonevmata*, 86.

14. Deliyannis, *Apomnimonevmata*, i, 163.

15. Fotakos, *Apomnimonevmata*, 84, 86.

16. Ibid., 146.

17. Deliyannis, *Apomnimonevmata*, i, 168–69; Protopsaltis, ed., *Panayiotou Papatsoni apomnimonevmata* (Athens, 1960), 63–64.

18. Moschopoulos, *Istoria*, 101–5, 156–57.

19. Ibid., 157–61; E. Kalogeropoulou, "Zitimata anefodiasmou kai peitharchias sto poliorkoumeno frourio tis Patras (1821–1825): i martyria tou stratiotikou dioikiti Yiousouf Mouchlis Pasa," in Dimitropoulos et al., eds., *Opseis tis epanastasis tou 1821*, 45–58.

20. Tzakis, "Polemos kai scheseis exousias," 165–69.

21. P. Green, *Sketches of the War in Greece* (London, 1827), 6; Il. Salafatinos, *Syntomoi paratiriseis epi tinon peristatikon anaferomenon eis ta legomena apomnimonevmata tou K. N. Spiliadou* (Athens, 1853), 12–13; Spiliades, *Apomnimonevmata*, i, 64.

22. Fotakos, *Apomnimonevmata*, 45.

23. F. Chrysanthopoulos, *Vios tou papa Flessas* (Athens, 1868), 20.

24. Kokkonas, *O politis Petros Skylitzis Omiridis*, 113.

25. Ypsilantis's proclamation in "Schimatismos tou protou en Elladi taktikou stratou," *Estia* (Jan.–June 1877), iii, 180–84; background in A. Daskalakis, "Ta topika politevmata kata tin epanastasin tou 1821," *Epistimoniki Epetiris tis Filosofikis Scholis tou Panepistimiou Athinon*, 15 (1964–65), 171–76.

26. Panayiotopoulos, *Dyo prinkipes*, here 72–73; "Avtoviografia Nikolaou Flogaïtou," *Ellinismos*, 1–2 (1898), 463–64; D. Gkinis, "O Dimitrios Ypsilantis

katevainei stin Ellada," *Eranistis*, 2 (1964), 187–89; Panayiotopoulos, *Konstantinos Kantiotis*, 87–93.

27. Panagiotopoulos, *Dyo prinkipes*, 91–93; J. C. Mazarakis-Ainian, L. Navari (trans.), *Greek Printing Presses and the Struggle for Independence, 1821–1827* (Athens, 2020), 20–35; Laios, ed., *Anekdotes epistoles*, 129, 140; cargo from "Schimatismos tou protou en Elladi taktikou stratou," *Estia* iii (Jan.–June 1877), 180–84.

28. Filemon, *Dokimion istorikon*, iii, 389.

29. Deliyannis, *Apomnimonevmata*, i, 238–39; Filemon, *Dokimion istorikon*, iv, 74–92.

30. C. Metaxas, *Souvenirs de la Guerre de l'Indépendance de la Grèce* (Paris, 1888), 38–43; Deliyannis, *Apomnimonevmata*, i, 238–39; Liata, "Oi anavathmoi tis apomnimonevsis," 219; "izpravnik" in Kokkonas, *O politis Petros Skylitzis Omiridis*, 109; Kantiotis in Filemon, *Dokimion istorikon*, iv, 86.

31. Filemon, *Dokimion istorikon*, iv, 89–90.

32. Negotiations and details in Daskalakis, *Keimena-pigai*, i, 212–18; also N. Kaltchas, *Introduction to the Constitutional History of Modern Greece* (New York, 1940), 43–45; see also the acute remarks of N. Rotzokos, "Topiki kai ethniki tavtotita sta apomnimonevmata ton Peloponnision agoniston tis epanastasis tou 1821," in D. Dimitropoulos et al., eds., *1821 kai apomnimonevma: istoriki chrisi kai istoriografiki gnosi* (Athens, 2020), 53–76.

33. Lignos, ed., *Archeia Lazarou*, 12–13, 20–25.

34. M. Raybaud, *Mémoires sur la Grèce pour servir à l'histoire de la guerre de l'indépendance*, 2 vols. (Paris, 1824), i, 393–95; S. Linnér, ed., *W. H. Humphreys "First Journal of the Greek War of Independence" (July 1821–February 1822)* (Stockholm, 1967), 26–28, 32–33.

35. Deliyannis, *Apomnimonevmata*, i, 249; Kokkonas, *O politis Petros Skylitzis Omiridis*, 116.

36. Raybaud, *Mémoires*, 430–31; Linnér, ed., *Humphreys "First Journal,"* 35.

37. Linnér, ed., *Humphreys "First Journal,"* 36; Raybaud, *Mémoires*, 432.

38. G. Kokkonas, "Poliorkia kai alosi tis Tripolitsas: i martyria tou Panayioti Anagnostopoulou yia tis diapragmatevseis kai to 'resalto,'" in D. Dimitropoulos et al., eds., *Opseis tis epanastasis tou 1821* (Athens, 2018), 21–44, here 28–29.

39. Raybaud, *Mémoires*, 454.

40. Ibid., 457.

41. Cited in the brilliant article by Giannis Kokkonas, "Poliorkia kai alosi tis Tripolitsas: i martyria tou Panayioti Anagnostopoulou yia tis diapragmatevseis kai to 'resalto,'" in Dimitropoulos et al., eds., *Opseis tis epanastasis tou 1821*, 21–44, here 42.

42. Raybaud, *Mémoires*, 465–66.

43. Deliyannis, *Apomnimonevmata*, i, 274–75.

44. Ibid., 275.

45. Fotakos, *Apomnimonevmata*, i, 257–59; on Necib: N. Clayer, *Mystiques, État et Société: les Halvetis dans l'aire balkanique de la fin du XVᵉ siècle à nos jours* (Paris, 1994), 222; John C. Alexander, "Yusuf bey al-Moravi on the siege and capture of Tripolitsa in 1821," in K. Lappas et al., eds., *Mnimi Penelopis Stathi; meletes istorias kai filologias* (Rethymnon, 2010), 152.
46. N. Veis, "Arkadika glossika mnimeia," in *Deltion Istorikis kai Ethnologikis Etaireias tis Ellados*, 6:22 (Aug. 1903), 232; E. Doxiadis, *State, Nationalism and the Jewish Communities of Modern Greece* (London, 2018), 33–37.
47. N. Kasomoulis, G. Vlachoyannis, ed., *Enthymimata stratiotika tis Epanastaseos ton Ellinon, 1821–1833*, 3 vols. (Athens, 1939), i, 152.
48. Veis, "Arkadika glossika mnimeia," 240.
49. Filemon, *Dokimion istorikon*, iv, 473.
50. Fotakos, *Apomnimonevmata*, i, 206.

CHAPTER 5: THE PISA CIRCLE

1. Laios, ed., *Anekdotes epistoles*, 206.
2. A.-P. de Candolle, *Mémoires et souvenirs de Augustin-Pyramus de Candolle écrits par lui-même publiés par son fils* (Geneva, 1862), 420–21: see the excellent discussion in Theodoridis, *Alexandros Mavrokordatos*, 113–14; on Karatzas, C. G. Patrinellis, "The Phanariots before 1821," *Balkan Studies* (2001), 177–98, here 191.
3. A source that reflects the Phanariot view of its subject and his milieu is A. C. Stourdza, *L'Europe orientale et le rôle historique des Maurocordato, 1660–1830* (Paris, 1913).
4. See A. Hatzis, "Establishing a revolutionary newspaper: transplanting liberalism in a pre-modern society," in L. Kiousopoulous et al., eds., *Human Rights in a Time of Illiberal Democracies* (Athens, 2020). Many thanks to Professor Hatzis for his guidance and help.
5. On Pisa, see: V. Panayiotopoulos, "Kati egine stin Piza to 1821," *Ta istorika*, 3:5 (June 1986), 177–82; Panayiotis Michailaris, "M'eipe pros toutois kai merikas eidiseis ton en Piza evriskomenon filon," in Katsardis-Hering, ed., *Oi poleis ton filikon*, 99–109; on Ignatios, see E. Protopsaltis, ed., *Ignatios Mitropolitis Oungrovlachias (1766–1828)* (Athens, 1959).
6. Laios, ed., *Anekdotes epistoles*, 251; E. Protopsaltis, ed., *Ignatios Mitropolitis Oungrovlachias (1766–1828)*, i: *Viografia* (Athens, 1959), 164–71; Theodoridis, *Alexandros Mavrokordatos*, 130–41; it is ironic that the first reaction of another Phanariot notable, the Ottoman minister in Vienna, Alexandros Mavroyeni, in March 1821 was to attribute the uprising in the Danubian Principalities, in his dispatch back to the Porte, to Karatzas and his circle: see T. Blancard, *Les Mavroyéni* (Paris, 1909), ii, 176. On the Pisa circle and the Etaireia, see Michailaris, "M'eipe pros toutois," 99–109.

7. Background in W. Bowers, *The Italian Idea: Anglo-Italian Radical Literary Culture, 1815–1823* (Cambridge, 2020), 148–51.

8. N. Fraistat and D. H. Reiman, eds., *Shelley's Poetry and Prose* (New York, 2002).

9. The text is provided, in French, in Theodoridis, *Alexandros Mavrokordatos*, 385–450.

10. Protopsaltis, ed., *Istorikon archeion Alexandrou Mavrokordatou*, i, 26–29.

11. Ibid., 30.

12. anon., "Ellinikai efimerides," *Pandora*, 443 (Sept. 1, 1868), 212–16, here 215.

13. Raybaud, *Mémoires*, i, 268–76.

14. Kasomoulis, *Enthymimata*, i, 393, cited by D. Tsiamalos, *Oi armatoloi tis Roumelis* (Athens, 2009), 204.

15. Cited in Protopsaltis, ed., *Istorikon archeion Alexandrou Mavrokordatou*, ii, 48.

16. On Makris, see A. Agapitos, *Oi endoxoi Ellines tou 1821, i oi Protagonistai tis Ellados* (Patras, 1877), 297–303.

17. Raybaud, *Mémoires*, i, 381–94.

18. On Varnakiotis, see K. Papageorgis, *Ta kapakia: Varnakiotis, Karaïskakis, Androutsos* (Athens, 2003), ch. 2; also the memoir by G. Gazis in K. Papado-poulos, *Ta kata G. Varnakiotin kai anaktisis tou Mesolongiou* (Mesolonghi, 1861), 116–18.

19. Dimos Tselios; Daskalakis, *Keimena-pigai*, i, 166–67.

20. Kasomoulis, *Enthymimata stratiotika*, i, 222; Rigas is discussed in D. Dimi-tropoulos, *Treis Filikoi, eparchoi stin Andro* (Athens, 2020).

21. Papageorgis, *Ta kapakia*, 48–51; Theodoridis, *Alexandros Mavrokordatos*, ch. 7, esp. 283ff.

22. N. Fysentzidis, *Anekdotoi avtografoi epistolai ton episimoteron ellinon oplarchigon kai diafora pros avtous engrafa tis dioikiseos meth'istorikon simeioseon* (Alexandria, 1893), 88–89.

23. On Varnakiotis, see the portrait in Papagiorgis; also Papadopoulos, *Ta kata G. Varnakiotin*, esp. 116–18; Fysentzidis, *Anekdotoi avtografoi*, 89–90.

24. Protopsaltis, ed., *Istorikon archeion Alexandrou Mavrokordatou*, i, 59; Papageorgis, *Ta kapakia*, 62.

25. Text in Gordon, *History of the Greek Revolution*, i, 322; cf. Mavrokordatos in Lignos, ed., *Archeia Lazarou*, i, 38–39; G. Finlay, *History of the Greek Revolution*, 2 vols. (Edinburgh, 1860), i, 292–93.

26. Protopsaltis, ed., *Istorikon archeion Alexandrou Mavrokordatou*, i, 71–72.

27. Ibid., 53, cited in Papageorgis, *Ta kapakia*, 107.

28. Theodoridis, *Alexandros Mavrokordatos*, 328–29 and passim.

29. Lignos, ed., *Archeia Lazarou*, i, 36–37; N. Alivizatos, "Assemblies and con-stitutions," in P. Kitromilides and K. Tsoukolas, eds., *The Greek Revolution: A Critical Dictionary* (Cambridge, MA, 2021), 439–52.

30. Finlay, *History of the Greek Revolution*, i, 295.

31. N. Alivizatos, *To syntagma kai oi echthroi tou stin neoelliniki istoria, 1800–2010* (Athens, 2011), 40–41; Kaltchas, *Introduction to the Constitutional History of Modern Greece*, 34–58.

32. F. Thiersch, *De l'état actuel de la Grèce et des moyens d'arriver à sa restauration*, ii (Leipzig, 1833), 251.

33. Alivizatos, *To syntagma kai oi echthroi*, 43–45. Forbearance against fellow Greeks was not total: there were assassinations of rivals, and executions of suspected spies and traitors.

34. Daskalakis, *Keimena-pigai*, i; Droulia, "Towards modern Greek consciousness," *Historical* Review, i (2004), 51–67, here 51; On the FLN, see M. J. Connelly, "Rethinking the Cold War and decolonisation: the grand strategy of the Algerian war of independence," *International Journal of Middle Eastern Studies*, 33 (2001), 221–45.

CHAPTER 6: KHURSHID PASHA'S HAREM

1. Inscription in T. Malavetas, "O, tafos tou Hoursid Pasa," *Thessalika grammata* 11 (Feb. 1935), 14.

2. J. Millingen, *Memoirs of the Affairs of Greece* (London, 1831), 34–35.

3. Ibid.

4. Papageorgis, *Ta kapakia*, 121.

5. Protopsaltis, ed., *Istorikon archeion Alexandrou Mavrokordatou*, ii, 37, 45.

6. Fysentzidis, *Anekdotoi autografoi*, 93–95. For the background see the Mapping Ottoman Epirus project at https://mapoe.stanford.edu/.

7. Protopsaltis, ed., *Istorikon archeion Alexandrou Mavrokordatou*, i, 69.

8. Makriyannis, *Memoirs*, 34. The contemporary report by the Greek secretary of Ismail Pasha, who passed it on firsthand to Praïdis, is in Protopsaltis, ed., *Istorikon archeion Alexandrou Mavrokordatou*, ii, 29.

9. On Ambatzis, see Lappas, *Athanasiou Lidoriki apomnimonevmata*, 24.

10. Makriyannis, *Memoirs*, 35; Prevelakis et al., eds., *Meyer*, 472.

11. Perraivos, *Apomnimonevmata polemika*, i, 91.

12. Makriyannis, *Memoirs*, 35; P. Mengous, *Narrative of a Greek Soldier, containing Anecdotes and Occurrences illustrating the Character and Manners of the Greeks and Turks in Asia Minor, and detailing Events of the Late War in Greece* (New York, 1830), 112, 121–22.

13. Perraivos, *Apomnimonevmata polemika*, i, 84–85; Prevelakis et al., eds., *Meyer*, 426–27.

14. Prevelakis et al., eds., *Meyer*, ii, 21ff.

15. S. Aravantinos, *Istoria Ali Pasa tou Tepelenli* (Athens, 1895), 326–32.

16. R. Walsh, *Narrative of a Journey from Constantinople to England* (Boston, 1828), 31–33. For another version of the charge sheet, see 259–60.

17. Aravantinos, *Istoria Ali Pasa*, 334 fn. 2, 337.

18. Prevelakis et al., eds., *Meyer*, 40.
19. Filemon, *Dokimion istorikon peri tis ellinikis epanastaseos*, iv, 471–72.
20. On the Stefanou family, see the excellent E. Voglis, *Erga kai imerai ellinikon oikogeneion, 1750–1940* (Athens, 2005), 205–66. On the handover: Germanos Palaion Patron, *Apomnimonevmata* (Athens, 1900), 113–14, which should now be modified in light of the documents in the Stefanou archive, ELIA (Greek: Logotechniko Istoriko Archeio); the date of the handover was April 16, according to the reimbursement claims submitted by those involved, *Archeia Ellinikis Paligenesias*, 15: 3, 24–25.
21. Prevelakis et al., eds., *Meyer*, ii, 74–75.
22. Prevelakis et al., eds., *Epirus*, 17.
23. Was Raybaud, who was in Tripolitsa, thinking of them when he mentions having seen Ottoman women "recount as among their greatest afflictions, surrounded as they were by cruel losses, being deprived of their jewels"? Raybaud, *Mémoires*, ii, 6.
24. Key documents on this affair may be found in the Stefanou archive, ELIA, fakellos 2: Haremia Khourshid Pasha (1821–1853). On the sequestration of harem property, see Protopsaltis, ed., *Istorikon archeion Alexandrou Mavrokordatou*, ii, 99.
25. Cf. E. Doxiadis, "Legal trickery: men, women and justice in late Ottoman Greece," *Past and Present*, 210 (Feb. 2011), 129–53.
26. Praïdes-Louriotis, 28 Jan. 1822, Protopsaltis, ed., *Istorikon archeion Alexandrou Mavrokordatou*, i, 119; Vatican, Zoras, ed., *Engrafa tou archeiou Vatikanou*, 212.
27. Makriyannis, *Memoirs*, 39.
28. On the massacres on Chios, see the next chapter.
29. Lignos, ed., *Archeia Lazarou*, i, 55; Moschopoulos, *Istoria*, 278–80.
30. Prevelakis et al., eds., *Meyer*, ii, 352–53; inscription in Malavetas, "O tafos," 14.
31. Prevelakis et al., eds., *Meyer*, ii, 337–40.
32. T. Prousis, *Lord Strangford at the Sublime Porte (1822): The Eastern Crisis* (Istanbul, 2012), 76–77; For an estimate by one of Ali Pasha's Greek secretaries, see Lappas, ed., *Athanasiou Lidoriki*, 25. Frantzis, *Epitomi tis istorias*, ii, 68 implausibly claims Khurshid Pasha, on being turned down by the sultan when he asked for financial help to redeem his family, turned for help to Ali Pasha, using G. Kitsos, Vasiliki's brother, as his agent, to suggest to the pasha that they work together. What is plausible is that Khurshid Pasha used some of Ali Pasha's wealth for the ransom.
33. I. Lampridis, *Epirotika meletimata* (Athens, 1887), 56; Moschopoulos, *Istoria*, 261–62.
34. T. Malavetas, "O tafos tou Hoursid Pasa," *Thessalika grammata*, ii (Feb. 1935), 13–14; N. Papatheodorou, "O tafos tou Hoursid Pasa sti Larisa," *Eleftheria* (April 15, 2018).

CHAPTER 7: THE WAR IN THE ISLANDS

1. Trikoupis, *Istoria tis ellinikis epanastaseos*, i, 170.
2. The classic work on the Greek sailors in the Ottoman navy is V. Sfyroeras, *Ta ellinika pliromata tou tourkikou stolou* (Athens, 1968); Lignos, *Istoria*, ii, 48–49; see also Prousis, *Lord Strangford at the Sublime Porte (1822)*, 121; on internal government, Trikoupis, *Istoria*, i, 172.
3. [E. Protopsaltis, ed.], D. Evmorfopoulos, *Apomnimonevmata* (Athens, 1957), 11.
4. D. I. Kriezis, *Epanorthosis esfalmenon tinon ek ton apomnimonevmaton peri tis ellinikis epanastaseos tou Fotakou* (Athens, 1874), 24; Fotakos, *Apomnimonevmata*, i, 113–16.
5. J. Emerson, G. Pecchio, and W. Humphreys, *A Picture of Greece in 1825*, 2 vols. (London, 1826), 177; Anargyros A. Hadzianargyrou, *Ta Spetsiotika, itoi syllogi istorikon engrafon kai ypomnimaton aforonton ta kata tin ellinikin epanastasin tou 1821 aristheisa ek ton archeion tis nisou Spetson*, 3 vols. (Athens, 1861), i, 149–51; D. Tzakis, D., "Apo tin Odysso sti Vostitsa" in O. Katsardis-Hering, ed., *Oi poleis ton Filikon* (Athens, 2018), 144–46; Lignos, *Archeia Lazarou*, i, 3–4.
6. A. Lignos, *Istoria tis nisou Ydras* (Athens, 1953), ii, 29; Kriezis, *Epanorthosis*, 24–27; Trikoupis, *Istoria*, i, 179–82; Filemon, *Dokimion istorikon*, iii, 108–14.
7. Deliyannis, *Apomnimonevmata*, i, 135; Kriezis, *Epanorthosis*, 28–29.
8. Trikoupis, *Istoria*, i, 170–84; A. Miaoulis, *Istoria tis Nisou Hydras* (Athens, 1874), 115–18.
9. On the now demolished Voulgaris mansion, see G. Prokopios, *To archontiko tou G. Voulgari stin Hydra* (Athens, 2001). On Voulgaris, see Sophia Laiou, "Patronage networks in the Aegean Sea, end of the 18th–beginning of the 19th century," in M. Sariyannis, ed., *New Trends in Ottoman Studies* (Rethymnon, 2014), 413–23.
10. E. Rothpletz, ed., *Lettres du Genevois Louis-André Gosse à sa mère pendant son séjour en Grèce (1826–1830)* (Paris, 1920), 21; Kriezis, *Epanorthosis*, 28.
11. Kriezis, *Epanorthosis*, 31; Miaoulis, *Istoria tis Nisou Hydras*, 92–93; cf. Lignos, *Istoria*, 32–34.
12. Lignos, *Istoria*, 183–85. For an excellent discussion, see E. Zei, *O agonas sti thalassa* (Athens, 2010), 51–63. My thanks to Antonis Hadzikyriakou for this source.
13. The essential work, product of an astonishing collaborative multi-archival research project, is G. Harlaftis and K. Papakonstantinou, eds., *Navtilia ton Ellinon, 1700–1821* (Athens, 2013), passim.
14. I am indebted to Gelina Harlaftis for her help. Her new edited volume on Greek shipping and 1821 affords a completely fresh understanding of this situation.
15. Lignos, *Istoria*, 46–47; H. Erdem, "'Do not think of the Greeks as agricultural labourers': Ottoman responses to the Greek war of independence," in F. Birtek

and T. Dragonas, eds., *Citizenship and the Nation-State in Greece and Turkey* (London, 2005), 75.

16. Orlandos, *Navtika*, 65–80; K. Nikodimos, *Ypomnima tis nisou Psaron*, i (Athens, 1862), 100–106.

17. Orlandos, *Navtika*, 61–66; *Précis des opérations de la flotte grecque durant la révolution de 1821 et 1822 écrit par un grec* (Paris, 1822), 51–52.

18. P. S. Omiridis, *Synoptiki istoria ton trion naftikon nison Ydras, Petson kai Psaron* (Nafplion, 1831), appendix, no. IA, "Prokyrigma tou Ellinikou Stolou," April 18, 1821; and doc. I: "Epistoli Spetsioton pros tous Hydraious," April 18, 1821; Orlandos, *Navtika*, i, 97, 263.

19. Mengous, *Narrative of a Greek Soldier*, 129–37; cf. the management of the Maniot privateer detailed in C. Swan, *Journal of a Voyage up the Mediterranean, principally among the Islands of the Archipelago and in Asia Minor, including Many Interesting Particulars relative to the Greek Revolution, especially a Journey through Maina to the camp of Ibrahim Pasha*, 2 vols. (London, 1826).

20. F. Pispiringkou, ed., *To imerologio tou "Kimonos"* (Athens, 2012), 65.

21. Moschopoulos, *Istoria*, 204–8; E. Liata, "*Ek tou ysterimatos armatosan*"; I fregata "*Timoleon*" stin epanastasi tou 1821 (Athens, 2020), 48–49; Filemon, *Dokimion istorikon*, iii, 319–20; W. Smiley, *From Slaves to Prisoners of War: The Ottoman Empire, Russia and International Law* (Oxford, 2018), 178.

22. A. de Voulx, "Recherches sur la coopération de la Régence d'Alger à la guerre de l'indépendance grecque," *Revue africaine*, 1 (1857), 134.

23. Orlandos, *Navtika*, 102; Liata, "*Ek tou ysterimatos armatosan*," passim.

24. C. D. Raffenel, *Histoire des événements de la Grèce, depuis les premiers troubles jusqu'à ce jour* (Paris, 1822), 115–20.

25. M. Malandrakis, *Sympliromatikai selides tis istorias tis Ellinikis Epanastaseos* (Athens, 1929), 4–5.

26. Stavrianos, *Pragmateia ton peripeteion*, 154–55; Raybaud, *Mémoires*, ii, 151–52.

27. Archives de la Ministère des Affaires Etrangères [Nantes], Smyrne, 36 [correspondence consulaire, 1821], Spadaro-David, May 28, 1821, 132–33; *Précis*, 25–31; Raffenel, *Histoire*, 122.

28. Orlandos, *Navtika*, i, 98–101.

29. Hadzianargyrou, *Ta Spetsiotika*, i, 431–2.

30. Decree in T. Prousis, "Smyrna in 1821: A Russian view," *Modern Greek Studies Yearbook*, 27 (1992), 153; Hadzianargyrou, *Ta Spetsiotika*, 436, 439, 443.

31. D. Polemis, *History of Andros* (Andros, 2016), 135; A. Drakakis, *Istoria tou oikismou tis Ermoupoleos (Syros)*, 2 vols. (Athens, 1979), i, 33.

32. D. Sofianos, "Enkyklioi (Avg. 1821–Ian. 1822) tou Oikoumenikou Patriarchou Evgeniou B' peri doulikis ypotagis ton Ellinon ston Othomano kataktiti," *Deltion tou Kentrou Erevnas tis Istorias tou Neoterou Ellinismou*

(2000), ii, 19–41; English translation in Prousis, "British embassy reports," 209 (letter of Feb. 11, 1822).

33. I. Moutzouris, *I armosteia ton nison tou aigaiou pelagous sta chronia tis ellinikis epanastaseos* (Athens, 1984), 11–12, 73–75 on Tinos; Malandrakis, *Sympliromatikai selides*, 47–55; Filemon, *Dokimion istorikon*, iii, 395–96.

34. See Dimitropoulos, *Treis Filikoi.*

35. Moutzouris, *I armosteia*, 42; Hadzianargyrou, *Ta Spetsiotika*, i, 434–37; Frantzis, *Epitomi*, iii, 210; Filemon, *Dokimion istorikon*, iii, 396.

36. A. Diamantaras, "En epeisodion tis ellinikis epanastaseos," *Deltion tis Istorikis kai Ethnologikis Etaireias tis Ellados*, 7:21 (August 1902), 51–57.

37. Hadzianargyrou, *Ta Spetsiotika*, i, 436, 439, 443.

38. Ibid., 434–35, 441.

39. Orlandos, *Navtika*, i, 73; Hadzianargyrou, *Ta Spetsiotika*, i, 447–48.

40. Cited by E. Jurien de la Gravière, "Les missions extérieures de la marine: III. La station du Levant," *Revue des Deux Mondes*, 103:4 (Feb. 15, 1873), 763–89, here 776.

41. K. P. Belsis, *Apo tin othomaniki nomimotita sto ethniko kratos: Lykourgos Logothetis, politiki viografia* (Athens, 2014), 88–89; Malandrakis, "Tou Dimitriou Themeli," *Sympliromatikai selides tis istorias tis Ellinikis Epanastaseos* (Athens, 1929), 47–55.

42. Raffenel, *Histoire*, 152–53.

43. De la Gravière, "Les missions extérieures de la marine," 770; Orlandos, *Navtika*, i, 156–58.

44. R. C. Anderson, *Naval Wars in the Levant, 1559–1853* (Liverpool, 1952); S. Laiou, "Entre les insurgés reaya et les indisciplinés ayan: la révolution grecque," in M. Hadjianastasis, ed., *Frontiers of the Ottoman Imagination: Studies in Honour of Rhoads Murphey* (Leiden, 2015), 213–28; Raffenel, *Histoire*, 150–51.

45. G. Vlachoyannis, *Chiakon archeion*, i (Athens, 1924), 5–6.

46. P. Argenti, ed., *The Massacres of Chios, described by contemporary diplomatic reports* (London, 1932), xvii.

47. Vlachoyannis, *Chiakon*, 322.

48. Ibid., 41, 341–42.

49. Ibid., 44–45.

50. Ibid., 321–28.

51. Cited in ibid., 29.

52. Ibid., 63, 67, 106.

53. Ibid., 111–12, 133–34, 194; Argenti, ed., *The Massacres of Chios*, passim.

54. Orlandos, *Navtika*, i, 254.

55. Vlachoyannis, *Chiakon*, 158.

56. C. Castanis, *The Greek Captive, a Narrative of the Captivity and Escape of Christophorus Plato Castanis* (Worcester, MA, 1845).

57. P.-J. Jourdain, *Mémoires historiques et militaires sur les événements de la Grèce*, 2 vols. (Paris, 1828), i, 68; M. Dimitriadis, ed., *"Archeio Agonos"*: *1806–1832: apo ta istorika archeia tou Mouseiou Benaki* (Athens, 2011), ii, 146–48, 151–52; Vlachoyannis, *Chiakon*, 93, 172.

58. Vlachoyannis, *Chiakon*, 174, 195, 234.

59. Malandrakis, *Sympliromatikai selides*, 78–79.

60. E. Stamatiadis, ed., *Samiaka, itoi istoria tis nisou Samou*, ii (Samos, 1881), 278.

61. Malandrakis, *Sympliromatikai selides*, 79–81.

62. Moutzouris, *I armosteia*, 10; S. Bozikis, "Dynamikes kai adraneies sti forologia kai sto forologiko mechanismo kata tin Epanastasi tou 1821," *Mnimon*, 31 (2010), 31–68.

63. Orlandos, *Navtika*, 245–46.

64. Moutzouris, *I armosteia*, 17.

65. S. Bozikis, "Dimosia oikonomia kai synkrotisi ethnikou kratous kata tin Elliniki Epanastasi tou 1821," PhD, Ionian University (2018), 161.

66. Moutzouris, *I armosteia*, 38.

67. Dimitriadis, ed., *"Archeio Agonos,"* 66; Moutzouris, *I armosteia*, 116, 172.

68. K. Lappas, "Proforikes paradoseis yia ton Beniamin Lesvios kai i chrisi tous stis viografies tou," *Mnimon*, 24:2 (2002), 85–105.

69. *Archeion Agonos*, 150, 183, 189; Metaxas, *Souvenirs*, 85–88.

70. Hadzianargyrou, *Ta Spetsiotika*, i, 456.

71. [Koudouriotis], A. Lignos, ed., *Archeia Lazarou kai Georgiou Koundouriotou, 1821–1832*, vol. 6 (Athens, 1927), 40.

72. Moutzouris, *I armosteia*, 82–85, 110-14; Dimitriadis, ed., *"Archeio Agonos,"* ii, 229, 110–14. Andros is now admirably discussed in Dimitropoulos, *Treis Filikoi*, passim.

73. *Archeion Agonos*, 149, 163, 170, 193.

74. Drakakis, *Istoria*, i, 46–49.

75. Ibid., 72.

76. Ibid., 83; G. Zoras, ed., *Engrafa tou archeiou Hagis peri ellinikis epanastaseos* (Athens, 1991), 423.

77. Cited in A. Delis, "A hub of piracy in the Aegean: Syros during the Greek war of independence," in D. Dimitropoulos, G. Harlaftis, and D. J. Starkey, eds., *Corsairs and Pirates in the Eastern Mediterranean, Fifteenth–Nineteenth Centuries* (Athens, 2016), 41–54; Prousis, *Lord Strangford*, 281.

78. Drakakis, *Istoria*, i, 51–95.

CHAPTER 8: ARMATOLES AND CONSTITUTIONS

1. Text of the secret veto in Fysentzidis, *Anekdotoi avtografoi epistolai ton episimoteron ellinon oplarchigon kai diafora pros avtous engrafa tis dioikiseos meth'istorikon simeioseon* (Alexandria, 1893), 127–28; Tsiamalos, 231: "Eis to exis kanenas armatolos den einai, oute rayias, all'eimetha oloi

Ellines." 232: "Dioikisi einai elefthera kai omoia me ekeinas tom pepolitev-
menon ethnon tis Evropis.".

2. Fysentzidis, *Anekdotoi avtografoi*, 135.

3. For more on the philhellenes, see ch. 10, passim.

4. Vryonis was also in touch with Mavrokordatos about an official guarantee
of his safety with the Greeks in the event that he fell into the disfavor of the
Sultan: Papageorgis, *Ta kapakia*, 128.

5. Fysentzidis, *Anekdotoi avtografoi*, 189.

6. A. Diakakis, "I poli tou Mesolongiou kata tin epanastasi tou 1821: polemos,
oikonomia, politiki, kathimerini zoi," PhD, Crete (2017), 89–90.

7. Gordon, *History of the Greek Revolution*, ii, 458.

8. [Brengeri], "Adventures of a foreigner in Greece: V," *London Magazine*, 6:24
(Dec. 1826), 536–38.

9. Ibid., 536; Raybaud, *Mémoires*, ii, 270.

10. Varnakiotis correspondence during and after the siege in Fysentzidis, *Anekdotoi avtografoi*, 190–93. His extraordinary apologia, undated, is in ibid.,
213–61. His 1824 denunciation of Mavrokordatos, ibid., 279–80..

11. Gordon, *History of the Greek Revolution*, i, 404–5; Papageorgis, *Ta kapakia*.

12. L. Papanikolaou, *I kathimerini istoria tou Eikosiena* (Athens, 2007), 218; on
Evvia, N. Ioannou, *Evvoïka, itoi istoria, periexousa tessaron eton polemous,
tis nisou Evvoias* (Ermoupolis, 1857), esp. 50–59.

13. Finlay, *History of the Greek Revolution*, i, 373.

14. Gordon, *History of the Greek Revolution*, i, 466–67.

15. Ibid., ii, xxx.

16. Fotakos, *Apomnimonevmata*, i, 472.

17. [Koundouriotis], A. Lignos, ed., *Archeia Lazarou kai Georgiou Koundouriotou, 1821–1832* (Athens, 1920), i, 158.

18. L. Tricha, *Spyridon: o allos Trikoupis, 1788–1873* (Athens, 2019), 164.

19. T. Kiousopoulou, "I tavtotita ton melon tis B' Ethnosynelefsis," in D. Dimitropoulos et al., eds, *I epanastasi tou 1821: meletes sti mnimi tis despoinas
Themeli-Katifori* (Athens, 2018), 63–92; Gordon, *History of the Greek Revolution*, ii, 6–7.

20. Gordon, *History of the Greek Revolution*, ii, 7.

21. *Archeia tis Ellinikis Palingenesias, 1821–1832* (Athens, 1971), i, 67.

22. See chapter 11.

23. Tricha, *Spyridon*, 172, citing A. Soutsos, "Peri satyras," in his *Elliniki Plastigx* (Athens, 1836), 150.

24. Hadzianargyrou, *Ta Spetsiotika*, i, 393–96; Gordon, *History of the Greek
Revolution*, 41–42.

25. Hadzianargyrou, *Ta Spetsiotika*, i, 400–402.

26. Ibid., i, 403–4.

27. Hydra cited by M. Sotiropoulos and A. Hadjikyriacou, "*Patris, Ethnos and
Demos*: representation and political participation in the Greek world," in J.

Innes and M. Philp, eds., *Re-Imagining Democracy in the Mediterranean, 1780–1860* (Oxford, 2018), 99–127, here 114.

28. *Ta Spetsiotika*, i, 144–45.
29. Protopsaltis, ed., *Ignatios Mitropolitis Oungrovlachias*, ii, 137; idem., *Istorikon archeion Alexandrou Mavrokordatou*, i, 224.
30. Kasomoulis, *Enthymimata stratiotika*, i, 225.
31. Millingen, *Memoirs*, 182.
32. B. Playainakou-Bekiaris and A. Stergellis, eds., *Archeion Ioanni Koletti*, 2 vols. (Athens, 1996–2002), i, 248.
33. Gordon, *History of the Greek Revolution*, i, 325.
34. S. Minta, "Letters to Lord Byron," *Romanticism on the Net*, 45 (2007), https://www.erudit.org/en/journals/ron/2007-n45-ron1728/015821ar; E. J. Trelawny, *Records of Shelley, Byron, and the Author* (New York, 2000), 253.
35. Finlay, *History of the Greek Revolution*, i, 299, cited in Kaltchas, *Constitutional History of Modern Greece*, 34; Protopsaltis, ed., *Istorikon archeion Alexandrou Mavrokordatou*, i, 137.

CHAPTER 9: THE NATURE OF THE STRUGGLE

1. C. C. Felton, *Greece: Ancient and Modern* (Boston, MA, 1867), 253.
2. Theodoridis, *Alexandros Mavrokordatos*, 408–9; Finlay, *History of the Greek Revolution*, i, 2–3; Kantakuzinos in Lignos, ed., *Archeia Lazarou kai Georgiou Koundouriotou*, i, 55. M. Palairet, *The Balkan Economies, c. 1800–1914* (Cambridge, 1997), 4–6, 18–21.
3. Veremis and Ilicak, *1821*, 84–90.
4. Ibid., *1821*, 112–35; Erdem, "Do not think of the Greeks as agricultural labourers," 69.
5. W. Smiley, *From Slaves to Prisoners of War: The Ottoman Empire, Russia and International Law* (Oxford, 2018), 176–78.
6. A. Daskalakis, *Keimena-pigai tis istorias tis ellinikis epanastaseos* (Athens, 1966), i, 443–46; A. Vakalopoulos, *Aichmalotoi ellinon kata tin epanastasin tou 1821* (Thessaloniki, 1941), 22.
7. Jourdain, *Mémoires*, i, 94; *The Narrative of J. Stephanini, a native of Arta in Greece* (Charleston, SC, 1829), 18–36; on Tsekouras, see Veis, "Arkadika glossika mnimeia," 230–32.
8. J. Schmidt, "The adventures of an Ottoman horseman: the autobiography of Kabudli Vasfi Efendi, 1800–1825," in *The Joys of Philology*, i (Istanbul, 2010), 165–286.
9. Gordon, *History*, i, 244–45. See too Linner, ed., *W. H. Humphreys "First Journal,"* 74–78.

10. A. Frantzis, *Epitomi tis istorias tis anagennitheisis Ellados archomeni apo tou etous 1715 kai ligousa to 1835* (Athens, 1839), i, 398–99; Vakalopoulos, *Aichmalotoi ellinon*, 40.

11. Filemon, *Dokimion Istorikon*, 155.

12. See the thoughtful S. Ploumidis, "I ennoia tou 'thanatou' stin elliniki epanastasi (1821–1832): ideologikes proslipseis kai politiki praktiki," *Mnimon*, 32 (2011–12), 59–86; Smiley, *From Slaves to Captives*, 178–79.

13. Hatzopoulos, "Saints in revolt," 246–76; N. Theotokas and N. Kotarides, *I oikonomia tis vias: paradosiakes kai veoterikes exousies stin Ellada tou 190u aiona* (Athens, 2006), ch. 1.

14. Papamichalopoulos, *Poliorkia kai alosis tis Monemvasias*, 91.

15. Daskalakis, *Keimena-pigai*, 443–46.

16. H. Lowry, *Ottoman Architecture in Greece* (Istanbul, 2009), 49–73.

17. N. Politis, *Eklogai apo ta tragoudia tou ellinikou laou* (Athens, 1914), 18–19; Fauriel, *Chants populaires*, ii, 62–63. A similar version in [n.a.], *Ethnika asmata tis Ellados, 1453–1821* (Athens, 1896); M. Alexiou, *The Ritual Lament in Greek Tradition* (Cambridge, MA, 1974), ch. 6.

18. D. Bartzis, "Ta palatia tou Kiamil Bey stin Korintho": https://argolikivivlio thiki.gr/tag/kiamel-beys-palaces-at-corinth; and G. Lois, "To pyrgospito tou Kiamil Bey stin Skykia Xylokastro" academia.edu; M. Dimitropoulou, "Pyrgospito Kiamil bey stin Sykia Korinthias," Patras University (2011). More generally, M. Kiel, "Corinth in the Ottoman period: (1458–1687) and (1715–1821)," *Shedet*, 3 (2016), 45–71.

19. S. Loukatos, "Tourko-Albanikou filellenismou eranisma kata tin ellinikin ethnoegersian," *Athina* (1973), 43–63.

20. Fotakos, *Apomnimonevmata*, ii, 307–8; Loukatos, "Tourko-Albanikou filellenismou," 43–63.

21. Frantzis, *Epitomi tis istorias*, i, 247; Kontakis, *Apomnimonevmata*, 52.

22. Ch. Loukos, "Erotikes scheseis kai sexoualikes pratikes kata tin epanastasi tou 1821," in D. Dimitropoulos et al., eds., *Opseis tis epanastasis tou 1821* (Athens, 2018), 385–402; F. Chrysanthopoulos [Fotakos], *Apomnimonevmata peri tis ellinikis epanastaseos*, 2 vols. (Athens, 1858), ii, 306–7; G. Cochrane, *Wanderings in Greece* (London, 1837), i, 42–43; D. Ainian, *Apomnimonevmata, kai viografia tou stratigou Georgiou Karaïskaki* (Athens, 2011), 209.

23. C. Reppas, *Ypotheseis kataskopias kata tin epanastasi tou 1821: archeiaka keimena* (Athens, 2012), 235–36.

24. Lignos, ed., *Archeia Lazarou kai Georgiou Koundouriotou*, vii (1827), 481.

25. Vakalopoulos, *Aichmalotoi ellinon*, 52–57.

26. Petros Mengous, 208–9; see too Dimitris Dimitropoulos, "Tiniakoi metanastes, thymata peiraton sta chronia tis Epanastasis. Oikonomia tis agoras kai oikonomias tis vias," in K. Danousis and K. Tsiknakis, eds., *Ministerium Historiae: timi ston pater Marko Foskolo* (Tinos, 2017), 153–75, here 153–55.

27. G. Harlaftis and K. Galanis, eds., *O emporikos kai polemikos stolos kata tin elliniki epanastasi, 1821–1831* (Crete, 2021), 42–43; M. Grenet, "La fabrique communauitaire: les grecs à Venise, Livourne et Marseille, c. 1770–c. 1830," PhD, EUI, Florence (2010), 446–47.

28. Reppas, *Ypotheseis kataskopias*, 232–34, 411–14.

29. Lappa, ed., *Athanasiou Lidoriki*, 31–32.

30. E. Driault, *L'expédition de Crète et de Morée (1823–1828)* (Cairo, 1930), 144–45.

31. L. I. Spiridonova, ed., *P. S. Nakhimov: dokumenti i materialy*, vol. 1 (St. Petersburg, 2003), 74–83 (my thanks to Gelina Harlaftis for showing me this source); A. Tsamados, *Istorika imerologia ton ellinikon navmachion tou 1821* (Athens, 1886), 8–12.

32. See Protopsaltis, ed., *Istorikon archeion Alexandrou Mavrokordatou*, ii..

33. T. Rigopoulos, "Anekdoton imerologion tou Agonos," in I. Theofanidis, ed., *Istorikon Archeion (1770–1836)*, (Athens, n.d.), iii, 108; on Gennaios: Rigopoulos (Fotopoulos, ed.), *Apomnimonevmata*, 57–59.

34. Androutsos in Protopsaltis, ed., *Istorikon archeion Alexandrou Mavrokordatou*, iv, 204, cited in the excellent E. Andriakaina, "To noima tou '21' sta apomnimonevmata tou Fotakou," PhD, Panteion (1999), 67–68.

35. "Archeion Georgiou Karaïskaki (1826–27)," *Naftiki Epitheorisis* 11:45 (July–Aug. 1924), 393; G. Tertsetis, *Exakolouthisis ton Prolegomenon eis ta ypomnimata tou Theodorou Kolokotroni* (Athens, 1852), 18.

36. Mengous, *Narrative of a Greek Soldier*, 115.

37. Howe (Richards, ed.), *Letters and Journals*, 66; Emerson et al., *A Picture of Greece in 1825*, i, 285; Fotakos, *Apomnimonevmata*, i, 350.

38. T. Gritsopoulos, ed., *Theodorou Kolokotroni diigisi ton symvanton tis Ellinikis fylis apo ta 1770 eos ta 1836* (Athens, 1981), 8; Protopsaltis, ed., *Istorikon archeion Alexandrou Mavrokordatou*, vi, 244.

39. Mengous, *Narrative of a Greek Soldier*, 123.

40. Emerson, *Picture*, 245–46; Schmidt, "The adventures of an Ottoman horse-man," 226.

41. Schmidt, "The adventures of an Ottoman horse-man," 266–67; Green, *Sketches of the War in Greece*, 132–36.

42. Millingen, *Memoirs on Greece*, 317.

43. Schmidt, "The adventures of an Ottoman horseman," 256; Fotakos, *Apomnimonevmata*, i, 296, 307.

44. Fotakos, *Apomnimonevmata*, i, 348–50; Ch. Andonov-Poljanski, ed., *British Documents on the History of the Macedonian People* (Skopje, 1968), i, 223; Prousis, *Lord Strangford at the Sublime Porte (1824)* (Istanbul, 2017), iv: 1824; Erdem, "'Perfidious Albanians' and 'zealous governors,'" 211–35.

45. R. R. Madden, *Travels in Turkey, Egypt, Nubia and Palestine in 1824, 1825, 1826 and 1827*, 2 vols. (London, 1829), ii, 379; from [D. Bürkli], *Die*

Flüchtlinge aus Griechenland (Zurich, 1823) trans. and cited by Ghekos, *I epistrofi*, 116.

46. Linner, ed., W. H. Humphreys *"First Journal of the Greek War of Independence,"* 24.

47. *Istorikon archeion tou stratigou Andreou Londou (1789–1847)*, 2 vols. (Athens, 1914–16), ii, 377–78; Playainakou-Bekiaris and Stergellis, eds., *Archeion Ioanni Koletti*, i, 502–3.

48. Protopsaltis, ed., *Istorikon archeion Alexandrou Mavrokordatou*, ii, 46.

49. G. Waddington, *A Visit to Greece in 1823 and 1824* (London, 1825), 138.

50. C. Loukos, "I ensomatosi mias paradosiakis archontikis oikoyeneias ston neo elliniko kratos: i periptosi ton Mavromihalaion," *Ta Istorika*, 1:2 (Dec. 1984), 283–97, here 284–85; Raybaud, *Memoires*, ii, 370–71.

51. J. Hamilton-Browne, "Narrative of a Visit, in 1823, to the Seat of War in Greece," *Blackwood's Edinburgh Magazine*, 36:226 (Sept. 1834), 404.

52. On Tripolitsa, see Fotakos, *Apomnimonevmata*, i, 513–14.

53. I. M. Hatzifotis, "To polemiko imerologio tou oplarchigou Ioannou Fouseki-Farmaki," *Parnassos* (July–Sept. 1972), 420–32.

54. Gritsopoulos, ed., *Diigisi symvanton*, 104–5; Fotakos, i, 329.

55. Millingen, *Memoirs of the Affairs of Greece*, 70.

56. T. Lappas, "Foresia kai armata stin Epanastasi tou 1821," *Nea Estia*, 546 (April 1950); R. Ellgood, *The Arms of Greece and her Balkan Neighbors in the Ottoman Period* (London, 2009).

57. Kolokotronis's pistols, in Protopsaltis, ed., *Kanellos Deliyannis: Apomnimonevmata*, ii, 130.

58. Millingen, *Memoirs of the Affairs of Greece*, 70; Pylia, ed., *Apo to 1821 sto 2012*, on Crete battlefield; Emerson et al., *A Picture of Greece in 1825*, 68–69.

59. Gordon, *History*, i, 481; Blancard, *Les Mavroyéni*, ii, 287–385.

60. Gazis, *Viografia*, 33.

61. "Imerologion tou Agonos tou Theodorou Rigopoulou," in *Istorikon Archeion I. Theofanidou* (Athens, n.d.), iii—separate paginations, here 102; on Panos, 105–6.

62. Rigopoulos, *Apomnimonevmata*, 110, cited in Voglis, *Erga kai imerai ellinikon oikogeneion*, 165–66; H. Angelomatis-Tsougarakis, "Women in the Greek War of Independence," in M. Mazower, ed., *Networks of Power in Modern Greece: Essays in Honour of John Campbell* (New York, 2008), 45–69.

63. Kasomoulis, *Enthymimata stratiotika*, ii, 341 n. 1; A. Tselali, ed., *Plapoutas* (Athens, 1952), i, 274; Fotakos, *Apomnimonevmata*, i, 474.

64. Kolokotronis to the villagers of Corinth, Feb. 24, 1824, in *Istorikon archeion tou stratigou Andreou Londou*, ii, 41–42; a recent treatment of the Kolokotronis myth is to be found in D. Dimitropoulos, "O 'geros tou Moria': ktizontas mia patriki figoura tou ethnous," in D. Dimitropoulos and K. Dede eds., *"I matia ton allon": proslipseis prosopon pou sfragisan treis aiones*

(180s–200s aiones) (Athens, 2012), 69–90; on Kolokotronis's character, G. Tertsetis (N. Konomos, ed.), *Anekdota keimena* (Athens, 1959), 105–10.

65. D. Loukopoulos, ed., *O Roumeliotis kapetanios tou 1821 Andritsos Safakas kai to archeio tou* (Athens, 1931), 93.

66. Makriyannis, *Memoirs*, 215.

67. Emerson et al., *A Picture of Greece in 1825*, 50–51.

68. Fotakos, *Apomnimonevmata*, ii, 306–7.

69. K. Karaman and S. Pamuk, "Ottoman state finances in European perspective, 1500–1914," *Journal of Economic History*, 70:3 (Sept. 2010), 612; H. Inalcik and D. Quataert, eds., *An Economic and Social History of the Ottoman Empire, 1300–1914* (Cambridge, 1994), 717, 968.

70. Erdem, "'Perfidious Albanians' and 'zealous governors,'" passim.

71. Moschopoulos, *Istoria*, 317.

72. Kasomoulis, *Enthymimata*, i, 161.

73. Schmidt, "The adventures of an Ottoman horseman," 237.

74. Fotakos, *Apomnimonevmata*, i, 525.

75. Ibid., 125; Lignos, ed., *Archeia Lazarou kai Georgiou Koundouriotou*, vii, 637; [Brengeri], "Adventures of a foreigner in Greece," 466.

76. T. Prousis, ed., *Lord Strangford at the Sublime Porte (1823)* (Istanbul, 2014), iii, 304–5.

CHAPTER 10: KNIGHTS ERRANT

1. G. G. Arnakis, ed., *George Jarvis: His Journal and Related Documents* (Thessaloniki, 1965), 6–10; Richards, ed., *Letters and Journals of Samuel Gridley Howe*, 29.

2. *Schweizerbote*, Sept. 13, 1821, cited in G. Ghekos, *I Epistrofi: agonistes tou A. Ypsilanti ston dromo yia tin Ellada, 1822/1823* (Athens, 2019), 53.

3. Charles Tennant, *A Tour through Parts of the Netherlands, Holland, Germany, Switzerland, Savoy and France in the Year 1821–22* (London, 1824), ii, 96–98.

4. Numbers in W. St. Clair, *That Greece Might Still Be Free* (Oxford, 1972), 356–58.

5. D. Barau, *La cause des Grecs: une histoire du mouvement philhellène, 1821–1829* (Paris, 2009), 193.

6. A. Massé, "French consuls and philhellenism in the 1820s: official positions and personal sentiments," *Byzantine and Modern Greek Studies*, 41:1 (April 2017), 103–18, here 106–8.

7. M. Grenet, "La fabrique communitaire: les grecs à Venise, Livourne et Marseille, c. 1770–c. 1830," PhD, EUI, Florence (2010), 433; also P. Échinard, *Grecs et Philhellènes à Marseille de la Révolution française à l'independence de la Grèce* (Marseille, 1973), 143.

8. Ibid., 146, 149.

9. Cited in P. Pakkanen, *August Myhrberg and North European Philhellenism* (Athens, 2006), 75.

10. P. Gaffarel, "Marseille et les Philhellènes en 1821 et 1822," *Revue historique*, 129:2 (1918), 263.

11. Échinard, *Grecs et Philhellènes à Marseille*, 141 and 136ff.

12. H. Mazurel, *Vertiges de la guerre: Byron, les philhellenes et le mirage grec* (Paris, 2013), 164–66.

13. Gaffarel, "Marseille et les Philhellènes," 251–52.

14. Échinard, *Grecs et Philhellènes à Marseille*, 156–57.

15. Barau, 52ff; C. Oikonomous, ed., *To tagma ton filellinon apo to imerologio tou Johanna Daniel Elster* (Athens, 2010), 43–44.

16. Gaffarel, "Marseille et les Philhellènes," 264–65; Mazurel, *Vertiges de la guerre*, 103.

17. See the useful biographies in https://www.eefshp.org/en/category/presentations.

18. St. Clair, *That Greece Might Still Be Free*, 32–33.

19. A. Lemaitre, *Musulmans et chrétiens: notes sur la guerre de l'indépendance grecque* (Paris, 1897), 1–3.

20. S. Hazareesingh, "Memory and political imagination: the legend of Napoleon revisited," *French History*, 18:4 (2004), 463–83; L. Murat, *L'homme qui se prenait pour Napoléon* (Paris, 2011).

21. L. S. Belloc, *Bonaparte et les Grecs* (Paris, 1826), avant-propos (n.p.).

22. E. Anceau, *Napoléon III* (Paris, 2012), 45–8; C. A. Sainte-Beuve, "La Grèce en 1863," *Nouveaux lundis*, v (Paris, 1884, revised ed.), 308–30.

23. Gaffarel, "Marseille et les Philhellènes," 266; E. About, *La Grèce contemporaine* (Paris, 1854), 80.

24. Échinard, *Grecs et philhellènes à Marseille*, 149; on Hastings, D. Dakin, *British and American Philhellenes during the War of Greek Independence, 1821–1833* (Thessaloniki, 1955), 36; Pakkanen, *August Myhrberg*, 28; Shelley, *Hellas*, preface.

25. I. Dimakis, "Ai katachriseis tou filellenismou en Evropi. Treis charakteristikai periptoseis," *Filellenika* (Athens, 1992), 107–29, relying on Anon., *Tagebuch und Erläuterungen über den Kampf der Philhellenen in Griechenland* (Dinkelsbühl, 1823) and F. A. Lessen, *Schilderung einer enthusiasmirten Reise nach Griechenland im Jahr 1822* (Görlitz, 1823).

26. F.-R. Schack, *Campagne d'un jeune Français en Grèce* (Paris, 1827), 2.

27. E. Dodwell, *A Classical and Topographical Tour through Greece during the Years 1801, 1805 and 1806*, 2 vols. (London, 1819), i, 291; R. B. Halbertsma, *Scholars, Travellers and Trade: The Pioneer Years of the National Museum of Antiquities in Leiden, 1818–1840* (London, 2003), ch. 5; also F. Bastet, *De drie collecties Rottiers te Leiden* (Leiden, 1987).

28. E. Gilmore Holt, *From the Classicists to the Impressionists: Art and Architecture in the 19th Century* (New Haven, CT, 1966), 15–17.

29. Q. de Quincy, *An Essay on the Nature, End and the Means of Imitation in the Fine Arts* (London, 1837), 390. The French original had been published in 1823 and was based on widely discussed lectures that had been delivered two years earlier; De Quincy, "Notice sur la statue antique de Venus, découverte dans l'île de Milo en 1820," lecture delivered in Paris at the Académie des Beaux-Arts, April 21, 1821: trans. in Gilmore Holt, *From the Classicists to the Impressionists*, 15–18.

30. L. de Bollmann, *Remarques sur l'État moral, politique et militaire de la Grèce* (Marseille, 1822), 5.

31. T. S. Perry, ed., *The Life and Letters of Francis Lieber* (Boston, MA, 1882), 35.

32. [Brengeri], "Adventures of a foreigner in Greece"; Lessen, *Schilderung*, 48, 6.

33. C. Müller, *Journey through Greece and the Ionian Islands in June, July and August 1821* (London, 1822), 5–6.

34. Perry, *Life and Letters*, 37–38.

35. [Brengeri], "Adventures of a Foreigner in Greece," *London Magazine* (Aug. 1826), 467–68.

36. Barau, *La cause des Grecs*, 508–9; Lessen, *Schilderung*, 6–8.

37. Linner, *W. H. Humphreys*, 39.

38. C. Vyzantios, *Istoria tou Taktikou Stratou tis Ellados* (Athens, 1837), 7.

39. [Brengeri], "Adventures of a Foreigner in Greece: II," *London Magazine* (Sept. 1826), 40.

40. An almost incredible story, but the author is generally reliable and claims to have had the account from Baleste himself. [Brengeri], ibid., 41–42.

41. St. Clair, *That Greece Might Still Be Free*, 88–91.

42. A few of the survivors reformed briefly under Tarella's successor, a long-serving Italian officer called Gubernatis until he too, at the end of 1822, had had enough: he left the Morea and sailed for Egypt where he became an instructor in the pasha's army.

43. Lessen, *Schilderung*, 27–28.

44. Perry, *Life and Letters*, 37–38.

45. Arnakis, *George Jarvis*, 110–11; C. W. J. Eliot, *Campaign of the Falieri and Piraeus in the Year 1827* (Princeton, NJ, 1992), 52–53; [Finlay], "An adventure during the Greek revolution," *Blackwoods Edinburgh Magazine* (Nov. 1842), 669–70; Oikonomous, ed., *To tagma ton filhellinon*, 195–96.

46. Lessen, *Schilderung*, 19.

47. Müller, *Journey through Greece*, 7–8, 10.

48. Barau, *La cause des Grecs*, 518; [Spiromilios], ed. G. Vlachoyannis, *Chroniko tou Mesolongiou, 1825–1826* (Athens, 1969), 28.

49. Barau, *La cause des Grecs*, 507.

50. [Brengeri], "Adventures of a Foreigner in Greece: IV," *London Magazine* (Nov. 1826), 345.

51. Lessen, *Schilderung*, 9.

52. Bollmann, *Remarques*, 12.

53. [Brengeri], "Adventures of a foreigner in Greece: II," 49–55.
54. Voutier cited in Barau, *La cause des Grecs*, 502.
55. Perry, *Life and Letters*, 43–44.
56. *John Bull*, 59, Jan. 28, 1822, 1.
57. Bollmann, *Remarques*, 3.
58. Ibid., 15.
59. [Brengeri], "Adventures of a foreigner in Greece," 177–95, esp. 179–81.
60. G. Schlumberger, ed., *Mémoires de Commandant Persat, 1806 à 1844* (Paris, 1910).
61. Barau, *La cause des Grecs*, 615–19.
62. Voutier in Barau, ibid., 445.
63. Barau, *La cause des Grecs*, 446–67.
64. Échinard, *Grecs et philhellènes à Marseille*, 164–70.
65. Polychroniades to Praides, *IAAM*, i, 87–96; also Thomas Gordon Papers, University of Aberdeen, MS 1160/20/144 memo: Joseph Thomas—High Commissioner of the Ionian Islands, Nov. 20, 1821. In the same archive, MS 1160/20/168, Persat—Gordon, Nov. 3, 1822, describes the background to Gordon's financial payments to Persat not to publish his memoir..
66. Data calculated from L. Droulia, *Philhellenisme: ouvrages inspirés par la guerre de l'indépendance grecque, 1821–1833* (Athens, 1974).

CHAPTER 11: ENGLISH GOLD

1. K. Manolopoulos, *Antimetopisis polemikon dapanon kata tin ethnergesian tou 1821* (Athens, 1973), 17–20.
2. A. Lignadis, *To proton daneion tis anexartesias* (Athens, 1970), 69; on the Zakynthos Committee, see Ch. Vlachopoulos, "Dionysios Romas kai i epitropi Zakynthou ston dromo yia tin ethniki synkrotisi," Univ. of Athens, PhD, 2015.
3. Bozikis, "Dimosia oikonomia," 537; S. Bozikis, "Dynamikes kai adraneies sti forologia kai sto forologiko michanismo kata tin epanastasi tou 1821," *Mnimon*, 31 (2010), 31–68.
4. Ottoman estimates from S. Pamuk, "The end of financial institutions in the Ottoman empire, 1600–1914," *Financial History Review*, 15:1 (2004), 7–32, esp. 23.
5. Lignadis, *To proton daneion*, 23–24.
6. Protopsaltis, ed., *Istorikon archeion Alexandrou Mavrokordatou*, i, 148.
7. Ibid., *Ignatios*, ii, 134; Lignadis, *To proton daneion*, 27–34.
8. Protopsaltis, ed., *Ignatios*, ii, 140–41.
9. Protopsaltis, ed., *Istorikon archeion Alexandrou Mavrokordatou*, i, 38–39.
10. Protopsaltis, ed., *Ignatios*, ii, 144–45; for the general background, see M. J. Turner, "'Arraying Minds against Bodies': Benthamite radicals and

revolutionary Europe during the 1820s and 1830s," *History*, 90:2 (298) (April 2005), 236–61; G. F. Bartle, "Bowring and the Greek loans of 1824 and 1825," *Balkan Studies*, 3:1 (1964), 61–74.

11. Lignadis, *To proton daneion*, 40–43.

12. G. F. Bartle, "Jeremy Bentham and John Bowring: a study in the relationship between Bentham and the editor of his *Collected Works*," *Bulletin of the Institute of Historical Research* (Oct. 1963), 27–35.

13. P. Bowring, *Free Trade's First Missionary: Sir John Bowring in Europe and Asia* (Hong Kong, 2014), 28.

14. Stanhope to Bentham, reporting a comment of Mavrokordatos, in L. O'Sullivan and C. Fuller, eds., *The Correspondence of Jeremy Bentham*, 12 (July 1824–June 1828) (Oxford, 2006), 10–11.

15. W. Hazlitt, "Jeremy Bentham," *The Spirit of the Age* (London, 1825), 3; "Parry's Last Days of Lord Byron," *Blackwood's Edinburgh Magazine*, 18:103 (Aug. 1825), 140.

16. W. Parry, *The Last Days of Byron* (London, 1825), 195–202, a book said to have been much admired by Goethe.

17. J. Harris, "Bernardino Rivadavia and Benthamite 'discipleship,'" *Latin American Research Review*, 33:1 (1998), 129–49.

18. "Mr. Blaquiere's Report on Greece," *Blackwood's Edinburgh Magazine*, 14:81 (Oct. 1823), 465–66.

19. On the role of the Crown and Anchor in radical politics, see C. Parolin, *Radical Spaces: Venues of Popular Politics in London, 1790–c. 1845* (Canberra, 2010), ch. 5; G. Tzourmana, *Bretanoi Rizospastes metarrythmistes* (Athens, 2015), 314–15.

20. Jourdain, *Mémoires*, i, 174–77, 178.

21. Ibid., 171.

22. U. Castignino-Berlinghieri, "Balance of power and legitimacy at the Congress of Vienna: the case study of the Order of Malta," in W. Telesko et al., eds., *Der Wiener Kongress 1814/1815: Band 1: Internationale Politik* (Vienna, 2019), 179–86.

23. Lignadis, *To proton daneion*, 154; D. Dakin, *British Intelligence of Events in Greece, 1824–1827: A Documentary Collection* (Athens, 1959).

24. F. Griffith Dawson, *The First Latin American Debt Crisis* (New Haven, CT, 1990), 40; Larry Neal and Lance Davis, "The evolution of the structure and performance of the London Stock Exchange in the first global financial market, 1812–1914," *European Review of Economic History*, 10:3 (Dec. 2006), 279–300.

25. M. Flandreau and J. Flores, "Bonds and brands: foundations of sovereign debt markets, 1820–1830," *Journal of Economic History*, 69: 3 (Sept. 2009), 646–84, esp. 656–58, 665–67.

26. On the Poyais scandal, see D. Sinclair, *The Land that Never Was: Sir Gregor MacGregor and the Most Audacious Fraud in History* (Boston, MA, 2003).

27. E. Blaquiere, *Report on the Present State of the Greek Confederation, and on its Claims to the Support of the Christian World, read to the Greek Committee on Saturday, September 13, 1823* (London, 1823), 4.

28. Hamilton-Browne, "Narrative of a visit," 400; Trelawny, *Records of Shelley, Byron and the Author,* 225.

29. Blaquiere, *Additional Facts, submitted to the Greek Committee by Mr. Blaquiere, on the Actual State of Affairs in the Morea and other points of the Confederation, read on Saturday, September 20th, 1823* (London, 1823).

30. R. Beaton, *Byron's War: Romantic Rebellion, Greek Revolution* (Cambridge, 2013), 120–33; South America in B. Eisler, *Byron, Child of Passion, Fool of Fame* (New York, 1999), 704.

31. Trelawny, *Records of Shelley, Byron and the Author,* 224; Parry records Byron telling him: "Talk of Don Juan, this Greek business, its disasters and mismanagement, have furnished me with matter for a hundred cantos. Jeremy Bentham and his scholar, Colonel Stanhope, shall be two of my heroes." "Last Days of Lord Byron," 148.

32. "Cephalonia Journal: Sept. 28, 1823," in L. Marchand, ed., *Byron's Letters and Journals,* ii (London, 1980), 32; Beaton, *Byron's War,* 175–81.

33. Cited in Beaton, *Byron's War,* 203.

34. Ibid., 186–207, 215.

35. For more on the impact of news of Byron's death in Europe, see the start of ch. 14.

36. J. Notopoulos, "New sources on Lord Byron at Missolonghi," *Keats–Shelley Journal,* 4 (Winter 1955), 31–45, here 34–36.

37. L. Stanhope, *Greece in 1823 and 1824* (London, 1824); Zaimis in K. Diamantis and E. Protopsaltis, eds., *Archeia Lazarou kai Georgiou Koundouriotou, 1821–1832,* vols. 6–10 (Athens, 1966–69), viii, 1,427, 515.

38. Stanhope, *Greece in 1823 and 1824,* 66, 117, 282; "Last Days of Lord Byron," 139, 148.

39. L. B. Bowring, ed., *John Bowring: Autobiographical Recollections* (London, 1877), 281–87; Protopsaltis, ed., *Istorikon archeion Alexandrou Mavrokordatou,* iii, 148–51 (Protocol of meeting on Feb. 23, 1823); W. L. Walker, "Recognition of belligerency and grant of belligerent rights," *Transactions of the Grotius Society,* 23 (1937), 177–210.

40. John Neal, *Wandering Recollections of a Somewhat Busy Life* (Boston, MA, 1869), 286.

41. Waddington, *A Visit to Greece,* 96; cited by V. Penn, "Philhellenism in England. II," *Slavonic and East European Review,* 14:42 (April 1936), 655, 658.

42. Bartle, "Bowring and the Greek loans"; Penn, "Philhellenism in England. II," 647–60; cited in St. Clair, *That Greece Might Still Be Free,* 222.

43. Gardika, "O Anastasios Polyzoidis," 35.

44. H. Lytton Bulwer, *An Autumn in Greece* (London, 1926), 131–37, for details of the commissioners' arrival and reception.

45. Finlay, *History of the Greek Revolution*, ii, 26–27; Stanhope, *Greece in 1823 and 1824*, 150, 275.

46. Playainakou-Bekiaris and Stergellis, eds., *Archeion Ioanni Koletti*, i, 319, 361–63; D. Kambouroglou, ed., *Istorikon archeion Dionysiou Roma*, 2 vols. (Athens, 1901–6), 730.

47. Playainakou-Bekiaris and Stergellis, eds., *Archeion Ioanni Koletti*, i, 402–3, 414, 427.

48. Orlandos, *Navtika*, ii, 29.

49. Stanhope, *Greece in 1823 and 1824*, 171.

50. S. S. Wilson, *A Narrative of the Greek Mission, or Sixteen Years in Malta and Greece* (London, 1839), 273.

51. Trelawny, *Records of Shelley, Byron and the Author*, 252; "Contents of the Journal of W. H. Humphreys," in Emerson et al., *A Picture of Greece in 1825*, ii, 261.

52. A. Palma, *Greece Vindicated* (London, 1826), 6.

53. Emerson et al., *A Picture of Greece in 1825*, ii, 108–9.

54. Bozikis, "Dimosia oikonomika," 537. The book based on this dissertation, S. Bozikis, *Elliniki epanastasi kai dimosia oikonomia: I synkrotisi tou ellinikou ethnikou kratous (1821–1832)* (Athens, 2020), appeared too late to be consulted.

55. Lignos, *Istoria tis nisou Hydras*, ii, 472.

56. Based on data in Bozikis, "Dimosia oikonomika," 520–30.

57. Data from Lignos, *Istoria tis nisou Hydras*, 471–75.

58. Finlay, *History*, ii, 40–41.

59. Wilson, *A Narrative of the Greek Mission*, 299, 401; Waddington, *A Visit to Greece in 1823 and 1824*, 135.

60. *Istorikon archeion tou stratigou Andreou Londou*, ii (1824), 341–54.

61. E. Liata, ed., *Archeion Kanellou Deliyianni: ta engrafa, 1779–1827* (Athens, 1993), 110–11; *Istorikon archeion tou stratigou Andreou Londou*, ii (1824), 393.

62. Gritsopoulos, ed., *Theodorou Kolokotroni*.

63. Rigopoulos, "Anekdoton imerologion tou Agonos," iii, 115–16.

64. Emerson et al., *A Picture of Greece in 1825*, ii, 50.

CHAPTER 12: MEHMED ALI INTERVENES

1. The standard work is now H. Lowry and I. Erünsal, *Remembering One's Roots: Mehmed Ali Pasha of Egypt's Links to the Macedonian Town of Kavala: Architectural Monuments, Inscriptions and Documents* (Istanbul, 2011); on the complex modern legal background, also K. Tsitselikis, *Old and New Islam in Greece: From Historical Minorities to Immigrant Newcomers* (Leiden, 2012), 359–65 ("The Egyptian Vakf").

2. E. Gouin, *L'Egypte au XIX siècle* (Paris, 1847), 150–52. There would appear to be no basis for the widespread belief that the family was Albanian.

3. K. Fahmy, *Mehmed Ali: From Ottoman Governor to Ruler of Egypt* (Oxford, 2009), chs. 1–4.

4. P.-X. Coste, *Mémoires d'un artiste: notes et souvenirs de voyages (1817–1877)*, 2 vols. (Paris, 1878), i, 25–30. There appears to be almost nothing on Coste and his engineering works except the excellent dissertation by K. M. Hill, "Pascale-Xavier Coste: a French architect in Egypt," PhD, MIT (1992); see also Eve-Marie Troelenberg, "Drawing knowledge, [re-] constructing history: Pascale Coste in Egypt," *International Journal of Islamic Architecture*, 4:2 (2015), 287–313.

5. Still unsurpassed is A. Politis, *L'Hellenisme et l'Egypte moderne*, 2 vols. (Paris, 1929–30), vol. 1; see also P. M. Glavanis, "Aspects of the economic and social history of the Greek community in Alexandria during the nineteenth century," PhD, University of Hull (1989), 91–92; see also C. Hadziiosif, "La colonie grecque en Egypte," PhD, Sorbonne: Paris IV (1980).

6. Glavanis, "Aspects," 95–96; P. Kontoyiannis, *Ethnikoi evergetai* (Athens, 1908), 45–46.

7. Politis, *L'Hellenisme*, i, 188–94; Glavanis, "Aspects," 100–103.

8. H. Sükrü Ilicak, "Ottoman context," in P. Kitromilides and C. Tsoukalas, eds., *The Greek Revolution: A Critical Dictionary* (Cambridge, MA, 2021), 66–71; A. L. Narotchnitzki, "La diplomatie russe et la préparation de la Conférence de St.-Petersbourg," Institute for Balkan Studies, *Les relations gréco-russes pendant la domination turque et la guerre d'indépendance grecque* (Thessaloniki, 1983), 87–97.

9. M. Sabry, *L'empire égyptien sous Mohamed-Ali et la question d'Orient (1811–1849)* (Paris, 1930), 92.

10. Gouin, *L'Égypte au dix-neuvième siècle*, 374–78.

11. For background, see S. Cronin, "Importing modernity: European military missions to Qajar Iran," *Comparative Studies in Society and History*, 50:1 (Jan. 2008), 197–226; A. Levy, "The officer corps in Sultan Mahud II's new Ottoman army, 1826–1839," *International Journal of Middle Eastern Studies*, 2:1 (Jan. 1971), 21–39; on Ibrahim in the Hijaz, a relatively under-studied episode, see G. F. Sadlier, "Account of a journey from Katif on the Red Sea to Tamboo on the Persian Gulf by Capt. G. F. Sadlier," *Transactions of the Literary Society of Bombay*, iii (London, 1823), 449–93.

12. H. Lauvergne, *Souvenirs de la Grèce pendant la compagne de 1825* (Paris, 1826), 46.

13. Coste, *Mémoires*, i, 30–39; A. Vingtrinier, *Soliman-pacha, colonel Sève, généralissime des armées egyptiennes* (Paris, 1886), 17–25.

14. F. Konrad, "Religion, political loyalty and identity: French and Egyptian perceptions of Suläyman Pasha Sève," in S. Jobs and G. Mackenthun, eds., *Agents of Transculturation* (Munich, 2013), 89–115.

15. K. Fahmy, "Mutiny in Mehmed Ali's new nizam army, April–May 1824," in J. Hathaway, ed., *Mutiny and Rebellion in the Ottoman Empire* (Madison, WI, 2002), 129–39.

16. Orlandos, *Navtika*, ii, 24–25.

17. Gordon, *History*, 2, 131–33; Orlandos, *Navtika*, ii, 27.

18. S. Lane-Poole, *The Life of the Right Honorable Stratford Canning*, 2 vols. (London, 1888), i, 390.

19. Driault, *L'Expédition*, 22–25.

20. Gordon, *History*, ii, 66–68.

21. Lignos, ed., *Archeia Lazarou kai Georgiou Koundouriotou*, iv: 1825: Jan.–June (Piraeus, 1926), 130–33.

22. *O Filos tou Nomou*, 88 (Jan. 16, 1825), 3.

23. Ibid., 97 (Feb. 16, 1825), 3; 99 (Feb. 23, 1825), 1.

24. Orlandos, *Navtika*, ii, 30.

25. K. Kotsonis, *O Ibraim stin Peloponniso* (Athens, 1999), ch. 3.

26. Lignos, ed., *Archeia Lazarou kai Georgiou Koundouriotou*, iv, 1929, 108–10 for the entire extraordinary letter.

27. Kotsonis, *O Ibraim*, ch. 4; Lignos, ed., *Archeia Lazarou kai Georgiou Koundouriotou*, iv, 1825: Jan.–June (Piraeus, 1929), 236–37, 242, 245.

28. Frantzis, *Epitomi tis istorias*, ii, 332.

29. Richards, ed., *Letters and Journals of Samuel Gridley Howe*, 57.

30. Driault, *L'Expédition*, 65–66.

31. Lignos, *Istoria tis nisou Ydras*, ii, 714–25: the numbers fell again in 1826 to five wounded and twenty killed, and thirty-two and seven killed in the last year, 1827. Many more sailors—nearly 250—seem to have died on land in various campaigns.

32. Trikoupis, *Istoria*, iii, 293; Emerson et al., *A Picture of Greece*; Lignos, *Istoria tis nisou Ydras*, ii, 506–9.

33. Dakin, ed., *British Intelligence*, 74, 85–87.

34. Gordon, *History*, ii, 215–16.

35. Richards, ed., *The Letters and Journals of Samuel Gridley Howe*, 69.

36. Emerson et al., *A Picture of Greece*, 166.

37. Fotakos, *Apomnimonevmata*, ii, 109; ibid., 78; Kotsonis, *O Ibraim*, 146.

38. Cited in Kotsonis, *O Ibraim*, 194; Frantzis, *Epitomi tis istorias*, ii, 341–73.

39. Richards, ed., *The Letters and Journals of Samuel Gridley Howe*, 106; Kotsonis, *O Ibraim*, 188.

40. Numbers of livestock and captives, in Gouin, *L'Egypte au XIX siècle*, 388–89.

41. On Mavromihalis's feelers with Mehmed Ali over submission, see Driault, *L'expédition*, 60.

42. C. Swan, *Journal of a Voyage up the Mediterranean, principally among the Islands of the Archipelago and in Asia Minor, including Many Interesting Particulars relative to the Greek Revolution, especially a Journey through Maina to the camp of Ibrahim Pasha*, 2 vols. (London, 1826), ii, 229–41.

43. See the almost contemporary account in Driault, *L'expédition*, 84–86; Richards, ed., *The Letters and Journals of Samuel Gridley Howe*, 114.

44. Trikoupis, *Istoria*, iii, 250–52; Richards, ed., *The Letters and Journals of Samuel Gridley Howe*, 110–11, gives another story of how the Greeks fooled the guards and got in.

45. Richards, ed., *The Letters and Journals of Samuel Gridley Howe*, 114.

46. Ibid., 116–24.

47. The best contemporary account is in Driault, *L'expedition*, 70–71; see also A. de Vaulabelle, *Histoire scientifique et militaire de l'expédition française en Egypte* (Paris, 1830–36), x, 334–35; M. du Camp, *Recollections of a Literary Life* (London, 1893), 376.

48. Driault, *L'expédition*, 70–72; E. Dodwell, *A Classical and Topographical Tour through Greece during the Years 1801, 1805 and 1806*, 2 vols. (London, 1819), 75–76.

49. Emerson et al., *A Picture of Greece*, 272; Green, *Sketches of the War in Greece*, 207.

CHAPTER 13: MESOLONGHI

1. Spiromilios, *Apomnimonevmata tis defteris poliorkias tou Mesolongiou* (Athens, 1926), 59; a wonderful portrait in D. Urquhart, *The Spirit of the East* (London, 1838), ii, 331–43.

2. Spiromilios, *Apomnimonevmata*, 5.

3. The key source, widely relied upon here, is Diakakis, "I poli tou Mesolongiou," 276–79. There is now a superb book based on this: A. Diakakis, *To Mesolonghi sto 1821: polemos, oikonomia, politiki, kathimerini zoi* (Athens, 2019).

4. Diakakis, "I poli tou Mesolongiou," 213–14.

5. Spiromilios, *Apomnimonevmata*, 24.

6. See Gordon, *History*, ii, 238–39; Spiromilios, *Apomnimonevmata*, 76.

7. Cited in de Vaulabelle, *Histoire*, x, 338; Gouin, *L'Egypte*, 391.

8. Spiromilios, *Apomnimonevmata*, 78, 82.

9. Diakakis, "I poli tou Mesolongiou," 283.

10. Finlay, *History of the Greek Revolution*, 97.

11. Diakakis, "I poli tou Mesolongiou," 307–17.

12. Driault, ed., *L'expédition de Crète*, 109, 115.

13. Cf. A. Balanika et al., "Medical care in free-besieged Messolonghi (1822–1826)," *Acta Med. Hist. Adriat.*, 14:1 (2016), 95–106.

14. Diakakis, "I poli tou Mesolongiou," 318–19, 357; T. Sklavenitis, ed., *Petros D. Stefanitsis: Apomnimonevmata (1821–1839)* (Athens, 2019), 14–15.

15. W. Black, *Narrative of Cruises in the Mediterranean in HMS "Euryalus" and "Chanticleer" during the Greek War of Independence (1822–1826)* (Edinburgh, 1900), 274.

16. Diakakis, "I poli tou Mesolongiou," 327–32.
17. Ibid., 328.
18. Ibid., 374–76.
19. The most reliable evaluation of the multiple accounts is in ibid., passim. One valuable anonymous contemporary account in G. Zoras, ed., *Mnimeia tis Ellinikis Istorias*, 10: *Engrafa tou archeiou Vatikanou peri tis ellinikis epanastaseos*, i, 1820–1826 (Athens, 1979), 604–10.
20. Driault, *L'expédition de Crète*, 172–73; report in Zoras, ed., *Mnimeia tis Ellinikis Istorias*, 532–35; overall, Diakakis, "I poli tou Mesolongiou," 358.
21. Diakakis, "I poli tou Mesolongiou," 358–59.
22. Stefanitsis, *Apomnimonevmata*, 22 and passim.
23. Diakakis, "I poli tou Mesolongiou," 360.
24. Figures in Zoras, ed., *Mnimeia tis Ellinikis Istorias*, 532.
25. A. N. Mauro, *La ruine de Missolonghi* (Paris, 1836), 12–13; Green, *Sketches*, 248–49.
26. Protopsaltis, ed., *Istorikon archeion Alexandrou Mavrokordatou*, vi, 1826, 36
27. Spiromilios, *Apomnimonevmata*, 111, 145.
28. Bozikis, "Dimosia oikonomika," 498, gives details.
29. Kambouroglou, ed., *Istorikon Archeion*, 104–11.
30. Spiromilios, *Apomnimonevmata*, 137.
31. A. Debidour, *Le Général Fabvier: sa vie militaire et politique* (Paris, 1904), 285.
32. C. Vyzantios, *Istoria tou taktikou stratou tis Ellados* (Athens, 1837), 57–72; Debidour, *Le Général Fabvier*, 292–94, 301–3.
33. S. Papageorgiou, "Vasos Mavrovouniotis, a Montenegrin chieftain on the threshold of modernity," *Mediterranea: ricerche storiche*, 32 (Dec. 2014), 463–81; T. Prousis, "Bedlam in Beirut: a British Perspective in 1826," *Chronos: Revue d'Histoire de l'Université de Balamand*, 15 (2007), 89–106; Frantzis, *Epitomi*, iii, 213.
34. Kambouroglou, ed., *Istorikon Archeion*, 104–7.
35. Green, *Sketches*, 232; Diakakis, "I poli tou Mesolongiou," 362.
36. G. Charitos, ed., *Archeion stratigou Georgiou Karaïskaki (1821–1835)* (Athens, 2009), 210, 237–38, 240–41; Fysentzidis, *Anekdotoi avtografoi*, 208.
37. Diakakis, "I poli tou Mesolongiou," 284.
38. Spiromilios, *Apomnimonevmata*, 38; Diakakis, "I poli tou Mesolongiou," 345–47.

CHAPTER 14: OUTSIDE THE NORMAL SPHERE OF FEELINGS

1. V. Hugo, "Sur George Gordon, Lord Byron," *La Muse française* (June 15, 1824), 327–39; Mazurel, *Vertiges de la Guerre*, passim.

2. J. Dimakis, "La 'Société de la Morale Chrétienne' de Paris et son action en faveur des Grecs lors de l'insurrection de 1821," *Balkan Studies*, 7:1 (1966), 27–47; N. Athanassoglou-Kallmyer, *French Images from the Greek War of Independence, 1821–1830* (New Haven, CT, 1989), 11; J.-C. Berchet, ed., *Mémoires de la comtesse de Boigne*, ii (*De 1820 à 1848*) (Paris, 1971), 176.

3. [Stendhal], K. G. McWatters, ed., *Chroniques pour l'Angleterre: contributions à la presse britannique*, 6 vols. (Grenoble, 1991), vi, 1826, 205–6; *Journal des dames et des modes*, 25 (May 5, 1826), 193.

4. McWatters, ed., *Chroniques pour l'Angleterre*, 205; Athanassoglou-Kallmyer, *French Images*, 38; A. Fabre, *Histoire du siège de Missolonghi* (Paris, 1827), 2.

5. A. Spanidis, "O Rossini kai I Ellada," unpublished paper; see also, A. Azevado, *G. Rossini: sa vie et ses oeuvres* (Paris, 1864), 248.

6. B. Walton, *Rossini in Restoration Paris: The Sound of Modernity* (Cambridge, 2007), 109.

7. Ibid., 147; see also M. Esse, "Rossini's noisy bodies," *Cambridge Opera Journal*, 21:1 (March 2009), 27–64.

8. L. Mébul, "L'aumòne d'un grand artiste," *Le guide musical* (Aug. 18/25, 1859).

9. Athanassoglou-Kallmyer, *French Images*, 13, 107.

10. M. Hannoosh, ed., *Eugène Delacroix: Journal*, i (Paris, 2009), 102, 112–13, 115, 156.

11. Athanassoglou-Kallmyer, *French Images*, 39.

12. Ibid., 101.

13. Cited by M. Bouyssy, "Women in philhellenism," in C. Fauré et al., eds., *Political and Historical Encyclopaedia of Women* (London, 2004), 253–69; data in Bozikis, *Elliniki epanastasi*, 460–67.

14. Bouyssy, "Women in philhellenism," 263, 265.

15. G. Douin, *Les premières frégates de Mohammed Aly (1824–1827)* (Cairo, 1926). On the French missions, the basic source is G. Douin, *Une mission militaire française auprès de Mohammed Aly* (Cairo, 1923); see also, J. P. Dunn, "Missions or mercenaries? European military advisors in Mehmed Ali's Egypt, 1815–1848," in D. Stoker, ed., *Military Advising and Assistance* (London, 2007), 11–25.

16. L. Frary, "Slaves of the Sultan: Russian ransoming of Christian captives during the Greek revolution, 1821–1830," in L. Frary and M. Kozelsky, eds., *Russian-Ottoman Borderlands: The Eastern Question Reconsidered* (Madison, WI, 2014), 101–30; Smiley, *From Slaves to Prisoners of War*, 182–84.

17. T. Prousis, *Lord Strangford at the Sublime Porte (1822): The Eastern Crisis* (Istanbul, 2012), 132–34; T. Proussis, "British embassy reports on the Greek uprising in 1821–1822: war of independence or war of religion?" *Archivum Ottomanicum*, 28 (2011), 212.

18. "People of colour," *Freedom's Journal*, 1:4 (Friday, April 6, 1827), 1.

19. E. G. Sideris and A. A. Konsta, "A letter from Jean-Pierre Boyer to Greek revolutionaries," *Journal of Haitian Studies*, 11:1 (Spring 2005), 167–71.

20. J. Martinez, *The Slave Trade and the Origins of International Human Rights Law* (Oxford, 2012). Interestingly, the role of this episode in the larger story has not been adequately told. A. Paliyenko, *Genius Envy: Women Shaping French Poetic History, 1801–1900* (Philadelphia, PA, 2016), 105–32.

21. Athanassoglou-Kallmyer, *French Images*, 40.

22. Fabre, *Histoire*, 14–15; D. G. Grigsby, *Extremities: Painting Empire in Post-Revolutionary France* (New Haven, CT, 2002), 304.

23. Kambouroglu, ed., *Istorikon archeion*, 226.

24. Ibid., 232, 624–25.

25. Ibid., 551–52. I have retained the Italianicized spelling of the Greek names in the original.

26. C. D. [Charles Deval], *Deux années à Constantinople et en Morée (1825–1826)* (Paris, 1828), 177–216.

27. K. S. Konstas, "Istorika engrafa Mesologgiton tis 'exodou' 1826–1833," *Epetiris Etaireia Stereoelladikon Meleton*, i (1968), 101–208, here 100, 120, 124–25, 147, 168, 183.

28. On the Ludolf family, see https://www.treccani.it/enciclopedia/giuseppe-costantino-ludolf_(Dizionario-Biografico). My thanks to Costas Kouremenos for his help.

29. A. Nuzzo, *La rivoluzione greca e la questione d'oriente, nella corrispondenza dei diplomatici napoletani (1820–1830)* (Salerno, 1934), 74–78. My thanks to Konstantina Zanou for help obtaining this book.

30. Lane-Poole, *Stratford Canning*, i, 395.

CHAPTER 15: THE SIEGE OF ATHENS

1. Fabvier in Protopsaltis, ed., *Istorikon archeion Alexandrou Mavrokordatou*, vi, *1826*, 102–3; Moretti, April 25, 1826, in G. Zoras, ed., *Mnimeia tis Ellinikis Istorias, x: Engrafa tou Archeiou Vatikanou* (Athens, 1979), i, 520.

2. Charitos, ed., *Archeion*, 260–62.

3. Ainian, *Apomnimonevmata*, 78; cf. Vlachoyannis, ed., *Enthymimata stratiotika*, ii, 333.

4. The wall is discussed in K. Biris, *Ai Athinai apo tou 19ou eis ton 20on aiona* (Athens, 1995), 10–14; background in A. M. Theocharakis, "The ancient circuit wall of Athens: its changing course and the phases of construction," *Hesperia*, 80:1 (Jan.–March 2011), 71–156; K. Stathis, "Putting Athens on the Ottoman map: preliminary observations," in M. Georgopoulou and K. Thanasakis, eds., *Ottoman Athens: Topography, Archaeology, History* (Athens, 2019), 213–27; see also S. Vryonis, "The ghost of Athens in Byzantine and Ottoman times," *Balkan Studies*, 43:1 (2002), 5–115.

5. E. D. Clarke, *Travels in Various Countries of Europe, Asia and Africa* (London, 1814), vi, 364; on the clock, see E. Theodosiou, S. Azzopardi, and V. Manimanis, "The first clock tower in Athens," *Horological Journal*, 145 (2003), 288–92.

6. Lidderdale, ed., *The Memoirs of General Makriyannis*, 96–97.

7. Emerson, "A Picture of Greece in 1825," 269.

8. Ibid., 56–57; Fotakos, *Apomnimonevmata*, ii, 6–7.

9. Ilicak, "Revolutionary Athens," 243–61.

10. Kasomoulis, *Enthymimata stratiotika*, ii, 288–89; A. Michos, eds. M. Ethymiou and V. Sarafis, *Apomnimomevmata tis devteras poliorkias tou Mesolongiou (1825-26)* (Athens, 2019), 91–92; Diakakis, "I poli tou Mesolongiou," 403ff.

11. Vlachoyannis, ed., *Enthymimata stratiotika*, ii, 339–41.

12. Lignos, ed., *Archeia Lazarou kai Georgiou Koundouriotou, 1826*, 147.

13. D. Kambouroglou, ed., *Theodoros Grivas: viografikon schediasma*, 44–47; Kasomoulis, *Enthymimata stratiotika*, ii, 343–45.

14. K. Paparrigopoulos, *Georgios Karaïskakis* (Athens, 1867), 70.

15. I have adapted the translation in Lidderdale, ed., *The Memoirs of General Makriyannis*, 121; original in S. Asdrachas, ed., *Makriyanni apomnimonevmata* (Athens, n.d.), 251.

16. Kasomoulis, *Enthymimata stratiotika*, ii, 344.

17. Kolokotronis, *Diigisi symvanton* (Athens, 1846), 176–77.

18. Protopsaltis, ed., *Istorikon archeion Alexandrou Mavrokordatou*, vi, 1826, 202–3.

19. Valtinos to Karaïskakis, August 10, 1826, in "To archeion tou G. Karaïskakis (1826–27)," *Navtiki Epitheorisis* (May–June 1924), 268–69.

20. Ilicak, "Revolutionary Athens," 250–56.

21. "Nikolaou Ant. Karori Imerologion Poliorkias Athinon," in E. Protopsaltis, ed., *Apomnimonevmata Athinaion Agoniston* (Athens, 1957), 68–69, 86.

22. Stavrianos, *Pragmateia*.

23. Paparrigopoulos, *Georgios Karaïskakis*, 79.

24. I. T. Kolokotronis, *Ellinika ypommimata itoi epistolai kai diafora engrafa aforonta tin ellinikin epanastasin apo 1824 mechri 1827* (Athens, 1856), 357, 386.

25. Protopsaltis, ed., *Istorikon archeion Alexandrou Mavrokordatou*, vi, 1826, 342–43; K. D. Diamantis, ed., *Archeia Lazarou kai Georgiou Kountouriotou* (Athens, 1967), vii, 427–28, 434–36; Cf. the information in Kolokotronis, *Ellinika ypommimata*, 388. Elmaz Bey was among the leaders of the Ottoman troops, the same individual who had made such an impression on Raybaud during the surrender negotiations outside Tripolitsa in 1821 and who had survived the sack and returned to western Greece. Karaïskakis reports him dead, but Gennaios Kolokotronis in his edition of the letters writes that he survived until 1850.

26. On the summer discussions of the need for a "new revolution," see Fotakos, *Apomnimonevmata*, ii, 298; Protopsaltis, ed., *Apomnimonevmata*, 42.

27. Paparrigopoulos, *Karaïskakis*, 110–11.

28. Millingen, *Memoirs*, 36–37.

29. Fotakos, *Apomnimonevmata*, ii, 299; Lignos, ed., *Archeia Lazarou kai Georgiou Koundouriotou, 1826*, 322.

30. M. Efthymiou, "Cursing with a message: the case of Georgios Karaïskakis," *Istorein* (2000), 173–82. Not only his enemies called him "Gypsy": Kolokotronis used the term affectionately toward him: see "Archeion Georgiou Karaïskaki (1826–27)," *Naftiki Epitheorisis*, 11:45 (July–Aug. 1924), 393

31. Data from St. Clair, *That Greece Might Still Be Free*, 357–59.

32. Lidderdale, ed., *The Memoirs of General Makriyannis*, 122, the original in Asdrachas, ed., *Makriyanni apomnimonevmata*, 252.

33. Lidderdale, ed., *The Memoirs of General Makriyannis*, 121, the original in Asdrachas, ed., *Makriyanni apomnimonevmata*, 251; C. W. J. Eliot, ed., *Campaign of the Falieri and Piraeus in the Year 1827, or Journal of a Volunteer, being the Personal Account of Captain Thomas Douglas Whitcombe* (Princeton, NJ, 1992), 64.

34. Eliot, ed., *Campaign*, 80; S. Papadopoulou, "Dionysios Vourvachis' (Denys Bourbaki): Enas gallos filenninas tou 1821 ellinikis katagogis," *Parnassos*, 5 (1963), 340–56.

35. Eliot, ed., *Campaign*, 97–99.

36. E. M. Church, *Chapters in an Adventurous Life: Sir Richard Church in Italy and Greece* (London, 1895), 307–8.

37. Cited by Dakin, *British and American Philhellenes*, 118.

38. Kolokotronis, *Ellinika ypomnimata*, 398; Dakin, *British and American Philhellenes*, 124–27.

39. Cochrane, *Wanderings in Greece*, i, 17–21, 32–35.

40. Gritsopoulos, ed., *Theodorou Kolokotroni*, 188.

41. Lidderdale, ed., *The Memoirs of General Makriyannis*, 132–33.

42. Dakin, *British and American Philhellenes*, 150–51.

43. Finlay, *History*, ii, 148.

44. Eliot, ed., *Campaign*, 140–49.

45. Debidour, *Le Général Fabvier*, 331–33.

46. Lidderdale, ed., *The Memoirs of General Makriyannis*, 140–41.

47. Ibid., 336.

48. Miller, *The Condition of Greece*, 183.

CHAPTER 16: THE INEXHAUSTIBLE PATIENCE OF THE PEOPLE

1. K. A. Diamantis, *Athinaikon Archeion* (Athens, 1971), 429.

2. Black, *Narrative of Cruises*, 245–54; Richards, ed., *Letters and Journals of Samuel Gridley Howe*, 194.

3. Miller, *The Condition of Greece*, 275–90.
4. Arnakis, ed., *George Jarvis*, 218.
5. Miller, *The Condition of Greece*, 218.
6. Ibid., 139.
7. Ibid., 242.
8. G. Kolokotronis, *Ellinika ypomnimata itoi epistolai kai diafora engrafa aforonta tin ellinikin epanastasin apo 1824 mechri 1827* (Athens, 1856), 397.
9. Miller, *The Condition of Greece*, 50.
10. Frantzis, *Epitomi tis istorias*, ii, 464–67.
11. Reppas, *Ypotheseis kataskopias*, 414–16.
12. Ibid., 418–23.
13. Ibid., 420–21.
14. Fotakos, *Apomnimonevmata*, ii, 341–51, for the entire story; cf. Frantzis, *Epitomi tis istorias*, ii, 467–68.
15. Kolokotronis, *Ellinika ypomnimata*, 477.
16. K. Papadopoulos, *Anaskevi ton eis tin istorian ton Athinon anaferomenon peri tou stratigou Odysseos Androutzou* (Athens, 1837), 17–18; also M. Karasarinis, "Rumeli," in Kitromilides and Tsoukalas, eds., *The Greek Revolution*, 308–9.
17. The minimum figure is estimated at well over 10,000: Nikolaou, "Islamisations," 397.
18. Kolokotronis, *Ellinika ypomnimata*, 273.
19. Veis, "Arkadika glossika mnimeia," 266; "O Agrioyiannis" at http://androni .blogspot.com/2012/09/blog-post.html.
20. Fotakos emphasizes the economic motive; Deliyannis the desire to free enslaved relatives. For the campaign of enslavement, see Nikolaou, "Islamisations," 390–407, esp. 398–99.
21. Cf. Spiliades, *Apomnimonevmata*, iii, 321ff; Fotakos, *Apomnimonevmata*, ii, 397–421.
22. Kolokotronis, *Ellinika ypomnimata*, 475; *Archeion Kanellou Deliyanni: ta eggrafa (1779–1827)* (Athens, 1993), 221–65, here 249.
23. Fotakos, 477, 485, 496; Hadzianargyrou, ed., *Ta Spetsiotika*, 1,093–97.
24. Ibid.
25. Spiliades, *Apomnimonevmata*, iii, 354; T. Stamatopoulos, *OI tourkoproskynimenoi kai o Kolokotronis* (Athens, 1974).
26. Frantzis, *Epitomi*, ii, 458–59; Hadzianargyrou, ed., *Ta Spetsiotika*, 1,046–50
27. Kolokotronis, *Ellinika ypomnimata*, 535.
28. Ibid., 550–52; Hadzianargyrou, ed., *Ta Spetsiotika*, 1,102–3.
29. Kolokotronis, *Ellinika ypomnimata*, 556.
30. J. Mangeart, *Souvenirs de la Morée* (Paris, 1830), 17; E. Quinet, *De la Grèce moderne et de ses rapports avec l'antiquité* (Paris, 1830), 13–14.
31. Kolokotronis, *Ellinika ypomnimata*, 564, 565.

CHAPTER 17: NAVARINO: THE FORCE OF THINGS

1. L. Cappon, ed., *The Adams-Jefferson Letters*, 2 vols. (Chapel Hill, NC, 1959), ii, 574.

2. T. Raikes, *A Portion of the Journal kept by T. Raikes, Esq. from 1831 to 1847*, 3 vols. (London, 1858), i, 64.

3. C. Crawley, "A forgotten prophecy (Greece 1820–21)," *Cambridge Historical Journal*, 1:2 (1924), 209–13; see too Grimsted, "Capodistrias and a 'New Order,'" 166–92.

4. L. Oeconomos, *Essai sur la vie du Comte Capodistrias depuis son départ de Russie en août 1822 jusqu'à son arrivée en Grèce en janvier 1828* (Paris and Toulouse, 1926), ch. 2.

5. C. W. Crawley, *John Capodistrias: Some Unpublished Documents* (Thessaloniki, 1970), 79–81.

6. Ibid., 81–82; on Capodistrias through the eyes of the Paris police, see Oeconomos, *Essai*, passim.

7. Woodhouse, *Capodistrias*, 245.

8. R. Blaufarb, "The western question: the geopolitics of Latin American independence," *AHR*, 112:3 (June 2007), 742–63; C. Webster, *Britain and the Independence of Latin America, 1812–1830: Selected Documents from the Foreign Office Archives* (London, 1938); H. Temperley, *The Foreign Policy of Canning, 1822–1827: England, the Neo-Holy Alliance and the New World* (London, 1925); W. S. Robertson, *France and Latin American independence* (Baltimore, MD, 1939); Stites, *Four Horsemen*. And see now the work by Gabriel Pacquette, notably his 2013 article in *Modern Intellectual History* and a special 2011 issue of the *European History Quarterly* devoted to European-South American relations in the 1820s.

9. Cited by W. S. Robertson, "The United States and Spain in 1822," *AHR*, 20:4 (July 1915), 781–800, here 798.

10. Cited in W. P. Cresson, "Chateaubriand and the Monroe Doctrine," *North American Review*, 217:809 (April 1923), 475–87.

11. For a detailed treatment of the entire story see the classic work by Temperley, *The Foreign Policy of Canning*.

12. Cousin d'Avalon, *Pradtiana* (Paris, 1820), 3, cited in Colonel Daupeyroux, "La curieuse vie de l'Abbé de Pradt," *Revue des études historiques*, 95 (1929), 295; On de Pradt and his possible influence on the Monroe Doctrine: T. R. Schellenberg, "Jeffersonian origins of the Monroe Doctrine," *Hispanic American Historical Review*, 14:1 (Feb. 1934), 1–31, and Laura Bornholdt, "The Abbé de Pradt and the Monroe Doctrine," *Hispanic American Historical Review*, 24:2 (May 1944), 201–21, for both sides of the argument.

13. De Pradt, *Vrai Système de l'Europe relativement à l'Amérique et à la Grèce* (Paris, 1825), 1–3, 13.

14. P. Quemeneur, "Chateaubriand et la Grèce," *Balkan Studies*, 3:1 (1962), 119–32.

15. J.-C. Berchet, *Chateaubriand* (Paris, 2012), 724–27.

16. Cited in G. Ioannidou-Bitsiadou, "L'attitude russe face a l'indépendance grecque (1821–1829) vue par deux diplomates français," in *Les relations gréco-russes pendant la domination turque et la guerre d'indépendance grecque* (Thessaloniki, 1983), 99–108, here 103; Abbé de Pradt, *De l'intervention armée pour la pacification de la Grèce* (Paris, 1828), 11: this work is dedicated to Capodistrias. On legitimacy, see Zanou, *Transnational Patriotism in the Mediterranean, 1800–1850: Stammering the Nation* (Oxford, 2018), 103–8, and above all Ghervas, *Réinventer la tradition*, passim.

17. R. Beaton, "Philhellenism," in P. Kitromilides and C. Tsoukalas, eds., *The Greek Revolution: A Critical Dictionary* (Cambridge, MA, 2021), 593–613, quotation from 604; Temperley, *The Foreign Policy of Canning*.

18. Temperley, *The Foreign Policy of Canning*, 326; W. Allison Phillips, "Greece and the Balkan Peninsula," in Lord Acton, ed., *The Cambridge Modern History*, x (New York, 1911), 187.

19. Chateaubriand, *Congrès de Vérone* (Brussels, 1852), 191.

20. Lane-Poole, *Stratford Canning*, i, 387–89.

21. Temperley, *The Foreign Policy of Canning*, 346–47.

22. Ibid., 349.

23. J. Bourchier, ed., *Memoir of the Life of Admiral Sir Edward Codrington: with selections from his public and private correspondence*, 2 vols. (London, 1873), ii, 58.

24. Douin, *L'expédition de Crète et de Morée*, 268–76; Driault, *L'expédition*, 244–58.

25. Bourchier, *Memoir*, ii, 17.

26. Ibid., ii, 7–10, 19, 49–50.

27. Ibid., 52; Driault, *L'expédition*, 247–50.

28. Bourchier, *Memoir*, ii, 60.

29. E. Ommanney, "Memories of Navarino," *World Wide Magazine*, i (1898), 48–52, here 49.

30. See the first account in Bourchier, *Memoir*, ii, 71–76; a Russian account from the *Azov* in L. I. Spridonova, ed., *P. S. Nakhimov: dokumenti i materialy*, 2 vols. (St. Petersburg, 2003), i, 74–83. My thanks to Gelina Harlaftis for this document.

31. *Life on Board a Man-of-War including a Full Account of the Battle of Navarino by a British Seaman* (Glasgow, 1829), 140–68, 173–75.

32. Bourchier, *Memoir*, ii, 77.

33. Anderson, *Naval Wars in the Levant*, 524–33.

34. Bourchier, *Memoir*, ii, 454–55.

35. J. Dimakis, *La presse française face à la chute de Missolonghi et à la Bataille navale de Navarin* (Thessaloniki, 1976), 102–40.

36. Bourchier, *Memoir*, ii, 116; Driault, *L'expedition*, 287; Bourchier, *Memoir*, ii, 84

37. On Ibrahim in the Hijaz, the best source is G. F. Sadlier, "Account of a journey from Katif on the Red Sea to Tamboo on the Persian Gulf by Capt. G. F. Sadlier," *Transactions of the Literary Society of Bombay*, iii (London, 1823), 449–93, esp. 473, 487–88.

38. Driault, *L'expédition*, 250–58, 289.

39. Woodhouse, *Capodistrias*, 336–39.

40. Ibid., 345.

41. A. Papadopoulos-Vretos, *Mémoires biographiques-historiques sur le président de la Grèce comte Jean Capodistrias* (Paris, 1837), i, 103.

42. Spiliades, *Apomnimonevmata*, iii (Athens, 1975), 541–43: *Theodorou Griva Viografiko Schediasma*.

43. Papadopoulos-Vretos, *Mémoires biographiques*, 103–5; G. Tolias, "La lanterne magique de Stamati Boulgari (1774–1842)," in M.-N. Bourguet et al., eds., *Enquêtes en Méditerranée: les expéditions françaises d'Égypte, de Morée et d'Algérie* (Athens, 1999), 57–69.

44. *Archeion Ioannou Kapodistrias*, 9 vols. (Kerkyra, 1986), vii, 294–304, here 294–95.

45. Anon., *Politikon systima tis Ellados* (Troezen, 1827), 45.

CHAPTER 18: LOVE, CONCORD, BROTHERHOOD, 1828–33

1. C. G. Pitcairn Jones, ed., *Piracy in the Levant, 1827–1828, selected from the Papers of Admiral Sir Edward Codrington KCB* (London, 1934), 183–86; J. A. Wombwell, "The long war against piracy: historical trends," Occasional Paper, no. 32, Fort Leavenworth, Kansas (2010), 79–80; D. Dimitropoulos, "Peirates sti steria: prosfyges, katadromeis kai kathimerinotita ton paraktion oikismon sta chronia tou Agona," Dimitropoulos et al., eds., *Opseis tis epanastasis tou 1821*, 87–105.

2. S. Bozikis, "Ta karavia estathisan gennitika," in G. Harlaftis and K. Galanis, eds., *O emporikos kai polemikos stolos kata tin elliniki epanastasi 1821–1831* (Rethymnon, 2021), 122; B. Gounaris, "Macedonia," in Koliopoulos and Tsoukalas, eds., *The Greek Revolution*, 232–47, here 245–46.

3. Cases from Pitcairn Jones, ed., *Piracy in the Levant*, passim.

4. Ibid., 218–19, 234–35.

5. Ibid., 240–63; "Gawen William Hamilton Esq.," in J. Marshall, ed., *Royal Naval Biography*: Supplement, Part 2 (London, 1828), 447–52.

6. G. Roux, *Histoire médicale de l'Armée Française en Morée pendant la campagne de 1828* (Paris, 1829).

7. G. Tolias, "La lanterne magique de Stamati Bulgari, (1782–1856)," in Bourguet et al., eds., *Enquêtes en Méditerranée*, 64–66.

8. E. Amaury-Duval, *Souvenirs (1829–1830)* (Paris, 1885), 80–81.

9. E. Chapuisat, *Élie-Ami Bétant, Secrétaire de Capodistria et ses Lettres inédites (1827–1829)* (Le Puy, 1926), 22–23.

10. L.-A. Gosse, *Relation de la Peste qui a regné en Grèce en 1827 et 1828* (Paris, 1838); see also Rothpletz, ed., *Lettres du Genevois Louis-André Gosse*; M. Bouvier-Bron, "La mission médicale de Louis-André Gosse pendant son séjour en Grèce (1827–1829)," *Gesnerus: Swiss Journal of the History of Medicine and Sciences*, 48:3–4 (1991), 343–57; Chapuisat, *Bétant*, 24.

11. See B. C. Gounaris, "Blood brothers in despair: Greek brigands, Albanian rebels and the Greek-Ottoman frontier, 1829–1831," *Cahiers balkaniques*, 45 (2018), 1–24.

12. My thanks to Kostis Karpozilos for this fundamental point.

13. G. Koulikourdi, *Aigina*, i (Athens, 1990), 68–87; Chapuisat, *Bétant*, 30–31.

14. See G. Kalpadakis, "Technocratic efforts in institution-building in the early modern Greek state," unpublished paper. My thanks to Dr. Kalpadakis for his assistance.

15. D. Themelis-Katiforis, "I dioxis tis peirateias kai to Thalassion Dikastirion, 1828–1829," PhD, National Capodistrian University, Athens (1973).

16. C. Loukos, "O kyvernitis I. Kapodistrias kai oi Mavromihalaioi," *Mnimon*, 4 (1974), 1–110.

17. Picture in I. A. Meletopoulos, *I istoria tis neoteras Elladas eis tin laikin eikonografian* (Athens, 1968), np.

18. Testimonies in Papadopoulos-Vretos, *Mémoires biographiques-historiques*, ii, 365–410; the best contemporary account is by an eyewitness, J. Pellion, *La Grèce et les Capodistrias pendant l'Occupation française de 1828 à 1834* (Paris, 1855), 242–50.

19. Cf. Ypsilantis to Kolokotronis (Jan. 29, 1821), in Kolokotronis, *Ellinika ypomnimata*, vi, and Filemon, *Dokimion Istorikon*, i, 309–10.

20. V. Kremmydas, "I dolofonia tou Kyberniti Ioanni Kapodistria," *Eranistis*, 14 (1977), 217–81.

21. Capodistrias remains a controversial if respected figure: see C. Koulouri and C. Loukos, *Ta prosopa tou Kapodistria: o protos kyvrnitis tis Elladas kai i neoelliniki ideologia (1831–1996)* (Athens, 1996), and G. Georgis, ed., *O Kyvernitis Ioannis Kapodistrias* (Athens, 2015).

22. Lt.-Col. Baker, "Memoir on the northern frontier of Greece," *Journal of the Royal Geographical Society*, 7 (1837), 81–94; on the border, J. Koliopoulos, *Brigands with a Cause* (Oxford, 1984).

23. See V. Gounaris, *"Den ein'o persinos kairos . . .": ellines kleftarmatoloi kai alvanoi stasiastes (1829–1831)* (Athens, 2020), passim.

24. K. Mendelssohn-Bartholdy, *Istoria tis Ellados apo tis en etei 1453* (Athens, 1876), ii, 598.

25. T. Evangelidis, *Istoria tou Othonos, vasileos tis Ellados (1832–1862)* (Athens, 1894), 38–39. My thanks to Costas Kouremenos for this reference. Also,

Finlay, *History*, ii, 290–92; L. Ross, *Erinnerungen und Mitteilungen aus Griechenland* (Berlin, 1863), 203; M. P. Vreto, "'Othon A': Vasileus tis Ellados," *Ethnikon Imerologion tou etous 1869* (Leipzig, 1869), 246.

26. Pellion, *La Grèce et les Capodistrias*, 371; Evangelidis, *Istoria tou Othonos*, 38–41.

27. The chief source is C. Neezer, *Apomnimonevmata to proton eton tis idryseos tou Ellinikou Vasileiou* (Istanbul, 1911); J. M. Hussey, ed., *The Journals and Letters of George Finlay, i: The Journals* (Camberley, Surrey, 1995), 66.

28. R. Carter, "Karl Friedrich Schinkel's project for a royal palace on the Acropolis," *Journal of the Society of Architectural Historians*, 38:1 (March 1979), 34–46.

29. F. Mallouchou-Tufanou, "The vicissitudes of the Athenian Acropolis," in [n.a.], *Great Moments in Greek Archaeology* (Athens, 2007), 37–41. The general background is presented by the classic work of the late lamented E. Bastea, *The Creation of Modern Athens: Planning the Myth* (Cambridge, 1999).

30. Cochrane, *Wanderings in Greece*, i, 146; E. Bastea, "Nineteenth-century travellers in the Greek lands: politics, prejudice and poetry in Arcadia," *Dialogos: Hellenic Studies Review*, 4 (1997), 47–69, here 53; generally, E. Stasinopoulos, *I Athina tou perasmenou aiona (1830–1900)* (Athens, 1963), 12–33.

31. Cited in W. McGrew, *Land and Revolution in Modern Greece, 1800–1881: The Transition in the Tenure and Exploitation of Land from Ottoman Rule to Independence* (Kent, OH, 1985), 77.

32. Pizanias, "Apo rayias Ellinas politis. Diafotismos kai epanastasi, 1750–1832," in Pizanias, ed., *Elliniki Epanastasi*, 43.

33. T. Kandiloros, *I diki tou Kolokotroni kai tou Dimitriou Plapouta* (Athens, 1960), 157.

34. See the excellent E. Tsakanika, *Agonistes tou 1821 meta tin epanastasi* (Athens, 2019), ch. 2.

35. Cochrane, *Wanderings*, i, 250–51; E. Giffard, *A Short Visit to the Ionian Islands* (London, 1837), 130, 138–44.

36. [Greek Parliament], *O logos tou Theodorou Koloktroni stin Pnyka* (Athens, 2008), 13. Note that in the Etaireia, "rain" was code for the Supreme Authority.

37. S. Marangou-Drygiannaki, "Orthodoxy and Russian policy towards Greece in the 19th century: the Philorthodox Society's conspiracy (1830–1840)," *Balkan Studies*, 41:1 (2000), 27–42; C. Papoulidis, "Un document caractéristique de Gabriel Catacazé tiré des archives de la politique extérieure de la Russie," *Balkan Studies*, 23:2 (1982), 1–7.

38. J. Koliopoulos, *Brigands with a Cause*, chs. 5–6.

39. D. Dawson, "The archduke Ferdinand Maximilian and the crown of Greece, 1863," *English Historical Review*, 37:145 (Jan. 1922), 107–14. My thanks to Simon Winder for information about Otto's retirement.

40. Maxime Du Camp, *Souvenirs littéraires* (Paris, 1893), i, 532–35.

41. Tertsetis, *Exakolouthisis*, 5; Du Camp, *Souvenirs*, i, 532–35, 549.

42. Anon., *The Notebooks of a Spinster Lady, 1878–1903* (London, 1919), 23–27.

43. S. Vios, *I sfagi tou Chiou eis to stoma tou Chiakou laou* (Chios, 1922); A. Chaldeos, "The Greek community in Tunis between 1805 and 1881: aspects of its demographics and its role in the local economic and political context," *Journal of North African Studies*, 24:6 (2019), 887–95.

44. J. Thompson, "Osman Effendi: a Scottish convert to Islam in early nineteenth-century Egypt," *Journal of World History*, 5:1 (Spring 1994), 99–123; "Edward William Lane: 1801–1876," *Oxford Dictionary of National Biography*.

45. Miller, *The Condition of Greece in 1827 and 1828*, 171.

46. M. Connors Santelli, *The Greek Fire: American-Ottoman Relations and Democratic Fervor in the Age of Revolutions* (Ithaca, NY, 2020), 152–54, 163–64.

47. C. Aliprantis, "Lives in exile: foreign political refugees in early independent Greece (1830–1853)," *Byzantine and Modern Greek Studies*, 43:2 (2019), 243–61.

48. J. Morley, *The Life of William Ewart Gladstone*, i (London, 1903), 30–31; Francis Lieber, "Guerrilla parties considered with reference to the laws and usages of war," in *The Miscellaneous Writings of Francis Lieber* (London: Lippincott & Co., 1881), ii, 275–92; General Orders No. 100: The Lieber Code: Instructions for the Government of Armies of the United States in the Field, prepared by Francis Lieber, LLD, Originally Issued as General Orders No. 100, Adjutant General's Office, 1863, Washington 1898: Government Printing Office, articles 81–85.

49. Blancard, *Les Mavroyeni*, ii, 683–700; Z. Papantoniou, "To iovilaion enos agonistou. To monon epizon ieron leipsanon tou Agonos," *Skrip* (1904), 287–92.

EPILOGUE: THE ECONOMY OF THE MIRACLE

1. I. Skylissis, *Molierou arista erga* (Trieste, 1871), 243.

2. Raybaud, *Mémoires*, ii, 124, 131–32.

3. The best source is G. Dorizas, *Viografia tis Ayias Monachis Pelagias tis Tinou* (Athens, 1978), passim.

4. *Evresis tis panseptou eikonos tou evangelismokou tis theotokou kai oikodomi tou ierou naou tis Evangelistrias eis tin nison Tinon* (Venice, 1833). My account follows the details given in this first 1833 edition; subsequent editions make changes.

5. H. A. Post, *A Visit to Greece and Istanbul in the Year 1827–8* (New York, 1830), 223–26; A. de Valon, *Une année dans le Levant* (Paris, 1846), I; H. Puckler Muskau (trans. Jean Cohen), *Entre l'Europe et l'Asie: Voyage dans*

l'Archipel (Brussels, 1840), ii, 41–42; "R," "A Panhellenic festival of today," *Macmillan's Magazine*, 48 (1883–84), 474–77.

6. G. Dorizas, *Oi ekklisies kai ta proskynimata tis Tinou* (Athens, n.d.), 22; Archives of the Catholic Archbishopric of Tinos [Xynara, Tinos], file 28/ 136–37, "Numerazione delle anime dei nostri cattolici di Tine fatta nel 1835."

7. C. Stewart, *Dreaming and Historical Consciousness in Island Greece* (Oxford, 2012), ch. 3, is a brilliant account of this extraordinary episode.

8. The best source for events on Tinos during the war is E. Georgantopoulos, *Tiniaka, itoi archaia kai neotera geografia kai istoria tis nisou Tinou* (Athens, 1889), esp. 136–7, 145–51.

9. F. Vitali, "O Tinou Gavriil Sylivos kai i symvoli tou eis tin ethnegersian tou 1821," *Epetiris Etaireia Kykadikon Meleton* (1971–73), 137–55; A. Lignos, ed., *Archeion tis koinotitos Hydras, 1778–1832*, 10 (Piraeus, 1928), 168; G. L. Dorizas, *I Tinos epi Tourkokratias kai kata ton Agona tou 1821* (Athens, 1978), 317; Archives of the Ministère des Affaires Étrangères (Nantes): Smyrne 36 (correspondence consulaire, 1821), 132–33.

10. I. Oikonomous, *O theos kai to 1821* (Athens, 2018), 18; Lane-Poole, *Stratford Canning*, i, 416.

11. Salafatinos, *Syntomoi paratiriseis*, 6; Cf. Capodistrias as cited in Oikonomos, *O theos kai to 1821*, 27.

12. Oikonomous, *O theos kai to 1821*, 27; for astute remarks on the trope of complaint, see R. Beaton, "Introduction," in Beaton and D. Ricks, eds., *The Making of Modern Greece: Nationalism, Romanticism and the Uses of the Past (1797–1896)* (Ashgate, 2009), 1–5.

13. Rothpletz, ed., *Lettres du Genevois Louis-André Gosse*, 46.

Index

Bathurst, Walter, 417
Bavarians, *see* Ludwig, King of Bavaria; Otto
  von Wittelsbach
Beecher Stowe, Harriet, 452
Beirut, 322, 323
Belgium, 434
Bellios, Constantine, 445
Belloc, Louise, 223
Benjamin of Lesvos, 159
Bentham, Jeremy, 247–50, 251, 260–61
besa (personal oath), 84–85, 209
Bessarabia, 9, 10, 20–21, 24, 31
Bétant, Élie-Ami, 432, 435
Black, William, 378
Blaquiere, Edward, 246, 251, 254–55, 266
Blouet, Abel, 431
Boeotia, 352–53
Boigne, Comtesse de, 328
Bolívar, Simón, 222, 232, 253
Bollmann, Louis de, 236, 237, 241
Bonaparte, Joseph, 365
Bonaparte, Prince Paul Marie, 223
Bosnians, xxix, xxxi, 304
Botsaris, Kitsos, 440
Botsaris, Kostas, 289
Botsaris, Markos, 117, 165, 167, 168, 174,
  209, 305
Botsaris, Notis, 196, 308, 316, 325
Boubouli, Eleni, 173
Bouboulina (Laskarina), 85, 173, 204
Boulgari, Stamati, 424, 431
Bourbaki, Constantin, 365–67
Bournias, Antonios, 149, 150
Bowring, John, 246–47, 249, 250, 251, 262,
  263, 264–65
Boyer, Jean-Pierre, 337, 338
Bozikis, Simos, 269, 271, 334
Bradford, Cornelius, 335
Brajović, Vaso (Vasos the Montenegrin),
  322–23, 447
Brazil, 434
Brengeri (Italian philhellene), 233, 234,
  237–39, 240, 241
Britain
  1st Regiment Greek Light Infantry,
    54, 367
  Alexandria occupied by (1807), 276
  Anglo-Russian negotiations, 406–7
  Codrington's naval force, 394–95, 407,
    409–15, 417, 418–19, 420–21,
    427, 461
  Greek distrust of, 179, 245–46, 260
  and Greek piracy, 428
  Greeks' growing orientation toward, 352,
    405–6

and Ionian Islands, xxxiii, 7, 54, 246, 312,
  367–68, 454
London Greek Committee, 247,
  248–51, 254–55, 256, 259, 261–64,
  368–69, 378
naval squadron in the Aegean, 297, 370–71
naval strength in the Levant, 252
recognizes Greeks as belligerents (1823),
  262, 404
sends fleet to enforce Treaty of London,
  409–18
senior officers arrive to lead Greeks (1827),
  367–70
shifting policy over Greeks, 262–63, 279,
  284, 346–47, 403–4
and slavery, 336
Browne, James Hamilton, 255, 257
Bulgarians, xxix
Byron, Lord, xxvii–xxviii, xxxi–xxxii
  admires Ottoman way of life, xxxi, 236,
    248, 256–57
  and Ali Pasha, xxxi, 37, 255
  arrival in Mesolonghi (January 1824), 259
  Chateaubriand's influence on, 402
  Childe Harold, 257
  corpse returns to London, 262, 266
  death of (1824), 223, 242, 259–60, 263,
    305, 326–27, 332, 402
  disdain for Benthamites, 248, 260
  Don Juan, 256, 257
  Ionian island base (1823), 256–59
  and London Greek Committee, 248, 251,
    255–56
  Millingen as doctor of, 115, 290
  and the Souliots, 199, 259, 380

Cambrian, HMS, 262, 295, 297, 352, 371,
  395, 412, 430, 458
camels, 192
Camp, Maxime Du, 450
Campbell, Thomas, 251
Candolle, Augustin Pyramus de, 92–93
Canning, George, 213, 261, 262–63, 346–47,
  404, 405–6, 453, 461
  death of (1827), 409, 419, 422
  and Ibrahim's "Barbarization" project,
    346, 407
Canning, Stratford, 284, 346, 352, 405–6, 461
Capodistrias, Agostino, 438
Capodistrias, Count Ioannis
  arrives in Nafplion, 423–24
  assassination of (1831), 437–38
  and candidates for postwar kingship,
    433–34, 438
  centralization attempts, 435, 436

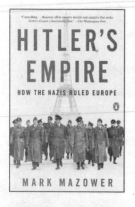

HITLER'S EMPIRE

How the Nazis Ruled Europe

Drawing on an unprecedented range and variety of original research, *Hitler's Empire* offers a chilling vision of what the world would have become had they won the war. Mark Mazower forces us to set aside timeworn opinions of the Third Reich, and instead shows how the party drew inspiration for its imperial expansion from America and Great Britain. A work as authoritative as it is unique, this is a surprising—and controversial—new appraisal of the Third Reich's rise and ultimate fall.

GOVERNING THE WORLD

The History of an Idea, 1815 to the Present

Governing the World tells the epic, two-hundred-year story of the reckoning with forces that have shaped the nature and destiny of the world's governing institutions. From the rubble of the Napoleonic empire in the nineteenth century, through the birth of the League of Nations and the United Nations in the twentieth century, and to the dominance of global finance at the turn of the millennium, Mazower masterfully explores the current era of international life as Western dominance wanes and a new global balance of powers emerges.

SALONICA, CITY OF GHOSTS

Christians, Muslims and Jews 1430-1950

Salonica, located in northern Greece, was long a fascinating crossroads metropolis of different religions and ethnicities, where Egyptian merchants, Spanish Jews, Orthodox Greeks, Sufi dervishes, and Albanian brigands all rubbed shoulders. As the acclaimed historian Mark Mazower follows the city's inhabitants through plague, invasion, famine, and the disastrous twentieth century, he resurrects a fascinating and vanished world.

PENGUIN BOOKS